Milton
New Hampshire
Vital Records
1888-1999

Richard P. Roberts

HERITAGE BOOKS
2011

HERITAGE BOOKS
AN IMPRINT OF HERITAGE BOOKS, INC.

Books, CDs, and more—Worldwide

For our listing of thousands of titles see our website
at
www.HeritageBooks.com

Published 2011 by
HERITAGE BOOKS, INC.
Publishing Division
100 Railroad Ave. #104
Westminster, Maryland 21157

Copyright © 2000 Richard P. Roberts

All rights reserved. No part of this book may be reproduced or transmitted in any form or by any means, electronic or mechanical, including photocopying, recording or by any information storage and retrieval system without written permission from the author, except for the inclusion of brief quotations in a review.

International Standard Book Numbers
Paperbound: 978-0-7884-1487-9
Clothbound: 978-0-7884-8934-1

Contents

Introduction 1
Births 4
Marriages 219
Deaths 445

INTRODUCTION

Early vital records of many New Hampshire towns can be located either through the State's Vital Records Department or on microfilms made available through LDS Family History Centers. Some, however, have been lost or are inaccessible for various reasons. A valuable, but time-consuming, source of information for events occurring after 1886 is the vital statistics which are provided in a section of the Annual Town Reports of many New Hampshire towns. Many of these town reports have been collected at the New Hampshire State Library in Concord, as well as more local repositories.

The amount of information published in these Annual Town Reports varies tremendously over time. Early records are far more detailed and comprehensive. Recent records are rather cursory, but issues of confidentiality and sensitivity to the privacy of those residents still living offsets the lack of information of genealogical value.

While the information provided is often very helpful, one must remember that it is not fool-proof or universally accurate, nor is it the primary source or the actual vital record itself. The fact that much of the data is self-reported suggests that it is reliable. However, errors in transcription, spelling (particularly with respect to French-Canadian and European families), and printing often are obvious. In addition, there may be, for example, two children listed as the third child of a particular couple, or the mother's maiden name, age or place of birth differs or is inconsistent from one entry to another. It is also important to note that a birth, marriage or death may have been reported in another town although the subject resided in Milton, or the entry may not have been made in the first place.

Despite these shortcomings, the information contained in the Annual Town Reports can be a valuable tool for the genealogist. Marriage and death records from the late 1800's often identify parents who were married nearly a century before. Finally, those families that have remained in Milton for several generations can be traced and connected to the present. The records for the year 1892 have not been located and are not included in this compilation.

Births - To the extent the information is available, the entries in the list of births are given as follows: child's name; date of birth; place of birth (Milton, unless otherwise indicated, although no place of birth is provided in recent years); the number of children in the family; father's name, place of birth, age and occupation; and the mother's maiden name, age and place of birth. The residence of the parents is sometimes given when it is shown as other than Milton. As noted above, the amount of information in earlier records is substantially greater.

At times, the given names of many children are missing from the early reports. In this case, the sex of the child is given and they are listed chronologically at the beginning of the surname heading. On occasion, the child's name can be determined from marriage or death records, as well as secondary sources. These names are shown in brackets where available.

Marriages - To the extent the information is available, the entries in the list of marriages follow this format: groom's name; groom's residence; bride's name; brides residence; date of marriage; place of marriage (Milton, unless otherwise indicated, although no place of marriage is given in recent years); H, signifying husband's information, and W, signifying wife's information, each in the following order - age, occupation, number of the marriage (if other than first), father's name, father's place of birth, father's occupation, mother's name, mother's place of birth, and mother's occupation. The name of the official conducting the marriage has been omitted but is generally provided in the original document. The records for several years do not provide the parents' surnames.

Deaths - To the extent available, the entries in the list of deaths contain the following information: name of decedent; place of death; date of death; age at death; cause of death; marital status; birthplace; father's name; father's place of birth; mother's name; and mother's place of birth. Later entries give the residence of the individual. Most of the entries listing a cause of death are self-explanatory.

In most recent years, the age at death was not provided in the report. That information is often available from the Social Security Death Benefits database and has not been provided.

There are additional resources which are certain to be useful in conjunction with the material contained in this book. A substantial effort to transcribe the cemetery inscriptions in the town of Milton has been conducted and is available at the Dover (N.H.) Public Library. In addition, many of the families listed in this volume may also be included in the prior works covering neighboring towns, particularly Wakefield, New Durham and Middleton.

BIRTHS

ADABAHR,
Ruth Evelyn, b. 12/23/1936 in Rochester; second; Harold Adabahr (mechanic, Espe'ce, NY) and Marie Anderson (Malden, MA)

ADAMS,
Angelina, b. 5/28/1989 in Rochester; Larry Adams and Sandra L. Marley
Anthony, b. 5/28/1989 in Rochester; Larry Adams and Sandra L. Marley
Kenneth L., Jr., b. 4/28/1950 in Lawrence, MA; second; Kenneth L. Adams (cleanser, Haverhill, MA) and Bertha Norman (Tuftonboro)

ADJUTANT,
Richard James, b. 8/22/1968 in Wolfeboro; Ronald H. Adjutant and Susan E. Kelly

AGRI,
Adam Joseph, b. 3/21/1984 in Rochester; Joseph M. Agri and Patricia L. Bernuth

AINSWORTH,
Jessica Lynn, b. 6/16/1979 in Dover; William J. Ainsworth, Jr. and Alice L. Currier

ALBERGHENE,
Naida Vincon, b. 3/27/1919; fourth; Oscar V. Alberghene (emp. ice co., Canton, MA) and Irene E. Connor (Woonsocket, RI)

ALBERTS,
Kayla Lynn, b. 4/2/1988 in Concord; Michael D. Alberts and Karyn Hagopian

ALDEN,
Gary Thomas, b. 5/24/1988 in Rochester; Mark C. Alden and Diane L. St. Ours

ALLARD,
Linda June, b. 3/25/1952 in Rochester; first; Paul A. Allard (mill worker, Canada) and Aileen L. Williams (Milton)

ALLEN,
Alyssa Elizabeth, b. 4/15/1991 in Rochester; William H. Allen and Lisa L. Cormier
Annie Elizabeth, b. 6/4/1908; second; George W. Allen (emp. in mill, 30, Wakefield) and Hattie M. Cook (20, Brookfield)
Dearborn, b. 9/3/1906; second; Harry Allen (ice man, 28, Brookfield) and Maude Dearborn (22, Laconia)
Jacob William, b. 11/2/1992 in Portsmouth; Daniel J. Allen and Cheryl L. Dufault
Mary Harriet, b. 11/3/1913; fourth; John M. Allen (foreman, Ireland) and Sadie Shackford (Gorham, ME)
Persis May, b. 12/1/1914; fifth; John M. Allen (emp. in mill, Ireland) and Sarah Shackford (Gorham, ME)

AMADON,
Muriel Louise, b. 8/25/1949 in Rochester; second; Clarence P. Amadon (teacher, Canada) and Florence S. Blanchard (ME)

AMAZEEN,
Alice Eloise, b. 10/23/1922; second; Walter Amazeen (shoemaker, Milton) and Lillian Parkhurst (Lynn, MA)
Laurel Marjorie, b. 1/6/1927; third; Walter Amazeen (shoemaker, Milton) and Lillian F. Parkhurst (Lynn, MA)
Warren Leonard, b. 5/23/1921; first; Walter Amazeen (shoe mfgr., Milton) and Lillian F. Parkhurst (Lynn, MA)

AMEY,
daughter, b. 9/21/1899; second; Harry B. Amey (lawyer, 30, Pittsburg) and Grace A. Norton (23, Island Pond, VT)

ANDERSON,
daughter, b. 6/12/1896; second; Peter Anderson (paper maker, 25, Scotland) and Mary Lindsay (30, Scotland)
Elaine Anna, b. 8/4/1923; third; Leslie W. Anderson (shoemaker, Stoneham, MA) and Hazel Perkins (Middleton)
Judith Gayle, b. 5/11/1946 in Rochester; third; Norris E. Anderson (farmer, Milton) and Meredith I. Goss (Sanford, ME); residence - West Milton

Karline Sandra, b. 11/8/1940 in Rochester; first; John A. Anderson (teacher, Cambridge, MA) and Iria V. Waris (Fitchburg, MA)
Nancy Ellen, b. 1/1/1941; fifth; Lesley W. Anderson (shoemaker, Stoneham, MA) and Hazel A. Perkins (Middleton)
Norris Elmer, b. 5/16/1918; first; Leslie W. Anderson (shoemaker, Stoneham, MA) and Hazel A. Perkins (Middleton)
Phyllis Emily, b. 1/10/1921; second; Leslie W. Anderson (laborer, Stoneham, MA) and Hazel Perkins (Middleton)

ANDES,
Richard Charles, b. 11/14/1979 in Portsmouth; Eugene B. Andes and Ellen D. Coleman
Robert Coleman, b. 7/31/1978 in Portsmouth; Eugene B. Andes and Ellen Coleman
Thomas Eugene, b. 8/7/1975 in Portsmouth; Eugene B. Andes and Ellen D. Coleman

ANDREWS,
son, b. 7/26/1899; second; Charles F. Andrews (painter, 25, Kennebunkport, ME) and Florence L. Thyng (19, Shapleigh, ME)

APPLETON,
Catherine Edith, b. 11/13/1961 in Rochester; Roland R. Appleton (beaterman's helper) and Merlyn E. Allen

ARLING,
Amanda Sue, b. 1/23/1989 in Dover; Richard N. Arling and Susan R. Crouse

ARMELL,
Rebecca Jane, b. 5/30/1986 in Dover; Eric M. Arnell and Irene L. Boulanger

ARNO,
Gerald LeRoy, b. 5/21/1925 in Milton Mills; fourth; Harold L. Arno (laborer, Wales, ME) and Bertha M. Danforth (Wales, ME); residence - Milton Mills

ASHWORTH,
son, b. 9/21/1905; first; John B. Ashworth (emp. in mill, 25, Sanford, ME) and Lillian Bean (25, Sanford, ME)

AUBERT,
Chesney Rae, b. 9/21/1989 in Rochester; David J. Aubert and Lisa Hutchins
Lindy Lee, b. 7/9/1981 in Wolfeboro; David J. Aubert and Shelby J. Bragg

AUCLAIR,
Joanne Doris, b. 9/15/1943 in Rochester; second; Frederic E. Auclair (navy yd. wkr., Middleton) and Doris M. Goodwin (Milton)
Leonard Albany, b. 6/18/1942 in Rochester; first; Frederick E. Auclair (mill employee, Middleton) and Doris M. Goodwin (Milton)

AVERY,
Craig Allen, b. 10/23/1988 in Dover; Brian A. Avery and Susan A. Shave
Gordon Mearl, b. 3/6/1947 in Rochester; seventh; Clifton A. Avery (logging, Rumney) and Phoebe H. Emery (Percy); residence - Milton Br.
Johnny B., b. 5/8/1986 in Dover; Brian A. Avery and Susan A. Shave
Louise P., b. 6/22/1897; second; Harry L. Avery (clerk, 34, Milton) and Hattie Pinkham (38, Milton)
Robert Harry, b. 8/17/1938 in Rochester; third; Theron W. Avery (fibre worker, Milton) and Emma L. Piper (Townsend, MA)
Theron W., b. 6/4/1895; first; Harry L. Avery (druggist, 31, Milton) and Hattie L. Pinkham (35, Milton)

AYER,
Charlotte Frances, b. 5/27/1937 in Wolfeboro; second; Richard E. Ayer (sch. bus dr., Newfield, ME) and Gertude V. Boisclair (Quincy, MA); residence - Milton Mills
Jane Elizabeth, b. 9/7/1944 in Rochester; first; Theodore H. Ayer (teacher, Milton Mills) and Priscilla H. Garrett (Rye); residence - Milton Mills
Rita Elizabeth, b. 3/19/1936 in Milton Mills; first; Richard E. Ayer (bus driver, Newfield, ME) and Gertrude V. Boisclair (Quincy, MA); residence - Milton Mills

AYERS,
Derick Stephen, b. 3/16/1987 in Rochester; Stephen E. Ayers and Lisa A. Moore

BABCOCK,
daughter, b. 7/18/1902; first; Raymond Babcock (shoemaker, 24, Falls Village) and Eva M. Gray (22, Brownfield, ME)

BADGER,
David F., Jr., b. 7/19/1947 in Dover; first; David F. Badger (landscaping, Oak Bluffs, MA) and Julienne T. Chaisson (Inverness, NS)

BAILEY,
Alice Faye, b. 9/16/1945 in Rochester; first; James B. Bailey (US Army, Erwin, TN) and Alice G. Tilton (Milton)
Bert Clifford, b. 1/8/1893; first; Clifford F. Bailey (shoe cutter, 21, Wells, ME) and Annie M. Dyer (22, Wakefield)
Clifton Irving, b. 9/10/1924; fourth; Alden H. Bailey (laborer, Hampstead) and Alice Wallingford (Milton)
Marion Estelle, b. 7/26/1916; first; Alden H. Bailey (laborer, Hampstead) and Alice Wallingford (Milton)
Melvin, b. 12/1/1918; third; Alden H. Bailey (laborer, Hampstead) and Alice Wallingford (Milton) (1924)
Michael Alan, b. 12/11/1974 in Rochester; Paul E. Bailey, Jr. and Stephanie J. Jacobs
Ralston Chester, b. 9/2/1917; second; Alden H. Bailey (emp. in mill, Hampstead) and Alice Wallingford (Milton)
Virginia Lynn, b. 10/14/1977 in Rochester; Paul E. Bailey, Jr. and Stephanie J. Jacobs

BAKER,
Andrew Edward, b. 4/2/1991 in Rochester; Harold A. Baker, Jr. and Penny J. Nason
Joelle Marlene Isabella, b. 8/23/1988 in Rochester; Lenard A. Baker and Brenda St. Hilaire
Kyle James, b. 8/18/1986 in Rochester; Harold A. Baker, Jr. and Penny J. Nason
Zachary Francis, b. 6/30/1991 in Rochester; John F. Baker and Kathleen A. Bouchard

BALL,
Abigail Edna-Elizabeth, b. 11/3/1998 in Dover; Robert Ball and Jody Ball

BALLANTINE,
Mabel F., b. 9/6/1891; second; Fred Ballantine (loom fixer, 27, Peabody, MA) and Maggie Fitzgerald (27, Peabody, MA)

BAMBERGER,
Katie Lynn, b. 10/28/1983 in Dover; Gary G. Bamberger and Alane Hollrock

BAMFORD,
Eric Ronald, b. 11/6/1977 in Rochester; Robert T. Bamford and Nancy E. Young

BANKS,
Arianna Alandra, b. 3/14/1995 in Rochester; Stanley D. Banks, III and Debora J. Banks
Daniel Joseph, b. 5/21/1970 in Kittery, ME; George J. Banks, Jr. and Virginia M. Potts
Kyle Stanley, b. 11/20/1987 in Rochester; Stanley D. Banks and Debora J. Huggard
Laura Anne, b. 6/2/1968 in Kittery, ME; George J. Banks, Jr. and Virginia M. Potts
Michael Joseph, b. 10/29/1964; sixth; George J. Banks (US Navy) and Virginia M. Potts
Shawnicee Marie, b. 6/6/1986 in Rochester; Stanley D. Banks, III and Deborah J. Huggard

BARCA,
David John, b. 5/1/1999 in Rochester; David Barca and Kelly Barca

BARKER,
Chaynna Lee, b. 5/9/1987 in Rochester; John A. Barker and Teena M. Seale
Robert Timothy, b. 8/23/1898; first; Robert S. Barker (shoecutter, 24, Stoneham, MA) and Alice B. Thompson (22, Boston, MA)
Ruth Morton, b. 8/21/1900; second; Robert S. Barker (shoe cutter, 27, Stoneham, MA) and Alice B. Thompson (25, Boston, MA)

BARLOW,
Thomas Patrick, b. 11/8/1907; third; Thomas J. Barlow (laborer, 37, Waltham, MA) and Mary M. McCormmack (23, Ireland)

BARRETT,
Carrie Ann, b. 2/14/1970 in Dover; James W. Barrett and Carole A. Provencher
Christina Alice, b. 7/9/1966 in Wolfeboro; James W. Barrett (factory worker) and Carole A. Provencher

BARRON,
Garrison Kade, b. 8/13/1999 in Rochester; Keith Barron and Janna Jerome

BARROW,
Irma Maralyn, b. 8/26/1920; first; Owen E. Barrow (laborer, Lyndon, CO) and Amy F. Hardy (Lyndeboro)

BARROWS,
Eleanor, b. 3/12/1911; first; Walter I. Barrows (civil engineer, Worcester, MA) and Lucy M. Hill (Charlton, MA)
Marjorie Lucille, b. 6/1/1919; third; Walter I. Barrows (civil engineer, Worcester, MA) and Lucy M. Hill (Charlton, MA)

BARTLETT,
Brian Edmon, b. 11/22/1967 in Rochester; first; Everette E. Bartlett (laborer) and Wanda J. Drew
Valerie Jean, b. 2/23/1971 in Rochester; Everett E. Bartlett and Wanda J. Drew

BASSETT,
daughter, b. 11/19/1900; first; Thomas B. Bassett (emp. in mill, 29, NB) and Lydia B. Young (18, Milton)
son, b. 5/21/1902; second; Thomas B. Bassett (mill, 30, Norton, NB) and Bessie L. Young (19, Milton)
son, b. 4/11/1903; third; Thomas B. Bassett (emp. in mill, 31, Norton, NB) and Bessie L. Young (20, Milton)
son, b. 4/18/1904; fourth; Thomas B. Bassett (shoemaker, 33, Norton, NB) and Bessie L. Young (21, Milton)

daughter, b. 10/2/1905; fifth; Thomas B. Bassett (shoemaker, 34, Norton, NB) and Bessie L. Young (22, Milton)

Clyde Franklin, b. 6/9/1896; third; Hazen Bassett (barber, 31, NB) and Nettie Cooley (27, Alton)

Jill Rebekah, b. 5/5/1979 in Rochester; Robert C. Bassett and Beverly J. McCarthy

Robert Charles, b. 3/12/1956 in Rochester; second; John L. Bassett (machinist, Peterborough) and Dorothy H. Pratt (Milford, MA)

BATES,
Arak Sebastian, b. 5/20/1999 in Rochester; Aubrey Bates and Kelly Guivens

BEAN[E],
son [Fred E.], b. 5/27/1899; third; Herbert L. Beane (RR sectionman, 39, Ossipee) and Iantha E. Knowles (32, Middleton)

daughter, b. 7/24/1902; second; Ernest C. Bean (mill, 21, Ossipee) and Ethel M. Brownell (21, Ossipee)

Alice Belle, b. 7/23/1901; fourth; Herbert L. Bean (mill hand, 42, Ossipee) and Iantha Knowles (35, Moultonboro)

Clayton Franklin, b. 3/1/1924; second; Henry E. Bean (boxmaker, Ossipee) and Ethel M. Ellis (Milton); residence - Rochester

Katherine Lois, b. 4/2/1946 in Rochester; Clayton F. Bean (mill worker, Milton) and Lucille M. Goodrow (New Durham)

Richard Francis, b. 1/18/1922; first; Henry E. Bean (laborer, Ossipee) and Ethel M. Ellis (Milton)

Roland Franklin, b. 8/28/1948 in Rochester; second; Clayton F. Bean (mill employee, Milton) and Lucille M. Goodrow (New Durham)

BEATON,
daughter, b. 6/17/1903; third; Hugh A. Beaton (telegraph operator, 29, Jefferson, OH) and Myrtle Hartshorne (27, Lunenburg, VT)

Leola, b. 2/4/1900; second; Hugh A. Beaton (telegraph operator, 26, Jefferson, OH) and Myrtle Hartshorne (25, Lunenburg, VT)

BEAUDOIN,
Kevin Joel, b. 10/28/1964 in Rochester; sixth; Gerard R. Beaudoin (self-employed) and Elaine M. Titus

Lydia Renee, b. 4/20/1995 in Dover; John R. Beaudoin and Vicki R. Beaudoin

BEAULIEU,
Joshua James, b. 6/28/1986 in Hanover; Joseph R. Beaulieu and Janet E. Tripp
Nikoma Michael, b. 4/9/1993 in Rochester; James M. Beaulieu and Rosita Cruz

BEGIN,
Lisa Ann, b. 7/12/1968 in Rochester; Wilfred J. O. Begin, Jr. and Andrea Zermani

BELANGER,
Deborah Lee, b. 2/14/1971 in Rochester; Louis J. Belanger, Jr. and Christine H. Canney
Edward Scott, b. 2/7/1972 in Rochester; Ronald A. Belanger and Kathleen M. Gautreau
Jeanine Ann, b. 3/2/1971 in Rochester; Ronald A. Belanger and Kathleen M. Gautreau

BELL,
Lena, b. 2/28/1913; fifth; Amedy Bell (laborer, Canada) and Phoebe Bonsent (Canada)
Mark Durand, b. 11/9/1967 in Dover; first; Philip D. Bell, Jr. (school principal) and Marlene A. Brigida

BELLEMENT,
Sofia, b. 1/13/1891; fourth; Charles Bellement (operative, 29, Canada) and Celina Jelenot (31, Canada)

BELLEMEUR,
Louise, b. 9/20/1920; third; William N. Bellemeur (laborer, Sanbornville) and Alta M. Jenness (Rochester)
Nellie, b. 10/2/1893; Charles Bellemeur (Canada) and Selina Gelinas (Canada) (1956)

BELLEVENCE,
son, b. 10/8/1916; eleventh; Joseph Bellevence (shoemaker, Canada) and Mary Thibault (Canada)

BELLMARE,
Travis Gary, b. 7/24/1982 in Rochester; Gary A. Bellmare and Susan C. Wells

BELLVILLE,
son, b. 2/6/1902; fifth; Fred Bellville (railroad, 38, Canada) and Celia Seymour (30, Canada)
Lillian, b. 10/22/1906; seventh; Fred Bellville (emp. on RR, 41, Canada) and Excila Seymore (34, Canada)
Theodore W. E., b. 2/13/1904; sixth; Fred Bellville (emp. on RR, 39, Canada) and Excila Seymore (32, Canada)

BENNETTE,
Ross John, b. 11/12/1989 in Laconia; John R. Bennette and Diane M. Baker

BENTLEY,
Travis Michael, b. 1/16/1985 in Rochester; Brian C. Bentley and Sandy L. Trask

BENTON,
Frances Alma, b. 4/11/1929 in Rochester; second; Edward Benton (truck driver, Sanbornton) and Lucilla Stillings (Wolfeboro)
Willard Edward, b. 4/7/1927; first; E. Maynard Benton (ice man, Sanbornton) and Lucilla M. Stillings (Wolfeboro)

BENTZLER,
Christopher Golden, b. 7/22/1975 in Rochester; Edward W. Bentzler and Donna L. Place

BERGER,
Brent Wheaton, b. 12/4/1991 in Rochester; Peter P. Berger and Gina R. Canney

BERGERON,
Patrick Dean, b. 6/8/1979 in Rochester; Christopher J. Bergeron and Sharon L. Canelas

BERNARD,
Krista Lee, b. 5/18/1984 in Dover; Donald E. Bernard and Michelle A. Mathews

BERRY,
son, b. 7/18/1891; second; Hiram H. Berry (horse dealer, 37, Milton) and Mary J. Hanson (40, Milton)
daughter [Beatrice], b. 10/10/1905; sixth; Jesse W. Berry (salesman, 28, Limington, ME) and Mabel M. Bodwell (26, Springvale, ME)
Alice, b. 8/21/1883 in Milton Mills; James E. Berry (S. Wakefield) and Abbie D. Buck (ME); residence - Milton Mills (1942)
Clifford Ashbel, b. 2/11/1880 in Milton Mills; third; Charles J. Berry (Milton) and Rosabelle Farnsworth (Rumney) (1932)
Nathan Miles, b. 10/22/1990 in Dover; Alfred M. Berry and Jill E. Aho
Sean Patrick, b. 9/3/1982 in Rochester; Scott Berry and Susan M. McNally

BESSON,
Felix, b. 3/2/1896; third; Frank Besson (laborer, 26, Canada) and Odelie Lochance (20, Canada)

BILL,
Susan Mabel, b. 5/12/1967 in Rochester; third; Edgar W. Bill (inspector) and Joyce A. Sweatt

BILODEAU,
Justin Andrew, b. 4/23/1986 in Rochester; Richard R. Bilodeau and Anne M. Foss
Lacey Leeanne, b. 11/10/1988 in Wolfeboro; Richard R. Bilodeau and Anne M. Foss

BINETTE,
Kristen Marie, b. 9/9/1995 in Rochester; Daniel P. Binette and Wendy E. Binette

BLACKMER,
Jacob Thomas, b. 5/29/1988 in Rochester; Thomas B. Blackmer and Janice Daykin

BLAIR,
Carol Ann, b. 4/14/1967 in Rochester; second; Leonard G. Blair (contractor) and Patricia M. Levesque
George Robert, b. 2/11/1934 in Rochester; first; Geneva Blair (VT)
Leonard Gould, b. 6/16/1928; second; Gould K. Blair (millwright, Laconia) and Rena D. Paey (Milton)
Pauline Dorothy, b. 3/29/1927; first; Gould K. Blair (carpenter, Laconia) and Rena D. Paey (Milton)
Wayne Leonard, b. 9/25/1963 in Rochester; Leonard G. Blair (carpenter) and Patricia M. Levesque

BLAISDELL,
Viola Belle, b. 3/4/1907; second; J. D. Blaisdell, Jr. (emp. in mill, 19, Lebanon, ME) and Bertha Cate (19, Durham)

BLANCHARD,
Earle Benjamin, Jr., b. 5/22/1970 in Dover; Earle B. Blanchard, Sr. and Virginia A. Phinney

BLANCHETTE,
Austin Nathaniel, b. 1/18/1990 in Portsmouth; Gerard A. Blanchette and Amy Beth Lashua

BLIER,
Timothy Michael, b. 8/25/1987 in Nashua; David M. Blier and Pierrette S. Viens

BLINN,
Jaime Beth, b. 6/30/1980 in Dover; Gregory J. Blinn and Joan E. Rousseau

BLOOD,
Ida Elizabeth, b. 12/20/1914; fourth; Alfred R. Blood (emp. in mill, E. Pepperell, MA) and Cora M. Blood (E. Pepperell, MA) (1915)

BLOUIN,
son [Onesime], b. 1/20/1900; first; James Blouin (emp. in mill, 27, Canada) and Emma Juyal (30, Canada)
daughter [Mary J. E.], b. 7/10/1903; third; Onesime Blouin (farmer, 30, Canada) and Emma Joyal (30, Canada)
son, b. 4/7/1906; fourth; James Blouin (farmer, 33, Canada) and Emma Joyal (36, Canada)
son, b. 1/27/1909; fifth; James Blouin (farmer, Canada) and Emma Joyal (Canada)
son, b. 9/17/1910; sixth; James Blouin (farmer, Canada) and Emma Joyal (Canada)
Albert, b. 1/1/1904; fifth; Joseph Blouin (shoemaker, 37, Canada) and Anna LaRochelle (31, Canada)
Joseph Fred Alexander, b. 5/10/1901; second; Onesime Blouin (mill hand, 28, Canada) and Emma Joyal (32, Canada)
Marie Emma, b. 5/10/1895; eleventh; Onesime Blouin (laborer, Canada) and Philomine Bisson (Canada) (1941)
Thea June, b. 6/10/1936 in Rochester; second; Victor Blouin (lea. b. wkr., Milton) and Marjorie Wallatedt (Boston, MA)

BOAK,
Robin Leslie, b. 11/16/1948 in Rochester; first; Robert S. Boak, Jr. (student, East Jaffrey) and Ruth P. Iovine (Boston, MA)

BODNAR,
Michelle Lynn, b. 5/13/1972 in Kittery, ME; James W. Bodnar and Rose Marie J. Gorlo

BODWELL,
son, b. 5/3/1911; second; Linwood C. Bodwell (laborer, Somersworth) and Myrtle G. Schofield (White Rock, NS)
Lindsey Jane, b. 5/24/1984 in Dover; Charles H. Bodwell and Sandra L. Taylor

BOGGS,
Eric Montgomery, b. 1/18/1964 in Rochester; sixth; Edwin K. Boggs (insurance agent) and Mary J. Richardson
Jefffrey Otis, b. 4/8/1960 in Rochester; fifth; Edwin K. Boggs, Jr. (insurance) and Mary J. Richardson

BOILEAU,
Heidi Ann, b. 7/14/1981 in Rochester; Raymond A. Boileau and Constance A. Cole

BOIS,
Marc Adrian, b. 9/27/1993 in Rochester; Randall M. Bois and Cheryl L. Allen

BOISVERT,
Christopher Michael, b. 7/3/1990 in Dover; David N. Boisvert and Gail L. Spencer
Roxann Marie, b. 4/12/1995 in Rochester; Paul J. Boisvert and Deborah J. Boisvert

BOLES,
Michael Alan, Jr., b. 10/3/1981 in Dover; Michael A. Boles, Sr. and Robin J. Sullivan
Nicholas Ryan, b. 1/30/1983 in Dover; Michael A. Boles, Sr. and Robin J. Sullivan
Rhonda Elaine, b. 5/14/1978 in Rochester; David M. Boles and Linda S. Ambrose
Tobi Lee, b. 8/17/1984 in Rochester; Michael A. Boles, Sr. and Robin J. Sullivan

BOLTON,
Edward Elliott, b. 12/1/1946 in Sanford, ME; fourth; Richard E. Bolton (lumberman, Concord) and Joyce G. Brown (Concord); residence - Milton Mills
Eric James, b. 8/9/1983 in Rochester; Charles R. Bolton and Rhonda J. Havu

BONNEY,
Carrie Lillian, b. 2/4/1881; Fred W. Bonney (Winthrop, ME) and Charlotte T. DeCoster (West Minot, ME) (1943)
George Herbert, b. 8/1/1957 in Wolfeboro; fifteenth; George H. Bonney (laborer, Townsend, MA) and Mamie Dunklee (Milford)

BOSTON,
Menola, b. 7/10/1890; third; Frederick B. Boston (day laborer, 34, North Berwick, ME) and Pauline Trafton (So. Berwick, ME)

BOSTROM,
Shana Elizabeth, b. 9/24/1988 in Rochester; Karl G. Bostrom, III and Jacqueline Pelletier

BOUCHARD,
Kyrie Ann, b. 8/30/1991 in Dover; Jay N. Bouchard and Melissa S. Martel
Lance Alexander, b. 12/12/1993 in Rochester; Jay N. Bouchard and Melissa S. Martel
Madison Belle, b. 9/24/1997 in Rochester; Jay N. Bouchard and Melissa S. Bouchard
Melanie Elizabeth, b. 6/11/1999 in Rochester; Jay Bouchard and Melissa Bouchard
Robert George, Jr., b. 12/26/1951 in Rochester; first; Robert G. Bouchard, Jr. (clerk, ME) and Helen E. Sceggell (Rochester)

BOUCHEE,
son, b. 12/11/1900; seventh; Sifrois Bouchee (emp. in mill, 45, Canada) and Julia Haggarty (36, Ireland)
stillborn son, b. 8/5/1903; eighth; Sifrais Bouchee (laborer, 46, Canada) and Julia Hagarty (45, Ireland)

BOUCHER,
Karen Kristine, b. 1/14/1977 in Dover; Phillip L. Boucher and Barbara R. Wampler
Nichole Ann, b. 5/16/1973 in Rochester; Phillip L. Boucher and Barbara R. Wampler

BOUGIE,
Andrew Allen, b. 1/14/1986 in Rochester; Roland P. Bougie and Jeannette N. Bilodeau

BOULANGER,
Brianna Marie, b. 4/8/1993 in Dover; Gary A. Boulanger and Donna M. Mulvey

BOULTON,
Ashleigh May, b. 12/2/1991 in Portsmouth; Conrad H. Boulton and
    Elizabeth A. Payne

BOURDEAU,
Alex Thomas, b. 9/2/1989 in Rochester; Thomas E. Bourdeau and
    Kathleen A. Cheney
Ashlee Maree, b. 4/20/1984 in Rochester; Robert W. Bourdeau and Lorrie
    L. Stuart
Erick Donald, b. 4/15/1991 in Rochester; Thomas E. Bourdeau and
    Kathleen A. Cheney

BOURGOIN,
Anthony Robert, b. 4/21/1982 in Rochester; Anthony E. Bourgoin and
    Sherolyn A. Keronen
Clifford Michael, b. 4/21/1982 in Rochester; Anthony E. Bourgoin and
    Sherolyn A. Keronen

BOURQUE,
Jacob Daniel, b. 9/21/1982 in Dover; Daniel C. Bourque and Suzanne M.
    Cantin
Tayla Marie, b. 12/4/1992 in Rochester; Paul J. Bourque and Patricia A.
    Young

BOURRE,
Christopher Scott, b. 2/28/1992 in Rochester; Jason S. Bourre and Sandra
    S. Colley

BOUSQUIN,
son, b. 10/10/1908; fourth; William Bonsquin (sic) (shoemaker, 27,
    Canada) and Leonia Stevens (29, Biddeford, ME)
Clarence E., b. 3/14/1904; second; William Bousquin (shoemaker, 26,
    Canada) and Leonia Stevens (23, Biddeford, ME)
Myrtle O., b. 1/22/1907; third; William Bosquin (sic) (shoemaker, 26,
    Canada) and Leonia Stevens (23, Biddeford, ME)

BOUTIN,
daughter, b. 2/21/1897; first; Joseph Bouten (sic) (fireman, 20, Canada)
    and Zelire Morin (20, Canada)

Joseph, b. 5/8/1899; second; Joseph Boutin (paper maker, 22, Canada) and Zalu Moren (23, Canada)

BOWDEN,
Sandra Jean, b. 12/23/1945 in Rochester; second; Pearl W. Bowden (mill worker, Penobscot, ME) and Hazel M. Tilton (Milton)
William Lee, b. 6/12/1949 in Rochester; fourth; Pearl W. Bowdin (sic) (mill employee, ME) and Hazel M. Tilton (NH)

BOWLEY,
Brenda Lee, b. 5/7/1956 in Rochester; first; Wayne Bowley (mach. opr., Rochester) and Barbara Lavalley (Sanford, ME); residence - Milton Mills
Leonard, b. 12/5/1959 in Rochester; third; Wayne H. Bowley (dyes leather, Rochester) and Barbara Lavalley (Sanford, ME); residence - Milton Mills
Michael Edward, b. 3/21/1962 in Rochester; Wayne H. Bowley (machine operator) and Barbara A. Lavalley
Pamela Jean, b. 12/17/1957 in Rochester; second; Wayne H. Bowley (research, Rochester) and Barbara Lavalley (Sanford, ME); residence - Milton Mills
Seth Rhea, b. 5/9/1977 in Wolfeboro; Freeman W. Bowley and Mary P. Alex
Sharon Ann, b. 12/31/1960 in Rochester; fourth; Wayne H. Bowley (tannery) and Barbara A. LaValley

BOYD,
Joseph Aratus, b. 7/2/1901; Joseph Boyd (Boston, MA) and Abby E. Shaw (Milton Mills) (1942)
Patricia Abbie, b. 12/20/1947 in Rochester; second; Joseph A. Boyd, Jr. (mechanic, Dover) and Thelma M. Murphy (Wilmington, DE)
Robert Ernest, b. 10/9/1965 in Rochester; William S. Boyd (engineer associate) and Evelyn M. Nason
William Joseph, b. 7/13/1961 in Rochester; William S. Boyd (US Navy) and Evelyn M. Nason
William Smith, b. 7/20/1940; fourth; Joseph A. Boyd (garage prop., Milton Mills) and Katherine R. Lougee (Rochester)

BOYERS,
Sarah Beth, b. 5/31/1983 in Wolfeboro; Brian G. Boyers and Kathryn J. Adams

Tyler Gage, b. 10/28/1986 in Exeter; Brian G. Boyers and Katheryn J. Adams

BRADEAU,
Emmeline, b. 12/12/1896; second; John Bradeau (mechanic, 23, St. John, NB) and Lizzie Bradeau (23, Kenzie, PQ)

BRAMWELL,
Jennie M., b. 4/12/1889; second; George H. Bramwell (spinner, 25, Franklin) and Emma A. Harris (19, Eastport, ME)

BRANNAN,
Betty Jean, b. 8/29/1959 in Rochester; first; George P. Brannan (shoeworker, Rochester) and Beverly A. Rouleau (W. Lebanon, ME)

BRANNON,
son, b. 7/19/1937 in Rochester; third; Norbert Brannon (disabled vet., E. Boston, ME) and Ruby Tufts (Middleton); residence - Milton Mills

BRAUDIS,
stillborn daughter, b. 8/30/1918; first; Arthur E. Braudis (emp. in mill, Rochester) and Bernis L. Page (Milton)

BRAWN,
Gordon, b. 11/30/1897; first; Fred L. Brawn (farmer, 31, Milton) and Edith M. Nute (23, Milton)

BREEDEN,
Kendrick Leigh, b. 2/1/1994 in Rochester; Arthur G. Breeden and Patricia J. Mellozzo

BREGY,
Marylynn Inez, b. 12/30/1989 in Rochester; David J. Bregy, Jr. and Sheryl P. Peak

BRETON,
Katelin Gabrielle, b. 10/18/1991 in Rochester; Michael Breton and Kathleen A. Doucette

BREWER,
Debra Ann, b. 1/11/1957 in Wolfeboro; third; Maurice H. Brewer (sealing, Royalston, MA) and Bertha Geary (Wolfeboro); residence - Milton Mills

Marvin Hollis, b. 1/10/1959 in Wolfeboro; fourth; Marcus H. Brewer (lumbering, Royalston, MA) and Bertha L. Geary (Wolfeboro); residence - Milton Mills

Tammie Lyn, b. 11/20/1955 in Rochester; second; Marcus Brewer (mill worker, NH) and Bertha Geary (NH); residence - Milton Mills

BROCHU,
Linda Yvonne, b. 7/18/1949; second; Leo P. Brochu (laborer, Sanford, ME) and June D. Durgin (Springvale, ME)

BROCK,
Derek Spencer, b. 10/25/1977 in Rochester; Alan J. Brock and Dorothy A. LaMontagne

Eunice Evelyn, b. 12/29/1909; second; Leslie C. Brock (engineer, Rochester) and Hattie E. Webber (No. Shapleigh, ME)

Harold Edison, b. 9/11/1908; first; Leslie C. Brock (fireman, 33, Rochester) and Hattie E. Webber (29, No. Shapleigh, ME)

Martha Annie, b. 7/9/1908; second; John B. Brock (laborer, 32, Pittsfield) and Annie M. Dyer (37, Sanbornville)

BRONSON,
Nicholas Gary, b. 2/4/1977 in Rochester; Gary L. Bronson and Jeanne M. Gregoire

BROOKS,
Andrea Jo, b. 5/22/1993 in Rochester; Gregory S. Brooks and Kimberly Jo Giguere

Michael Christopher, b. 5/11/1979 in Rochester; Samuel C. Brooks and Sylvia A. Amsler

Michael Ray, b. 3/22/1970 in Dover; Lee D. Brooks and Jeanette L. Cole

Samantha Nichole, b. 7/5/1992 in Rochester; Samuel C. Brooks and Coreen M. Taliaferro

BROWN,
Ambrose Minard, b. 9/11/1923; fourth; Ambrose M. Brown (mill hand, Brighton, MA) and Ora Blouin (Springvale, ME)
Amy Lynn, b. 8/13/1974 in Rochester; Keith M. Brown and Edith G. Cosgrove
Ashley Nicole, b. 3/14/1985 in Rochester; Howard M. Brown and Sharon R. Ivone
Bonnie Lee, b. 2/12/1950 in Rochester; second; William R. Brown (checker, MA) and Ramona Burroughs (NH)
Brady George, b. 7/12/1990 in Rochester; Robert L. Brown and Karen J. Goodell
Brianna Cea, b. 2/24/1989 in Rochester; Robert L. Brown and Karen J. Goodell
Brittney Jean, b. 9/13/1984 in Rochester; Robert L. Brown and Karen J. Goodell
Bryan Philip, b. 12/12/1986 in Rochester; Robert L. Brown and Karen J. Goodell
Cody Keith, b. 1/7/1997 in Portsmouth; Jason E. Brown and Wendy P. Brown
Erwin Maxwell, b. 1/18/1922; fourth; Lloyd E. Brown (laborer, Glenburn, ME) and Josephine E. Fabian (Mapleton, ME)
Gordon James, b. 4/2/1974 in Rochester; Dana E. Brown and Charlotte D. Hicks
Grace Emma A., b. 9/6/1932 in Rochester; fourth; Ambrose Brown (mill hand, Brighton, MA) and Ora Blouin (Springvale, ME)
Helen Ingeborg, b. 6/11/1960 in Rochester; second; Orlando W. Brown (sporting goods) and Joan O. Batchelor
Jason Tyler, b. 3/7/1986 in Rochester; James R. Brown and Diane M. Carpenter
John Victor, b. 8/12/1918; second; Ambrose M. Brown (emp. in mill, Brighton, MA) and Ora M. Blouin (Springvale, ME)
Joseph Michael, b. 10/25/1983 in Rochester; Howard M. Brown and Sharon R. Ivone
Joshua Wendell, b. 4/12/1987 in Dover; Wendell M. Brown and Priscilla DiPrizio

Joyce Elizabeth, b. 2/29/1920; third; Lloyd E. Brown (emp. in mill, Glenburn, ME) and Josephine E. Fabian (Mapleton, ME)

Kayla Mary, b. 7/19/1997 in Dover; Lee A. Brown, Sr. and Janice M. Brown

Kevin James, b. 6/29/1987 in Rochester; James R. Brown and Diane M. Carpenter

Lois Ernell, b. 1/31/1924; fifth; Lloyd E. Brown (mill hand, Glenburn, ME) and Josephine E. Fabian (Mapleton, ME)

Margaret Frances, b. 10/29/1916; fourth; Leslie M. Brown (machinist, Glenburn, ME) and Amy Nichols (Dover, ME)

Marie Olsen, b. 11/18/1958 in Rochester; first; Orlando Brown, Jr. (store owner, Sanford, ME) and Joan O. Batchelder (Brookline, MA)

Matthew Peter, b. 10/31/1987 in Rochester; Howard M. Brown and Sharon R. Ivone

Matthew Shane, b. 11/27/1986 in Wolfeboro; Mark W. Brown and April F. King

Michael Scott, b. 7/20/1983 in Rochester; Arthur R. Brown and Nancy J. Downs

Nicholas Robert, b. 12/2/1986 in Rochester; Arthur R. Brown and Nancy J. Downs

Ora M., b. 7/1/1915; first; Ambrose M. Brown (ice man, Brighton, MA) and Ora M. Blouin (Springvale, ME)

Philip Edward, b. 10/8/1920; fifth; Leslie M. Brown (machinist, Glenburn, ME) and Amy M. Nichols (Dover, ME)

Rick Matthew, b. 8/12/1988 in Rochester; Arthur R. Brown and Nancy J. Downs

Russell B., b. 1/20/1896; first; Russell B. Brown (shoemaker, 23, Cheshire, MA) and Mary T. Hubbard (20, Westfield, MA)

Thomas Howard, b. 2/26/1971 in Rochester; O. Wendell Brown and Joan O. Batchelder

William R., Jr., b. 12/10/1955 in Rochester; third; William R. Brown (laborer, MA) and Ramona Burroughs (Milton)

BRUCE,

Carolyn Lee, b. 3/17/1952 in Rochester; second; Kenneth R. Bruce (tool maker, Milton) and Marion A. Cole (Rochester)

David Kenneth, b. 5/20/1949 in Rochester; first; Kenneth R. Bruce (carpenter, ME) and Marion A. Cole (NH)

Donald Raymond, b. 6/22/1953 in Rochester; third; Kenneth Bruce (tool maker, Milton) and Marion Cole (East Rochester)
Douglas Paul, b. 6/21/1957 in Rochester; fifth; Kenneth Bruce (cable maker, Milton) and Marion Cole (East Rochester)
Harold Lincoln, b. 11/1/1897; first; Charles P. Bruce (shoemaker, 25, Boston, MA) and Emma Brown (19, Augusta, ME)
Jessie Elizabeth, b. 6/2/1991 in Wolfeboro; David K. Bruce and Colleen E. Lavertue
Kendra Jean, b. 5/3/1955 in Rochester; fourth; Kenneth Bruce (simplex co., Milton) and Marion A. Cole (East Rochester)
Kimberly Marion, b. 10/28/1988 in Wolfeboro; David K. Bruce and Colleen Lavertue

BRUNELLE,
Stephanie Diane, b. 2/17/1999 in Dover; John Brunelle and Georgia Brunelle

BUBAR,
Mary Elizabeth, b. 6/22/1946 in Rochester; first; Joseph B. Bubar (minister, Weston, ME) and Ruth E. Hughey (Waterboro, ME); residence - Milton Mills

BULLEMAN,
Kayla Marie, b. 4/11/1997 in Rochester; Corey M. Bulleman and Deanna M. Bulleman

BURBANK,
daughter, b. 2/19/1903; first; Harry L. Burbank (butcher, 26, Newfield, ME) and Sophronia Daniels (24, Newfield, ME)

BURBINE,
David H., b. 8/14/1919; third; David H. Burbine (emp. ice co., Wakefield, MA) and Marietta Doucette (NS)
David Henry, b. 4/11/1917; second; David H. Burbine (ice man, Wakefield, MA) and Marietta Doucette (NS)
John Alexander, b. 3/18/1927; sixth; David H. Burbine (laborer, Wakefield, MA) and Mary E. Doucette (Yarmouth, NS)
Joseph W., b. 6/13/1916; first; David H. Burbine (emp. ice house, Wakefield, MA) and Marietta Doucette (NS)

Louis Francis, b. 1/19/1922; fourth; David H. Burbine (laborer, Wakefield, MA) and Mary E. Doucette (Yarmouth, NS)
William Earl, b. 6/1/1924; fifth; David H. Burbine (laborer, Wakefield, MA) and Mary E. Doucette (Yarmouth, NS)

BURGESS,
Andrew Garrett, b. 3/26/1984 in Portsmouth; Kurt D. Burgess and Frankie L. McMahan

BURKE,
son, b. 8/18/1900; sixth; Edwin A. Burke (emp. in mill, 29, Wolfeboro) and Ethel Rollins (26, Wolfeboro)
Dana, b. 8/21/1894; third; Edwin A. Burke (shoemaker, 23, Wolfeboro) and Ethel Rollins (21, Wolfeboro)
Robert James, b. 2/10/1975 in Portsmouth; Russell K. Burke and Mary M. Christensen

BURNETT,
Kyle David, b. 3/12/1995 in Rochester; Walter A. Burnett, Jr. and Patricia A. Burnett
Ryan Allan, b. 4/21/1992 in Rochester; Walter A. Burnett, Jr. and Patricia A. Couch

BURNHAM,
Emily Jane, b. 2/23/1999 in Rochester; Gary Burnham and Claudine Burnham

BURNS,
Michael William, b. 10/13/1962 in Rochester; James J. Burns (veterinarian) and Lola A. Tanner
Peter Kirk, b. 12/31/1965 in Rochester; James Burns (veterinarian) and Lola A. Tanner
Susan Gail, b. 5/8/1950 in Sanford, ME; second; Robert I. Burns (mill spinner, Gorham, ME) and Sarah Ridlon (Sweden, ME)

BURROUGHS,
son, b. 4/28/1939; second; Wilfred W. Burroughs (shoe worker, Brookfield) and Emily E. Wallingford (Berwick, ME)

Eleanor Joyce, b. 7/14/1953 in Rochester; second; Warren Burroughs, Jr. (pipe fitter, Dover) and Rosamond Pecunies (Wolfeboro)
Eugene Wilbur, b. 7/19/1925; first; Warren D. Burroughs (ice man, Wolfeboro) and Madelene G. White (Rochester)
Eugene Wilbur, b. 5/4/1951 in Rochester; first; Warren D. Burroughs (lumber worker, Dover) and Rosamond Pecunies (Wolfeboro)
Jessica Jeanne, b. 5/19/1997 in Dover; Eugene W. Burroughs and Brenda L. Burroughs
Melody Irene, b. 2/7/1949 in Rochester; first; W. D. Burroughs, Jr. (veteran, NH) and Barbara J. Colby (MA)
Norma Rose, b. 5/18/1937 in Rochester; first; Wilfred Burroughs (shoe worker, Brookfield) and Emily Wallingford (Berwick, ME)
Ramona Isadore, b. 9/10/1926; second; Warren D. Burroughs (laborer, Wolfeboro) and Madeline G. White (N. Rochester)
Thelma Juanita, b. 5/21/1930; eighth; Carl M. Burroughs (sic) (laborer, Middleton) and Marion G. Rand (Milton)

BURROWS,
daughter [Martha A.], b. 11/10/1905; second; Will S. Burrows (teamster, 35, Milton) and Emma S. Knowles (35, Middleton)
Allen Michael, b. 4/6/1986 in Rochester; Jeffrey A. Burrows and Cheryl J. Hemenway
Anna Alberta, b. 9/26/1935 in Rochester; twelfth; Carl M. Burrows (lea. b. wkr., Middleton) and Marion G. Rand (Milton)
Carline, b. 10/13/1928; seventh; Carl M. Burrows (laborer, Middleton) and Marion G. Rand (Milton)
David Lloyd, b. 5/11/1972 in Rochester; Lloyd A. Burrows and Nancy L. Henderson
Edgar Eugene, b. 1/2/1933; tenth; Carl M. Burrows (mill hand, Middleton) and Marion G. Rand (Milton)
Eva May, b. 6/29/1890; second; Hevain J. Burrows (blacksmith, 35, Lebanon, ME) and Sarah E. Burrows (Cornish, ME)
Evelyn Mae, b. 11/18/1958 in Rochester; fifth; George D. Burrows (adm. & tech. sup., Milton) and Edna M. Scranton (Goshen)
Frances I., b. 3/10/1919; second; Carl M. Burrows (emp. in mill, Middleton) and Marion G. Rand (Milton)
George David, b. 3/26/1921; fourth; Carl L. Burrows (laborer, Middleton) and Marion G. Rand (Milton)

Kathryn Inez, b. 8/17/1966 in Rochester; George D. Burrows (mechanic) and Edna M. Scranton
Lincoln, b. 2/12/1923; fourth; Carl M. Burrows (mill hand, Middleton) and Marion G. Rand (Milton)
Lincoln, b. 1/4/1959 in Rochester; second; Luman K. Burrows (laborer, Milton) and Ruth A. Blanchard (Brentwood)
Lloyd Arthur, b. 2/25/1944 in Rochester; first; Ruth M. Burrows (Milton)
Luman Kenneth, b. 5/5/1934; eleventh; Carl M. Burrows (mill emp., Middleton) and Marion G. Rand (Milton)
Mary Ann, b. 8/30/1950 in Rochester; second; Daniel Burrows (student, NH) and Lucille Goodnow (NH)
Maud L., b. 5/31/1893; first; Will S. Burrows (shoe trimmer, 22, Milton) and Emma S. Knowles (22, Middleton)
Paul Edward, b. 11/22/1926 in Rochester; fifth; Carl M. Burrows (laborer, Middleton) and Marion G. Rand (Milton)
Rebecca Jane, b. 11/13/1962 in Rochester; George D. Burrows (A.S.T. Nat'l Guard) and Edna M. Scranton
Ruth Marion, b. 1/22/1924; fifth; Carl M. Burrows (laborer, Middleton) and Marion G. Rand (Milton)
Scott Alan, b. 9/27/1967 in Rochester; second; Lloyd A. Burrows (draftsman) and Nancy L. Henderson
Stephanie Lee, b. 6/6/1989 in Rochester; Steven R. Burrows and Karen Taatjes
Steven Richard, b. 8/8/1964 in Rochester; first; Lloyd A. Burrows (electrician) and Nancy L. Henderson
Susan Jill, b. 4/21/1961 in Rochester; George D. Burrows (adm. supply tech.) and Edna M. Scranton
Willard Carl, b. 8/17/1917; second; Carl M. Burrows (fireman, Middleton) and Marion G. Rand (Milton)

BUSH,
Lisa Lynn, b. 4/15/1966 in Rochester; Roger W. Bush (laster) and Alice F. Bailey

BUSQUE,
Michele Geraldine, b. 1/21/1973 in Rochester; Paul E. Busque and Bernice J. Blanchard

BUTLER,
son, b. 8/7/1927; ninth; Edward T. Butler (fireman, Hingham, MA) and Margaret J. Burbine (Wakefield, MA)
Ada Elizabeth, b. 2/3/1924; seventh; Edward T. Butler (laborer, Hingham, MA) and Margaret J. Burbine (Wakefield, MA)
Conrad Valentine, b. 12/8/1933; thirteenth; Edward T. Butler (fireman, Hingham, MA) and Margaret J. Burbine (Wakefield, MA)
Elizabeth Anne, b. 2/10/1945 in Manchester; first; Grace A. Butler (Milton)
Emily Skye, b. 2/25/1995 in Rochester; William M. Butler and Michelle L. Butler
George Fenton, b. 12/28/1929; eleventh; Edward T. Butler (fireman, Hingham, MA) and Margaret J. Burbine (Wakefield, MA)
Grace Ann, b. 8/7/1928; tenth; Edward T. Butler (fireman, Hingham, MA) and Margaret Burbine (Wakefield, MA)
John Pierce, b. 10/5/1919; fourth; Edward T. Buttler (sic) (emp. ice co., Hingham, MA) and Margaret J. Burbine (Wakefield, MA)
Margaret Ellen, b. 9/6/1917; third; Edward T. Butler (laborer, Hingham, MA) and Margaret Burbine (Wakefield, MA)
Maynard Erwin, b. 8/27/1931; twelfth; Edward T. Butler (leatherboard mill, Hingham, MA) and Margaret Burbine (Wakefield, MA)
Patrick, b. 8/2/1922; sixth; Edward T. Butler (laborer, Hingham, MA) and Margaret J. Burbine (Wakefield, MA)
Thomas V., b. 6/11/1926; eighth; Edward T. Butler (laborer, Hingham, MA) and Margaret J. Burbine (Wakefield, MA)
Walter Francis, b. 2/18/1921; fifth; Edward T. Butler (laborer, Hingham, MA) and Margaret J. Burbine (Wakefield, MA)

BYRNE,
Alice Marie L.O., b. 9/22/1905; first; Thomas Byrne (emp. in mill, 23, England) and Zenaide Therien (28, Canada)

CALDWELL,
Ryan Thomas, b. 10/29/1980 in Dover; Walter L. Caldwell, Jr. and Emily S. Royce

CALKINS,
daughter, b. 2/20/1891; fourth; Henry G. Calkins (29, Lubec, ME) and Emma M. Lancaster (27, Lubec, ME)

CALL,
Myles Garritt, b. 10/1/1997 in Rochester; Wayne E. Call and Kelley L. Call

CAMLIN,
Sean David, b. 7/20/1990 in Rochester; David R. Camlin and Carole L. Condon

CAMPBELL,
Inez E., b. 12/10/1893; first; Ernest C. Campbell (shoe cutter, Barnard, VT) and Mary E. Perkins (Acton, ME)

CANNEY,
Alan Richard, b. 4/16/1967 in Rochester; second; John B. Canney (machine tender) and Roberta C. Marcoux

CARIGNAN,
Benjamin Venuto, b. 3/22/1978; John O. Carignan and Patricia A. Browne

CARINDON,
Goldie Earlene, b. 2/17/1953 in Rochester; third; Stanley Carindon (plumber, unknown) and Alfreda M. Smith (Rochester)

CARLE,
Jessica Anne, b. 5/25/1974 in Wolfeboro; Richard N. Carle and Anita L. Buonocore
Nathan James, b. 12/20/1976 in Wolfeboro; Richard N. Carle and Anita L. Buonocore

CARNEY,
Alison Lane, b. 7/10/1983 in Rochester; Thomas J. Carney and Tracy A. Wadsworth

CARON,
son, b. 4/17/1903; second; Conrad J. Caran (sic) (emp. in mill, 32, Canada) and Mary L. Caron (28, Canada)
Joseph C.P.E., b. 11/19/1906; fourth; Conrad Caron (emp. in mill, 36, Canada) and Marie L. Caron (32, Canada)

Joseph Louis George, b. 12/6/1908; fifth; Conrad Caron (emp. in mill, 38, Canada) and Marie L. Caron (34, Canada)

M.J.L. David P., b. 7/24/1905; third; Conrad Caran (sic) (emp. in mill, 35, Canada) and Marie Louise Caran (31, Canada)

CARPENTER,
Ernest Arthur, b. 11/23/1923; first; Roland Carpenter (mill hand, Rollinsford) and Hazel Trumbull (Webster)

Richard Dale, b. 3/18/1936 in Rochester; second; Harold Carpenter (foreman, Rollinsford) and Ethel Randlett (Littleton)

Sylvia Corinne, b. 11/11/1932 in Rochester; first; Harold Carpenter (foreman, Rollinsford) and Ethel Randlett (Littleton)

CARR,
Dylan Steven, b. 1/16/1991 in Rochester; Edward F. Carr and Susan M. Perry

CARRIER,
Thomas Roger, b. 6/22/1986 in Dover; Dennis R. Carrier and Pamela J. Pennell

CARSWELL,
Brian Lee, b. 1/21/1963 in Rochester; Fred E. Carswell (antiques) and Dorothy L. Wilder

Elizabeth Ann, b. 12/5/1961 in Rochester; Fred E. Carswell (self employed) and Dorothy L. Welder

Fred Eugene, b. 7/1/1925 in Rochester; second; Fred Carswell (merchant, Denver, CO) and Frances E. Ayer (Maplewood, ME); residence - Milton Mills (1926)

Neil William, b. 5/16/1953 in Rochester; third; Fred E. Carswell, Jr. (millworker) and Dorothy L. Wilder (1960)

Robert Eugene, b. 11/21/1949 in Rochester; second; Fred E. Carswell (clerk, Rochester) and Dorothy L. Wilder (Fitchburg, MA)

CARTER,
Jeanne Marie, b. 11/11/1949 in Rochester; second; Donald L. Carter (store keeper, Plainfield, NJ) and Martha A. Tablar (Honduras)

Joshua Cyril, b. 4/29/1991 in Exeter; Duncan E. Carter and Laura A. Baldasaro

Phillip Ian, b. 8/28/1987 in Rochester; Kevin J. Carter and Deborah L. Gelinas

CARY,
Ingrid Helen, b. 7/15/1984 in Rochester; Raymond J. Cary and Beverly G. Hellman
Laurinda Ruth, b. 3/6/1964 in Rochester; third; John R. Cary (woodsman) and Dorothy M. Atkinson

CASAVANT,
Walter James, b. 5/4/1938 in Rochester; first; Joseph W. Casavant (shoe worker, Middleton) and Mary D. Fosset (E. Boston, MA)

CASEY,
William Edward, b. 11/12/1935; fifth; William E. Casey (farmer, Ireland) and Hazel M. Emery (N. Gloucester, ME)

CATALDO,
Adam William, b. 12/27/1974 in Rochester; Albert W. Cataldo, Jr. and Roberta T. Permatteo
Diane Marie, b. 2/24/1970 in Rochester; Albert W. Cataldo, Jr. and Roberta T. Permatteo
Donna Linda, b. 10/29/1976 in Rochester; Albert W. Cataldo, Jr. and Roberta T. Permatteo

CATES,
Alfred Tibby, b. 4/29/1906; first; Alfred A. cates (teamster, 33, Harrison, ME) and Florence Richardson (28, Wentworth's Location)

CAUCHEE,
son, b. 11/4/1903; first; Joseph Cauchee (emp. in mill, 25, Canada) and Lydia Therrian (22, Canada)

CERNIAUSKAS,
Julia Elizabeth, b. 12/19/1991 in Rochester; Vytas A. Cerniauskas and Teresa L. Bell
Kristina May, b. 5/15/1997 in Rochester; Vytas A. Cerniauskas and Teresa L. Cerniauskas

CHABOT,
Mindy Jo, b. 4/28/1981 in Rochester; Henry J. Chabot and Mary A. Hanson

CHADWICK,
Emily Kristine, b. 9/12/1990 in Portsmouth; Bruce A. Chadwick and Anne E. Murphy

CHAMBERL[A]IN,
Elizabeth Jane, b. 4/12/1952 in Rochester; second; Howard Chamberlain (machine oper., Brockton, MA) and Eleanor K'yzanowski (Dickson City, PA)
Gardiner S., b. 7/3/1909; second; Guy H. Chamberlain (laborer, Wakefield) and Elizabeth E. Cunningham (Scotland)
M. E., b. 12/23/1891; first; Telesford Chamberlain (teamster, 24, Canada) and Eugenie Marchand (22, Canada)
Mark Howard, b. 10/2/1954 in Rochester; third; Howard Chamberlain (foreman, Brockton, MA) and Eleanor K'sanowski (Dickson City, PA)
Muriel, b. 8/18/1917; sixth; Guy H. Chamberlain (ice man, Union) and Elizabeth Cunningham (Scotland)
Pearl, b. 11/14/1893; second; Fred M. Chamberlin (hotel keeper, 34, Milton) and Grace M. Dicey (26, Wakefield)

CHANDLER,
daughter, b. 3/10/1891; first; Albert E. Chandler (shoe cutter, Lynn, MA) and Ruth Hartford (Rochester)
stillborn son, b. 2/10/1921; first; Joseph L. Chandler (laborer, Groton) and Gladys A. Hoyt (Rochester)

CHANDRONAIS,
Belzimire, b. 3/22/1880 in Milton Mills; second; Clovis Chandronais (mill worker, Canada) and Beatrice Morin (Canada); residence - Milton Mills (1938)

CHAPMAN,
stillborn daughter, b. 8/16/1937 in Rochester; third; Fred Chapman (engineer, Haverhill) and Irene Acton (Laconia)

stillborn daughter, b. 6/25/1938; fourth; Fred A. Chapman, Jr. (stationary eng., Haverhill) and Irene Acton (Laconia)

CHASE,
Amanda Elizabeth, b. 8/4/1993 in Rochester; James F. Chase and Kellie-Ann Pomeroy
Arthur Leonard, b. 2/10/1912; third; George H. Chase (shoemaker, 31, Cambridge, MA) and Addie G. Willey (26, Wakefield)
Betty Joanne, b. 7/17/1933 in Rochester; sixth; George H. Chase (laborer, Cambridge, MA) and Adeline Willey (Wakefield)
Carol Ann, b. 12/11/1979 in Rochester; Charles E. Chase and Carol A. Sullivan
Cheryl Ann, b. 6/7/1963 in Rochester; Richard W. Chase (salesman) and Joan E. McQuade
George Albert, b. 8/2/1946 in Rochester; third; Leslie O. Chase (A. Supt. M., East Rochester) and Doris L. Fortier (Chocorua)
Kelly Ivie, b. 9/16/1980 in Portsmouth; Robert L. Chase and Jennifer E. Brawn
Leslie Oliver, b. 1/26/1935 in Rochester; first; Leslie O. Chase (office clerk, Milton) and Doris L. Fortier (Chocorua)
Leslie Oliver, III, b. 6/22/1959 in Rochester; first; Leslie O. Chase, 2nd (electrician, Rochester) and Marilyn R. Hoadley (Concord)
Melissa May, b. 3/25/1983 in Rochester; Charles E. Chase and Carol A. Sullivan
Nancy Weymouth, b. 4/21/1937 in Rochester; second; Leslie O. Chase (foreman, Milton) and Doris Fortier (Tamworth)
Olive A., b. 5/9/1914; fourth; George H. Chase (shoemaker, Cambridge, MA) and Addie G. Willey (Wakefield)
Randall Arthur, b. 7/1/1953 in Rochester; second; Arthur L. Chase (carpenter, Milton) and Dorothy Gathmann (Oak Park, IL)
Richard White, IV, b. 2/27/1982 in Dover; Richard W. Chase, III and Joan E. O'Brien
Roger Eugene, b. 1/2/1951 in Rochester; first; Arthur L. Chase (carpenter, Milton) and Dorothy L. Gathman (Oak Park, IL)
Theresa Olivia, b. 4/17/1919; fifth; George H. Chase (shoemaker, Cambridge, MA) and Addie G. Willey (Wakefield)

CHASSE,
Chris Michael, b. 6/1/1963 in Rochester; Gilbert A. Chasse (supply clerk) and Gail E. Columbus
Michael Keith, b. 2/1/1965 in Rochester; Gilbert A. Chasse (office clerk) and Gail E. Columbus

CHENEY,
Colleen Jayne, b. 7/24/1962 in Rochester; Donald A. Cheney (construction) and Diane L. Varney
Donald Arthur, b. 8/17/1941 in Rochester; fourth; Richard H. Cheney (lea'bd worker, Whitefield) and Doris V. Brock (Boston, MA)
Helen Doris, b. 3/22/1931; first; Richard H. Cheney (leatherboard mill, Whitefield) and Doris V. Brock (Boston, MA)
Irene Frances, b. 5/8/1933; second; Richard H. Cheney (mill hand, Whitefield) and Doris Brock (Boston, MA)
Joyce Lucille, b. 3/14/1938 in Rochester; third; Richard H. Cheney (lea. worker, Whitefield) and Doris V. Brock (Boston, MA)
Karen Lee, b. 9/7/1966 in Rochester; Donald A. Cheney (equipment operator) and Dianne L. Varney
Kathleen Ann, b. 11/22/1963 in Rochester; Donald A. Cheney (const. worker) and Diane L. Varney
Mary Ida, b. 2/17/1923; first; Walter L. Cheney (laborer, Gonic) and Velena M. Ellis (Milton)
Robert Arthur, b. 5/21/1927; fourth; Walter L. Cheney (laborer, Gonic) and Valena M. Ellis (Milton)

CHESLEY,
Evelyn Gertrude, b. 7/11/1880 in Milton Mills; George L. Chesley (NH) and Mary A. Archibald (NH); residence - Milton Mills (1942)

CHICK,
Jamie Michael, b. 4/26/1982 in Portsmouth; Brian M. Chick and Donna L. Fernald

CHIKREOTIS,
James, b. 11/8/1914; first; Michael Chikreotis (baker, C'ts'p'd'n, Greece) and Deni Mikrees (Budeay, Greece)

CHIPMAN,
daughter, b. 6/25/1906; fifth; Edward Chipman (shoemaker, 39, Natick, MA) and Bertha M. Drew (40, Milton)
Alta, b. 9/16/1895; third; Edward Chipman (mill operative, 28, Natick, MA) and Bertha M. Drew (29, Milton)
Clara Eleanor, b. 2/12/1904; fourth; Edward Chipman (emp. in mill, 37, Natick, MA) and Bertha M. Drew (37, Milton)
Ralph, b. 6/28/1893; second; Edward S. Chipman (leatherboard office, 26, Natick, MA) and Bertha M. Drew (27, Milton)

CHRISTENSEN,
Stephen Roy, b. 11/27/1963 in Rochester; Arthur R. Christensen (minister) and Joan B. Elms
Thomas Jacob, b. 4/13/1965 in Rochester; Arthur R. Christensen (minister) and Joan B. Elms

CHRISTIE,
Arthur Willard, b. 9/20/1962 in Dover; Paul H. Christie (truck driver) and Marilyn C. Hamilton
John William, b. 10/18/1961 in Dover; Paul H. Christie (truck driver) and Marilyn C. Hamilton
Paul Harold, Jr., b. 11/18/1960 in Dover; first; Paul H. Christie (truck driver) and Marilyn C. Hamilton

CIBEL,
Aaron Christopher, b. 1/12/1973 in Bitburg, Germany; Stanley A. Cibel, Jr. and Veronica Morits

CICCOTELLI,
Brenton Paul, b. 4/19/1990 in Dover; Paul S. Ciccotelli and Joyce E. Cook

CICIRELLI,
Anthony Joseph, b. 9/21/1984 in Dover; Joseph S. Cicirelli and Kelli D. Magowan

CLARK,
Benjamin Nicholas, b. 9/16/1997 in Dover; Steven A. Clark and Christine E. Clark

Mabel F., b. 9/21/1893; first; George P. Clark (spinner, 22, Great Falls) and Katie E. Lewis (22, England)

CLAYTON,
Carlyne Melvina, b. 1/8/1918; second; George W. Clayton (shoe cutter, Truro, NS) and Emma V. Columbus (Wakefield); residence - East Rochester
Graham O., b. 8/22/1916; first; George W. Clayton (shoe cutter, Truro, NS) and Emma V. Columbus (Wakefield); residence - East Rochester

CLEAVES,
Donna Lee, b. 2/13/1952 in Wolfeboro; first; James S. Cleaves (machinist, MA) and Marguerite Titcomb (MA)
Frances Elizabeth, b. 1/10/1914; fifth; Thomas L. Cleaves (emp. in mill, Boston, MA) and Stella C. Flagg (Perry, ME)
Harold L., b. 3/1/1915; sixth; Thomas L. Cleaves (emp. in mill, Boston, MA) and Stella Flagg (Perry, ME)
James Anthony, b. 8/8/1943 in Rochester; first; Walter T. Cleaves (marine driver, Lynn, MA) and Elaine D. Haase (Jamaica, W. Indies)
Margaret Isabel, b. 10/10/1922; fourth; George N. Cleaves (laborer, Milton, MA) and Vivian P. McGregor (Roxbury, MA)
Robert Wayne, b. 10/28/1946 in Rochester; second; Walter T. Cleaves (mar. diver, Lynn, MA) and Elaine D. N. Haase (Jamaica, BWI)

CLEMENT,
George W., b. 4/30/1894; first; James W. Clement (spinner, 22, Gorham) and Lena King (21, Wartes, PQ)
Kathelene Lula, b. 10/22/1924 in Milton Mills; sixth; Ralph W. Clement (teaming, Moultonboro) and Kathelene Hagan (Lawrence, MA); residence - Milton Mills
Norman Joseph, b. 6/11/1923; fifth; Ralph W. Clement (lumberman, Moultonboro) and Catherine Hennigan (Lawrence, MA)

CLEMENTS,
daughter, b. 7/4/1896; second; Charles Clements (laborer, 25, Wakefield) and Harriett Goodwin (21, Milton)

CLEVELAND,
Elizabeth R., b. 4/24/1949 in Rochester; stillborn; first; Raymond L. Cleveland (lab. tech., NH) and Lucille M. Pontbriand (ME); residence - Rochester
Raymond Lester, b. 9/1/1920; first; Willard C. Cleveland (laborer, Otisfield, ME) and Ruth O. Stillings (Boston, MA)

CLICHE,
Alison Rae, b. 6/7/1978 in Rochester; Stephen P. Cliche and Diane L. Hobbs
Derek Stephen, b. 10/17/1980 in Rochester; Stephen P. Cliche and Diane L. Hobbs

CLIFFORD,
Sandi Marie, b. 11/15/1971 in Kittery, ME; Loren O. Clifford and Teresa R. Elliott

CLOUGH,
Darrin Jay, b. 3/30/1977 in Wolfeboro; David J. Clough, Sr. and Terri L. Goodwin
Fred Ellsworth, b. 5/29/1924 in Milton Mills; second; Warren C. Clough (laborer, Effingham) and Marguerite Weeks (Milton Mills); residence - Milton Mills
Fred Ellsworth, Jr., b. 1/27/1952 in Rochester; third; Fred E. Clough (mill worker, Milton) and Janette E. Houston (N. Shapleigh, ME)
Gerald Herbert, b. 12/17/1953 in Rochester; second; Herbert E. Clough (Milton) and Colleen J. Morrill (Brookfield)
Gloria, b. 12/24/1930 in Milton Mills; third; Dennis F. Clough (woolen mill, Berwick, ME) and Mamie V. Marsh (Acton, ME); residence - Milton Mills
Gordon Wayne, b. 3/27/1959 in Rochester; third; Leon E. Clough (inspector, Milton Mills) and Eleanor L. Gordon (Acton, ME); residence - Milton Mills
Gregory Leon, b. 11/4/1951 in Rochester; second; Leon E. Clough (store mgr., Milton Mills) and Eleanor Gordon (Acton, ME)
Herbert Eugene, b. 7/24/1930 in Milton Mills; third; Warren C. Clough (weaver, Effingham) and Marguerite Weeks (Milton Mills); residence - Milton Mills

Herman Franklin, b. 3/27/1908; first; Dennis Clough (shoemaker, 21, Milton) and Elsie M. Tinker (16, Wolfeboro)

Juanita, b. 9/17/1933 in Milton Mills; fourth; Warren C. Clough (weaver, Effingham) and Marguerite D. Weeks (Milton Mills); residence - Milton Mills

Leon Edward, b. 9/16/1922; first; Warren C. Clough (laborer, Effingham) and Marguerite Weeks (Milton)

Sandra Lee, b. 10/26/1949 in Rochester; first; Leon E. Clough (mill employee, NH) and Eleanor L. Gordon (ME)

Valerie Lynn, b. 6/23/1963 in Rochester; Leon E. Clough (sorter, tannery) and Eleanor L. Gordon

CLOUTIER,

Heidi Maria, b. 1/31/1996 in Rochester; Jeffrey J. Cloutier and Maria C. Cloutier

CLUFF,

Lulu R., b. 9/4/1899; second; Asa W. Cluff (laborer, 38, Alfred, ME) and Lizzie E. Morton (44, Augusta, ME)

COLBATH,

John Sumner, b. 2/26/1912; second; John S. Colbath (shoemaker, 26, Dover) and Annie B. Jellison (22, N. Berwick, ME)

Morgan Marsh, b. 1/8/1997 in Rochester; Jeremiah G. Colbath and Amy L. Colbath

COLBY,

Stacey Ann, b. 2/2/1991 in Rochester; Barry A. Colby and Christine M. Ronayne

COLLINS,

daughter, b. 12/13/1889; first; Stephen Collins and Sadie L. Shortridge (18, Brookfield)

Alice Thelma, b. 1/4/1921; second; Lester E. Collins (emp. in mill, Alton) and Hazel A. Grace (Tamworth)

Jake Merrill, b. 10/18/1937 in Rochester; eighth; Raymond Collins (lumberman, S. Berwick, ME) and Alice Bailey (Belfast, ME)

Patrick Virgil, b. 8/20/1963 in Rochester; Warner V. Collins (shoe worker) and Lorrette A. Roy

COLSON,
Shannon Elizabeth, b. 10/29/1997 in Rochester; David J. Colson and Sheila B. Colson

COLTON,
Estelle, b. 3/23/1891; fifth; Cyrus S. Colton (mill operative, 39, Ossipee) and Lucy A. Lang (32, Brookfield)

COLUMBUS (see Coulombe),
Albert Francis, b. 7/29/1942 in Rochester; third; Albert H. Columbus (mach. oper., Milton) and Marjorie Benner (Jamaica Plain, MA)
Charles, b. 11/7/1902; eighth; Adelon W. Columbus (laborer, 39, Canada) and Melvina Howle (33, Milton)
Emily Alice, b. 12/15/1912; second; Arthur N. Columbus (shoemaker, 25, Milton) and Flora H. Boisvert (27, Somersworth)
Emily Mabel, b. 4/28/1905; ninth; William O. Columbus (laborer, 42, Canada) and Melvina Hall (35, Milton)
Jennette Louise, b. 8/16/1915; third; Arthur Columbus (truckman, Milton) and Flora Boisvert (Somersworth)
Joanne Elizabeth, b. 1/25/1942 in Rochester; second; Raynold G. Columbus (truck driver, Newton, MA) and Florence R. Pheault (Berwick, ME)
Marie Thelma, b. 6/29/1919; fifth; Arthur N. Columbus (truckman, Milton) and Florence H. Boisvert (Somersworth)
Ruth, b. 12/11/1916; fourth; Arthur N. Columbus (truckman, Milton Mills) and Flora H. Boisvert (Somersworth)
Thelma Louise, b. 8/19/1940 in Rochester; first; Reynold G. Columbus (truck driver, Somersworth) and Florence R. Pheault (Berwick, ME)

CONNELL,
Maynard Arthur, b. 6/1/1920; second; Edward A. Connell (laborer, Littleton, MA) and Ione E. Beaton (Lunenburg, VT)
Phyllis M., b. 7/4/1917; first; Edward A. Connell (ice man, Littleton, MA) and Ione E. Beaton (Lunenburg, VT)
Shirley Elaine, b. 1/30/1923; third; Edward A. Connell (ice man, Tyngsboro, MA) and Ione E. Beaton (Lunenburg, VT)

CONNELLY,
daughter, b. 3/17/1889; fourth; T. Connerly (sic), Jr. (cloth finisher, 33, Union) and Clara Lowd (28, Acton, ME)
Raymond, b. 3/24/1891; fifth; Timothy Connelly, Jr. (operative, 36, Union) and Clara Lord (31, Acton, ME)

CONNERS, [see Connor, O'Connor]
Harold Henry, b. 5/11/1901; seventh; Michael A. Conners (mill hand, 38, Salem, MA) and Carrie Schroeder (27, Boston, MA)
Rudolph Augustus, b. 1/30/1905; eighth; Michael A. Conners (laborer, 42, Ireland) and Carrie F. Schroeder (32, Boston, MA)

CONNOR, [see Conners, O'Connor]
Henry F., b. 9/5/1906; ninth; Michael Connor (emp. in mill, 46, Ireland) and Carrie Schroeder (34, Boston, MA)

CONRAD,
daughter, b. 3/15/1908; eighth; John F. Conrad (shoemaker, 35, St. George, NB) and Lelia McLaughlin (30, NB)

CONTOIS,
Mona Elizabeth, b. 5/10/1959 in Rochester; stillborn; Carl Contois (teacher, Lebanon) and Arlene Abbott (Ossipee); residence - Candia

COOK,
Amy Louise, b. 5/14/1986 in Dover; Raymond N. Cook and Merle L. Stowe
James Edward, b. 9/9/1991 in Rochester; James E. Cook and Melissa I. Perkins
Kyanna Nicole, b. 1/9/1999 in Rochester; David Cook and Jolene Cook

COOKSON,
Murial Elaine, b. 4/30/1919 in Madison, ME; second; Leon M. Cookson (electrician, Mt. Vernon, ME) and Hazel G. Porter (Farmington, ME)

COOPER,
Patricia Rose, b. 2/14/1996 in Wolfeboro; Dale H. Cooper and Patricia A. Cooper

Sarah Alexandra, b. 9/5/1982 in Rochester; Dale H. Cooper and Sarah R. Brown

COPLEY,
Betty Dianne, b. 8/14/1948 in Rochester; third; Henry W. Copley (junk dealer, Lynn, MA) and Nancy E. Ferguson (Georgetown, MA)

COPP,
Thelma Althea, b. 4/20/1920; sixth; Arthur L. Copp (emp. in mill, Bangor, ME) and Rena V. Bean (Ossipee)

CORMIER,
Chelsea Marie, b. 3/4/1992 in Rochester; Jeffery C. J. Cormier and Sandra Berge
David Joseph, b. 3/27/1989 in Dover; James J. Cormier and Wendi A. Matteson
Drake Cameron, b. 5/12/1991 in Dover; Dale G. Cormier and Deborah A. Labrie
Rachel Anne, b. 3/16/1988 in Dover; James J. Cormier and Wendi Matteson

CORRIVEAU,
Heather Marie, b. 5/17/1995 in Dover; Thomas A. Corriveau and Martha Corriveau
Jessica Ann, b. 7/22/1998; Thomas A. Corriveau and Martha Corriveau
Ryan Henry, b. 11/18/1997 in Dover; Roger A. Corriveau and Linda M. Corriveau

CORSON,
daughter, b. 9/9/1888; Leroy F. Corson (shoe operative, Milton) and Winora J. Corson (Lebanon, ME)
son, b. 9/5/1893; fifth; Leroy F. Corson (McKay stitcher, Milton) and Winora Jones (Lebanon, ME)
daughter [Mary L.], b. 1/2/1901; fourth; John M. Corson (mill hand, 28, Dover) and Eva M. Postleton (23, Acton, ME)
Annie, b. 4/18/1907; fifth; John M. Corson (laborer, 34, Milton) and Eva M. Postleton (30, Acton, ME)
Bessie M., b. 7/20/1877; third; James M. Courson (sic) (shoe worker, Lisbon, ME) and Emma F. Rand (New Durham) (1940)

Draxa, b. 2/12/1911; first; George N. Corson (drug clerk, Milton) and Bessie M. Laskey (Milton)
Edwin, b. 8/30/1896; sixth; Leroy F. Corson (laborer, 39, Milton) and Winora W. Jones (35, Lebanon, ME)
Gladys F., b. 10/20/1897; first; John M. Corson (shoe cutter, 24, Dover) and Eva M. Postleton (21, Acton, ME)
Leo Henry, b. 3/6/1899; third; John M. Corson (farmer, 26, Dover) and Eva M. Postleton (21, Acton, ME)
Leon Monroe, b. 3/6/1899; second; John M. Corson (farmer, 26, Dover) and Eva M. Postleton (21, Acton, ME)

COTA,
Ava Lynn, b. 8/12/1999 in Rochester; Shawn Cota and Maryann Guyer

COTE,
Dorothy, b. 10/6/1927 in Milton Mills; second; Joseph Cote (farmer, Fall River, MA) and Marie A. Gagne (Sandy Bay, Canada); residence - Milton Mills
Edith, b. 6/16/1929; third; Joseph Cote (farmer, Fall River, MA) and Marie A. Gagne (Sandy Bay, Canada)

COTTON,
daughter, b. 1/26/1897; fourth; Benjamin D. Cotton (laborer, 40, Milton) and Phoebe L. Tibbetts (24, Rochester)

COUCH,
Randy William, Jr., b. 1/28/1987 in Rochester; Randy W. Couch and Susan M. Ranagan
Zackary David, b. 9/8/1991 in Dover; Randy W. Couch and Misty J. Fisher

COULOMBE (see Columbus),
Albert Henry, b. 7/1/1910; tenth; Odilon Coulombe (farmer, Canada) and Malvina Haule (Milton)

COURIER,
child, b. 7/10/1893; fourth; Simeon J. Courier (mill hand, 38, Canada) and Mary Hall (30, Canada)

Alfred, b. 7/10/1893; fifth; Simeon J. Courier (mill hand, 38, Canada) and Mary Hall (30, Canada)

COUSINS,
Janice Fay, b. 2/12/1946 in Rochester; second; Leo B. Cousins (teamster, Monroe, ME) and Beverly A. Gagne (Oxford, ME); residence - Milton Mills

COUTURE,
Alex Joshua, b. 4/11/1990 in Dover; Mark A. Couture and Geraldine A. Trainor
Delia, b. 10/26/1894; third; Pierre Conture (sic) (laborer, 26, Canada) and Phelomena Blouin (24, Canada)
Ledia, b. 8/30/1896; fourth; Pierre Couture (laborer, 27, Canada) and Philomena Blouin (28, Canada)
Marie Areine, b. 5/18/1901; seventh; Pierre Couture (mill hand, 30, Canada) and Philomena Blouin (29, Canada)
Mark Allen, b. 5/26/1987 in Dover; Mark A. Couture and Geraldine A. Trainor
Owen David, b. 7/10/1997 in Wolfeboro; Earl D. Couture and Christina L. Couture

COX,
Carmen Antoinette, b. 2/15/1970 in Rochester; George A. Cox and Elmira E. Frost

CRABTREE,
Glaydis E., b. 5/20/1896; first; Albert Crabtree (dyer, England) and Edith M. Lewis (21, Milton)

CROSBY,
Benjamin Paul, b. 10/10/1991 in Portsmouth; Merrill R. Crosby and Anita J. Searles

CRUZ,
Alexander Michael, b. 10/11/1996 in Portsmouth; Peter A. Cruz and Lesley D. Cruz
Nicholas Adam, b. 2/28/1998; Peter A. Cruz and Lesley D. Cruz

CUDDY,

Barbara Ann, b. 6/5/1934; third; William B. Cuddy (laborer, Winterport, ME) and Helen F. Curtis (Boston, MA)

Charles Edward, b. 7/25/1929 in Rochester; first; William Cuddy (laborer, Winterport, ME) and Helen Curtis (Boston, MA)

CUMMER,

Annessa Angelee, b. 6/18/1997 in Dover; Brian L. Cummer and Kerry A. Cummer

CUMMINGS,

daughter, b. 1/8/1890; sixteenth; A. V. Cummings (carpenter, 47, Kingsley, Canada) and Rovey J. Cummings (St. Johns, Canada)

CURLL,

Dorothy Caroline, b. 1/14/1927; fifth; John E. Curll (mill operative, Lunenburg, NS) and Helen F. Burbine (Wakefield, MA)

Helen Frances E., b. 10/18/1925; fourth; John E. Curll (clerk, Lunenburg, NS) and Helen Burbine (Wakefield, MA)

Herbert Kenneth, b. 6/25/1924; third; John E. Curll (clerk, Lunenburg, NS) and Helen F. Burbine (Wakefield, MA)

John William, b. 3/16/1922; first; John E. Curll (laborer, Lunenburg, NS) and Helen F. Burbine (Wakefield, MA)

Robert Frederick, b. 4/20/1923; second; John E. Curll (clerk, Lunenburg, NS) and Helen F. Burbine (Wakefield, MA)

CURRAY,

Annie M., b. 5/26/1889; sixth; John F. Curray (carpenter, 37, Leicester) and Ida E. Ricker (31, Dover)

CURRIER,

Adam Mark, b. 9/27/1985 in Rochester; Mark R. Currier and Deborah A. Moore

Arline, b. 5/17/1929; second; Henry S. Currier (laborer, Providence, RI) and Elfreda M. Bragg (Shapleigh, ME)

David Alan, b. 9/15/1943 in Wolfeboro; second; Ralph R. Currier (mule spinner, Milton) and Irma J. Hutchinson (Greenfield, MA)

Elizabeth Victoria, b. 2/18/1949 in Rochester; second; James W. Currier (army chaplain, Canada) and Edith C. V. Serberg (MA)

Joseph Lawrence, b. 6/11/1906; third; George W. Currier (shoemaker, 32, Albany, VT) and Mary A. Delaney (27, Lisbon)
Lawrence L., Jr., b. 10/15/1950 in Wolfeboro; first; Lawrence L. Currier, Sr. (milkman, Milton) and Mary Long (Wolfeboro)
Ralph Raymond, Jr., b. 9/2/1942 in Rochester; first; Ralph R. Currier (woolen wkr., Milton Mills) and Irma S. Hutchinson (Greenfield, MA); residence - Milton Mills
Ronald Wayne, b. 7/30/1937 in Sanford, ME; seventh; Henry Currier (mill hand, Providence, RI) and Alfreda Bragg (Shapleigh, ME)
Scott Robert, b. 11/21/1983 in Rochester; Mark R. Currier and Deborah A. Moore
Tyler Ryan, b. 5/23/1987 in Rochester; Mark R. Currier and Deborah A. Moore
Virginia Lee, b. 7/1/1954 in Wolfeboro; second; Lawrence Currier (laborer, Sanford, ME) and Mary S. Long (Wolfeboro)

CURRY,
daughter [Eva May], b. 4/13/1902; second; William J. Curry (shoemaker, 25, Stratham) and Hattie Goodwin (27, Milton)
Everett W., b. 2/15/1900; first; William S. Curry (shoemaker, 22, Milton) and Hattie F. Goodwin (22, Milton)

CURTIN,
Ethan David, b. 2/19/1993 in Dover; George Curtin and Maureen F. Maitland

CURTIS,
Cynthia Pauline, b. 12/17/1945 in Rochester; second; Reginald W. Curtis (shoe shop, Farmington) and Pauline S. Emerson (Berwick, ME)
Kate Stephanie, b. 12/5/1988 in Rochester; Stephen P. Curtis and Barbara A. Wing
Katie Elaine, b. 8/26/1986 in Rochester; Garry D. Curtis and Marie R. Day
Sylvia Louise, b. 12/13/1946 in Rochester; third; Reginald W. Curtis (bed laster, Farmington) and Pauline S. Emerson (Berwick, ME)

CUSHING,
Kelly Jane, b. 11/4/1981 in Portsmouth; George A. Cushing and Donna M. Gloski

CUSTEAU,
daughter [Emma], 10/29/1905; first; Aldege Custeau (emp. on RR, 29, Canada) and Lizzie Blouin (23, Canada)
Delia Marion, b. 3/31/1909; third; Aldege Custeau (emp. in mill, Canada) and Lizzie Blouin (Canada)
Eldredge, b. 3/16/1907; second; Eldredge Custeau (emp. in mill, 30, Canada) and Lizzie Blouin (25, Canada)
George Arthur, b. 1/14/1911; fourth; Aldege Custeau (emp. in mill, Canada) and Lizzie Blouin (Canada)
Patricia Ann, b. 1/18/1943 in Rochester; first; George A. Custeau (mach. helper, Lebanon, ME) and Mildred B. Witham (Lebanon, ME)

CUTTER,
Travis Edward, b. 7/17/1992 in Rochester; James A. Cutter and Kam L. Canney

DAHL,
Lisa Anne, b. 10/31/1977 in Rochester; John S. Dahl and Sandra G. Parisi

DALESSANDRI,
David Anthony, b. 8/18/1970 in Rochester; John D. Dalessandri and Sylvia L. Curtis

DALEY,
George Lawrence, IV, b. 4/25/1986 in Rochester; George L. Daley, III and June B. Rand

DAME,
Andrea Lyn, b. 8/30/1963 in Rochester; Howard P. Dame (shoe worker) and Elinore F. Kraus
Melissa Ann, b. 3/22/1968 in Rochester; Howard P. Dame and Elinore F. Kraus

DAMON,
Deborah Jean, b. 10/7/1952 in Rochester; third; Sheldon W. Damon (mill worker, Meredith) and Mary E. Garnett (Rochester)
James Robert, b. 3/12/1951 in Rochester; second; Sheldon W. Damon (mill worker, Meredith) and Mary E. Garnett (Rochester)

Sheldon Ralph, b. 5/9/1949 in Rochester; first; Sheldon W. Damon (shoe factory, NH) and Mary E. Garnett (NH)

DARLING,
Ruth, b. 6/28/1926 in Rochester; third; Herbert C. Darling (farmer, RI) and Lola Durell (Kennebunk, ME); residence - Milton Mills

DAUDELIN,
Gail Patricia, b. 10/25/1944 in Rochester; second; Alfred O. Daudelin, Jr. (US Army, Northwood) and Lorraine E. Howard (Rochester); residence - Milton Mills

DAVIDSON,
Daniel Edward, b. 6/16/1960 in Rochester; third; James S. Davidson (teacher) and Helen F. Keane
Joel Robert, b. 2/6/1959 in Manchester; second; James S. Davidson (teacher, Claremont) and Helen F. Keane (Manchester)
Justin Tyler, b. 4/6/1984 in Dover; John E. Davidson, Jr. and Wanda L. Heald
Sarah Elizabeth, b. 5/2/1993 in Dover; Dineen M. Davidson and Vicki M. Rohwer

DAVIS,
stillborn daughter, b. 10/2/1939 in Rochester; third; Daniel Davis (mill worker, Newfield, ME) and Helen Colby (Springvale, ME); residence - Milton Mills
Alison Marie, b. 2/26/1991 in Rochester; Thomas J. Davis and Stacey A. Thompson
Bryan Glenn, b. 7/26/1936 in Milton Mills; second; Daniel Davis (mill hand, Newfield, ME) and Helen Colby (Springvale, ME); residence - Milton Mills
Cheryl Lynn, b. 9/11/1943; fifth; Daniel N. Davis (machinist, Newfield, ME) and Helen R. Colby (Springvale, ME)
Daniel James, b. 12/20/1968 in Rochester; Daniel R. Davis and Barbara L. Wallingford
Daniel Roland, b. 4/14/1945 in Milton Mills; Daniel R. Davis (welder, Newfield, ME) and Helen R. Colby (Springvale, ME); residence - Milton Mills

Lora May, b. 11/1/1891; second; John F. Davis (shoemaker, 49, Farmington) and Ida May Place (21, Farmington)

Roxana Jean, b. 8/22/1957 in Rochester; first; Roger B. Davis (merchant marine, Rochester) and Janet Rouleau (W. Lebanon, ME)

Sandra Jean, b. 11/14/1935 in Rochester; first; Harold Davis (clerk, Newfield, ME) and Evelyn Randlett (Littleton); residence - Milton Mills

Sharon Diann, b. 12/10/1941 in Rochester; fourth; Daniel N. Davis (lea'bd worker, Newfield, ME) and Helen R. Colby (Springvale, ME); residence - Milton Mills

Thomas Michael, b. 5/8/1963 in Rochester; Wendell J. Davis (elec. engineer) and Demetria Baras

Walter Francis, Jr., b. 12/27/1984 in Rochester; Walter F. Davis and Debra A. Grant

Wendy Christine, b. 11/17/1961 in Rochester; Wendell J. Davis (elect. engineer) and Demetria Baras

DAWSON,
Harold Cleveland, b. 4/5/1913; second; S. Frank Dawson, Jr. (leatherboard mf'r, Lawrence, MA) and Edith W. Ackerman (Warsaw, NY)

DAY,
son, b. 6/16/1896; first; Freeman Day (leather board, 35, Brownfield, ME) and Esther E. Hamden (23, Fryeburg, ME)

son [Everett H.], b. 11/12/1901; third; Frank B. Day (shoemaker, 33, Shapleigh, ME) and Addie F. Hooper (20, Acton, ME)

son [Frank C.], b. 7/17/1904; fourth; Frank B. Day (shoemaker, 36, Shapleigh, ME) and Addie F. Hooper (23, Acton, ME)

Phillip, b. 9/20/1897; first; Sylvester Day (laborer, 29, Porter, ME) and Nano F. Donnell (27, Milford, MA)

DEANGELIS,
Edward Christopher, Jr., b. 8/3/1969 in Rochester; Edward C. DeAngelis and Jean A. Hutchins

DEARBORN,
David Alan, b. 10/22/1938 in Rochester; Charles H. Dearborn (shoe worker, W. Lebanon, ME) and Bertha P. Longley (Kingfield, ME)

DEBUTTS,
John Mitchell, III, b. 10/1/1985 in Rochester; John M. Debutts, Jr. and Cynthia A. Price

DELAND,
Jody Ann, b. 1/5/1972 in Rochester; Mark H. DeLand and Sandra L. Henderson

DELASIERRA,
Austin Jameson, b. 6/12/1993 in Rochester; Rafael N. DeLasierra and Kristina L. Young

DELLACHIAIE,
Judith Mary, b. 9/27/1965 in Rochester; John F. DellaChiaie (mgr. part owner) and Eleanor R. Mells
Liza Marie, b. 11/23/1966 in Rochester; John F. DellaChiaie (dix heel mgr.) and Eleanor R. Mello

DELPONTE,
Alicia Joan, b. 5/5/1987 in Dover; David W. DelPonte and Christine J. Hayward

DEMARY,
Jamie Lee, b. 2/24/1987 in Portsmouth; Raymond E. Demary, Jr. and Diane E. Farrugo
Jessica Arin, b. 4/5/1988 in Portsmouth; Raymond E. Demary, Jr. and Diane E. Farrugo

DEMERITT,
son [Bertie], b. 7/30/1899; fourth; Berthold I. Demeritt (foreman, 24, Newfield, ME) and Musetta A. Dorr (24, Milton)
son [Bruce R.], b. 3/25/1903; fifth; Berthold I. Demeritt (foreman, 28, Newfield, ME) and Musetta A. Dorr (28, Milton)
child [Rosbert E.], b. 6/1/1905; sixth; Berthold I. Demeritt (shoemaker, 30, Newfield, ME) and Musetta A. Dorr (29, Milton)
stillborn daughter, b. 3/26/1941; sixth; Delphin G. DeMeritt (laborer, Milton) and Carrie S. Tobey (Dover)
Adel Ruth, b. 10/13/1934 in Rochester; second; Delphin G. DeMeritt (shoe wkr., Milton) and Carrie S. Toby (Kittery, ME)

Bonibelle, b. 9/20/1894; second; Berthold I. Demeritt (shoeforeman, 19, Newfield, ME) and Muzetta A. Dorr (18, Milton)

Bruce Raith, b. 4/10/1921; first; Bruce R. DeMeritt (draughtsman, Milton) and Mary E. Hunter (Roslindale, MA)

Carolyn June, b. 5/22/1933; first; Delphin G. DeMeritt (shoe work, Milton) and Carey Tobey (Dover, MA)

Delphin Gage, b. 5/1/1907; seventh; Berthold I. Demeritt (foreman, 32, Newfield, ME) and Musetta A. Dorr (32, Milton)

Delphin Gage, b. 11/4/1936; third; Delphin DeMerritt (sic) (shoe worker, Milton) and Carrie Toby (Dover, MA)

Hannah Ethelma, b. 12/18/1909; eighth; Berthold I. Demeritt (foreman, Newfield, ME) and Musetta A. Dorr (Milton)

James Calvin, b. 5/18/1938; fourth; Delphin G. DeMeritt (shoe worker, Milton) and Carrie S. Tobey (Dover)

Lloyd A., b. 5/28/1896; third; Berthold I. Demeritt (shoe foreman, 21, Newfield, ME) and Musetta A. Dorr (21, Milton)

Merribell, b. 8/6/1893; first; Berthold I. Demeritt (shoe packer, 18, Newfield, ME) and Musetta Dorr (18, Milton)

Vera Dorothea, b. 10/26/1911; ninth; Berthold I. Demeritt (supt. shoe fac., Newfield, ME) and Musetta A. Dorr (Dover)

William F., b. 5/21/1939; fifth; Delphin G. DeMeritt (shoe worker, Milton) and Carrie S. Tobey (Dover)

DEMERS,
Kimberly Anne, b. 10/23/1994 in Rochester; Anthony G. Demers and Cindy L. Garland

DENNEY,
George, b. 4/29/1893; eighth; Almon A. Denney (sawyer, 39, Newport, NJ) and Clara L. Hubbard (28, Centre Harbor); residence - Centre Harbor

DEPALMA,
Tracy Lynn, b. 12/6/1966 in Rochester; first; Michael L. DePalma (laborer) and Gail L. Hayes

DERBY,
William Theodore, b. 9/19/1931 in Rochester; second; William T. Derby (millworker, Lebanon, ME) and Arlene Steele (Barre, VT); residence - Milton Mills

DESAULNIER,
daughter [Celia], b. 4/6/1904; fourth; Joseph Deseulnier (sic) (laborer, 24, MI) and Mary O. Custeau (25, Lawrence, MA)
Charles, b. 9/8/1908; sixth; Joseph Desaulnier (shoemaker, MI) and Mary A. Custeau (Lawrence, MA) (1923)
Henry, b. 6/25/1907; sixth; Joseph Desaulnier (laster, 27, MI) and Mary A. Custeau (29, Lawrence, MA)

DESMARAIS,
Jennifer Rose, b. 5/4/1977 in Rochester; Paul H. Desmarais and Claudette C. Boulay
Lydia June, b. 6/16/1975 in Rochester; Paul H. Desmarais and Claudette C. Boulay

DESROSIER,
Jay Paul, b. 2/25/1978 in Hanover; Dennis K. Desrosier and Vicki L. Marsh

DEVEAU,
Edward Alexander, b. 3/18/1988 in Rochester; Leon E. Deveau and Susan J. Cleary

DEWOLF,
Helen, b. 1/23/1891; first; Charles DeWolf (machinist, 23) and Hattie Hayes (23, Milton)

DEXTER,
Geneva May, b. 4/2/1928; first; Gilwin W. Dexter (mill operative, Dover, ME) and Amy F. Betts (Lebanon, ME)
Jean Althea, b. 6/15/1931; second; Gilwin W. Dexter (leatherboard mill, Dover, ME) and Amy F. Betts (Lebanon, ME)
Lisa Whiting, b. 12/24/1970 in Rochester; Fred E. Dexter, Jr. and Elsie A. Tufts

DEZAN,
Shelley Beatrice, b. 12/11/1972 in Rochester; Douglas F. Dezan and Patricia G. Ellingwood

DIACO,
Michelle Marie, b. 1/25/1986 in Dover; Eugene Diaco and Suzanne K. Smith

DICEY,
Dana M., b. 10/18/1891; first; Dana M. Dicey (laborer, 21, Union) and Winnie M. Duntley (-6, Milton)
Eleanor, b. 3/13/1914; second; Dana M. Dicey (emp. in mill, Milton) and Marion M. Dixon (Lebanon, ME)
Helen Agnes, b. 7/2/1911; first; Dana M. Dicey (emp. in mill, Milton) and Marion M. Dixon (Lebanon, ME)

DICKIE,
Jared Julien, b. 10/3/1993 in Dover; Brian J. Dickie and Leslie J. Reynolds
Paige Danielle, b. 2/25/1992 in Dover; Brian J. Dickie and Leslie J. Reynolds

DICKSON,
son [Ernest], b. 4/11/1900; first; Ernest F. Dickson (emp. in mill, 20, Lunenburg, MA) and Allie M. Corson (18, Milton)
son [Franklin B.], b. 12/14/1901; second; Ernest F. Dickson (mill hand, 22, Lunenburg, MA) and Allie M. Corson (20, Milton)
son [Charles Leroy], b. 5/18/1904; third; Ernest F. Dickson (emp. in mill, 25, Lunenburg, MA) and Allie M. Corson (23, Milton)
Carlyne Phyllis, b. 4/5/1908; third; William A. Dickson (supt. leatherboard mill, 34, Lunenburg, MA) and Hattie M. Newell (33, Still River, MA)
Ernest Franklin, b. 2/17/1944 in Rochester; first; Franklin B. Dickson (mill worker, Milton) and Mary E. Timmins (Petersburg, VA)
Hazel, b. 8/18/1904; second; William A. Dickson (supt. of mill, 30, Lunenburg, MA) and Hattie M. Newell (29, Still River, MA)
John Charles, b. 11/15/1947 in Rochester; third; Charles L. Dickson (supt., Milton) and Ruby E. Snow (NB)

Mary Elizabeth, b. 8/13/1947 in Rochester; second; Franklin B. Dickson (foreman, Milton) and Mary E. Timmins (Petersburg, VA)

William Alden, b. 3/31/1944 in Rochester; first; Charles L. Dickson (mill supt., Milton) and Ruby E. Snow (Boris Town, NB)

DIXON,

Amy Thelma, b. 10/8/1910; fifth; Stephen E. Dixon (emp. in mill, Milton) and Georgie M. Moody (Ossipee)

Elizabeth Elaine, b. 4/7/1925 in Rochester; first; Elwood M. Dixon (lea. bd. mill, Milton) and Gladys M. St. John (Rochester) (1926)

Elmer T., b. 4/10/1907; third; Stephen E. Dixon (emp. in mill, 43, Milton) and Georgie M. Moodey (20, Ossipee)

Elwood, b. 2/13/1902; first; Stephen E. Dixon (clerk, 38, Milton) and Georgie B. Moody (17, Ossipee)

Paul J., b. 7/2/1904; second; Stephen E. Dixon (laborer, 40, Ossipee) and Georgie M. Moody (19, Ossipee)

Ruth Anna, b. 2/23/1922; sixth; Stephen E. Dixon (watchman, Milton) and Georgia M. Moody (W. Ossipee)

Virginia Irene, b. 11/28/1921; fourth; Marion M. Dixon (Lebanon, ME)

Wayne Rodney, b. 10/22/1908; fourth; Stephen E. Dixon (emp. in mill, 44, Milton) and Georgie M. Moody (22, Ossipee)

DODDRELL,

Lynlee Grace, b. 1/13/1990 in Rochester; Jeffrey V. Doddrell and Cheryl L. Foss

DODGE,

Tracy Ann, b. 8/11/1969 in Rochester; Philip C. Dodge and Lady A. Boudreau

DODIER,

Brenda Darlene, b. 8/19/1948 in Rochester; first; Donald R. Dodier (painter, Somerville, MA) and Ruth E. Valley (Milton Mills)

Diana Rita, b. 8/27/1949 in Rochester; second; Donald R. Dodier (laborer, MA) and Ruth E. Valley (NH)

DOE,

son [Chester A.], b. 10/2/1898; second; James F. Doe (farmer, 26, Milton) and Edith Witham (24, Brookfield) son [Arthur N.], b. 11/19/1899; third; James F. Doe (farmer, 27, Milton) and Edith Witham (25, Brookfield)

Rachel, b. 2/13/1906; first; James F. Doe (farmer, 33, Milton) and Etta F. Martin (32, Brockton, MA)

Ralph A., b. 6/18/1897; first; James F. Doe (farmer, 25, Milton) and Edith Witham (23, Brookfield)

DOHERTY,

Annie Gertrude, b. 4/11/1916; second; Philip D. Doherty (machinist, Franklin, MA) and Iva L. Hoyt (Rochester) (1918)

Edna E., b. 5/7/1914; first; Philip Doherty (loom fixer, Franklin, MA) and Ina Hoyt (Rochester)

Helen Frances, b. 8/10/1918; third; Philip D. Doherty (machinist, Franklin, MA) and Iva L. Hoyt (Rochester)

DOLAN,

Eva Eileen, b. 10/6/1958 in Wolfeboro; second; Thomas J. Dolan (teacher, Passaic, NJ) and Clara L. Blalock (Neptune, NJ)

DONLON,

James Louis, b. 7/14/1985 in Rochester; James A. Donlon and Marie S. Russo

DORE,

daughter, b. 10/11/1902; first; Blanche Dore (17, Farmington)

son, b. 5/15/1932; first; Charles E. Dore (laborer, Milton) and Blanch Nickerson (Milton)

Barbara Evelyn, b. 7/16/1933; second; Charles E. Dore (laborer, Milton) and Blanche Nickerson (Milton)

Dean Edward, b. 6/9/1967 in Rochester; second; Ivan E. Dore (machinist) and Leona M. Kean

Deborah Ann, b. 3/2/1966 in Rochester; Ivan E. Dore (machinist) and Leona M. Kean

Ivan Edward, b. 4/20/1936; third; Charles E. Dore (laborer, Milton) and Blanche Nickerson (Milton)

Joshua John, b. 12/18/1989 in Rochester; Jeffrey L. Dore and Mary A. Katwick

Sonya Rose, b. 10/15/1960 in Wolfeboro; first; Ivan E. Dore (mechanic) and Carolyn E. Haley

Tony John, b. 7/27/1973 in Rochester; Lyford R. Dore and Marie A. Trivigno

DORR,
son [Charles E.], b. 5/5/1893; second; Charles H. Dorr (laborer, 36, Milton) and Winnie Duntley (17, Milton)
son [Scott L.], b. 8/6/1895; third; Charles H. Dorr (laborer, 38, Milton) and Winnie Duntley (19, Milton)
daughter, b. 11/28/1913; first; William W. Dorr (emp. in mill, Milton) and Ruth M. Edwards (Temple)
Alta May, b. 6/15/1904; sixth; Charles H. Dorr (farmer, 51, Milton) and Mary W. Duntley (29, Milton)
Althea L., b. 8/25/1872; Charles C. Dorr (Milton) and Melissa E. Jones (Milton) (1955)
Blanche Marion, b. 10/21/1922; third; William W. Dorr (laborer, Milton) and Ruth M. Edwards (Temple)
Clifford Walton, b. 9/13/1917; third; William W. Dorr (emp. in mill, Milton) and Ruth M. Edwards (Temple)
Edwin Francis, b. 6/25/1915; second; William W. Dorr (emp. in mill, Milton) and Ruth M. Edwards (Temple)
Franklin, b. 4/18/1907; seventh; Charles H. Dorr (laborer, 54, Milton) and Mary W. Duntley (32, Milton)
Norman William, b. 7/26/1929; fourth; William W. Dorr (clerk, Milton) and Ruth M. Edwards (Temple)
Ray, b. 4/21/1889; tenth; Charles C. Dorr (farmer, 59, Milton) and Melissa Jones (34, Milton)
Theodore Lyman, b. 4/14/1897; fourth; Charles H. Dorr (laborer, 45, Milton) and Winnie Duntley (21, Milton)
Theodore Lyman, b. 3/25/1899; fifth; Charles H. Dorr (laborer, 46, Milton) and Mary W. Duntley (23, Milton)

DOUGHTY,
Tyler Wayne, b. 2/10/1987 in Rochester; Lyle W. Doughty and Karen L. George

DOUGLAS,
Deborah Ann, b. 8/10/1959 in Rochester; first; Kenneth Douglas (navy yard, Dover) and Claire E. Connerton (Melrose, MA)

Justin Daniel, b. 10/5/1982 in Rochester; Ronald M. Douglas and Darlene A. Richards

Kenneth, Jr., b. 1/4/1961 in Rochester; Kenneth Douglas (navy yard) and Claire E. Connerton

Khali Lynn, b. 8/18/1999 in Rochester; Heath Douglas and Kathleen Sullivan

DOUGLASS,

Emily Joy, b. 8/9/1999 in Rochester; Neil Douglass and Crystal Douglass

Esther Florence, b. 4/28/1906; fourth; Edward P. Douglass (blacksmith, 29, Bridgton, ME) and Mabel Taylor (22, Parsonsfield, ME)

DOUQUETTE,

Helen Elizabeth, b. 10/18/1905; fourth; Leon Dauquette (sic) (emp. in mill, 36, Canada) and Emma Hall (33, Canada)

Olena Alice, b. 6/3/1907; fifth; Leon Douquette (emp. in mill, 37, Canada) and Emma Hall (35, Canada)

DOWNING,

child, b. 10/8/1902; first; George A. Downing (railroad, 30, Farmington) and Alice Hodgdon (Rochester)

son, b. 3/15/1908; first; Llewellyn Downing (laborer, 26, Milton) and Fanny Lavill (30)

son, b. 2/23/1910; tenth; Lewis C. Downing (laborer, Milton) and Tessie M. Leavitt (No. Conway)

son, b. 9/18/1911; second; Llewellyn Downing (laborer, Milton) and Katherine Leavitt (No. Conway)

Edna May, b. 4/3/1935 in Rochester; second; Robert Downing (lumber mkr., Rochester) and Anna Flanigan (Ireland)

Hazel Louise, b. 12/1/1912; sixth; Lewis C. Downing (wood cutter, 31, Milton) and Katresia M. Leavitt (33, No. Conway)

Lillian May, b. 2/5/1909; ninth; Lewis E. Downing (laborer, Milton) and Tressie M. Leavitt (No. Conway)

Violet Jane, b. 11/18/1914; sixth; Charles L. Downing (laborer, Milton) and Katresia M. Leavitt (North Conway)

DOWNS,

son [Roy M.], b. 5/21/1893; first; John A. Downs (laborer, 30, Rochester) and May A. Thompson (22, Auburn, ME) daughter [Ethel G.], b. 8/26/1894; second; Frank L. Downs (farmer, 34, Milton) and Augusta O. Kimball (30, Middleton)

daughter [Flora M.], b. 12/6/1897; second; John A. Downs (laborer, 37, Rochester) and Lizzie Thompson (28, Auburn, ME)

son, b. 8/15/1900; first; Perley E. Downs (laborer, 21, Eaton) and Lena M. Thompson (16, Ossipee); residence - Madison

daughter, b. 2/11/1908; third; Fred C. Downs (emp. in mill, 30, Lebanon, ME) and Eva M. West (23, Wakefield)

Arthur, b. 3/19/1905; first; Fred C. Downs (shoemaker, 27, Lebanon, ME) and Eva M. West (20, Wakefield)

Arthur William, b. 3/27/1937 in Rochester; first; Herbert Downs (lea. worker, Barnstead) and Wilma Warnecke (Milton)

Blanche, b. 5/13/1896; first; George A. Downs (laborer, 27, Milton) and Ada Tanner (21, Farmington)

Christopher Dean, b. 3/25/1966 in Rochester; Herbert A. Downs, Jr. (mechanic) and Susan K. Irish

David Wayne, b. 9/11/1964 in Wolfeboro; second; Raymond F. Downs (molding operator) and Helen L. Kraus

Doris Eva, b. 5/22/1919; fifth; Charles F. Downs (laborer, Milton) and Eva M. West (Sanbornville)

Hattie Ella, b. 1/24/1871; second; Albert F. Downs (shoe maker, Milton) and Dora Tuttle (Strafford) (1939)

Hazel May, b. 2/17/1907; second; Fred C. Downs (shoemaker, 29, Lebanon, ME) and Eva M. West (22, Wakefield)

Herbert A., Jr., b. 3/25/1947 in Rochester; third; Herbert A. Downs (mechanic, Barnstead) and Wilma F. Warnecke (Milton)

Josie M., b. 11/27/1877; fifth; Albert F. Downs (shoe maker, Milton) and Dora Tuttle (Strafford) (1939)

Leah Marie, b. 5/19/1973 in Dover; Herbert A. Downs, Jr. and Nancy M. Pelletier

Louis Philip, b. 5/13/1940 in Rochester; second; Raymond F. Downs (mill worker, Milton) and Ruby J. Clifford (Wolfeboro)

Mabel Sabrina, b. 2/7/1904; third; Frank L. Downs (shoemaker, 43, Milton) and Augusta O. Kimball (39, Middleton)

Marie Ann, b. 2/12/1949 in Rochester; third; Raymond F. Downs (mill employee, NH) and Ruby J. Clifford (NH)

Raymond Franklin, b. 4/11/1914; fourth; Fred C. Downs (laborer, Lebanon, ME) and Eva M. West (Brookfield)

Raymond Franklin, b. 3/25/1938 in Rochester; first; Raymond F. Downs (lea. worker, Milton) and Ruby J. Clifford (Wolfeboro)
Raymond Leonard, b. 8/23/1961 in Rochester; Raymond F. Downs (laborer) and Helen L. Kraus
Sharon Elizabeth, b. 2/9/1940 in Rochester; second; Herbert A. Downs (mach. tender, Barnstead) and Wilma F. Warnecke (Milton)
Winona, b. 2/16/1921; third; Perley E. Downs (laborer, Madison) and Helena Thompson (Madison)

DRAPEAU,
Scott Henry, b. 5/14/1981 in Dover; David E. Drapeau and Jo-Anne Marion

DRAWBRIDGE,
stillborn son, b. 6/28/1899; first; Edward Drawbridge (clerk, 27, Worcester, MA) and Bertha E. Cook (24, Milton)

DREW,
Alice Jeanne, b. 5/11/1940 in Rochester; second; Elmer E. Drew (mill worker, Middleton) and Helen E. Pike (Farmington)
Arthur N., b. 12/19/1932 in Milton Mills; fourth; Frank P. Drew (lumberman, Ossipee) and Bessie Morrison (Stowe, ME)
Catherine Marie, b. 9/7/1966 in Rochester; Thomas E. Drew (comm. artist) and Nancy M. Joos
Charles Maurice, Jr., b. 9/8/1934 in Milton Mills; first; Charles M. Drew (laborer, Union) and Katherine Gordon (Acton, ME)
Clifford T., b. 7/10/1890; seventh; Horace Drew (hotel prop., 41, Eaton) and Maggie A. Walker (Ireland)
Clifton H., b. 7/10/1890; sixth; Horace Drew (hotel prop., 41, Eaton) and Maggie A. Walker (Ireland)
Florence Lizzie, b. 6/5/1892; Albert R. Drew and Abbie I. Tilton (1952)
George W., b. 9/12/1893; first; Samuel E. Drew (edge setter, 24, Stoneham, MA) and Ina F. Wentworth (19, Milton)
Heidi Lee, b. 6/24/1964 in Rochester; second; Thomas E. Drew (side wall app.) and Nancy M. Joos
Kristen Lee Marie, b. 6/3/1982 in Rochester; Michael O. Drew and Katherine M. Hall
Shannon Marie, b. 11/10/1972 in Rochester; Ralph H. Drew and Shirley M. Perry

Thelma, b. 6/26/1896; second; Samuel E. Drew (butcher, Stoneham, MA) and Ina F. Wentworth (Milton)

Thomas Elmer, b. 10/16/1943 in Rochester; fourth; Elmer E. Drew (navy yard, Middleton) and Helen E. Pike (Farmington)

William, b. 4/9/1904; second; William F. Drew (shoemaker, 26, Tamworth) and Kate M. Hardy (23, Tamworth)

DUBE,
Pauline Blanche, b. 1/24/1947 in Rochester; first; Roger E. Dube (wd. h. emp., Quebec, Can.) and Rita L. Plante (Somersworth)

DUBERGER,
Edgar Frances E., b. 9/10/1914; second; Edgar W. Duberger (engineer, Springfield, MA) and Una P. Giguere (Holyoke, MA)

DUCHANNE,
Marilla, b. 11/13/1890; Benjamin Duchanne (laborer, 28, Canada) and Melvina Tetro (VT)

DUCHANO,
Denise Elaine, b. 12/4/1964 in Rochester; second; Norman P. Duchano (laborer) and Barbara J. Laskey

DUCHARME,
Michael Joseph, b. 6/5/1982 in Rochester; Joel A. Ducharme and Christine M. Vachon

DUCHESNEAU,
Stephen Daniel, b. 8/16/1987 in Rochester; David G. Duchesneau and Andrea J. Camann

DUDA,
Thomas Lee Holton, b. 3/13/1985 in Dover; Thomas J. Duda and Victor L. Holton

DUFORD,
Lisa Marie, b. 1/20/1969 in Rochester; Roger E. Duford and Rita V. Chase

DUGGAN,
Timothy Edward, b. 6/27/1988 in Rochester; Frank S. Duggan and Brigid O'Brien

DUMAIS,
Casey Joseph, b. 6/30/1983 in Dover; Gary A. Dumais and Vivian R. McGrath

DUNTON,
Christopher Katwick, b. 5/16/1961 in Rochester; Charles D. Dunton (student) and Bonnie A. Katwick
Jennifer Anne, b. 8/27/1969 in Rochester; Charles D. Dunton and Bonnie A. A. Katwick

DUPLESSIS,
Daniel, b. 10/15/1964 in Dover; Louis A. DuPlessis (mgr. com. relations) and Jane M. Haynes

DUPUIS,
Euclide R., Jr., b. 5/13/1931; first; Euclide R. Dupuis (leatherboard mill, Milton) and Mary N. Wiggin (Milton)
James Albert, b. 10/4/1932; second; Clyde R. Dupuis (mill hand, Milton) and Mary N. Wiggin (Milton)
James Albert, b. 3/13/1954 in Rochester; first; James A. Dupuis (mechanic, Milton) and Jean K. Lapington (England)
Jeanne Louise, b. 1/10/1944 in Rochester; second; Norman M. Dupuis (mill worker, Milton) and Doris E. Downs (Milton)
Lorraine Frances, b. 7/1/1946 in Rochester; first; Clyde R. Dupuis (mill worker, Milton) and Ellen H. Wyatt (Milton)
Louise Theresa, b. 3/26/1931; fourth; Wilfrid Dupuis (leatherboard mill, Milton) and Gertrude Harrity (Rochester)
Margaret Mary, b. 9/7/1953 in Rochester; first; Norman L. Dupuis (weaver, Union) and Marguerite Nadeau (Pembroke, MA)
Michael Gordon, b. 12/3/1955 in Rochester; second; James A. Duplis (sic) (lineman, Milton) and Jean Lapington (England)
Norman Bernard, b. 2/14/1935 in Rochester; sixth; Wilfred Dupuis (mill worker, Milton) and Gertrude Harrity (Rochester)
Norman Leroy, b. 5/27/1935 in Rochester; third; Euclide R. Dupuis (mill worker, Milton) and Mary N. Wiggin (Milton)

Norman Richard, b. 3/19/1957 in Rochester; third; Norman Dupuis (mechanic, Rochester) and Margaret Nadeau (Rochester)

Paul Robert, b. 6/12/1958 in Rochester; fourth; Norman L. Dupuis (mechanic, Rochester) and Margaret Nadeau (Rochester)

Raymond Franklin, b. 11/3/1936 in Rochester; seventh; Wilfred Dupuis (fibre worker, Milton) and Gertrude Harrity (Rochester)

Robert Richard, b. 3/12/1929; third; Wilfred L. Dupuis (lea. worker, Milton) and Gertrude T. Harrity (Rochester)

Roland Joseph, b. 11/28/1932; fifth; Wilfred Dupuis (laborer, Milton) and Gertrude Harrity (Rochester)

Ronald Norman, b. 7/12/1940 in Rochester; first; Norman M. Dupuis (mill worker, Milton) and Doris E. Downs (Milton)

Tammie Sue, b. 9/23/1963 in Dover; Norman L. Dupuis (shoe cutter) and Sheila M. Vachon

DURAND,
Brandon James, b. 10/7/1987 in Dover; James R. Durand, Sr. and Brenda L. Bernard

DURKEE,
David Brian, b. 6/14/1955 in Rochester; third; Donald Durkee (machinist, Farmington) and Lorraine Benton (Hinsdale)

Kevin Donald, b. 2/9/1953 in Rochester; second; Donald P. Durkee (machinist, Farmington) and Lorraine M. Benton (Hinsdale)

DUROCHER,
Louise, b. 1/24/1898; fifth; Joseph O. Durocher (shoemaker, 32, Canada) and Sarah J. Conners (26, Lynn, MA)

DYER,
Dorotha Eva, b. 1/27/1920; first; Harry R. Dyer (laborer, Cape Elizabeth, ME) and Bernice Garland (Wolfeboro)

Ellen May, b. 12/2/1921; second; Harry R. Dyer (laborer, Cape Elizabeth, ME) and Bernice M. Garland (Wolfeboro); residence - S. Portland, ME

EARL,
daughter, b. 10/1/1900; third; George M. Earl (emp. in mill, 27, NB) and Grace L. Tucker (25, Lubec, ME)

EASTMAN,
Stephanie Lynn, b. 11/23/1991 in Rochester; John A. Eastman and Cheryl A. Balomenos

EBARE,
Jennifer Rose, b. 7/20/1976 in Rochester; Gene M. Ebare and Deborah A. Pennell
Jessica Marie, b. 10/31/1972 in Rochester; Robert L. Ebare and Rosemary J. Pennell

ELDRIDGE,
Amy Michelle, b. 1/26/1977 in Dover; David A. Eldridge and Patricia R. Semprebon
Barbara Ann, b. 5/1/1933; sixth; Melvin Eldridge (laborer, Ossipee) and Delia Custeau (Milton)
Carlton D., b. 6/15/1924; second; Carlton S. Elbridge (sic) (laborer, Ossipee) and Esther M. Haley (Tuftonboro)
Carlyne Wilma, b. 10/19/1928; third; Carlton S. Eldridge (mill operative, Ossipee) and Esther M. Haley (Tuftonboro)
Donald Edgar, b. 2/6/1941; third; Moses O. Eldridge (mill worker, Ossipee) and Lillian M. Johnson (W. Lebanon, ME)
Everett Harold, b. 11/22/1941; third; Chauncey J. Eldridge (lea'bd. worker, Ossipee) and Esther L. Adjutant (Wolfeboro)
Geraldine Gertrude, b. 8/8/1934; seventh; Melvin Eldridge (laborer, Ossipee) and Delia Custeau (Milton)
Helen Lorraine, b. 10/23/1942 in Rochester; fourth; Chauncey S. Eldridge (mill emp., Ossipee) and Esther L. Adjutant (Wolfeboro)
Homer Francis, b. 4/9/1927; second; Milton Eldridge (machinist, So. Berwick, ME) and Laura Marcoux (Milton)
Jeanne Carole, b. 11/13/1944 in Rochester; second; Fred R. Eldridge (machinist, Ctr. Ossipee) and Isabelle M. Hoyt (Milton)
Lucille Emily, b. 7/31/1942 in Rochester; fourth; Moses O. Eldridge (mill hand, Ossipee) and Lillian Johnson (W. Lebanon, ME)
Nancy Elaine, b. 8/3/1942 in Rochester; first; Fred R. Eldridge (mill employee, Wolfeboro) and Isabel M. Hoyt (Milton)
Raymond Emile, b. 5/15/1931 in Rochester; fifth; Melvin H. Eldridge (leatherboard mill, Ossipee) and Delia Custeau (Milton)
Royal Gene, b. 6/27/1945 in Rochester; fifth; Moses O. Eldridge (mill worker, Ossipee) and Lillian M. Johnson (W. Lebanon, ME)

Russell Newell, b. 11/11/1933; first; Moses O. Eldridge (mill op., Ossipee) and Lillian Johnson (W. Lebanon, ME)
Ruth Evelyn, b. 1/26/1937; second; Moses Eldridge (mill hand, Ossipee) and Lillian Johnson (W. Lebanon, ME)

ELLIOT,
Jerrica Marie, b. 5/6/1989 in Exeter; James Edward Elliot and Lora Lee Vandenbussche

ELLIOTT,
Benjamin Robert, b. 4/26/1986 in Rochester; John P. Elliott, Jr. and Ann Lomasney
Hannah Ellen, b. 7/17/1990 in Rochester; Chad S. Elliott and Ruth A. Armstrong
Mayghen Noelle, b. 12/15/1987 in Rochester; Chad S. Elliott and Ruth A. Armstrong
Michelle Dee, b. 3/5/1984 in Dover; Steven J. Elliott and Donna E. Snyder

ELLIS,
stillborn daughter, b. 1/25/1895 in Wolfeboro; first; George E. Ellis (laborer, 25, Wolfeboro) and Inez G. Duntley (15, Milton)
son [Lloyd F.], b. 4/17/1896; second; George Ellis (laborer, 27, Wolfeboro) and Inez G. Duntley (17, Milton)
daughter [Ethel M.], b. 4/18/1900; fourth; George E. Ellis (emp. in mill, 30, Wolfeboro) and Inez G. Duntley (21, Milton)
daughter [Nellie B.], b. 7/8/1903; sixth; George E. Ellis (laborer, 34, Wolfeboro) and Inez G. Duntley (24, Milton)
daughter, b. 11/15/1903; first; Elmer A. Ellis (shoemaker, 25, Malone, NY) and Abbie Trickey (26, Lebanon, ME)
Brian M., b. 3/4/1955 in Rochester; fourth; Russell E. Ellis (mach. oper., Wolfeboro) and Thelma Verville (Portsmouth)
Charles Francis, b. 4/7/1929; first; Lloyd F. Ellis (laborer, Milton) and Eleanor G. Londo (Wolfeboro)
Cory Allen, b. 1/19/1985 in Rochester; Leon L. Ellis and Cindy L. Patnode
Crystal Lee, b. 7/19/1957 in Rochester; third; Edward G. Ellis (mach. tender, Milton) and Lois Bowers (Pittsfield, ME)

David Arthur, b. 5/14/1953 in Rochester; third; Russell E. Ellis (fibre mill, Wolfeboro) and Thelma Verville (Portsmouth)

Delores Elaine, b. 10/7/1956 in Rochester; fifth; Russel E. Ellis (mach. opr., Wolfeboro) and Thelma L. Verville (Portsmouth)

Edward G., b. 4/6/1915; eleventh; George E. Ellis (emp. in mill, Wolfeboro) and Inez G. Duntley (Milton)

Erwin Ernest, b. 11/13/1943 in Rochester; fifth; Lloyd F. Ellis (fibr. mill emp., Milton) and Eleanor G. Londo (Wolfeboro)

Evelyn May, b. 12/15/1898; third; George E. Ellis (laborer, 29, Wolfeboro) and Inez G. Duntley (19, Milton)

Evodia Ellen, b. 7/23/1946 in Rochester; sixth; Lloyd F. Ellis (roller, Milton) and Eleanor G. Londo (Wolfeboro)

James Robert, b. 1/26/1952 in Rochester; second; Russell E. Ellis (millwright, Wolfeboro) and Thelma L. Verville (Portsmouth)

Jeffrey Richard, b. 2/9/1972 in Rochester; James R. Ellis and Carleen E. Nicholson

Kenneth Raymond, b. 8/23/1935; fourth; Lloyd F. Ellis (mill hand, Milton) and Eleanor Londo (Wolfeboro)

Leon Louis, b. 11/28/1959 in Rochester; seventh; Russell Ellis (bleach room, Wolfeboro) and Thelma Verville (Portsmouth)

Lillian Rose, b. 12/22/1908; eighth; George E. Ellis (laborer, 39, Wolfeboro) and Gertrude I. Duntley (29, Milton)

Lloyd George, b. 5/9/1961 in Rochester; Russell E. Ellis (laborer) and Thelma L. Verville

Marie Jean, b. 1/14/1958 in Rochester; sixth; Russell E. Ellis (mach. opr., Wolfeboro) and Thelma L. Verville (Portsmouth)

Myrtle May, b. 5/21/1907; seventh; George E. Ellis (shoe laster, 38, Ossipee) and Gertrude I. Duntley (28, Milton)

Nettie, b. 11/9/1910; ninth; George E. Ellis (emp. ice co., Wolfeboro) and Inez G. Duntley (Milton)

Pauline Louise, b. 2/26/1964 in Rochester; ninth; Russell E. Ellis (machine tender) and Thelma L. Verville

Philip Landon, b. 10/11/1971 in Rochester; Russell E. Ellis, Jr. and Clarissa C. Jones

Robert E., b. 3/15/1870; fifth; Ephraim Ellis (farmer, Middleton) and Hannah ----- (Middleton) (1939)

Roger, b. 4/12/1931; second; Lloyd F. Ellis (leatherboard mill, Milton) and Eleanor T. Londo (Wolfeboro)

Rosalie Arline, b. 7/15/1913; tenth; George E. Ellis (shoe worker, Wolfeboro) and Inex G. Duntley (Milton)

Ruby, b. 5/3/1905; sixth; George E. Ellis (shoemaker, 36, Wolfeboro) and Gertrude I. Duntley (26, Milton)

Russell E., Jr., b. 4/24/1948 in Rochester; first; Russell E. Ellis (shoe shop, Wolfeboro) and Thelma L. Verville (Portsmouth)

Tommy Lee, b. 6/5/1986 in Rochester; Leon L. Ellis and Cindy L. Patnode

Vilena Maude, b. 9/3/1904; first; Robert E. Ellis (papermaker, 34, Milton) and Nettie M. Dyer (28, Wakefield)

ELMORE,

Brittany Nicole, b. 9/19/1994 in Rochester; Jeremy R. Elmore and Lynn A. Glidden

ELWELL,

Cassandra Leigh, b. 10/24/1992 in Dover; Kenneth L. Elwell and Sandra C. Colby

Heather Dawne, b. 1/29/1982 in Wolfeboro; William D. Elwell and Donna J. Cranmore

Holly Jeanne, b. 12/26/1969 in Rochester; Wilfred A. Elwell and Shirley M. Perry

Holly Shetland, b. 12/24/1983 in Wolfeboro; William D. Elwell and Donna J. Cranmore

Michael Andrew, b. 11/16/1966 in Rochester; Wilfred A. Elwell (shoe worker) and Shirley M. Perry

EMERSON,

Chevonne Lee, b. 9/23/1970 in Wolfeboro; Clark B. Emerson and Patricia A. Haines

Jason Scott, b. 7/13/1975 in Rochester; Harold A. Emerson and Carol J. Ellingwood

Jennifer, b. 1/15/1945 in Rochester; first; Robert B. Emerson (US Army, Dorchester, MA) and Margaret Carmichael (Greenwich, CT); residence - Milton Mills

Kayla Rose, b. 4/3/1992 in Portsmouth; Charles E. Emerson and Karen R. Larochelle

Nancy Joan, b. 1/22/1942; first; Beatrice E. Emerson (Haverhill, MA)

EMMONS,
son, b. 3/26/1906; first; Jerome E. Emmons (laborer, 24, Shapleigh, ME) and Ida L. Connors (16, Sanford, ME)

ENMAN,
Minerva Jane, b. 5/16/1933 in Milton Mills; fourth; Russell R. Enman (laborer, Bangor, ME) and Inzy E. Farren (Errol); residence - Milton Mills

ERNST,
Sarah Elizabeth, b. 9/25/1986 in Rochester; Mark A. Ernst and Peggy L. Seamans

ESSAFF,
Logan Stephen, b. 5/17/1999 in Portsmouth; Peter Essaff and Adrienne Greenlaw

ESTEVAO,
Theodore Demetrius, b. 2/18/1998; Elias L. Estevao and Jessica R. Estevao

EVANS,
daughter, b. 2/5/1904; first; Clarence D. Evans (farmer, Wakefield) and Gertrude L. Perry (Topsfield, MA)
daughter [Carrie May], b. 3/16/1904; first; Calvin J. Evans (farmer, 29, Wakefield) and Flora B. Rines (29, New Durham)
daughter [Marion], b. 8/29/1905; second; Joseph C. Evans (farmer, 30, Wakefield) and Flora B. Rhines (31, New Durham)
Andrea Elaine, b. 7/8/1968 in Dover; David C. Evans and Geraldine R. Swett
Cynthia Ann, b. 9/20/1962 in Rochester; David C. Evans (USMC) and Geraldine R. Swett
Florence Mabel, b. 11/5/1917; first; Robert C. Evans (boxmaker, Middleton) and Marion L. Whitehouse (Berwick, ME)
Katelyn Cecille, b. 1/6/1993 in Dover; Jacob J. Evans and Carlene M. Hirsch
Seth Jordon, b. 2/1/1998; Frank J. Evans and Sherry L. Gorney
Sumner, b. 5/23/1894; second; Charles H. Evans (laborer, 28, Alton) and Alice Tebbetts (18, Rochester)

Sumner William, b. 12/10/1917; first; Sumner L. Evans (foreman, Milton) and Blanche I. O'Brian (Masonville, PQ)

Yvonne, b. 1/14/1934 in Rochester; first; Richard Evans (mill emp., Wakefield) and Miriam Paschal (Boston, MA); residence - Milton Mills

FALL,

Arnold, Jr., b. 12/29/1931 in Milton Mills; second; Arnold Fall (laborer, Rollinsford) and Bernice Brown (Attleboro, MA); residence - Milton Mills

Erwin Arnold, b. 12/5/1930 in Salem, MA; first; Arnold Fall (laborer, Rollinsford) and Bernice Brown (N. Attleboro, MA); residence - Milton Mills

FANSLAU,

Carol MaryJean, b. 3/12/1985 in Rochester; Gene H. Fanslau and Mary E. Record

FARLEY,

Eva Louise, b. 10/13/1913; second; Charles E. Farley (laborer, Mt. Desert, ME) and Mary L. Tebbetts (East Rochester)

FAUCHER,

Melissa Rachelle, b. 10/13/1984 in Rochester; Denis H. Faucher and Rachel M. Thibodeau

FECTEAU,

Jerad Ronald, b. 10/12/1983 in Dover; Ralph A. Fecteau and Beverly J. Lord

Meredith Ellen, b. 5/10/1981 in Dover; Ralph A. Fecteau and Beverly J. Lord

FEENEY,

Thelma Winona, b. 12/22/1917; first; Preston H. Feeney (lumberman, Saugus, MA) and Minnie E. Hersom (Lebanon, ME)

Willard Guild, b. 8/23/1922; second; Preston Feeney (card room, Saugus, MA) and Minnie Hersom (Sanford, ME) (1923)

FERGUSON,
Jacob Scott, b. 2/23/1985 in Rochester; Scott J. Ferguson and Anne M. Duggan
Jonathan Edward, b. 2/8/1987 in Rochester; Scott J. Ferguson and Anne M. Duggan
Scott James, b. 1/25/1957 in Sanford, ME; fifth; Frederick Ferguson (mechanic, Sanford, ME) and Helen Neary (Brooklyn, NY); residence - Milton Mills

FERRELLI,
Mariah Elizabeth, b. 10/18/1995 in Dover; James M. Ferrelli and Karyn L. Ferrelli

FERRIS,
Stacy Lee, b. 4/8/1969 in Rochester; Dennis G. Ferris and Judith A. Hutchins

FEYLER,
Dwight Wayne, b. 11/26/1951 in Rochester; fourth; Harlan Feyler (beater man, Waldoboro, ME) and Louise Garland (Wolfeboro)

FIELDS,
Keith Alan, b. 3/28/1960 in Rochester; third; Henry C. Fields (rigger) and Arlene M. Sceggell
Lorraine Carol, b. 7/8/1964 in Rochester; fifth; Henry C. Fields (navy yard) and Arlene M. Sceggell
Nancy Ann, b. 4/7/1962 in Rochester; Henry C. Fields (rigger) and Arlene M. Sceggell

FIFIELD,
Danielle Elizabeth, b. 7/30/1988 in Rochester; James K. Fifield and Diane Buskey
Danielle Jean, b. 5/9/1981 in Wolfeboro; David A. Fifield and Debra A. Sprague
Denise Tisha, b. 2/25/1985 in Rochester; Kenneth G. Fifield and Jeanne E. Huppe
Erik Shawn, b. 8/15/1987 in Rochester; James K. Fifield and Diane L. Buskey

Georgieanna, b. 4/4/1963 in Rochester; George R. Fifield (laborer) and Lavina Brewer

Rena Elizabeth, b. 7/25/1961 in Rochester; George R. Fifield (laborer) and Lavina Brewer

Robert Henry, b. 3/10/1952 in Rochester; second; Francis H. Fifield (shoe worker, NH) and Marjorie V. Woodes (Rochester)

Virginia Lee, b. 8/23/1946 in Rochester; first; Francis H. Fifield (shoe worker, Wakefield) and Marjorie V. Woodes (Rochester)

FILGATE,
William P., Jr., b. 4/25/1930; second; William P. Filgate (laundry man, Plymouth) and Margaret Lover (Wakefield); residence - Laconia

FINEGAN,
Rosalie Brenda, b. 7/12/1906; third; Herbert F. Finegan (bookkeeper, 37, Rindge) and Clara B. Wakefield (31, Townsend, MA)

FLANAGAN,
Abigale Meghan, b. 2/10/1995 in Dover; James R. Flanagan and Sandra L. Flanagan

Alisha Mae, b. 7/19/1997 in Rochester; James R. Flanagan and Sandra L. Flanagan

Darlene Marie, b. 11/8/1965 in Rochester; Dennis M. Flanagan (salesman) and Jeanette D. Marcoux

David Brian, b. 12/5/1960 in Rochester; fourth; Dennis B. Flanagan (salesman) and Jeanette D. Marcoux

Denise, b. 8/27/1959 in Rochester; second; Dennis M. Flanagan (shoeworker, Berwick, ME) and Jeannette D. Marcoux (Milton)

Dennis Matthew, b. 8/27/1959 in Rochester; third; Dennis M. Flanagan (shoeworker, Berwick, ME) and Jeannette D. Marcoux (Milton)

Kevin Wesley, b. 4/11/1981 in Dover; Dennis M. Flanagan, Jr. and Theresa F. Anderson

Michael John, b. 12/26/1969 in Rochester; Dennis M. Flanagan and Jeanette Marcoux

Nichole Annie, b. 7/10/1999 in Dover; James Flanagan and Sandra Flanagan

FLETCHER,
stillborn son, b. 8/19/1925 in Rochester; fourth; Harry Fletcher (clerk, Caribou, ME) and Laura E. Young (Milton Mills); residence - Milton Mills (1926)
Daniel Hartwell, b. 12/4/1926; sixth; Harry Fletcher (clerk, Caribou, ME) and Laura Young (Acton, ME); residence - Milton Mills
Harvey R., Jr., b. 3/9/1948 in Rochester; first; Harvey R. Fletcher (store clerk, Rochester) and Lois M. Hardesty (Phoenix, AZ)

FLOYD,
Edward James, b. 3/12/1915; second; Melvin Floyd (teamster, Conway) and Marie Russell (Rumford, ME)

FOGG,
Keith Edward, b. 8/19/1958 in Sanford, ME; third; George L. Fogg (leather opr., Sanford, ME) and Shirley L. Laskey (Wolfeboro); residence - Milton Mills

FOLGER,
Richard Martin, III, b. 8/3/1985 in Wolfeboro; Richard M. Folger, Jr. and Tammy A. Nisbet

FORCIER,
Jennifer Anne, b. 12/21/1987 in Dover; Robert L. Forcier and Brenda J. Mundy

FORTIER,
Deborah Lee, b. 11/4/1951 in Rochester; stillborn; first; William K. Fortier (laborer, Tamworth) and Rena L. Drew (Pittsfield)
Dwight Keith, b. 11/6/1953 in Rochester; second; William K. Fortier (mill worker, Tamworth) and Rena L. Drew (Pittsfield)
Leslie Walter, b. 5/11/1956 in Rochester; second; William K. Fortier (mach. tender, Tamworth) and Rena Drew (Pittsfield)

FOSS,
Shirley Diane, b. 1/30/1950 in Wolfeboro; second; Walter C. Foss (shoe shop, Rochester) and Margaret Clifford (Wolfeboro)

FOSTER,
Merissa Ann Rishay, b. 3/27/1975 in Rochester; Richard C. Foster and Susan E. Boothby
Richard Carl, II, b. 3/2/1976 in Rochester; Richard C. Foster and Susan E. Boothby

FOX,
Edwyna E., b. 8/1/1893; first; Charles D. Fox (hotel keeper, 37, Milton) and Hattie M. Fox (33, Milton)
Lillian E., b. 7/13/1893; fourth; John E. Fox (station agent, 43, Tuftonboro) and Abbie F. Woodman (41, Tamworth)

FRANCQ,
Joseph, stillborn, b. 8/2/1927 in Rochester; fourth; J. Victor Francq (poultryman, Lowell, MA) and Alida Jacmain (Canada); residence - Milton Mills

FREEMAN,
Emily Louise, b. 12/28/1905; first; George L. Freeman (civil engineer, 25, W. Gray, ME) and Annie B. Kimball (22, Milton)

FRENCH,
Jeffrey David, b. 4/24/1988 in Rochester; Deane N. French and Judyth Roberts
Kristen Alaine, b. 8/26/1983 in Rochester; Deane N. French and Judyth Roberts
Merilyn Elizabeth, b. 5/3/1930; Forrest French (garage man, Roxbury, MA) and Gladys L. Laskey (Milton)
Suzanne, b. 1/13/1945 in Milton Mills; second; Forrest S. French (garage owner, Porter, ME) and Gladys L. Laskey (Milton); residence - Milton Mills

GAGNE,
Arthur Joseph Leo, b. 5/30/1915; first; Frank Gagne (emp. in mill, Canada) and Blanche McNicoll (Canada)
Harold Prentice, 3d, b. 2/20/1952 in Rochester; second; Harold P. Gagne, Jr. (US Army, ME) and Frances M. Weeman (Rochester)
Kayla Marie, b. 12/17/1985 in Rochester; Steven P. Gagne and Cherie L. Chenette

Sandra Louise, b. 3/22/1951 in Rochester; first; Harold P. Gagne, Jr. (shoe worker, ME) and Frances M. Weeman (Union)

Sharon Lee, b. 1/4/1947 in Wolfeboro; Harold P. Gagne (woodsman, Oxford, ME) and Fayelyn M. Cousins (Lewiston, ME); residence - Milton Mills

Wallace Eugene, b. 5/4/1948 in Rochester; first; Thelma I. Gagne (Lyman)

GAGNON,
Benjamin Ernest, b. 2/5/1982 in Rochester; James J. Gagnon and Penny C. Cox

Jason Adam, b. 11/28/1989 in Rochester; Paul E. Gagnon, Jr. and Debra A. Jackunchuck

Steven Joseph, b. 1/7/1982 in Dover; David A. Gagnon and Kathy A. Lamper

GALARNEAU,
Bryanna Catherine, b. 12/1/1995 in Rochester; Mark A. Galarneau and Stephanie K. Galarneau

Mark Alan, b. 7/27/1958 in Rochester; third; Milford L. Galarneau (machinist, Union) and Madeline MacIlvaine (Milton)

Milford Lauren, Jr., b. 10/1/1942 in Rochester; first; Milford L. Galarneau (navy yard, Union) and Madelyn MacIlvaine (Milton)

Peter Jay, b. 2/5/1949 in Rochester; second; Milford L. Galarneau (shoe factory, NH) and Madeline E. MacIlvaine (NH)

GALPIN,
Elmer Lewis, b. 1/28/1904 in Milton Mills; first; Lewis P. Galpin (Torrrington, CT) and Annie E. Wentworth (Ossipee); residence - Milton Mills (1938)

GARCELON,
Casey Catrina, b. 1/9/1995 in Rochester; Richard M. Garcelon and Kristine Garcelon

GARCIA,
Peter Anthony, Jr., b. 8/17/1990 in Rochester; Peter A. Garcia and Kristen A. Cooper

GARD,
John H., 3d, b. 10/31/1936 in Milton Mills; first; John H. Gard, Jr. (driller stone, Tilton) and Margaret O. Munsey (Gilmanton)

GARDNER,
Richard L., b. 6/29/1911; second; Harry W. Gardner (architect, Dover) and Celia M. Brophy (Philadelphia, PA)

GARLAND,
daughter, b. 10/1/1888; A. W. Garland (clerk, Bartlett) and Minnie E. Colbath
child [Nellie M.], b. 8/7/1904; first; Clarence E. Garland (farmer, 31, Wakefield) and Verna Reynolds (21, Sanford, ME)
stillborn daughter, b. 2/5/1923; fourth; Bernice Garland (Wolfeboro)
Chad Dakota, b. 11/24/1998 in Rochester; Robert Garland and Nancy Garland
Eva Mildred, b. 4/5/1920; first; Aldo B. Garland (fireman, Wolfeboro) and Bessie B. Glass (Portsmouth)
Jessie Priscilla, b. 9/8/1910; first; Joseph S. Garland (civil engineer, Wakefield) and Josie M. Calkins (Milton)

GARNETT,
Mary Elizabeth, b. 9/14/1929 in Rochester; first; Reynard Garnett (bookkeeper, Lebanon, ME) and Isabel McBride (Watertown, NY)

GARVEY,
Patricia Louise, b. 9/11/1950 in Wolfeboro; first; Louis J. Garvey (mach. op., CT) and Myrtle Saunders (NS); residence - Boston, MA

GARVIN,
son, b. 7/27/1894; eighth; Edward Garvin (mechanic, 35, No. Andover, MA) and Maggie Mahony (32)

GARYAIT,
Barbara Ann, b. 8/18/1935 in Rochester; Arthur Garyait (mill hand, Lebanon, ME) and Charlotte Wiggin (Milton)
Mark Alan, b. 9/27/1956 in Rochester; fifth; Richard Garyait (US Navy, Union) and Evelyn McCoy (MI)

Sherrie Jean, b. 8/15/1954 in Rochester; fourth; Richard Garyait (US
Navy, Union) and Evelyn L. McCoy (Ionia, MI)

GAUDETTE,
Charles Edward, b. 7/30/1915; sixth; Charles N. Gaudette (Supt. Boston
Ice, Hudson City, NY) and Sarah A. O'Donnell (Belfast, Ireland)
Pauline, b. 4/1/1910; fourth; Charles N. Gaudette (laborer, Hudson, NY)
and Sarah A. McDaniel (Belfast, Ireland) (1914)

GAUTHIER,
Aaron Sky, b. 6/1/1974 in Rochester; Paul R. Gauthier and Lynne C.
Papatones
Michael Raymond Alexander, b. 2/6/1981 in Rochester; Paul R. Gauthier
and Lynne C. Papatones

GAUTREAU,
Anthony David, b. 4/15/1980 in Rochester; Michael W. Gautreau and
Evelyn M. Burrows
Chad Edward, b. 9/13/1980 in Dover; Craig E. Gautreau and Vivian E.
Cutter
Pauline Jane, b. 7/1/1984 in Rochester; Mark G. Gautreau and Jean
Worster

GEARWAR,
Jacob Michael, b. 12/9/1980 in Dover; Michael W. Gearwar and Marcia
A. Frost

GEARY,
Helen Carolene, b. 6/7/1911; first; Anthony W. Geary (emp. sawmill,
Waterboro, ME) and Alice R. Perkins (Wolfeboro)
Richard James, b. 8/9/1936 in Limerick, ME; Paul Geary (plumber, S.
Wolfeboro) and Lorna Dall (Portland, ME)

GENTES,
Ethan Charles, b. 5/31/1991 in Tokyo, Japan; Steven C. Gentes and Jane
Lucier

GEORGE,
Bert Dutton, Jr., b. 12/3/1981 in Wolfeboro; Bert D. George, Jr. and Jeanne A. Goddard

GERMAIN,
Anne Marie, b. 12/28/1962 in Rochester; Clifford Germain (teacher) and Gwendolyn M. Turner
Kathleen Ann, b. 6/6/1960 in Rochester; third; Clifford P. Germain (school teacher) and Gwendolyn M. Turner
Timothy Robert, b. 6/29/1961 in Rochester; Clifford P. Germain (gas att. & teacher) and Gwendolyn Turner

GERMON,
Bruce, b. 11/7/1960 in Rochester; third; Richard H. Germon (steel worker) and Lorraine Whitehouse

GERO,
Jessica Carolyn, b. 11/8/1995 in Dover; Steven E. Gero and Tamara Grant-Gero
Zachary Steven, b. 5/10/1989 in Dover; Steven E. Gero and Tamara S. Grant

GERONAITIS,
Amy Elizabeth, b. 2/26/1993 in Dover; William V. Geronaitis and Teresa A. Melanson
John William, b. 10/1/1990 in Dover; William V. Geronaitis and Teresa A. Melanson

GIBSON,
Nicole Jennie, b. 10/6/1989 in Dover; Michael A. Gibson and Diane R. McDuffee
Robert Gordon, b. 3/24/1933 in Rochester; first; William E. Gibson (chef, Plainfield) and Stella Tomilson (Stanley, NB); residence - Milton Mills

GILBERT,
son [John I.], b. 12/13/1901; fourth; Daniel Gilbert (laborer, 37, Farmington) and Ida M. Duntley (30, Farmington)

stillborn daughter, b. 7/11/1910; seventh; Daniel Gilbert (farmer, Farmington) and Ida M. Duntley (Milton)

Ada, b. 3/29/1893; second; Daniel Gilbert (shoemaker, 28, Farmington) and Ida M. Duntley (22, Milton)

Alma, b. 8/11/1908; sixth; Daniel Gilbert (farmer, 46, Farmington) and Ida Duntley (39, Milton)

Darrell Elroy, b. 7/29/1912; eighth; Daniel Gilbert (laborer, 49, Farmington) and Ida M. Duntley (41, Milton)

Evelyn, b. 8/3/1906; fifth; Daniel Gilbert (farmer, 41, Farmington) and Ida M. Duntley (37, Milton)

Raymond, b. 4/18/1891; first; Daniel Gilbert (shoemaker, 26, Farmington) and Ida M. Duntley (20, Farmington)

Walter, b. 12/2/1899; third; Thomas Gilbert (paper maker, 28, Canada) and Annie Valley (26, Barrington)

Wilfred, b. 6/2/1896; third; Daniel Gilbert (laborer, 31, Farmington) and Ida Duntley (25, Milton)

GILES,
Jesse Henry, b. 9/9/1909; first; Charles F. Giles (Springvale, ME) and Philomen Sturgeon (Canada) (1911)

GILMAN,
John Lake, b. 5/19/1935 in Laconia; first; John G. Gilman (farmer, Lisbon) and Mildred Lake (Lincoln)

GILMORE,
stillborn son, b. 5/27/1933; first; William E. Gilmore (hosp. orderly, Worcester, MA) and Doris N. Goodwin (Laconia)

Nancy Louise, b. 10/17/1934 in Rochester; first; William E. Gilmore (laborer, Worcester, MA) and Doris M. Goodwin (Laconia)

GIORDANO,
Frederick, III, b. 3/17/1993 in Rochester; Frederick Giordano, Jr. and Liliam Collazo

GLADWIN,
Thelma Irene, b. 3/14/1917; first; Chester A. Gladwin (ice man, Halifax, NS) and Jennie M. Spooner (Wilksport, ON)

GLAUDE,
Wilfrid, b. 1/10/1884 in Milton Mills; first; Alexie Glaude (bleacher, Canada) and Marie Hamel (St. George, PQ); residence - Milton Mills (1938)

GLIDDEN,
Catherine Gertrude, b. 10/21/1913; thirteenth; Charles A. Glidden (laborer, Gonic) and Winnie M. Duntley (Milton)
Frank Elmer, b. 7/16/1916; second; George W. Glidden (emp. in mill, Farmington) and Maude A. Nickless (Hooksett)
Ruth Agnes, b. 10/14/1917; third; George W. Glidden (emp. in mill, Farmington) and Maude A. Nickless (Hooksett)
Thurlo Wilton, b. 2/5/1914; first; George W. Glidden (emp. in mill, Farmington) and Maud A. Nickolass (Hooksett)
Vaughn Dale, b. 10/4/1970 in Rochester; Franklin S. Glidden and Alice E. Gibb

GOFF,
Amanda Jane, b. 1/4/1982 in Exeter; Kevin M. Goff and Laurie J. Forcier
Shannan Elizabeth, b. 11/23/1980 in Exeter; Kevin M. Goff and Laurie J. Forcier

GOGGIN,
William Haines, b. 6/12/1975 in Rochester; Jerome N. Goggin and Gloria J. Haines

GOLDEN,
Josh Van, b. 1/24/1997 in Dover; Todd M. Golden and Polly A. Golden
Judith Kay, b. 9/19/1946 in Rochester; second; William H. Golden (shoe maker, Ctr. Barnstead) and Marion A. Wyatt (Farmington)

GOLDENBERG,
Elijah Kai, b. 9/22/1992 in Rochester; Ari B. Goldenberg and Kristen Caswell
Zachariah Nathaniel, b. 8/1/1990 in Dover; Ari B. Goldenberg and Kristen M. Caswell

GOLDTHWAIT,
Lillian Frances, b. 8/20/1928; fifth; Herbert Goldthwait (laborer, Lynn, MA) and Marilla Prescott (Acton, ME); residence - Milton Mills

GOODBEAM,
son, b. 4/6/1888; Joseph Goodbeam (laborer, Canada) and Mary Jeffers (Canada)

GOODRICH,
Katherine A., b. 7/9/1928 in Rochester; second; James F. Goodrich (lumber oper., Berwick, ME) and Katherine Redlon (Berwick, ME)

GOODSON,
Arlyne Frances, b. 12/29/1912; first; Francis Goodson (chauffeur, Gonic) and Ethel Birch (Parsonsfield, ME) (1913)

GOODWIN,
daughter, b. 8/25/1927 in Milton Mills; sixth; Charles H. Goodwin (laborer, Milton Mills) and Stella D. Hamilton (Milton Mills); residence - Milton Mills
Anna, b. 3/18/1917; fourth; Clarence G. Goodwin (shoemaker, Dover) and Agnes M. Mulligan (Lynn, MA)
Annie R., b. 8/22/1874; fourth; Benjamin F. Goodwin and Emma A. Wentworth (1939)
Arlyne Doris, b. 6/11/1919; third; Charles H. Goodwin (napper in mill, Milton) and Stella D. Hamilton (Milton) (1920)
Brittney Lynn, b. 9/24/1991 in Dover; Wayne E. Goodwin and Linda E. Winship
Clayton Lawrence, b. 3/3/1935 in Wolfeboro; first; Howard W. Goodwin (laborer, Milton Mills) and Frances Curry (ME); residence - Milton Mills
Doris Margaret, b. 7/29/1920; fifth; Clarence G. Goodwin (laborer, Dover) and Agnes M. Mulligan (Lynn, MA)
Dorothy Phyllis, b. 7/29/1920; sixth; Clarence G. Goodwin (laborer, Dover) and Agnes M. Mulligan (Lynn, MA)
Frank Shepard, b. 3/31/1913; third; Clarence G. Goodwin (shoe trimmer, Milton) and Agnes M. Mulligan (Lynn, MA)

Gloria Phillis, b. 11/15/1925 in Milton Mills; fifth; Charles H. Goodwin (laborer, Milton Mills) and Stella D. Hamilton (Milton Mills); residence - Milton Mills
Harriett F., b. 6/4/1875; fourth; Benjamin F. Goodwin and Emma A. ----- (1939)
James Robert, b. 7/31/1951 in Rochester; third; Lloyd E. Goodwin (shoe worker, Farmington) and Barbara J. Tufts (Milton)
Karen Alice, b. 12/6/1959 in Rochester; fifth; Lloyd E. Goodwin (cementer, Farmington) and Barbara Tufts (Milton)
Keith Allan, b. 11/12/1955 in Rochester; fourth; Lloyd E. Goodwin (shoe worker, Farmington) and Barbara J. Tufts (Milton)
Lois Ida, b. 10/22/1923; fourth; Charles H. Goodwin (napper, Milton) and Stella Hamilton (Milton)
Mary Jane, b. 6/14/1911; second; Clarence G. Goodwin (shoemaker, Milton) and Agnes M. Morgan (Lynn, MA)
Sandra Jean, b. 5/14/1948 in Rochester; second; Lloyd E. Goodwin (shoe shop, Farmington) and Barbara J. Tufts (Milton)
Warren Henry, b. 3/20/1913; first; Charles H. Goodwin (shoemaker, Milton) and Stella D. Hamilton (Milton)
William Howard, b. 4/21/1915; second; Charles H. Goodwin (napper, Milton) and Stella D. Hamilton (Milton)

GORDON,
Aaron Matthew, b. 9/27/1991 in Rochester; Glenn A. Gordon and Wendy A. Foss
Alyssa Nicole, b. 5/5/1994 in Rochester; Glenn A. Gordon and Wendy A. Foss
Ansel Francis, b. 1/20/1914; first; Almon F. Gordon (blanket folder, Shapleigh, ME) and Nellie Cronin (Acton, ME) (1915)
Deborah Mary, b. 11/1/1953 in Rochester; first; Leo E. Gordon (US Army, Acton, ME) and Agnes E. Ryan (Pittsfield)
Ellsworth Franklin, b. 9/3/1918; fifth; Almon F. Gordon (laborer, Shapleigh, ME) and Nellie Cronin (Acton, ME) (1920)
Evelin A., b. 4/8/1915; second; Almon F. Gordon (blanket folder, Shapleigh, ME) and Nellie Cronin (Acton, ME)
Tarrya Louise, b. 2/19/1949 in Rochester; fifth; Ansel F. Gordon (woodsman, NH) and Beatrice M. Dalphond (NH)

GORNEY,
Molly Kathryn, b. 6/26/1998; Keith G. Gorney and Betsy L. Gorney

GORTON,
Zachary Joseph, b. 6/18/1990 in Dover; Michael C. Gorton, Sr. and Annette Rowe

GOSSELIN,
daughter [Beatrice E.], b. 5/17/1907; second; Joseph A. Gosselin (emp. in mill, 24, Canada) and Lucy E. Bellemer (21, Canada)
Albert Abathol, b. 9/30/1913; fourth; Joseph A. Gosselyn (sic) (foreman, Canada) and Lucy E. Belmer (Canada)
Kathleen Marie, b. 1/8/1984 in Wolfeboro; Robert R. Gosselin, II and Catherine J. Carlin
Mark Alan, b. 2/10/1972 in Dover; Alfred M. Gosselin and Lila M. Goodwin
Mary Blanche, b. 10/9/1908; third; Joseph A. Gosselin (emp. in mill, 26, Canada) and Lucy E. Bellemeur (23, Canada)
Matthew Robert, b. 8/26/1982 in Wolfeboro; Robert R. Gosselin, II and Catherine J. Carlin
Michael John, b. 9/25/1985 in Wolfeboro; Robert R. Gosselin, II and Catherine J. Carlin

GOURLAY,
Eben James, b. 6/21/1999 in Dover; Robert Gourlay and Joanne Gourlay

GOWEN,
stillborn son, b. 12/10/1904; ninth; George W. Gowen (laborer, 51, Berwick, ME) and Eva A. Baker (36, Gloucester, MA)
Dorothy E., b. 8/29/1908; tenth; George W. Gowen (laborer, 55, Berwick, ME) and Eva A. Baker (38, Gloucester, MA)
George, b. 7/25/1903; eighth; George W. Gowen (teamster, 50, Berwick, ME) and Eva M. Baker (34, Gloucester, MA)
Ida M., b. 4/16/1889; first; George W. Gowen (farmer, 36, North Berwick, ME) and Eva M. Baker (20, Gloucester, MA)
John F., b. 11/4/1894; fourth; George W. Gowen (farmer, Gloucester, MA) and Eva Baker (S. Berwick, ME)

GRACE,
daughter, b. 5/11/1915; first; Mary E. Grace (Tamworth)
Helen Louise, b. 10/14/1919; first; John A. Grace (farmer, Maidstone, VT) and Flora M. Grace (Albany)

GRANT,
David Franklin, b. 12/12/1963 in Wolfeboro; David R. Grant, Sr. (set-up man) and Jeanine C. Fontaine
Ethel, b. 2/1/1891; second; Walter B. Grant (butcher, Milford, MA) and Gertrude G. Howard (Canada)
Muriel Rose, b. 7/26/1899; third; Hugh D. Grant (blacksmith, 29, NS) and Bessie McLarcee (33, NS)

GRAY,
Albert Lord, b. 8/5/1954 in Rochester; first; William A. Gray (laster, Alton) and Rita J. King (Alton)
Angela Marie, b. 7/10/1987 in Rochester; Stephen C. Gray and Sharon Appleton
Brandi Lee, b. 9/17/1979 in Rochester; David B. Gray and Lorna A. Morgan
Craig Robert, b. 7/27/1969 in Rochester; John D. Gray and Diane G. Colbath
Sean Michael, b. 10/15/1973 in Dover; Thomas A. Gray and Claudia Harmon
Steven Douglas, b. 12/10/1968 in Rochester; Wilbur M. Gray and Gloria M. King
William Russell, b. 6/25/1985 in Rochester; Stephen C. Gray and Sharon A. Appleton

GREEN,
Christopher Nathaniel, b. 3/26/1981 in Rochester; Laurice B. Green, Jr. and Gloria J. Pied

GREENE,
Christopher Bruce, b. 12/14/1963 in Wolfeboro; James L. Greene (tanner) and Patricia L. Ferguson
Erin Suzanna, b. 3/4/1971 in Wolfeboro; Douglas A. Greene and Genevieve P. Frase

Frederick Sumner, b. 4/5/1960 in Wolfeboro; third; James L. Greene (tanner) and Patricia L. Ferguson
George Andrews, b. 10/31/1938 in Rochester; fifth; Harold G. Greene (lumber wkr.) and Margaret L. Ellison (E. Barrington)
Molly Jennifer, b. 3/13/1969 in Wolfeboro; Douglas A. Greene and Genevieve P. Frase
Rebecca Malina, b. 9/30/1975 in Rochester; Douglas A. Greene and Genevieve P. Frase

GREGOIRE,
Clara Irene, b. 11/18/1959 in Rochester; fifth; Adelard Gregoire (trimmer, Somersworth) and Irene Duchano (Sanbornville)
Jeanne Marie, b. 12/12/1954 in Rochester; third; Adelard Gregoire (tannery, Somersworth) and Irene Duchano (Sanbornville)
Susanne Beatrice, b. 6/27/1956 in Rochester; fourth; Adelard Gregoire (emp. in tannery, Somersworth) and Irene Duchano (Sanbornville)

GRENIER,
Ina Celia, b. 6/30/1897; fifth; Peter Grenier (laster, 39, Stoneham, MA) and Rose Tracey (39, Southboro, MA)
Louis Wilfred, b. 8/12/1898; first; Joseph Grenier (mill operative, 28, Canada) and Alphonaine Croteau (25, Canada)

GREY,
Eva Lydia, b. 6/4/1908; fifth; George H. Grey (clergyman, 45, Sheffield, VT) and Eva Gray (35, Sheffield, VT)

GRIFFIN,
Anthony George, b. 12/12/1963 in Rochester; Thomas G. Griffin (beater man) and Terri E. Sanborn
Jean, b. 3/12/1963; John J. Griffin (mechanic) and Janet L. York
Kathryn Ella, b. 9/3/1971 in Wolfeboro; Thomas G. Griffin and Terri E. Sanborn

GRISKOWITZ,
Kathy Lynn, b. 8/21/1963 in Rochester; Anthony Griskowitz (shoe worker) and Sharron L. Titcomb

GRODEN,
stillborn son, b. 6/10/1891; first; Frank Groden (section hand, 36, Canada) and Ory Provencher (28, Canada)

GRONDEN,
son, b. 12/6/1961 in Rochester; Sterling L. Gronden (machine operator) and Geraldine Landeen

GROVER,
stillborn son, b. 9/23/1905; first; Harry C. Grover (hotel prop., 33, Barrington) and Mary F. Emerson (36, Wakefield)

GUINDON,
Michelle Elizabeth, b. 11/2/1996 in Dover; Gary P. Guindon and Diane E. Guindon
Nicole Elaine, b. 9/15/1989 in Dover; Gary P. Guindon and Diane Beattie

GUSTAFSON,
Carl William, b. 1/3/1907; eighth; Nicholas H. Gustafson (laborer, 43, Sweden) and Sarah A. F. Lord (3-, Hingham, MA)
Helen Gertrude, b. 8/14/1908; ninth; Nicholas H. Gustafson (laborer, 45, Sweden) and Sarah A. F. Lord (38, Hingham, MA)
Herman Lawrence, b. 6/15/1905; eighth; Nicholas H. Gustafson (laborer, 41, Wiesbe, Sweden) and Sarah A. F. Lord (35, Hingham, MA)

HAGEMIKE,
Dana Anthony, b. 12/13/1984 in Rochester; Anthony C. Hagemike and Catherine E. Appleton
Tina Marie, b. 4/20/1981 in Dover; Anthony C. Hagemike and Catherine E. Appleton

HALDERMAN,
Jeremy Steven, b. 5/4/1985 in Portsmouth; Richard D. Halderman and Brenda G. Jones

HALE,
Margaret Rebecca, b. 9/19/1926 in Milton Mills; Albert Hale (mill operative, Laconia) and Mamie Day (W. Newfield, ME); residence - Milton Mills

HALEY,
Chris-Ann, b. 7/3/1967 in Rochester; first; Roy C. Haley (set-up man) and
   Carlene E. Gould
Marjory Alice, b. 12/21/1925 in Rochester; Ralph S. Haley (lumberman,
   Tuftonboro) and Gladys Doying (Nashua) (1926)

HALL,
daughter, b. 3/18/1891; third; Fred Hall (laborer, 25, Canada) and Mary
   Duquette (24, Canada)
son, b. 2/13/1899; fifth; John Hall (mill hand, 37, Canada) and Marceline
   Moro (38, Canada)
daughter, b. 8/20/1899; eighth; Fred Hall (laborer, 24, Canada) and Mary
   Duquett (23, Canada)
daughter, b. 12/14/1900; ninth; Fred Hall (laborer, 35, Canada) and Mary
   Douquette (34, Canada)
Annmarie Patricia, b. 8/15/1993 in Portsmouth; Stewart C. Hall and
   Dianne M. Gilblair
Brandon Phillip, b. 3/1/1984 in Rochester; Gregory A. Hall and Sheila A.
   Downs
Christopher Weyland, b. 5/1/1968 in Rochester; Gary A. Hall and Sue I.
   Moody
Eric Kenneth, b. 4/5/1976 in Rochester; Kenneth H. Hall and Deborah A.
   Whitten
Harold Reginald, b. 9/27/1908; first; Clarence W. Hall (clerk, 22, No.
   Shapleigh, ME) and Georgie M. Dorr (21, Milton)
Helen Pearl, b. 2/24/1910; second; Clarence W. Hall (teamster, No.
   Shapleigh, ME) and Georgie M. Dorr (Milton)
Hugh Norman, b. 3/12/1947 in Rochester; second; Hugh N. Hall (log
   chopper, Oakland, GA) and Lee A. Drew (Providence, RI); residence
   - Milton Mills
Jereme Michael, b. 5/7/1971 in Rochester; Gary A. Hall and Sue I. Moody
John Andrews, Jr., b. 11/20/1918; second; John A. Hall (farmer,
   Wakefield) and Laura E. Willey (Milton)
Josephine M., b. 6/4/1912; first; John A. Hall (heel cutter, Wakefield) and
   Laura Willey (Milton) (1914)
Kimberly Constance, b. 1/6/1969 in Rochester; Kenneth W. Hall, Jr. and
   Brenda J. Sanborn
Scott Michael, b. 12/20/1979 in Dover; Kenneth H. Hall and Deborah A.
   Whitten

HAM,
daughter, b. 9/4/1893; third; Charles Ham (laborer, Farmington) and
    Phoebe Tibbetts (21, Rochester)
Barbara Mabel, b. 8/18/1932; first; Francis H. Ham (laborer, Milton) and
    Mabel G. Ritchie (Newfield, ME)
Bernard William, b. 9/17/1917; fifth; James J. Ham (emp. in mill, Dover)
    and Blanche C. Drew (Brookfield)
Edwin, b. 2/9/1901; second; Charles E. Ham (mill hand, 31, Farmington)
    and Lena Varney (24, Milton)
Frank, b. 2/24/1909; first; James J. Ham (emp. in mill, Dover) and
    Blanche C. Drew (Brookfield)
George W., b. 6/2/1891; second; Charles E. Ham (farmer, 30,
    Farmington) and Phoebe Tibbetts (21, Rochester)
James J., b. 12/17/1914; fourth; James J. Ham (emp. in mill, Dover) and
    Blanche C. Drew (Brookfield)
Katherine B., b. 3/14/1911; second; James J. Ham (emp. in mill, Dover)
    and Blanche C. Drew (Brookfield)
Lawrence Richard, b. 10/11/1922; sixth; James J. Ham (laborer, Dover)
    and Blanche C. Drew (Brookfield)
Mildred Teresa, b. 1/29/1913; third; James J. Ham (emp. in mill, Dover)
    and Blanch C. Drew (Brookfield)
Robert Francis, b. 9/11/1935; second; Francis H. Ham (mill hand, Milton)
    and Mabel G. Ritchie (Newfield, ME)

HAMILL,
Thomas Boyd, b. 9/22/1896; first; Thomas B. Hamill (ice dealer, 32, PEI)
    and Francis A. Rayner (28, PEI)

HAMILTON,
son [Ralph C.], b. 9/17/1902; first; Harry Hamilton (shoemaker, 26,
    Rochester) and Minnie G. Remick (20, Milton)
daughter [Rena], b. 8/3/1904; second; Harry Hamilton (shoemaker, 28,
    Rochester) and Minnie G. Remick (22, Milton)
daughter, b. 1/13/1908; fourth; Harry Hamilton (shoemaker, 31,
    Rochester) and Minnie G. Remick (25, Milton)
Beatrice, b. 6/21/1906; third; Harry Hamilton (shoemaker, 30, Rochester)
    and Minnie G. Remick (23, Milton)
Beatrice, b. 7/29/1910; fifth; Harry R. Hamilton (shoemaker, East
    Rochester) and Minnie G. Remick (Milton) (1911)

Stella Doris, b. 9/28/1894; first; Edgar F. Hamilton (laborer, 38, Milton) and Carrie A. Hooper (18, Milton)

HAMMOND,
Hazel P., b. 3/7/1914; seventh; Joseph Hammond (mill hand, Acton, ME) and Lizzie Williams (Wakefield)
Phillip Stephen, b. 2/4/1976 in Dover; Warren G. Hammond and Kathleen E. White

HANEY,
Cheri Lee, b. 9/20/1973 in Rochester; David W. Haney and Barbara A. Bilodeau
David Wayne, b. 9/27/1972 in Rochester; David W. Haney and Barbara A. Bilodeau
Katrina Elizabeth, b. 3/29/1989 in Portsmouth; James F. Haney and Margaret A. Trout

HANNIGAN,
Patrick Michael, b. 6/3/1999 in Dover; Joseph Hannigan and Rachel Hannigan

HANSEN,
Aimee Lynn, b. 1/13/1988 in Dover; Gerald B. Hansen and Dawn D. Marquis

HANSON,
daughter, b. 11/3/1906; fourth; John H. Hanson (emp. in mill, 34, Gonic) and Emma A. Pulsifer (31, Rochester)
Mariana Jean, b. 7/10/1945 in Rochester; second; Richard H. Hanson (air corps, Barnstead) and Natalie L. Wyatt (Farmington)

HARGRAVES,
Juanita Cutts, b. 6/29/1904; first; Carlton J. Hargraves (barber, 19, Milton) and Lillian R. Prescott (18, Acton, ME)

HARNDEN,
Mabel Esther, b. 3/29/1911; second; Esther E. Harnden (Denmark, ME)

HARRIMAN,
son, b. 6/13/1898; seventh; James W. Harriman (farmer, 38, Somersworth) and Abbie E. Berry (33, Waltham, MA)
son, b. 6/13/1898; eighth; James W. Harriman (farmer, 38, Somersworth) and Abbie E. Berry (33, Waltham, MA)
son, b. 5/1/1902; ninth; James W. Harriman (farmer, 42, Somersworth) and Abbie E. Berry (38, Waltham, MA)
Breanna Lee, b. 5/24/1999 in Rochester; Michael Harriman and Nicole Harriman
Carl Edward, 3d, b. 4/8/1963 in Rochester; Carl F. Harriman, Jr. (instructor) and Faith E. Brooks
Dorothy Lucille, b. 10/29/1960 in Rochester; fourth; Carl E. Harriman (radio mechanic) and Faith E. Brooks
Kirk Eugene, b. 11/9/1894; fifth; James Wm. Harriman (farmer, 34, Somersworth) and Abbie E. Berry (26, Waltham, MA)
Sandra Jean, b. 5/21/1958 in Rochester; third; Carl E. Harriman (radio mechanic, Concord) and Faith E. Brooks (Dover)

HARRINGTON,
Bonnie Ruth, b. 12/16/1952 in Rochester; third; Bradford Harrington (shoe worker, MA) and Annie R. Lamper (Wolfeboro)
Diana Linda, b. 9/7/1951 in Rochester; first; Frederick Harrington (machine oper., New Bedford, MA) and Arlene Campbell (New Hampton)

HARRIS,
Fannie L., b. 12/1/1896; second; Henry E. Harris (laborer, Woburn, MA) and Blanche E. Downs (21, Dover)
Hazen, b. 10/25/1895; first; Henry E. Harris (shoecutter, Woburn, MA) and Blanche E. Downs (Milton)

HART,
son, b. 4/2/1893; second; Malcom A. H. Hart (physician, 31, Milton) and Estella L. Draper (29, Fair Haven, VT)
daughter, b. 9/13/1895; eleventh; Lewis P. Hart (laborer, 43) and Adelia Whitehouse (39)
stillborn daughter, b. 9/25/1896; thirteenth; Lewis P. Hart (laborer, 44, Grafton, MA) and Adella Whitehouse (40, Wolfeboro)
Bernice Maude, b. 6/28/1887; Dana B. Hart and Martha J. Stevens (1952)

Ezra Draper, b. 5/12/1896; third; M. A. H. Hart (physician, 34, Milton) and Estelle L. Draper (32, Fair Haven, VT)
Jessica Nicole, b. 9/10/1985 in Dover; James N. Hart and Donna L. Hillsgrove

HARTE,
Caitlin Mary, b. 5/19/1985 in Rochester; Kevin J. Harte and Colleen J. Cheney
Cori Lynn, b. 3/2/1983 in Rochester; Kevin J. Harte and Colleen J. Cheney
Joseph Michael, b. 7/29/1986 in Rochester; Kevin H. Harte and Colleen J. Cheney
Kelly Shannon, b. 10/2/1987 in Rochester; Kevin J. Harte and Colleen J. Cheney

HARTFORD,
Helen M., b. 11/21/1925; fourth; Lewis M. Hartford (laborer, East Rochester) and Ruby L. Labby (East Rochester)

HATCH,
son, b. 2/13/1896; second; Frank Hatch (farmer, 34, Lyman, ME) and Susan A. Staples (28, Milton); residence - Lyman, ME
Ernest, b. 11/27/1894; first; Francis W. Hatch (teamster, 33, Lyman, ME) and Susie A. Staples (24, Milton); residence - Lyman, ME
Joshua Edward, b. 6/7/1989 in Dover; Jeffrey E. Hatch and Teresa L. McKay
Matthew Jeffrey, b. 3/29/1993 in Rochester; Jeffrey E. Hatch and Teresa L. McKay

HAYES,
son, b. 9/20/1890; fifth; Charlie Hayes (farmer, Milton) and ----- (Farmington)
son [Norman H.], b. 10/12/1899; sixth; S. Lyman Hayes (mail agent, 37, Milton) and Annie F. Corson (34, Milton)
daughter [Helen F.], b. 6/29/1901; seventh; S. Lyman Hayes (mail clerk, 38, Milton) and Annie F. Corson (36, Milton)
daughter [Arlene], b. 6/28/1902; second; James H. Hayes (farmer, 39, Lebanon, ME) and Ida Willey (37, Wolfeboro)

daughter [Ethel M.], b. 2/3/1903; second; Guy L. Hayes (carpenter, 25, Milton) and Myrta Clements (29, Lebanon, ME)

stillborn daughter, b. 3/20/1906; fourth; Guy L. Hayes (carpenter, 27, Milton) and Myrta Clements (32, Lebanon, ME)

Alice E., b. 3/14/1901; first; Guy L. Hayes (carpenter, 23, Milton) and Myrta E. Clements (27, Lebanon, ME)

Blanche, b. 1/29/1896; fifth; S. Lyman Hayes (postal clerk, 33, Milton) and Annie Corson (30, Milton)

Evelyn Myrtle, b. 2/15/1913; second; William H. Hayes (laborer, Northwood) and Flora M. Shattuck (Amesbury, MA); residence - East Rochester

Freeman, b. 6/13/1890; second; Richard B. Hayes (farmer, 24, Lebanon, ME) and Annie Downs (Milton)

Mabel Eliza, b. 3/8/1907; fifth; Guy L. Hayes (carpenter, 29, Milton) and Myrta E. Clements (34, Lebanon, ME)

Marion, b. 3/27/1890; third; William O. Hayes (shoemaker, 36, Rochester) and Ella Knox (Milton)

Marjorie Edna, b. 9/20/1905; third; James H. Hayes (farmer, 43, Lebanon, ME) and Ida Willey (40, Wolfeboro)

Maurice L., b. 6/22/1893; fourth; S. Lyman Hayes (mail clerk, 31, Milton) and Annie Corson (28, Milton)

Milton Ware, b. 6/10/1905; eighth; S. Lyman Hayes (mail clerk, 42, Milton) and Annie F. Corson (39, Milton)

Pamela Townsend, b. 1/29/1946 in Rochester; first; Paul T. Hayes (blank. mfr., Haverhill, MA) and Caroline E. Wiegman (Norfolk, VA); residence - Milton Mills

Philip George, b. 4/22/1904; third; Guy L. Hayes (carpenter, 26, Milton) and Myrta E. Clements (31, Lebanon, ME)

HEBERT,

Nathan Scott, b. 3/22/1984 in Wolfeboro; Edward J. Hebert and Melodie A. Hill

Travis Edward, b. 6/5/1986 in Wolfeboro; Edward J. Hebert and Melodie A. Hill

HEDLAND,

son, b. 8/27/1907; second; Guy E. Hedland (theatricals, 23, Portland, CT) and Edith A. Randall (22, Kilderm'r, England)

HEIDLER,
George Albert, III, b. 7/12/1968 in Rochester; George A. Heidler, II and Madeline E. Anderson

HELIE,
Michael Everett, b. 9/11/1973 in Rochester; Everett C. Helie and Carol A. Marcoux

HEMINGWAY,
Leo, b. 10/3/1921; fourth; Leo Hemingway (lumberman, Milton Plantation, ME) and Myra E. Downing (Lebanon, ME)

HENDERSON,
Charlene Evelyn, b. 10/17/1961 in Rochester; Franklin C. Henderson (truck driver) and Leona M. Herrick

Franklin Calvin, Jr., b. 7/19/1959 in Rochester; first; Franklin Henderson (farmer, Rochester) and Leona M. Herrick (Springfield, VT)

Richard Edwin, b. 5/2/1986 in Rochester; Robert B. Henderson and Barbara J. Hunter

Roland Earl, b. 10/23/1935 in Rochester; first; Earl Henderson (shoe worker) and Frances Tatro (Penacook)

Sandra Louise, b. 7/3/1950 in Rochester; second; Clifford Henderson (weaver, ME) and Geraldine Horton (NH)

Stanley Warren, Jr., b. 4/2/1986 in Rochester; Stanley W. Henderson and Mary M. Vachon

HENNER,
Alice May, b. 9/9/1956 in Rochester; third; Roland Henner (service station, New Bedford, MA) and Lillian Normandin (New Bedford, MA)

Gayle Helene, b. 9/9/1956 in Rochester; fourth; Alfred Henner (service station, Osterville, MA) and Jeanne Manderville (New Bedford, MA)

Keith Alan, b. 1/9/1965 in Rochester; Roland J. Henner, Jr. (mechanic) and Shirley L. Smith

Meagan Nicole, b. 7/20/1998; Todd Henner and Laurie Henner

Raymond J., b. 10/18/1957 in Rochester; fifth; Alfred Henner (self employed, Osterville, MA) and Jeanne Mandeville (New Bedford, MA)

Robert Jean, b. 7/27/1966 in Rochester; Roland Henner, Jr. (mechanic) and Shirley L. Smith

HEON,
Megan Alexis, b. 8/31/1998; Dale P. Heon and Michelle L. Heon

HERSCHEL,
Corey Lee, b. 3/17/1993 in Rochester; Richard L. Herschel and Beatrice L. Horn
Gregory Harris, b. 12/5/1986 in Rochester; Richard L. Herschel and Beatrice L. Horn
Nathaniel Allen, b. 7/11/1990 in Rochester; Richard L. Herschel and Beatrice L. Horn

HERSEY,
Adam Joel, b. 10/8/1984 in Rochester; Roland D. Hersey and Marie J. Ellis
Nicole Marie, b. 3/30/1987 in Rochester; Roland D. Hersey and Marie J. Ellis

HERSOM,
Clifton Frank, b. 11/9/1920; first; Clifton E. Hersom (laborer, Sanford, ME) and Mildred R. Weeks (Ossipee)
George Russell, b. 4/13/1916; first; Everett L. Hersom (emp., B&M RR, Milton) and Christie Ann Hill (Lebanon, ME)

HIBBARD,
Adrian James, b. 4/8/1984 in Portsmouth; Gary M. Hibbard and Sharon L. Lavertue

HICKS,
Lucinda Ellen, b. 10/11/1956 in Rochester; third; Clifford H. Hicks (restaurant owner, Jefferson) and Dorothy E. Willette (Manchester)

HICKSON,
Gloria Jean, b. 8/4/1945 in Rochester; first; Glen Hickson (farm laborer) and Ramona I. Burroughs (Milton)

HILDRETH,
Cynthia Ruth, b. 2/11/1957 in Rochester; first; Frederick Hildreth (grocer, Boothbay Harbor, ME) and Virginia Livingston (Alton Bay)

HILL,
daughter, b. 9/17/1913; fourth; James Hill (sawyer, Strafford) and Margaret Gray (Barnstead)
Aaron Taylor, b. 8/24/1994 in Rochester; Craig Hill and Lorna L. Smith
Alicia Rose, b. 12/20/1994 in Dover; James E. Hill, Jr. and Michele A. Lirette
James Edward, III, b. 4/14/1992 in Dover; James E. Hill, Jr. and Michele A. Lirette
Patricia Marjorie, b. 4/17/1942 in Rochester; first; Winfred L. Hill (mill worker, Newton, MA) and Marjorie L. Clough (Acton, ME); residence - Milton Mills

HILLS,
Courtney Emily, b. 4/8/1992 in Rochester; Peter R. Hills and Susan L. Lambert

HOBIN,
Joseph Robert, b. 2/10/1996 in Rochester; Timothy F. Hobin and Ourania N. Hobin

HOBLER,
Aidan James, b. 7/21/1999 in Rochester; Christopher Hobler and Jennifer Hobler

HODGDON,
Mary A., b. 5/20/1872; second; George F. Hodgdon (painter, Boston, MA) and Lucinda J. Jones (Boston, MA) (1940)

HODGES,
daughter [Alice M.], b. 2/10/1898; second; Edgar C. Hodges (shoemaker, 28, Moultonville) and Carrie L. Corson (25, Lebanon, ME)
Ruth H., b. 9/20/1895; first; Edgar C. Hodges (shoemaker, 26, Ossipee) and Carrie L. Corson (21, Lebanon, ME)

HODGKINS,
Melissa Ann, b. 6/2/1989 in Dover; Gregory J. Hodgkins and Cyndy J. Mahoney

HODSON,
Alana Joy, b. 6/18/1997 in Portsmouth; Paul D. Hodson and Teri J. Hodson

HOGAN,
Melissa Kelly, b. 10/9/1982 in Rochester; Kelly D. Hogan and Marie L. LaPierre

HOLMAN,
Beverly Ann, b. 6/22/1953 in Rochester; fifth; Winfield Holman (SS missionary, Denmark, ME) and Verna Merrill (Northfield)
Donna Belle, b. 3/21/1952 in Rochester; fourth; Winfield Holman (minister, ME) and Verna H. Merrill (Northfield)
Lois Karlene, b. 4/9/1950 in Rochester; third; Winfield Holman (rural pastor, ME) and Verna Merrill (NH)
Pauline Eva, b. 9/9/1947 in Rochester; first; Winfield H. Holman (missionary, Denmark, ME) and Verna H. Merrill (Northfield)
Vera Jane, b. 2/10/1949 in Rochester; second; Winfield H. Holman (missionary, ME) and Verna H. Merrill (NH)

HOLMES,
daughter [Pauline W.], b. 5/17/1906; first; Clarence W. Holmes (teacher, 28, Buxton, ME) and Winnie Dore (24, Milton)

HOLT,
Evelyn Fenn, b. 11/30/1978 in Rochester; Richard T. Holt, II and Jane D. Chace
Joshua Charles, b. 12/30/1980 in Rochester; Brian B. Holt and Susan M. Duggan

HOMOLISKI,
Edwin Herbert, b. 11/21/1925 in Nashua; second; Alexander Homoliski (ice man, Russia) and Ethel Taylor (Brookline)

HOOD,
Pamela Lee, b. 10/21/1945 in Rochester; first; Leslie J. Hood, Jr. (foreman, Springfield, MA) and Madeline R. Davis (Acton, ME)

HOOPER,
son, b. 4/13/1906; first; John W. Hooper (B&M emp., 23, Wakefield) and Grace L. Connolly (21, Milton)

HOPKINS,
Carole Ann, b. 10/6/1945 in Rochester; first; Donald A. Hopkins (weaver, Peterborough) and Frances H. Chase (Rochester)

HORN[E],
daughter [Lorita A.], b. 3/31/1903; second; John E. Horne (merchant, 24, Acton, ME) and Olive A. Moulton (25, Newfield, ME)
son, b. 1/2/1905; first; Orril F. Horne (shoemaker, 24, Rochester) and Elsie M. Varney (19, Milton)
son, b. 4/7/1906; second; Frank O. Horne (shoemaker, 26, Rochester) and Elsie M. Varney (20, Milton)
Alfred Neil, b. 1/22/1936; third; Clyde W. Horne (laborer, Milton) and Ethel F. Cleaves (Lynn, MA); residence - W. Milton
Alice Pearl, b. 8/31/1897; second; Rufus Horne (shoemaker, 28, Wakefield) and Mary Conniff (24, England)
Beatrice Laura, b. 9/21/1964 in Rochester; ninth; Clyde H. Horn (marine machinist) and June E. Runnels
Clyde Benjamin, b. 11/20/1925; first; Clyde W. Horne (laborer, Milton) and Ethel F. Cleaves (Lynn, MA) (1932)
Dale Marie, b. 11/21/1960 in Rochester; seventh; Clyde H. Horn (machinist) and June E. Runnells
David Alan, b. 4/20/1931 in Milton Mills; Herman J. Horne (clerk, Milton) and Mildred Dow (Dover); residence - Milton Mills
Doris M., b. 10/4/1900; first; John E. Horne (clothing dealer, 22, Acton, ME) and Olive A. Moulton (22, Newfield, ME)
Grace Louise, b. 6/15/1926; first; Raymond F. Horne (mill operative, Milton) and Eva A. McIntire (Rochester)
Herman Julian, b. 10/26/1904; third; John E. Horne (merchant, Acton, ME) and Olive A. Moulton (Newfield, ME) (1911)
John Everand, b. 3/7/1917; fourth; John E. Horne (merchant, Acton, ME) and Olive Moulton (Newfield, ME)

June Meroa, b. 6/8/1934; second; Clyde W. Horne (laborer, Milton) and Ethel F. Cleaves (Lynn, MA)

Michael Christopher Harris, b. 10/24/1985 in Rochester; Vaun E. Horn and Deborah L. Cheney

Pamela Ann, b. 5/14/1936 in Rochester; third; Herman J. Horne (lineman, Milton Mills) and Mildred Dow (Dover); residence - Milton Mills

Patricia Olive, b. 12/13/1933 in Rochester; second; Herman J. Horne (electrician, Milton Mills) and Mildred E. Dow (Dover); residence - Milton Mills

Peter Julian, b. 5/14/1936 in Rochester; fourth; Herman J. Horne (lineman, Milton Mills) and Mildred Dow (Dover); residence - Milton Mills

Raymond Franklin, b. 7/11/1927; second; Raymond F. Horne (emp. in mill, Milton) and Eva A. McIntire (Rochester)

Richard Chandler, b. 9/13/1929 in Rochester; third; Raymond F. Horne (mach. oper., Milton) and Eva McIntire (Rochester)

Vaun Eugene, b. 1/5/1962 in Rochester; Clyde H. Horn (machinist) and June E. Runnels

HORNING,

Holly Marie, b. 12/18/1988 in Dover; Joel L. Horning and Tami L. Rouleau

Jace Andrew, b. 7/3/1990 in Dover; Joel L. Horning and Tami L. Rouleau

HOWARD,

Benjamin Casey, b. 6/13/1996 in Dover; Casey R. Howard and Patricia A. Howard

HOYT,

Eric Brian, b. 12/28/1966 in Rochester; third; John F. Hoyt (laborer) and Emelia J. Dion

Garrick Anthony, b. 6/20/1991 in Rochester; Robert A. Hoyt and Donna Fadley

Isabella Melissa L., b. 3/14/1919; first; George L. Hoyt (farmer, Milton) and Laura E. Jones (Milton)

Kevin Owen, b. 7/10/1968 in Rochester; John F. Hoyt and Gertrude M. Paul

Linda Anne, b. 9/3/1956 in Rochester; third; John F. Hoyt (b't'man's helper, Belmont) and Gertrude Paul (Rochester)

HUBBARD,
Kyle Alexander, b. 6/19/1991 in Rochester; Shawn L. Hubbard and Deborah A. Sherman

HUGHES,
Caleb Moody, b. 7/17/1988 in Rochester; Mark A. Hughes and Kimberly Campbell
Cody Clinton, b. 7/30/1985 in Rochester; Mark A. Hughes and Kimberly A. Campbell

HUNTER,
Bruce James, b. 1/13/1969 in Rochester; James B. Hunter and Maureen R. Leighton
Frank Carlino, b. 8/8/1939 in Rochester; eighth; Charles O. Hunter (dis. veteran, Charlestown, MA) and Jennie E. Magee (Arlington, MA); residence - W. Milton
James Baxter, b. 10/11/1935; seventh; Charles O. Hunter (retired, Charlestown, MA) and Jennie E. McGee (Arlington, MA)
Margaret Louise, b. 4/18/1966 in Rochester; James B. Hunter (laborer) and Maureen R. Leighton
Phillip James, b. 2/26/1965 in Rochester; James B. Hunter (laborer) and Maureen R. Leighton
Rockie James, b. 12/20/1961 in Rochester; James B. Hunter (laborer) and Maureen R. Leighton
Rosemarie Darline, b. 7/24/1963 in Rochester; James B. Hunter (laborer) and Maureen R. Leighton

HUNTRESS,
Charles Herbert, b. 4/11/1951 in Rochester; sixth; Donald R. Huntress (wood chopper, Haverhill, MA) and Virginia Pollard (Farmington)

HURD,
son, b. 3/30/1898, first; Arthur L. Hurd (carder, 18, Lebanon, ME) and Lizzie M. Webber (16, Milton)
stillborn son, b. 11/18/1937 in Sanford, ME; fourth; Mervyn Hurd (store owner, Milton Mills) and Alice Stevens (Middleton); residence - Milton Mills

Elizabeth Anne, b. 6/4/1933 in Milton Mills; third; Mervyn F. Hurd
(window dec., Milton Mills) and Alice E. Stevens (Middleton);
residence - Milton Mills
John Clifford, b. 10/9/1915; second; Ralph H. Hurd (emp. in mill, Milton)
and Florence Tuttle (Wakefield) (1918)
Marion, b. 5/15/1910; first; Ralph H. Hurd (emp. woolen mill, Acton,
ME) and Florence Tuttle (Wakefield)
Richard Franklin, b. 10/12/1931 in Milton Mills; second; Mervyn F. Hurd
(window dsr., Milton) and Alice E. Stevens (Middleton); residence -
Milton Mills

HURLBURT,
Raymond, b. 3/22/1916; fifth; Forrester R. Hurlburt (emp. in mill, NS)
and Blauda M. Churchill (NS)

HURLEY,
Conor Kashnig, b. 1/26/1980 in Dover; Mark E. Hurley and Pamela A.
Kashnig

HUTCHINS,
stillborn daughter, b. 1/8/1888; Frank H. Hutchins (sawyer, Wakefield)
and A. D. Hutchins (Wakefield); residence - Wakefield
David Alan, b. 11/17/1957 in Rochester; sixth; Edwin H. Hutchins
(machinist, Wolfeboro) and Gloria Clough (Milton Mills); residence
- Milton Mills
Dianne Lynn, b. 3/24/1968 in Rochester; Edwin H. Hutchins and Gloria J.
Clough
James Edwin, b. 2/17/1956 in Rochester; fifth; Edwin H. Hutchins (mach.
oper., Wolfeboro) and Gloria Clough (Milton Mills); residence -
Milton Mills
Jean Ann, b. 11/18/1950 in Rochester; third; Edwin H. Hutchins (farmer,
Wolfeboro) and Gloria Clough (Milton)
Judith Ann, b. 8/6/1948 in Rochester; first; Edwin H. Hutchins (farmer,
Wolfeboro) and Gloria J. Clough (Milton Mills)
Lisa Ann, b. 1/5/1965 in Rochester; Edwin H. Hutchins (set-up man) and
Gloria J. Clough
Pamela Jean, b. 7/8/1949 in Rochester; second; Edwin H. Hutchins
(herdsman, NH) and Gloria J. Clough (NH)

Richard Wayne, b. 5/6/1966 in Rochester; Edwin Hutchins (set-up man) and Glora J. Clough

Sandra Deane, b. 9/2/1959 in Rochester; seventh; Edwin H. Hutchins (machinist, Wolfeboro) and Gloria Clough (Milton Mills); residence - Milton Mills

Shirley Jane, b. 8/11/1953 in Wolfeboro; fourth; Edwin H. Hutchins (farmer, NH) and Gloria J. Clough (NH)

INGALLS,
Dawn Marie, b. 2/17/1976 in Rochester; Arthur Ingalls, III and Kathleen P. Perrotta

Lynn Marie, b. 10/29/1974 in Rochester; Arthur Ingalls III and Kathleen P. Perrotta

ISRAEL,
Cassy Lynn, b. 12/18/1971 in Kittery, ME; Norman L. Israel and Joan C. Cook

JACOBS,
David Joel, b. 2/1/1979 in Rochester; David W. Jacoibs and Lauren J. Joos

David Wayne, b. 9/27/1955 in Rochester; second; Stephen Jacobs (pumpman, E. Rochester) and Betty Chase (Rochester)

Denise Ann-Marie, b. 3/10/1956 in Rochester; first; Joseph E. Jacobs (laborer, Rochester) and Mary J. Ward (Milton)

Stephanie Joan, b. 9/27/1953 in Rochester; first; Stephen N. Jacobs (navy yard, Lebanon, ME) and Betty J. Chase (Milton)

JEFFREY,
Robert, b. 8/7/1909; second; Charles A. Jeffrey (hotel prop., Yarmouth, NS) and Leona G. Coyne (St. Paul, MN)

JENKINS,
Ralph Chester, b. 9/14/1885; Henry A. Jenkins and Emma F. Smith (1952)

JENNESS,
son, b. 12/31/1889; sixth; Edwin P. Jenness (laborer, 32, Wakefield) and Alma J. Kawkins (29, Dover)

Edgar Joseph, b. 8/16/1921; fifth; Joseph C. Jenness (mill hand, Milton) and Sarah M. Allen (Brookfield)
Ella M., b. 3/18/1895; eighth; Calvin P. Jenness (farmer, 38, Wakefield) and Alma J. Hawkins (33, Dover)
Judith Lee, b. 7/29/1947 in Rochester; first; Leland H. Jenness (tool, die mkr., Brookline) and Iris M. Coles (Australia)

JENNINGS,
Lee Brian, b. 7/11/1973 in Exeter; William B. Jennings and Mary C. Hall

JEWETT,
daughter, b. 9/10/1890; fourth; Haven R. Jewett (farmer, 34, Milton) and Mary V. Sibley (Watertown, MA)
Dana Clayton, b. 10/2/1972 in Wolfeboro; Clayton G. Jewett and Narma R. Burroughs
Haven Furber, b. 11/9/1899; fifth; Haven R. Jewett (farmer, 43, Milton) and Nellie M. Sibley (38, Watertown, MA)

JOHNSON,
Aleta Barbara, b. 7/18/1991 in Rochester; David L. Johnson and Karen A. Goodwin
Amos Lee, b. 6/27/1988 in Rochester; David L. Johnson and Karen Goodwin
Asa David, b. 8/20/1989 in Rochester; David L. Johnson and Karen A. Goodwin
Charles Ellsworth, b. 2/12/1928; second; Clarence E. Johnson (mill operative, Rochester) and Josephine Gosselin (Milton)
Clarence W., b. 4/15/1903; second; Ralph Johnson (salesman, 23, Lowell, MA) and Rosa Delnge (22, Nashua)
H. Raymond, b. 8/12/1888; Henry R. Johnson (carpenter, Wolfeboro) and Lillian M. Pinkham (Milton) (1939)
Heather Marie, b. 11/22/1983 in Dover; Irvin M. Johnson and Shirley J. Hersom
Jason Aaron, b. 11/20/1974 in Rochester; Norman H. Johnson and Darlene L. Joy
Jeffrey Matthew, b. 8/21/1968 in Rochester; Milton A. Johnson, Jr. and Norma F. Beckman
Jeremy Mark, b. 10/27/1970 in Rochester; Rev. Milton Johnson, Jr. and Norma F. Beckman

John Martin, b. 10/7/1966 in Rochester; Milton Johnson, Jr. (minister) and Norma F. Beckman

Mark Lester, b. 12/16/1967 in Rochester; Richard W. Johnson and Anna M. Chretien

Peggy Ann, b. 3/11/1971 in Rochester; Richard W. Johnson and Anna M. Chretien

William Lawrence, b. 6/27/1952 in Rochester; Charles B. Johnson (teacher, Manchester) and Jean G. Gleason (Winchester, MA)

JONES,

Alice Varney, b. 6/23/1896; fifth; Fred P. Jones (farmer, 37, Milton) and Emma J. Cowell (37, Lebanon, ME)

Elizabeth, b. 8/21/1894; fourth; Fred P. Jones (farmer, 34, Milton) and Emma J. Cowell (35, Lebanon, ME)

Hanson Varney, b. 10/7/1899; fourth; Charles D. Jones (merchant, 36, Milton) and Pauline Hart (34, Milton)

Joshua, b. 4/24/1980 in Rochester; Harold F. Jones and Debra Dickinson

Levi D., b. 6/1/1891; second; Charles D. Jones (druggist, 28, Milton) and Pauline Hart (26, Milton)

Lucy J., b. 10/1/1899; first; Charles A. Jones (farmer, 47, Milton) and Nellie M. Crocker (30, Hyde Park, MA)

Marjorie, b. 3/15/1899; sixth; Fred P. Jones (farmer, 39, Milton) and Emma J. Cowell (39, Lebanon, ME)

Mary, b. 6/10/1891; second; Ira W. Jones (hydraulic engineer, 37, Milton) and Lucia C. Wentworth (24, Milton)

Norman Humphrey, b. 4/13/1907; first; Frank Jones (shoemaker, 26, East Rochester) and Annie L. Burrison (21, So. Boston, MA)

Philip C., b. 8/31/1891; third; Fred S. Jones (farmer, 32, Milton) and Emma J. Cowell (32, Lebanon, ME)

Russell Hart, b. 10/30/1893; third; Charles D. Jones (pharmacist, 30, Milton) and Pauline Hart (28, Milton)

Ruth Marion, b. 6/21/1921; first; Moulton R. Jones (farmer, Lebanon, ME) and Erma Hemingway (Milton) (1923)

JOOS,

Chandra Mei Ling, b. 9/9/1974 in Rochester; Victor J. Joos, Jr. and Annie Thien

Ethan Shiong, b. 3/12/1973 in Rochester; Victor J. Joos, Jr. and Annie Thien

JORDAN,
stillborn daughter, b. 3/24/1890; first; Frank H. Jordan (shoemaker, 21, Milton) and Sadie Pinkham (Milton)

JORDON,
Lisa Ann, b. 3/10/1965 in Rochester; Thomas M. Jordon (laborer) and Judith A. Lindemeyer

JOY,
Denise Elizabeth, b. 11/1/1960 in Rochester; first; Douglas E. Joy (truck driver) and Cheryl L. Davis

JUBINVILLE,
Kristen Marie, b. 4/25/1988 in Rochester; Michael J. Jubinville, Sr. and Linda A. Seale

JUDKINS,
Barbara Lena, b. 1/22/1931 in Rochester; third; Esburn O. Judkins (headmaster, Upton, ME) and Lena Estey (Fitchburg, MA)
Robert Oscar, b. 10/16/1929 in Rochester; second; Esburn O. Judkins (headmaster, Upton, ME) and Lena Estey (Fitchburg, MA)

JULIN,
Arnold Milton, b. 12/23/1936 in W. Milton; second; Arnold S. Julin (farmer, E. Boston, MA) and Elsie E. Williams (Boston, MA)
Eunice Williams, b. 9/25/1934; first; Arnold S. Julin (farmer, E. Boston, MA) and Elsie E. Williams (Boston, ME)
Gwyn Allen, b. 5/21/1940; third; Arnold S. Julin (farmer, WPA, Boston, MA) and Elsie E. Williams (Boston, MA)

KAICHEN,
Kristen Michaela, b. 11/14/1998 in Dover; Michael Kaichen and Lynette Kaichen

KANE,
Heather Carolyn, b. 9/27/1985 in Rochester; Larish E. Kane and Susan G. Small

KATWICK,
Arthur David, b. 11/30/1954 in Rochester; fourth; Robert T. Katwick (floor sander, W. Bridgewater, MA) and Mary P. Lortie (Hingham, MA)
Candace Lynn, b. 3/19/1970 in Rochester; John W. Katwich (sic) and Pauline A. Laskey
Ginger Marie, b. 10/2/1974 in Rochester; John W. Katwick and Pauline A. Laskey

KEAN,
Carrie Ann, b. 9/20/1978 in Rochester; Gerald L. Kean and Charlotte R. Farrington
Edwina Natalie, b. 5/26/1953 in Wolfeboro; fourteenth; William H. Kean (laborer, MA) and Mamie Dunklee (NH)
Gerald Louis, b. 8/16/1954; fourteenth; William H. Kean (laborer, Ayer, MA) and Mamie Dunklee (Milford)
Rodney Allen, b. 12/16/1951; twelfth; William H. Kean (laborer, Ayer, MA) and Mamie E. Dunklee (Milford)
Thomas, b. 8/23/1950; eleventh; William H. Kean (laborer, Ayer, MA) and Mamie Dunklee (Milford)
Walter Raymond, b. 10/6/1948 in Milton Mills; eleventh; William H. Kean (laborer, Ayer, MA) and Mamie E. Dunklee (Milford)

KEAY,
Joseph Francis, b. 5/5/1918; first; William F. Keay (electrician, Dover) and Alma M. Lessard (Springvale, ME)
Sharon Anne, b. 5/23/1939; first; Joseph F. Keay (mill worker, Milton) and Dorothy P. Goodwin (Milton)
Shirley Alma, b. 5/23/1939; second; Joseph F. Keay (mill worker, Milton) and Dorothy P. Goodwin (Milton)

KEDDIE,
Lois, b. 2/12/1912; second; Arthur W. Keddie (mill operative, 20, Beverly, MA) and Clara B. Wentworth (24, Milton)

KEENAN,
Robert Matthew, b. 1/27/1975 in Dover; Robert E. Keenan and Marilyn J. Bottisti

KEENE,
Sandra Ruth, b. 12/15/1938 in Rochester; first; Nelson B. Keene (mill worker, Boston, MA) and Arlene M. Stanhope (Claremont)

KELLEY,
daughter, b. 11/30/1899; first; William S. Kelley (lumber surveyor, 29, Sandown) and Lizzie A. Virtue (20, St. Johns, NB); residence - Sandown

KENAJOS,
Helen, b. 4/19/1917; second; Appostolos Kenajos (emp. in mill, Carinth's, Greece) and Stevanola Pavilis (Plaza, Greece)

KENDALL,
Kristin Marie, b. 7/26/1983 in Rochester; Steven J. Kendall and Diane M. Tanner

KENNERSON,
daughter, b. 7/11/1896; second; Everett Kennerson (shoemaker, 31, Tamworth) and Tinnie Lyman (25, Madison)

KENNEY,
son, b. 10/30/1911; third; Frank A. Kenney (laborer, Burlington, MA) and Nettie M. Dyer (Brookfield)
Abbie A., b. 2/27/1908; second; Frank A. Kenney (emp. in mill, 30, Burlington, MA) and Nettie M. Dyer (32, Sanbornville)
Alice Gertrude, b. 8/10/1907; third; Herbert N. Kenney (emp. in mill, 28, Farmington) and Grace Yeaton (24, New Durham)
Beatrice May, b. 6/11/1913; fourth; Frank A. Kenney (farmer, Burlington, MA) and Nettie M. Dyer (Sanbornville)

KERDUS,
Adam Robert, b. 7/1/1987 in Rochester; Daniel W. Kerdus and Tamara J. Runnels

KERSHAW,
Breeana Ruth, b. 11/28/1978 in Malden, MA; Stephen Kershaw and Nancy S. Plummer

KILGORE,
son, b. 1/27/1897; third; George L. Kilgore (farmer, 28, Norway, ME) and Elizabeth Witham (25, Acton, ME); residence - Acton, ME
daughter, b. 1/27/1897; fourth; George L. Kilgore (farmer, 28, Norway, ME) and Elizabeth Witham (25, Acton, ME); residence - Acton, ME

KIMBALL,
son [Ralph W.], b. 5/2/1899; second; Ralph M. Kimball (shoemaker, 39, Rochester) and Carrie E. Willey (32, Middleton)
Elizabeth, b. 4/30/1922; first; Ralph W. Kimball (laborer, Milton) and Gladys M. Wingate (Rochester)
Jean Emily, b. 11/29/1930; third; N. Thurston Kimball (farmer, Rochester) and Clara E. Chipman (Milton)
John, b. 1/30/1940 in Rochester; first; John P. Kimball (drug clerk, Wolfeboro) and Mary E. A. LeVangie (Brookline, MA)
Paul Adams, b. 6/8/1941 in Rochester; second; John P. Kimball (clerk, Wolfeboro) and Mary E. LeVangie (Brookline, MA)
Richard Henry, b. 7/21/1920; third; Charles A. Kimball, Jr. (laborer, South Boston, MA) and Anna A. Daley (Salem, MA); residence - Peabody, MA
Robert Jewett, b. 5/4/1926; second; N. T. Kimball, Jr. (farmer, Rochester) and Clara E. Chipman (Milton)
Thurston Chipman, b. 9/22/1924; first; N. Thurston Kimball (farmer, Rochester) and Clara E. Chipman (Milton)

KINEZIS,
Karline, b. 2/22/1921; fourth; Apostolos Kinezis (laborer, Corinthus, Greece) and Stavanola Pavlens (Plaza, Greece)

KING,
Guerdon Earl, b. 10/4/1941 in Rochester; second; Guerdon E. King (woodsman, Kentsville, NS) and Marjorie H. Plumer (Boston, MA); residence - Milton Mills
Holly Ann, b. 8/14/1965 in Rochester; Guerdon E. King (wheel man) and Marjorie J. Drew
Ronald E., b. 6/7/1937 in Rochester; fifth; Guerdon King (teamster, NS) and Lucille Williams (Farmington); residence - Milton Mills
Ronald Earl, b. 8/14/1973 in Rochester; Ronald E. King and Ernestine G. Boford

KINGSTON,
daughter, b. 5/1/1890; eighth; George Kingston (RR sect. hand, 39, Ireland) and Nellie Sullivan (Ireland)
Jeremiah David, b. 5/3/1877; George Kingston (Cork, Ireland) and Ellen Sullivan (Cork, Ireland) (1942)

KINNEY,
Martha Ann, b. 7/28/1948 in Rochester; first; Arthur R. Kinney (railroad man, Newburyport, MA) and Helen M. Burrows (Kittery, ME)

KINTNER,
Alexander Oliver, b. 11/3/1991 in Dover; Russell W. Kintner and Maryann Deforte

KINVILLE,
Carter Russell, b. 3/25/1998; Christopher M. Kinville and Kate L. Kinville
Curtis Robert, b. 3/25/1998; Christopher M. Kinville and Kate L. Kinville

KIRK,
Jacob Dylan, b. 4/8/1980 in Rochester; Kirk A. Kirk and Lorrie L. Stuart
Jeffrey Alan, b. 8/19/1967 in Rochester; first; Elwin R. Kirk (meter dept. GE) and Susan B. Logan
Sarah Beth, b. 9/12/1974 in Wolfeboro; Elwin R. Kirk and Susan B. Logan
Shannon Kathleen, b. 10/15/1969 in Rochester; Elwin R. Kirk and Susan B. Logan
Sheena Jean, b. 4/20/1984 in Rochester; Stephen J. Kirk and Shirley J. Hutchins
Stephen Jerome, II, b. 10/1/1975 in Rochester; Stephen J. Kirk and Shirley J. Hutchins

KLEPPER,
Timothy Michael, b. 3/6/1977 in Rochester; David J. Klepper, Sr. and Deborah L. Crawford

KLUTZ,
Paul Louis, b. 12/5/1948 in Rochester; first; Jacob A. Klutz (mill worker, Blowing R., NC) and Rita B. Dupuis (Rochester)

Richard Allen, b. 9/3/1952 in Rochester; third; Jacob A. Klutz (mill worker, NC) and Rita B. Dupuis (Rochester)
Robert Allen, b. 1/2/1950 in Rochester; second; Jacob A. Klutz (mill, NC) and Ritta Dupuis (Rochester)
Theresa Juanita, b. 2/7/1956 in Rochester; fourth; Jacob A. Klutz (mill worker, NC) and Rita B. Dupuis (Rochester)

KNIGHT,
son, b. 11/22/1914; second; Wilbert C. Knight (machinist, Milton) and Sarah B. Maddox (N. Shapleigh, ME)
Elizabeth Joan, b. 8/2/1959 in Rochester; second; Ronald M. Knight (salesman, Rochester) and Bessie Zerinopoulos (Dover)
Judith, b. 2/1/1944 in Rochester; second; John L. Knight (teacher, Topsham, ME) and Jane C. Staggus (Fairmont, WV)
Lawrence Henry, b. 7/3/1899; first; Wilbur C. Knight (shoemaker, 27, Milton) and Sarah B. Maddox (22, No. Shapleigh, ME)
Lorraine, b. 4/15/1940 in Melrose, MA; second; Roland W. Knight (garage bus., Milton) and Christine Souter (Somerville, MA)
Norma Jean, b. 10/29/1951 in Rochester; third; John W. Knight (lumber jack, Portsmouth) and Matilda Hoyt (Dover)
Ronald Maxwell, II, b. 12/12/1966 in Rochester; third; Ronald M. Knight (salesman) and Bessie Zerbinopoulos

KNOWLES,
Marion Helen, b. 1/27/1899; first; Charles Knowles (shoemaker, 24, Middleton) and Bessie I. Keyes (20, No. Conway)

KNOX,
Melissa Marie, b. 9/12/1975 in Rochester; Richard E. Knox and Janet L. Drouin

KOEHLER,
Alyssa Marie, b. 6/29/1990 in Rochester; Michael J. Koehler and Susan M. Wilson

KRASNOW,
Jessica Wish, b. 11/9/1984 in Dover; Stephen J. Krasnow and Susan M. Valdina

KRESSLER,
Justin Tyler, b. 10/31/1989 in Portsmouth; Robert J. Kressler and Heather D. Carter

KUCZWARA,
Sarah Rose, b. 12/22/1995 in Rochester; Paul A. Kuczwara and Cindy I. Kuczwara

KURBEL,
Kevin Cameron, b. 11/4/1977 in Rochester; Robert H. Kurbel and Candace L. Cameron

KURTZ,
William Willis, b. 2/3/1943 in Rochester; first; William E. Kurtz (navy, Meriden, CT) and Noreen K. Willis (Milton)

LABBE,
Derek Alan, b. 12/13/1980 in Rochester; David A. Labbe and Celeste M. Quinn

LABRECQUE,
Aimee Nicole, b. 3/9/1972 in Dover; Norman R. LaBrecque and Christina Pasol
Ashley Ann, b. 9/25/1996 in Dover; Brian O. Labrecque and Jennifer L. Labrecque

LABRIE,
Bayly Chays, b. 6/20/1996 in Rochester; Maurice G. Labrie and Barbara A. Labrie
Christine Anne, b. 11/20/1970 in Rochester; Leo M. Labrie and Anita Lavoie
Devan Layn, b. 7/21/1992 in Rochester; Maurice G. Labrie and Barbara A. Provencher
Gabriel Dominic, b. 10/4/1973 in Rochester; Stephen M. Labrie and Cheryl A. Byrd
Joseph Anthony, b. 7/12/1957 in Rochester; third; Leo M. Labrie (mechanic, Wakefield) and Anita Lavoie (Canada)
Maurice Gerard, b. 8/2/1963 in Rochester; Leo M. Labrie (self-employed, garage) and Anita V. Lavoie

Michael John, b. 10/27/1960 in Rochester; fourth; Leo M. Labrie (filling sta. owner) and Anita V. Lavoie

Michelle Anne, b. 5/22/1976 in Rochester; Stephen M. Labrie and Cheryl A. Byrd

Stephen Maurice, b. 1/6/1953 in Rochester; first; Leo M. Labrie (mechanic, Wakefield) and Anita V. Lavoie (Canada)

LACHANCE,
Bruce David, b. 2/13/1951 in Rochester; third; Robert G. LaChance (shoe worker, Rochester) and Daisy B. Drew (Union)

LAFRANCE,
Charity Rae, b. 1/27/1998; Michael LaFrance and Andrea LaFrance

Sarah Elisabeth, b. 5/26/1990 in Rochester; Michael J. LaFrance and Andrea G. Demary

LAJOIE,
Teaghan Sage, b. 11/4/1993 in Dover; Troy A. LaJoie and Donna M. Hamilton

LAMARRE,
Ronald William, b. 10/6/1963 in Rochester; Leon G. LaMarre (elec. engineer) and Bonnie L. Hasting

LAMBERT,
Cameron Robert, b. 7/8/1991 in Dover; Robert E. Lambert and Michele S. Faulhaber

Joshua Michael, b. 6/9/1982 in Rochester; Michael L. Lambert and Dawna M. Woodill

Tasha Lynn, b. 4/4/1989 in Dover; Robert E. Lambert and Michele S. Faulhaber

LAMONTAGNE,
son, b. 10/10/1912; fourth; Joseph Lamontagne (21, Ossipee) and Lenora Arling (25, Tamworth)

LAMPER,
George Frank, b. 2/16/1921; first; Harland A. Lamper (laborer, Alton) and Annie Leighton (Middleton)

LAMSON,
son, b. 12/1/1904; first; Joseph C. Lamson (shoemaker, 20, Manchester) and Jane Meikle (20, Wakefield)

LANDRY,
Zachery Judson, b. 8/29/1987 in Portsmouth; Jeffrey G. Landry and Patricia A. de Rochemont

LANG,
Dana Miranda, b. 12/20/1983 in Dover; Philip J. Lang and Lisa B. Tremblay

LANGLEY,
daughter, b. 3/16/1902; second; Hiram W. Langley (shoemaker, 29, Fairfield, ME) and Mamie F. Lewis (21, Milton)
James Wallace, b. 9/24/1979 in Rochester; Wallace J. Langley and Susan M. Carlson
Katy Mae, b. 8/30/1987 in Rochester; Wallace J. Langley and Susan M. Carlson

LAPANNE,
Tammy Ann, b. 10/19/1976 in Dover; Francis R. LaPanne and Joline M. Morin

LAROCHELLE,
Aleck A., b. 9/19/1907; first; Arthur F. Larochelle (shoemaker, 2-, Canada) and Lena M. Columbus (18, Milton)
Raymond Arthur, b. 5/30/1909; second; Arthur A. Larochelle (shoemaker, Canada) and Lena M. Columbus (Milton)

LASKEY,
son, b. 3/21/1888; Allie J. Laskey (farmer, Milton) and Rosa A. Barker (New Vineyard, ME)
daughter, b. 11/5/1890; second; Allie Laskey (farmer, 32, Milton) and Rose A. Barker (New Vineyard, ME)
Alan Lee, b. 7/7/1948 in Wolfeboro; third; Clyde Laskey (trucking, Milton) and Eva M. Richards (Wakefield)
Arline Rose, b. 9/30/1916; third; Ralph D. Laskey (Milton) and Maud Philbrick (Milton) (1918)

Barbara Jean, b. 8/26/1948 in Rochester; first; Kenneth M. Laskey
(garage owner, Milton Mills) and Arlene F. Bumford (Sanbornville)
Brackett W., b. 11/10/1907; third; Allie J. Laskey (farmer, 48, Milton)
and Lizzie A. Weeks (28, Brookfield)
Gladys, b. 8/29/1904; first; Allie J. Laskey (farmer, 41, Milton) and Lizzie
A. Weeks (26, Wakefield)
Kenneth Marten, b. 3/14/1915; second; Ralph D. Laskey (teamster,
Milton) and Maude Philbrick (Milton)
Ralph Diah, b. 10/1/1893; third; Allie J. Laskey (farmer, 34, Milton) and
Rose A. Barker (32, New Vineyard, ME)
Robert P., b. 9/11/1911 in Milton Mills; first; Ralph D. Laskey (laborer,
Milton) and Maude Philbrick (Milton) (1941)
Ronald Dale, b. 10/21/1959 in Rochester; third; Roger C. Laskey
(machine operator, Acton, ME) and Mildred Hersom (Easton, ME);
residence - Milton Mills
Ronald Ellwyn, b. 8/8/1939 in Rochester; first; Charles H. W. Laskey
(mill hand, Acton, ME) and Roberta E. Littlefield (Sanford, ME);
residence - Milton Mills
Shirley Louise, b. 5/12/1937 in Wolfeboro; first; Clyde Laskey (trucking,
Milton) and Eva Mae Richards (Wakefield)
Virginia, b. 12/26/1922; fourth; Ralph D. Laskey (teamster, Milton) and
Maude Philbrick (Milton) (1923)
Walter Allie, b. 6/6/1942 in Wolfeboro; second; Clyde Laskey (trucking,
Milton) and Eva M. Richards (Wakefield)

LAUGHLIN,
son, b. 6/20/1890; ninth; John Loughlin (sic) (46, Ireland) and Ellen
Callahan (Ireland)
stillborn son, b. 1/6/1895; John Laughlin (foreman ice co., 50, Ireland)
and Ellen Callyhan (46, Ireland)
son, b. 10/19/1901; first; Cecelia Laughlin (23, North Cambridge, MA)

LAURENT,
Joshua Matthew, b. 9/21/1987 in Rochester; Dennis P. Laurent and
Gwendolyn S. Brierley
Scott Aaron, b. 3/9/1986 in Rochester; David W. Laurent and Susan D.
Boles

LAVALLEY,
Charlyne Ann, b. 11/14/1946 in Rochester; first; Philip D. LaValley (water dept., Concord) and Eunice C. Burnette (Chattanooga, TN)

LAVERTUE,
Colleen Estelle, b. 10/29/1965 in Rochester; John F. Lavertue (shoe laster) and Phyllis L. Morrill
Florence Pearl, b. 1/17/1938; fourth; Ralph R. Lavertue (mach. tender, Rochester) and Kathryn Cathcart (Farmington)
Fred J., b. 6/16/1930; second; Ralph R. Lavertue (laborer, Rochester) and Alice K. Cathcart (Farmington)
John Louis, b. 10/20/1942 in Rochester; fifth; Ralph R. Lavertue (mach. helper, Rochester) and Alice K. Cathcart (Farmington)
Karla Eunice, b. 11/23/1961 in Rochester; John F. Lavertue (foreman) and Phyllis L. Morrill
Sallee Lou, b. 9/5/1934; third; Ralph R. Lavertue (mill emp., Rochester) and Kathryn Cathcart (Farmington)

LAVOYE,
daughter, b. 5/27/1913; first; Edward T. Lavoye (wood chopper, New Durham) and Mary Harrison (England)

LAWSON,
Mary Autumn, b. 12/11/1937 in Rochester; first; Henry Lawson (garageman, IA) and Audrey Tanner (Wakefield)

LEARY,
Erin Tracey, b. 11/30/1970 in Rochester; John E. Leary and Gloria Burroughs
Heather Dawn, b. 8/30/1972 in Rochester; John E. Leary, Jr. and Gloria J. Burroughs
Hollie Jean, b. 3/2/1968 in Rochester; John E. Leary and Gloria J. Burroughs
John Edward, III, b. 3/20/1974 in Rochester; John E. Leary and Gloria J. Burroughs
Shannon Kelly, b. 5/26/1969 in Rochester; John E. Leary, Jr. and Gloria J. Burroughs

LEBLANC,
Robert James, III, b. 5/19/1993 in Rochester; Robert J. LeBlanc, Jr. and Christine Camerato

LECLAIR,
Brian Amos, b. 2/21/1989 in Rochester; Amos R. Leclair and Nancy L. Lesure
Carl W., Jr., b. 3/27/1940 in Rochester; first; Carl W. LeClair (lumberman, Epping) and Margaret E. Butler (Milton)
Richard Robert, b. 7/7/1985 in Rochester; Amos R. Leclair and Nancy L. Lesure
Shana Lee, b. 9/19/1983 in Rochester; Amos R. Leclair and Nancy L. Lesure

LEEMAN,
Dennis Arthur, b. 6/26/1952 in Dover; first; George H. Leeman (moulder, Milton) and Pauline Maglaras (Dover)
Donna Lynn, b. 8/13/1960 in Rochester; third; George H. Leeman (moulder) and Pauline Maglaras
Dorothy Mildred, b. 7/28/1917; second; Milledge G. Leeman (electrical worker, Eatsport, ME) and Helen DeWolfe (Milton)
George Hazen, b. 3/2/1925; third; Milledge G. Leeman (mill hand, Eastport, ME) and Helen M. DeWolfe (Milton)
Paula Joe, b. 10/3/1954 in Rochester; second; George H. Leeman (moulder, Milton) and Pauline Maylaras (Dover)
Ruth, b. 7/4/1913; first; Milledge G. Leeman (moulder, Eastport, ME) and Helen M. DeWolfe (Milton)

LEFE[B]VRE,
daughter, b. 5/27/1911; second; Joseph Lefevre (laborer, Canada) and Louisa Saymore (Concord)
Charlotte Beatrice, b. 7/17/1953 in Rochester; first; Robert R. Lefebvre (brush factory, Rochester) and Thelma J. Titcomb (Beverly, MA)
Heather Marie, b. 8/20/1986 in Rochester; Mark G. Lefebvre and Tina M. Nesbitt

LEIGHTON,
Evelyn May, b. 8/7/1923; first; Presco F. Leighton (laborer, Middleton) and Gladys E. Russell (Danvers, MA)

Kelly Ann, b. 8/20/1968 in Rochester; Herbert F. Leighton and Mildred
A. Ross
Kenneth Allen, b. 12/25/1960 in Rochester; third; Herbert F. Leighton
(gen. helper) and Mildred A. Ross
Michael H., b. 8/5/1957 in Rochester; second; Herbert F. Leighton
(laborer, Middleton) and Mildred Ross (W. Lebanon, ME)
Roberta Abbie, b. 6/7/1947; second; Edwin P. Leighton (mill emp.,
Middleton) and Abbie J. Armstrong (Dunbarton); residence - Milton
Mills

LEMIEUX,
son, b. 4/13/1907; second; Homer J. Lemieux (emp. in mill, 21, So.
Berwick, ME) and Ellen C. Minahane (31, So. Berwick, ME)
Alfred Edgar, b. 11/4/1910; fourth; Homer J. Leminaux (sic) (teamster,
So. Berwick, ME) and Ellen Minahane (So. Berwick, ME)
Catherine Cecelia, b. 11/20/1908; third; Homer J. Lemineux (sic) (emp. in
mill, 23, So. Berwick, ME) and Ellen C. Minahane (31, So. Berwick,
ME)
Linda Louise, b. 7/20/1962 in Rochester; Preley A. Lemieux (blocker) and
Lucille A. Wood
Robin Lee, b. 5/15/1957 in Rochester; first; Perley Lemieux (buffer,
Sanford, ME) and Lucille Wood (Lebanon, ME); residence - Milton
Mills
Susan Lynn, b. 3/10/1960 in Rochester; second; Perley A. Lemieux
(machine operator) and Lucille A. Wood

LEMIRE,
Brandon Mills, b. 4/26/1974 in Laconia; Kevin M. Lemire and Ellen M.
Harris

LESSARD,
son, b. 8/30/1896; third; Joseph Lessard (shoemaker, 40, Canada) and
Delvina Dion (28, Canada)
daughter, b. 6/13/1900; sixth; Benoni Lessard (emp. in mill, 43, Canada)
and Delvina Dion (32, Canada)
Harry, b. 4/18/1899; sixth; Belaine Lesard (shoemaker, 43, Canada) and
Delvina Dion (32, Canada)
Joseph Arthur, b. 2/4/1914; first; Eva May Lessard (Rochester)

Leo Everett, b. 5/1/1950 in Rochester; first; Norman Lessard (shoe worker, NH) and Beatrice Wyman (MA)
Linda Lee, b. 6/14/1955 in Rochester; third; Norman Lessard (GE, Rochester) and Beatrice Wyman (Revere, MA)
Marie Cecelia, b. 2/25/1898; fifth; Belaine Lessard (shoemaker, 41, Canada) and Delvina Dion (30, Canada)
Marion Louise Alice, b. 7/24/1911; tenth; Joseph B. Lessard (shoemaker, Canada) and Delvina Dion (Canada)
Norman Edward, b. 4/15/1954 in Rochester; second; Norman A. Lessard (machine oper., Rochester) and Beatrice T. Wyman (Revere, MA)
Sarah Rachel, b. 3/19/1984 in Rochester; Norman E. Lessard and Claudette C. Boulay

LEWIS,
Edward Walter, b. 5/4/1898; second; Walter J. Lewis (shoemaker, 23, Lebanon, ME) and Mary P. Couture (21, Canada)

LIBB[E]Y,
daughter, b. 8/7/1893; second; Aubrey Libby (RR conductor, 21, Berwick, ME) and Fannie F. Gerrish (20, W. Lebanon, ME)
daughter, b. 8/16/1902; first; Willard F. Libbey (farmer, 23, St. Stephens) and Elsie M. Peterson (19, Limington, ME)
son, b. 3/28/1929; eighth; Robert M. Libby (laborer, Tuftonboro) and Helen S. Eldridge (Ossipee); residence - Ossipee
Alfred K., b. 12/3/1924; sixth; Robert W. Libbey (laborer, Tuftonboro) and Helen S. Eldridge (Ossipee); residence - Ossipee
Brian Keith, b. 1/15/1957 in Rochester; first; Donald Libby (mach. opr., Milton) and Josephine Paul (Rochester)
Leroy Ernest, b. 3/15/1931 in Milton Mills; first, Ernest L. Libby (pic. oper., Wolfeboro) and Ruth M. Libby (Portsmouth); residence - Ossipee
Mary Alice, b. 3/17/1923; fifth; Robert M. Libbey (laborer, Tuftonboro) and Helen S. Eldridge (Ossipee); residence - Tuftonboro
Robert Carlton, b. 4/12/1921; fourth; Robert M. Libby (farmer, Tuftonboro) and Helen S. Eldridge (Ossipee); residence - Tuftonboro

LIBERI,
Christopher Vincent, b. 7/25/1989 in Rochester; Bernard Liberi, III and Susan L. Gilman

LIEBERMAN,
Christopher Edward, b. 6/5/1985 in Rochester; Peter L. Lieberman and Patricia B. Daigle

LILLJEDAHL,
Denise Ann, b. 12/20/1957 in Rochester; second; C. H. Lilljedahl, Jr. (US Army, Lynn, MA) and Thelma Dumont (Rochester)
Robert Alan, b. 4/17/1959 in Rochester; third; Carl H. Lilljedahl, Jr. (contractor, Lynn, MA) and Thelma I. Dumont (Rochester)
Shirley May, b. 3/6/1936 in Rochester; Henry Lilljedahl (shoe worker, Lynn, MA) and Dorothy Varney (Lowell, MA)

LINDSAY,
Warren S., b. 11/14/1907; second; Arthur R. Lindsay (shoemaker, 25, Milton) and Myrtle E. Stevens (20, Brookfield)

LINDSEY,
Silvia May, b. 4/30/1922; first; Bruce Lindsey (marine, St. Johnsbury) and ----- (Waterboro, VT) (1923)

LINES,
Bradley Theodore, b. 2/8/1960 in Rochester; fifth; Bradley T. Lines (minister) and Alberta J. Welch

LIRETTE,
Karrie Lynn, b. 1/3/1979 in Dover; Douglas E. Lirette and Linda M. Chick
Kelly Renee, b. 5/28/1982 in Dover; Douglas E. Lirette and Linda M. Chick

LISTNER,
Maria Lynn, b. 10/25/1970 in Rochester; Joseph Listner and Diane N. Gibb

LIVINGSTON,
Evangeline Juanita, b. 3/15/1916; fourth; Fred A. Livingston (emp. in mill, Hampstead) and Katherine M. Jones (Haverhill, MA)
Geraldine Faith, b. 4/13/1912; first; Fred A. Livingstone (sic) (teamster, 24, Hampstead) and Katherine M. Jones (25, Haverhill, MA)

Meredith Elmer, b. 9/4/1913; second; Fred A. Livingston (emp. in mill, Hampstead) and Katherine M. Jones (Haverhill, MA)
Sylvia Ramona, b. 2/16/1918; fifth; Fred A. Livingston (emp. in mill, Hampstead) and Katherine M. Jones (Haverhill, MA)
Warner Carlyle, b. 12/15/1914; third; Fred A. Livingston (emp. in mill, Hampstead) and Katherine M. Jones (Haverhill, MA)

LOCKE,
James Willis, b. 7/15/1899; first; Arthur Locke (laborer, 23, Concord) and Mabel Wiggin (20, Brookfield)

LOCKHART,
Kimberly Ellen, b. 9/19/1970 in Rochester; Charles F. Lockhart and Lorraine F. Dupuis

LODGE,
Eric Scott, b. 4/15/1976 in Dover; Bruce J. Lodge and Claudia M. Dow

LOGAN,
Aaron Michael, b. 4/9/1975 in Rochester; Charles M. Logan and Bonnie I. Byrd
Charles Harry, b. 10/21/1922; second; Charles W. Logan (laborer, Lynxville, WI) and Florence Y. Welch (Ossipee)
Charles Michael, b. 7/16/1954 in Rochester; third; Charles H. Logan (office worker, Milton) and Patricia M. Parsons (East Rochester)
Kathie Jean, b. 7/31/1948 in Rochester; first; Charles H. Logan (barber, Milton) and Patricia M. Parsons (East Rochester)
Kelly Anne, b. 3/20/1959 in Rochester; fifth; Charles H. Logan (draftsman, Milton) and Patricia M. Parsons (East Rochester)
Patrick Shawn, b. 2/2/1957 in Rochester; fourth; Charles H. Logan (draftsman, Milton) and Patricia Parsons (Rochester)
Susan Beth, b. 9/4/1950 in Rochester; second; Charles H. Logan (barber, NH) and Patricia Parsons (NH)

LOMBARDO,
Kali Ann, b. 4/14/1987 in Rochester; Steven E. Lombardo and Ann M. Pike

LONG,
Donald Andrew, b. 12/21/1957 in Rochester; fourth; John H. Long, Sr. (cook, Wolfeboro) and Catherine Perkins (New Durham); residence - Milton Mills

Mary Sylvea, b. 9/26/1932 in Wolfeboro; second; Dennis W. Long (H.S. Prin., ME) and Virginia LaCross (VT); residence - Milton Mills

Sharon Elaine, b. 12/22/1943 in Rochester; second; Frank L. Long (laborer, army, Bowdoinham, ME) and Janice R. Gervais (Haverhill, MA)

LOPES,
Christopher Micheal, b. 9/24/1993 in Rochester; Micheal J. Lopes and Lorraine J. Tessier

LORD,
stillborn son, b. 1/27/1936; eighth; J. Edwin Lord (electrician, W. Lebanon, ME) and Ruth G. Wentworth (E. Lebanon, ME)

Beatrice Vivian, b. 6/8/1924; second; James E. Lord (merchant, W. Lebanon, ME) and Ruth G. Wentworth (E. Lebanon, ME)

Bertie W., b. 2/11/1901; fifth; Hiram Lord (sawyer, 38, Acton, ME) and Lilla M. Temple (39, Shapleigh, ME)

Earl Melvin, b. 12/3/1925; third; James E. Lord (electrician, W. Lebanon, ME) and Ruth G. Wentworth (E. Lebanon, ME)

Ernest Alonzo, Jr., b. 9/29/1942 in Rochester; second; Ernest A. Lord (clerical work, Rollinsford) and Dorothy S. Hall (Haverhill, MA)

Ethelyn Rose, b. 9/16/1933 in Sanford, ME; second; Leslie F. Lord (mill op., Acton, ME) and Elsie Burnham (Acton, ME)

Frank Kendall, b. 12/24/1939 in Rochester; first; Ernest A. Lord (clerk, Salmon Falls) and Dorothy J. Hall (Haverhill, MA)

Henry, b. 9/3/1931; seventh; James E. Lord (electrician, W. Lebanon, ME) and Ruth Wentworth (E. Lebanon, ME)

Ida Josephine, b. 12/6/1928; fifth; J. Edwin Lord (electrician, W. Lebanon, ME) and Ruth Wentworth (E. Lebanon, ME)

John, b. 9/2/1931; sixth; James E. Lord (electrician, W. Lebanon, ME) and Ruth Wentworth (E. Lebanon, ME)

Philip Edwin, b. 6/22/1922; first; James Edwin Lord (salesman, Lebanon, ME) and Ruth G. Wentworth (Lebanon, ME)

Raymond Everett, b. 9/5/1944 in Rochester; third; Leslie F. Lord (mill worker, Acton, ME) and Elsie E. Burnham (Sanford, ME)

Richard Wentworth, b. 1/13/1927; fourth; J. Edwin Lord (electrician, W.
Lebanon, ME) and Ruth G. Wentworth (E. Lebanon, ME)
Robert Leslie, b. 8/29/1931; first; Leslie F. Lord (leatherboard mill,
Acton, ME) and Elsie E. Burnham (Sanford, ME)

LOUBIER,
Jesse Carroll, b. 3/14/1984 in Rochester; Roland L. Loubier and Nancy A.
Carlson

LOVER,
Richard Augustine, b. 7/18/1910; third; Peter J. Lover (RR section man,
Union) and Alice M. Downs (Sanbornville)
Richard Peter, b. 7/7/1949 in Rochester; first; William C. Lover
(carpenter, NH) and Merle V. Derby (NH)
Valna I., b. 8/15/1907; second; Peter J. Lover (RR section, 26, Wakefield)
and Alice M. Downs (18, Wakefield)
Wilbur, b. 4/24/1914; fourth; Peter J. Lover (fireman, Wakefield) and
Alice M. Downs (Wakefield)

LOVIE,
daughter, b. 11/15/1890; first; Octadie Lovie (moulder, Canada) and
Helen Pelkey (NY)

LOWRY,
Leslie Erwin, 3d, b. 8/5/1951 in Nashua; second; Leslie E. Lowry, Jr.
(school teacher, IL) and Jane Hill (MA)

LUCEY,
Shayne Curtis, b. 1/14/1999 in Dover; Kevin Lucey and Linda Lucey

LUCIER,
Jane Ann, b. 2/25/1957 in Rochester; second; John Lucier (surveyor,
Hartford, CT) and Paula A. Regan (Rochester)
John Andrew, b. 9/20/1958 in Rochester; third; John Max Lucier (civil
engineer, Hartford, CT) and Paula Ann Regan (Rochester)
Judith Lorraine, b. 1/23/1961 in Rochester; John M. Lucier (surveyor) and
Paula A. Regan
Linda Lee, b. 5/18/1955 in Rochester; first; John M. Lucier (state h. dept.,
CT) and Paula A. Regan (Rochester)

LUND,
Amanda Marie, b. 6/28/1985 in Rochester; Gary S. Lund and Lorraine E. Provencher
Brian Carroll, b. 8/21/1963 in Rochester; Herbert C. Lund (office clerk) and Margaret M. Sanborn
Gary Steven, b. 7/18/1958 in Rochester; sixth; Herbert C. Lund (foreman, Strafford) and Margaret M. Sanborn (Whitefield)
Jessica Lyn, b. 8/15/1983 in Rochester; Gary S. Lund and Lorraine E. Provencher

LURVEY,
Zachary Allen, b. 10/29/1997 in Dover; Gerald A. Lurvey and Valerie A. Lurvey

LUSCOMB,
Cindy Gayle, b. 5/24/1957 in Rochester; fourth; Kenneth Luscomb (roller, Lynn, MA) and Juanita Clough (Milton Mills); residence - Milton Mills
Helen Marguerite, b. 8/31/1949 in Wolfeboro; first; Kenneth K. Luscomb (lumberjack, MA) and Juanita Clough (NH)
Joshua James, b. 7/21/1976 in Rochester; Kenneth K. Luscomb and Roxanne M. LeClair
Kenneth K., Jr., b. 10/4/1954 in Rochester; third; Kenneth K. Luscomb (roller, Lynn, MA) and Juanita Clough (Milton)
Wanda Jean, b. 3/6/1964 in Rochester; fifth; Kenneth K. Luscomb (molder presser) and Juanita Clough

LYGREN,
Karl M., b. 10/4/1960 in Wolfeboro; first; John Lygren (ass't engineer) and Janice L. Greene
Kirsten Elizabeth, b. 9/18/1964 in Wolfeboro; second; John Lygren (electrical engineer) and Janice L. Greene

LYONS,
Daniel Twomey William, b. 10/6/1993 in Dover; Michael W. Lyons and Terri E. Mullarkey

LYTTLE,
stillborn son, b. 8/6/1895; first; William Lyttle (carpenter, 58, NS) and Ida Hill (28, Bartlett)

MACE,
Joshua Bartlett, b. 7/2/1996 in Dover; Joseph E. Mace and Peggy J. Mace

MACGOWN,
Randi Jessica, b. 6/3/1989 in Rochester; Darren J. Macgown and Ellen K. Brock

MACILVAINE,
Madeline Esther, b. 8/21/1922; third; George H. MacIlvaine (plumber, Antrim) and Esther L. Fielder (Beverly, MA)

MACISAAC,
Shanna Lynn, b. 8/27/1983 in Portsmouth; Shaun A. MacIsaac and Cindy L. Riley

MACK,
Rachel Dee, b. 7/7/1971 in Rochester; Gregory E. Mack and Betsy R. Pugh
Terrence Gordon, b. 5/4/1968 in Rochester; Gregory Mack and Betsy R. Pugh

MACLEAN,
John Howard, b. 6/23/1912; first; John D. MacLean (contractor, 27, PEI) and Effie L. MacLean (21, Long Branch, NJ); residence - New York City
Roy David, b. 9/4/1973 in Rochester; Clare A. MacLean and Evelyn Noke

MADDEN,
Phyllis Irma, b. 8/24/1923, first; William J. Madden (laborer, England) and Beulah Marsh (Acton, ME)

MAKI,
Nicole Jean, b. 2/26/1982 in Portsmouth; Roland K. Maki and Roxann J. Gargulak

MALO,
Beverley Adrian, b. 3/25/1918; second; Wilfred P. Malo (shoemaker, Leominster, MA) and Clara E. Columbus (Wakefield); residence - Auburn, ME
Clayton Richard, b. 10/14/1920; third; Wilfred P. Malo (shoe cutter, Leominster, MA) and Clara E. Columbus (Union); residence - Rochester

MALSBURY,
Bruce Aubrey, b. 12/2/1947 in Rochester; fifth; Job A. Malsbury (wood chop., Gilmanton) and Audrey L. Hagerman (Littleton)

MANN,
Louann, b. 6/30/1943 in Rochester; third; Orman Mann (transportation, Berlin) and Germaine Maxfield (Rochester)

MANNETTE,
Kevin Thomas, b. 2/14/1978 in Dover; Thomas R. Mannette and Deborah M. Kennedy

MANNING,
Michael James, b. 9/12/1988 in Hanover; James B. Manning and Deborah J. Wing

MANSFIELD,
Shame Kahrle, b. 8/17/1998; Ronald J. Mansfield and Cynthia J. Mansfield

MARCH,
Cris William, b. 10/15/1963 in Rochester; Clifton L. March (clerk) and Patricia L. Parker
Lauri May, b. 10/1/1962 in Rochester; Clifton L. March (clerk) and Patricia L. Parker
Sandra Dianne, b. 5/2/1955 in Rochester; second; Robert E. March (unemployed, Rochester) and Marian March (Rochester)
Vicki Leigh, b. 9/6/1961 in Rochester; Clifton L. March (clerk) and Patricia L. Packer

MARCHAND, [see Marshall]
daughter [Florence M.], b. 8/30/1898; fourth; Arthur Marchand (mill operative, 25, Canada) and Fanny Valley (23, Canada)
son [Edgar P.], b. 10/6/1899; fifth; Arthur Marchand (RR sectionman, 26, Canada) and Fanny Valley (24, Canada)
Alphonse, b. 7/5/1897; third; Arthur Marchand (laborer, 24, Canada) and Fanney Valley (22, Canada)
Alphonzo, b. 12/17/1891; second; Oscar Marchand (paper maker, 23, Canada) and Emma Pouliotte (19, Great Falls)
Aurea, b. 10/15/1897; fourth; Oscar Marchand (paper maker, 29, Canada) and Emma Pouliot (25, Somersworth)
Blanche Alice, b. 7/9/1907; ninth; Arthur Marchand (barber, 34, Canada) and Fanny Valley (32, Canada)
George Ernest, b. 9/19/1903; seventh; Arthur Marchand (emp. in mill, 30, Canada) and Fanny Valley (28, Canada)
Gladys, b. 1/3/1906; eighth; Arthur Marchand (emp. in shop, 32, Canada) and Fanny Valley (30, Canada)
Louis Oscar, b. 4/29/1896; second; Arthur Marchand (laborer, 23, Canada) and Fanny Valley (21, Canada)
Lucille, b. 10/23/1895; third; Oscar Marchand (paper maker, 27, Canada) and Emma Puibit (23, Somersworth)
Manuel, b. 1/25/1900; first; Mary Marchand (19, Canada)

MARCOUX,
daughter, b. 7/15/1901; eighth; Archie Marcoux (farmer, 35, Canada) and Rose Storne (25, Canada)
son [Charles], b. 10/31/1927; fourth; Napoleon Marcoux (mill operative, Wakefield) and Hazel M. Downs (Milton)
Archie Philip, b. 3/11/1925; second; Napoleon Marcoux (mill hand, Wakefield) and Hazel M. Downs (Milton)
Brenda Lee, b. 6/11/1962 in Rochester; Raymond A. Marcoux (truck driver) and Mary J. Nadeau
David Brian, b. 8/25/1956 in Rochester; third; Archie Marcoux (laborer, Milton) and Beverly Young (Rochester)
Deborah Ann, b. 11/8/1952 in Rochester; second; Joseph R. Marcoux (machine tender, Milton) and Janet M. Chapman (Laconia)
Dora, b. 5/7/1909; twelfth; Archie Marcoux (laborer, Canada) and Rosa Storm (Canada)

Edna Lura, b. 4/8/1924; first; Napoleon E. Marcoux (laborer, Wakefield) and Hazel M. Downs (Milton)
Harry, b. 3/1/1907; second; Joseph E. Marcoux (shoemaker, 27, Canada) and Annie Dubois (23, Somersworth)
James Phillip, b. 2/2/1948 in Rochester; second; Archie P. Marcoux (mill employee, Milton) and Beverly M. Young (Rochester)
Jeanette, b. 8/15/1935; eighth; Napoleon E. Marcoux (mill hand, Wakefield) and Hazel M. Downs (Milton)
Joseph, b. 9/4/1904; tenth; Archie Marcoux (farmer, 40, Canada) and Rosa Storm (28, Canada)
Joseph E., b. 6/8/1906; eleventh; Archie Marcoux (emp. in mill, 41, Canada) and Rosie Storm (29, Canada)
Joseph R., Jr., b. 10/15/1950 in Rochester; first; Joseph R. Marcoux (mach. op., NH) and Janet Chapman (Laconia)
Joseph Richard, b. 8/26/1926; third; Napoleon E. Marcoux (mill operative, Wakefield) and Hazel M. Downs (Milton)
Lorraine Lyn, b. 6/13/1969 in Rochester; James P. Marcoux and Wendy L. Horn
Louis Odelord, b. 8/30/1902; ninth; Archie Marcoux (laborer, 36, Canada) and Rose Storne (26, Canada)
Mary Jane, b. 3/31/1956 in Rochester; first; Raymond Marcoux (dryman, Milton) and Mary-Jane Nadeau (Dover)
Mary Kathleen, b. 9/30/1930; fifth; Napoleon E. Marcoux (leatherboard mill, Wakefield) and Hazel M. Downs (Milton)
Melody Ann, b. 10/10/1970 in Rochester; James P. Marcoux and Wendy L. Horn
Michael Joseph, b. 9/29/1965 in Rochester; Raymond A. Marcoux (laborer) and Mary Jane Nadeau
Patricia Annette, b. 5/10/1957 in Rochester; third; Joseph Marcoux (mach. opr., Milton) and Janet Chapman (Laconia)
Raymond Arthur, b. 2/25/1933; eighth; Napoleon E. Marcoux (mill hand, Wakefield) and Hazel M. Downs (Milton)
Raymond Richard, b. 10/22/1960 in Rochester; second; Raymond A. Marcoux (truck driver) and Mary Jane Nadeau
Rita Alice, b. 2/11/1932; sixth; Napoleon E. Marcoux (mill hand, Wakefield) and Hazel M. Downs (Milton)
Robert David, b. 2/25/1937; tenth; Napoleon Marcoux (mill hand, Sanbornville) and Hazel Downs (Milton)

Robert David, b. 11/30/1958 in Rochester; first; Robert D. Marcoux (dryer dept., Milton) and Mary A. Smith (Seabrook)

Roberta Caroline, b. 2/25/1937; ninth; Napoleon Marcoux (mill hand, Sanbornville) and Hazel Downs (Milton)

Rose Ora, b. 3/23/1924; first; Albert C. Marcoux (laborer, Wakefield) and Delvina A. Jalbert (So. Berwick, ME)

Seana Frances, b. 1/18/1994 in Milton; Francis J. Marcoux and Amber L. Pike

Selina Florence, b. 2/7/1926; second; Albert C. Marcoux (mill operative, Wakefield) and Delvina L. Jalbert (So. Berwick, ME)

Walter J., b. 12/19/1904; first; Joseph E. Marcoux (shoemaker, 25, Canada) and Annie D. Dubois (20, Somersworth)

MARDAS,
Erin Lisa, b. 9/1/1990 in Dover; Thomas A. Mardas and Susan E. Darling

MARIOTTI,
Shannon Lee, b. 10/25/1976 in Dover; Robert D. Mariotti and Jeanne L. Durand

MARRONE,
Melissa Pat, b. 3/13/1990 in Rochester; Vincent W. Marrone, Jr. and Susan M. Varnum

MARSH,
Andrew Joseph, b. 3/15/1994 in Dover; Richard S. Marsh and Justine M. Bombria

Colby Harrison, b. 4/30/1984 in Rochester; Paul C. Marsh and Martha J. Raymond

Dorris L., b. 6/2/1901; first; Forrest L. Marsh (lawyer, Milton) and Mildred J. Tibbetts (Newfield, ME) (1911)

Eva May, b. 2/14/1936 in Rochester; third; Ithiel Marsh (mill worker, Milton Mills) and Mary Whitehouse (Lebanon, ME)

Robert Edward, b. 4/13/1932 in Rochester; first; Ithiel E. Marsh (mill hand, Acton, ME) and Mary Whitehouse (Lebanon, ME)

Ronald T., b. 12/11/1909; second; Forrest L. Marsh (lawyer, Milton) and Mildred J. Tibbetts (Newfield, ME) (1911)

MARSHALL, [see Marchand]
son, b. 12/26/1890; first; Oscar Marshall (mill operative, Canada) and ---- (Canada)
Amore, b. 10/28/1894; first; Arthur Marshall (laborer, 22, Canada) and Fannie Valley (20, Canada)
Arthur G., b. 8/27/1901; sixth; Arthur Marshall (mill hand, 28, Canada) and Fanny Valley (26, Canada)
Blanche, b. 8/24/1900; sixth; Louis Marshall (emp. in mill, 45, Canada) and Ellen Theoret (43, Canada)
Doris Antoinette, b. 7/18/1909; tenth; Arthur Marshal (sic) (barber, Canada) and Fannie M. Valley (Canada)
Edward Lothrop, b. 11/13/1906; first; George B. Marshall (supt. shoe shop, 32, N. Easton, MA) and Rosalie B. Tozin (31, Waldo, ME)
Louise Philomina, b. 10/6/1909; second; Lewis Marshal (sic), Jr. (emp. in mill, Wakefield) and Philomena Hamil (Minneapolis, MN)

MARTIN,
Amy Lynne, b. 1/30/1982 in Rochester; David D. Martin and Debra E. Reid
Meagan Leigh, b. 3/26/1979 in Rochester; Michael F. Martin and Angelica Brooks
William Clyde, IV, b. 1/5/1987 in Rochester; William C. Martin, III and Cheryl L. Brown

MARTINEAU,
Leon Edward, Jr., b. 1/27/1946 in Rochester; first; Leon E. Martineau (mill worker, Rochester) and Norma M. Tilton (Milton)

MASON,
Edward F., b. 1/3/1888; Charles E. Mason (clergyman, ME) and Mary M. Files (ME)
Eva Virginia, b. 7/18/1983 in Wolfeboro; Mitchell K. Mason and Rhonda L. Bushway

MATHER,
Andrew Nathan, b. 2/16/1985 in Rochester; David A. Mather and Donna J. Berry
Christopher Lee, b. 7/14/1982 in Dover; David A. Mather, Sr. and Joyce A. Bennett

Jamie Lynn, b. 4/30/1980 in Dover; David A. Mather, Sr. and Joyce A. Bennett

Laurel Elizabeth, b. 6/15/1987 in Dover; Donald R. Mather and Kimberley A. Moreau

MATHES,

son, b. 7/–/1891; first; Samuel Mathes (lawyer, Berwick, ME) and Lottie Leonard (Great Falls)

MAT[T]HEWS,

Elizabeth, b. 4/23/1895; second; Samuel Matthews (lumberman, 33, Berwick, ME) and Lottie Learned (25, Somersworth)

Mildred V., b. 3/14/1908; fifth; black; Oscar S. Mathews (barber, Brunswick, ME) and Hattie A. Jackson (Fall River, MA) (1911)

Nelson, b. 7/15/1897; third; Samuel Mathews (lumberman, 36, Berwick, ME) and Lottie Leonard (27, Somersworth)

Sarah Rae, b. 12/28/1989 in Dover; Dewey F. Mathews and Karen S. Bickert

Thelma T., b. 8/8/1912; sixth; black; Oscar S. Mathews (barber, 41, Brunswick, ME) and Hattie A. Jackson (40, Fall River, MA)

Wilbur L., b. 2/3/1893; second; Samuel S. Mathews (lumber business, 31, Berwick, ME) and Lottie L. Leonard (23, Great Falls)

MATTRESS,

Barbara Ann, b. 11/6/1935 in Sanford, ME; second; Harold Mattress (mill hand, Milton Mills) and Marie Boutti (Brooklyn, NY); residence - Milton Mills

Cheryl Elaine, b. 6/8/1945 in Rochester; first; Jesse Mattress (lumberman, Acton, ME) and Elmida D. Baulch (Bakersfield, VT); residence - Milton Mills

Jason Eric, b. 8/2/1963 in Rochester; Jesse Mattress (Greene tannery) and Elmida Balch

Jeanette Ann, b. 5/31/1937 in Rochester; third; Harold Mattress (machinist, Milton Mills) and Marie Botti (Brooklyn, NY); residence - Milton Mills

John Harold, b. 1/25/1973 in Wolfeboro; John E. Mattress and Linda L. Colby

Michel Scott, 2d, b. 6/16/1977 in Rochester; Michel S. Mattress and Kim E. Moody

Rose Marie, b. 11/18/1934 in Rochester; first; Harold Mattrass (sic) (machinist, Milton Mills) and Marie Botti (Brooklyn, NY); residence - Milton Mills

MAXFIELD,
Mark Leland, b. 12/18/1941 in Rochester; first; Leland L. Maxfield (minister, Rochester) and Elizabeth Z. Bronson (Durham, NY)

MAYRAND,
Mary Pearl, b. 3/15/1921; first; Samuel J. Mayrand (laborer, Canada) and Mavis L. Page (Milton)

McCALLISTER,
Steven Lee, b. 7/21/1969 in Rochester; John R. McCallister and Simonne Y. Vigneault
Susan Lee, b. 4/28/1967 in Rochester; first; John R. McCallister (tool & die maker) and Simonne Y. Vigneault

McCARTHY,
Shawn Wayne, b. 10/6/1983 in Rochester; Wayne E. McCarthy and Patricia A. Trask

McCLEARY,
April Leah, b. 7/14/1984 in Portsmouth; James H. McCleary and Sandra M. Berry
Crystal Margaret, b. 7/14/1984 in Portsmouth; James H. McCleary and Sandra M. Berry

McCONNELL,
Kayla Chanel, b. 4/27/1997 in Rochester; Keith J. McConnell and Tina M. McConnell

McDOWELL,
Claire Ellen, b. 9/21/1951 in Rochester; second; James McDowell (machine oper., Milton) and Katherine Malone (Jamaica Plain, MA)
James Henderson, b. 3/30/1923; first; William McDowell (US Navy, Boston, MA) and Marion Henderson (Edinboro, Scotland); residence - Boston, MA

James Henderson, 2d, b. 1/12/1947 in Rochester; first; James H. McDowell (shoe shop, Milton) and Katherine M. Malone (Boston, MA); residence - West Milton

McGEE,
Marie Juliette H., b. 8/10/1931; third; Louis A. McGee (laborer, Win. Mls., Canada) and Fedora Labrie (Biddeford, ME)

McGINLEY,
Melissa Kay, b. 6/7/1990 in Dover; Neal H. McGinley and Christine A. Ayotte

McGLONE,
Hannah Lynn, b. 6/25/1999 in Rochester; Bernie McGlone and Veronica Tallard

McGRATH,
Kathleen Teresa, b. 5/6/1928; second; Thomas J. McGrath (mill operative, Tipperary, Ireland) and Mary J. McCarten (Downpatrick, Ireland)
Mary Jeanette, b. 6/17/1926; first; Thomas J. McGrath (mill operative, Tipperary, Ireland) and Mary J. McCarten (Downpatrick, Ireland)
Shawn Michael, b. 11/14/1973 in Kittery, ME; John M. McGrath and Susan M. Rock

McINTIRE [see McIntyre],
stillborn son, b. 3/28/1937 in Rochester; first; Everett McIntire (shoe worker, Rochester) and Marie McKeagney (Ossipee)
Amy Marie, b. 9/10/1978 in Rochester; Charles N. McIntire and Patricia A. Swebilius
Charles Norman, b. 5/17/1942 in Rochester; fourth; Frank E. McIntire (navy yard, Rochester) and Marie E. McKeagney (Ossipee)
Laura Ann, b. 11/20/1974 in Rochester; Charles N. McIntire and Patricia A. Swebilius
Neil Eugene, b. 9/20/1943 in Rochester; fifth; Frank E. McIntire (navy yard, Rochester) and Marie E. McKeagney (Ossipee)
Robert Everett, b. 6/5/1939 in Rochester; third; Frank E. McIntire (lea. worker, Rochester) and Marie E. McKeagney (Ossipee)
Sara Elizabeth, b. 9/10/1978 in Rochester; Charles N. McIntire and Patricia A. Swebilius

Stephen Robert, b. 6/6/1960 in Rochester; second; Robert E. McIntire (US Navy) and Lena I. Smith

Walter Gordon, b. 4/8/1938 in Rochester; second; Frank E. McIntire (lea. worker, Rochester) and Marie E. McKeagney (Ossipee)

McINTOSH,
Irma, b. 4/7/1900; second; Robert A. McIntosh (shoemaker, 30, Calais, ME) and Addie C. Duntley (33, Milton)

Robert Duntley, b. 1/31/1898; first; Robert A. McIntosh (shoemaker, 24, Calais, ME) and Addie C. Duntley (29, Milton)

McINTYRE [see McIntire],
Lori Lee, b. 11/29/1961 in Rochester; Robert E. McIntyre (mechanic) and Lena I. Smith

McKAY,
Kristen Marie, b. 5/7/1982 in Rochester; Gerald W. McKay and Mary E. Maciejko

McKENNA,
Michael Patrick, b. 8/23/1982 in Dover; Michael P. McKenna, Sr. and Denise M. Breton

McMULLEN,
Stephen Patrick, Jr., b. 9/19/1994 in Rochester; Stephen P. McMullen and Katherine R. Currier

McPHERSON,
Brian Allen, b. 3/22/1980 in Rochester; Russell E. McPherson and Dianne H. Lowell

Joshua Scott, b. 10/15/1993 in Rochester; Kevin M. McPherson and Tammy L. Thibedau

MEADER,
James L., b. 5/31/1893; first; Fred P. Meader (piano tuner, Durham) and Emma Raynolds (Dover); residence - Washington, DC

Stephen James, b. 11/15/1990 in Dover; James D. Meader and Sandra L. Gelinas

MEE,
Linda Elaine, b. 6/11/1946 in Rochester; first; George W. Mee (carpenter, Newfield, ME) and Virginia R. Laskey (Milton); residence - Milton Mills

MEIKLE,
son, b. 8/16/1888; George D. Meikle (shoemaker, Saugus, MA) and Emma E. Fox (Milton); residence - Haverhill, MA
Marjorie Dorris, b. 11/4/1898; first; William Meikle, Jr. (shoecutter, 24, Wakefield) and Clara E. Googins (20, Milton)

MELOON,
Harold Clifford, II, b. 5/18/1971 in Wolfeboro; Harold C. Meloon and Anna L. Schlegel
Michael Shane, b. 10/18/1972 in Dover; Harold C. Meloon and Anna L. Schlegel

MENARD,
David Richard, b. 11/20/1950 in Rochester; second; Alfred W. Menard (mach. helper, Rochester) and Olivine Rouleau (Lebanon, ME)

MENEGONI,
Paula Ann, b. 1/16/1956 in Rochester; fourth; Frank J. Menegoni (storekeeper, Richmond, MA) and Antoinette Konsevich (Millers Falls, MA)

MERCER,
Clara I., b. 6/14/1914; second; Henry T. Mercer (carpenter, Newfoundland) and Sarah J. Deering (Newfoundland)

MERCIER,
Ashley Marie, b. 7/11/1991 in Dover; Andre E. Mercier and Lynn A. Perron
Brittany Marlene, b. 11/11/1986 in Rochester; Andre E. Mercier and Lynn A. Perron

MERRIAM,
Benjamin Chad, b. 2/11/1990 in Rochester; Thomas K. Merriam and Kathleen G. Kimball

MERRILL,
daughter [Marthena L.], b. 5/25/1903; third; Allie E. Merrill (shoemaker, 28, Albany) and Nettie Stevens (24, Milton)
Deborah Ann, b. 7/18/1949 in Rochester; second; Herbert O. Merrill (shoe factory, ME) and Gladys E. Rouleau (NH)
Edna E., b. 10/27/1900; Allie Merrill and Nettie Stevens (1963)
Lucy Norma, b. 8/24/1919; first; Frank W. Merrill (emp. in mill, Saco, ME) and Beryl M. White (Lebanon, ME)
Nancy Alice, b. 1/11/1961 in Rochester; Edward S. Merrill (shoe worker) and Alice E. Amazeen
Richard Steven, b. 5/2/1957 in Rochester; tenth; Edward S. Merrill (edge trimmer, Salem, MA) and Alice Amazein (Milton)
Robert Alan, b. 8/16/1951 in Rochester; second; Wilson R. Merrill (meat cutter, Glencliff) and Margaret Stevens (Norwood, MA)
Steven Kent, b. 11/21/1958 in Rochester; eleventh; Edward S. Merrill (edge trimmer, Salem, MA) and Alice E. Amazeen (Milton)
Wilmerth A., b. 12/18/1910; fourth; Herbert L. Merrill (teamster, Freedom) and Della M. Wilcox (Houghton, ME)

MERROW,
son, b. 1/26/1888; James W. Merrow (Milton) and Ida S. Ricker (Milton)
son, b. 9/15/1891; second; Wilbur S. Merrow (shoemaker, 24, Moultonville) and Lizzie Mitchell (25, New Durham)
Carrol T., b. 8/11/1894; fourth; Wilbur S. Merrow (shoelaster, 30, Moultonville) and Lizzie Mitchell (31, New Durham)

MERYWEATHER,
Zacharia Rocsten, b. 5/23/1986 in Portsmouth; Rodney G. Meryweather and Diane M. Carlson

MESERVE,
Connie Lee, b. 8/30/1948 in Rochester; first; Irving E. Meserve (mill worker, Milton) and Joan B. Dodge (Providence, RI)
Irvin Edwin, b. 11/4/1928; first; Ralph E. Meserve (lumberman, Saco, ME) and Celia E. Edridge (Ossipee); residence - Berwick, ME

MESSER,
Milton Robert, b. 8/9/1922; seventh; William I. Messer (telegrapher, Troy) and Blanche Weatherwax (Glenville, NY)

MEYER[S],
Carl Hugo, Jr., b. 10/28/1947 in Rochester; sixth; Carl H. Meyer (carpenter, Dover, MA) and Agnes B. Rowgaut (Dorchester, MA)
Frederick Augustus, III, b. 5/23/1953 in Rochester; third; Frederick Meyers, Jr. (General Electric, Needham, MA) and Irma J. Hutchinson (Greenfield, MA); residence - Milton Mills (1959)
Krista Kaylin, b. 6/13/1988 in Rochester; Warren F. Meyer and Jacqueline D. Highland
Peter John, b. 9/8/1955 in Rochester; fourth; Frederick Meyer (GE, Needham, MA) and Irma Hutchinson (Greenfield, MA); residence - Milton Mills
Warren Frederick, b. 7/21/1959 in Rochester; fifth; Frederick A. Meyer (carpenter, Needham, MA) and Irma J. Hutchinson (Greenfield, MA); residence - Milton Mills

MICHAUD,
Diane Marie, b. 12/21/1975 in Rochester; Joseph R. Michaud and Mary L. Pelletier
Julia Mary, b. 9/6/1990 in Milton; Mark R. Michaud and Lauren L. Munroe
Lynn Marie, b. 5/9/1980 in Rochester; Joseph R. Michaus (sic) and Mary-Paul L. Pelletier
Taylor Mark, b. 9/29/1988 in Rochester; Mark R. Michaud and Lauren Munroe

MILLER,
Brandy-Lynn Douglas, b. 8/1/1995 in Rochester; Brad D. Miller and Laura J. Miller
Cameron Christopher, b. 2/12/1996 in Rochester; Christopher D. Miller and Jennifer A. Miller
Christine Aili, b. 9/12/1989 in Dover; Stephen P. Miller and Frances A. Galasyn
Danielle Marie, b. 1/26/1991 in Rochester; Scott W. Miller and Carol A. Hatch
Edward Deal, III, b. 5/3/1973 in Rochester; Edward D. Miller, Jr. and Diane J. Leyden
Hilda, b. 3/4/1904; sixth; John C. Miller (laborer, 46, Richmond, VT) and Annie Miller (34, Hingham, MA)

James Edward, b. 6/3/1914; second; James W. Miller (emp. in mill, Dover) and Katherine M. Ham (Dover)
Josie E., b. 8/10/1880 in Milton Mills; Elias L. Miller (farmer, Acton, ME) and Mary J. Pinkham (Milton Mills); residence - Milton Mills (1937)
Laura-Anne Douglas, b. 6/3/1994 in Dover; Brad D. Miller and Laura J. Hastings
Melissa Anne, b. 4/11/1992 in Portsmouth; Stephen P. Miller and Frances A. Galasyn
Rebecca Ann, b. 6/3/1979 in Rochester; John L. Miller and Lucinda M. Wood
Walter Francis, b. 2/17/1916; third; James W. Miller (emp. in mill, Dover) and Katherine M. Ham (Dover)

MILLS,
son, b. 11/12/1898; first; Fred W. Mills (farmer, 23, Strafford) and Annie L. Eaton (23, Brookfield)
Bruce Robert, b. 1/18/1960 in Rochester; first; Garold W. Mills (shoe cutter) and Lois E. Barnes
Deborah Lee, b. 8/22/1966 in Rochester; Garold W. Mills (shoe cutter) and Lois E. Barnes
Kelly Sue, b. 3/19/1964 in Rochester; third; Edward L. Mills (machine operator) and Constance L. Rogers
Stephanie Jeanne, b. 5/29/1987 in Dover; Jeffrey E. Mills and Margaret J. D'Acquisto

MITCHELL,
stillborn daughter, b. 4/27/1900; first; George A. Mitchell (emp. in mill, 33, Fitchburg, MA) and Gertrude A. Tucker (25, Tuscott, ME)
Flora M., b. 8/18/1891; second; Walter Mitchell (laborer, 24, New Durham) and Mertie Johnson (23, Brookfield)

MOLLICA,
Matthew John, b. 5/17/1985 in Rochester; Philip M. Mollica and Linda L. Lucier
Philip Michael, II, b. 1/19/1984 in Rochester; Philip M. Mollica and Linda L. Lucier

MONAHAN,
Katherine Harriet, b. 9/3/1925; tenth; Frank T. Monahan (electrician, Cambridge, MA) and Lumina D. Lavoie (Union)

MONTEFUSCO,
Melissa L., b. 5/7/1956 in Rochester; third; Louis Montefusco (field rep., NJ) and Cynthia Moore (PA)

MOODEY,
Walter E., b. 8/6/1902; second; Edwin H. Moodey (lumberman, 38, Meredith) and Flora E. Densmore (30, Exeter)

MOODY,
daughter [Virginia], b. 12/9/1929 in Rochester; first; Alfred Moody (ship. clerk, Ossipee) and Alice Phinney (Lynn, MA)
Carrie Elaine, b. 8/7/1943 in Rochester; eighth; Alfred H. Moody (machinist, Tamworth) and Alice M. S. Phinney (Lynn, MA)
Chris Aileen, b. 2/23/1964 in Rochester; eleventh; Theodore J. Moody (maintenance) and Ruth B., Golden
Colleen Ruth, b. 3/14/1949 in Rochester; fourth; Theodore J. Moody (mill employee, NH) and Ruth B. Goldin (NH)
Daniel Patrick, b. 6/15/1966 in Rochester; Theodore Moody (maintenance foreman) and Ruth B. Golden
Erin Sue, b. 7/16/1967 in Rochester; thirteenth; Theodore J. Moody (laboratory) and Ruth B. Golden
Jamie David, b. 6/21/1959 in Rochester; eighth; Theodore J. Moody (maintenance, Tamworth) and Ruth B. Golden (Barnstead)
Karrie Ann, b. 1/17/1971 in Rochester; Ronald D. Moody and Karen J. Stevens
Kathleen Lea, b. 12/9/1945 in Rochester; second; Theodore J. Moody (lunchman, Tamworth) and Ruth B. Golden (Ctr. Barnstead)
Kim Elaine, b. 8/13/1960 in Rochester; ninth; Theodore J. Moody (maintenance) and Ruth B. Golden
Linda Eileen, b. 12/8/1952 in Rochester; sixth; Theodore J. Moody (Spauld. fibre, Tamworth) and Ruth B. Golden (Barnstead)
Michael Shawn, b. 8/6/1955 in Rochester; seventh; Theodore J. Moody (Spaulding F., Tamworth) and Ruth Golden (Barnstead)
Nancy Lee, b. 12/9/1940; seventh; Alfred H. Moody (lea. worker, Tamworth) and Alice M. S. Phinney (Lynn, MA)

Patricia Anne, b. 2/26/1938 in Rochester; sixth; Alfred H. Moody (shoe worker, Tamworth) and Alice M. Phinney (Lynn, MA)

Peggy Ann, b. 12/17/1944 in Rochester; first; Theodore Moody (clerk, Tamworth) and Ruth B. Golden (Ctr. Barnstead)

Ronald Anthony, b. 5/3/1950 in Rochester; fourth; Walter Moody (mill worker, NH) and Margaret Golden (NH)

Sandra Annette, b. 3/6/1941 in Rochester; first; Walter L. Moody (fibre worker, Ossipee) and Margaret E. Golden (Barnstead)

Sue Ileen, b. 1/9/1947 in Rochester; second; Walter L. Moody (fibre mill, Ossipee) and Margaret E. Golden (Barnstead)

Tami Jean, b. 8/21/1961 in Rochester; Theodore J. Moody (foreman) and Ruth B. Galden

Tausha Marie, b. 9/27/1975 in Rochester; Terrence A. Moody and Susan E. Smith

Terrence Aaron, b. 3/9/1947 in Rochester; third; Theodore J. Moody (hand molder, Tamworth) and Ruth B. Golden (Barnstead)

Theodore Joseph, b. 11/2/1977 in Wolfeboro; Jamie D. Moody and Deborah L. Bodwell

Thomas Walter, b. 6/12/1949 in Rochester; third; T. Walter Moody (mill employee, NH) and Margaret E. Golden (NH)

Timothy John, b. 12/31/1951 in Rochester; fifth; Theodore J. Moody (beater man, Tamworth) and Ruth B. Golden (Ctr. Barnstead)

MOOERS,

Leon Wayne, b. 7/20/1950 in Rochester; first; Fred L. Mooers (electrician, ME) and Arlene Currier (NH)

Rodney Scott, b. 10/16/1953 in Rochester; second; Fred L. Mooers (US Army, Acton, ME) and Arlene M. Currier (Chelsea, MA)

MOORE,

son, b. 8/5/1890; William E. Moore (farmer, MA) and Sarah Downs (Milton)

Edward Kenneth, b. 1/25/1918; first; Lyle K. Moore (laborer, Milton) and Hannah C. Curley (Roslindale, MA)

MORAN,

Clyde Patrick, b. 6/27/1945 in Rochester; first; Clyde P. Moran (coast guard, Chicago, IL) and Evora M. Reagan (Lynn, MA)

Evora May, b. 6/3/1946 in Rochester; second; Clyde P. Moran (mill worker, Chicago, IL) and Evora M. Reagan (Lynn, MA)

MORANN,
Amanda Lynn, b. 6/17/1992 in Rochester; Tom William Henry Morann and Deborah L. Hescock

MOREAU,
Michelle Lyn, b. 9/16/1991 in Rochester; Roland J. Moreau and Diana L. Higgins

MORGAN,
Charles Kenneth, b. 4/11/1931; first; Charles O. Morgan (Montreal, Canada) and Florence Remick (Milton)
Peggy Ellen, b. 7/10/1962 in Rochester; Maynard A. Morgan (shoe worker) and Florence J. Brown
Willard Thomas, b. 12/8/1925; third; Willard T. Morgan (laborer, Seaford, DE) and Loulia M. Fabian (Presque Isle, ME)
William Rice, Jr., b. 5/23/1979 in Rochester; William R. Morgan, Sr. and Debra Pappagallo

MORIN,
Ellen, b. 5/15/1893; sixth; Antoine Morin (laborer, 31, Canada) and Belzemer DeMers (27, Canada)
Frank Herbert, b. 9/10/1931; first; Stephen H. Morin (shoeworker, Alfred, ME) and Beatrice Kenney (Milton)
Louis John, b. 1/7/1933; second; Stephen H. Morin (shoeworker, Alfred, ME) and Beatrice Kenney (Milton)
Robyn Kelly, b. 3/21/1964 in Rochester; third; Maurice R. Morin (laborer) and Sharon E. Long
Stella Olida, b. 6/29/1918; second; Samuel L. Morin (emp. in mill, Ashland) and Ora P. Dyer (Sanbornville)

MORRILL,
Fred Raymond, III, b. 1/31/1984 in Rochester; Fred R. Morrill, Jr. and Denise A. Provencher
Matthew Stewart, b. 12/8/1987 in Rochester; Fred R. Morrill, Jr. and Denise A. Provencher

Michael Paul, b. 4/11/1975 in Rochester; David W. Morrill and Cindy-Lu
   Bean
Stuart Alan, b. 1/16/1962 in Rochester; Fred R. Morrill (truck driver) and
   Eva C. Meyer

MORRISON,
Arlene Frances, b. 8/19/1926 in Rochester; first; Harry A. Morrison
   (bookkeeper, Milton) and Frances Smith (Boston, MA)
Chester Eugene, b. 5/14/1928 in Rochester; second; Harry A. Morrison
   (shipper, Milton) and Frances Smith (Milton) (1934)
Franklin Ellsworth, b. 9/16/1909; second; Harry B. Morrison (emp. in
   mill, Eastport, ME) and Vinie R. Leighton (Milton)
Harry Adelbert, b. 7/30/1907; first; Harry B. Morrison (emp. in mill, 3-,
   Eastport, ME) and Vernie R. Leighton (19, Milton)

MOSES,
Barbara Betty, b. 3/13/1950 in Rochester; Sylvanus Moses (sawyer, MA)
   and Loretta Dukette (NH)

MOULTON,
daughter [Lorna A.], b. 9/13/1904; first; Seth A. Moulton (mech.
   engineer, 28, Lowell, MA) and Elfrida M. Peacock (23, Solon, ME)
Elijah Raymond, b. 10/8/1993 in Rochester; Lawrence L. Moulton, Jr. and
   Jodi R. Reichert
Olena Ria, b. 4/8/1907; second; Seth A. Moulton (mech. engineer, 31,
   Lowell, MA) and Elfrida M. Peacock (25, Solon, ME)
Spencer Lawrence, b. 9/3/1990 in Rochester; Lawrence L. Moulton, Jr.
   and Jodi R. Reichert

MUCCI,
daughter [Ellen], b. 3/14/1907; seventh; Nicolo Mucci (grocer, 38, Italy)
   and Theresa Lorenzi (36, Italy)
son, b. 2/25/1911; sixth; Nicolo Mucci (grocer, Italy) and Theresa
   Lorenzo (Italy)
Alice M. S., b. 2/3/1899; fourth; N. Mucci (fruit dealer, 28, Italy) and
   Zoresia Leorenzi (26, Italy)
Arlene R., b. 2/11/1912; eighth; Nicolo Mucci (merchant, Italy) and
   Theresa Lorenzi (Italy) (1915)

James Osborne Nicholas, b. 11/17/1917; first; Iacapino Mucci (shoemaker, Italy) and Dorothy E. Wootton (Harrow, England) (1918)

MUGFORD,
Kirsten Megan, b. 5/6/1997 in Rochester; Rohn W. Mugford and Tamara L. Mugford

MURPHY,
Helen Veronica, b. 7/31/1922; second; James D. Murphy (laborer, Albertson, PEI) and Jane Wright (Boston, MA)
James Edward, b. 8/20/1921; first; James D. Murphy (laborer, Albertson, PEI) and Jane Wright (Boston, MA)
John Alfred, b. 5/30/1924; seventh; James D. Murphy (laborer, PEI) and Jennie Wright (Boston, MA)
Karli, b. 12/19/1978 in Rochester; Joseph J. Murphy and Glenda J. Walsh

MUSE,
Marion, b. 3/20/1909; first; James R. Muse (ice man, Yarmouth, NS) and Marion C. Marshall (Wakefield)

MYERS,
Noah Greer, b. 6/10/1985 in Dover; Stephen R. Myers and Nancy M. Brooks
Stephen Brooks, b. 3/23/1983 in Dover; Stephen R. Myers and Nancy M. Brooks

MYHR,
May, b. 8/14/1922; second; Oscar Myhr (machinist, Norway) and May Bernier (Dover); residence - Dover

NADEAU,
Audie James, b. 7/2/1962 in Rochester; Richard A. Nadeau (shoe worker) and Grace M. Tanner
Holly Anne, b. 4/20/1960 in Rochester; second; Richard A. Nadeau (shoe worker) and Grace Tanner
Kyle Audie, b. 6/8/1991 in Rochester; Audie J. Nadeau and Kris D. Morrill

Marie Adele, b. 8/21/1963 in Rochester; Richard A. Nadeau (shoe worker) and Grace M. Tanner

Nicole Lyn, b. 2/24/1987 in Exeter; Conrad H. Nadeau and Rhonda K. Lewis

Richard Jason, b. 5/24/1961 in Rochester; Richard A. Nadeau (shanking) and Grace M. Tanner

Richard Leroy, b. 7/31/1981 in Rochester; Richard J. Nadeau and Sandra J. Cox

NARESKI,
Joseph Andrew, Jr., b. 10/4/1946 in Rochester; first; Joseph A. Nareski (Milton Mills) and Margaret R. Hale (Milton Mills); residence - Milton Mills

NARY,
Edward Allan, Jr., b. 11/2/1952 in Rochester; first; Edward A. Nary (mechanic, MA) and Ann M. DesRoches (VT)

Elizabeth Jeanne, b. 3/28/1950 in Rochester; third; Elmer E. Nary, Jr. (RR engineer, MA) and Elizabeth Osborne (Canada)

NASON,
Denise M., b. 12/27/1957 in Rochester; first; Ronald Nason (laborer, Gorham, ME) and Sharon Downs (Rochester)

Gerald Almon, Jr., b. 12/15/1964 in Wolfeboro; second; Gerald A. Nason (machine operator) and Mary E. Trites

Joshua Ronald, b. 12/30/1982 in Rochester; Ronald W. Nason and Cynthia M. Monteith

Matthew Rodney, b. 11/27/1996 in Dover; Dave R. Nason and Karen M. Nason

Michelle Lee, b. 2/4/1969 in Wolfeboro; Gerald A. Nason and Mary E. Trites

Rodney Edward, b. 3/13/1958 in Rochester; first; Rodney E. Nason (USAF, Wolfeboro) and Betty F. Provencher (Milton)

Ronald Wayne, Jr., b. 2/13/1959 in Rochester; second; Ronald W. Nason (laborer, Gorham, ME) and Sharon E. Downs (Rochester)

Shania Marie, b. 12/3/1996 in Dover; James E. Nason and Karen M. Nason

Thomas Dave, b. 7/9/1994 in Dover; Dave R. Nason and Karen M. Lamper

NELSON,
Joshua Allen, b. 3/15/1989 in Rochester; Charles T. Nelson, Jr. and Beth A. Cutler

NESBITT,
Alyssa Marie, b. 6/10/1998; James M. Nesbitt, IV and Jami-Lynn Nesbitt

NEWELL,
Harold Ralph, b. 7/22/1925; first; Milford W. Newell (ice man, Clark's Har., NS) and Vera A. Craig (Bradford)
James Isaiah, b. 3/15/1928; second; Milford Newell (mill operative, Clark's Hbr., NS) and Vera A. Craig (Bradford)

NICKERSON,
stillborn son, b. 7/30/1895; first; James T. Nickerson (laborer, 26, NS) and Lillian Mason (21, Milton)
stillborn son, b. 11/4/1898; third; James T. Nickerson (laborer, 28, NS) and Lillian Mason (26, Milton)
son [Maurice W.], b. 2/8/1902; fifth; James T. Nickerson (sawmill, 31, NS) and Lillian M. Mason (30, Milton)
Blanche, b. 7/25/1904; sixth; James T. Nickerson (sawyer, 34, NS) and Lillian M. Mason (32, Milton)
Carrie, b. 12/24/1906; seventh; James T. Nickerson (sawyer, 36, NS) and Lillian M. Mason (35, Milton)
Willis E., b. 12/16/1896; second; James T. Nickerson (laborer, 26, NS) and Lillian M. Mason (25, Milton)

NIELSEN,
Scott Allen, b. 6/3/1972 in Rochester; Paul B. Nielsen and Marjorie J. Goodwin

NIVEN,
Eileen Rose, b. 12/2/1996 in Rochester; Michael R. Niven and Sarah A. Niven

NIX,
Staci Jean, b. 8/16/1970 in Manchester; Richard E. Nix and Joan Ann Carter

NOBLE,
daughter, b. 10/15/1902; first; John C. Noble (paper maker, 31, Lawrence, MA) and Minnie E. Richards (23, Belfast, ME)

NOLAN,
Mildred Arleen, b. 11/25/1912; first; Robert E. Nolan (contractor, 37, Middleboro, MA) and Mildred L. Bragdon (33, Milton)

NORRISH,
Cassandra Jean, b. 5/8/1991 in Rochester; Stephen E. Norrish and Tammy A. Champy
Stephen Earl, II, b. 9/9/1988 in Rochester; Stephen E. Norrish and Tammy Champy

NORTON,
stillborn son, b. 7/21/1898; seventh; Frank E. Norton (foreman, 32, Lawrence, MA) and Maggie E. Ivers (31, Lawrence, MA)
Harvard, b. 12/24/1891; second; William K. Norton (teacher, 27, Boston, MA) and Eliza M. Norton (26, Burlington, MA)
John Leighton, b. 8/14/1899; eighth; Frank E. Norton (foreman, 33, Lawrence, MA) and Maggie E. Ivers (32, Lawrence, MA)
Joseph A., b. 7/22/1896; sixth; Frank E. Norton (leather board, 30, Lawrence, MA) and Maggie E. Ivers (29, Lawrence, MA)
Lawrence Ivers, b. 7/6/1907; ninth; Frank E. Norton (supt. of mill, 42, Lawrence, MA) and Margaret Ivers (41, Lawrence, MA)

NOWILL,
Randall William, Jr., b. 11/22/1985 in Portsmouth; Randall W. Nowill and Henrietta G. Loveday

NUTE,
Aubrey Y., b. 2/20/1899; second; Harry Y. Nute (shoemaker, 24, Milton) and Christie B. Goodwin (23, Acton, ME)
Audrey B., b. 2/20/1899; third; Harry Y. Nute (shoemaker, 24, Milton) and Christie B. Goodwin (23, Acton, ME)
Norma Arline, b. 8/24/1924; first; Ray H. Nute (farmer, Milton) and Doria M. Ferland (Rochester)
Rubie, b. 8/7/1895; first; Harry Nute (shoemaker, 19, Milton) and Christie Goodwin (18, Acton, ME)

Ruth Eliza, b. 10/15/1923; first; Charles E. Nute (laborer, Milton) and Ella M. Jenness (Milton)

NUTTER,
Addis Calvin, b. 4/26/1942 in Rochester; second; Malcolm H. Nutter (mill worker, Milton) and Grace E. Grey (Barnstead Ctr.)
Addis S., b. 2/19/1895; first; Hartley Nutter (laborer, 21, Milton) and Ada Huntress (20, Athens, ME)
Annie Florence, b. 1/18/1896; first; Roscoe C. Nutter (shoemaker, 20, Milton) and May E. Johnson (25, Greenland)
Donna Jean, b. 7/16/1943 in Rochester; first; Frank R. Nutter (radio service, Milton) and Ernestine F. Witham (Portsmouth)
Evelyn Ruth, b. 7/15/1906; first; Frank Nutter (shoemaker, 23, Sanford, ME) and Gertrude E. Wentworth (19, Milton)
Francina I., b. 2/24/1902; third; Hartley A. Nutter (ice man, 28, Milton) and Ada M. Huntress (27, Athens, ME)
Frank R., b. 8/20/1914; second; Frank J. Nutter (shoemaker, Sanford, ME) and Gertrude E. Wentworth (Milton)
Malcolm Hartley, b. 1/8/1915; first; Addis S. Nutter (laborer, Milton) and Marion G. Rand (Milton)
Nelson T., b. 3/23/1894; first; Jacob Nutter (shoemaker, 37, Milton) and Kate M. Perkins (25, Jackson)

NYE,
Joshua Philip, b. 6/15/1990 in Rochester; Philip R. Nye and Linda E. Timmins

O'BRIEN,
Niall Joseph, b. 4/17/1991 in Rochester; Scott D. O'Brien and Pearl M. Burke

O'CONNOR, [see Conners]
Alice, b. 6/2/1897; fifth; Michael O'Connor (mill hand, 35, Ireland) and Carrie Schroeder (24, Boston, MA)

O'LAUGHLIN,
son [Ronald M.], b. 2/13/1902; second; James G. O'Laughlin (paper mill, 34, Stoneham, MA) and Addie F. Knight (27, Milton)

Leon W., b. 8/2/1895; first; James G. O'Laughlin (shoemaker, 28, Stoneham, MA) and Addie F. Knight (21, Milton)

O'ROURKE,
Kristen Leigh, b. 8/31/1985 in Rochester; James H. O'Rourke and Nancy E. Weyland

OLIVER,
William Eugene, b. 10/25/1948 in Rochester; second; William W. Oliver (towerman, Portland, ME) and Marion E. Dudley (Hartford, CT)

OLMES,
Hannah Elizabeth, b. 8/2/1999 in Portsmouth; Philip Olmes and Kathleen Olmes

OSBORN,
daughter, b. 9/2/1901; fourth; Charles B. Osborn (clergyman, 30, Rochester) and Cora Meyer (34, Andover, MA)
Jesse Ryne, b. 6/8/1991 in Rochester; Michael D. Osborn and Michele A. St. Hilaire

OUELLETTE,
Leah Marie, b. 3/12/1981 in Dover; Gary A. Ouellette and Jeanne M. Walker

PAEY,
son, b. 7/11/1905; second; George W. Paey (shoemaker, 33, Stoneham, MA) and Josie M. Downs (28, Milton)
Charles Edward, b. 2/12/1940 in Rochester; second; Bernard G. Paey (shoe worker, Milton) and Irene C. Otis (Somersworth)
Clyde Wilfred, b. 3/4/1912; fourth; George W. Paey (shoemaker, 34, Stoneham, MA) and Josephine M. Downs (39, Milton)
Cynthia Ruth, b. 6/8/1939 in Rochester; second; Clyde W. Paey (fibre worker, Milton) and Louise C. Huntress (Haverhill, MA)
Darrell Eugene, b. 2/16/1966 in Wolfeboro; David G. Paey (road maintenance operator) and Dorothy M. Bickford
David Gene, b. 7/31/1936 in Rochester; first; Clyde Paey (clerk, Milton) and Louise Huntress (Haverhill, MA)

David Gene, Jr., b. 10/16/1964 in Wolfeboro; second; David G. Paey (truck driver) and Dorothy M. Bickford

Evelyn, b. 1/3/1910; third; George W. Paly (sic) (shoemaker, Stoneham, MA) and Josephine M. Downs (Milton)

Laronda Ann, b. 10/20/1962 in Wolfeboro; David G. Pacy (sic) (US Navy) and Dorothy M. Bickford

Rena D., b. 4/3/1903; first; George W. Paey (shoemaker, 30, Stoneham, MA) and Josie M. Downs (25, Milton)

PAGE,

daughter [Doris M.], b. 12/7/1894; fifth; George W. Page (laborer, 35, Sandwich) and Nettie Rines (23, Milton)

son, b. 11/23/1899; first; Robert Page (barber, 22, Milton) and Ida Sibley (25, Boston, MA)

daughter [M. Norma], b. 10/17/1902; second; Robert Page (barber, 26, Milton) and Ida F. Sibley (28, Boston, MA)

Charlene A., b. 2/2/1915; sixth; Robert Page (barber, Milton) and Ida Sibley (Boston, MA)

Frank, b. 10/25/1895; first; Edward Page (laborer, 26, W. Gardiner, ME) and Vina Roy (21, Canada)

Irma, b. 7/31/1908; third; Robert Page (barber, Milton) and Ida Sibley (Boston, MA) (1911)

Robert W., b. 10/31/1910; fourth; Robert Page (barber, Milton) and Ida Sibley (Boston, MA) (1911)

Ruth, b. 6/11/1912; fifth; Robert Page (barber, 35, Milton) and Ida F. Sibley (38, Boston, MA)

PAGEAU,

Joan Marie, b. 12/20/1960 in Rochester; sixth; Rolland A. Pageau (treer shoe shop) and Reta M. McFarland

John Rolland, b. 8/10/1952 in Rochester; fourth; Rolland A. Pageau (shoe worker, Canada) and Rita M. McFarland (Groveton)

PAINTER,

Joseph Michael, b. 9/26/1981 in Portsmouth; Eugene Painter, Jr. and Christine A. Karkavelas

PALMER,
daughter, b. 3/10/1901; third; Benjamin F. Palmer (laborer, 38, Newfield, ME) and Eva B. Burke (26, Somersworth)
Christopher William, b. 10/1/1985 in Wolfeboro; David W. Palmer and Pamela A. Stock
Robert, Jr., b. 9/8/1937 in Rochester; fourth; Robert Palmer (boss packer, Rochester) and Evelyn Young (Acton, ME); residence - Milton Mills
Roberta Beth, b. 4/16/1951 in Rochester; sixth; Robert B. Palmer (counterman, Rochester) and Evelyn I. Young (Acton, ME)
Rodney Wayne, b. 7/10/1936 in Rochester; third; Robert Palmer (mill worker, Rochester) and Evelyn Young (Acton, ME); residence - Milton Mills
Ronald Alan, b. 9/6/1945 in Rochester; fourth; Robert B. Palmer (fireman, Rochester) and Evelyn I. Young (Acton, ME); residence - Milton Mills

PANAGOS,
Philip Stephen, b. 9/21/1982 in Rochester; John J. Panagos and Joanne Drummond

PAPPAS,
Anthony Maurice, b. 12/14/1971 in Rochester; Ronnie L. Pappas and Loraine Y. Dallaire

PAQUIN,
John, b. 2/6/1952 in Rochester; stillborn; sixth; Henry Paquin (laborer, MI) and Henrietta Brewer (MA)

PARE,
Justin Philip, b. 5/18/1988 in Dover; Robert G. Pare and Betty L. John

PARKER,
Albert Lauren, b. 9/19/1953 in Rochester; third; Lauren E. Parker, Jr. (US Navy, East Rochester) and Rita Boucher (Rochester)
David Vickery, b. 4/21/1981 in Dover; Robert L. Parker and Elaine A. Vickery
Elaine Theresa, b. 5/25/1951 in Rochester; third; Earl S. Parker (weaver, NH) and Loretta B. Boucher (Pembroke, MA)

Jaclyn Maureen, b. 1/3/1987 in Rochester; William E. Parker and Cathy L. Bluemer
Stephanie Alice, b. 6/1/1983 in Dover; Robert L. Parker and Elaine A. Vickery
Wayne William, Jr., b. 7/19/1978 in Portsmouth; Wayne W. Parker and Sharon L. McManus
William Paul, b. 9/12/1991 in Rochester; William E. Parker and Cathy L. Bluemer

PARON,
daughter, b. 9/1/1908; first; Joseph A. Paron (shoemaker, 20, Canada) and Cecelia Lapoint (16, Wakefield)

PARSONS,
Elizabeth Anne, b. 1/18/1930; third; Bernard F. Parsons (shoeworker, East Rochester) and Mary E. Regan (Milton); residence - East Rochester

PASQUALE,
Stephanie Marie, b. 9/29/1970 in Dover; Stephen M. Pasquale and Kathleen J. Poisson

PATCH,
son [John], b. 7/24/1900; second; John Patch (laborer, 26, Newfield, ME) and Gertrude M. Clark (22, Wolfeboro)
stillborn daughter, b. 2/7/1946 in Rochester; first; Alfred G. Patch (truck driver, Milton Mills) and Margaret M. Rouleau (Milton)
Alan Wayne, b. 8/12/1953 in Rochester; fourth; Alfred G. Patch (mill worker, Acton, ME) and Margaret Rouleau (Milton)
Charles, b. 3/5/1903; John Patch (NH) and Gertrude Clark (NH) (1953)
Dixie Lee, b. 11/4/1950 in Rochester; third; Alfred G. Patch (woodsman, ME) and Margaret Rouleau (NH)
Eileen Marie, b. 6/15/1982 in Rochester; Dale F. Patch and Lucila Gonzales
Emily Elizabeth, b. 3/21/1986 in Rochester; Dale F. Patch and Lucila Gonzales
Laurie Ann, b. 10/28/1974 in Rochester; Bruce R. Patch and Beverly A. Brierley

Robert Alfred, b. 3/10/1948 in Rochester; first; Alfred G. Patch (teamster, Milton Mills) and Margaret M. Rouleau (Milton)

PATTERSON,
Patricia Lee, b. 8/30/1942 in Rochester; first; Harold L. Patterson (clergyman, Altoona, PA) and Inez Peterson (Detroit, MI); residence - Milton Mills

PAUL,
Ada Arline, b. 4/20/1923; fourth; George H. Paul (laborer, Lynn, MA) and Winifred M. Lord (Acton, ME)
Beatrice Winifred, b. 11/13/1920; third; George H. Paul (laborer, Lynn, MA) and Winifred M. Lord (Acton, ME)
Henry Harrison, b. 5/26/1898; second; George H. Paul (farmer, 32, Lynn, MA) and Alice E. Lord (33, Acton, ME)
Theodore Oscar, b. 9/5/1926 in Rochester; fifth; George H. Paul (laborer, Lynn, MA) and Winnie Lord (Acton, ME)

PEABODY,
Elizabeth Joan, b. 8/21/1995 in Rochester; William S. Peabody and Cheryl A. Peabody

PEACOCK,
son [Alfred G.], b. 11/4/1898; fourth; Robert M. Peacock (clergyman, 50, Canada) and Ada M. Lee (39, Vassalboro, ME)
Ruth A., b. 5/21/1902; fifth; Robert M. Peacock (clergyman, 53, Ontario) and Afa M. Lee (42, Riverside, ME)

PEARCE,
George Michael, b. 8/3/1969 in Sanford, ME; John M. Pearce and Emily J. Pillsbury (1973)
John Morgan, Jr., b. 5/9/1971 in Sanford, ME; John M. Pearce and Emily J. Pillsbury (1973)

PEARSON,
Sawyer Richard, b. 1/27/1993 in Rochester; Craig S. Pearson and Karen L. Cheney
Sierra Naomi, b. 10/25/1990 in Rochester; Craig S. Pearson and Karen C. Cheney

Zachary Sanders, b. 9/3/1989 in Rochester; Craig S. Pearson and Karen L. Cheney

PECK,
Frederick William, Jr., b. 4/14/1934; second; Frederick W. Peck (mill emp., Ware, MA) and Lillian Katan (Westford, VT)

PELLETIER,
Michael John, b. 10/16/1979 in Dover; Donald J. Pelletier and Patricia A. Marcoux
Stacy Paul, b. 9/21/1964 in Rochester; first; Norman E. Pelletier (laborer) and Paula D. Moulton

PENNELL,
son, b. 8/18/1901; second; Willis J. Pennell (mill hand, 25, St. Albans, VT) and Zenaide Bilodeau (20, Canada)
stillborn daughter, b. 2/8/1927; seventh; Edward Pennell (B. & M. RR, Tamworth) and Dora Williams (Tamworth); residence - Tamworth
Alston Edward, b. 9/26/1944 in Rochester; fourth; Reginald E. Pennell (woolen mill, Tamworth) and Helen J. Remick (Milton)
Brenda Lee, b. 10/12/1964; sixth; Reginald E. Pennell (laborer) and Marie B. Parks
Deborah Ann, b. 4/29/1956 in Rochester; seventh; Reginald Pennell (steamer, Milton, MA) and Helen Remick (Milton)
Edwin C., b. 12/22/1924; sixth; Edwin A. Pennell (laborer, Tamworth) and Dora L. Williams (Tamworth); residence - Tamworth
Helen Louise, b. 12/27/1942 in Rochester; third; Reginald E. Pennell (mill employee, Tamworth) and Helen J. Remick (Milton)
James Michael, b. 5/13/1985 in Rochester; James E. Pennell and April L. Young
John William, b. 4/6/1951 in Rochester; fifth; Reginald E. Pennell (machine oper., NH) and Helen Remick (Milton)
John William, b. 3/10/1962 in Rochester; John E. Pennell (mill worker) and Marie B. Parks
Julie Ann, b. 4/2/1963 in Rochester; Reginald E. Pennell (machine operator) and Marie B. Parks
June Marie, b. 7/1/1941 in Rochester; second; Reginald E. Pennell (mill employee, Ossipee) and Helen J. Remick (Milton)

June Marie, b. 2/6/1960 in Rochester; second; Reginald E. Pennell (laborer) and Marie B. Parks

Margaret Louise, b. 9/22/1920; third; Edwin A. Pennell (railroad, Tamworth) and Dora Williams (Tamworth); residence - Tamworth (1938)

Pamela Jean, b. 4/9/1961 in Rochester; Reginald E. Pennell (laborer) and Marie B. Parks

Reginald E., b. 3/22/1919; second; Edwin A. Pennell (railroad, Tamworth) and Dora Williams (Tamworth); residence - Tamworth (1938)

Reginald Edwin, III, b. 1/13/1997 in Rochester; Reginald E. Pennell, Jr. and Pamela A. Pennell

Ryan Alston, b. 12/29/1998; Reginald E. Pennell, Jr. and Pamela A. Pennell

Virginia Frances, b. 8/6/1922; fifth; Edward A. Pennell (RR sect. hand, Tamworth) and Dora L. Williams (Tamworth); residence - Tamworth

PENNEY,
Dylan Scott, b. 8/26/1990 in Rochester; Robert S. Penney and Kelly M. Brooks

Jasmine Marie, b. 3/16/1992 in Rochester; Robert S. Penney and Keely M. Brooks

PENNO,
David Lee, b. 8/3/1985 in Rochester; Arthur A. Penno and Laurie R. Joyal

PERKINS,
Adam Gordon, b. 5/4/1909; third; Harry O. Perkins (sawyer, Milton) and Lena G. Willey (Middleton)

Ai Juan, b. 3/21/1997 in Rochester; Edward J. Perkins and Erline M. Perkins

Charles Edward, b. 11/17/1955 in Rochester; fifth; Otis Perkins (laborer, Wolfeboro) and Hattie Twombly (Wolfeboro)

Edith Geneva, b. 2/2/1938 in Farmington; third; Otis Perkins (laborer, Milton Mills) and Hattie E. Twombly (Wolfeboro); residence - Milton Mills

Emily Lauren, b. 9/15/1993 in Dover; Patrick S. Perkins and Lisa M. Kern

George Henry, b. 7/3/1916; first; Lester Perkins (mill hand, Wolfeboro) and Lizzie Lord (Acton, ME) (1917)
Henry Otis, b. 7/28/1933 in Milton Mills; second; Otis I. Perkins (laborer, Wolfeboro) and Hattie E. Twombly (Wolfeboro); residence - Milton Mills
Jerimiah Robert, b. 2/16/1995 in Rochester; Edward J. Perkins and Erline M. Perkins
Lloyd A., b. 11/24/1909; fifth; A. A. Perkins (shoemaker, New Durham) and Bertha E. Kimball (Wolfeboro)
Molly Anne, b. 9/17/1965 in Rochester; Lloyd A. Perkins (lineman) and Mary A. Lawson
Patrick Stephen, b. 3/9/1968 in Rochester; Lloyd A. Perkins and Mary A. Lawson
Paul Vincent, b. 12/30/1942 in Rochester; fourth; Otis I. Perkins (saw mill emp., Wolfeboro) and Hattie E. Twombly (Wolfeboro)
Stanley Reginald, b. 7/10/1919; first; James A. Perkins (laborer, Wakefield) and Margarette E. Swinerton (Milton); residence - Wakefield

PERRY,
Caroline Joyce, b. 5/25/1936 in Wolfeboro; first; Henry W. Perry (mill worker, Brewster, MA) and Sarah E. Robie (Wakefield); residence - S. Milton
Delores Wanda, b. 11/15/1937 in Wolfeboro; third; John Perry (ass't dyer, PEI) and Hazel May Drew (Union); residence - Milton Mills
Dorothy Louise, b. 1/3/1924; fifth; Charles E. Perry (farmer, W. Brewster, MA) and Ruth W. Perry (Marstons Mills, ME)
Elsie Jeanet, b. 8/1/1931; seventh; Charles E. Perry (laborer, Brewster, MA) and Ruth W. Perry (Marstons Mills, ME)
Francis Willard, b. 7/3/1922; fourth; Charles E. Perry (farmer, Brewster, MA) and Ruth W. Perry (Marstons Mills, ME)
James Clinton, b. 12/17/1933; eighth; Charles E. Perry (laborer, Brewster, MA) and Ruth W. Perry (Marstons Mills, ME)
John Willard, b. 10/24/1948 in Rochester; second; Charles E. Perry, Jr. (US Army, Walpole) and Eva M. Pearson (Tamworth)
John Willard, Jr., b. 9/17/1971 in Rochester; John W. Perry and Lena M. Cullen
Mildred Edith, b. 3/24/1921; second; James E. Perry (laborer, Brookfield) and Lilla F. Doyer (Lawrence, MA)

Rebecca Caroline, b. 12/8/1969 in Dover; Otis E. Perry and Caroline L. French

Ronald Clinton, b. 7/25/1947 in Rochester; first; Charles E. Perry, Jr. (leather mill, Walpole) and Eva M. Pearson (Tamworth)

Shirley May, b. 10/4/1935; ninth; Charles E. Perry (farmer, Brewster, MA) and Ruth W. Perry (Marston's M., ME)

Susan Lee, b. 7/9/1953 in Rochester; fifth; Charles E. Perry, Jr. (leatherboard mill, Walpole) and Eva M. Pearson (Tamworth)

Timothy David, b. 3/28/1946; first; Vianna R. Perry (Milton); residence - West Milton

Vianna Rosa, b. 2/28/1926; sixth; Charles E. Perry (farmer, Brewster, MA) and Ruth M. Perry (Marstons Mills, ME)

PERT,
Elyse Katherine, b. 1/8/1989 in Rochester; Edmund K. Pert and Joyce A. Moore

PETERSON,
Alan Carrol, II, b. 8/10/1977 in Rochester; Alan C. Peterson and Patricia G. Weed

Ali Caitlin, b. 11/17/1982 in Rochester; Alan C. Peterson and Patricia G. Weed

Amanda Carrol, b. 8/17/1974 in Rochester; Alan C. Peterson and Patricia G. Weed

Andy Charles, b. 3/13/1979 in Rochester; Alan C. Peterson and Patricia G. Weed

Angie Carole, b. 1/12/1976 in Rochester; Alan C. Peterson and Patricia G. Weed

Bobbi Lynne, b. 9/7/1987 in Rochester; Geoffrey D. Peterson and Debra E. Reid

Chandler Ross, b. 3/11/1996 in Dover; Thomas O. Peterson and Dianne E. Peterson

Curtis Taylor, b. 2/28/1988 in Rochester; Christopher R. Peterson and Judith L. Lucier

Justin Ronald, b. 6/21/1991 in Dover; Thomas O. Peterson and Dianne E. Hancock

Marissa L., b. 9/16/1984 in Rochester; Christopher R. Peterson and Judith L. Lucier

Matthew Thomas, b. 2/14/1989 in Dover; Thomas O. Peterson and
Dianne E. Hancock

PETROCCIA,
Makenzie Rachel, b. 2/25/1997 in Rochester; Thomas D. Petroccia and
Edith I. Petroccia

PEVEAR,
Drew Devan, b. 9/9/1994 in Portsmouth; George A. Pevear, Jr. and
Angela M. Goddard

PHILBRICK,
daughter, b. 7/10/1891; first; Charles S. Philbrick (farmer, 31, Freedom)
and Jennie H. Applebee (27, Milton Mills)

PHILIBERT,
Arthur James, b. 1/7/1919; sixth; Augustine Philibert (lthr. bd. mfgr.,
Barre, VT) and Florence Greenwood (Grasmere)
Janet Murial, b. 1/21/1920; seventh; Augustine Philibert (laborer, Barre,
VT) and Florence Greenwood (Grassmere)

PHILIPPI,
Brianna Mae, b. 1/5/1997 in Rochester; Todd L. Philippi and Michelle M.
Philippi

PHILLIPS,
Brian Daniel, b. 8/4/1988 in Rochester; Daniel A. Phillips and Laura J.
Moore
Brian David, b. 5/4/1987 in Dover; David B. Phillips and Denise A.
Lilljedahl
Erik Robert, b. 12/7/1989 in Rochester; Daniel S. Phillips and Laura J.
Moore
Jeffrey Lynne, b. 2/2/1949 in Rochester; third; Paul S. Phillips (mill
employee, MA) and Priscilla M. Pratt (MA)

PHILPOT,
Judith Emily, b. 9/13/1939 in Rochester; second; J. Frank Philpot
(laborer, Windham, ME) and Janet L. Columbus (Milton); residence
- Lebanon, ME

PIERCE,
Beverly Ann, b. 1/9/1948 in Rochester; fourth; Carl H. Pierce (mill worker, Cornish, ME) and Mary E. Drew (Union)
Carl Henry, Jr., b. 4/2/1944 in Rochester; first; Carl H. Pierce (spray painter, Cornish, ME) and Mary E. Drew (Union); residence - Milton Mills
Carl Henry, III, b. 5/16/1967 in Rochester; third; Carl H. Pierce, Jr. (meat cutter) and Bernadette M. Routhier
Charles Arthur, b. 10/3/1945 in Rochester; second; Carl Henry Pierce (farmer, Cornish, ME) and Mary E. Drew (Union)
Joseph Louis, b. 6/4/1968 in Rochester; Carl H. Pierce, Jr. and Bernadette M. Routhier
Joyce Elaine, b. 9/19/1946 in Rochester; third; Carl H. Pierce (teamster, Cornish, ME) and Mary E. Drew (Union)

PIKE,
daughter [Lenore Elizabeth], b. 11/30/1912; first; Philip G. Pike (butcher, 24, Milton) and Rosamond Piper (24, Wakefield)
son, b. 4/21/1959 in Rochester; second; Lloyd G. Pike (oven operator, Rochester) and Marylin L. Williams (Milton)
Amber Lee, b. 11/29/1964 in Rochester; second; Lloyd G. Pike (maintenance) and Marylin L. Williams
Christi Elizabeth, b. 2/21/1989 in Dover; Philip W. Pike and Catherine E. Black
Frank A., b. 2/18/1861; first; James D. Pike (New Durham) and Susan L. Cloutman (Middleton) (1940)
Franklin R., b. 5/7/1923 in Wolfeboro; first; Ralph Pike (bookkeeper, Milton Mills) and Marion Brierly (Everett, MA); residence - Milton Mills (1939)
Kevin Roland, b. 12/31/1949 in Rochester; second; Roland S. Pike (mechanic, Milton) and Carolyn M. Drew (Union)
Kimberly Ann, b. 6/22/1968 in Rochester; Kevin R. Pike and Sherrylee M. Gauthier
Lloyd Gerry, Jr., b. 12/20/1956 in Rochester; first; Lloyd G. Pike (dryerman, Rochester) and Marylin Williams (Milton)
Nicholas Scott, b. 12/11/1984 in Dover; Lloyd G. Pike, Jr. and Carol A. Randall
Pamela Ann, b. 6/3/1948 in Rochester; first; Roland S. Pike (mechanic, Milton Mills) and Carolyn M. Drew (Union)

Philip Damon, b. 1/31/1915; second; Philip G. Pike (butcher, East
Rochester) and Rosamond E. Piper (Sanbornville)
Philip Walter, b. 8/9/1963 in Rochester; Weyland P. Pike (mechanic) and
Sandra A. Moody
Ralph W., b. 8/4/1893; fourth; Robert S. Pike (butcher, 33, Middleton)
and Fannie Roberts (34, Milton)
Richard Charles, Jr., b. 1/22/1990 in Rochester; Richard C. Pike and Lisa
May Brown
Roger Leslie, b. 11/29/1926 in Rochester; third; Ralph W. Pike
(bookkeeper, Milton Mills) and Marion Brierley (Roxbury, MA);
residence - Milton Mills
Roland Seth, b. 7/11/1924 in Milton Mills; second; Ralph W. Pike (clerk,
Milton Mills) and Marion Brierley (Everett, MA); residence - Milton
Mills
Scott Wade, b. 4/12/1966 in Rochester; Lloyd G. Pike (machine operator)
and Marylin L. Williams
Shaun Damon, b. 7/19/1968 in Rochester; Richard A. Pike and Jessica L.
Mattress
Stephen Roger, b. 5/2/1952 in Sanford, ME; third; Roger L. Pike (textile
ind., Rochester) and Phyllis R. Merrill (Everett, MA)
Theresa Lynn, b. 6/13/1965 in Rochester; Richard A. Pike (barber) and
Jessica L. Mattress
Weyland Philip, b. 6/3/1939 in Rochester; first; Philip D. Pike (mill
worker, Milton Mills) and Beatrice Van Buskirk (Chelsea, MA);
residence - Milton Mills

PINA,
Stanley Arthur, b. 12/26/1951 in Rochester; second; Antone Pina
(machine oper., Taunton, MA) and Thelma Columbus (Milton)
Steven Anthony, b. 9/21/1950 in Rochester; first; Anthony Pina (shoe
worker, MA) and Thelma Columbus (Milton)

PINKERTON,
Brian Edward, b. 4/23/1990 in Dover; Arthur D. Pinkerton and Kathy Jo
Timmreck
Keith Emery, b. 9/15/1988 in Dover; Arthur D. Pinkerton and Kathy Jo
Timmreck

PINKHAM,
daughter, b. 11/16/1913; third; Harry W. Pinkham (farmer, Milton) and Fannie I. Hayes (Milton)
Bernard Bertrand, b. 1/22/1908; second; Thomas H. Pinkham (painter, 41, Cliftondale, MA) and Mary F. Cushman (25, Orford)
David Richard, b. 9/21/1939 in Rochester; first; Harold B. Pinkham (writer, Milton) and Edith P. Wiggin (Milton Mills)
Edward James, b. 9/1/1959 in Kittery, ME; Harry W. Pinkham (USAF) and Joyce E. Sanborn (Rochester)
Harold, b. 6/16/1894; third; James D. Pinkham (shoelaster, 26, Milton) and Sarah McGonigle (29, Ireland)
Harry Wilbur, b. 4/16/1938 in Rochester; first; Winston H. Pinkham (shoe worker, Milton) and Muriel E. Pinkham (Milton)
Henry C., b. 7/21/1906; first; Thomas H. Pinkham (painter, 40, Cliftondale, MA) and Mary F. Cushman (23, Orford)
Judy Lynn, b. 6/20/1958 in Rochester; first; Harry W. Pinkham (USAF, Rochester) and Joyce E. Sanborn (Rochester)
Shirley, b. 8/20/1911; second; Harry W. Pinkham (farmer, Milton) and Fannie I. Hayes (Milton)
Winston Hayes, b. 8/20/1910; first; Harry W. Pinkham (farmer, Milton) and Fannie I. Hayes (Milton)

PIPER,
Edwin Charles, b. 2/11/1911; first; Charles E. Piper (telephone op., Wakefield) and Helen Pray (Dover)
Gerine June, b. 6/6/1945 in Rochester; second; Edwin C. Piper (mill worker, Milton) and Dorothy M. Gray (Sanbornville)
Margaret Jean, b. 11/30/1945 in Rochester; second; Lewis P. Piper (mill worker, Union) and June E. Ferguson (Georgetown, MA)
Merrianne, b. 1/23/1950 in Rochester; third; Edwin C. Piper (mill worker, Milton) and Dorothy M. Gray (Sanbornville)
Naomi Lee, b. 3/22/1941 in Rochester; first; Edwin C. Piper (lea'bd. worker, Milton) and Dorothy M. Gray (Sanbornville)
Rita E., b. 3/20/1911; second; James A. Piper (farmer, Newfield, ME) and Laura A. Evans (Wakefield)

PLACE,
Marilyn Esther, b. 12/27/1938; third; Percy Place (shoe worker, Farmington) and Esther Dore (Milton)

Peter Paul, b. 1/28/1962 in Rochester; Lawrence E. Place (shoe worker) and Lillian P. Tarlton

PLOURDE,
Tiffany Renee, b. 4/7/1976 in Rochester; Samuel F. Plourde, Jr. and Dale N. Wilkins

PLUM[M]ER,
daughter, b. 9/15/1891; fourth; George L. Plumer (farmer and lumber dealer, 45, Milton) and Ada E. Burrows (36, Milton)
son [Dwight H.], b. 12/25/1896; third; Moses B. Plumer (farmer, 48, Milton) and Lizzie Hussey (39, Acton, ME)
Agnes H., b. 10/29/1873; first; George L. Plumer (farmer, Milton) and Ada E. Burroughs (Milton) (1933)
Bard, b. 4/27/1911; third; Bard B. Plummer, Jr. (farmer, Milton) and Ruth L. Fall (Milton)
Bard B., b. 10/22/1879; third; Bard B. Plummer (farmer, Milton) and Eliza Wentworth (Jamaica Plain, MA) (1939)
Bard Burge, b. 7/23/1954 in Rochester; first; Bard Plummer (laborer, Milton) and Martha E. Hefler (Newton, MA)
Caroline Fall, b. 4/15/1947 in Rochester; first; Lyman Plummer (mot. v. insp., Milton) and Ruth E. Whitehouse (Farmington)
Dorothy, b. 6/9/1918; fifth; Bard B. Plummer, Jr. (farmer, Milton) and Ruth L. Fall (Milton)
Elizabeth, b. 1/7/1909; first; Bard B. Plummer, Jr. (farmer, Milton) and Ruth L. Fall (Milton)
Elizabeth, b. 2/9/1957 in Rochester; third; Bard Plummer (road worker, Milton) and Martha Hefler (Newton, MA)
Etta A., b. 3/17/1880; third; George L. Plumer (farmer, Milton) and Ada E. Burroughs (Milton) (1933)
Francis B., b. 5/3/1891; first; Moses B. Plumer (farmer, 43, Milton) and Elizabeth J. Hussey (34, Acton, ME)
Joseph, b. 8/22/1894; second; Moses B. Plummer (farmer, 46, Milton) and Lizzie Hussey (37, Acton, ME)
Joseph Henry, b. 11/14/1909; second; Jay B. Plummer (farmer, Billerica, MA) and Annie B. Miner (Riverside, NB)
Lillian Carrie, b. 7/4/1908; first; Jay B. Plummer (farmer, 24, Billerica, MA) and Annie B. Miner (24, Riverside, NB)

Lyman, b. 8/3/1912; fourth; Bard B. Plummer, Jr. (farmer, 33, Milton) and Ruth L. Fall (25, Milton)

Marion, b. 7/12/1893; second; Hazen Plummer (McKay stitcher, 27, Milton) and Nettie E. Pike (29, Middleton)

Nancy Jane, b. 1/31/1956 in Rochester; second; Bard Plummer (mach. oper., Milton) and Martha E. Hefler (Newton, MA)

Ray, b. 8/2/1895; third; Hazen Plummer (traveling agent, 29, Milton) and Nettie Pike (31, Middleton)

Ruth, b. 4/19/1910; second; Bard B. Plummer, Jr. (farmer, Milton) and Ruth L. Fall (Milton)

POFF,
Erin Michele, b. 9/28/1981 in Dover; David M. Poff and Janine G. Hammond

POLAND,
John Robert, b. 11/6/1950 in Rochester; second; Milton W. Poland (student, MA) and Audette Turner (SC)

POLLOCK,
Mara Catherine, b. 10/30/1970 in Rochester; Albert T. Pollock and Caroline Schmucker

POMEROY,
Kellie Ann, b. 4/9/1966 in Rochester; William J. Pomeroy (moulder) and Patricia A. Thompson

Mary Margaret, b. 6/18/1963 in Rochester; William J. Pomeroy (moulder) and Patricia A. Thompson

Randy William, b. 9/24/1961 in Rochester; William Jos. Pomeroy (moulder) and Patricia A. Thompson

Samantha Kellie, b. 6/12/1991 in Dover; Randy W. Pomeroy and Sally E. Leclair

Thomas Michael, b. 10/2/1970 in Wolfeboro; William J. Pomeroy and Patricia A. Thompson

PORTER,
Casey George, b. 12/16/1998 in Rochester; Brian Porter and Sandra Porter

POULIOT,
Nathan David, b. 12/23/1998; Robert Pouliot and Charity Pouliot

POWELL,
Daryll George, b. 6/14/1980 in Rochester; George T. Powell and Carol L. Barr

POWER,
Burton Russell, b. 10/16/1908; first; Lewis R. Power (ice man, 26, Marblehead, MA) and Georgie W. Quint (17, Milton)
Marion Esther, b. 11/17/1909; second; Lewis R. Power (ice man, Marblehead, MA) and Georgie W. Quint (Milton)
Ruth, b. 10/10/1911; third; Lewis R. Power (ice man, Marblehead, MA) and Georgie W. Quint (Milton)

PRATT,
Harvey Bruce, b. 3/21/1941; second; George R. Pratt (laborer, Haverhill, MA) and Myrtle A. Titcomb (W. Newbury, MA)

PREBLE,
stillborn son, b. 8/21/1915; third; Stephen E. Preble (civil engineer, Portsmouth) and Jessie N. Calkins (Trescott, ME); residence - Lebanon, ME
Barbara Phyllis, b. 8/13/1918; fourth; Stephen E. Preble (civil engineer, Portsmouth) and Jessie A. Calkins (Trescott, ME)
Eglantine Louise, b. 3/26/1908; first; Stephen E. Preble (draughtsman, 23, Portsmouth) and Jessie A. Calkins (21, Trescott, ME)

PREEPER,
Antoinette Serena, b. 9/26/1911; fifth; William C. Preeper (painter, Boston, MA) and Carrie B. Hurd (Acton, ME)
William C., b. 6/25/1916; seventh; William Preeper (mill hand, Boston, MA) and Carrie Hurd (Acton, ME) (1917)

PRESCOTT,
son, b. 6/20/1889; third; Crosby H. Prescott (hotel keeper, 37, Acton, ME) and Annie M. Hurd (34, Acton, ME)
daughter, b. 11/29/1900; third; Charles E. Prescott (laborer, 27, Milton) and Mary E. Evans (18, Nottingham)

Hattie E., b. 1/2/1901; third; Charles E. Prescott (Milton) and Mary E. Evans (Nottingham)
Joseph, b. 12/30/1877; Aaron Prescott (farmer, Barrington) and Susan E. Foss (Dover) (1939)
LeRoy Merle, b. 3/25/1914; fourth; Benjamin F. Prescott (farmer, Madbury) and May E. Wicks (Providence, RI) (1938)
Marion Marilla, b. 11/7/1887 in Milton Mills; Crosby H. Prescott (ME) and Annie F. Hurd (ME); residence - Milton Mills (1942)
Mark Evans, b. 3/18/1992 in Wolfeboro; Steven W. Prescott and Nancy M. Salisbury
Ruth H., b. 10/29/1891; fourth; Crosby H. Prescott (hotel keeper, 41, Acton, ME) and Annie F. Hurd (37, Acton, ME)
Zackary Francis, b. 7/29/1997 in Rochester; Dennis L. Prescott, II and Victoria L. Prescott

PRESSIMONE,
Tracy-Lee, b. 3/13/1965 in Wolfeboro; Walter T. Pressimone (laborer) and Candise E. Clough

PRINCE,
son, b. 1/25/1894; first; George H. Prince (laborer, 27, Sparta, WI) and Mary E. Moore (18, Milton)
stillborn son, b. 7/18/1895; second; George H. Prince (laborer, 29, Sparta, WI) and Mary E. Moore (20, Milton)
son [Hermon L.], b. 9/2/1900; fifth; George H. Prince (emp. in mill, 34, Sparta, WI) and Mary E. Moore (25, Milton)
daughter [Mamie], b. 11/5/1902; sixth; George H. Prince (mill, 34, Sparta, WI) and Mary E. Moore (27, Milton)
Annie, b. 8/15/1896; third; George H. Prince (laborer, 29, Sparta, WI) and Mary E. Moore (21, Milton)
Cecil May, b. 4/1/1906; eighth; George H. Prince (emp. in mill, 39, Sparta, WI) and Mary E. Moore (29, Milton)
George William, b. 11/5/1898; fourth; George H. Prince (laborer, 30, Sparta, WI) and Mary Edna Moore (23, Milton)
Kenneth Alton, b. 9/29/1911; eighth; George H. Prince (emp. in mill, Sparta, WI) and Mary E. Moore (Milton)

PROVENCHER,
Betty Faith, b. 4/21/1938; fifth; Antonio Provencher (bed laster, Sanbornville) and Draxa Corson (Milton)
Carole Alice, b. 8/9/1946; sixth; Edward A. Provencher (shoe worker, Sanbornville) and Draxa Corson (Milton)
Dale Anthony, b. 5/8/1936; fourth; Antonio E. Provencher (shoe worker, Sanbornville) and Draxa Corson (Milton)
Dennis Edward, b. 4/9/1933; second; Antonio E. Provencher (fish dealer, Sanbornville) and Draxa Corson (Milton)
Dorinda Lynn, b. 6/25/1966 in Rochester; Norris Provencher (shoe worker) and Dorothy Guy
Lorraine Ella, b. 11/1/1964 in Rochester; sixth; Norris L. Provencher (bed laster) and Dorothy E. Guy
Norrene Lee, b. 10/2/1963 in Rochester; Norris L. Provencher (shoe worker) and Dorothy E. Guy
Norris Lee, b. 5/29/1935; third; Antonio Provencher (shoe worker, Sanbornville) and Draxa Corson (Milton)
Norris Lee, II, b. 8/21/1967 in Rochester; eighth; Norris L. Provencher (bed laster) and Dorothy E. Guy

PUGH,
Ralph W., Jr., b. 5/5/1940 in Rochester; second; Ralph W. Pugh (beaterman, Lynn, MA) and Rachel M. Dow (Milton)
Shirley Ann, b. 7/17/1936 in Rochester; first; Ralph Pugh (garage mech., Lynn, MA) and Rachel Doe (Milton)

PUGLIA,
Maurisa Rose, b. 2/21/1978 in Portsmouth; Vincent S. Puglia and Susan R. Ebel

PUTNEY,
Cris Alan, b. 9/17/1966 in Rochester; Warren C. Putney (laborer) and Christine Williams
Ernest Wray, b. 9/5/1965 in Rochester; Wray A. Putney (maintenance) and Patricia A. Witham
Gary Warren, b. 6/14/1961 in Rochester; Warren C. Putney (laborer) and Christine Williams
Lisa Jean, b. 4/21/1963 in Rochester; Warren C. Putney (dryer room) and Christina Williams

Lloyd Wray, b. 2/28/1963 in Rochester; Wray A. Putney (maintenance) and Patricia A. Witham

Lori Anne, b. 7/1/1959 in Rochester; second; Warren C. Putney (dryerman, Derry) and Christine Williams (Rochester)

Lynn Marie, b. 6/28/1958 in Rochester; first; Warren C. Putney (scaler, Derry) and Christine Williams (Rochester)

Peter Scott, b. 3/27/1965 in Rochester; Warren C. Putney (machine tender) and Christine Williams

QUARTARONE,
Anthony James, b. 10/22/1977 in Dover; Frank T. Quartarone and Sandra M. Russell

QUILLAN,
James, b. 1/8/1899; fifth; John Quillan (shoemaker, 33, Milton, ME) and Catherine Dannahay (30, Stoneham, MA)

Mary, b. 12/2/1897; fourth; J. H. Quillin (sic) (laster, 30, Milton, MA) and Catherine Donnahay (27, Stoneham, MA)

QUINN,
Heather Dawn, b. 11/15/1975 in Rochester; James S. Quinn and Judith I. Manson

Ryan James, b. 2/19/1978 in Rochester; James S. Quinn and Judith Manson

QUINT,
Georgie Wilhelmina, b. 1/17/1891; first; George B. Quint (ice house, Ossipee) and Wilhelmina Forsythe (Kentville, NS) (1938)

RAAB,
Tiffany, b. 9/21/1978 in Rochester; Bruce P. Raab and Linda A. Horne

RAIFSNIDER,
Alexandria Sarah, b. 10/20/1997 in Dover; John M. Raifsnider, Jr. and Kimberly A. Raifsnider

RAMSEY,
Alice Sophie, b. 9/8/1949 in Rochester; first; Charles E. Ramsey (shoe factory, ME) and Adelia E. Jenness (NH)

Bruce Charles, b. 11/11/1955 in Rochester; second; Charles E. Ramsey
(GE, Saco, ME) and Adelia Jenness (Nashua)
Judith Ann, b. 8/5/1939 in Rochester; first; Lawrence S. Ramsey (lea.
worker, Thompson, CT) and Ruth E. Stevens (Northwood)
Larry Jay, b. 6/4/1947 in Rochester; second; Lawrence S. Ramsey
(foreman, Thompson, CT) and Ruth E. Stevens (Northwood)

RAND,
son [Ernest W.], b. 8/6/1894; first; George W. Rand (laborer, 28,
Cambridge, MA) and Ida Moore (24, Milton)
daughter, b. 10/2/1895; second; George W. Rand (laborer, 25, Cambridge,
MA) and Ida E. Moore (24, Milton)
stillborn son, b. 5/1/1919; first; Earl K. Rand (emp. ice co., Milton) and
Hazel A. Hoyt (Rochester)
Alice Susan, b. 6/16/1899; fourth; George W. Rand (machine tender, 29,
Cambridge, MA) and Ida E. Moore (28, Milton)
Arthur Hartwell, b. 2/14/1911; first; Arthur H. Rand (shoemaker,
Wilmington, MA) and Vera F. Cooley (Boston, MA)
Earle, b. 8/1/1897; third; George W. Rand (laborer, 27, Cambridge, MA)
and Ida E. Moore (26, Milton)
Edwin Stanley, b. 7/30/1939 in Rochester; first; Kenneth Rand
(woodsman, New Durham) and Frances I. Burrows (Milton)
Harold F., b. 11/23/1903; fifth; George W. Rand (emp. in mill, 33,
Cambridge, MA) and Ida E. Moore (32, Milton)
Leo Edward, b. 5/19/1910; sixth; Wilotte G. Rand (emp. ice co.,
Cambridge, MA) and Ida E. Moore (Milton)
Sterling Foster, b. 12/28/1912; second; Arthur H. Rand (emp. in mill, 27,
Wilmington, MA) and Vera F. Cooley (26, Boston, MA)

RANDALL,
Amanda Rae, b. 9/27/1988 in Rochester; Jerry L. Randall and Mary J.
Marcoux
Derek Miles, b. 4/11/1977 in Rochester; Roger M. Randall, Jr. and Jayne
F. Bishop
Jerry Lee, II, b. 7/11/1984 in Rochester; Jerry L. Randall and Mary J.
Marcoux

RANKIN,
Judson William, b. 5/14/1904; first; James E. Rankin (sawyer, 25, Houlton, ME) and Clara A. Brackett (17, Acton, ME)

RANSON,
Katie Melissa, b. 7/24/1985 in Dover; Dennis J. Ranson and Mary V. Rustici
Kristen Nicole, b. 3/30/1983 in Dover; Dennis J. Ranson and Mary V. Rustici

RAWSKI,
Peter, b. 12/12/1986 in Rochester; Donald J. Rawski and Patricia I. Brown

REAGAN,
Richard Alan, b. 12/5/1966 in Rochester; fourth; Ronald M. Reagan (set-up man) and Donna G. Stepp

REARICK,
Haylee Elizabeth, b. 1/6/1992 in Dover; Thomas W. Rearick and Sheila A. Tierney

REED,
Christopher James, b. 9/28/1981 in Dover; James C. Reed and Susan E. Parmenter

REGAN,
George Vincent, b. 7/24/1908; third; Jeremiah J. Regan (emp. on railroad, 35, Ireland) and Mary Mahoney (33, Ireland)
James V., b. 7/27/1906; second; Jeremiah J. Regan (emp. on RR, 34, Ireland) and Mary Mahoney (31, Ireland)
James Victor, Jr., b. 6/5/1934 in Rochester; first; James V. Regan (mill emp., Milton) and Dorothy Otis (Farmington)
James Victor, 3d, b. 8/25/1961 in Rochester; James V. Regan (teacher) and Teresa Dolan
Jerome Raymond, b. 2/25/1916; fifth; Jerome John Regan (emp. in mill, Ireland) and Mary T. Mahoney (Ireland)
Margaret Cataline, b. 10/18/1911; fourth; Jeremiah J. Regan (emp. on RR, Ireland) and Mary Mahoney (Ireland)

Margaret Mary, b. 7/4/1957 in Rochester; first; James V. Regan (student, Rochester) and Teresa Dolan (Ireland)

Mary E., b. 9/9/1904; first; Jeremiah J. Regan (emp. in mill, 32, Ireland) and Mary Mahoney (29, Ireland)

Michael Bruce, b. 9/19/1963 in Rochester; James V. Regan, Jr. (teacher) and Teresa Dolan

Paula Ann, b. 8/15/1936 in Rochester; second; James V. Regan (shoe worker, Milton) and Dorothy Otis (Farmington)

Robert Arthur, b. 4/23/1940 in Rochester; third; James V. Regan (clerk, Milton) and Dorothy A. Otis (Farmington)

Sean, b. 11/24/1959 in Rochester; stillborn; James Regan, Jr. (teacher, Rochester) and Theresa Dolan (Ireland); residence - Sunapee

REMICK,

son, b. 3/20/1893; first; Charles E. Remick (laster, 30, Farmington) and Lula E. Wentworth (32, Farmington)

daughter [Christine], b. 12/25/1903; first; William Remick (farmer, 35, Milton) and Carrie B. Hurd (20, Acton, ME)

son [Howard M.], b. 6/19/1905; second; Willie Remick (farmer, 36, Milton) and Carrie B. Hurd (21, Acton, ME)

son [Alfred], b. 7/15/1906; third; Willie Remick (farmer, 37, Milton) and Carrie B. Hurd (23, Acton, ME)

daughter, b. 10/19/1924; third; Edgar Remick (shoe operator, Milton) and Carrie Grace (Albany)

Anly Dorothea, b. 6/4/1911; first; Arthur F. Remick (emp. in mill, Tamworth) and Angie E. Page (Milton)

Bessie May, b. 6/23/1918; fourth; Arthur F. Remick (laborer, Tamworth) and Angie E. Page (Milton)

Elsie C., b. 6/23/1909; fourth; Willie Remick (farmer, Milton) and Carrie B. Hurd (Acton, ME) (1911)

Florence May, b. 8/1/1913; second; Arthur F. Remick (emp. in mill, Tamworth) and Angie M. Page (Milton)

Harold Leslie, b. 4/12/1921; second; Edgar B. Remick (shoemaker, Milton) and Carrie E. Grace (Albany)

Helen Janette, b. 10/31/1922; fifth; Arthur F. Remick (truckman, Tamworth) and Angie Page (Milton)

Marguerite, b. 7/18/1916; third; Arthur F. Remick (emp. in mill, Tamworth) and Angie E. Page (Milton)

RENDALL,
son, b. 9/1/1893; first; Herman Rendall (spinner, 25, Great Falls) and Abbie Batchelder (22, Shapleigh, ME)

REYNOLDS,
Addie G., b. 5/13/1890; first; Winfield Reynolds (carpenter, 28, So. Berwick, ME) and Mary M. Reynolds (Ireland)
Eric Verne, b. 6/14/1970 in Rochester; Verne M. Reynolds and Paula A. Richards
Jesse Aaron, b. 8/22/1992 in Rochester; Richard W. Reynolds, Jr. and Heather J. Audet
Rodney Warren, b. 8/4/1971 in Rochester; Verne M. Reynolds and Paula A. Richards

RHODES,
Charles Harry, b. 4/7/1951 in Rochester; second; Harry C. Rhodes (machine oper., East Rochester) and Virginia White (Lebanon, ME)
Norman Allen, b. 10/12/1902; first; Joseph Rhodes (mill, 28, Medford, MA) and Helen Meikle (23, Wakefield); residence - Lowell, MA

RICHARD,
Ashlynne Renee, b. 12/23/1989 in Rochester; Joseph A. Richard and Audrey A. Rawls

RICHARDS,
Abigail Jordan, b. 10/17/1995 in Dover; Dean L. Richards and Suzette L. Richards
Meghan Jennifer, b. 10/15/1993 in Dover; Michael J. Richards and Sandra D. Hutchins

RICHARDSON,
Neil Malcolm, b. 6/12/1922; fifth; Frank Richardson (laborer, Worcester, VT) and Bessie Urquhart (Abroath, Scotland)

RICKER,
daughter, b. 7/16/1903; first; Asa J. Ricker (mail carrier, 23, Lebanon, ME) and Dorothy Danforth (20, Littleton, MA)
Emily Kate, b. 5/24/1979 in Dover; William B. Ricker and Mary E. Collay

Meghan Ruth, b. 2/21/1979 in Hanover; Edward R. Ricker and Karen R. Schubarth
Robert Maurice, b. 3/17/1934 in Rochester; first; George M. Ricker (farmer, Berwick, ME) and Bertha Wiggin (Milton Mills); residence - Milton Mills

RILEY,
Neil William, b. 2/3/1981 in Dover; Francis E. Riley and Pamela L. Hanchett

RINES,
stillborn son, b. 10/24/1915; first; Bessie C. Rines (Brookfield)
Ada M., b. 1/10/1891; second; Mark Rines (carpenter,47, Milton Mills) and Mary Horne (43, Brookfield)
Vanessa Rae, b. 9/7/1978 in Dover; Chester O. Rines and Deborah A. Lacasse

RIOUX,
Gabrille Kathleen, b. 1/30/1997 in Dover; Roger J. Rioux and Carrie A. Rioux

ROBERGE,
Emily Paige, b. 9/16/1998; Scott Roberge and Robin Roberge
Steven Arthur, b. 7/24/1954 in Rochester; second; Gerard Roberge (teacher, Groveton) and Christine Blodgett (Stratford)

ROBERTS,
daughter, b. 3/10/1894; second; Lena Roberts
daughter, b. 8/9/1898; third; Albert Roberts (shoemaker, 27, Raymond) and Carrie E. Nutter (20, Milton); residence - Merrimack
daughter, b. 10/17/1900; fourth; Wellington M. Roberts (paper maker, 28, Winterport, ME) and Lizzie Smart (22, Newburg, ME)
son, b. 10/9/1901; fifth; Wellington N. Roberts (mill hand, 29, Frankfort, ME) and Lizzie H. Smart (23, Newburg, ME)
son, b. 11/6/1907; first; William Roberts (laborer, 38, Farmington) and Sarah Page (15, NH)
Albert Burton, b. 9/5/1925; first; Alvin B. Roberts (mill hand, Raymond) and Marion L. Downing (Milton)
Kirk Norman, b. 9/23/1891; first; Lena M. Roberts (18, Alton)

ROBINSON,
Casey Robert, b. 6/23/1983 in Exeter; Robert H. Robinson and Bonnie L. Bullis
Connor William, b. 3/5/1997 in Dover; Lance W. Robinson and Karen M. Robinson
Craig Brandon, b. 6/3/1982 in Exeter; Robert H. Robinson and Bonnie L. Bullis
Ericka Jane, b. 4/17/1972 in Rochester; Richard A. Robinson and Janice C. Dame
Scot Ira, b. 8/27/1973 in Rochester; Stephen J. Robinson and Rena L. Drew

RODNEY,
Amber Michelle, b. 11/24/1992 in Rochester; Mark A. Rodney and Kristen A. Leclair
Daniel Richard, b. 8/21/1987 in Rochester; Richard W. Rodney and Lisa M. Bodge
Mark Allan, b. 1/20/1968 in Rochester; George R. Rodney and Sharone E. Downs

RODRIGUE,
Jennifer Ann, b. 4/30/1971 in Rochester; Richard L. Rodrigue and Elaine D. Savoie

ROGERS,
Jessica Alvina, b. 6/30/1989 in Rochester; Francis Rogers and Paula T. Beaulieu

ROLFE,
Jennifer Lynn, b. 10/7/1972 in Rochester; Melvin A. Rolfe and Theresa A. Hoffman

ROLLINS,
Tadd Arnold, b. 5/19/1978; Arnold D. Rollins and Denise R. Winne

RONAYNE,
Caitlin Ann, b. 11/15/1991 in Dover; John J. Ronayne and Kathie J. Terry

ROODE,
stillborn daughter, b. 3/9/1935 in Rochester; first; Robert Roode (packer, Yarmouth, NS) and Wilhelmina Bousley (Newburyport, MA)

ROOTS,
Isabel Vivian, b. 12/4/1916; fifth; William S. Roots (emp. in mill, Winchester, MA) and Maude V. Livingstone (Rochester)

ROSEBERRY,
Amanda Marie, b. 7/26/1987 in Rochester; Steven M. Roseberry and Michele S. Gagne
Joshua Steven, b. 4/18/1984 in Rochester; Steven M. Roseberry and Michele S. Gagne

ROSIN,
Belinda Leigh, b. 11/22/1967 in Rochester; first; Eugene Rosin (trooper, NH State Police) and Mary Ann E. Zelasny

ROSS,
Jennifer Lorraine, b. 7/2/1986 in Portsmouth; Brian T. Ross and Vanessa G. Adkins

ROUKEY,
son, b. 2/13/1916; seventh; George E. Roukey (teamster, New Zealand) and Mary M. Labille (Rollinsford)

ROULEAU,
stillborn son, b. 4/20/1895; first; Albert Rouleau (laborer, 25, Canada) and Delia Blouin (20, Canada)
son [Joseph], b. 6/11/1896; second; Albert Rouleau (laborer, 26, Canada) and Delia Blouin (22, Canada)
son, b. 4/28/1907; fifth; Etienne Rauleau (sic) (shoemaker, 40, Canada) and Kelda Lacasse (34, Canada)
stillborn son, b. 9/4/1921; first; Louis H. Rouleau (emp. ice house, Lebanon, ME) and Josephine Burbine (Wakefield, MA)
Dorothy Ann, b. 6/28/1933; fourth; Louis H. Rouleau (laborer, Lebanon, ME) and Mary J. Burbine (Wakefield, MA)
Edmonde, b. 4/2/1927; second; Alfred J. Rouleau (ice man, Lebanon, ME) and Helen E. Douquette (Milton)

Jimmy Norman, b. 7/21/1947 in Rochester; first; Norman A. Rouleau (lumberman, Milton) and Audrey B. Merrill (Lebanon, ME)
Josephine Louise, b. 12/6/1922; second; Louis H. Rouleau (laborer, Lebanon, ME) and Josephine Burbine (Wakefield, MA)
Margaret Mary, b. 3/31/1924; third; Louis H. Rouleau (laborer, Lebanon, ME) and Mary J. Burbine (Wakefield, MA)
Norman Alfred, b. 10/9/1928 in Rochester; third; Alfred Rouleau (ice man, Lebanon, ME) and Helen Duquette (Milton)
Rose Marie, b. 9/20/1935; fourth; Samuel Rouleau (laborer, Lebanon, ME) and Mar'rita Lavertue (Rochester); residence - Lebanon, ME
Samuel, Jr., b. 8/10/1928; first; Samuel Rouleau (ice man, Lebanon, ME) and Marg'ta Lavertue (Rochester); residence - Lebanon, ME

ROWE,
Christina Lee, b. 2/15/1984 in Dover; Jerry L. Rowe and Deborah L. Wietzel
David James, b. 2/1/1983 in Rochester; Jerry L. Rowe and Deborah L. Wietzel
Roxanne Ellen, b. 3/8/1971 in Rochester; Robert J. Rowe and Deanna J. Simmons

ROY,
Joseph A., b. 11/30/1895; first; Napoleon Roy (laborer, 20, Canada) and Clauris Blagon (28, Canada)
Kaitlin Gene, b. 4/9/1981 in Portsmouth; David M. Roy and Susan E. Fritz
Megan Elizabeth, b. 11/6/1977 in Portsmouth; David M. Roy and Susan E. Fritz
Michael Vincent, b. 3/12/1987 in Rochester; Richard E. Roy, Jr. and Kathy M. Pelletier

RUDD,
daughter [Marion E.], b. 8/9/1903; first; Alfred F. Rudd (blacksmith, 22, Richmond, PQ) and Flossie B. Gray (17, Brownfield, ME)
daughter, b. 2/6/1908; second; Alfred T. Rudd (blacksmith, 27, Richmond, PQ) and Flossie D. Gray (21, Brownfield, ME)

RUNNEL[L]S,
Antoinette Lee, b. 2/1/1962 in Rochester; Robert D. Runnels (truck driver) and Virginia S. Smith
Brenda Lorraine, b. 4/18/1953 in Rochester; third; Robert D. Runnels (Air Force, Wakefield) and Virginia Smith (Huntington, MA)
Donna Jean, b. 7/16/1943 in Rochester; third; Othello D. Runnells (mill operator, Acton, ME) and Pearl E. Wilkinson (Salem, MA)
June Estelle, b. 6/26/1928 in Milton Mills; first; Othello D. Runnels (weaver, Acton, ME) and Pearl Wilkinson (Salem, MA); residence - Milton Mills
Lynette Pearl, b. 12/18/1951 in Rochester; second; Robert D. Runnels (USAF, Milton) and Virginia S. Smith (MA)
Randall Dean, b. 6/14/1974 in Wolfeboro; Robert D. Runnels and Karen R. Hill
Robert D., Jr., b. 2/10/1955 in Rochester; fourth; Robert D. Runnels (USAF, Wakefield) and Virginia Smith (MA); residence - Milton Mills
Robert Dean, b. 1/30/1932 in Wakefield; second; Othello Runnels (mill hand, Acton, ME) and Pearl Wilkinson (Salem, MA); residence - Milton Mills
Tamara Jean, b. 7/19/1960 in Rochester; fourth; Robert D. Runnels (tannery) and Virginia S. Smith
Tracie Lynn, b. 10/22/1964 in Rochester; sixth; Robert D. Runnels (truck driver) and Virginia S. Smith
Vickie Jolene, b. 12/1/1964 in Rochester; first; Glenn E. Runnels (plumbing supply) and Marie E. Roberts

RUSS,
Adam Christopher, b. 8/25/1986 in Dover; David A. Russ and Kathy J. Ecker
Danielle Kay-Gail, b. 10/13/1989 in Dover; Stephen A. Russ and Stephanie M. Juckett
David A., b. 8/15/1957 in Rochester; first; Alfred F. Russ (plumber, Rollinsford) and Jane Wentworth (Rochester); residence - West Milton
Kevin Andrew, b. 5/9/1988 in Dover; David A. Russ and Kathy J. Ecker
Paula Gail, b. 8/8/1958 in Rochester; second; Alfred F. Russ (plumber, Rollinsford) and Jane Wentworth (Rochester); residence - West Milton (1959)

Stephen Alfred, b. 3/15/1961 in Rochester; Alfred F. Russ (heating & plumbing) and Jane G. Wentworth

RUSSO,
Nina Rose, b. 7/11/1969 in Rochester; Louis R. Russo, Jr. and Marie F. Geyer
Richard Lee, b. 1/9/1972 in Kittery, ME; Jay E. Russo and Margaret T. Richardson
Stacie Ann, b. 6/1/1972 in Rochester; Raymond E. Russo and Betty-mae Arigo

ST. CYR,
Albert, b. 10/25/1901 in Milton Mills; ninth; Albert St. Cyr (lumberman, Canada) and Belzemire Morin (Canada); residence - Milton Mills (1941)
Samuel Simeon, b. 10/30/1878 in Milton Mills; John St. Cyr (Canada) and Rosie Cummings (Exeter); residence - Milton Mills (1944)

ST. GERMAINE,
James Arthur, b. 11/17/1912; third; Nelson St. Germaine (emp. in mill, Haverhill, MA) and Beulah St. Germaine (Beverly, MA)

ST. HILAIRE,
Gail Ann, b. 7/21/1972 in Rochester; Richard L. St. Hilaire and Eleanor G. Hurley

SANBORN,
Amie Lee, b. 12/7/1985 in Rochester; William E. Sanborn and Tammy L. Foss
Brenda Jeanne, b. 11/23/1942 in Rochester; second; Carleton I. Sanborn (worker, Farmington) and Myrtle M. Nute (Wakefield)
Carlyn Ellen, b. 10/29/1936 in Rochester; first; Carlton Sanborn (mill foreman, Farmington) and Myrtle Nute (Wakefield)
Carole Lea, b. 9/2/1953 in Rochester; fifth; Ivory M. Sanborn (fibre mill, Farmington) and Dorothy Grace (Boston, MA)
Clifton Ivory, b. 8/12/1937 in Rochester; first; Ivory Sanborn (fibre worker, Farmington) and Dorothy Grace (Boston, MA)
Dale Francis, b. 6/9/1940 in Rochester; second; Fred W. Sanborn (fibre worker, Union) and Isabel E. Weeman (Union)

Dennis William, b. 10/2/1938 in Wolfeboro; first; Fred W. Sanborn
(beater oper., Milton) and Isabelle Weeman (Union)
Dennis William, Jr., b. 3/26/1967 in Boston, MA; first; Dennis W.
Sanborn (leather worker) and Angela Devaney
Eva May, b. 6/12/1898; second; Walter L. Sanborn (farmer, 25, Milton)
and Hattie A. Rines (22, New Durham)
Fred William, b. 7/27/1912; third; Walter L. Sanborn (farmer, 39, Milton)
and Esther E. Harnden (39, Denmark, ME)
Harry Bruce, b. 11/1/1958 in Rochester; stillborn; sixth; Ivory M. Sanborn
(foreman, Farmington) and Dorothy C. Grace (Boston, MA)
Ivory M., Jr., b. 8/2/1947 in Rochester; fourth; Ivory M. Sanborn
(foreman, Farmington) and Dorothy C. Grace (Boston, MA)
James Henry, b. 6/15/1939 in Wolfeboro; third; William H. Sanborn
(mach. tender, Farmington) and Doris M. Bean (Eaton)
Jocelyn Nicole, b. 8/20/1988 in Rochester; James W. Sanborn and
Elizabeth Rodrigue
Martin W., b. 2/15/1896; first; Walter L. Sanborn (farmer, 23, Milton)
and Hattie A. Rines (20, New Durham)
Meghan Laura, b. 9/30/1990 in Rochester; James W. Sanborn and
Elizabeth A. Rodrigue
Robert Carl, b. 12/23/1938; second; Ivory M. Sanborn (lea. worker,
Farmington) and Dorothy Grace (Boston, MA)
Robin Jean, b. 12/13/1965 in Rochester; James Sanborn (toggler) and
Donna E. St. Pierre
Terri Evelyn, b. 4/30/1945 in Rochester; fourth; Fred W. Sanborn (mill
worker, Milton) and Isabel E. Weeman (Union)

SANDERS,
Evelyn Linnea, b. 3/21/1937 in Rochester; third; Ernest Sanders
(carpenter, Sweden) and Linnea Sundin (Sweden); residence -
Milton Mills

SANFACON,
Abigail Janet, b. 11/8/1993 in Dover; Scott R. Sanfacon and Kyle E.
Krasnow
Jacob Daniel, b. 2/12/1999 in Rochester; Donald Sanfacon and Gayle
Sanfacon
Molly Germaine, b. 10/2/1991 in Rochester; Richard P. Sanfacon and
Madelyn Y. Melanson

Tyler Gerald, b. 6/26/1985 in Rochester; Gerald L. Sanfacon and Dianne M. Lamoreaux

SARGENT,
Aldo L., b. 3/26/1918; first; Adan L. Sargent (RR roundhouse, Franklin) and Bertha F. Garland (Wolfeboro); residence - Plymouth

SAUFLEY,
Julie Marie, b. 6/21/1996 in Rochester; Samuel M. Saufley and Kim M. Saufley

SAVOIE,
stillborn son, b. 12/21/1922; first; Fred J. Savoie (laborer, Dover) and Ruby Ellis (Milton)
son, b. 12/21/1922; second; Fred J. Savoie (laborer, Dover) and Ruby Ellis (Milton)
stillborn son, b. 11/18/1955 in Rochester; third; Maurice Savoie (loader oper., Milton) and Helen Cheney (Milton)
Deborah Joyce, b. 6/1/1954 in Rochester; second; Maurice M. Savoie (lumberman, Milton) and Helen D. Cheney (Milton)
Elaine Marilyn, b. 2/11/1928; fifth; Fred J. Savoie (mill operative, Dover) and Rubie G. Ellis (Milton)
Jacqueline, b. 8/21/1948 in Rochester; second; Elaine M. Savoie (Milton)
Jacqueline Phyllis, b. 12/24/1924; third; Fred J. Savoie (laborer, Dover) and Ruby Ellis (Milton)
Marie Elaine, b. 8/21/1948 in Rochester; first; Elaine M. Savoie (Milton)
Marlene Elaine, b. 5/24/1951 in Rochester; first; Maurice Savoie (shoe worker, Milton) and Helen D. Cheney (Milton)
Maurice Maxwell, b. 9/5/1926; fourth; Fred J. Savoie (mill operative, Dover) and Ruby Ellis (Milton)

SCEGGELL,
Amy Rebecca, b. 3/15/1974 in Rochester; Forrest L. Sceggell and Mary J. Coddington
Arline May, b. 5/2/1932; first; Howard J. Sceggell (mill hand, Ossipee) and Anna F. McIntire (Rochester)
Benjamin Perley, b. 5/29/1934 in Rochester; second; Forrest B. Sceggell (mill emp., Ossipee) and Ruth H. Leeman (Milton)

David A., b. 5/2/1955 in Rochester; first; H. J. Sceggell, Jr. (press oper., Rochester) and Shirley M. Littlefield (Rochester)

Forrest Luther, b. 4/24/1944 in Rochester; third; Forrest B. Sceggell (navy yard, Ossipee) and Ruth H. Leeman (Milton)

George Osborne, b. 6/6/1947 in Rochester; fourth; Forrest B. Sceggell (fireman, Ossipee) and Ruth H. Leeman (Milton)

Howard Jefferson, b. 5/28/1935 in Rochester; Howard J. Sceggell (printer, Ossipee) and Anna F. McIntire (Rochester)

Jennifer Kristin, b. 12/25/1971 in Rochester; Forrest L. Sceggell and Mary J. Coddington

Joy Pearl, b. 5/18/1985 in Rochester; David A. Sceggell and Doreen P. Joy

Peter Benjamin, b. 3/13/1978 in Rochester; Forrest L. Sceggell and Mary J. Coddington

Sarah Elizabeth, b. 1/1/1976 in Rochester; Forrest L. Sceggell and Mary J. Coddington

Stephen Howard, b. 11/4/1957 in Rochester; second; H. J. Sceggell, Jr. (finisher, Rochester) and Shirley M. Lilljedahl (Rochester)

SCOFIELD,
Adeline Irene, b. 1/20/1917; fourth; William D. Scofield (foreman, Newark, NJ) and Adeline E. Hall (Barrington)

SCOTT,
Dale Allen, III, b. 2/15/1973 in Kittery, ME; Dale A. Scott, Jr. and Kristie K. Kelchner

John Jacob, Jr., b. 9/27/1975 in Rochester; John J. Scott and Kathleen M. Gautreau

Melinda Dawn, b. 4/5/1971 in Rochester; John J. Scott and Linda E. Moody

Orrel, b. 6/23/1906; third; Joseph W. Scott (shoemaker, 29, Springfield, MA) and Adaline Davis (27, Windsor, MA)

SCRUTON,
daughter, b. 7/6/1904; second; Russell G. Scruton (emp. in mill, 33, Farmington) and Helen A. Cotton (19, Farmington)

stillborn son, b. 10/31/1905; third; Russell G. Scruton (emp. in mill, 34, Farmington) and Helen A. Cotton (20, Farmington)

Eileen, b. 5/15/1902; first; Russell G. Scruton (teamster, 31, Farmington) and Helen A. Cotton (17, Farmington)

SCULLY,
Christopher Ryan, b. 5/19/1986 in Dover; Timothy J. Scully and Deborah A. Collins
Justin Tyler, b. 1/10/1990 in Dover; Timothy James Scully and Deborah Ann Collins

SEALE,
Kimberly Anne, b. 1/6/1984 in Rochester; Edmund D. Seale and Darlene A. Young
Michael Aaron, b. 8/30/1987 in Rochester; Edmund D. Seale and Darlene A. Young

SEAMANS,
Peggy Lee, b. 7/7/1963 in Wolfeboro; Earl H. Seamans (laborer) and Katherine Brewer

SEARS,
Wyatt Joseph, b. 5/5/1994 in Rochester; Eric J. Sears and Wendy A. Lampros

SEVENEY,
Evelyn E., b. 12/13/1914; first; William Seveney (Salmon Falls) and Vera E. Belleville (Somersworth)

SHACKLEY,
daughter, b. 11/20/1890; first; Walter Shackley (laborer, 19) and Eva Pinkham (Dover); residence - Dover

SHARPE,
son, b. 11/29/1911; second; Frank Sharpe (teamster, Milton) and Ethel Cook (Wolfeboro)

SHAULL,
Kathryn W., b. 11/23/1961 in Laconia; Ben. E. Shaull (Navy) and Mary A. Swett

SHAVE,
Samantha Jeanne, b. 7/11/1987 in Rochester; Edward F. Shave, Jr. and Wendy L. Sirois

SHAW,
Devin Taylor, b. 7/30/1993 in Dover; Kevin T. Shaw and Barbara M. Mahoney
Jaime Frances, b. 1/18/1978 in Exeter; James S. Shaw and Shelley M. Keyser
Jillian Marie, b. 1/16/1981 in Rochester; James S. Shaw and Shelley M. Keyser

SHERBURNE,
John Taylor, b. 12/23/1992 in Dover; Fred W. Sherburne and Rebecca A. Kohut

SHERMAN,
Shirley Marie, b. 10/19/1946 in Rochester; second; Harold L. Sherman (spinner, RI) and Marie A. Butler (Allenton, RI); residence - Milton Mills

SHUTE,
Karen Rachel, b. 10/28/1977 in Rochester; Douglas H. Shute and Nancy L. Desilets
Sarah Jean, b. 6/30/1980 in Rochester; Douglas H. Shute and Nancy L. Desilets

SIGOUIN,
Henry Rene, b. 10/20/1948 in Rochester; sixth; Leopold F. Sigouin (foreman, Sherbrooke, Can.) and Yvette M. Joyal (Laconia)
John Louis, b. 2/14/1950 in Rochester; seventh; Leopold Sigouin (foreman s.s., Canada) and Yvette Joyal (NH)
Philippe Allan, b. 9/9/1947; fifth; Leopold F. Sigouin (sole cutter, Quebec, Can.) and Yvette M. Joyal (Laconia)

SIMES,
Harold Edward, b. 12/25/1888 in Milton Mills; first; Fred H. Simes (superintendent, Milton) and Mary A. Smith (Somersworth); residence - Milton Mills (1941)

SIMS,
Katherine Fisher, b. 2/4/1991 in Dover; David L. Sims and Mary Woolverton

Nathan Cobb, b. 4/17/1988 in Dover; David L. Sims and Mary
Woolverton

SINCERE,
son, b. 12/19/1888; Charles Sincere (woodchopper, Canada) and Harriet
Sincere (Canada)

SINCLAIR,
daughter [Arline M.], b. 5/1/1901; first; Milo M. Sinclair (mill hand, 22,
Stow, ME) and Minnie F. Johnson (32, Milton)

SIROIS,
Morgan Leigh, b. 5/31/1986 in Rochester; Scott A. Sirois and Leslie C.
McMahon

SKELLEY,
stillborn daughter, b. 7/14/1899; fifth; Frank Skelley (shoemaker, 32,
England) and Eunice Ordway (38, Lowell, MA)

SKELTON,
Hannah Lee, b. 8/17/1990 in Rochester; Benjamin E. Skelton and Bonnie
L. Bullis

SLEEPER,
daughter, b. 10/31/1889; first; May Sleeper (24, Alton)
daughter [Pauline D.], b. 6/17/1898; first; Fred B. Sleeper (shoemaker, 23,
Alton) and Stella E. Dicey (21, Wakefield)
daughter [Beatrice M.], b. 5/21/1900; second; Fred B. Sleeper (laborer,
25, Alton) and Stella E. Dicey (23, Wakefield)

SLINEY,
Melvin Everard, b. 1/7/1922; second; Francis A. Sliney (US Army, Lynn,
MA) and Violet M. DeVoll (Skowhegan, ME); residence - Lynn,
MA

SLOAN,
stillborn son, b. 5/12/1894; first; B. B. Sloan (druggist, 24, Barre, VT)
and Adelaide C. Waldron (22, Milton)

SMALL,
Byrle Virginia, b. 5/11/1908; first; Chester W. Small (shoemaker, 23, Boston, MA) and Elsie M. Nute (20, Farmington)

SMART,
Glenn Kolin, b. 8/30/1941 in Sanford, ME; first; Beverly Smaty (Hooksett); residence - Milton Mills

SMITH,
son, b. 4/17/1925; first; LaForrest Smith (mechanic, Barrington) and Gladys Laskey (Milton); residence - Barrington
Alfreda May, b. 5/6/1929 in Rochester; thirteenth; William A. Smith (laborer, Alton) and Iona B. Smith (Norton Mills, VT)
Alyce Irene, b. 7/5/1951; sixth; William S. Smith, Jr. (painter, Rochester) and Rhoda I. Gervais (Exeter)
Beverly Lorraine, b. 12/23/1969 in Rochester; Marshall W. Smith and Eleanor J. Eldridge
Brandon Michael, b. 3/24/1997 in Rochester; Joshua A. Smith and Shaeanna M. Smith
Brett Ryde, b. 12/2/1988 in Dover; James A. Smith and Lenore Ekwurtzel
Carrie Lynn, b. 3/19/1978 in Rochester; Ernest R. Smith and Karen K. Doherty
Connor Merris, b. 5/27/1993 in Concord; Donald M. Smith and Suzanne L. Williams
Dale Wilbur, b. 2/9/1975 in Rochester; John C. Smith and Linda L. Ellsworth
Dana, b. 6/10/1986 in Rochester; Michael R. Smith and Brenda J. Wessell
David Ellmon, b. 12/17/1948 in Rochester; second; Cecil E. Smith (shoe worker, Union) and Josephine Scarpignato (Fitchburg, MA)
David Ronald, Jr., b. 3/13/1979 in Rochester; David R. Smith, Sr. and Draxine M. Provencher
David Ross, b. 7/27/1976 in Rochester; Ernest R. Smith and Karen K. Doherty
Donna Lee, b. 12/26/1962 in Rochester; George H. Smith, Jr. (constr. worker) and Linda L. Goodwin
Dorothy Ardell, b. 9/3/1936; first; Edmund Smith (shoe worker, Farmington) and Hannah DeMerritt (Milton)
Edmund Lincoln, b. 11/8/1938; third; Edmund L. Smith (shoe fac., Farmington) and Hannah DeMeritt (Milton)

Elizabeth Louise, b. 12/12/1941; first; George H. Smith (laborer, Farmington) and Janet S. Williams (Milton)

Erica Dawn, b. 6/3/1945 in Rochester; third; William S. Smith, Jr. (painter, Rochester) and Rhoda Fervais (Exeter)

Ernest Randall, b. 12/22/1940; fourth; Hazel S. Smith (Nottingham)

Gregory Dennison, b. 10/19/1964 in Rochester; first; Warren H. Smith (construction work) and Sandra L. Dennison

Guy Alexander, b. 7/14/1987 in Rochester; Randy D. Smith, Sr. and Jeannette L. Pridham

Harry Robert, b. 4/9/1939 in Rochester; first; Guy R. Smith (lea. worker, Union) and Myrtle L. Derby (Barnstead)

Harry Robert, Jr., b. 10/23/1963 in Rochester; Harry R. Smith (tacker) and Patricia M. Hill

John Calvin, Jr., b. 8/28/1942 in Sanford, ME; third; John C. Smith (ship yd. wkr., Newfield, ME) and Mary Bernudez (Puerto Rico); residence - Milton Mills

John Lewis, b. 1/21/1898; second; Julius L. Smith (painter, Somersworth) and Mary A. Clark (33, Dublin, Ireland)

John Robert, Jr., b. 12/21/1972 in Rochester; John R. Smith and Toan T. Nguyen

Joshua Allen, b. 12/26/1986 in Rochester; Harry R. Smith, Jr. and Tammy J. Whitten

Lena Iona, b. 6/5/1940; fourth; Edmund L. Smith (shoe worker, Farmington) and Hannah DeMeritt (Milton)

Lena May, b. 9/11/1948 in Rochester; second; Alfreda M. Smith (Rochester)

Leona May, b. 9/10/1948 in Rochester; first; Alfreda M. Smith (Rochester)

Marion, b. 5/18/1894; first; Oscar C. Smith (shoecutter, 28, Berwick, ME) and Mary A. Hodgdon (25, Milton); residence - Beverly, MA

Marlene Alma, b. 6/25/1949 in Rochester; fifth; William S. Smith, Jr. (mill employee, NH) and Rhoda I. Jarvis (NH)

Marshall Weldon, b. 2/5/1924; twelfth; William A. Smith (laborer, Alton) and Iona B. Knights (Norton Mills, VT)

Michael Joseph, b. 11/24/1947 in Rochester; first; Cecil E. Smith (mechanic, Union) and Josephine Scarpignato (Fitchburg, MA)

Michel Leroy, b. 2/3/1947 in Rochester; third; William S. Smith, Jr. (truck driver, Rochester) and Rhoda I. Gervais (Exeter)

Nicholas William, b. 11/1/1988 in Concord; Donald M. Smith and
    Suzanne Williams
Patrick Harry, b. 9/29/1962 in Rochester; Harry R. Smith (tacker) and
    Patricia M. Hill
Randy Dale, b. 12/29/1967 in Rochester; Harry R. Smith and Patricia M.
    Hill
Raymie Marie, b. 12/29/1987 in Rochester; Patrick H. Smith and Pamela
    J. Foster
Richard Arthur, b. 8/23/1948 in Rochester; seventh; Edmund L. Smith
    (mill worker, Farmington) and Hannah DeMerritt (Milton)
Richard Henry, b. 9/25/1954 in Rochester; seventh; William S. Smith
    (painter, Rochester) and Rhoda Gervais (Exeter)
Samantha Marie, b. 6/30/1987 in Rochester; Michael R. Smith and
    Brenda J. Wessell
Shirley Jean, b. 3/29/1945 in Rochester; fourth; George H. Smith (box
    shop, Farmington) and Janet S. Williams (Milton)
Sylvia Lorraine, b. 11/3/1937; second; Edmund L. Smith (shoe worker,
    Farmington) and Hannah DeMeritt (Milton)
Tamara Marjorie, b. 6/30/1989 in Rochester; Patrick H. Smith and
    Pamela J. Foster
Victoria Lorene, b. 3/3/1965 in Rochester; William J. Smith (floorman)
    and Lorene V. Wilkinson

SNELL,
Joan Mildred, b. 4/27/1933 in Rochester; first; Frank H. Snell (minister,
    Fall River, MA) and Doris Hapgood (Lynn, MA); residence - Milton
    Mills

SNYDER,
Asia Leigh, b. 7/13/1984 in Dover; Glen P. Snyder and Fawn S. Choate
Barbara Anna, b. 2/6/1948 in Rochester; third; James H. Snyder (farmer,
    Rector, AR) and Josephine L. Eaton (Wells, ME)
Elizabeth Louise, b. 3/29/1949 in Wolfeboro; fourth; James H. Snyder
    (mill worker, Rector, AR) and Josephine L. Eaton (Wells, ME)
Jason Wayne, b. 4/30/1974 in Rochester; Arthur W. Snyder and Patricia
    E. Post
John Henry, b. 2/7/1947 in Rochester; second; James H. Snyder (mill
    worker, Rector, AR) and Josephine L. Eaton (Wells, ME); residence
    - Milton Mills

SODANO,
Shane Elise, b. 8/17/1981 in Portsmouth; Alfred L. Sodano and Shawn M. Lampson

SOUCY,
Gary Joseph, b. 6/25/1962 in Rochester; Oscar J. Soucy, Jr. (trimmer) and Roberta C. Marcoux
Matthew Paul, b. 11/12/1981 in Portsmouth; David P. Soucy and Elaine J. Bourassa
Monica Mae, b. 1/6/1984 in Rochester; Frederick J. Soucy and Judy I. Lyons
Sonya Lou, b. 2/22/1979 in Hanover; Frederick J. Soucy and Judy L. Lyons

SPENCER,
son, b. 6/16/1896; second; William Spencer (shoe foreman, 29, Charlestown, MA) and Annie McDonald (24, NS); residence - Lynn, MA

SPEROPOLOUS,
Timothy Zachariah, b. 3/31/1998; Peter R. Speropolous and Debora A. Speropolous

SPICER,
Emily Kate, b. 2/18/1995 in Rochester; Michael A. Spicer and Tina M. Spicer

SPINALE,
Francesco Nicholas, b. 1/4/1993 in Dover; Frank D. Spinale and Susan M. Murphy
Gina Marie, b. 2/23/1991 in Dover; Frank D. Spinale and Susan M. Murphy

SPINNEY,
Bruce Osborn, b. 1/17/1933 in Rochester; second; Ernest Spinney (poultryman, Kittery, ME) and Ida Cotton (Wolfeboro); residence - Milton Mills

Leona Frances, b. 5/10/1931 in Rochester; first; Ernest O. Spinney (poultryman, Portsmouth) and Ida Cotton (Wolfeboro); residence - Milton Mills

SPRAGUE,
Cynthia Louise, b. 10/6/1959 in Rochester; stillborn; Louis R. Sprague (machinist, Rochester) and Cynthia Paey (Rochester)
David Anthony, b. 9/6/1952 in Rochester; seventh; Bernard G. Sprague (ME) and Virginia Smith (VA)
Diane Lynn, b. 12/22/1957 in Rochester; second; Richard Sprague (US Navy, Boston, MA) and Jeanne Thompson (Rochester)
Jessica Ann, b. 2/23/1981 in Dover; Richard E. Sprague and Linda A. Lamper
Kayla Jeanne, b. 4/18/1991 in Rochester; William C. Sprague and Tammy J. McKay
Loretta Ann, b. 5/15/1957 in Rochester; tenth; Bernard Sprague (laborer, Waterboro, ME) and Virginia Smith (Richmond, VA); residence - Milton Mills
Mary Leona, b. 9/14/1934 in Milton Mills; second; Fred E. Sprague (laborer, Newfield, ME) and Louise J. Paul (Acton, ME); residence - Milton Mills
Richard Edwin, b. 11/21/1978 in Rochester; Richard E. Sprague and Linda A. Lamper
Rooky Gene, b. 9/7/1956 in Rochester; first; Louis Sprague (mach. opr., Rochester) and Cynthia Paey (Rochester)
Ryan William, b. 4/12/1989 in Rochester; William C. Sprague and Tammy J. McKay
William Cornelius, b. 9/14/1962 in Rochester; Richard E. Sprague (machine tender) and Jeanne E. Thompson

STACY,
Henry M., b. 11/17/1894; first; William R. Stacy (bookkeeper, 24, Cambridge, MA) and Georgiella Marston (20, Deerfield)

STANHOPE,
Marguerite E., b. 4/18/1915; first; Otis C. Stanhope (shoemaker, Whiting, ME) and Harriet B. Coran (Athol, MA)

STANLEY,
stillborn child, b. 7/18/1911; first; Irving Stanley (shoemaker, ME) and Emma S. Roberts (Exeter)
Alison Elizabeth, b. 3/11/1992 in Rochester; William C. Stanley and Debra A. Brooks

STAPLES,
Joseph Allan, Jr., b. 10/8/1990 in Rochester; Joseph A. Staples and Tonda L. Cumpton
Neil E., b. 8/14/1904; first; Isabel M. Staples (20, Glenburn, ME)
Ruth Elsie, b. 9/23/1903; first; Harry W. Staples (teamster, 31, Milton) and Henrietta M. Sigler (18, New York, NY)

STARKEY,
David Paul, b. 12/2/1954 in Rochester; first; Paul Starkey (beater man, Athol, MA) and Beverly Drew (Wolfeboro)

STARUCH,
Theresa Catherine, b. 5/25/1986 in Rochester; George J. Staruch and Gerarda A. Leaden

STEADMAN,
Amber Leigh, b. 10/10/1985 in Rochester; Charles L. Steadman and Cindy L. Garland
Katie Lynn, b. 11/19/1979 in Rochester; Charles L. Steadman and Cindy L. Garland

STEER,
Stephen Wilfred, b. 7/20/1999 in Rochester; Paul Steer and Maureen Steer

STETSON,
Gordon Drury, b. 3/12/1920; second; Louis O. Stetson (grocer, Piermont) and Bessie Drury (Worcester, MA)

STEVENS,
son [Gerald F.], b. 8/2/1907; third; John H. Stevens (shoemaker, 27, Milton) and Winifred V. Keegan (28, Solon, ME)
Anna Isabel, b. 2/6/1911; second; Charles Stevens (fruit peddler, Armenia) and Clara Downing (Middleton)

Carl D., b. 6/6/1944 in Sanford, ME; third; Chester Stevens (engineer, Acton, ME) and Louise Teel (Arlington, MA); residence - Milton Mills

Donald Vernette, b. 1/20/1898; first; Frank D. Stevens (chauffeur, Milton) and Marguerite Meikle (Union) (1911)

Edwin M., b. 11/6/1902; seventh; William F. Stevens (mill, 33, Kennebunkport, ME) and Addie Daniels (34, Kennebunkport, ME)

Robert D., b. 6/6/1944 in Sanford, ME; fourth; Chester Stevens (engineer, Acton, ME) and Louise Teel (Arlington, MA); residence - Milton Mills

Sally Rose, b. 5/1/1935 in Rochester; first; Chester Stevens (farmer, Acton, ME) and Louise Teel (Arlington, MA); residence - Milton Mills

STEWART,
Mark Daniel, b. 10/6/1966 in Rochester; Daniel T. Stewart (US Army) and Betty Ann Berry

STONEBRAKER,
David Ward, b. 9/4/1948 in Rochester; fourth; Louis V. Stonebraker (asst. manager, Ada, MI) and Leslie M. Underhill (Boston, MA)

Marion Lee, b. 2/18/1947 in Rochester; third; Louis V. Stonebraker (prod. engr., Ada, MI) and Leslie M. Underhill (Boston, MA); residence - Milton Mills

STONEHOUSE,
Charles Benjamin, b. 2/15/1971 in Dover; Robert C. Stonehouse and Jeanne T. Todoro

STORM,
Joseph, b. 5/3/1909; fourth; Isadore Storm (sawyer, Canada) and Marie Imbralt (Canada)

STORMS,
Gary Allen, b. 1/11/1973 in Rochester; Allen H. Storms and Bernice J. Blanchard

STORY,
Suzanne Lee, b. 3/29/1949 in Rochester; first; Raymond W. Story (carpenter, MA) and Eleanor L. Ryder (MA)

STOWE,
Donald Williams, b. 9/14/1918; second; Merle L. Stowe (emp. in mill, Dover, ME) and Ruth A. Williams (Alma, NB)
Kenneth, b. 7/19/1922; third; Merle L. Stowe (RR section hand, Dover, ME) and Amy R. Williams (Alma, NB)
Leroy Douglas, b. 12/3/1916; first; Merle L. Stowe (emp. in mill, Dover, ME) and Amy R. Williams (Alma, NB)
Merle Louise, b. 8/25/1949 in Rochester; first; Donald W. Stowe (civil service, NH) and Muriel A. Ramsey (CT)

STOWELL,
Donald Irving, b. 7/5/1936; second; Leon Stowell (truck driver, Antrim) and Mary Hall (Milton)
Theresa Leona, b. 10/1/1934 in Rochester; first; Leon C. Stowell (truck driver, Antrim) and Mary J. Hall (Milton)

STRACHAN,
Bernadette Carole, b. 10/27/1967 in Rochester; third; George C. Strachan (carpenter) and Lola E. Drew
Malessa Ann, b. 6/20/1962 in Rochester; George C. Strachan (painter) and Lola E. Drew
Wendy Lea, b. 6/14/1960 in Rochester; first; George C. Strachan (US Navy) and Lola E. Drew

STRONG,
Daniel Joseph, b. 7/17/1996 in Rochester; Christopher S. Strong and Stacy L. Strong

STUART,
Bethany Marie, b. 12/21/1987 in Dover; James E. Stuart and Joyce M. Johnson

STURGEON,
Dorothy Valna, b. 6/29/1909; third; Fred H. Sturgeon (shoemaker, Milton) and Emma Wood (Eaton) (1914)

John Henry, b. 1/13/1903; first; Fred H. Sturgeon (shoemaker, Milton) and Emma Wood (Eaton) (1914)
Vinar Orlando, b. 7/13/1904; second; Fred H. Sturgeon (shoemaker, Milton) and Emma Wood (Eaton) (1914)

SWANSON,
Matthew John, b. 7/7/1994 in Dover; David A. Swanson and Michielle L. Moss

SWASEY,
Katheryn Elizabeth, b. 11/9/1985 in Rochester; Richard H. Swasey and Martha L. Hillyer
Sean Patrick, b. 10/3/1984 in Rochester; Richard H. Swasey and Martha L. Hillyer

SWEENEY,
Henry Leo, b. 4/27/1912; third; Colton H. Sweeney (laborer, 30, NY) and Maude Burke (27, Somersworth)

SWEET,
Carrol Whitney, b. 3/28/1896; first; Samuel G. Sweet (shoecutter, 28, Marblehead, MA) and Harriet J. Bodge (25, Wolfeboro)

SWINERTON,
daughter, b. 6/11/1891; third; Charles Swinnerton (sic) (farmer, 27, Milton) and Addie Peverly (22, Middleton)
daughter [Margaret E.], b. 7/9/1900; Jacob M. Swinerton (shoemaker, 30, Rochester) and Emma A. Melville (27, New Braintree)
son [Reginald C. V.], b. 4/26/1903; fourth; Jacob M. Swinerton (shoemaker, 44, Rochester) and Emma L. Melville (29, Dawson, MA)
son, b. 9/3/1908; fifth; Jacob M. Swinerton (shoemaker, 49, Rochester) and Emma A. Melvill (34, So. Braintree, MA)
son, b. 6/17/1911; seventh; Jacob N. Swinerton (shoemaker, Rochester) and Emma A. Melville (New Braintree, MA)
daughter, b. 6/17/1911; eighth; Jacob N. Swinerton (shoemaker, Rochester) and Emma A. Melville (New Braintree, MA)
daughter, b. 9/28/1917; tenth; Jacob M. Swinerton (shoemaker, Rochester) and Emma A. Mellville (Braintree, MA)

Barbara Ann, b. 11/25/1936 in Rochester; first; Lawrence Swinerton (relief wkr., Milton) and Anna Adjutant (E. Wolfeboro); residence - W. Milton

Jacob M., Jr., b. 1/17/1906; fifth; Jacob M. Swinerton (McKay stitcher, 46, Rochester) and Emma Melville (31, New Braintree, MA)

Jane Elizabeth, b. 4/13/1940 in Wolfeboro; second; Lawrence Swinerton (road com., Milton) and Anna M. Adjutant (Wolfeboro)

Lawrence A. F., b. 5/11/1913; ninth; Jacob M. Swinerton (shoemaker, Rochester) and Emma A. Melville (Braintree, MA) (1924)

Lawrence A. F., b. 7/11/1944 in Wolfeboro; third; Lawrence Swinerton (laborer, Milton) and Anna May Adjutant (East Wolfeboro); residence - West Milton

SYLVESTER,

Lindsey Kathryn, b. 6/3/1993 in Rochester; Paul G. Sylvester and Lisa M. Brown

Meagan Lisa, b. 5/13/1985 in Rochester; Paul G. Sylvester and Lisa M. Brown

Sarah Ann, b. 3/15/1988 in Rochester; Paul G. Sylvester and Lisa M. Brown

SZIRBIK,

Adam Thomas, b. 4/14/1978 in Dover; George H. Szirbik and Josephine T. Gallinoto

TAATJES,

Adam Michael, b. 12/7/1998 in Rochester; Michale Taatjes and Amy Taatjes

Donald Alan, b. 12/22/1966 in Rochester; fourth; Robert D. Taatjes (electrical engineer) and Norma F. Simes

Karen Lee, b. 6/21/1964 in Rochester; third; Robert D. Taatjes (electrical eng.) and Norma F. Simes

Kelsey Beth, b. 3/21/1997 in Rochester; Michael R. Taatjes and Amy B. Taatjes

Michael Robert, b. 1/1/1969 in Rochester; Robert D. Taatjes and Norma F. Simes

Nicole Fae, b. 6/6/1985 in Rochester; Brian S. Taatjes and Kathleen M. Fennell

Tyler Scott, b. 1/2/1989 in Rochester; Brian S. Taatjes and Kathleen M. Fennell

TABLER,
William James, b. 2/24/1987 in Derry; Robert W. Tabler and Wendy J. Hodgkins

TABORY,
Sarah Kathleen, b. 9/21/1973 in Rochester; Paul L. Tabory and Anne E. O'Neill

TANNER,
son, b. 11/16/1906; first; Herbert E. Tanner (farmer, 31, Farmington) and Marie E. Devarney (23, Ireland)
stillborn daughter, b. 11/21/1935; second; Hervey C. Tanner (barber, Wakefield) and Yvonne Lessard (Rochester)
Dawn Sylvia, b. 6/25/1963 in Rochester; Hervey C. Tanner, Jr. (millwright) and Georgette St. Cyr
Deborah Rose, b. 11/30/1957 in Rochester; first; H. C. Tanner, Jr. (US Navy, Milton) and Georgette St. Cyr (Westbrook, ME)
Diane Marie, b. 3/11/1959 in Rochester; second; Harvey C. Tanner, Jr. (cementer, shoe sh., Milton) and Georgette M. St. Cyr (Westbrook, ME)
Donna Leigh, b. 3/14/1961 in Rochester; Hervey C. Tanner, Jr. (maintenance) and Georgette M. St. Cyr
Ella Celia, b. 10/9/1939 in Rochester; third; Waldo P. Tanner (mill worker, Lebanon, ME) and Grace M. Corliss (Laconia); residence - Lebanon, ME
George Lawrence, b. 9/5/1933 in Rochester; second; George L. Tanner (garage owner, Farmington) and Rita Piper (Milton)
Grace Marie, b. 6/9/1937 in Dover; first; Waldo Tanner (lea. mill e., W. Lebanon, ME) and Grace Corliss (Laconia)
Hervey Cornelius, b. 8/19/1934; first; Hervey C. Tanner (barber, Wakefield) and Yvonne Lessard (Rochester)
Laura Lynn, b. 3/23/1988 in Portsmouth; Phillip J. Tanner and Jessica Pitman
Lola Amelia, b. 9/20/1932 in Rochester; George L. Tanner (garage man, Farmington) and Rita Piper (Milton)

Norman Stanley, b. 1/20/1943 in Rochester; fourth; Hervey C. Tanner
(navy yd. emp., Wakefield) and Yvonne M. Lessard (Rochester)
Patrick Phillip, b. 10/29/1936; third; Hervey Tanner (barber, Wakefield)
and Yvonne Lessard (Rochester)
Philip Joseph, b. 2/14/1962 in Rochester; Hervey C. Tanner, Jr.
(maintenance) and Georgette M. St. Cyr
Ruth Anne, b. 1/30/1945 in Rochester; first; Vincent A. Tanner (shoe
worker, Lebanon, ME) and Ruth M. Ramsey (Berwick, ME)

TARDIFF,
Willard Andrea, b. 3/23/1926; first; Andrea Tardiff (laborer, Somerset,
Canada) and Victoria M. Douquette (Milton)

TASKER,
daughter, b. 2/21/1889; second; Charles W. Tasker (shoe cutter, 33,
Lebanon) and Ida B. Shattuck (32, Rochester)
Andrew Franklin, b. 1/17/1951; second; F. Bruce Tasker (farmer,
Brighton, MA) and Gladys E. Farris (Brighton, MA)
Katrina Ann, b. 7/11/1986 in Rochester; Theodore L. Tasker, III and
Theresa M. Whelan

TATRO,
Clare Henrietta, b. 7/4/1918; ninth; Francis A. Tatro (laborer, No. Adams,
MA) and Mary S. Ducharme (S. Berwick, ME)
Dora Leona, b. 9/13/1919; third; Leon M. Tatro (emp. in mill, Athol,
MA) and Blanch M. Burgess (Bolton, MA)
Edna Irene, b. 1/20/1917; eighth; Francis A. Tatro (emp. in mill, No.
Adams, MA) and Mary L. Ducharne (So. Berwick, ME)

TEBBETTS,
Jason Robert, b. 2/2/1988 in Dover; Robert F. Tebbetts and Constance A.
Rouillard
Ryan Grey, b. 3/15/1986 in Dover; Robert F. Tebbetts and Constance A.
Rouillard

TERCYAK,
Angela Joyce, b. 4/10/1980 in Rochester; Michael F. Tercyak and
Deborah J. Savoie

TETREAULT,
Zachary Paul, b. 5/1/1974 in Rochester; Paul R. Tetreault and Theresa A. Gagnon

THAYER,
David Samuel, b. 4/1/1980 in Wolfeboro; Richard P. Thayer and Diane J. Cardinal
Jasper Cardinal, b. 3/26/1977 in Wolfeboro; Richard P. Thayer and Diane J. Cardinal

THERRIAULT,
Jaime Elizabeth, b. 12/26/1989 in Portsmouth; James Adrien Therriault and Mary Elizabeth Delisle
Jessica Marie, b. 11/2/1991 in Portsmouth; James A. Therriault and Mary E. Delisle

THIBADAU,
Frank E., Jr., b. 12/5/1949 in Rochester; second; Frank E. Thibidau (sic) (woodsman, NH) and Thelma I. Gagne (NH)
Lawrence Arthur, b. 12/3/1950 in Rochester; third; Frank E. Thibadau (woodsman, Wolfeboro) and Thelma Gagne (Lyman)

THIBEAULT,
Daniel Benjamin, b. 11/26/1980 in Rochester; Bruce W. Thibeault and Barbara A. Goyette

THIBODEAU,
James Henry, b. 6/6/1979 in Rochester; James W. Thibodeau and Jean D. Lamoreux
Mandy Margaret, b. 11/17/1975 in Rochester; James W. Thibodeau and Jean D. Lamoureaux

THOMAS,
Charles Allen, b. 10/3/1959 in Wolfeboro; first; Charles L. Thomas (US Army) and Kazuko Nakahara (1960)
Charles LeRoy, b. 11/18/1937 in Rochester; first; Wilfred Thomas (lea. worker, Middletown, NS) and Blanche Dadmun (Allston, MA)

THOMPSON,
stillborn daughter, b. 6/24/1927; fifth; Mark L. Thompson (painter, Jay, ME) and Mary E. Smith (Brookline, MA)
Charles E., b. 9/9/1906; first; Cornelius Thompson (laborer, 33, PEI) and Nellie T. Sullivan (28, Ireland)
Dennis Timothy, b. 3/7/1936 in Rochester; second; Edwin Thompson (mill worker, Milton) and Thelma Warnecke (Milton)
Doris Elizabeth, b. 11/3/1906; first; Fred C. Thompson (shoemaker, 34, Wayne, ME) and Gertrude M. Knox (18, Lebanon, ME)
Edwin Cornelius, b. 5/5/1909; third; Cornelius Thompson (emp. in mill, PEI) and Nellie T. Sullivan (Ireland)
Jeanne Elizabeth, b. 12/5/1934 in Rochester; first; Edwin C. Thompson (machinist, Milton) and Thelma Warnecke (Milton)
John Fenton, b. 9/5/1910; fourth; Cornelius Thompson (emp. in mill, PEI) and Nellie T. Sullivan (Ireland)
Josephine Elizabeth, b. 5/15/1908; second; Cornelius Thompson (emp. in mill, 36, PEI) and Nellie T. Sullivan (30, Ireland)
Leah Melissa, b. 10/21/1982 in Rochester; Barry J. Thompson and Pamela J. Beaudoin
Mary C., b. 2/27/1920; second; Mark L. Thompson (engineer, East Jay, ME) and Mary E. Smith (Brookline, MA); residence - Beverly, MA

THURLO,
Malcolm Delano, b. 9/5/1936 in Rochester; first; Perley Thurlo (laborer, Amesbury, MA) and Bertha Delano (Berkley, MA)
Pearl Christine, b. 5/31/1926; first; Perley E. Thurlo (laborer, Newburyport, MA) and Dorothy C. Kenney (Manchester)

THURSTON,
daughter, b. 9/17/1897; first; Charles H. Thurston (stable keeper, 35, Gilmanton) and Eubie Leighton (19, Farmington)
daughter, b. 11/23/1903; eighth; Josiah W. Thurston (emp. saw mill, 39, Effingham) and Silvia A. ----- (39, Wells, ME)
Donald Herbert, b. 9/16/1930 in Rochester; third; Milton H. Thurston (barber, Plymouth) and Beatrice Hartford (East Rochester)
Milton Herbert, b. 8/2/1954 in Rochester; first; Donald Thurston (stitching, Rochester) and Geraldine Avery (Rumney)

THYNG,
son [Raymond E.], b. 11/15/1899; first; John S. Thyng (leatherboard, 29, Shapleigh, ME) and Nellie G. Trafton (28, Shapleigh, ME)

TIBBETTS,
son [Verne P.], b. 8/20/1907; second; John Tibbetts (shoemaker, 26, Portsmouth) and Jennie B. Sanborn (17, Acton, ME)
son, b. 6/17/1916; second; Chris H. Tibbetts (farmer, Milton) and Theresa V. Stevens (Boston, MA)
Arthur Philip, b. 8/4/1906; first; John Tibbetts (shoe maker, Portsmouth) and Jennie Sanborn (Acton, ME) (1920)
Christopher H., b. 3/11/1888; Walter S. Tibbetts (NH) and Harriet A. Downing (NH) (1953)
Frank P., b. 11/1/1911; second; Grace M. Tibbetts (Milton); residence - Farmington
Grace May, b. 4/9/1888; Phoebe E. Tibbetts (Rochester) (1955)
Hailey Marie, b. 5/4/1998; Lester G. Tibbetts and Ginger D. Tibbetts
Helen Agnes, b. 9/13/1908; third; John Tibbetts (shoemaker, Portsmouth) and Jennie Sanborn (Acton, ME) (1911)
James Everett, b. 11/20/1944 in Rochester; second; Louis E. Tibbetts (grocer, Brookfield) and Arlene R. Laskey (Milton)
Janet, b. 9/6/1934 in Rochester; first; Louis E. Tibbetts (farmer, Brookfield) and Thelma Peabody (Lynn, MA)
Karla Rose, b. 8/2/1941 in Rochester; first; Leon E. Tibbetts (superintendent, Wakefield) and Arlene R. Laskey (Milton)
Leola, b. 2/5/1895; third; Thomas Tibbetts (laborer, 36, Wolfeboro) and Etta Hamilton (36, Conway)
Mathew Alan, b. 6/30/1999 in Rochester; Lawrence Tibbetts and Carrie Tibbetts

TILTON,
Alice Glenice, b. 10/31/1926; second; Glen W. Tilton (ice man, East Rochester) and Matilda M. Whitehouse (Farmington)
Cindy Lou, b. 8/8/1960 in Rochester; fifth; Glen W. Tilton (painter) and Yvonne R. Long
Deborah Jane, b. 3/31/1956 in Rochester; first; Glen W. Tilton, Jr. (mechanic, Lebanon, ME) and Yvonne Long (Rochester)
Hazel Margee, b. 4/8/1922; first; Glen W. Tilton (laborer, East Rochester) and Matilda Whitehouse (Farmington)

Margaret Norma, b. 4/7/1926; second; Norman V. Tilton (ice man, Lebanon, ME) and Margaret E. Trask (Yarmouth, NS)

Michael Kelly, b. 2/25/1957 in Rochester; second; Glen W. Tilton, Jr. (woodsman, Lebanon, ME) and Yvonne R. Long (Rochester)

Ruth Alice, b. 4/27/1916; first; Earlon C. Tilton (laborer, Lebanon, ME) and Grace E. Babb (Farmington)

TIRRELL,

Debra Sylvia, b. 7/2/1957 in Rochester; second; Carleton Tirrell (brakeman, Dover) and Sylvia Merrill (Lebanon, ME)

Earl, b. 3/13/1899; ninth; Charles W. Tirrell (shoemaker, 47, Boston, MA) and Annie J. Tuttle (38, Newmarket)

Penney Candy, b. 11/11/1961 in Rochester; Carleton W. Tirrell (shoe worker) and Sylvia J. Merrill

TITCOMB,

George Benjamin, Jr., b. 8/29/1954 in Rochester; second; George B. Titcomb (sheet m. wkr., W. Newbury, MA) and Dorothy Stanhope (Lynn, MA)

TOMPSON,

Michael Andrew, b. 7/11/1968 in Rochester; Wayne A. Tompson and Martha A. Kinney

TONGKALAKE,

George, b. 7/24/1914; third; James Tongkalake (emp. in mill, Greece) and Vasilika Tongkalake (Greece)

TOOF,

Jonathan A., b. 9/5/1946 in Dover; second; Herman W. Toof (coppersmith, Dover) and Muriel E. Columbus (Milton)

TOPLIFFE,

Whitney Jean, b. 2/19/1986 in Rochester; David B. Topliffe and Amy A. Fitch

TOSTEVIN,

Alison Lucretia, b. 6/25/1977 in Dover; Edward H. Tostevin and Andree A. Benoit

TOUSSAINT,
Brent Michael, b. 6/25/1970 in Rochester; Rene L. Toussaint and Lucille M. Desmarais
Kelly Ann, b. 7/9/1972 in Rochester; Rene L. Toussaint and Lucille M. Desmarais
Nichole Lynn, b. 7/9/1972 in Rochester; Rene L. Toussaint and Lucille M. Desmarais

TOWLE,
Alex Paul, b. 12/30/1987 in Rochester; Scott R. Towle and Darlene R. Bye
Alyson Paige, b. 12/31/1992 in Rochester; Kevin P. Towle and Kathy L. Johnson
Angela Marie, b. 2/10/1975 in Rochester; Joseph A. Towle and Ann M. Turmelle
Daniel Everett, b. 3/31/1989 in Rochester; Thomas S. Towle and Susan M. Nesbitt
Griffin Paul-Scott, b. 10/22/1998; Kevin P. Towle and Kathy L. Towle
Jared Andrew, b. 11/2/1992 in Rochester; Scott R. Towle and Darlene R. Bye
Jordan Scott, b. 2/20/1991 in Rochester; Scott R. Towle and Darlene R. Bye
Morgan Eileen, b. 10/11/1989 in Rochester; Kevin P. Towle and Kathy L. Johnson
Thomas James, b. 12/1/1984 in Rochester; Thomas S. Towle and Susan M. Nesbitt

TOWNSEND,
Agnes Melissa, b. 5/25/1900; second; John E. Townsend (manufacturer, Milton) and Eda B. Lowd (Acton, ME) (1913)
Henry Albert, b. 1/1/1898; first; John E. Townsend (manufacturer, 27, Milton) and Eda Lowd (27, Acton, ME)
Robert William, b. 7/15/1946 in Rochester; first; Ralph V. Townsend (minister, Barnard, VT) and Edythe M. Trimmer (Buffalo, NY)
Thomas Ralph, b. 12/18/1948 in Rochester; second; Ralph V. Townsend (minister, Bethel, VT) and Edythe M. Trimmer (Buffalo, NY)

TOY,
April Dawn, b. 4/13/1975 in Wolfeboro; Harold E. Toy and Brenda L. Bowley

Nicole Barbara, b. 4/13/1975 in Wolfeboro; Harold E. Toy and Brenda L. Bowley

TOZER,
William E., b. 3/28/1910; first; Granville E. Tozer (teamster, Danvers, MA) and Annie M. Wiggin (Milton) (1911)

TRAFTON,
son, b. 2/23/1916; fifth; Ashton R. Trafton (emp. in mill, Wakefield) and Bertha M. Lord (Shapleigh, ME)
Denise Marie, b. 1/8/1967 in Dover; first; Eugene C. Trafton (mechanic) and Marion E. Maleham
Lisa Ann, b. 1/8/1967 in Dover; second; Eugene C. Trafton (mechanic) and Marion E. Maleham

TREADWELL,
Allison Marie, b. 2/27/1994 in Dover; Stacy P. Treadwell and Tammy J. Pilotte
Christopher Michael, b. 5/9/1991 in Dover; Stacy P. Treadwell and Tammy J. Pilotte

TREPANIER,
Kayleigh Marie, b. 10/29/1993 in Rochester; Alain C. Trepanier and Kristen M. Powers

TRIPP,
Arley J., b. 11/5/1890; first; Edwin Tripp (shoemaker, 30, Sanford, ME) and Lucy Howe (Milton)
Jeremiah Jon, b. 9/14/1976 in Rochester; Edwin W. Tripp and Anne L. Twitchell

TUCK,
David Louis, b. 10/22/1942 in Rochester; fourth; Donald L. Tuck (bus driver, Ware, MA) and Helen M. Chadbourne (Rochester)

TUCKER,
Avis Lancaster, b. 1/28/1912; second; Charles W. Tucker (emp. in mill, 35, Rochester) and Edna N. Calkins (29, Trescott, ME)

Raymond Calkins, b. 4/22/1907; first; Charles W. Tucker (laborer, 30, Rochester) and Edna N. Calkins (24, Trescott, ME)
Richard Stephen, Jr., b. 4/25/1986 in Portsmouth; Richard S. Tucker and Jean E. Momberg

TUFTS,
Barbara, b. 11/18/1921; second; John D. Tufts (farmer, Middleton) and Alice M. Hodges (Milton); residence - Middleton
Gladys Ruth, b. 2/14/1925; second; Herbert G. Tufts (farmer, Middleton) and Mary E. Grace (Albany); residence - Middleton
Gloria Merilyn, b. 5/19/1931 in Sanford, ME; first; Orrie Tufts (mill oper., Middleton) and Iris Shepard (Acton, ME); residence - Milton Mills
Jae-Lynn Annie, b. 7/3/1984 in Rochester; Wilson W. Tufts and Debra Ebert
Maurice Wright, b. 5/23/1929; second; Moses D. Tufts (farmer, Middleton) and Evelyn R. Nutter (Milton); residence - Middleton
Patricia Ruth, b. 10/18/1927; first; Moses D. Tufts (farmer, Middleton) and Evelyn R. Nutter (Milton); residence - Middleton
Phyllis Elizabeth, b. 9/9/1919; first; John D. Tufts (farmer, Middleton) and Alice Maude Hodges (Milton); residence - Middleton
Taralie Ann, b. 2/2/1957 in Rochester; third; Lauriston Tufts (carpenter, Farmington) and Elizabeth Pomerleau (Pittsfield, MA)

TULLY,
Brian Keith, b. 5/23/1963 in Rochester; Thomas L. Tully (USAF) and Judith K. Golden
Connie Jean, b. 11/1/1965 in Rochester; Thomas L. Tully (USAF) and Judith K. Golden

TURCOTTE,
Lee Arthur, b. 4/4/1998; Arthur J. Turcotte and Mary J. Turcotte

TUTTLE,
daughter, b. 7/24/1890; second; Charles Tuttle (laborer, 40, Farmington) and Rosetta Dorr (Milton)
son, b. 5/29/1916; third; Fred L. Tuttle (machinist, Wakefield) and Ruth Dickson (Boston, MA)
Cameron Alan, b. 6/18/1999 in Rochester; Jason Tuttle and Christy Tuttle

Ernest A., b. 5/5/1898; third; Willie M. Tuttle (laborer, 28, Rochester) and Ida M. Kent (26, Wolfeboro)

Helen Elizabeth, b. 7/26/1928 in Milton Mills; seventh; Fred L. Tuttle (laborer, Wakefield) and Ruth Dixon (Boston, MA); residence - Milton Mills

TWEEDIE,

Nicholas David, b. 1/20/1991 in Rochester; Michael L. Tweedie and Stacy J. Dunn

TWOMBLY,

son, b. 5/8/1909; second; Bertrand E. Twombly (farmer, Milton) and Bessie A. Plummer (Milton)

Christine Roxie, b. 5/3/1907; second; James L. Twombly (farmer, 66, Milton) and Olivia E. McLean (28, PEI)

James Lewis, b. 8/12/1905; first; James L. Twombly (farmer, 64, Milton) and Olivia E. MacLean (26, PEI)

Leslie B., b. 5/26/1904; first; Bertram E. Twombly (emp. in mill, 26, Milton) and Bessie A. Plumer (24, Milton)

Robert Malcolm, b. 7/9/1909; third; James L. Twombly (farmer, Milton) and Olivia E. MacLean (PEI)

Sarah J., b. 6/19/1879; James H. Twombly (farmer, Milton) and Ellen M. Wentworth (Milton) (1937)

UNFONAK,

James Dean, b. 11/22/1971 in Rochester; James E. Unfonak and Beverly I. Haynes

URNESS,

Ezekiel Andrew, b. 4/1/1972 in Rochester; David A. Urness and Sharon M. Kimmons

UTZ,

Traci Dianne, b. 7/10/1972 in Rochester; William L. Utz and Cheryl A. Lane

VACHON,

Austin Gage, b. 10/5/1993 in Rochester; Valmore R. Vachon and Donna M. Breeden

Dorothy Amanda, b. 7/23/1974 in Dover; Thomas R. Vachon and Judith L. Joy
Homer Ernest, b. 6/22/1932; fifth; Emile J. Vachon (mill hand, Somersworth) and Emma P. Custeau (Milton)
Jennifer Lynn, b. 8/30/1976 in Dover; Thomas R. Vachon and Vivian C. Couture
Joseph Amede, b. 8/1/1/1926; first; Emile J. Vachon (mill operative, Somersworth) and Emma P. Custeau (Milton)
Lisa Marie, b. 9/21/1977 in Dover; Thomas R. Vachon and Vivian C. Couture
Marie Therese, b. 4/26/1952 in Rochester; second; Roger A. Vachon (woodsman, Rochester) and Theresa M. Duchano (Wolfeboro)
Paula Jean, b. 8/23/1954 in Rochester; fourth; Robert A. Vachon (bulldozer oper., Milton) and Theresa Duchano (Wolfeboro)
Richard Emile, b. 12/22/1930; fourth; Emile J. Vachon (leatherboard mill, Somersworth) and Emma P. Custeau (Milton)
Robert Aldege, b. 12/3/1927; second; Emil J. Vachon (laborer, Somersworth) and Emma P. Custeau (Milton)
Theresa Yvonne, b. 1/7/1929; third; Emil J. Vachon (ice man, Somersworth) and Emma P. Custeau (Milton)
Thomas Robert, b. 3/15/1951 in Rochester; first; Robert A. Vachon (mechanic, Milton) and Theresa M. Duchano (Wolfeboro)
Valmore Raymond, b. 11/25/1972 in Dover; Thomas R. Vachon and Judith L. Joy
Virginia Anne, b. 6/11/1953 in Rochester; third; Robert A. Vachon (self-employed, Milton) and Theresa Duchano (Wolfeboro)

VAILLANCOURT,
Michelle Marie, b. 10/27/1986 in Rochester; Armand P. Vaillancourt and Marie A. Pappagallo

VALLEY,
son, b. 4/16/1903; first; Godfrey Valley (emp. in mill, 27, Canada) and Josephine Britton (17, Wolfeboro)
son, b. 9/20/1926; third; Paul G. Valley (weaver) and Mildred Weeks (Moultonville); residence - Milton Mills
Audrey Elaine, b. 11/17/1946 in Sanford, ME; first; Paul G. Valley (spinner, Milton Mills) and June K. Sprague (Acton, ME); residence - Milton Mills

Norman E., Jr., b. 12/11/1952 in Rochester; first; Norman E. Valley (General Elec., Milton) and Blanche E. Williams (Union)

Paul G., b. 6/6/1932 in Milton Mills; fourth; Paul G. Valley (mechanic, Ossipee) and Mildred Weeks (Moultonville); residence - Milton Mills (1940)

Paul G., Jr., b. 3/14/1924 in Milton Mills; first; Paul G. Valley (mechanic, Ossipee) and Mildred Weeks (Moultonville); residence - Milton Mills (1940)

Ruth Emma, b. 1/14/1930 in Milton Mills; Paul J. Valley (mechanic, Ossipee) and Mildred Weeks (Moultonville); residence - Milton Mills

VAN VLIET,
Franklin Elforest, b. 9/24/1922; second; Henry J. Van Vliet (S.A. for blind, Long Island City, NY) and Ethel T. Downs (Milton); residence - Manchester

Harold Henry, b. 7/19/1921; first; Henry J. Van Vliet (S.A. dep. blind, L.I. City, NY) and Ethel T. Downs (Milton); residence - Manchester

VANROSSUM,
Finn Mulkern, b. 5/3/1999 in Dover; Red Vanrossum and Kathleen Mulkern

VARNEY,
Dianne Lois, b. 10/2/1941; fourth; George W. Varney (shoe worker, Lynn, MA) and Evelyn B. Tufts (Alton)

Eric Steven, b. 4/30/1983 in Dover; Brad R. Varney and Elaine A. Tufts

Franklin Parker, b. 8/29/1912; second; Gerald G. Varney (brass finisher, 23, Wakefield) and Eliza J. Jenness (20, Milton)

Heather Ann, b. 10/3/1984 in Rochester; Brad R. Varney and Elaine A. Tufts

Jane Louise, b. 8/15/1944; fourth; George W. Varney (shoe worker, Lynn, MA) and Evelyn B. Tufts (Alton)

Mabel, b. 12/31/1910; first; Gerald G. Varney (brass finisher, Wakefield) and Eliza J. Jenness (Milton)

Nancy Lee, b. 5/29/1943; fifth; George W. Varney (shoeworker, Lynn, MA) and Evelyn B. Tufts (Alton)

Stanley Maurice, b. 3/3/1915; third; Gerald G. Varney (brass finisher, Wakefield) and Eliza J. Jenness (Milton) (1919)

VASHEY,
Dennis Alan, b. 12/4/1948 in Wolfeboro; first; Henry E. Vashey (chef, Pawtucket, RI) and Mary E. Drown (Wakefield)

VENO,
Deanna Lee, b. 6/2/1978 in Rochester; Ernest W. Veno and Deborah J. Laurent
Irving Woodrow, b. 1/8/1919; third; Samuel A. Veno (wood chopper, Brookfield) and Mary G. Burke (Buffalo, NY)

VERNAL,
Eugene Anson, b. 12/24/1919; third; Chester F. Vernal (foreman, ice house, Richford, VT) and Olivette M. Rogers (Somerville, MA)
Winona May, b. 11/5/1917; second; Chester F. Vernal (foreman ice house, VT) and Olivette Rogers (Somerville, MA)

VIEN,
Ernest, b. 10/21/1900; fourth; Benjamin Vien (emp. railroad, 34, Canada) and Arthemise Drapeau (30, Canada)
Louis, b. 9/15/1897; second; Benjamin Vien (laborer, 30, Canada) and Arthemise Drapeau (27, Canada)

VIGUE,
Timothy James, b. 7/25/1987 in Dover; Thomas J. Vigue and Barbara J. Schelling

WACHOWIAK,
Mark Anthony, Jr., b. 2/7/1992 in Rochester; Mark A. Wachowiak and Julie A. Leonard

WADE,
Ronald Edward, b. 5/3/1950 in Rochester; third; Alston M. Wade (laborer, NH) and Ruth Eastman (Middleton)

WADLEIGH,
Joseph Elijah, b. 10/25/1918; first; Joseph Elijah Wadleigh (undertaker, Lynn, MA) and Edwina E. Fox (Milton) (1919)

WALBRIDGE,
June Louise, b. 6/2/1937 in Rochester; first; Charles H. Walbridge (salesman, Peterboro) and Mary Lessard (Milton)

WALDRON,
Elsie G., b. 11/23/1891; first; Fred E. Waldron (spinner, 19, Newfield, ME) and Annie Pinkham (17, Milton Mills)

WALKER,
daughter, b. 12/31/1941 in Rochester; first; Gertrude M. Walker (Haverhill, MA)
Burton Moses, b. 9/12/1912; first; Allie F. Walker (farmer, 25, Limerick, ME) and Blanch Chamberlain (19, Milton)
Michael Allen, b. 12/18/1987 in Dover; James A. Walker and Jessica L. Oliver

WALLACE,
daughter, b. 9/20/1889; third; Charles F. Wallace (laborer, 31, Middleton) and Dora Perkins (29, Middleton)
Lisa Marie, b. 3/26/1964 in Rochester; first; Vinton W. Wallace (laborer) and Judith E. Moore
Sarah Ann, b. 11/30/1974 in Rochester; Paul W. Wallace and Sandra L. Dahl
Vinton Wesley, III, b. 11/28/1974 in Rochester; Vinton W. Wallace, Jr. and Judith A. Hutchins
Virginia Louise, b. 6/1/1978 in Rochester; Paul W. Wallace and Sandra L. Dahl

WALLINGFORD,
Amos, b. 1/4/1889; first; C. M. Wallingford (farmer, 34, Milton) and Ida Downs (33, Milton)
Debra Elaine, b. 4/27/1971 in Rochester; Forrest A. Wallingford and Carolyn Dow
Eleanor Capen, b. 12/18/1910; first; Amos D. Wallingford (farmer, Milton) and Edith A. Medcalf (Rochester, NY)
Jaye Lynn, b. 3/15/1987 in Dover; Sterling K. Wallingford and Mary L. Lemay

WALSH,
Chelsea Jolene, b. 6/17/1991 in Dover; James W. Walsh and Donna K. Radcliffe
Gail Agnes, b. 11/23/1954 in Rochester; second; Glenn I. Walsh (dryer, S. Lebanon, ME) and Myrtle E. Durkee (Salem, MA)
James William, b. 6/6/1966 in Rochester; Glen I. Walsh (machine operator) and Myrtle E. Durkee
Katherine Margaret, b. 3/18/1993 in Rochester; James W. Walsh and Donna K. Radcliffe
Marilyn, b. 11/10/1923; second; Earl L. Walsh (mechanic, Lebanon, ME) and Jessie Tinker (Wolfeboro)

WALTERS,
Brea Dawn, b. 9/21/1987 in Rochester; Jeff R. Walters and Sharon E. Steeves
Corinn Elizabeth, b. 1/11/1985 in Rochester; Jeff R. Walters and Sharon E. Steeves

WARBURTON,
Brian Thomas, b. 7/2/1990 in Rochester; Robert E. Warburton, Jr. and Rebecca J. Burrows

WARD,
John Errington, III, b. 3/21/1997 in Dover; John E. Ward, Jr. and Donna J. Ward
Mary Jeanette, b. 11/13/1933; first; Donald F. Ward (mill op., Rochester) and Jeanette E. Blouin (Lebanon, ME)
Rachel Catherine, b. 4/2/1999 in Dover; J. Ward and Donna Ward

WARNECKE,
stillborn daughter, b. 6/12/1947 in Rochester; second; W. H. Warnecke, Jr. (foreman, Milton) and Ruth A. Dixon (Milton)
Billie Donna, b. 5/20/1944 in Rochester; first; William H. Warnecke, Jr. (US Marines, Milton) and Ruth A. Dixon (Milton)
Cheryle Ann, b. 5/10/1946 in Rochester; first; Donald S. Warnecke (mill worker, Milton) and Marion L. Rouleau (West Ossipee)
Donald Sidney, b. 10/31/1923; fourth; William H. Warnecke (ice man, Groneau, Germany) and Francina Nutter (Milton)

Linda Lee, b. 5/27/1947 in Rochester; second; Donald S. Warnecke (mill wright, Milton) and Marion L. Rouleau (W. Ossipee)

Thelma Addie, b. 2/21/1916; first; William H. Warnecke (ice man, Gronan, Germany) and Francina I. Nutter (Milton)

William H. O. L., b. 2/17/1920; third; William H. Warnecke (laborer, Gronan, Germany) and Francina I. Nutter (Milton)

Wilma F., b. 4/5/1918; second; William H. Warnecke (ice man, Gronan, Germany) and Francina I. Nutter (Milton)

WARREN,

Brittany Teal, b. 2/7/1980 in Dover; Mark T. Warren and Susan R. Hanley

Tara Brooke, b. 11/16/1977 in Dover; Mark T. Warren and Susan R. Hanley

WASHBURNE,

Paul Ivan, b. 12/7/1975 in Wolfeboro; Ivan Washburne and Claire G. Chandronait

WATSON,

Marvin Keith, b. 7/13/1953 in Rochester; second; Richard E. Watson (fibre mill, Farmington) and Frances A. Benton (Rochester)

Richard E., Jr., b. 4/7/1951 in Rochester; first; Richard E. Watson (machine tender, Farmington) and Frances Benton (Rochester)

WATTERS,

Matthew Andrew, b. 6/15/1991 in Dover; William S. Watters and Michele A. Trainor

WEARE,

Jacqueline Sharon, b. 9/5/1939 in Rochester; second; Scott A. Weare (machinist, Rochester) and Blanche A. Grenier (Berwick, ME); residence - Lebanon, ME

WEBB,

Karen Susan, b. 10/22/1963 in Rochester; George L. Webb (striker) and Elizabeth L. Smith

Kimberly Ann, b. 8/2/1968 in Rochester; George L. Webb and Elizabeth L. Smith

WEBBER,
Clarence, b. 5/10/1891; second; Everett Webber (carpenter, 28, N. Shapleigh, ME) and Ina E. Ross (27, N. Shapleigh, ME)
Marguerite, b. 11/30/1897; third; E. S. Webber (carpenter, 34, N. Shapleigh, ME) and Ina E. Ross (33, N. Shapleigh, ME)
Valdemar G., b. 3/19/1900; first; William G. Webber (painter, 21, Newfield, ME) and Helen M. Corson (17, Lebanon, ME)

WEBSTER,
Marguerite Francis, b. 12/1/1912; first; Ralph S. Webster (draftsman, 27, Lakeport) and Elva M. Gowen (22, Milton)

WEEKS,
Josephine, b. 3/26/1904; first; Albert Weeks (farmer, 23, Wakefield) and Phylura Dame (26, Rochester)
Kenneth Willard, b. 3/24/1923; first; Maud L. Weeks (Ossipee)

WEEMAN,
Jennifer Julie, b. 5/22/1979 in Rochester; Guy A. Weeman and Judy E. Bradley

WELCH,
daughter, b. 4/21/1903; fifth; Horace M. Welch (shoemaker, 42, Shapleigh, ME) and Carrie L. Brown (26, Barrington)
daughter, b. 12/26/1904; sixth; Horace M. Welch (emp. in mill, 43, Shapleigh, ME) and Carrie L. Brown (27, Barrington)
son [Wilfred L.], b. 3/20/1905; first; Fred Welch (emp. in mill, 23, So. Berwick, ME) and Lydia Marchand (21, Wakefield)
son [Clyde R.], b. 3/20/1906; second; Fred Welch (laborer, 24, So. Berwick, ME) and Lydia Marchand (22, Wakefield)
Barzilla H., b. 3/10/1899; second; H. M. Welch (shoemaker, 38, Shapleigh, ME) and Carrie L. Brown (23, Barrington)
Charles W., b. 2/5/1907; second; Charles J. Welch (emp. in mill, 22, So. Berwick, ME) and Lydia Marcoux (22, Canada)
Emily Lillian, b. 11/12/1909; fourth; Fred Welch (emp. in mill, So. Berwick, ME) and Lydia Marshall (Wakefield)
Evelyn Louise, b. 2/1/1921; first; Leon J. Welch (laborer, Ossipee) and Mertie A. Williams (Tamworth)

Evelyn Louise, b. 10/6/1925; fourth; Leon J. Welch (laborer, Ossipee) and Mertie A. Williams (Tamworth); residence - Ossipee
Joseph, b. 9/22/1909; third; Charles J. Welch (laborer, So. Berwick, ME) and Lydia M. Marcoux (Canada)
Lucy M., b. 11/11/1901; fourth; Horace M. Welch (shoemaker, 40, Shapleigh, ME) and Carrie L. Brown (26, Barrington)
Lyndsey Lee, b. 12/7/1991 in Dover; Joel E. Welch and Joanne M. Lee
Mackenzie Joel, b. 12/13/1993 in Dover; Joel E. Welch and Joanne M. Lee
Norman M., b. 9/8/1914; fifth; Fred Welch (millwright, So. Berwick, ME) and Lydia A. Marshall (Sanbornville)
Odell, b. 3/20/1907; third; Fred Welch (emp. in mill, 25, So. Berwick, ME) and Lydia Marchand (23, Wakefield)
Raymond, b. 1/23/1905; first; Charles Welch (laborer, 21, Salmon Falls) and Lydia Marcoux (21, Canada)

WENTWORTH,
son, b. 9/26/1890; first; Charles E. Wentworth (24, Milton) and Carrie S. Place (Middleton)
daughter [Eleanor H.], b. 9/1/1893; Charles Wentworth (laborer, 26, Milton) and Hattie Patch (24, Newfield, ME)
daughter [Lilla M.], b. 11/10/1894; sixth; Charles Wentworth (laborer, 34, Milton) and Hattie B. Patch (28, Newfield, ME)
son, b. 7/2/1896; seventh; Charles S. Wentworth (laborer, 37, Wakefield) and Hattie B. Patch (29, Newfield, ME)
son, b. 10/30/1899; fourth; Martin G. Wentworth (farmer, 36, Milton) and Georgia E. Gerrish (34, Lebanon, ME)
daughter, b. 1/19/1901; third; Elroy E. Wentworth (shoemaker, 22, Milton) and Ethel M. Hargrave (20, Somersworth)
son, b. 1/1/1903; third; George E. Wentworth (butcher, 35, Milton) and Lillian M. Maddox (30, N. Shapleigh, ME)
son, b. 6/17/1909; fifth; Charles E. Wentworth (emp. in mill, Sebago, ME) and Lizzie M. Smith (Sebago, ME)
daughter, b. 12/26/1915; third; Linwood J. Wentworth (section hand, Lebanon, ME) and Carrie S. Wentworth (Acton, ME)
daughter, b. 11/22/1924; fourth; Grover C. Wentworth (laborer, Milan) and Lena L. Miles (Bethlehem)
stillborn son, b. 9/13/1925; fifth; Grover C. Wentworth (mill hand, West Milan) and Lena Miles (Bethlehem)

Alicia Ann, b. 10/5/1960 in Rochester; seventh; Harry Wentworth (machinist) and Martha L. Tuttle

Andrea Lynn, b. 12/12/1956 in Rochester; sixth; Harry Wentworth (machinist, N. Rochester) and Martha L. Tuttle (Rochester)

Clara Belle, b. 1/8/1888; fourth; Hiram Wentworth (carpenter, Milton Mills) and Clara J. Hart (Milton Mills); residence - Milton Mills (1937)

Clark, b. 8/23/1950 in Rochester; stillborn; second; Earl Wentworth (foreman, NH) and Virginia Kimball (NH)

Craig, b. 8/23/1950 in Rochester; stillborn; third; Earl Wentworth (foreman, NH) and Virginia Kimball (NH)

Daniel Paul, b. 6/19/1980 in Rochester; Daniel L. Wentworth and Karmen A. Sanborn

David Lyon, Jr., b. 2/26/1964 in Wolfeboro; first; David L. Wentworth (mill work) and Dolores A. Virgue

Edward E., b. 2/25/1899; first; Elroy E. Wentworth (laborer, 20, Milton) and Ethel M. Goodwin (19, Somersworth)

Edward Roland, b. 6/18/1893; third; Ernest L. Wentworth (laborer, Milton) and Florence Lucas (IA)

Erlan Carl, b. 10/15/1935 in Sanford, ME; second; Norman Wentworth (mill hand, Acton, ME) and Helen Dunnells (Newfield, ME); residence - Milton Mills

Eva, b. 4/7/1914; second; Linwood J. Wentworth (laborer, Lebanon, ME) and Carrie S. Wentworth (Acton, ME)

Eva M., b. 3/20/1889; fourth; Charles S. Wentworth (laborer, 28, Acton, ME) and Hattie Patch (22, Newfield, ME)

Everett Linwood, b. 6/17/1909; fifth; Charles E. Wentworth (emp. in mill, Sebago, ME) and Lizzie M. Smith (Sebago, ME) (1958)

Harlan Eugene, b. 10/15/1935 in Sanford, ME; third; Norman Wentworth (mill hand, Acton, ME) and Helen Dunnells (Newfield, ME); residence - Milton Mills

Harry, b. 10/1/1925; first; Horace A. Wentworth (mill hand, Albany) and Sarah A. Pomfret (Preston, England)

Hattie Belle, b. 10/14/1886 in Milton Mills; John E. Wentworth (Milton Mills) and Sarah B. Hussey (Great Falls); residence - Milton Mills (1942)

Hazel, b. 7/26/1898; second; George E. Wentworth (butcher, 30, Milton) and Lillian Maddox (24, No. Shapleigh, ME)

Ianen Harry, b. 11/15/1984 in Rochester; Daniel L. Wentworth and Astra K. Sanborn

Jane Augusta, b. 7/1/1890 in Milton Mills; John E. Wentworth (Milton Mills) and Sarah B. Hussey (Great Falls); residence - Milton Mills (1942)

John Andrew, b. 9/25/1966 in Rochester; Harry Wentworth (die maker) and Martha L. Tuttle

John W., b. 7/31/1893; first; George E. Wentworth (butcher, 26, Milton) and Lillian Maddox (21, No. Shapleigh, ME)

Margaret, b. 1/29/1901; first; Hiram Wentworth (carpenter, 57, Milton) and Clara E. Pierce (38, Shapleigh, ME) (1912)

Max, b. 7/4/1891; second; Luther H. Wentworth (salesman, 47, Milton) and Flora Nelson (36, E. Hardwick, VT)

Paul Norman, b. 6/21/1947 in Rochester; second; Lloyd R. Wentworth (mill wright, Union) and Mariam L. Corson (East Rochester)

R. G., b. 4/16/1891; second; Ernest L. Wentworth (shoemaker, 27, Milton) and Florence A. Lucas (IA)

Stephen Barnabas, b. 6/25/1982 in Rochester; Daniel L. Wentworth and Astra K. Sanborn

Tiffany Marie, b. 7/7/1982 in Dover; Merle P. Wentworth and Sharon L. Gearwar

WESSELL,

Heather Marie, b. 3/15/1991 in Dover; Robert W. Wessell and Andrea S. Williamson

Jennifer Jean, b. 5/8/1987 in Rochester; Robert W. Wessell and Andrea S. Williamson

Shannon Nicole, b. 11/5/1986 in Rochester; Alan D. Wessell and Lisa M. Cameron

WEST,

Corey Bruce, b. 12/29/1974 in Rochester; Carl B. West and Marie T. Vachon

WETTSTEIN,

Ashley Brianna, b. 4/25/1997 in Rochester; Michael C. Wettstein and Stefanie A. Wettstein

Katherine Amber, b. 7/16/1995 in Rochester; Michael C. Wettstein and Stefanie A. Wettstein

WHALEN,
Steven Gardner, b. 10/4/1972 in Rochester; Gardiner A. Whalen, Sr. and Phyllis M. Adams

WHEELER,
daughter, b. 10/8/1960 in Laconia; third; Gerald R. Wheeler (unemployed) and Geneva M. Wentworth
Kayla Hope, b. 2/18/1992 in Rochester; Kevin N. Wheeler and Becky L. Plickert
Santana Paige, b. 2/18/1992 in Rochester; Kevin N. Wheeler and Becky L. Plickert

WHELDON,
Michael Frank, b. 7/17/1967 in Rochester; first; Frank W. Wheldon (supply dept. Pease AFB) and Bettyann Chapman
Michelle Ann, b. 3/4/1970 in Rochester; Frank W. Wheldon and Bettyann Chapman

WHETNALL,
Colleen Marion, b. 10/14/1931 in Rochester; second; Leroy E. Whetnall (steeplejack, Constitution, OH) and Eleanor Tanner (Wakefield)
Palma Louise, b. 6/27/1934 in Rochester; third; Leroy E. Whetnall (steel wkr., Constitution, OH) and Eleanor Tanner (Wakefield)

WHIPPLE,
Meredith Lee, b. 7/1/1958 in Rochester; first; Stuart K. Whipple (prin. & teacher, Claremont) and Elizabeth L. Bernard (Medford, MA)

WHITE,
Allison Marie, b. 12/22/1993 in Dover; Mark D. White and Jacqueline M. Pouliot
Brenda L., b. 2/13/1955 in Rochester; second; Earle R. White (tannery, Taunton, MA) and Mary Sprague (Milton Mills); residence - Milton Mills
Jared Michael, b. 3/31/1981 in Rochester; Michael P. White and Gale A. Johnson
Michaela Erin, b. 6/9/1984 in Rochester; Michael P. White and Gale A. Johnson

Rachel Sarah, b. 6/9/1984 in Rochester; Michael P. White and Gale A. Johnson

WHITEHOUSE,
son, b. 5/23/1910; tenth; Nicholas W. Whitehouse (laborer, Middleton) and Maggie Cassidy (Boston, MA)
Daniel Herbert, b. 8/13/1937 in Rochester; first; Daniel Whitehouse (mechanic, Lebanon, ME) and Pauline Baker (Moultonboro)
Elizabeth Katherine, b. 1/23/1996 in Dover; Eugene W. Whitehouse and Michele A. Whitehouse
Flora E., b. 7/16/1914; seventh; Harry F. Whitehouse (painter, Somersworth) and Gertrude L. Blake (Belfast, ME)
Florence, b. 6/15/1908; eighth; Nicholas W. Whitehouse (laborer, 38, Middleton) and Maggie Cassidy (38, Boston, MA)
Irene Louise, b. 2/7/1924; second; Charles R. Whitehouse (foreman, Portsmouth) and Ruth Elsie Staples (Milton)
Jamie Lyn, b. 8/15/1978 in Rochester; Ralph T. Whitehouse and Arleen L. Thivierge
Jenny Lynn, b. 10/25/1981 in Dover; Eugene W. Whitehouse, Jr. and Nancy J. Lund
Jill Ann, b. 10/22/1976 in Rochester; Eugene W. Whitehouse and Nancy J. Lund
Katherine Ann, b. 8/9/1962 in Rochester; Herbert D. Whitehouse (electrician) and Gloria A. Vincent
Kelly Ann, b. 5/28/1958 in Rochester; fourth; Eugene Whitehouse (laborer, Brockton, MA) and Valerie F. Dickson (Boston, MA)
Lillian Mattie, b. 8/25/1916; eighth; Harry F. Whitehouse (emp. in mill, Somersworth) and Gertrude L. Baker (Belfast, ME)
Margaret Ina, b. 9/18/1921; first; Charles R. Whitehouse (emp. ice house, Portsmouth) and Ruth Elsie Staples (Milton)
Ralph Theodore, b. 5/23/1910; ninth; Nicholas W. Whitehouse (laborer, Middleton) and Maggie Cassidy (Boston, MA)
Richard Louis, b. 11/1/1935; third; Wingate Whitehouse (laborer, Farmington) and Anna Peachey (Newburyport, MA)

WHITTEN,
Courtney Dee, b. 3/18/1993 in Rochester; Carl L. Whitten and Constance I. Dubois

Crystal Leane, b. 2/13/1992 in Rochester; Carl L. Whitten and Constance I. Dubois

Sherry Lynn, b. 11/29/1971 in Dover; Thomas E. Whitten and Barbara A. Toussaint

WIGGIN,

daughter, b. 12/23/1908; fourth; Albert E. Wiggin (overseer, 35, Acton, ME) and Cora B. Day (36, Newfield, ME)

son, b. 4/16/1909; third; Harvey F. Wiggin (teamster, Wakefield) and Mira L. Witham (Milton)

Albert Luther, b. 2/24/1934; first; Luther D. Wiggin (mill worker, Milton) and Irene E. Tatro (Milton) (1938)

Annie M., b. 4/12/1889; first; E. M. Wiggin (mill hand, 20, Acton, ME) and Susie Day (23, Shapleigh, ME)

Arline Victoria, b. 2/22/1915; ninth; Harry L. Wiggin (ice man, Tuftonboro) and Mabel Drown (Ossipee)

Carrie I., b. 3/23/1889; first; Charles S. Wiggin (cloth finisher, 27, Acton, ME) and Elen G. Waldron (20, Rollinsford)

Edith Pearl, b. 2/4/1899; first; Albert E. Wiggin (mill hand, 26, Acton, ME) and Cora B. Day (38, Newfield, ME)

Evelyn Louise, b. 5/8/1927; second; Raymond W. Wiggin (mill operative, No. Rochester) and Anita L. Gerry (Kingston, MA)

Harold, b. 11/8/1902; second; Arthur D. Wiggin (teacher, 28, Barton, VT) and Edith M. Buggy (26, Potton, PQ)

James Edgar, b. 11/15/1919; fifth; William E. Wiggin (laborer, Lee) and Isabell McIntire (Lebanon, ME)

Luther D., b. 8/23/1916; tenth; Harry L. Wiggin (emp. in mill, Tuftonboro) and Mabel Drown (Center Ossipee)

Marjorie E., b. 3/22/1907; fourth; Harry L. Wiggin (emp. in mill, 26, Tuftonboro) and Mabel E. Drown (23, Ossipee)

Mary Nutter, b. 8/18/1913; Harry L. Wiggin (emp. ice co., Tuftonboro) and Mabel E. Drown (Ossipee)

Minnie F., b. 3/12/1907; first; William A. Wiggin (laborer, 27, Wolfeboro) and Alice A. McMullen (21, England)

Wayne Robert, b. 11/26/1942 in Rochester; first; Leroy C. Wiggin (mill worker, N. Rochester) and Dorothy J. Wiggin (Dover)

WIGHT,
Nikia Marie, b. 4/9/1999 in Rochester; Thomas Wight and Tammy Sprague

WILK,
Joshua William, b. 12/4/1987 in Dover; William W. Wilk and Jennie L. Smith

WILKINS,
Alan Roy, b. 12/21/1948 in Rochester; fourth; Ralph W. Wilkins (poultry farm., Beverly, MA) and Virginia B. Wade (Salem, MA)
Cheryl Lynn, b. 1/19/1955 in Rochester; seventh; Ralph W. Wilkins (mach. oper., Beverly, MA) and Virginia Wade (Salem, MA); residence - Milton Mills
Dana Ralph, b. 6/6/1950 in Rochester; fifth; Ralph W. Wilkins (poultryman, Beverly, MA) and Virginia Wade (MA)
Fernand Marion, b. 5/14/1924; fourth; Arthur W. Wilkins (laborer, Acton, ME) and Violet Sliney (Skowhegan, ME)
Sarah Marie, b. 5/28/1992 in Rochester; Michael S. Wilkins and Suzanne C. Forcier
Teresa May, b. 3/19/1923; third; Arthur Wilkins (laborer, Acton, ME) and Violet Devall (Skowhegan, ME)
Tyler Bentley, b. 5/7/1947 in Rochester; first; Loring P. Wilkins (minister, Beverly, MA) and Thelma A. Bentley (Manchester, ME); residence - Milton Mills

WILKINSON,
Carolyn Ann, b. 9/29/1942 in Rochester; first; Wilfred A. Wilkinson (ship fitter, East Wakefield) and Yvonne F. Bullis (Haverhill, MA); residence - Milton Mills
Mahala J., b. 5/27/1949 in Rochester; fourth; M. A. Wilkinson (carpenter, NH) and Edwina N. Young (NH)
Stephanie Alice, b. 3/4/1967 in Wolfeboro; first; Durwood F. Wilkinson (construction business) and Linda M. Worster

WILLEY,
stillborn daughter, b. 6/8/1924 in Milton Mills; fourth; Edwin F. Willey (locomotive eng., Wakefield) and Marion P. Hinkley (Gloucester, MA); residence - Milton Mills

stillborn son, b. 6/16/1925 in Milton Mills; fifth; E. Farnham Willey (RR engineer, Wakefield) and Marian Hinckley (Gloucester, MA); residence - Wakefield

Arline Maralyn, b. 4/2/1924; third; Leon M. Willey (laborer, Brookfield) and Flora M. Downs (Milton)

Catherine, b. 9/24/1895; second; Joseph D. Willey (grocer, 41, Wakefield) and Annie O. Roberts (35, N. Berwick, ME)

Eunice, b. 8/8/1925; fourth; Leon M. Willey (laborer, Brookfield) and Flora M. Downs (Milton)

Frances Elizabeth, b. 5/9/1925 in Rochester; second; J. Herbert Willey (druggist, Rollinsford) and Grace C. Fletcher (York, ME) (1939)

Glendon Nelson, b. 6/26/1950 in Rochester; third; Nelson F. Willey (mill worker, NH) and Haroldine Gagne (ME)

Herbert Fletcher, b. 8/9/1920; first; J. Herbert Willey (druggist, Rollinsford) and Grace C. Fletcher (Cape Neddick, ME)

Nelson Forrest, Jr., b. 11/19/1952 in Wolfeboro; fourth; Nelson F. Willey (sawmill, Wakefield) and Haroldine Gagne (ME)

Norma Miriam, b. 3/24/1923; second; Leon M. Willey (ice man, Brookfield) and Flora M. Downs (Milton)

Richard Morrison, b. 2/2/1920; first; Leon M. Willey (laborer, Brookfield) and Flora M. Downs (Milton)

Sadie H., b. 6/12/1879; Joseph F. Willey (farmer, Brookfield) and Mary J. Laskey (Milton) (1938)

WILLIAMS,

son, b. 8/1/1905; second; Edson M. Williams (emp. in mill, 23, Westbrook, ME) and Fannie R. Abbott (22, Provincetown, MA)

Agnes Susie, b. 5/16/1924; third; Charles J. Williams (laborer, Tamworth) and Lilla M. Pennell (Tamworth)

Amy Laurel, b. 9/28/1986 in Dover; Mark A. Williams and Madolyn L. Warner

Arnold, b. 6/21/1936 in Rochester; third; Shaber W. Williams (P.W.A. wkr., Tamworth) and Myrtle Ellis (Milton)

Benjamin Fred, b. 6/26/1991 in Rochester; William E. Williams and Lisa M. Verville

Charles J., b. 1/25/1922; first; Charles J. Williams (woodsman, Tamworth) and Lilla M. Pennell (Tamworth)

Christine, b. 7/31/1935 in Rochester; second; Shaber W. Williams (mill hand, Tamworth) and Myrtle M. Ellis (Milton)

Clayton William, b. 1/15/1934 in Rochester; first; Shaber Williams (mill emp., Tamworth) and Myrtle Ellis (Milton)

Debra Jean, b. 6/4/1957 in Rochester; first; Clifford Williams (truck driver, Rochester) and Rose M. Rouleau (Milton)

Eileen Lillian, b. 12/8/1928; fourth; Ralph J. Williams (mill operative, Tamworth) and Lillian McCarten (Belfast, Ireland)

Janet Susan, b. 5/2/1925; second; Ralph J. Williams (laborer, Tamworth) and Lillian J. McCarten (Belfast, Ireland)

Lillian Lee, b. 4/18/1954 in Rochester; first; Ralph A. Williams (tree expert, Milton) and Jacqueline Marcou (Rochester)

Mark Alan, b. 6/17/1960 in Rochester; second; Clifford J. Williams (highway dept.) and Rose Marie Rouleau

Marylin Loretta, b. 4/17/1936; seventh; Ralph J. Williams (mill hand, Tamworth) and Lillian J. McCarten (Belfast, Ireland)

Matthew Allan, b. 9/1/1989 in Dover; Mark A. Williams and Madolyn L. Warner

Pamela Ann, b. 6/2/1963 in Rochester; Clifford J. Williams (truck driver) and Rose M. Rouleau

Ralph Alston, b. 11/12/1923; first; Ralph J. Williams (mill hand, Tamworth) and Lillian McCartan (Belfast, Ireland)

Richard William, b. 6/19/1923; second; Charles J. Williams (mill hand, Tamworth) and Lilla M. Pennell (Tamworth)

Shirley Lucille, b. 7/18/1938; eighth; Ralph J. Williams (lea. worker, Tamworth) and Lillian J. McCartan (Belfast, Ireland)

Thomas Marcial, b. 8/7/1999 in Rochester; John Williams and Mariecris Williams

Timothy Andrew, b. 12/4/1991 in Dover; Mark A. Williams and Madolyn L. Warner

William Irving, b. 11/6/1926; third; Ralph J. Williams (mill operative, Tamworth) and Lillian J. McCarten (Belfast, Ireland)

WILLIS,

Gladys Barbara, b. 10/25/1926; second; Perley Willis (laborer, St. Albans, VT) and Alice O. Douquette (Milton)

Noreen Katherine, b. 8/21/1925; first; Perley Willis (ice man, St. Albans, VT) and Alice O. Douquette (Milton)

WILSON,
Caitlin Nicole, b. 1/26/1991 in Dover; Gary A. Wilson and Molly A. Perkins
Corey Alan, b. 5/1/1995 in Dover; Gary A. Wilson and Molly A. Wilson
Danny Richard, b. 7/30/1964 in Rochester; second; Lester A. Wilson (laborer) and Joanne L. Dupuis
Dorothy Margaret, b. 11/25/1919; fourth; Charles W. Wilson (foreman, gravel pit, Portland, ME) and Florence E. Blake (Peaks Island, ME)
Gary Allen, b. 7/18/1963 in Rochester; Lester A. Wilson (laborer) and Joanne L. Dupuis
Kathleen Marie, b. 12/13/1989 in Rochester; Ronald R. Wilson and Elizabeth K. Bodenstedt
Kristen Marie, b. 11/6/1988 in Dover; Gary A. Wilson and Molly A. Perkins
Michael James, b. 8/15/1966 in Rochester; Lester A. Wilson (Dietz operator) and Joanne L. Dupuis
Robert Milton, b. 5/29/1926; fifth; Charles W. Wilson (manager, Portland, ME) and Florence E. Blake (Peak's Island, ME)

WINGATE,
Kevin Ronald, b. 12/28/1989 in Rochester; Bradley J. Wingate and Lori J. Copp

WINTERS,
Jeremiah Jay, b. 9/28/1977 in Rochester; Darryl C. Winters and Linda L. Lessard
Jesse Lee, b. 9/28/1977 in Rochester; Darryl C. Winters and Linda L. Lessard

WISHART,
Michael, b. 1/9/1926; second; John B. Wishart (farmer, Lawrence, MA) and Alice G. Aproyd (Maynard, MA); residence - Milton Mills

WITHAM,
daughter, b. 10/21/1915; second; Perley D. Witham (laborer, Milton) and Florence P. Locke (Boston, MA)
son, b. 10/21/1917; third; Perley D. Witham (shoemaker, Milton) and Florence P. Locke (Boston, MA) (1918)

Clifford Milton, b. 2/6/1902; fourth; Perley D. Witham (laborer, Milton) and Florence P. Locke (Boston, MA)

Norris Herbert, b. 6/10/1922; eighth; Edward J. Witham (laborer, Acton, ME) and Nettie M. Merrill (Saco, ME)

Raymond Orlon, b. 2/22/1917; seventh; Edward J. Witham (emp. in mill, Acton, ME) and Nettie M. Merrill (Saco, ME)

WOOD,

Timothy Fred, b. 3/22/1962 in Rochester; Herbert F. Wood (color wheel) and Mary K. Porter

Vicky Ann, b. 10/9/1964 in Rochester; second; Herbert F. Wood (color wheel) and Mary C. Porter

WOODBURY,

Ann, b. 12/15/1924; first; William E. Woodbury (poultryman, Hudson, MA) and Doris M. Horne (Milton Mills); residence - Milton Mills

Jane, b. 1/13/1928 in Milton Mills; third; William E. Woodbury (poultryman, Hudson) and Doris A. Horne (Milton Mills); residence - Milton Mills

Stephen Horne, b. 1/13/1928 in Milton Mills; second; William E. Woodbury (poultryman, Hudson) and Doris A. Horne (Milton Mills); residence - Milton Mills

Susan, b. 9/25/1931 in Milton Mills; fourth; William E. Woodbury (poultry kpr., Hudson) and Doris M. Horne (Milton Mills); residence - Milton Mills

WOODILL,

Erin Marie, b. 7/25/1982 in Rochester; Rodney J. Woodill and Dolores E. Ellis

Sharyne Ann, b. 9/20/1962 in Rochester; George H. Woodill (meter dept.) and Sandra R. Keene

WOODWARD,

Steven Richard, b. 2/1/1973 in Rochester; Frederick W. Woodward and Lucille E. Desrocher

WORCESTER [see Worster],

Jean, b. 6/20/1961 in Rochester; Harland Worcester (comm. pilot) and Pauline Rodis

WORSTER [see Worcester],

Jane, b. 6/10/1959 in Rochester; third; Harland S. Worster (instructor, Rochester) and Pauline Rodis (Somersworth)

WORTHING,

Elizabeth Anne, b. 5/4/1981 in Exeter; Stuart R. Worthing and Margaret A. Fogg

Lorissa Marie, b. 12/25/1978 in Rochester; Stuart R. Worthing and Margaret A. Fogg

WRIGHT,

E. A. [son], b. 4/10/1910; second; Albert Wright (carpenter, NS) and Harriet R. Preeper (Roxbury, MA) (1911)

WYATT,

Clarence T., Jr., b. 1/13/1945 in Rochester; first; Clarence T. Wyatt (lumberman, Barrington) and Pearl C. Thurlow (Milton)

Dolores Jean, b. 7/23/1950 in Rochester; third; Clarence Wyatt (mill worker, Barrington) and Pearl Thurlow (Milton)

Ellen Hayes, b. 8/16/1913; third; Edgar J. Wyatt (emp. ice co., Haverhill, MA) and Hattie E. Hayes (Milton)

Harriet Frances, b. 10/17/1907; first; Edgar J. Wyatt (iceman, 34, Haverhill, MA) and Hattie E. Hayes (3-, Milton)

Luther Asa, b. 11/5/1910; second; Edgar J. Wyatt (emp. ice co., Farmington) and Hattie E. Hayes (Milton)

Robert Arnold, b. 9/26/1946 in Rochester; first; Clarence T. Wyatt (mill worker, Barrington) and Pearl C. Thurlow (Milton)

YACHANIN,

David Alan, b. 5/17/1984 in Portsmouth; Edward Yachanin and Ladessa R. Logan

YOUNG,

daughter, b. 6/27/1896; eighth; Herbert Young (laborer, 28, Alton) and Susan Pettigrew (32, Farmington)

son, b. 7/11/1905; third; William H. Young (shoemaker, 29, Dover) and Hattie M. Pearson (30, NS)

son, b. 2/2/1906; first; Alvah H. Young (fireman, 19, Farmington) and Gertrude M. Swinerton (16, Worcester, MA)

Annie F., b. 12/25/1890; fifth; Horace F. Young (minister, Candia) and Annie Remick (Lewiston, ME)

Carol Anne, b. 9/7/1944 in Rochester; first; Beverly M. Young (Rochester)

Eugene Leo, b. 10/31/1898; stillborn; first; James C. Young (blacksmith, 26, Wakefield) and Annie G. Cameron (20, Lagonia, ME)

Heather Michelle, b. 5/12/1988 in Dover; David E. Young and Michelle Goodine

Judith Elaine, b. 1/8/1945 in Rochester; second; Willard J. Young (US Army, Farmington) and Beatrice L. Wilkinson (East Wakefield); residence - Milton Mills

Willard A., b. 7/23/1941 in Rochester; Willard J. Young (truckman, Farmington) and Beatrice L. Wilkinson (E. Wakefield); residence - Milton Mills

ZERBINOPOULOS,

Alexis Rae, b. 7/22/1996 in Dover; Lance T. Zerbinopoulos and Holly A. Zerbinopoulos

ZINK,

Jonathan Adric, b. 3/3/1985 in Rochester; George E. Zink and Pauline T. Harrison

MARRIAGES

ABBOTT,
Clifton O. of Milton m. Alice **Miles** of Boston, MA 10/9/1931; H - 26, truck driver, b. Ossipee, s/o Wilbur F. Abbott (Wolfeboro, laborer) and Florence Cook (Tamworth, housewife); W - 21, housekeeper, b. Gd. Pre, NS, d/o Alex Miles (Gd. Pre, NS, laborer) and Violetta Hutchinson (Lockville, NS, housewife)
George O. of Manchester m. Sadie M. **Guptill** of Milton 3/23/1896; H - 24, shoemaker, b. Manchester, s/o Milton A. (Manchester) and Josephine (NY); W - 23, weaver, b. Milton, d/o George (Milton) and Sarah F. (Wolfeboro)

ADAMS,
Larry of Milton m. Sandra L. **Marley** of Milton 1/2/1989

ADJUTANT,
Bruce C. of N. Rochester m. Bonnie L. **Brown** of Milton 8/15/1974 in Somersworth; H - b. 1/27/1947; W - b. 2/12/1950
Eli E. of Milton m. Carrie **Elkins** of Farmington 7/27/1905; H - 34, shoemaker, 2nd, b. Tuftonboro, s/o John F. Adjutant (Ossipee, farmer) and Augusta F. Garland (Ossipee); W - 34, housekeeper, 2nd, b. No. Berwick, ME, d/o Albert H. Joy (No. Berwick, ME, farmer) and Cynthia Hilton (Wells, ME)
Ervin F. of Milton m. Claudia N. **Richards** of Limerick, ME 1/12/1967 in No. Rochester; H - 49, machine tender; W - 25, homemaker
Kenneth R. of Milton m. Dorothy F. **Perkins** of Farmington 7/18/1961 in West Milton; H - 20, Army; W - 18, at home
Robert A. of Milton m. Donna J. **Parker** of Dover 3/29/1970; H - b. 7/23/1944; W - b. 6/21/1950
Ronald H. of Milton m. Susan E. **Kelly** of Wakefield 10/23/1965; H - 16, carpenter; W - 17, at home

ADREY,
Jerry G. of Haverhill, MA m. Claire M. **Hallissy** of Milton 6/28/1992

AHERN,
Floyd W. of Milton m. Marna E. **Grusheck** of Milton 12/23/1990

AIKEN,
David E. of Farmington m. Nancy J. **Gilman** of Milton 10/12/1962; H - 29, student; W - 21, teacher

AKERLEY,
Freeburn H. of Milton m. Laura F. **Ratcliffe** of Milton 11/25/1903 in Boston, MA; H - 21, shoemaker, b. NS, s/o James H. Akerley (NS) and Martha E. Hazel (NS); W - 25, shoe stitcher, b. Boston, MA, d/o William E. Ratcliffe (England, upholsterer) and Julia -----

ALDEN,
Mark C. of Milton m. Diana L. **LaFrance** of Milton 11/21/1987
Weston E. of Alton m. Dorothy G. **Piper** of Milton 6/21/1957 in Lebanon, ME; H - 36, garage, 2nd, b. Alton, s/o Herbert T. Alden (MA) and Lois I. Presley (NH); W - 40, housewife, 2nd, b. NH, d/o Robert Gray (NH) and Merion Morrison (MA)

ALEXANDER,
Francis L. of Franklin m. Cathy A. **Perkins** of Milton 6/25/1983 in Wolfeboro

ALLAIN,
Daniel G. of Springvale, ME m. Kimberley A. **Stacey** of Springvale, ME 10/1/1983 in Milton Mills

ALLAIRE,
Robert J. of Milton m. Jacqueline A. **Wheeler** of Rochester 9/21/1985 in Wakefield
Robert J. of Milton m. Beverly T. **Wyatt** of Milton 1/23/1988
Robert J. of Milton m. Jeannine L. **Collins** of Milton 1/9/1994

ALLARD,
John P. of Milton m. Julie A. **Pennell** of Milton 12/28/1980
Paul A. of Milton m. Aileen L. **Williams** of Milton 9/21/1950 in W. Lebanon, ME; H - 19, textile wkr., b. Montreal, Canada, s/o Paul Allard (NY) and Antoinette Descary (PA); W - 21, at home, b. Milton, d/o Ralph J. Williams (Tamworth) and Lillian McCartan (Ireland)

ALLEN,
George W. of Milton m. Hattie E. **Cook** of Milton 4/28/1906 in Rochester; H - 27, emp. in mill, b. Wakefield, s/o William H. Allen (Wakefield) and Lizzie B. Nichols (Wakefield); W - 18, at home, b. Brookfield, d/o Frank E. Cook (Milton, shoemaker) and Ida C. Hatch (Wolfeboro)

Paul N. of So. Lebanon, ME m. Mary E. **Dickson** of Milton 6/1/1968; H - 20; W - 20

ALLEY,
Royce F. of Rochester m. Diana M. **Brochu** of Milton Mills 3/31/1979

ALLFREY,
Dennis G. of Milton m. Tricia L. **Grondin** of Milton 10/26/1995

AMAZEEN,
Walter of Farmington m. Lillian F. **Parkhurst** of Milton 5/11/1920 in Farmington; H - 39, shoe worker, 2nd, b. Milton, s/o Charles Amazeen (Farmington) and Emma Rollins (Standish, ME); W - 27, shoe worker, b. Lynn, MA, d/o Frank Parkhurst (machinist) and Isabelle Dunn

AMES,
Frank H. of East Rochester m. Ida M. **March** of Milton 7/6/1959 in Conway; H - 64, retired, 2nd, widower, b. Rochester, s/o William P. Ames (NH) and Lydia York (Canada); W - 49, at home, 2nd, widow, b. Dover, d/o Elmer V. Junkins (ME) and Jessie C. Remick (NH)

ANCTIL,
David M. of Falls Church, VA m. Rebecca A. **Allen** of Loveland, OH 7/5/1975; H - b. 5/13/1951; W - b. 1/29/1956

ANDERSON,
Cory of Milton m. Brenda L. **Gaines** of Milton 8/26/1989 at Pease AFB

Leslie W. of Milton m. Maude I. **Jones** of Medway, MA 11/21/1962 in Farmington; H - 67, shoe shop; W - 67, at home

Norris E. of Forestdale, MA m. Olive H. **Rice** of Saugus, MA 11/3/1990

ANDREWS,
Leonard of Biddeford, ME m. Henrietta M. **Leavitt** of Biddeford, ME 8/23/1901; H - 62, carriagesmith, 3rd, b. Boston, MA, s/o Ira Andrews and Sarah Wentworth; W - 55, lady, b. Saco, ME, d/o Seth Guiney and Francis Neal

ANDUJAR,
Jose, Jr. of Milton m. Kellie A. **Poulin** of Milton 4/25/1992

APPLEBEE,
Arthur F. of Milton m. Carrie M. **Pinkham** of Dover 7/16/1891 in Great Falls; H - 22, shoemaker, b. Dover, s/o Theodore (Milton, shoemaker) and Augusta (Farmington, housekeeper); W - 21, lady, b. Dover, d/o George (dead) and Olive (housekeeper)

C. A. of Milton m. Mattie **Barstow** of Tilton 5/23/1937 in Tilton; H - 74, laborer, 2nd, b. Milton, s/o William Applebee (Milton) and Susan Miller (Acton, ME); W - 64, housewife, 3rd, b. Canada, d/o John Montrose and Mary Angevin (Canada)

ARCHER,
John S. of ME m. Rita J. **Gray** of Milton 12/14/1998

ARMSTEAD,
Roger A., Jr. of San Antonio, TX m. Sheree J. **Rowell** of West Lebanon, ME 6/14/1975; H - b. 11/16/1955; W - b. 10/18/1956

ARNOLD,
Alan D. of Kittery, ME m. Stacey R. **Todd** of Kittery, ME 9/23/1990
John D. of Milton m. Margaret J. **Beach** of East Lebanon, ME 4/15/1972 in Farmington; H - b. 5/14/1949; W - b. 4/9/1952

ASCHOFF,
Frederick O. V. of Brooklyn, NY m. Alice Gertrude **Butler** of Brooklyn, NY 8/23/1894; H - 27, cashier, b. Bremen, Germany, s/o Emil Aschoff (merchant) and Elizabeth; W - 26, b. Portland, ME, d/o Jay Frank Butler (merchant) and Celia

ATHERTON,

Edwin W. of Milton m. Sadie May **Pease** of Newfields 1/8/1924 in Newfields; H - 25, mill hand, b. Newmarket, s/o Edwin Atherton (mill hand) and Sadie Roberts (Raymond); W - 19, clerk, b. Newfields, d/o Frank Pease (Farmington) and Helen ----- (Exeter)

ATWATER,

Walter R. of Milton m. Eva May **Horne** of Lebanon, ME 5/18/1935; H - 63, laborer, b. Steuben, ME, s/o William Atwater (Picton, NS, farmer) and Priscilla Leighton (Steuben, ME, housewife); W - 59, housekeeper, 3rd, b. Dover, d/o Nathaniel Burke (Wolfeboro, farmer) and Mary Brown (Wolfeboro, housewife)

AUBERT,

David J. of Milton Mills m. Lisa A. **Hutchins** of Milton Mills 4/2/1988 in Milton Mills

Richard F. of Milton m. Donna T. **McQueen** of Milton 8/23/1980 in Manchester

AVERY,

Clifton A. of Milton m. Mary O. **Allen** of Rumney 7/14/1956 in Rumney; H - 48, lumberman, 2nd, b. Rumney, s/o Arthur W. Avery and Florence -----; W - 53, at home, 2nd, b. Warren, d/o William Shortt and Mabel M. Gould

Harry L. of Milton m. Hattie L. **Pinkham** of Milton 11/15/1894; H - 31, clerk, b. Milton, s/o Brackett F. Avery (Wolfeboro, farmer) and Susan V. (Milton); W - 35, clerk, b. Milton, d/o Nathaniel G. Pinkham (Milton, post master) and Emily C. (Sandwich)

John W. of Milton m. Emma **Getchell** of Milton 6/23/1889 in Rochester; H - 19, shoemaker, b. Wolfeboro, s/o Brackett (Wolfeboro) and Susan (Milton); W - 22, shoe stitcher, b. ME, d/o Edward (ME) and Syntha (ME)

Theron W. of Milton m. Emma L. **Piper** of Milton 5/18/1919; H - 23, manager, b. Milton, s/o Harry L. Avery (Milton, merchant) and Hattie L. Pinkham (Milton); W - 20, mill hand, b. Townsend, MA, d/o Everett E. Piper (Townsend Harbor, MA, teamster) and Stella R. Wakefield (Townsend, MA)

AYER,
Richard E. of Milton Mills m. Gertrude V. **Boisclair** of Milton Mills 11/27/1935 in Sanbornville; H - 50, bus driver, b. Newfield, ME, s/o Harry E. Ayer (Newfield, ME, retired) and Charlotte Hanson (NY, housewife); W - 23, at home, b. Quincy, MA, d/o Peter Boisclair (Quincy, MA, carpenter) and Annie Calibert (Quincy, MA, housewife)

AYERS,
Stephen E. of Milton m. Lisa A. **Moore** of Milton 8/12/1986

AYLARD,
John D. of Farmington m. Jean M. **Paquette** of Milton 5/11/1996

BABCOCK,
Collins of Milton m. Aletha A. **Preeper** of Milton 12/25/1903 in Acton, ME; H - 21, shoemaker, b. Lenox, MA, s/o Alvin Babcock (Falls Village, CT) and Nellie Ames (Falls Village, CT); W - 22, weaver, b. Boston, MA, d/o William C. Preeper (NS, farmer) and Matilda McDonald (PEI)
Raymond W. of Milton m. Eva M. **Gray** of Milton 3/25/1902 in Acton, ME; H - 24, shoemaker, b. Falls Village, CT, s/o Alvin Babcock and Nellie Ames (Falls Village, CT); W - 22, shoe operative, b. Brownfield, ME, d/o Anjavine W. Gray (Bangor, ME, farmer) and Fannie M. Bickford (Lewiston, ME)

BACON,
Osciola F. of Milton m. Alice E. **Lewis** of Milton 7/18/1888; H - 28, agent, b. Newport; W - 21, b. England

BADGER,
David F. of Milton m. Julianne **Chaisson** of Alton Bay 10/11/1942 in Alton Bay; H - 20, nursery fmn., b. Oak Bluffs, MA, s/o Charles E. Badger (Winchester, MA, laborer) and Hattie D. Baird (N. Sydney, NS, housewife); W - 19, dye house, b. NS, d/o Simon Chaisson (NS, unemployed) and Matilda Roach (NS, housewife)

BAILEY,
Alden H. of Milton m. Alice **Wallingford** of Milton 9/28/1915; H - 26, farmer, b. Methuen, MA, s/o Isaiah Bailey (Salem) and Ida Hoyt (Sandown); W - 23, emp. laundry, b. Milton, d/o Clarence M. Wallingford (Milton, farmer) and Ida E. Downs (Milton)

Clifford F. of Milton m. Annie M. **Dyer** of Milton 7/16/1891; H - 19, shoe cutter, b. Lynn, MA, s/o Frank (dead) and Lydia (dead); W - 17, housekeeper, b. W. Junction, d/o Charles (mill operative) and Martha (housekeeper)

Clifton I. of Milton m. Joan **Garvin** of Wakefield 5/31/1947 in Sanbornville; H - 22, mike oper., b. Milton, s/o Alden H. Bailey (Hampstead, mill emp.) and Alice Wallingford (Milton, housewife); W - 20, clerk, b. Wakefield, d/o Josiah D. Garvin (Wakefield, high. p'man) and Annie J. Perkins (New Durham, housewife)

Paul E., Jr. of Rochester m. Stephanie J. **Jacobs** of Milton 6/1/1974; H - b. 5/1/1954; W - b. 9/27/1953

Ralston C. of Milton m. Christina L. **White** of Lebanon, ME 2/18/1949 in Rochester; H - 31, mill wkr., b. Milton, s/o Alden H. Bailey (Hampstead) and Alice Wallingford (Milton); W - 28, shoe wkr., b. Lebanon, ME, d/o Orman V. White (East Rochester) and Ardys C. Clark (East Rochester)

BAKER,
Harold A., Jr. of Rochester m. Penny J. **Nason** of Milton 6/27/1981
Lenard A. of Charleston, SC m. Brenda A. **St. Hilaire** of Milton 3/29/1984 in Concord

BALD,
John A. of Somersworth m. Cynthia J. **Lord** of Milton 6/15/1985 in East Rochester

BALENDER,
Fred of Milton m. Margaret **Fitzgerald** of Milton 1/21/1888; H - 23, operative, b. MA; W - 23, b. Salem, MA

BALL,
Robert B. of Milton m. Joan T. **Tasker** of Milton 10/17/1984

BALSER,
Christopher S. of Milton m. Stephanie A. **Podolec** of Lebanon, ME 11/7/1987 in Rochester
Steven M. of Scottsdale, AZ m. Eileen L. **Russo** of Scottsdale, AZ 4/9/1994

BALUKONIS,
John M. of Exeter m. Olive M. **Smart** of Milton 9/27/1958; H - 40, shoe worker, 2nd, b. Exeter, s/o John Balukonis (Lithuania) and Skolda Resiziane (Lithuania); W - 25, machine oper., 2nd, b. MA, d/o Halford O. Bent (MA) and Ruth M. Ormes (MA)

BANKS,
Dennis P., Sr. of Milton m. Joy L. **Bostrom** of Rochester 10/20/1984
James F. of Milton m. Renee **Shanklin** of Dover 10/2/1989 in Portsmouth
Stanley D. of Milton Mills m. Debora J. **Huggard** of Milton Mills 8/4/1984
William G. of Milton m. Jean A. **Olsen** of Milton 1/18/1986

BARBER,
Charles J. of Milton m. Elizabeth V. **Galbraith** of Milton 12/4/1922 in Farmington; H - 23, laborer, b. Burlington, VT, s/o William Barber (Burlington, VT, shoemaker) and Melvina S. Babbitt (Canada); W - 18, emp. in mill, b. Downpatrick, Ireland, d/o Joseph Galbraith (Downpatrick, Ireland, laborer) and Susanna McCarten (Rathmullen, Ireland)
Charles R. of Farmington m. June **Wentworth** of Milton 3/18/1944 in Wakefield; H - 26, inspector, b. Franklin, s/o Maurice A. Barber (Wheelock, VT, farmer) and Viotti M. Ingalls (Walden, VT, housewife); W - 19, unemployed, b. Wakefield, d/o Homer Wentworth (Wakefield, stockman) and Margie V. Drown (Ossipee, housewife)
Charles R., Jr. of Milton m. Linda J. **Ealy** of Rochester 6/5/1971 in Greenland; H - b. 1/10/1945; W - b. 4/15/1948

BARBIN,
Richard O. of Lynnfield, MA m. Gail F. **McLaughlin** of Wakefield, MA 4/4/1970; H - b. 11/26/1948; W - b. 2/10/1948

BARCA,
David J. of Milton m. Kelly A. **Logan** of Milton 11/22/1997

BARKER,
Robert S. of Milton m. Alice B. **Thompson** of Milton 11/29/1897 in Rochester; H - 24, shoecutter, b. Stoneham, MA, s/o Timothy B. Barker (E. Boston, MA); W - 21, shoe stitcher, b. Boston, MA, d/o Frank H. Thompson (Ossipee, laborer)

BARNER,
Christian of Portland, ME m. Jennifer E. **Thayer** of Milton 8/12/1989

BARNES,
Edwin O. of Chelsea, MA m. Laura A. **Booth** of Milton 8/13/1890 in Wakefield; H - 64, accountant, 2nd, b. Boston, MA, s/o Edwin (dead) and Betsey L. (dead); W - 26, lady, b. Milton, d/o George (dead) and Belle

BARRETT,
Barrie G. of Milton m. Sharon E. **Morin** of Milton 1/31/1969; H - b. 7/20/1940; W - b. 12/22/1943
Charles W. of Milton m. Carolyn E. **Genest** of Milton 2/22/1986
James W. of Milton m. Carole A. **Provencher** of Milton 6/19/1965; H - 18, farmer; W - 18, waitress
James W. of Milton m. Patricia C. **Edmands** of Milton 7/23/1992

BARROWS,
Arthur O. of Berlin m. Alice **Burnside** of Stratford 6/20/1910; H - 23, laborer, b. Fort Williams, NS, s/o Charles Barrows (Fort Williams, NS, laborer) and Carrie ----- (England); W - 24, housework, b. Stratford, d/o Daniel Burnside (Stratford, farmer) and Cora Stone (Stratford)

BARRY,
Joseph A. of Berwick, ME m. Kathleen M. **Thurlow** of Kittery, ME 11/11/1995

BARTSCH,
David T. of Milton m. Linda R. **Guldbrandsen** of Milton 10/11/1980

BASFORD,
Thomas W. of Providence, RI m. Ruth **Plummer** of Milton 8/15/1948; H - 45, chef, 2nd, b. Stafford, England, s/o Thomas W. E. Basford (England, engine fitter) and Harriet Lees (England, housewife); W - 38, dietitian, b. Milton, d/o Bard B. Plummer (Milton, farmer) and Ruth L. Fall (Milton, housewife)

BASSETT,
John L. of Milton m. Dorothy H. **Gatchell** of Milton 5/21/1955 in Farmington; H - 43, machinist, 2nd, b. Peterborough, s/o Alston Bassett and Irene Chapman; W - 37, housewife, 2nd, b. Milford, MA, d/o Everett Pratt and F. Hazel Lavers
John N. of Milton m. Patricia G. **Griffin** of Milton 8/30/1969; H - b. 6/26/1945; W - b. 7/31/1949
Robert C. of Milton m. Beverly J. **McCarthy** of Rochester 6/1/1974 in Rochester; H - b. 3/12/1956; W - b. 6/5/1957
Thomas B. of Milton m. Bessie **Young** of Milton 4/2/1900 in Rochester; H - 23, paper maker, b. Norton, NB, s/o William H. Bassett (Norton, NB, carpenter) and Wealthy A. ----- (Norton, NB); W - 17, housekeeper, b. Milton, d/o Horace F. Young (clergyman) and Annie -----

BEACH,
John S. of Kittery, ME m. Rose B. **Gerry** of Kittery, ME 5/8/1985

BEAN,
Henry E. of Milton m. Ethel M. **Remick** of Milton 12/18/1920 in Moultonville; H - 20, laborer, b. Ossipee, s/o Fred Bean (Eaton, laborer) and Anna Nichols (Ossipee); W - 20, emp. in mill, 2nd, b. Milton, d/o George E. Ellis (Wolfeboro, laborer) and Inez G. Duntley (Milton)
Michael A. of Milton m. Cathy A. **Ricker** of Milton 6/30/1990 in Milton Mills

BEAUDETTE,
Raymond J. of Milton m. Lisa M. **Norton** of Milton 1/1/1994

BEAUDOIN,
John R. of Milton m. Vicki R. **Twombly** of Milton 5/20/1989 in Rochester

BEAULIEU,
Kerry P. of Milton m. Elizabeth A. **Lapierre** of Milton 7/1/1995

BECK,
George W. of Salem, MA m. Jeanette E. **LaFrancois** of Salem, MA 8/31/1979

BEGIN,
Raymond J. of Milton m. Joan S. **Kimball** of Wakefield 3/30/1974 in Wakefield; H - b. 11/13/1944; W - b. 12/1/1954

BEINHORN,
Alan I. of New York, NY m. Joan C. **Lord** of Milton 5/6/1972; H - b. 1/4/1948; W - b. 6/30/1951

BELANGER,
Roger M. of Milton m. Cathleen S. **Colwell** of Milton 7/31/1982

BELIVEAU,
Raymond S. of Worcester, MA m. Patricia M. **Beliveau** of Worcester, MA 9/25/1954; H - 38, machinist, 2nd, b. Worcester, MA, s/o Charles Beliveau and Blanche Kimball; W - 33, at home, 2nd, b. Worcester, MA, d/o George O'Malley and Rosamond McCue

BELLEMEUR,
William N. of Milton m. Alta Mae **Jenness** of Rochester 11/27/1915; H - 28, teamster, 2nd, b. Sanbornville, s/o Charles Bellemeur (Canada, watchman) and Celanire Jelleneau (Canada); W - 16, moulder, b. Rochester, d/o Isaac B. Jenness (Barrington, farmer) and Sarah J. Howard (Rochester)

BENNETT,
Stillman J. of Sanford, ME m. Florence M. **Burnham** of Sanford, ME 12/24/1902; H - 21, machinist, b. Sanford, ME, s/o Justus P. Bennett and Harriette Ricker (Lebanon); W - 18, lady, b. Milton, d/o Henry M. Burnham (Wakefield, carpenter) and Sarah A. Miles (Milton)

BENNINGTON,
Brian R. of Acton, ME m. Melissa A. **Dame** of Acton, ME 5/2/1992

BENO,
Charles R. of Milton m. Susan L. **Stevens** of Concord 11/30/1968 in Concord; H - 24; W - 20

BENTON,
Maynard of Lebanon, ME m. Lucilla M. **Stillings** of Milton 6/26/1926; H - 22, ice man, b. Sanbornton, s/o Albert Benton (Gilford, farmer) and Alma Morse (Campton); W - 19, student, b. Wolfeboro, d/o Charles O. Stillings (Ossipee, mill operative) and Susie F. Newell (Clarks Harbor, NS)

BENTZLER,
Edward W. of Milton m. Donna L. **Place** of Rochester 12/27/1974; H - b. 12/23/1936; W - b. 5/1/1951

BERGER,
Peter P. of Milton m. Gina C. **Rosende** of Milton 7/1/1990

BERGERON,
Christopher J. of Milton m. Sharon L. **Canelas** of Milton 12/16/1978; H - b. 3/26/1957; W - b. 7/20/1957

BERNIER,
Gary R. of Milton m. Rae Ann **DesRoches** of Milton 10/3/1987 in Newmarket
Kenneth A. of Nottingham m. Judi E. **Pomroy** of Milton 10/22/1988

BERRY,
George E. of Milton m. Mabel **Turbin** of Marlboro, MA 7/2/1920 in Union; H - 33, carpenter, b. Milton, s/o Hiram H. Berry (Milton, farmer) and Mary J. Hanson (Milton); W - 22, hairdresser, b. NS, d/o James Turbin (Halifax, NS, contractor) and Irene Lyons (NS)
Jessie W. of Springvale, ME m. Mabel M. **Bodwell** of Milton 11/25/1896; H - 19, brakeman, b. Limington, ME, s/o Edmund D. (Limington, ME) and Martha A. (Gorham); W - 18, lady, b. Springvale, ME, d/o Charles L. (hotel prop.) and Etta M.
Paul A. of Milton m. Joyce A. **Komar** of Milton 7/30/1995

BETSCH,
Joseph C. of Milton m. Agnes **MacFarland** of Milton 6/30/1908; H - 22, papermaker, b. Dayton, KY, s/o Martin Betsch (Germany, retired) and Mary ----- (Dayton, KY); W - 19, stenographer, b. Lockport, NY, d/o William MacFarland (Scotland, supt. paper mill) and Margaret Wilson

BICKFORD,
Robert E., Jr. of Milton m. Robin M. **Downs** of Milton 4/14/1984 in Rochester

BIENEK,
David E. of Milton m. Roxanne S. **Drapeau** of Milton 10/18/1997

BILODEAU,
Jay J. of Milton m. Janet I. **Jarest** of Milton 5/18/1996
Richard R. of Milton m. Anne M. **Foss** of Milton 10/19/1985
Ronal J. of Milton m. Rhonda S. **Howard** of Rochester 1/5/1991
Wayne J. of Milton m. Joyce L. **Ricker** of Milton 4/13/1990

BIRON,
Wilfrid A. of Manchester m. Grace A. **Butler** of Milton 7/3/1948 in Manchester; H - 22, presser, b. Manchester, s/o Wilfred Biron (Manchester) and Mary F. Gagnon (Manchester, housekeeper); W - 19, nurse's aid, b. Milton, d/o Edward T. Butler (Hingham, MA, fireman) and Margaret J. Burbine (Malden, MA, housewife)

BISHOP,
William P. of Milton m. Esther M. **Upton** of Camden, ME 3/19/1897; H - 24, shoemaker, b. Camden, ME, s/o Fred A. Bishop (Walpole, MA); W - 22, dressmaker, b. Millbridge, d/o George L. Upton (Greenhurst, NY)

BLACK,
Kenneth D. of Portland, ME m. Marjorie **Murch** of Portland, ME 10/19/1936 in W. Milton; H - 25, stock clerk, b. Newton, MA, s/o Arthur A. Black (Orr's Is., ME, treasurer) and Ruby E. Stover (Harpswell, ME, housewife); W - 21, salesgirl, b. Portland, ME, d/o

Karl Murch (S. Casco, ME, a. mgr. bak.) and Isabel Brown (Raymond, ME, housewife)

BLAIR,
Alfred C. of Milton m. Elaine A. **Anderson** of Milton 9/8/1942; H - 19, mechanic, b. Laconia, s/o Harry A. Blair (Laconia, carpenter) and Amelia M. Clifford (Newark, NJ, housewife); W - 19, office clerk, b. Milton, d/o Leslie Anderson (Stoneham, MA, wood heeler) and Hazel A. Perkins (Middleton, housewife)
Gould K. of Milton m. Rena D. **Paey** of Milton 4/3/1926 in Rochester; H - 23, ice man, b. Laconia, s/o Leon B. Blair (Canada, farmer) and Phoebe Foote (Canada); W - 22, at home, b. Milton, d/o George W. Paey (Stoneham, MA, shoe operative) and Josie M. Downs (Milton)
Harry E. of Milton m. Margaret I. **Whitehouse** of Milton 8/3/1953; H - 28, oil dealer, b. Laconia, s/o Henry A. Blair and Amelia Clifford; W - 31, office worker, b. Milton, d/o Charles R. Whitehouse and R. Elsie Staples
Leonard G. of Milton m. Patricia M. **Levesque** of Somersworth 5/18/1962; H - 33, carpenter; W - 24, shoe worker

BLAISDELL,
Samuel of Milton m. Ethel M. **Bean** of Milton 10/23/1943 in Rochester; H - 64, janitor, 2nd, b. Somersworth, s/o Edward Blaisdell (Cambridge, MA, mill hand) and Katherine Morey (Cambridge, MA, housewife); W - 43, housewife, 2nd, b. Milton, d/o George E. Ellis (Tuftonboro, ice man) and Inez G. Duntley (Milton, housewife)
Samuel G. of Milton m. Flora A. **Hersom** of Milton 5/2/1903; H - 30, steam fitter, b. Somersworth, s/o Edward Blaisdell (Somersworth, emp. in mill) and Kate Morey (Edgecomb, ME); W - 36, housekeeper, 2nd, b. Lebanon, ME, d/o Lorenzo D. Goodwin (Lebanon, ME, farmer) and Mary E. Butler (Lebanon, ME)

BLANCHETTE,
E. A. of Rochester m. M. I. **Merrill** of Milton 6/26/1948 in Rochester; H - 28, cook, b. Biddeford, ME, s/o Edward D. Blanchette (Canada, mill emp.) and Clara Jarvais (Peterborough, matron); W - 25, at home, 2nd, b. Barnstead Ctr., d/o Albert B. Gray (Strafford, mill worker) and Bessie J. Brown (Durham, housewife)

BLOOD,
Byron A. of Milton m. Drusilla M. **Dudley** of Milton 9/22/1897 in Rochester; H - 26, shoemaker, b. Bucksport, ME, s/o Lewis M. Blood (Bucksport, ME, farmer); W - 26, shoe finisher, b. Rochester, d/o Samuel Dudley

BLOUIN,
Lewis of Milton m. Eva **Langlois** of Tewksbury, MA 9/7/1909 in Lowell, MA; H - 32, ice man, b. Canada, s/o Onesime Blouin (Canada, farmer) and Philomen Beson (Canada); W - 20, emp. in mill, b. Lowell, MA, d/o Frank Langlois (emp. in mill)

BOAK,
Robert S., Jr. of Portsmouth m. Ruth P. **Iovine** of Milton 10/27/1946 in Dover; H - 25, radio an., b. E. Jaffrey, s/o Robert S. Boak (Red Lake, MN, Navy Yard) and Marion B. Kelley (Providence, RI, housewife); W - 27, teacher, b. Boston, MA, d/o Adam Iovine (Dover, auto salesman) and Ruth H. Swenson (Malden, MA, public welfare)

BODWELL,
Charles H. of Milton m. Sandra L. **Taylor** of Milton 4/14/1979
Lance G. of Milton Mills m. Andrea L. **Dame** of Milton Mills 6/26/1982 in Union
Linwood C. of Milton m. Myrtle G. **Schofield** of Milton 2/5/1910; H - 21, laborer, b. Somersworth, s/o Charles L. Bodwell (Acton, ME, farmer) and Etta M. Murry (Sanford, ME); W - 15, b. White Rock, NS, d/o Clarence Schofield (Fort Williams, NS, teamster) and Mary C. Ellis (White Rock, NS)

BOGGS,
Eric M. of Milton m. Amanda L. **Huggard** of Milton Mills 12/10/1983

BOIS,
Randall M. of Milton m. Cheryl L. **Allen** of Durham 8/22/1992

BOISVERT,
Joseph O. of Milton m. Angelina E. **Labrie** of Rochester 8/16/1927 in Rochester; H - 21, RR worker, b. Somersworth, s/o George Boisvert (Canada, RR worker) and Marie Rouleau (Canada); W - 23, shoe

oper., b. Rochester, d/o Louis Labrie (Canada, mason) and Obeline Turmelle (Canada)

BOLES,
David M. of Milton m. Linda S. **Ambrose** of Somersworth 6/19/1976 in Rochester; H - b. 9/28/1956; W - b. 4/4/1956
Michael A. of Milton m. Robin J. **Sullivan** of Milton 2/7/1981

BONNEY,
George H., Jr. of Milton m. Sharon M. **Lachance** of Rochester 6/30/1978 in Rochester; H - b. 8/1/1957; W - b. 7/14/1960

BOOMA,
Scott C. of Milton m. Annie M. **Stevens** of Milton 1/18/1906; H - 23, shoemaker, b. Lancaster, s/o Frank E. Booma (Lancaster, printer) and Martha Fields (Lancaster); W - 20, bookkeeper, b. Milton, d/o Freeman E. Stevens (Wakefield, farmer) and Sarah E. Howe (Newfield, ME)

BOSSIE,
Mark S. of Milton m. Lisa M. **Jones** of Milton 5/29/1999

BOSTICK,
Harold N. of Pittsburg, TX m. Janet F. **Davis** of W. Lebanon, ME 7/1/1961; H - 27, Air Force; W - 24, assembler

BOSTON,
Victor L. of Milton m. Blanche W. **Wakefield** of Milton 10/22/1916; H - 22, clerk, b. Wells, ME, s/o Edward Boston (Wells, ME, farmer) and Hattie I. Hilton (Wells Depot, ME); W - 19, b. Townsend, MA, d/o Mary S. Wakefield (Townsend, MA)

BOSTROM,
Karl G., III of Milton Mills m. Jacqueline A. **Pelletier** of Milton Mills 3/29/1980 in Milton Mills

BOUCHER,
James L. of Milton m. Brenda L. **Pennell** of Milton 7/7/1984 in Gonic

BOURDEAU,
Robert W. of Milton m. Lorrie L. **Kirk** of Milton 9/11/1982
Thomas E. of Milton m. Kathleen A. **Cheney** of Milton 3/14/1987

BOURGOINE,
Anthony E. of Rochester m. Sherolyn A. **Keronen** of Milton 7/21/1979

BOUTSIANIS,
Richard J. of Milton m. Wendy J. **Attanasio** of Milton 12/23/1985 in Portsmouth

BOWLEY,
Ralph E. of Milton Mills m. Sarah C. **Leech** of Milton Mills 7/8/1961; H - 24, Navy; W - 18, at home
Scott J. of Milton Mills m. Dianne L. **Hutchins** of Milton Mills 7/5/1988
Wayne H. of Milton m. Barbara A. **Lavalley** of Rochester 12/16/1955 in Rochester; H - 19, tannery, b. Rochester, s/o Ralph Bowley and Lydian Coolidge; W - 20, shoe worker, b. Sanford, ME, d/o Henry Lavalley and Hazel Mattress
Wayne H. of Milton m. Barbara A. **Bowley** of Milton 5/25/1957 in Dover; H - 21, mach. opr., 2nd, b. Rochester, s/o Ralph M. Bowley (VT) and Lydian Coolidge (MA); W - 21, marker, 2nd, b. Sanford, ME, d/o Henry Lavalley (VT) and Hazel Mulleur (Acton, ME)

BOYD,
John B. of Milton m. Pauline A. **Wiggin** of Rochester 8/5/1942 in Lebanon, ME; H - 19, truck driver, b. Dover, s/o Joseph A. Boyd (Milton, mechanic) and Katherine Lougee (Milton, housewife); W - 18, shoe worker, b. Lebanon, d/o Harry L. Wiggin (lea'b'd mill) and Mabel Drowns (Ossipee, lea'b'd mill)
Joseph of Milton m. Abbie E. **Shaw** of Milton 12/9/1899 in Milton Mills; H - 26, student, b. Boston, MA, s/o Joseph Boyd; W - 24, milliner, b. Milton, d/o Aratus B. Shaw (Newfield, ME, carpenter)
William S. of Milton m. Evelyn M. **Nason** of Wakefield 10/15/1960 in Wakefield; H - 20, US Navy; W - 20, at home

BOYER,
William R., II of RI m. Ginger M. **Katwick** of Milton 1/3/1998

BOYERS,
Brian G. of Milton Mills m. Kathryn J. **Adams** of Exeter 10/18/1980 in Exeter

BOYLE,
Michael P. of Milton m. Lisa A. **Drew** of Milton 12/20/1991

BRADLEY,
Earl M. of Milton m. Lillian M. **West** of Brookfield 5/18/1930 in N. Salem; H - 23, farmer, b. Lynn, MA, s/o Joseph H. Bradley (Haverhill, MA, shoe worker) and Myrtle V. Carter (W. Pembroke, ME, wd. hl. wkr.); W - 23, at home, b. Brookfield, d/o George E. West (Brookfield, farmer) and Lillian M. Brown (Brookfield, housewife)
Norris A. of Dover m. Beatrix A. **Meunier** of Milton Mills 1/17/1966 in Rochester; H - 40, painter; W - 61, restaurant business

BRADSTREET,
Timothy S. of Milton m. Diane M. **Tarmey** of Milton 2/15/1980

BRANNAN,
Thomas V. of Milton m. Donna L. **Conway** of Milton 2/25/1984 in Farmington
Thomas V. of Milton m. Sandra L. **Currier** of Milton 6/15/1991

BRAWN,
Gordon N. of Milton m. Martha N. **Rodgers** of No. Rochester 12/24/1917; H - 20, machinist, b. Milton, s/o Fred L. Brawn (Altoona, PA, machinist) and Edith M. Nute (Milton); W - 20, emp. in mill, b. Bridgeton, Scotland, d/o Robert Rodgers (Glasgow, Scotland) and Janett Taylor (Glasgow, Scotland)

BRENNAN,
Bruce D. of Milton m. Christine M. **Labrie** of Milton 8/27/1988

BREWER,
Newell G. of Milton m. Terry A. **Locke** of Milton 2/7/1995

BRIDGES,
Robert L. of Milton m. Elizabeth A. **Nute** of Milton 3/20/1989 in Chichester

BRIERLEY,
Leroy T. of Acton, ME m. Hattie E. **Webber** of Milton 2/13/1898; H - 23, merchant, b. Acton, ME, s/o E. J. Brierley (Lowell, MA, merchant); W - 18, seamstress, b. N. Shapleigh, ME, d/o Parker G. Webber (Shapleigh, ME, carpenter)

BRIGGS,
Maynard W. of Manchester, CT m. Ruth E. **Avery** of Milton 10/5/1946; H - 30, electrician, b. Bingham, ME, s/o John W. Briggs (Briggs L., ME, deceased) and Susie E. Lathrop (S. Windsor, CT, housewife); W - 24, teacher, b. Laconia, d/o Theron W. Avery (Milton, clerk) and Emma L. Piper (Townsend, MA, housewife)

BROCHU,
Gary L. of Milton Mills m. Beatrace A. **Colwell** of Rochester 11/10/1984
Oneil L. of Milton m. Joyce E. **Pierce** of Milton 7/20/1968; H - 29; W - 21
Russell N. of Milton m. Noreen E. **Stanley** of Manchester 7/25/1994

BROCK,
Alan J. of Milton m. Laurel J. **Lindsay** of Milton 11/25/1994
Charles C. of Milton m. Grace Ella **Betts** of Lebanon, ME 6/7/1934; H - 21, mill op., b. Boston, MA, s/o John B. Brock (Pittsfield, laborer) and Annie M. Dyer (Sanbornville, housewife); W - 20, at home, b. Lebanon, ME, d/o Ralph Betts (Lebanon, ME, laborer) and Myrtie McIntire (Lebanon, ME, housewife)
John B. of Milton m. Annie M. **Bailey** of Milton 4/26/1908; H - 32, shoemaker, b. Pittsfield, s/o John Brock (Barnstead) and Rosina Leighton (St. Johnsbury, VT); W - 37, housekeeper, 2nd, b. Sanbornville, d/o Charles Dyer (Brownfield, ME, farmer) and Martha A. Drew (Brookfield)

BRONSON,
Gery L. of Milton m. Jean M. **Gregoire** of Milton 9/1/1973; H - b. 7/18/1955; W - b. 12/12/1954

BROOKS,
Norman E., Jr. of Milton m. Karie A. **Richards** of Milton 9/3/1994

BROWN,
Ambrose M. of Milton m. Marie A. **Blouin** of Milton 9/8/1914; H - 28, emp. ice co., b. Brighton, MA, s/o John M. Brown (Kings Co., NS, foreman ice co.) and Margaret Fahey (Brighton, MA); W - 18, shoe stitcher, b. Springvale, ME, d/o Onesime Blouin (Canada, farmer) and Heline Lessard (Canada)

Ernest F. of Milton m. Ida M. **[illegible]** of Gilmanton 1/4/1894; H - 25, shoemaker, b. Sandwich, s/o Warren J. Brown (Tamworth, farmer) and Nettie; W - 19, shoe stitcher, b. Gilmanton, d/o William A. (blacksmith) and Mary

James G. of Middleton m. Jean A. **Merrill** of Milton 12/7/1974 in Farmington; H - b. 7/6/1956; W - b. 3/23/1956

Jason E. of Milton m. Wendy P. **Carter** of East Lebanon, ME 1/1/1994

John V. of Milton m. Helen A. **Whitehouse** of Milton 5/10/1936 in Farmington; H - 17, shoe worker, b. Milton, s/o Ambrose M. Brown (Brighton, MA, emp. mill) and Ora M. Blouin (Milton, housewife); W - 18, at home, b. Milton, d/o Perley Whitehouse (Farmington, shoe cutter) and Victoria Douquette (Milton, housewife)

Lee A. of Milton m. Janice M. **Newhall** of Milton 10/19/1996

Philip E. of Milton m. Constance **Perkins** of Orange, MA 11/14/1942 in Farmington; H - 22, machinist, b. Milton, s/o Leslie M. Bown (sic) (Glenburn, ME, machinist) and Amy M. Nichols (Dover, ME, housewife); W - 19, unemployed, b. Farmington, d/o Herbert S. Perkins (New Durham, shoe maker) and Roseanna Pouliot (Rochester, housewife)

Raymond A. of Milton m. Margaret E. **Bourdeau** of Rochester 5/8/1970 in Wakefield; H - b. 10/29/1936; W - b. 3/24/1935

Walter of New York, NY m. B. Bernice **Hart** of Milton 10/12/1908 in Farmington; H - 44, salesman, 2nd, b. St. John, NB, s/o Silas Brown (St. John, NB) and Sarah Burns (St. John, NB); W - 32, bookkeeper, b. Milton, d/o John F. Hart (Milton) and Mary A. Twombly (Milton)

William A., Jr. of Milton m. Jeanne L. **York** of Milton 4/14/1979

William R., Jr. of Milton m. Gail L. **Labrecque** of Barrington 12/31/1983

BROWNELL,
Lawrence R. of Milton m. Maxine A. **Boulanger** of Milton 2/18/1978; H - b. 3/18/1933; W - b. 9/22/1948

BROZEAU,
David A. of Milton m. Denise A. **Jacobs** of Milton 4/21/1979

BRUCE,
Charles P. of Milton m. Emma **Brown** of Milton 8/30/1896 in Lebanon, ME; H - 23, shoemaker, b. Boston, MA, s/o Henry J. (S. Boston, MA) and Mary F. (Ossipee); W - 18, teacher, b. Lebanon, ME, d/o John

David K. of Milton m. Colleen E. **Lavertue** of Milton Mills 6/11/1988

Donald R. of Milton m. Pamela J. **Cross** of Rochester 11/29/1975; H - b. 6/22/1953; W - b. 11/29/1955

Douglas P. of Milton m. Marjorie B. **Hayward** of Wakefield 6/1/1974 in Union; H - b. 6/21/1957; W - b. 4/28/1957

Edgar B. of Lebanon, ME m. Gladys M. **Beaton** of Milton 6/27/1931 in Chocorua; H - 24, teacher, b. Lebanon, ME, s/o Charles P. Bruce (Boston, MA, machinist) and Emma Brown (Augusta, ME, housewife); W - 28, teacher, b. Milton, d/o Hugh A. Beaton (Jefferson, OH, station agt.) and Myrtle Hartshorn (Lunenburg, VT, housewife)

Kenneth R. of Milton m. Marion A. **Cole** of East Rochester 7/10/1947; H - 30, carpenter, b. Lebanon, ME, s/o Fred Bruce (Boston, MA, shoemaker) and Affie Guptill (Berwick, ME, housewife); W - 22, mill wkr., b. East Rochester, d/o Charles W. Cole (East Rochester, mill worker) and Thelma M. Sinclair (Dover, housewife)

BRUNELLE,
Craig R. of Rollinsford m. Kathleen M. **Sullivan** of Milton Mills 7/16/1988 in Rollinsford

Dennis W. of Milton m. Janet L. **Irving** of Milton 2/14/1999

BUCKLEY,
James J. of Milton m. M. Eula **Hussey** of Milton 8/12/1903 in Manchester; H - 26, physician, b. Dover, s/o Daniel Buckley (Ireland, mill overseer) and Catherine McCarthy (Ireland); W - 25,

lady, b. Acton, ME, d/o Benjamin Hussey (Acton, ME, musician) and Charlotte E. Huff (Charlestown, MA)

Robert C. of Berwick, ME m. Theresa J. **Horn** of Milton 7/16/1966; H - 22, maint. man; W - 18, at home

BUCZEK,
Theodore J. of Dover m. Linda L. **Warnecke** of Milton 12/21/1963; H - 20, mach. opr.; W - 16, student

BUDDENHAGEN,
Otto H. of Milton m. Effie **Howard** of Milton 11/9/1908 in Rochester; H - 27, papermaker, b. Germany, s/o William Buddenhagen (Germany, tailor) and Johana Martin (Germany); W - 21, milliner, b. Rochester, d/o Fred Howard (Rochester, shoemaker) and Costella Scruton (Strafford)

BUMFORD,
Rexford W. of Rochester m. Dora Pearl **Burke** of Milton 7/12/1918; H - 23, soldier, b. Rochester, s/o Herbert Bumford (Barrington) and Gertrude L. Wallace (Rochester); W - 19, emp. in mill, b. Wolfeboro, d/o Edwin A. Burke (Wolfeboro) and Ethel L. Rollins (Wolfeboro)

BURKE,
Charles L. of Milton m. Ida E. **Hood** of Milton 5/2/1942 in Sanford, ME; H - 59, barber, 2nd, b. Wolfeboro, s/o Charles F. Burke (Milton, deceased) and Hattie Tibbetts (Wolfeboro, deceased); W - 38, housewife, 2nd, b. Milton, d/o Oscar B. Dixon (Milton, deceased) and Nellie Down (Ossipee, deceased)

Gary M. of Milton m . Denise A. **Kladder** of Milton 10/13/1990

Gary M. of Milton m. Louise M. **Currier** of Milton 6/26/1999

Jeremy S. of Milton m. Andrea L. **Hammond** of Milton 8/15/1998

John E. of Lebanon, ME m. Mary **Cohen** of Lebanon, ME 11/8/1913; H - 21, shoeworker, b. Buffalo, NY, s/o James Burke (Buffalo, NY) and Delia Donahue (Buffalo, NY); W - 25, housework, 2nd, b. Ireland, d/o Daniel Cohen (Ireland) and Johanna Haley (Ireland)

William E. of Milton m. Mary J. **Raynor** of Milton 6/28/1899 in Rochester; H - 25, shoemaker, b. Wolfeboro, s/o Charles F. Burke

(Milton, laborer); W - 22, shoe stitcher, b. PEI, d/o John W. Raynor (PEI, farmer)

BURNETT,
Walter A., Jr. of Milton m. Patricia A. **Goodwin** of Milton 8/10/1991

BURNS,
James G. of Milton m. Lois A. **Tanner** of Rochester 7/2/1955; H - 24, clerk, b. NJ, s/o W. Frank Burns and Anna Peck; W - 22, teacher, b. Rochester, d/o George L. Tanner and Rita E. Piper
Michael W. of Milton m. Tracy L. **Donato** of Milton 10/21/1989 in Wolfeboro
William F. of Perth Amboy, NJ m. Sherlie M. **Taylor** of Woodbridge, NJ 6/14/1975; H - b. 6/14/1925; W - b. 6/29/1925

BURROUGHS,
Eugene W. of Milton m. Paula C. **Donlon** of Gonic 6/14/1974 in Gonic; H - b. 5/4/1951; W - b. 11/21/1954
Eugene W. of Milton m. Brenda L. **Marcoux** of Milton 7/28/1990
Howard of Milton m. Evelyn N. **Tufts** of Milton 7/22/1944 in Dover; H - 39, lea'b'd wkr., b. Brookfield, s/o Howard Burroughs (Brookfield, farmer) and Mercy Kimball (Wolfeboro, housewife); W - 38, shoe worker, 2nd, b. Milton, d/o Frank J. Nutter (Sanford, ME, mill wkr.) and Gertrude Wentworth (Milton, housewife)
W[arren]., Jr. of Milton m. Barbara J. **Colby** of Milton 1/2/1948; H - 18, US Army, b. Dover, s/o W. D. Burroughs (Wolfeboro, state highway) and Madeline G. White (No. Rochester, housewife); W - 17, housewife, b. Worcester, MA, d/o William I. Colby (Bow, textile worker) and Lois J. Heddie (Milton Mills, textile worker)
Warren D. of Brookfield m. Madeline G. **White** of Milton 10/9/1924 in Lebanon, ME; H - 24, laborer, b. Wolfeboro, s/o Howard W. Burroughs (Brookfield, farmer) and Mercy M. Kimball (Wolfeboro); W - 18, at home, b. Rochester, d/o William F. White (Boston, MA, mill hand) and Isadore Howard (Berwick, ME)
Warren D., Jr. of Milton m. Rosamond J. **Pecunies** of Wolfeboro 1/14/1951 in Wolfeboro; H - 21, machinist, 2nd, b. Dover, s/o Warren D. Burroughs (Wolfeboro) and Madeline White (Rochester); W - 23, nurse's aid, b. Wolfeboro, d/o Otto Pecunies (Portsmouth) and Eleanor Fernald (Wolfeboro)

BURROWS,
Carl M. of Middleton m. Marion G. **Nutter** of Milton 2/3/1917 in Rochester; H - 22, fireman, b. Middleton, s/o David E. Burrows (Middleton, farmer) and Nina E. Pinkham (Middleton); W - 21, emp. in mill, 2nd, b. Milton, d/o George W. Rand (Cambridge, MA, emp. in mill) and Ida E. Moore (Milton)

Daniel H. of Milton m. Lucille M. **Goodnow** of Rochester 6/17/1950 in Farmington; H - 23, student, b. NH, s/o Carl M. Burrows (NH) and Marion G. Rand (NH); W - 22, at home, b. NH, d/o Andrew Goodnow (NH) and Jessie Colbath (NH)

Daniel H. of Milton m. Marie L. **Cullen** of Rochester 1/12/1952 in Rochester; H - 25, USAF, 2nd, b. NH, s/o Carl M. Burrows and Marion G. Rand; W - 23, shoe worker, 3rd, b. ME, d/o Mathurin J. Robichaud and Irene M. Lamontagne

David L. of Milton m. Lisa M. **Dube** of Milton 5/27/1995

Edwin S. of Milton m. June M. **Pennell** of Milton 6/20/1959; H - 19, shoe shop, b. Rochester, s/o Francis Burrows (NH); W - 17, student, b. Rochester, d/o Reginald Pennell (NH) and Helen Remick (NH)

George D. of Milton m. Janet M. **Reed** of Middleton 7/3/1947 in Farmington; H - 26, store mgr., b. Milton, s/o Carl M. Burrows (Milton, mill worker) and Marion G. Rand (housewife); W - 20, clerk, 2nd, b. Haverhill, MA, d/o Eric A. Bullis (Westminster, MA, shoe cutter) and Viola F. Griffin (Haverhill, MA, housewife)

George D. of Milton m. Edna M. **Hagen** of Farmington 3/22/1958 in Rochester; H - 36, Nat. Guard, 2nd, b. Milton, s/o Carl M. Burrows (Middleton) and Marion G. Rand (NH); W - 31, shoe worker, 3rd, b. Goshen, d/o Ivan E. Scranton (Goshen) and Doris L. Lewis (Groveland, MA)

Kenneth R. of Milton m. Christine L. **Skillings** of Milton 5/16/1986

Lloyd A. of Milton m. Nancy L. **Henderson** of Milton 8/24/1963; H - 19, electrician; W - 18, clerical

Luman K. of Milton m. Ruth-Ann **Blanchard** of Milton 6/16/1956 in So. Tamworth; H - 22, mill worker, b. Milton, s/o Carl M. Burrows and Marion C. Rand; W - 16, at home, b. Brentwood, d/o Theodore Blanchard and Ruth Hoyt

Steven R. of Milton m. Karen L. **Taatjes** of Milton 9/6/1986

Willis of Sanford, ME m. Edna G. **Boothby** of So. Acton, ME 9/13/1909; H - 20, teamster, b. Alfred, ME, s/o Lemuel Burrows and Annie F.

Littlefield (Alfred, ME); W - 17, housework, b. Lynn, MA, d/o Frank M. Boothby (farmer) and Mary E. Demant

BUTLER,
Charles E. of Attleboro, MA m. Rose E. **Almeida** of Attleboro, MA 8/15/1959; H - 45, crane operator, 2nd, b. MA, s/o Edward Butler (MA) and Margaret Burbine (MA); W - 48, inspector, 2nd, b. Boston, MA, d/o John H. Shea (MA) and Helen McCarthy (MA)
J. Pierce of Milton m. D. Margaret **Wilson** of Milton 11/25/1939; H - 20, mill worker, b. Milton, s/o Edward T. Butler (Hingham, MA, fireman) and Margaret Burbine (Wakefield, MA, housewife); W - 19, at home, b. Milton, d/o Charles W. Wilson (Portland, ME, machinist) and Florence Blake (Peaks I., ME, housewife)
Maynard E. of Milton m. Lillian A. **Roberts** of Wolfeboro 10/27/1951; H - 20, st. h. dept., b. Milton, s/o Edward T. Butler (MA) and Margaret J. Burbine (MA); W - 19, laundry, b. Wolfeboro, d/o Horace Roberts (Wolfeboro) and Blanche Sprague (ME)
William M. of Milton m. Michelle L. **Campbell** of Milton 9/24/1994

BUZUZINSKI,
James J. of Lebanon m. Cynthia G. **Foster** of Milton 6/20/1955 in Rochester; H - 24, teacher, b. Lebanon, s/o Jacob Buzuzinski and Adella Androwski; W - 20, student, b. Dover, d/o Walter J. Foster and Leona Priest

BUZZELL,
George A. of Acton, ME m. Lovey A. **Day** of Milton 4/1/1914 in Milton Mills; H - 37, farmer, 2nd, b. Acton, ME, s/o Lyman Buzzell (Acton, ME, farmer) and Jane Lord (Acton, ME); W - 31, weaver, b. Newfield, ME, d/o John L. Day (Shapleigh, ME, laborer) and Susan Patch (Newfield, ME)

BYNUM,
Nathaniel L. of Union m. Beth A. **Emerson** of Milton 7/11/1998

BYRNE,
Thomas of Milton m. Zenaide **Therien** of Manchester 4/1/1904 in Manchester; H - 21, emp. in mill, b. England, s/o Patrick Byrne and

Mary Cartland; W - 26, weaver, b. Canada, d/o Herbert Therien (Canada) and Emelie Boisvert (Canada)

BYRON,
Raymond of Milton m. Alta L. **Dodge** of Farmington 2/27/1911 in Rochester; H - 23, shoemaker, b. Weedon, PQ, s/o Moses Byron (Weedon, PQ, laborer) and Virginia Dansgram (Weedon, PQ); W - 19, shoe stitcher, b. Barrington, d/o Frank S. Dodge (New Durham) and Roselle Pearl (Rochester)

CALIRI,
Columbus H. of Lawrence, MA m. Catherine D. **Spaziano** of Lawrence, MA 7/20/1926; H - 21, law student, b. Milford, MA, s/o Vincent Caliri (Italy, jeweler) and Anna Bolami (Italy); W - 18, student, b. Lawrence, MA, d/o Antonio Spaziano (Italy, merchant) and Josephine Reboldo (Italy)

CAMERON,
Steven S. of Berwick, ME m. Denise L. **Young** of Berwick, ME 6/24/1995

CAMPBELL,
Richard D. of Rochester m. Lorraine M. **Benton** of Milton 6/6/1947 in Rochester; H - 18, shoe wkr., b. W. Ossipee, s/o Forrest F. Campbell (Brookfield, truck driver) and Winifred M. Eldridge (W. Ossipee, mill worker); W - 18, student, b. Hinsdale, d/o Edward M. Benton (Laconia, foreman) and Lucilla M. Stillings (NS, housewife)
Sidney S. of Bangor, ME m. M. Inez **McNeil** of Bangor, ME 9/1/1934 in Milton Mills; H - 36, foreman, b. Mt. Hersey, ME, s/o Loren Campbell (Patten, ME, storekeeper) and Elizabeth Getchell (Patten, ME, prac. nurse); W - 24, nurse, b. Quebec, Canada, d/o Michael J. McNeil (Quebec, Canada, contractor) and Margaret E. Dow (Quebec, Canada, housewife)

CANNEY,
Carl B. of Milton m. Alice M. **Brownell** of Dover 6/28/1911 in Dover; H - 25, salesman, b. Milton, s/o George D. Canney (Dover, farmer) and Addie B. Hatch (No. Berwick, ME); W - 24, teacher, b. Dover, d/o William A. Brownell (Dover, police officer) and Sarah S. Brown (Barrington)

John B. of Rochester m. Roberta C. **Soucy** of Milton 8/20/1966; H - 25, mach. attendant; W - 29, shoe worker

Lawrence E. of Milton m. Kelly A. **Leighton** of Milton 8/23/1986 in Rochester

Ralph Wilson of Farmington m. Ethel Maud **Hayes** of Milton 9/18/1921; H - 25, farmer, b. New Durham, s/o Henry Canney (New Durham, drover) and Mary Wilson (Rochester); W - 18, teacher, b. Milton, d/o Guy L. Hayes (Milton, carpenter) and Myrta E. Clements (Lebanon, ME)

Robert B. of Milton m. Constance J. **March** of East Rochester 1/28/1952 in Rochester; H - 23, clerk, b. ME, s/o Victor T. Canney and Isadora Canney; W - 22, artist, b. NH, d/o Clifton L. March and Ida M. Junkins

Victor T. of Lebanon, ME m. Isadore **Tanner** of Lebanon, ME 4/22/1926; H - 25, mechanic, b. Rochester, s/o Benjamin L. Canney (Rochester, flagman) and Ella M. Hoyt (Barrington); W - 18, at home, b. Farmington, d/o Herbert E. Tanner (Farmington, farmer) and Marie E. Devaney (Ireland)

CAPEN,
Ralph L., Sr. of Milton m. Christina M. **Capen** of Milton 10/22/1988 in Rochester

CAPLETTE,
Norman E. of Rochester m. Deborah L. **Nason** of Milton 9/15/1982 in Rochester

CAREY,
Daniel M. of Milton m. Michele J. **Batiste** of Milton 6/10/1989

CARIGNAN,
Roger M. of Somersworth m. Candise E. **Pressimone** of Milton Mills 10/28/1967 in Sanbornville; H - 26, truck driver; W - 18, machine oper.

CARMICHAEL,
George E. of Greenwich, CT m. Helen G. **Fox** of Milton 12/25/1912; H - 37, teacher, b. Rockville, MA, s/o James T. Carmichael (Pixton, NS)

and Susan Roberts (PEI); W - 31, b. Milton, d/o Everett F. Fox (Acton, ME, merchant) and Carrie B. Ricker (Somersworth)

CARPENTER,
Harold of Milton m. Ethel R. **Randlett** of E. Lebanon, ME 10/30/1931 in Dover; H - 23, bookkeeper, b. Rollinsford, s/o John Carpenter (Somersworth, shoemaker) and Annie M. Jenkins (Stoneham, MA); W - 19, at home, b. Littleton, d/o Charles W. Randlett (Somersworth, storekeeper) and Ida Condon (NS, housewife)
John H. of Milton m. Lydia M. **Dixon** of Milton 11/16/1914; H - 29, shoemaker, 2nd, b. S. Berwick, ME, s/o Ernest L. Carpenter (Portland, ME, carpenter) and Jennie V. Hooper (Portland, ME); W - 22, shoe stitcher, b. Winchester, MA, d/o Oscar B. Dixon (Milton, laborer) and Nellie F. Doe (Ossipee)
John H. of Milton m. Louise C. **Burbank** of Milton 12/7/1931; H - 46, shoeworker, 3rd, b. S. Berwick, ME, s/o Ernest Carpenter (S. Berwick, ME, carpenter) and Jennie I. Hooper (Woodsfords, ME, housewife); W - 28, housekeeper, b. Milton, d/o Harry L. Burbank (Parsonsfield, ME, laborer) and Sophronia Dunnells (Newfield, ME, housewife)
Joseph W., Jr. of Ipswich, MA m. Gloria A. **Belanger** of W. Lebanon, ME 8/1/1992
Roland of Milton m. Hazel B. **Trumbull** of Milton 2/27/1923; H - 28, laborer, b. Rollinsford, s/o Ernest Carpenter (Rollinsford, carpenter) and Jennie Eager (Portland, ME); W - 18, domestic, b. Webster, d/o Arthur Trumbull (Gilmanton, laborer) and Junie Woods (Sunapee)

CARR,
James W., Jr. of Milton m. Deborah G. **Burns** of Milton 11/12/1994
Walter C. of Milton m. Emma F. **Dorr** of Milton 8/13/1904 in Rochester; H -60, fruit dealer, 3rd, b. Holderness, s/o Jacob Carr (Holderness) and Harriet Beede (Gilmanton); W - 40, shoe stitcher, b. Milton, d/o Stephen D. Dorr (Milton, farmer) and Melvina Staples (Farmington)

CARROLL,
Joseph P. of Limerick, ME m. Marguerite **Remick** of Milton 5/28/1938 in Sanbornville; H - 27, mill worker, b. England, d/o William T. Carroll (England, mill worker) and Marion Fox (Ireland, deceased);

W - 21, at home, b. Milton, d/o Arthur Remick (Tamworth, laborer) and Angie E. Page (Milton, deceased)

CARSON,
Leon M. of Milton m. Hazel D. **Ricker** of Rochester 12/31/1922 in Exeter; H - 23, mill operative, b. Milton, s/o John M. Carson (Milton, farmer) and Eva M. Postleton (Acton, ME); W - 32, tel. supervisor, b. Rochester, d/o John S. Ricker (Milton, farmer) and Augusta R. Tappan (Sandwich)

CARSWELL,
Fred E. of Milton m. Frances E. **Ayer** of Milton 2/4/1914 in Manchester; H - 22, druggist, b. Denver, CO, s/o Luther E. Carswell (foreman brass finisher, Manchester) and Jennie E. Titus (Manchester); W - 21, telephone op'r, b. Newfield, ME, d/o Harry E. Ayer (Newfield, ME, expressman) and Charlotte Hanscom (New York City)
Fred E. of Milton Mills m. Natalie B. **Ahearn** of Milton Mills 10/25/1969; H - b. 7/1/1925; W - b. 6/26/1920
Peter A. of Milton m. Dawn E. **Worden** of Dover 9/19/1964 in Rochester; H - 23, draftsman; W - 21, IBM operator

CARTER,
Duncan E. of Milton m. Laura A. **Baldasaro** of Milton 10/8/1988 in Newfields

CASEY,
Robert H. of Milton m. Grace L. **Horne** of Milton 8/7/1948; H - 20, woodsman, b. Boston, MA, s/o William E. Casey (Ireland, farmer) and Hazel Emery (N. Gloucester, ME, stitcher); W - 22, secretary, b. Milton, d/o Raymond F. Horne (Milton, Navy Yard) and Eva McIntire (Rochester, office worker)

CASSELL,
Peter of Roxbury, MA m. Agatha C. **Armstead** of West Lebanon, ME 6/21/1975; H - b. 9/18/1895; W - b. 9/2/1903

CATE,
Aaron J. of Milton m. Mary E. **Wentworth** of Milton 10/27/1904; H - 31, machinist, b. Salem, MA, s/o Adoniram J. Cate (Haverhill, MA) and

Henrietta W. Batchelder (Salem, MA); W - 38, lady, b. Milton, d/o John A. Wentworth (Milton) and Hannah E. Gray (Strafford)

Aaron J. of Milton m. Maud E. **Hamilton** of Gouldsboro, ME 8/5/1943 in Ellsworth, ME; H - 69, 2nd, s/o Adoniram J. Cate (Haverhill, MA, watchmaker) and Henrietta Batchelder (Salem, MA, housekeeper); W - 65, 2nd, d/o Lindsey Tracey (Gouldsboro, ME, farmer) and Eliza Stevens (Rockland, ME, housekeeper)

Harry R. of Rochester m. Norma M. **Willey** of Milton 3/26/1943; H - 26, US Army, b. Gray, ME, s/o Raymond M. Cate (Brookfield, fireman) and Mertie Small (Gray, ME, deceased); W - 20, shoe worker, b. Milton, d/o Leon M. Willey (Brookfield, Navy Yard) and Flora M. Downs (Milton, Navy Yard)

CATHCART,

Herbert of Farmington m. Pauline **Laney** of New Durham 11/20/1937 in Alton; H - 25, pipe f. helper, b. Farmington, s/o Fred Cathcart (Farmington, unknown) and Bernice Haddock (Farmington, shoe worker); W - 21, shoe stitcher, b. Alton, d/o George Laney (Skowhegan, ME, laborer) and Hazel Nutter (Dover, shoe stitch.)

CERNIAUSKAS,

Vytas A. of Milton m. Teresa L. **Bell** of Boothbay Harbor, ME 10/27/1990

CHALMERS,

Albert R. of Rochester m. Addie C. **Pike** of Milton 6/24/1914; H - 28, shoemaker, b. Rochester, s/o David Chalmers (Avon, Scotland, florist) and Mabel C. Cushing (Rochester); W - 30, clerk, b. Wakefield, d/o Freeman D. Pike (Brookfield, carpenter) and Sophia Ricker (Milton)

CHALOUX,

Daniel L. of Milton Mills m. Kelly A. **Charron** of Milton Mills 9/21/1985 in Wakefield

CHAMBERL[A]IN,

Ernest of Alton m. Winifred **Marsh** of Milton 2/14/1898; H - 20, shoemaker, b. Alton, s/o Charles H. Chamberlin (shoemaker); W - 19, weaver, b. Milton, d/o John E. Marsh

G. S. of Milton m. Hazel **Sheehan** of Bangor, ME 9/26/1931 in Dover; H - 22, mill worker, b. Milton, s/o Guy Chamberlain (Union, hospital wkr.) and Elizabeth Cunningham (Scotland, housewife); W - 20, at home, b. Bangor, ME, d/o Joseph Sheehan (Albany, NS, lumberman) and Eliza A. Smith (Hemison, PQ, housewife)

Guy H. of Milton m. Verna M. **Woodman** of Ossipee 8/27/1921 in Dover; H - 34, ice man, 2nd, b. Wakefield, s/o Fred M. Chamberlain (Milton, laborer) and Grace M. Dicey (Effingham); W - 17, domestic, b. Ossipee, d/o Fred Woodman (NS, laborer) and Etta M. Colby (Ossipee)

Henry E. of Lakeside, NE m. Annie H. **Wentworth** of Milton 4/18/1891; H - 20, stock grower, b. Union, s/o George W. (Brookfield, farmer) and Emily E. (Wakefield, housekeeper); W - 18, teacher, b. Milton, d/o Henry H. (Milton, truckman) and Louisa (Milton, housekeeper)

Telesphore of Milton m. Eugene **Marshall** of Manchester 6/23/1890 in Manchester; H - 23, teamster, b. Canada, s/o Joseph and Hermine; W - 20, mill operative, b. Canada, d/o Elzeare and Celanive

CHAMBERS,
Rodney R. of Milton Mills m. Ellen L. **Bussiere** of Berwick, ME 6/16/1979

CHAMPY,
David, II of Milton m. Laurie M. **Hill** of Milton 8/24/1996

CHANDLER,
Clarence E. of Acton, ME m. Mary E. **McDaniels** of Acton, ME 2/7/1914 in Acton, ME; H - 45, shoemaker, 2nd, b. Chicago, IL, s/o Jonathan Chandler (Chicago, IL) and Harriet McFarland (Scotland); W - 42, housekeeper, 2nd, b. East Wakefield, d/o Charles Sanborn (Wakefield) and Abbie Day (Wakefield)

CHAPDELAINE,
Normand J. of Gonic m. Eileen M. **Bartlett** of Milton 11/11/1972; H - b. 3/24/1944; W - b. 7/31/1947

CHAPIN,
Thomas S. of Milton m. Geraldine L. **Stillman** of Milton 10/20/1972; H - b. 11/26/1945; W - b. 5/10/1943

CHAPMAN,
Fred A. of Milton m. Eunice M. **Reagan** of Milton 3/3/1945 in Farmington; H - 39, fitter, 2nd, b. Haverhill, s/o Fred Chapman (Haverhill, fireman) and Harriett Heath (Corinth, VT, housewife); W - 30, shoe worker, 2nd, b. Sanbornville, d/o Bert Gilbert (painter) and Gretchen Waycott (Lynn, MA, housewife)

CHARTRAND,
Douglas J. of Sanford, ME m. Lucille S. **Poutry** of Sanford, ME 9/2/1967; H - 25, shipper; W - 27, grinder oper.

CHASE,
Charles E. of Milton m. Carol A. **Sullivan** of Milton 6/30/1979
George A. of Milton m. Lynette M. **Lindsay** of E. Kingston 9/3/1977 in Plaistow; H - b. 8/2/1946; W - b. 1/6/1951
James F. of Milton m. Wendy J. **Silvia** of Farmington 2/14/1981 in Rochester
James F. of Milton m. Kellie-Ann **Pomeroy** of Milton 7/14/1990 in Somersworth
Leslie O. of Milton m. Doris L. **Fortier** of Chocorua 5/20/1934 in Sanbornville; H - 23, shipper, b. E. Rochester, s/o George H. Chase (Cambridge, MA, shoe cutter) and Adeline Willey (Sanbornville, housewife); W - 22, school tchr., b. Chocorua, d/o Albert J. Fortier (Ossipee, road patrol) and Nellie W. Hobbs (Conway, housewife)
Leslie O., II of Milton m. Marilyn R. **Hoadley** of Farmington 7/19/1958 in Farmington; H - 23, Navy Yard, b. Rochester, s/o Leslie O. Chase (Rochester) and Doris Fortier (Chocorua); W - 20, bank teller, b. Concord, d/o J. Emery Hoadley (MA) and Virginia B. Douglas (Farmington)
Leslie O., III of Milton m. Wendy V. **Gagnon** of Newmarket 5/18/1985 in Newmarket
Mark G. of Milton m. Debra L. **Ferris** of Milton 2/14/1987
Richard W., III of Milton m. Joan E. **O'Brien** of Dover 11/6/1981
Timothy R. of Milton m. Debra J. **Fortin** of West Lebanon, ME; H - b. 11/13/1956; W - b. 11/24/1959

CHASSE,
Gilbert A. of Somersworth m. Gail E. **Columbus** of Milton 6/24/1961 in Rochester; H - 22, Navy Yard; W - 21, office work

CHENEY,
Donald A. of Milton m. Dianne L. **Varney** of Milton 9/23/1961; H - 20, cons't; W - 19, shoe shop

Walter L. of Milton m. Valena M. **Ellis** of Milton 8/12/1922 in Rochester; H - 23, laborer, b. Rochester, s/o Arthur Cheney (Halifax, NS, laborer) and Marie Duchane (Berwick, ME); W - 18, shoe stitcher, b. Milton, d/o Robert E. Ellis (Milton, machine tender) and Nettie M. Dyer (Sanbornville)

CHESLEY,
Charles F. of Alton m. Ada **Johnson** of Milton 12/24/1904 in Rochester; H - 30, shoemaker, 2nd, b. Barnstead, s/o Herbert L. Chesley (Barnstead, farmer) and Ida F. Pickering (Barnstead); W - 23, housekeeper, b. Wolfeboro, d/o Frank Johnson (Wolfeboro, farmer) and Elizabeth Sanborn (Gilmanton)

Christopher J. of Milton m. Lynn M. **Boles** of Milton 10/5/1996

CHIARELLA,
John J. of Sunapee m. Maureen E. **Rodrigue** of Milton Mills 8/22/1987

CHICK,
Brian S. of Wakefield m. Barbara **Eugley** of Milton 7/16/1974 in Milton Mills; H - b. 5/14/1956; W - b. 12/28/1955

Everett A. of Rochester m. Abbie B. **Randall** of Rochester 9/8/1923; H - 52, carpenter, 2nd, b. Shapleigh, ME, s/o Winslow O. Chick (Shapleigh, ME, shoemaker) and Sarah A. Murray (Shapleigh, ME); W - 52, shoe stitcher, 2nd, b. Shapleigh, ME, d/o Samuel Batchelder (Shapleigh, ME, farmer) and Lucy Trafton (Shapleigh, ME)

CHORBA,
Stephen J., Jr. of Milton m. Cheryl A. **Morrill** of Milton 7/20/1991

CHRISTENSEN,
George of Westerly, RI m. Grace M. **Olsen** of Westerly, RI 9/2/1933; H - 33, steel worker, b. Penn Yan, NY, s/o Martin Christensen (Denmark, farmer) and Mary Jensen (Denmark, at home); W - 37, upholsterer, 2nd, b. Goshen, VT, d/o Edward Baker (For't Dale, VT, farmer) and Emma A. Madison (Rutland, VT, at home)

CICCOTELLI,
Paul S. of Milton m. Joyce E. **Cook** of Milton 7/12/1987

CILLEY,
Irving H. of Milton Mills m. Lena J. **Sidney** of Milton Mills 12/31/1946 in Sanford, ME; H - 57, tex. overseer, 3rd, b. NH, s/o Anthony Cilley (NH, deceased) and Rosetta Foss (ME, housewife); W - 52, housewife, 2nd, b. D. Green, VT, d/o George E. Rollins (deceased) and Blanche Darcy (Cabot, VT, deceased)

CLARK,
John J. of Milton m. Christine L. **Honnon** of Milton 3/21/1986
T. H. of Haverhill, MA m. Nellie B. **Perkins** of Haverhill, MA 11/12/1894; H - 24, shoemaker, b. Rossep't, NY, s/o W. A. Clark (Rossep't, NY, wheelwright) and Charlotte; W - 21, lady, b. Waterboro, ME
Thomas E. of East Moline, IL m. Sherry L. **Velkovich** of Milton 12/25/1964; H - 23, US Navy; W - 19, factory worker
Walter C. of Dover, MA m. Mary A. **Batchelder** of Boston, MA 10/26/1899; H - 50, carpenter, 2nd, b. Barre, MA, s/o Nelson Clark; W - 51, lady, 2nd, b. Wolfeboro, d/o John C. Corliss

CLAY,
Bradley T. of Milton m. Mechelle A. **Genest** of Milton 6/28/1986

CLAYTON,
George W. of East Rochester m. Emma V. **Columbus** of Milton 6/17/1912; H - 26, shoe cutter, b. Truro, NS, s/o James G. Clayton (NS, farmer) and Minnie Patton (NS); W - 21, shoe stitcher, b. Milton, d/o Odilon Columbus (Quebec, Canada, farmer) and Malvina Hall (Milton)

CLEAVES,
Frank H. of Milton m. Alta D. **Chipman** of Milton 9/3/1916; H - 23, machinist, b. Milton, MA, s/o Thomas L. Cleaves (Mattapan, MA, carpenter) and Mary E. McNamara (Dorchester, MA); W - 20, bookkeeper, b. Milton, d/o Edward S. Chipman (Natick, MA, leatherboard finisher) and Mary B. Drew (Milton)

James S. of Milton m. Marie **Tanner** of Lebanon, ME 4/4/1931 in Berwick, ME; H - 23, hot house, b. Lynn, MA, s/o Benjamin Cleaves (Beverly, MA, motorman) and Flossy Jones (Lynn, MA, housewife); W - 17, at home, b. Lebanon, ME, d/o Herbert Tanner (Farmington, farmer) and Marie Devaney (Ireland, housewife)

James S. of Milton m. Marguerite **Titcomb** of Farmington 9/22/1944 in Wolfeboro; H - 37, garage mech., 2nd, b. Lynn, MA, s/o Benjamin B. Cleaves (Beverly, MA, retired) and Flossie H. Jones (Lynn, MA, at home); W - 24, shoe worker, b. W. Newbury, MA, d/o Charles L. Titcomb (W. Newbury, MA, carpenter) and Charlotte M. Gile (Conway, at home)

CLEMENT,

Charles of Milton m. Hattie **Goodwin** of Farmington 7/6/1894 in Wakefield; H - 23, spinner, b. Victory, VT, s/o James Clement (farmer) and Annie; W - 20, lady, b. Milton, d/o Benjamin Goodwin (Lebanon, ME, farmer) and Augusta

James W. of Milton m. Laura **King** of Acton, ME 7/22/1893 in Wakefield; H - 19, spinner, b. Gorham, s/o James Clement (farmer) and Annie; W - 18, weaver, b. St. Johnsbury, VT, d/o Jonathan King (farmer) and Annie

CLEMENTS,

Hanson E. of Milton m. Mattie B. **Keyes** of Milton 11/25/1896; H - 44, carpenter, 2nd, b. Berwick, ME, s/o Hanson (Berwick, ME) and Lydia (Berwick, ME); W - 39, shoe stitcher, 2nd, b. Farmington, d/o Paul (Farmington) and Melinda A. Twombly (Rochester)

John B. of Milton m. Addie M. **Houghton** of Nashua 6/16/1903; H - 39, farmer, 2nd, b. Milton, s/o Leander Clements (Milton, farmer) and Susan Stevens (Tuftonboro); W - 33, seamstress, 2nd, b. Groton, MA, d/o William P. Lee (Douglas, MA) and Rhodia M. Bryant (Irasburg, VT)

CLEVELAND,

Raymond of Milton m. Lucille **Pontbriand** of Dover 5/28/1943 in Dover; H - 22, machine oper., b. Milton, s/o Willard Cleveland (Otisfield, ME, machinist) and Ruth O. Stillings (Boston, MA, housewife); W - 22, machine oper., b. Dexter, ME, d/o Henry Pontbriand (Nashua, machinist) and Josephine M. Deay (Dover-Foxcroft, ME, housewife)

Willard C. of Milton m. Ruth O. **Stillings** of Milton 8/20/1919 in Rochester; H - 20, shoemaker, b. Otisfield, ME, s/o John A. Cleveland (Otisfield, ME, mill hand) and Elizabeth A. Walker (Lynn, MA); W - 18, bookkeeper, b. Boston, MA, d/o Charles O. Stillings (Ossipee, mill hand) and Susie F. Newell (West Head, NS)

Willard C. of Milton m. Louise C. **Carpenter** of Milton 11/8/1951 in East Rochester; H - 52, machinist, 2nd, b. Otisfield, ME, s/o John A. Cleveland (Otisfield, ME) and Elizabeth Walker (Lynn, MA); W - 48, housekeeper, 2nd, b. Milton, d/o Harry L. Burbank (Newfield, ME) and Sophronia Dunnels (Newfield, ME)

CLICHE,
Stephen P. of Somersworth m. Diane L. **Hobbs** of Milton 7/6/1974 in Rochester; H - b. 4/4/1954; W - b. 10/3/1956

CLIFFORD,
Gregory L. of Milton m. Karin A. **Stella** of Milton 1/1/1990

CLOUGH,
David J. of Milton Mills m. Terri L. **Goodwin** of Milton 5/19/1972; H - b. 2/19/1951; W - b. 11/12/1953

Fred E. of Milton m. Janette E. **Huard** of Shapleigh, ME 11/20/1948 in N. Shapleigh, ME; H - 24, b. Milton Mills, s/o Warren Clough (Effingham, weaver) and Margaret Weeks (Milton Mills, weaver); W - 20, at home, 2nd, b. Shapleigh, ME, d/o Kenneth Houston (Sanford, ME, overseer) and Evelyne Sciggell (Gorham, ME, housewife)

Fred E., Jr. of Milton Mills m. Rebecca **Nason** of Union 12/23/1972; H - b. 1/27/1952; W - b. 1/7/1954

Gerald H. of Milton Mills m. Joanne M. **Beaulieu** of Gilford 9/25/1999

Herbert E. of Milton m. Colleen J. **Morrill** of Wakefield 7/15/1950 in Wakefield; H - 20, mill emp., b. NH, s/o Warren Clough (NH) and Marguerite Weeks (NH); W - 16, at home, b. NH, d/o Harry W. Morrill (NH) and Phyllis L. Grant (NH)

Jon M. of Milton m. Christine I. **Spinney** of Milton 6/29/1996

Leon E. of Milton m. Eleanor L. **Gordon** of Milton 9/20/1947 in Acton, ME; H - 25, logger, b. Milton, s/o Warren C. Clough (Effingham, weaver) and Marguerite Weeks (Milton, housewife); W - 19, at home, b. Acton, ME, d/o Almon F. Gordon (Shapleigh, ME, fireman) and Nellie Cronin (Acton, ME, housewife)

Warren C. of Effingham m. Marguerite D. **Weeks** of Milton 12/24/1921 in Milton Mills; H - 21, mill hand, b. Effingham, s/o Fred E. Clough (Wolfeboro, lumberman) and Dillie B. Chick (Effingham); W - 13, weaver, b. Milton, d/o Frank S. Weeks (Porter, ME, physician) and Minnie L. Alley (Kezar Falls, ME)

Warren C. of Milton m. Grace L. **Twombley** of E. Rochester 6/25/1967 in E. Rochester; H - 66, retired; W - 76, retired

COATE,
Michael W. of Milton m. Lois M. **Peterson** of Milton 3/25/1995

COFFEY,
Michael A. of Milton m. Athena L. **Anderson** of Milton 12/13/1985

COHEN,
Donald S. of Peekskill, NY m. Carolyn L. **Bruce** of Milton 3/6/1976; H - b. 10/13/1950; W - b. 3/17/1952

COLBATH,
Robert N., III of Milton m. Priscilla E. **Lodge** of W. Lebanon, ME 7/1/1967 in Sanbornville; H - 20, clerk; W - 20, receptionist

William E. of Lebanon, ME m. Grace L. **Champion** of Lebanon, ME 6/10/1909; H - 30, clerk, 2nd, wid., b. Lebanon, ME, s/o John Colbath (Lebanon, ME, farmer) and Elmira Emery (Sanford, ME); W - 26, housekeeper, b. Milton, d/o Clarence Champion (Effingham) and Ella M. Quimby (Newfield, ME)

COLBROTH,
Steven P., Sr. of Milton m. Katherine A. **Jarest** of Milton 9/5/1987

COLBY,
Barry A. of Rochester m. Christine M. **Ronayne** of Milton 3/12/1977; H - b. 10/3/1957; W - b. 9/1/1957

George E. of East Bridgewater, MA m. Sandra J. **Bill** of Milton 8/14/1971; H - b. 2/7/1949; W - b. 7/15/1951

COLE,
John B. of Milton m. Marion L. **Emerson** of Milton 4/19/1980

Tracy L. of Milton m. Tracey A. **Wiseman** of Rochester 8/4/1997

COLELL,
Michael P. of Milton m. M. M. **McCarthy** of Dover 9/15/1948 in Farmington; H - 35, salesman, 2nd, b. Dover, s/o Peter Colell (Syria, salesman) and Annie Kamel (Syria, housewife); W - 27, housewife, b. Dover, d/o Cornelius McCarthy (Ireland, highway worker) and Margaret Austin (Dover, housewife)

COLEMAN,
Glenn R. of Milton m. Deanna G. **Butler** of Milton 8/28/1977; H - b. 6/6/1956; W - b. 8/18/1958

COLLINS,
Brian A. of Milton m. Pauline L. **Ellis** of Milton 2/16/1985
Ernest L. of Lebanon, ME m. Eunice L. **Sawyer** of Lebanon, ME 5/24/1924; H - 23, teamster, b. Alton, s/o James Z. Collins (Alton, painter) and Alice Hatch (Augusta, ME); W - 20, telephone op., b. Lebanon, ME, d/o Eugene A. Sawyer (Wolfeboro, papermaker) and Mary J. Yeaton (Wolfeboro)
Jake M. of Rochester m. Thelma L. **Columbus** of Milton 11/30/1963; H - 26, teacher; W - 23, teacher
James Z. of Milton m. Van Etta B. **Young** of Newington 11/11/1933; H - 59, painter, 2nd, b. Alton, s/o Lewis D. Collins (farmer) and Mary H. Young (Alton, housewife); W - 60, housekeeper, 2nd, b. Belfast, ME, d/o Phineas Moody (Belfast, ME, horseman) and Lucy Ann Lawton (Searsmont, ME, housewife)
Norman A. of Milton m. Janet L. **Chick** of Milton 7/1/1983
Patrick V. of Milton m. Jennifer R. **Adams** of Dover 6/28/1986 in Dover

COLSON,
David J. of Milton m. Sheila B. **Callaghan** of Rochester 7/25/1992

COLUMBUS [see Coulombe],
Albert H. of Milton m. Marjorie M. **Benner** of Milton 8/18/1934 in Farmington; H - 24, laborer, b. Milton, s/o Odilon Columbus (Canada, farmer) and Melvina Hall (Milton, housewife); W - 19, at home, b. Boston, MA, d/o Howard Benner (Eastport, ME, mill emp.) and Esther J. Hurd (Portland, ME, housewife)
Albert H. of Milton m. Jeanne **Glasz** of Rochester 4/4/1970; H - b. 7/1/1910; W - b. 3/18/1917

Arthur N. of Milton m. Esther J. **Benner** of Milton 12/2/1933 in Farmington; H - 46, truckman, 2nd, b. Acton, ME, s/o Odilon Columbus (Canada, farmer) and Melvina Hall (Milton Mills, housewife); W - 36, housekeeper, 2nd, b. Portland, ME, d/o Arthur E. Hurd (Rochester, shoemaker) and Cora Gray (Farmington, housewife)

Reynold of Milton m. Florence **Rheault** of Somersworth 9/22/1939 in Berwick, ME; H - 29, truck driver, b. Somersworth, s/o Arthur Columbus (Acton, ME, truckman) and Flora Boisvert (Somersworth, housewife); W - 19, milll oper., b. Berwick, ME, d/o Jeffrey Rheault (Canada, laborer) and Eva Lemelin (S. Berwick, ME, housewife)

COMEAU,
Herbert J., Jr. of E. Lebanon, ME m. Leah B. **Gonthier** of Berwick, ME 2/17/1991

COMPTON,
William F. of Milton m. Etta **Hadlock** of Manchester 10/18/1913 in Manchester; H - 45, carpenter, 2nd, b. Saco, ME, s/o William F. Compton (NJ) and Mary J. Wood (Saco, ME), W - 43, housework, 2nd, b. Troy, VT, d/o James Lake (Richford, VT) and Maria E. Lake (Richford, VT)

CONDON,
Franklin A., III of Milton m. Patricia M. **Dugan** of Rochester 2/13/1993

CONGRAM,
Timothy E. of Milton m. Betty J. **Tufts** of Milton 6/30/1979

CONNOLLY,
Timothy of Milton Mills m. Mary J. **Hawksworth** of Milton Mills 2/16/1933 in Milton Mills; H - 76, painter, 2nd, b. Wakefield, s/o Timothy Connolly (Ireland) and Annie Trindles (Ireland); W - 74, at home, 2nd, b. Acton, ME, d/o Lyman R. Buzzell (Acton, ME) and Jane Lord (Shapleigh, ME)

CONRAD,
David P., Jr. of Milton m. Lee A. **Walk** of Milton 9/18/1999

CONTOIS,
Carl M. of Grafton m. Arlene M. **Abbott** of Milton 5/31/1958 in W. Lebanon; H - 24, teacher, b. Lebanon, s/o Aurele Contois (NH) and Victoria Dutile (VT); W - 23, teacher, b. Ossipee, d/o Clifton Abbott (NH) and Alice Miles (NS)

COOK,
Dennis C. of Milton m. Deena L. **Boyle** of Milton 9/14/1994
James E. of Milton m. Melissa L. **Perkins** of Milton 9/9/1989 in Barrington
Raymond N. of Dover m. Merle L. **Fereira** of Milton 5/22/1983 in Conway
Walter E., Jr. of Milton m. Maureen **Merner** of Newton 4/12/1985 in Newton

COOKE,
Chester E., III of Salem, MA m. Rose A. **MacDonald** of Milton 1/25/1975 in Sanbornville; H - b. 10/1/1957; W - b. 1/23/1956

COOPER,
Dale H. of Milton m. Sarah R. **Brown** of Milton 3/20/1982 in Rochester
Dale H. of Milton Mills m. Patricia A. **Swanson** of Milton Mills 5/20/1995

COPE,
David P. of Rochester m. Julie M. **Haskins** of Milton Mills 8/18/1984
Edward D. of Milton m. Marilyn A. **Stubbs** of Milton 12/24/1989

COPP,
Thomas B. of Milton m. Josephine **Rouleau** of Milton 1/1/1942; H - 21, mill worker, b. Ctr. Ossipee, s/o Maynard D. Copp (Orrington, ME, garage owner) and Nora F. Eldridge (Center Ossipee, shoe worker); W - 19, shoe worker, b. Milton, d/o Louis H. Rouleau (Lebanon, ME, mill worker) and Josephine Burbine (Wakefield, MA, housewife)
William R. of Rochester m. Beverly A. **Pierce** of Milton 5/27/1967; H - 18, factory worker; W - 19, at home

CORBIN,
Bruce J. of Milton m. Terri L. **Truman** of Milton 8/15/1998

CORINDON,
Stanley A. of Milton m. Hefreda M. **Smith** of Milton 11/23/1950 in Wolfeboro; H - 40, plumber, b. Rochester, s/o Unknown and Jennie Judd; W - 21, housewife, b. Rochester, d/o William A. Smith (Alton) and Iona B. Knight (VT)

CORLISS,
Richard L. of Somersworth m. Charlotte R. **Douglas** of Milton 10/16/1965 in Piermont; W - 23, tannery wk.; W - 20, shoe worker

CORMIER,
Dale G. of Milton m. Deborah A. **LaBrie** of Milton 8/11/1990 in Dover
Jeffrey C. J. of Milton m. Sandra **Berge** of Rollinsford 6/4/1988 in Somersworth
Richard E. of Milton m. Carol A. **Dustin** of Milton 12/19/1970 in Conway; H - b. 11/19/1929; W - b. 6/25/1939

CORNELISSEN,
Ronald F. of Milton Mills m. Cynthia M. **Hart** of Milton Mills 2/14/1998

CORSON,
George N. of Milton m. Bessie M. **Laskey** of Milton 11/10/1910; H - 28, clerk, b. Milton, s/o George M. Corson (Lebanon, ME, laborer) and Draxa H. Pierce (Lebanon, ME); W - 20, housekeeper, b. Milton, d/o Allie J. Laskey (Milton, farmer) and Rose A. Barker (New Vineyard, ME)
John M. of Milton m. Eva M. **Postleton** of Milton 4/11/1896; H - 23, shoe cutter, b. Milton, s/o George M. (Lebanon, ME, RR foreman) and Draca (Lebanon, ME); W - 19, housekeeper, b. Acton, ME, d/o Joseph H. (Providence, RI) and Francina (Acton, ME)
Leo H. of Milton m. Nellie M. **Thompson** of Rochester 4/11/1926 in Rochester; H - 27, foreman, b. Milton, s/o John M. Corson (Milton, farmer) and Eva M. Postleton (Acton, ME); W - 32, stenographer, b. St. Elizabeth, NJ, d/o Fred H. Thompson (Hartford, CT, car. painter) and Georgianna Farr (Orange, NJ)
Ronald N. of Milton m. Sheila M. **Haselton** of Rochester 11/4/1955 in Acton, ME; H - 26, laborer, b. Derry, s/o Draxa Corson; W - 20, housewife, b. Rochester, d/o William Haselton and Marie Tanner

CORT,
Alan R. of Milton Mills m. Rhonda M. **Wallace** of Milton Mills 7/19/1997

COSTA,
Alexander J. of Penacook m. Barbara S. **Atherton** of Milton 11/12/1949 in Wakefield; H - 32, b. Penacook, s/o Alexander J. Costa (Albania) and Mary Vassalion (Albania); W - 25, at home, 3rd, b. Franklin, d/o Otis F. Ayer (NH) and Florence M. Brayley (NH)

COSTER,
Donald R. of Milton m. Betty J. **Eastman** of Milton 6/21/1975 in Barnstead; H - b. 6/4/1938; W - b. 12/29/1946

COTTON,
Benjamin D. of Milton m. Phebe **Ham** of Milton 6/6/1895; H - 38, laborer, b. Milton, s/o Richard R. (Lebanon, ME, laborer); W - 23, housekeeper, b. Rochester, d/o Luke Tibbetts (Sanford, ME, housekeeper)

COUCH,
Randy W. of Milton m. Misty J. **Fisher** of Milton 8/25/1990 in Wolfeboro

COULOMBE,
Arthur N. of Milton m. Flora **Boisvert** of Somersworth 5/31/1909 in Somersworth; H - 21, shoemaker, b. Milton, s/o Odilon Coulombe (Canada, farmer) and Melvina Haule (Canada); W - 23, weaver, b. Somersworth, d/o George Boisvert (Canada, stone mason) and Marie Rouleau (Canada)

COUTURE,
Andre P. of Milton m. Simone O. **Couture** of Milton 2/20/1983
Earl D. of Milton m. Christine I. **Gregg** of Milton 6/15/1996
Ernest P., Jr. of Milton m. Jennifer A. **Randall** of Milton 11/15/1991

COVELL,
Mark D. of Milton m. Marlene C. **Boyle** of Milton 6/22/1991

COWAN,
Wayne B. of Milton m. Janice N. **Connell** of Milton 5/1/1983

COWELL,
Allen E. of Lebanon, ME m. Sarah I. **Hayes** of Lebanon, ME 4/19/1900 in Rochester; H - 37, farmer, b. Lebanon, ME, s/o Edmund E. Cowell (Beverly, MA) and Elizabeth J. Chamberlin (Milton); W - 33, lady, b. Lebanon, ME, d/o Cyrus W. Hayes (Lebanon, ME, farmer) and Lydia Furbush (Lebanon, ME)

COX,
Timothy P. of Marcy, NY m. Deborah L. **Cox** of Marcy, NY 6/21/1986

CREPEAU,
Peter O. J. of Portland, ME m. Rita J. **Boyle** of Portland, ME 6/30/1967; H - 20, US Army; W - 19, laborer

CROMEENES,
Darryl J. of Milton m. Debbie **Lee** of Milton 5/14/1988 in Dover

CRONIN,
John J. of Park Ridge, IL m. Theresa Y. **Vachon** of Milton 9/2/1950; H - 22, salesman, b. IL, s/o Frank J. Cronin (Lockport, IL) and Marguerite Owens (Chicago, IL); W - 21, receptionist, b. Milton, d/o Emile Vachon (Somersworth) and Emma Custeau (Milton)

CRUMP,
Bernard R., Jr. of Plattsburgh, NY m. Sherry L. **Cooper** of Milton 7/14/1990

CUMMER,
Brian L. of Jackson, MI m. Kerry A. **Buchanan** of Milton 10/29/1994

CUMMINGS,
Albert of Milton m. Lizzie **Remick** of Milton 8/31/1889; H - 26, shoemaker, b. MA, s/o Eustace (MA) and Angie (MA); W - 23, shoe stitcher, b. Milton, d/o Charles

Thomas F. of Milton m. Margaret F. **Doran** of Milton 9/7/1901; H - 40, laborer, 2nd, b. Ireland, s/o Thomas F. Cummings and Bridget Casey;

W - 38, housekeeper, 2nd, b. England, d/o Thomas Doran and Julia Brophy

William P. of Milton m. Helen L. **Held** of Rochester 8/22/1999

CURLL,

John E. of Milton m. Helen E. **Burbine** of Milton 8/30/1922 in Farmington; H - 21, laborer, b. Lunenburg, NS, d/o Leander Curll (Lunenburg, NS, laborer) and Lucy Veniotte (Mahone, NS); W - 17, at home, b. Wakefield, MA, d/o John Burbine (Argyle, NS, foreman) and Margaret Muse (Quinnin, NS)

CURRIE,

John M. M. of Auburn, ME m. Margaret P. **Patterson** of Milton 6/8/1898; H - 23, salesman, b. Bay City, s/o John J. Currie (Strathray, ON, salesman); W - 20, lady, b. Minden, IA, d/o John Patterson (Scotland, miller)

CURRIER,

Joseph of Milton m. Edna G. **Nason** of Acton, ME 6/29/1929 in East Rochester; H - 32, laborer, b. Ossipee, s/o Joseph Currier (Canada, laborer) and Delia Mattress (Ossipee); W - 30, at home, b. Acton, ME, d/o Elmer E. Nason (Acton, ME, farmer) and Abbie L. Abbott (Shapleigh, ME)

Lawrence L. of Milton m. Mary S. **Long** of Milton 10/22/1949; H - 22, mechanic, b. Milton, s/o Henry S. Currier (RI) and Elfreda Bragg (ME); W - 18, at home, b. Wolfeboro, d/o Dennis W. Long (ME) and Virginia LaCross (VT)

Mark R. of Milton Mills m. Deborah A. **Moore** of Milton 8/14/1982 in Atkinson

Michael F. of Milton m. Kathleen M. **Taatjes** of Milton 11/9/1996

CURRY,

William S. of Milton m. Hattie **Clement** of Milton 10/11/1899 in Acton, ME; H - 22, shoemaker, b. Stratham, s/o John T. Curry (Stratham, carpenter); W - 21, shoe stitcher, 2nd, b. Acton, ME, d/o Benjamin Goodwin (Norway, ME, painter)

CURTIS,
Reginald W. of Milton m. Pauline **Emerson** of Rochester 1/19/1940 in Berwick, ME; H - 33, shoe worker, 2nd, b. Farmington, s/o William B. Curtis (Farmington, ME, retired) and Bessie J. Gilman (Hallowell, ME, housewife); W - 22, stenographer, b. Berwick, ME, d/o Cleon H. Emerson (Berwick, ME, com. artist) and Ruth Crampsey (Beverly, MA, nurse)

CUSHING,
Arthur R. of Milton m. Michelle R. **Rennebu** of Dover 9/14/1996

CUSTEAU,
Aldege of Milton m. Lizzie **Blouin** of Milton 3/6/1905 in Gonic; H - 28, RR employee, b. Canada, s/o George Custeau (Canada, lumberman) and Mary Marcoux (Canada); W - 23, shoe stitcher, b. Canada, d/o Onesime Blouin (Canada, farmer) and Phelomen Beson (Canada)

CUTTER,
Mearl L. of Farmington m. Norma M. **Drew** of Milton 6/20/1953; H - 22, lumbering, b. Orange, MA, s/o Frank M. Cutter and Margaret Phillips; W - 21, shoe worker, b. Pittsfield, d/o Dwight Drew and Eunice Downs

D'ANNA,
Robert A. of Milton m. Carol A. **Parks** of Milton 8/24/1989 in Portsmouth

DADMUN,
Carl F. of Cambridge, MA m. Luella C. **Seltsam** of Milton 2/2/1941; H - 22, meat cutter, b. Allston, MA, s/o Alex Dadmun (Baltimore, MD, deceased) and Elizabeth L. Guilford (Thornton, nurse); W - 23, nurse, b. E. Foxboro, MA, d/o Fred L. Seltsam (Hartford, CT, conductor) and Luella Burke (Shelton, CT, housewife)

DADSON,
Cleon M. of Medford, MA m. Mabel D. **Davis** of Medford, MA 1/12/1956; H - 70, retired, 2nd, b. NY, s/o John Dadson and Addie Bain; W - 62, housewife, 2nd, b. NB, d/o George L. Dinsmore and Annie Ferguson

DAIGLE,
Jerome N. of Milton m. Sherolyn A. **Bourgoine** of Milton 11/11/1983

DALE,
Robert D. of Freeport, ME m. Lynda B. **Tabor** of Bath, ME 8/11/1962; H - 20, brdg. const.; W - 18, at home

DALEY,
George L., III of East Rochester m. June B. **Tufts** of Milton 2/9/1985

DALZELL,
Heath W. of Milton m. April D. **Damon** of Milton 9/4/1999

DAME,
Howard P. of Wakefield m. Elinore F. **Kraus** of Milton 8/13/1960 in Wakefield; H - 19, shoe worker; W - 18, shoe worker

DAMON,
James R. of Milton m. Kathie E. **Nason** of Wakefield 9/22/1972 in Union; H - b. 3/12/1951; W - b. 10/11/1951
Sheldon W. of Farmington m. Mary E. **Garnett** of Milton 12/16/1948 in Rochester; H - 18, shoe worker, b. Meredith, s/o Sheldon Damon (Hancock, rest. owner) and Beatrice Chase (Ctr. Harbor, housewife); W - 19, at home, b. Rochester, d/o Raymond Garnett (E. Rochester, Navy Yard) and Isabel McBride (Watertown, NY, shoe worker)

DANA,
Frank A. of Lebanon, ME m. Grace F. **Horne** of Waterboro, ME 3/20/1911; H - 27, farmer, b. Alfred, ME, s/o James F. Dana (Middleton, farmer) and Idella Corson (Bridgton, ME); W - 18, housekeeper, b. Waterboro, ME, d/o Arthur Horne (Wakefield, lumber surveyor) and Ada Cook (Bethlehem)

DANIELSON,
Roger C. of Chelsea, MA m. Linda J. **Geyer** of Chelsea, MA 2/26/1972; H - b. 12/29/1945; W - b. 9/2/1950

DANIS,
Kurt J. of Rochester m. Dawn M. **Semprebon** of Milton 7/2/1988 in Rochester

DANSEREAU,
John D. of Brookfield m. Susan M. **Guilmette** of Milton 8/1/1992

DASKEY,
Michael W. of Milton m. Cindi A. **Robitille** of Rochester 12/3/1988 in Rochester

DAVIDSON,
Dineen M. of Somersworth m. Vicki M. **Rohwer** of Portsmouth 5/24/1991
John E. of Farmington m. Theresa L. **Stowell** of Milton 7/4/1954; H - 22, US Air Force, b. Dover, s/o Walter Davidson and Corinne Thurston; W - 19, at home, b. Rochester, d/o Leon C. Stowell and Mary J. Hall
John E., Jr. of Milton m. Wanda L. **Libby** of Milton 6/25/1983 in Somersworth

DAVIS,
Charles O. of Lebanon, ME m. Flora A. **Meserve** of Lebanon, ME 5/10/1896; H - 40, carpenter, 2nd, b. Conway, s/o Ozem (Gilford) and Elmira (Conway); W - 30, housekeeper, 2nd, b. Somerville, MA, d/o William and Elmira Merrow (Somerville, MA)
Daniel N. of Milton Mills m. Pearl E. **Joy** of Milton Mills 3/12/1966; H - 54, shaver; W - 43, tannery worker
Daniel R. of Milton Mills m. Barbara L. **Wallingford** of Charlestown 8/9/1968 in Rochester; H - 23; W - 21
Daniel R. of Milton m. Jacqueline A. **Keating** of Wakefield 7/1/1972 in Wakefield; H - b. 4/14/1945; W - b. 1/2/1950
Floyd Y. of Northfield m. Grace E. **Pike** of Milton Mills 12/23/1931 in Northfield; H - 34, weaver, b. Tilton, s/o Frank M. Davis (Laconia, weaver) and Eva J. Reed (Tilton, housewife); W - 27, housework, b. Wakefield, d/o David C. Pike (Middleton, butcher) and May Miller (Lawrence, MA, housework)
Frank M. of Milton m. Sadie **Shortridge** of Milton 12/24/1895; H - 29, shoe stitcher, b. Milton, s/o Sewell (Norwich, VT); W - 24, laborer, d/o George

Harry of Milton m. Clara E. **Hurd** of Milton 6/19/1920; H - 33, farmer, b. Harpoot, Armenia, s/o David Davis (Harpoot, Armenia, merchant) and Mary Stone (Harpoot, Armenia); W - 22, housekeeper, b. Farmington, d/o Will G. Hurd (Farmington, teamster) and Nellie E. Varney (Farmington)

Merton E. of Acton, ME m. Mary E. **Parsons** of Milton 5/29/1936 in Farmington; H - 20, emp. mill, b. Newfield, ME, s/o Frank E. Davis (Amesbury, MA, painter) and Rose Auger (Haverhill, MA, housewife); W - 31, bookkeeper, 2nd, b. Milton, d/o Jerome Regan (Ireland, emp. mill) and Mary A. Mahoney (Ireland, housewife)

Robert C. of Amherst m. Ann **Woodbury** of Milton 7/1/1950; H - 29, clerk, b. NY, s/o Roy W. Davis (CT) and Marietta Cowles (CT); W - 25, sec'y, b. NH, s/o William E. Woodbury (NH) and Doris Horne (NH)

Roger B. of Milton m. Janet F. **Rouleau** of Lebanon, ME 2/15/1957 in Rochester; H - 23, unemployed, b. Rochester, s/o Daniel Davis (Newfield, ME) and Helen Colby (Springvale, ME); W - 19, factory worker, b. Lebanon, ME, d/o Alfred Rouleau (Milton) and Helen Duquette (Milton)

Roger B. of Milton Mills m. Patricia L. **Forbes** of Milton Mills 11/13/1983 in Wakefield

Sidney B. of Sullivan m. Norma L. **Paul** of Milton 6/16/1951 in East Rochester; H - 24, forester, b. Keene, s/o Leston F. Davis (NH) and Bessie V. Barrett (NH); W - 24, teacher, b. Cranston, RI, d/o Joseph L. Paul (MA) and Angeline McNeil (RI)

Walter F. of Milton m. Debra A. **Grant** of Milton 1/2/1984 in Rochester

DAWSON,

Seth F. of Milton m. Ruth H. **Iovine** of Waco, TX 9/5/1936 in Rochester; H - 57, manufacturer, 3rd, b. Lawrence, MA, s/o Seth F. Dawson (England, manufacturer) and Lizzie A. Cutting (Potsdam, NY, housewife); W - 42, school tch., 3rd, b. Boston, MA, d/o Svante Swanson (Sweden, clergyman) and Hilda Lundgren (Sweden, housewife)

DAY,

Alden B. of Milton m. Sarah M. **Allen** of Brookfield 3/6/1909 in Brookfield; H - 20, emp. in mill, b. W. Newfield, ME, s/o John L. Day (W. Newfield, ME, farmer) and Susan Patch (W. Newfield,

ME); W - 20, emp. in mill, b. Brookfield, d/o Samuel M. Allen (Brookfield, farmer) and Emma Cummings (Brookfield)
Frank B. of Milton m. Addie F. **Hooper** of Acton, ME 10/19/1898; H - 30, shoemaker, b. Shapleigh, ME, s/o Benjamin Day (Waterboro, ME); W - 18, shoe stitcher, b. Acton, ME, d/o Charles F. Hooper (Brockton, MA, engineer)
Leslie F. of Milton m. Myrtle I. **Farnham** of Rochester 4/11/1931 in Rochester; H - 35, box mill, b. Milton, s/o Freeman Day (Porter, ME, teamster) and Esther Harnden (Denmark, ME, housewife); W - 32, stenographer, b. Rockland, ME, d/o Ansel Farnham (Rockland, ME, box mill) and Lizzie M. Brown (Rockland, ME, housewife)
Lewis J. of Milton m. Lizzie E. **Nason** of No. Berwick, ME 9/18/1890 in Somersworth; H - 23, teamster, b. Lyman, ME, s/o Porter (Alfred, ME, farmer) and Mary A. (Wells, ME, dead); W - 20, weaver, b. Lyman, ME, d/o Charles E. (No. Berwick, ME, watchman) and Elmira (Alfred, ME, housekeeper)
Sylvester of Milton m. Nano **Donnell** of Milford, MA 12/24/1896; H - 29, laborer, b. Brownfield, ME, s/o James (Brownfield, ME, farmer) and Lydia J. (Hiram, ME); W - 26, shoe stitcher, b. Milford, MA, d/o Philip P. (Ireland) and Elizabeth (Milford, MA)

DEANGELIS,
Edward C. of Chelsea, MA m. Jean A. **Hutchins** of Milton Mills 4/26/1969; H - b. 10/12/1947; W - b. 11/18/1950

DEE,
Raymond H. of Milton m. Nancy L. **Dean** of Rochester 7/4/1970 in Sanbornville; H - b. 10/23/1951; W - b. 5/27/1952

DEHART,
Damon H. of Wakefield, MA m. Judith H. **Swope** of Milton Mills 8/23/1980 in Exeter

DELAND,
Mark H. of Monson, MA m. Sandra L. **Henderson** of Milton 5/22/1971; H - b. 7/17/1950; W - b. 7/3/1950

DELLAS,
Athanasios of Forestville, CT m. LeeAnn M. **Johnson** of Milton 11/23/1985 in Somersworth

DEMERITT,
Bruce R. of Milton m. Mary E. **Hunter** of Roslindale, MA 9/6/1920; H - 17, hyd. surveyor, b. Milton, s/o Berthold I. Demeritt (Newfield, ME, foreman) and Musetta A. Dorr (Dover); W - 19, stenographer, b. Roslindale, MA, d/o John Hunter (Scotland, collector) and Margaret Hannah (Scotland)
Delphine of Milton m. Carrie S. **Tobey** of Kittery, ME 11/30/1928; H - 21, shoemaker, b. Milton, s/o Berthold DeMeritt (W. Newfield, ME, shoemaker) and Musetta A. Dorr (Dover); W - 24, school tchr., b. Kittery, ME, d/o Thomas C. Tobey (Portsmouth, mason) and Rosabel Tobey (Dover)
Philip O., Jr. of Sanford, ME m. Christine M. **Buxton** of Sanford, ME 9/2/1995
Robert G., Sr. of Milton m. Sharon J. **Therrien** of Rochester 9/17/1994
Rossbert of Milton m. Mildred A. **Willard** of Beverly, MA 11/22/1941; H - 36, shoe worker, b. Milton, s/o Berthold DeMeritt (Newfield, ME, retired) and Musetta A. Dorr (Dover, housewife); W - 45, shoe worker, 2nd, b. Beverly, MA, d/o Albert W. Fielder (Beverly, MA, photographer) and Alice M. Caswell (Beverly, MA, nurse)

DEMERS,
Anthony G. of Milton Mills m. Cindy L. **Garland** of Milton Mills 7/24/1993

DEPALMA,
Anthony of Milton m. Keri L. **Koopman** of Milton 2/4/1989

DESHARNAIS,
Ronald H. of Somersworth m. Jeanne M. **Bronson** of Milton 5/26/1979

DESMARIS,
Robert R. of Rochester m. Billie D. **Warnecke** of Milton 7/4/1964 in Rochester; H - 18, filling sta. worker; W - 20, clerk

DEVOID,
Clarence E. of Milton m. Edna F. **Whitten** 1/22/1961 in Farmington; H - 60, retired vet.; W - 63, housewife

DEWOLF,
Charles T. of North Adams, MA m. Hattie E. **Hayes** of Milton 11/30/1890; H - 22; W - 22, lady, b. Milton, d/o Luther and Sarah D.

DEXTER,
Gilwin W. of Milton m. Amy F. **Betts** of W. Lebanon, ME 7/2/1927; H - 24, laborer, b. Dover, ME, s/o Leslie Dexter (Dover, ME, farmer) and Amy M. Nichols (Dover, ME); W - 19, domestic, b. Lebanon, ME, d/o Ralph H. Betts (Lebanon, ME, farmer) and Myrtie McIntire (Lebanon, ME)

DIACO,
Eugene of Milton m. Suzanne K. **Smith** of Milton 10/19/1984

DICEY,
Dana M. of Milton m. Marion M. **Dixon** of Milton 12/26/1910; H - 20, shoemaker, b. Milton, s/o Dana Dicey (Wakefield, conductor) and Winnie M. Duntley (Milton); W - 17, shoe stitcher, b. Lebanon, ME, d/o Oscar B. Dixon (Milton, laborer) and Nellie F. Doe (Ossipee)

DICKEY,
Myron P. of Kennebunk, ME m. Nellie M. **Wentworth** of Milton 1/12/1910; H - 57, clergyman, 2nd, wid., b. Derry, s/o David W. Dickey (Londonderry) and Sarah A. Campbell (Windham); W - 35, teacher, b. Milton, d/o John A. Wentworth (Milton) and Hannah E. Gray (Strafford)

DICKSON,
C. LeRoy of Milton m. Ruby Elise **Snow** of Dover 5/29/1941 in Dover; H - 36, superintendent, b. Milton, s/o Ernest F. Dickson (Lunenburg, MA, foreman) and Allie M. Corson (Milton, housewife); W - 36, nurse, b. Boiestown, NB, d/o John G. Snow (Dover, retired) and Elsie A. Munn (Dover, housewife)

Ernest F. of Milton m. Allie May **Corson** of Milton 10/28/1899; H - 20, engineer, b. Lunenburg, MA, s/o William F. Dickson (Charleston,

MA, mach. tender); W - 18, lady, b. Milton, d/o George M. Corson (Lebanon, ME, RR foreman)

Franklin of Milton m. Mary E. **Timmins** of Brentwood 8/10/1935 in Brentwood; H - 33, mill worker, b. Milton, s/o Ernest Dickson (Lunenburg, MA, foreman) and Allie M. Corson (Milton, housewife); W - 26, teacher, b. Petersburg, VA, d/o Henry Timmins (NB, carpenter) and Hannah S. Tuck (Brentwood, housewife)

William A. of Milton m. Grace E. **Harwood** of Milton 5/21/1918 in East Rochester; H - 43, superintendent, b. Lunenburg, MA, s/o William F. Dixon (sic) (Charlestown, MA, emp. in mill) and Matilda L. Lancy (Lunenburg, MA); W - 35, teacher, b. Boston, MA, d/o Walter H. Hardwood (sic) (Malden, MA) and Anna M. Brenham (Manchester)

William A. of Milton m. Patricia A. **Knowlton** of Dover 9/4/1964 in Dover; H - 20, stk. clerk; W - 18, secretary

William A. of Milton m. Judith L. **Richard** of Dover 3/6/1971 in Rochester; H - b. 3/31/1944; W - b. 4/27/1950

DIEMER,

George S. of Milton m. Anne Mary **Hall** of Rochester 4/25/1959 in Rochester; H - 69, shoe shop, 2nd, widower, b. Albania; W - 60, shoe shop, 2nd, widow, b. Canada, d/o James Boutoir (Canada) and Margaret McCann (Canada)

DILLIHUNT,

Charles E. of Malden, MA m. Mildred E. **Brown** of Somerville, MA 11/15/1927; H - 25, conductor, 2nd, b. Boston, MA, s/o Charles Dillihunt (NS, inspector) and Lillian F. Annable (Boston, MA); W - 22, at home, b. Boston, MA, d/o Charles H. Brown (Germany, engineer) and Helen T. Wickham (Ireland)

DION,

Roger J., Jr. of Germany m. Marie S. **Donlon** of Milton 9/6/1996

DISTASIO,

Peter of Saugus, MA m. Jane J. **Claflin** of Saugus, MA 8/18/1973; H - b. 3/28/1940; W - b. 1/16/1949

DIXON,
Elwood M. of Milton m. Gladys M. **St. John** of Milton 6/27/1923; H - 21, emp. in mill, b. Milton, s/o Stephen E. Dixon (Milton, watchman) and Georgia M. Moody (Ossipee); W - 23, stenographer, b. Rochester, d/o Napoleon St. John (Hudson, MA, emp. in mill) and Elizabeth A. Manning (Hudson, MA)
Oscar B. of Lebanon, ME m. Rosie L. **Jenkins** of Meredith 10/13/1906; H - 45, farmer, 2nd, b. Milton, s/o Ichabod Dixon (Lebanon, ME) and Nancy J. Harmon (Cornish, ME); W - 32, housekeeper, 3rd, b. Meredith, d/o John L. Lawrence (Meredith) and Martha E. Crockett (Meredith)
Stephen E. of Milton m. Georgia **Moodey** of Lebanon, ME 8/24/1901; H - 37, clerk, b. Milton, s/o Ichabod Dixon and Nancy J. Harmond; W - 17, lady, b. Ossipee, d/o George B. Moodey and Nellie R. Doe (Ossipee)

DOANE,
Barry W. of Milton m. Leslie N. **Holland** of Milton 3/20/1993

DOBLE,
Henry L. P. of Milton m. Cecilia M. **Loughlin** of Milton 8/23/1910 in Sanbornville; H - 21, iceman, b. S. Weymouth, MA, s/o George H. Doble (S. Weymouth, MA, shoemaker) and Eva Humble (Abington, MA); W - 30, milliner, b. N. Cambridge, MA, d/o John Loughlin (Ireland, foreman) and Ellen Callaghan (Ireland)

DODDRELL,
Jeffrey V. of Sanbornville m. Cheryl L. **Foss** of Milton Mills 10/8/1988

DODGE,
Carl L. of Lebanon, ME m. Loretta G. **Guertin** of Lebanon, ME 8/17/1921; H - 34, clerk, b. Lowell, MA, s/o Charles S. Dodge (Portsmouth, clerk) and Mary A. Lampson (Exeter); W - 42, boxmaker, 2nd, b. Hudson, MA, d/o John J. Welch (Waltham, MA, RR clerk) and Mary L. Fay (Marlboro, MA)

DODIER,
Donald R. of Wakefield m. Ruth E. **Valley** of Milton 1/14/1948; H - 20, emp. in mill, b. Somerville, MA, s/o Frank J. Dodier (Sanbornville,

cook) and Evangeline C. Young (housekeeper); W - 18, at home, b. Milton Mills, d/o Paul G. Valley (Ossipee) and Mildred R. Weeks (Ossipee, weaver)

Robert A. of Rollinsford m. Virginia A. **Richardson** of Milton 1/27/1973 in Rollinsford; H - b. 2/27/1951; W - b. 8/6/1951

Stanley L. of Wakefield m. Deborah A. **Inman** of Milton 8/17/1974; H - b. 7/21/1953; W - b. 6/13/1953

DOE,

Arthur E. of Milton m. Ruby R. **Hitchcock** of Milton 7/23/1983 in Rochester

James F. of Milton m. Edith M. **Witham** of Brookfield 9/6/1896 in Brookfield; H - 24, farmer, b. Milton, s/o Mark D. (Newfield, ME, farmer) and Rachel (Milton); W - 21, housekeeper, b. Brookfield, d/o Charles (Milton) and Rose (Newport, VT)

James F. of Milton m. Etta F. **Martin** of Somersworth 7/28/1904; H - 32, farmer, 2nd, b. Milton, s/o Mark D. Doe (Newfield, ME, farmer) and Rachel Horne (Milton); W - 30, teacher, b. Brockton, MA, d/o Bartholomew Martin (Newburyport, MA) and Margaret Henderson (Milton)

DOHERTY,

Philip of Milton m. Iva L. **Hoyt** of Milton 11/22/1913; H - 37, loom fixer, b. Franklin, MA, s/o Michael Doherty (Ireland) and Annie Nangle (Ireland); W - 25, weaver, b. Rochester, d/o Alonzo L. Hoyt (Rochester, teamster) and Lillian G. Edgerly (Wolfeboro)

DONLON,

James A. of Milton m. Marie S. **Russo** of Milton 2/2/1985 in Rochester

DONNELLY,

John J., Jr. of Irvington, NJ m. Ella C. **Tanner** of Lebanon, ME 7/4/1959; H - 20, Air Force, b. Newark, NJ, s/o John J. Donnelly (NJ) and Grace Lupton (NJ); W - 19, student, b. Rochester, d/o Waldo Tanner (NH) and Grace Corlis (NH)

DONOVAN,

Michael P. of Milton m. Diane L. **Jackson** of Bath, ME 3/21/1983

DORE,
Charles E. of Milton m. Blanch **Nickerson** of Milton 11/25/1931; H - 38, laborer, 2nd, b. Milton, s/o Charles H. Dore (Milton, laborer) and Mary W. Duntley (Milton, housekeeper); W - 27, at home, b. Milton, d/o James T. Nickerson (NS, sawyer) and Mary L. Mason (Milton, housekeeper)

Everett F. of Milton m. Addie B. **Tuck** of Milton 12/21/1904; H - 20, clerk, b. Wolfeboro, s/o Henry F. Dore (Ossipee, mill oper.) and Sarah A. Hanson (Wolfeboro); W - 20, housekeeper, b. Washington, ME, d/o Lewis C. Tuck (Parsonsfield, ME) and Clara D. Todd (Maysville, ME)

Franklin W. of Milton m. Ethelyn R. **Lord** of Milton 11/18/1952 in Rochester; H - 23, Spaldo, b. Wolfeboro, s/o Frank Dore and Harriet Crennan; W - 19, shoe worker, b. Sanford, ME, d/o Leslie F. Lord and Elsie Burnham

Ivan E. of Milton m. Carolyn E. **Haley** of Melvin Village 12/13/1959 in Wolfeboro; H - 23, mechanic, b. Milton, s/o Charles E. Dore (NH) and Blanche E. Nickerson (NH); W - 19, at home, b. Wolfeboro, d/o Lawrence Haley and Francis Thibedeau (NH)

Ivan E. of Milton m. Leona M. **Kean** of Rochester 2/22/1964; H - 26, foreman; W - 21, shoe worker

Ivan E. of Milton m. Shirley H. **Lavertue** of Milton 4/21/1979

Ivan E. of Milton m. Jane E. **Boisvert** of Milton 6/19/1993

Jeffrey L. of Milton m. Kathy L. **Aubin** of Milton 8/10/1985

Jeffrey L. of Milton m. Mary A. **Katwick** of Milton 9/4/1987

DORR,
Alfonzo F. of Milton m. Augusta M. **Burke** of Milton 12/28/1895; H - 21, shoemaker, b. Milton, s/o Stephen Dorr (Milton, farmer); W - 19, shoe stitcher, b. Wolfeboro, d/o Charles Burke (Wolfeboro, laborer)

Charles E. of Haverhill, MA m. Bertha C. **Lessard** of Milton 1/28/1918; H - 24, machinist, b. Milton, s/o Charles H. Dorr (Milton, laborer) and Mary W. Duntley (Milton); W - 17, domestic, b. Milton, d/o Belaine Lessard (Canada, farmer) and Delvina Dion (Canada)

Charles H. of Milton m. Winnie M. **Duntley** of Milton 3/9/1893; H - 34, laborer, b. Milton, s/o Amasa Dorr (Milton) and Sarah A.; W - 17, housekeeper, b. Milton, d/o John H. Duntley (shoemaker) and Elizabeth A.

Charles H. of Milton m. Katherine **Deveau** of Milton 9/8/1918; H - 65, laborer, 2nd, b. Milton, s/o Amasa Dorr (Middleton) and Sarah A. Ellis (Middleton); W - 25, housekeeper, 2nd, b. Milton, d/o William Cronin (Portsmouth, laborer) and Katherine Lynch (Charlestown, MA)

Hervey W. of Milton m. Catherine M. **Keene** of Milton 10/28/1903 in Berwick, ME; H - 29, farmer, b. Milton, s/o Charles C. Dorr (Milton, farmer) and Melissa Jones (Milton); W - 33, housekeeper, 2nd, b. Newfoundland, d/o James J. McKenzie (Newfoundland) and Anna M. Folly (Newfoundland)

William W. of Milton m. Ruth M. **Edwards** of Temple 10/21/1913 in Lyndeboro; H - 32, mill operative, b. Milton, s/o Stephen D. Dorr (Milton) and Melvina F. Staples (Farmington); W - 20, b. Temple, d/o Edwin B. Edwards (Temple, farmer) and Sarah E. Walton (Temple)

DOUCETTE,
Lucien of Somersworth m. Cheryl A. **Perry** of Milton 12/13/1969; H - b. 11/6/1951; W - b. 1/11/1951

DOUGLAS,
James E. of Dover m. Nina R. **Russo** of Milton 5/30/1992
Kenneth of Dover m. Claire E. **Sweeney** of Milton 10/23/1955 in Dover; H - 50, real estate, b. Dover, s/o William Douglas and Lillian Lancaster; W - 33, inspector, 2nd, b. Melrose, MA, d/o William Connorton and Hilda Hulsman
Ronald M. of Milton m. Darlene A. **Richards** of Rochester 5/17/1980 in Rochester

DOW,
Donald D. of Old Orchard, ME m. Diane G. **Pinette** of W. Orlando, FL 12/15/1961; H - 22, student; W - 18, at home

DOWNES,
Leonard of Milton m. Donna M. **Tweedy** of Milton 7/2/1988

DOWNING,
Charles L. of Milton m. Tressie May **Leavitt** of Milton 8/15/1917; H - 35, laborer, b. Milton, s/o Charles W. G. Downing (Milton, laborer) and

Sarah Page (Milton); W - 38, housekeeper, 2nd, b. No. Conway, d/o Frank Leavitt (Biddeford, ME, carpenter) and Sadie E. Adams (New Bedford, MA)

George A. of Milton m. Fannie I. **Pinkham** of Milton 3/18/1926; H - 53, sect. foreman, 2nd, b. Farmington, s/o George T. Downing (Farmington, farmer) and Anna R. Aikens (Barnstead); W - 44, housekeeper, 2nd, b. Milton, d/o Charles Hayes (Farmington, farmer) and Nelle M. Parmenter (Farmington)

DOWNS,

Arthur F. of Milton m. Ethel O. **Hanson** of Rochester 10/22/1927 in East Rochester; H - 23, mac. tender, b. Milton, s/o Fred C. Downs (Waltham, MA, mac. tender) and Eva M. West (Sanbornville); W - 26, shoe oper., 2nd, b. Lyman, ME, d/o William Bousquin (Canada, shoe oper.) and Leona Stevens (Biddeford, ME)

Arthur W. of Milton m. Joan M. **Lambert** of Milton 10/21/1961; H - 24, mechanic; W - 20, el. test.

Charles H. of Lebanon, ME m. Sarah **Gorman** of Lebanon, ME 5/10/1900; H - 55, hotel prop., b. Milton, s/o Moses Downs and Lavina Hanson; W - 25, housekeeper, b. Ireland, d/o Peter Gorman (Ireland, farmer) and Mary -----

Chester K. of Milton m. Hannah M. **Boyce** of Barrington 7/9/1970; H - b. 10/26/1892; W - b. 6/28/1880

Chester R. of Milton m. Eliza A. **Marshall** of Newton, MA 3/29/1923; H - 30, broom maker, b. Milton, s/o Frank L. Downs (Milton, janitor) and Augusta Kimball (Middleton); W - 44, dressmaker, b. Paradise, NS, d/o Melbourne Marshall (Paradise, NS, farmer) and Lydia C. Weston (Yarmouth, NS)

Frank L. of Milton m. Augusta O. **Kimball** of Rochester 5/21/1891; H - 24, farmer, b. Milton, s/o John T. (farmer) and Olive A. (housekeeper); W - 23, shoe stitcher, b. Middleton, d/o John B. (dead) and Sabrina (housekeeper)

Fred of Milton m. Ina Anna **Come** of Milton 6/7/1916; H - 36, shoemaker, b. Milton, s/o Albert F. Downs (Milton) and Dora M. Tuttle (Strafford); W - 21, shoe stitcher, 2nd, b. Roxbury, VT, d/o Joseph Bell (Montreal, Canada, farmer) and Hattie M. Gushea (Worcester, VT)

Fred C. of Milton m. Eva M. **West** of Wakefield 12/21/1901; H - 23, laborer, b. Lebanon, ME, s/o Arthur F. Downs and Eva M. Williams

(Portsmouth); W - 17, housekeeper, b. Wakefield, d/o Charles West (Wakefield, laborer) and Betsy Whitehouse

Fred W. of Milton m. Leonie M. **Cote** of Dover 9/11/1939 in Dover; H - 22, mach. tender, b. Barnstead, s/o Arthur L. Downs (Barnstead, farmer) and Maud Welch (Barnstead, housewife); W - 24, top stitcher, b. Dover, d/o Etienne Cote (Canada, retired) and Marie Gregorie (Canada, housewife)

George A. of Milton m. Ada R. **Tanner** of Milton 12/23/1895; H - 26, clerk, b. Milton, s/o Albert F. (Milton); W - 21, housekeeper, b. Farmington, d/o Frank (Farmington, farmer)

Hazen W. of Milton m. Martha G. **Cushman** of Milton 8/13/1910 in Athol, MA; H - 62, truckman, 2nd, wid., b. Milton, s/o Joshua H. Downs (Milton) and Emily P. Duntley (Farmington); W - 53, housekeeper, 2nd, wid., b. Fairlee, VT, d/o Samuel L. Granger (Fairlee, VT) and Hannah G. Pierce (Fairlee, VT)

Herbert A. of Milton m. Wilma T. **Warnecke** of Milton 5/1/1936; H - 21, mill worker, b. C. Barnstead, s/o Arthur L. Downs (C. Barnstead, farmer) and Maude Welch (Tunbridge, VT, housewife); W - 18, bookkeeper, b. Milton, d/o W. L. Warnecke (Gronan, Germany, machinist) and Francina I. Nutter (Milton, housewife)

Raymond of Milton m. Ruby **Clifford** of Wolfeboro 6/26/1937; H - 23, mach. tend., 2nd, b. Milton, s/o Fred C. Downs (Lebanon, ME, laborer) and Eva M. West (Wakefield, moulder); W - 21, at home, b. Wolfeboro, d/o Walter Clifford (Pontford, VT, laborer) and Edith Glidden (Alton, WPA proj.)

Raymond F. of Milton m. Margaret O. **Brown** of Milton 9/10/1934; H - 20, mill emp., b. Milton, s/o Fred C. Downs (Lebanon, ME, laborer) and Eva M. West (Wakefield, mill emp.); W - 19, housekeeper, b. Milton, d/o Ambrose M. Brown (Brighton, MA, mill emp.) and Ora M. Blouin (Springvale, ME, housewife)

Roy M. of Milton m. Anna L. **Shaw** of Dover 7/5/1948 in Rochester; H - 55, mill worker, b. Milton, s/o John A. Downs (laborer) and May L. Thompson (Lebanon, housewife); W - 53, cook, 2nd, b. S. P'm'th, KY, d/o Thomas R. Adams (Portsmouth, OH, farmer) and Lydia N. Rice (housewife)

DOYLE,

William J. of Milton m. Bessie **Whitton** of Lebanon, ME 10/15/1906 in Gonic; H - 22, shoemaker, b. Ireland, s/o James Doyle (Ireland) and

Ellen Molloy (Ireland); W - 17, at home, b. Lebanon, ME, d/o Hiram
Whitton (flagman) and Alice Tucker

DRAPEAU,
David N. of Milton m. Wendy M. **Sawyer** of Milton 11/29/1985 in
Rochester

DRAPER,
Loren W., Jr. of Milton m. Toni M. **Barbaro** of Portsmouth 1/17/1985 in
Rochester

DRAWBRIDGE,
Edward F. of Middleton m. Bertha **Cook** of Milton 6/11/1899 in
Wakefield; H - 26, clerk, b. Worcester, MA, s/o George D.
Drawbridge (England, painter); W - 22, milliner, b. Milton, d/o
Martin V. B. Cook

DREW,
Charles M. of Milton Mills m. Katherine **Gordon** of Milton Mills
1/28/1934 in Somersworth; H - 21, mill op., b. Wakefield, s/o
Charles A. Drew (Wakefield, chim. clnr.) and Iva M. Reed
(Wakefield, housewife); W - 18, housekeeper, b. Acton, ME, d/o
Almon F. Gordon (Acton, ME, fireman) and Nellie Cronin (Sanford,
ME, housewife)

Charles M. of Milton m. Pearl L. **Ryan** of Rochester 7/10/1953 in
Wakefield; H - 41, engineer, 2nd, b. Wakefield, s/o Charles A. Drew
and Iva Reed; W - 52, shoe worker, 2nd, b. Acton, ME, George
Muchmore and Hervie Horne

Clarence L. of Milton m. Ida L. C. **Russell** of Milton 11/16/1936 in W.
Milton; H - 49, laborer, 2nd, b. Wakefield, s/o John W. Drew
(Brookfield, laborer) and Addie Thibbedeaux (Oldtown, ME,
housewife); W - 49, prac. nurse, 3rd, b. Belleville, ON, d/o Richard
N. Cornell (Belleville, ON, laborer) and Isabelle Brown (PEI,
housewife)

Ralph H. of Portsmouth m. Shirley M. **Elwell** of Milton 6/10/1972; H - b.
2/23/1925; W - b. 10/4/1935

Thomas B. of Milton m. Minnie **Ellis** of Rochester 5/1/1914; H - 38,
stable keeper, 2nd, b. Brookfield, s/o William H. Drew (Dover) and

Emerline Dyer (Brookfield); W - 39, housework, 2nd, d/o James
Shattuck (Rowley, MA) and Martha ----- (Rowley, MA)

DROUIN,
Armand L. of East Lebanon, ME m. Justina **Guzman** of Milton 4/4/1964;
H - 21, shoe worker; W - 27, assembly
Michael J. of Milton m. Gloria A. **Belanger** of Milton 11/20/1983

DUBE,
Dennis D. of Milton m. Cynthia A. **Kinkaid** of Rochester 11/27/1971; H -
b. 6/5/1951; W - b. 6/2/1955
Joseph N. of Milton m. Shirley C. **Davis** of Rochester 8/28/1971; H - b.
7/17/1947; W - b. 10/28/1948
Lionel A., Jr. of Milton m. Doreen P. **Joy** of Union 7/27/1974 in
Rochester; H - b. 4/5/1950; W - b. 7/6/1956
Lionel A., Jr. of W. Lebanon, ME m. Marie J. **Fortin** of W. Lebanon, ME
11/28/1981

DUCHARME,
Joel A. of Milton m. Christine M. **Vachon** of Milton 12/5/1981

DUGGAN,
Dennis J. of Milton m. Cindy K. **Hill** of Milton 1/10/1992

DUMONT,
Albert L. of Milton m. Patricia L. **Ward** of Milton 9/18/1994

DUNBAR,
Charles W. of Somerville, MA m. Eva E. **Douquette** of Milton 11/9/1913;
H - 22, timekeeper, b. Milford, s/o Edson L. Dunbar (Nobleboro,
ME) and Martha E. White (Westboro, MA); W - 22, housework, b.
Milton, d/o Leon Douquette (Canada, laborer) and Emma Houle
(Canada)

DUNPHY,
Barry W. of Dover m. Rosamond S. **Gray** of Milton 6/11/1965 in
Rochester; H - 23, acct.; W - 22, clerical wk.

DUNTLEY,
Herbert R. of Milton m. Anabel **Robbins** of Milton 12/26/1916; H - 36, laborer, b. Milton, s/o John H. Duntley (Milton) and Elizabeth A. Downs (Milton); W - 45, housekeeper, 2nd, b. Wolfeboro, d/o John Yeaton (Alfred, ME) and Eunice S. Black (Gray, ME)

DUNTON,
Charles D. of Portsmouth m. Bonnie A. A. **Katwick** of Milton 10/21/1960 in Portsmouth; H - 21, student; W - 20, student
Erik C. of Milton m. Rebecca A. **Rowe** of Milton 9/17/1986 in Rye

DUPREY,
Daniel P. of Milton m. Sandy-Jo **Menard** of E. Lebanon, ME 11/14/1992

DUPUIS,
Clyde R. of Milton m. Carrie G. **Niblock** of Milton 11/29/1969; H - b. 3/20/1906; W - b. 12/27/1901
Euclyde of Milton m. Ellen H. **Wyatt** of Milton 8/31/1944; H - 38, leatherb'd mill, 2nd, b. Milton, s/o Fred Welch (S. Berwick, ME, counter mill) and Lydia Marchand (Wakefield, housewife); W - 31, leatherb'd mill, b. Milton, d/o Edgar J. Wyatt (Haverhill, MA, retired) and Hattie E. Hayes (Milton, housewife)
James A. of Milton m. Jean K. **Lapington** of Milton 4/3/1953; H - 20, unemployed, b. Milton, s/o Euclide Dupuis and Mary N. Wiggin; W - 19, at home, b. England, d/o Albert Lapington and Edith Norman
Mark A. of Rochester m. Penny L. **Bullis** of Milton 6/15/1991
Norman of Milton m. Doris E. **Downs** of Milton 9/25/1937; H - 22, mill hand, b. Milton, s/o Alfred Dupuis (S. Berwick, ME, moulder) and Ledia Marchand (Sanbornville, dead); W - 18, shoe packer, b. Milton, d/o C. Fred Downs (Lebanon, ME, laborer) and Eva M. West (Sanbornville, moulder)
Norman L. of Milton m. Marie M. **Nadeau** of Somersworth 2/28/1953 in Somersworth; H - 17, shoe worker, b. NH, s/o Euclide Dupuis and Mary N. Wiggin; W - 18, shoe worker, b. NH, d/o Benedict P. Nadeau and Marie Jacques
Norman M. of Milton m. Marilyn A. **Columbus** of Milton 10/16/1954; H - 19, US Navy, b. Rochester, s/o Wilfred Dupuis and Gertrude Harrity; W - 19, at home, b. Jersey City, NJ, d/o Albert Columbus and Marjorie Benner

Roland N. of Milton m. Irene J. **Belleville** of Rochester 9/17/1960 in Rochester; H - 20, draftsman; W - 20, at home

Wilfred of Milton m. Gertrude **Harrity** of Rochester 5/23/1925 in Rochester; H - 20, leatherboard mill, b. Milton, s/o Fred Dupuis (So. Berwick, ME, machinist) and Lydia Marshall (Wakefield); W - 20, shoe operative, b. Rochester, d/o Peter Harrity (Salmon Falls, telegraph oper.) and Phoebe Sylvain (Canada)

DURGIN,

George Frank of Milton m. Helen W. **Stanton** of Lebanon, ME 1/29/1890; H - 29, minister, b. Oxford, ME, s/o Joseph H. (Portland, ME) and Emma L. (Otisfield, ME, housekeeper); W - 26, teacher, b. Lebanon, ME, d/o James (RI, farmer) and Catherine (RI, housekeeper)

Henry I. of Effingham m. Alta M. **Knox** of Milton 12/3/1890; H - 26, physician, b. Freedom, s/o Joshua (Eaton, farmer) and Mary E. (Effingham, housekeeper); W - 26, lady, b. Milton, d/o Ira S. (Lebanon, ME, RR rep'm) and Susan A. (Milton, housekeeper)

DURKEE,

Donald P. of Durham m. Lorraine M. **Campbell** of Milton 2/11/1950; H - 21, student, b. Farmington, s/o Porter J. Durkee (Danvers, MA) and Estelle Swinerton (Farmington); W - 20, shoe shop, 2nd, b. Hinsdale, d/o Edward M. Benton (Sanbornton) and Lucilla M. Stillings (Ossipee)

DUROST,

Christopher R. of Milton m. Erica K. **Woodruff** of Milton 11/25/1998

DYER,

Herman C. of Milton m. Susie A. **Staples** of Milton 5/19/1888; H - 19, laborer, b. Brookfield; W - 20, b. Milton

EASON,

Robert E. of Farmington m. Shirley M. **Perry** of Milton 11/16/1955; H - 26, box maker, b. Portland, ME, s/o Walter Eason and Mary A. Shapleigh; W - 20, at home, b. Milton, d/o Charles E. Perry and Ruth W. Perry

EASTMAN,
John A., Jr. of Milton m. Cheryl A. **Balomenos** of Milton 11/24/1990

EATON,
Frank L. of Milton m. Cynthia A. **Hauser** of Milton 9/6/1980 in Wakefield

Henry O. of Milton m. Pauline R. **Allard** of Milton 9/3/1955; H - 27, mach. oper., b. Wells, ME, s/o Daniel Eaton and Gertrude Russell; W - 16, at home, b. Canada, d/o Paul F. Allard and Antoinette Descary

John I. of Brookline, MA m. Stephanie D. **Curtis** of Brookline, MA 12/16/1962; H - 23, mechanic; W - 20, housework

EAVES,
Timothy R. of Milton m. Donna M. **Washburne** of Milton 8/9/1975; H - b. 4/15/1957; W - b. 5/6/1958

EAYRES,
George T. of Milton m. Theresa A. **Menegoni** of Milton 8/24/1963; H - 23, gas sta. att'n; W - 22, secretary

EBARE,
Gene M. of Milton m. Debra A. **Pennell** of Milton 7/5/1975; H - b. 1/29/1955; W - b. 4/29/1956

EDGERLY,
Roy A. of Milton m. Lisa A. **Desmarais** of Milton 4/20/1991

EDMUNDS,
Garth C. of Milton m. Dorothy G. **Perkins** of Milton 9/7/1991

ELDRIDGE,
Carlton S. of Milton m. Esther M. **Haley** of Tuftonboro 9/2/1922; H - 20, laborer, b. Ossipee, s/o Orodon J. Eldridge (Ossipee, laborer) and Lucy C. Welch (Ossipee); W - 18, domestic, b. Tuftonboro, d/o George H. Haley (Tuftonboro, carpenter) and Edith C. Ayers (Tuftonboro)

David A. of Milton m. Patricia R. **Semprebom** of Milton 6/10/1976; H - b. 12/3/1953; W - b. 3/23/1959

Moses O. of Milton m. Lillian M. **Johnson** of W. Lebanon, ME 8/23/1933; H - 33, mill op., b. Ossipee, s/o Arodon J. Eldridge (Ossipee, retired) and Lucy C. Welch (Ossipee, shoe worker); W - 28, shoe worker, b. Lebanon, ME, d/o L. Ed. Johnson (Strafford, farmer) and Josephine H. Desc'y (Stoneham, MA, housewife)

Russell N. of Milton m. Nancy K. **Dyer** of Berwick, ME 7/2/1955 in Berwick, ME; H - 21, shoe worker, b. Milton, s/o Moses Eldridge and Lillian Johnson; W - 17, student, b. Ashfield, MA, d/o Theodore Dyer and Amy Brown

Willis C. of Milton m. Maybelle E. **Knox** of Milton 8/3/1927 in Ctr. Ossipee; H - 24, farmer, b. Ossipee, s/o Plummer Eldridge (Ossipee, farm foreman) and Emma Welch (Tuftonboro); W - 32, laundress, 2nd, b. Ossipee, d/o L. Laburton White (Haverhill, MA, bag. master) and Elizabeth A. Pascoe (Freedom)

ELLINGWOOD,

Maynard A. of Milton m. Mary J. **Sexton** of Milton 8/19/1972 in Rochester; H - b. 8/17/1951; W - b. 4/30/1954

Maynard A. of Milton m. Margaret E. **Lessard** of Middleton 4/4/1974 in Chichester; H - b. 8/17/1951; W - b. 5/5/1954

ELLIOTT,

Erlon H. of Milton m. Sandra L. **Kohl** of Rochester 5/21/1999

Harold R. of Groveton m. Mary **Alexander** of Milton 5/4/1916 in Milton Mills; H - 22, loom fixer, b. Island Pond, VT, s/o David Elliott (Canada, RR conductor) and Selina Moore (Canada); W - 20, b. Keene, d/o Lester E. Alexander (Fitzwilliam, clergyman) and Carrie E. Webster (Walpole)

Michael of Milton m. Renee **Carignan** of Milton 9/30/1989

Steven J. of Rochester m. Donna E. **Snyder** of Milton 8/2/1980

ELLIS,

Arthur G. of Milton m. Georgie A. **Herrick** of Revere, MA 6/27/1906 in Revere, MA; H - 25, shoemaker, b. Milton, s/o Ephraim Ellis (Middleton) and Hannah A. Jones (Middleton); W - 35, clerk, b. E. Boston, MA, d/o Hiram H. Herrick (NY) and Mary A. V. Gomes (Salem, MA)

Charles F. of Milton m. Rachel **Letourneau** of Rochester 11/24/1955 in Rochester; H - 26, state hwy., b. Milton, s/o Lloyd Ellis and Eleanor

Londo; W - 18, shoe worker, b. S. Berwick, ME, d/o Alphonse Letourneau and Blanche Langevin

David A. of Milton m. Jeannette E. **Provencal** of Rochester 5/9/1977; H - b. 5/14/1953; W - b. 2/2/1957

George E. of Milton m. Inez G. **Duntley** of Milton 10/7/1894; H - 25, laborer, b. Wolfeboro, s/o Moses Ellis (Sandwich) and Hannah (Somersworth); W - 15, housekeeper, b. Milton, d/o John H. Duntley (Milton, shoe operative) and Elizabeth A. (Dover)

Herbert F. of Lebanon, ME m. Carrie D. **McDaniels** of Lebanon, ME 8/22/1888; H - 20, shoemaker, b. Alton; W - 18, b. Hollis, ME

James R. of Milton m. Carleen E. **Nicholson** of Wakefield 8/7/1971; H - b. 1/26/1952; W - b. 12/2/1951

John T. of Milton m. Minnie F. **Johnson** of Milton 9/27/1890; H - 24, carpenter, b. Middleton, s/o Ephraim (dead) and Abbie H. (housekeeper); W - 23, housekeeper, b. Milton, d/o James W. (farmer) and Julia (dead)

Kenneth R. of Milton m. Barbara E. **Thibidou** of Lee 1/3/1957; H - 21, laborer, b. Milton, s/o Lloyd Ellis (Milton) and Eleanor Londo (Wolfeboro); W - 18, at home, b. Wolfeboro, d/o Arthur Thibidou (Wolfeboro) and Mabel Adams (Rochester)

Kenneth R. of Milton m. Mary E. **Seale** of Farmington 6/10/1964; H - 29, farmer; W - 20, at home

Kenneth R. of Milton m. Heather A. **Barnes** of Milton 10/9/1984

Leon L. of Milton m. Cindy L. **Patnode** of Milton 8/3/1985

Lloyd F. of Milton m. Eleanor G. **Londo** of Middleton 1/16/1928 in Sanford, ME; H - 31, ice man, b. Milton, s/o George Ellis (Wolfeboro, ice man) and Gertrude Duntley (Milton); W - 17, at home, b. Wolfeboro, d/o Nelson Londo (Topsham, MA, laborer) and Mildred Corson (Wolfeboro)

Robert of Milton m. Nettie **Dyer** of Milton 12/25/1901; H - 32, papermaker, b. Milton, s/o Ephraim Ellis and Abbie Jones (Middleton); W - 26, shoe stitcher, b. Wakefield, d/o Charles H. Dyer (Brownfield, ME, laborer) and Martha A. Drew (Brookfield)

Roger of Milton m. Betty E. **Gerry** of Rochester 3/6/1954 in Rochester; H - 22, shoe worker, b. NH, s/o Lloyd F. Ellis and Eleanor Londo; W - 20, shoe worker, b. NH, d/o Elmer Gerry and Gertrude Witham

Russell E. of Milton m. Thelma L. **Verville** of Rochester 7/12/1947 in Rochester; H - 20, mill wkr., b. Wolfeboro, s/o Floyd E. Wentworth (S. Berwick, ME, laborer) and Eleanor G. Londo (Wolfeboro, housewife); W - 20, shoe wkr., b. Portsmouth, d/o Ernest L. Collins (Alton, welder) and Eunice Sawyer (Lebanon, ME, housewife)

EMERSON,
Harry L. of Milton m. Sadie W. **Sinnott** of Milton 7/1/1947; H - 60, sawyer, 2nd, s/o Daniel M. Emerson (Candia, millman) and Sylvania Hazelton (Candia, housewife); W - 63, housewife, 2nd, b. Milton, d/o Joseph F. Willey (Brookfield, farmer) and Mary J. Laskey (Milton, housewife)

ENDICOTT,
Phillip D. of CA m. Jonette M. **Rettig** of CA 8/29/1997

ERNST,
Mark A. of Albany, NY m. Peggy L. **Seamans** of Milton 12/9/1982 in Farmington

EVANS,
David C. of East Rochester m. Geraldine R. **Swett** of Milton 11/11/1961; H - 26, US Marines; W - 20, at home
Francis J., Jr. of Milton m. Sherry L. **Ham** of Milton 8/26/1995
Francis J., Sr. of Milton m. Phyllis J. **Pelletier** of Milton 4/18/1992
Joseph C. of Milton m. Laura **Hall** of Milton 11/27/1924 in Rochester; H - 50, farmer, 2nd, b. Wakefield, s/o John W. Evans (Wakefield, farmer) and Melvina Farnham (Wakefield); W - 42, housekeeper, 2nd, b. Milton, d/o Joseph F. Willey (Brookfield, farmer) and Mary J. Laskey (Milton)
Richard of Milton m. Miriam J. **Paschal** of Milton 10/8/1933 in Rochester; H - 24, mill op., b. Wakefield, s/o Victor C. Evans (Wakefield, laborer) and Mattie C. Weeks (Wakefield, housewife); W - 19, at home, b. Boston, MA, d/o Benjamin F. Paschal (Antigonish, NS, sea captain) and Emma F. Bray (Bar Harbor, ME, housewife)
Robert C. of Milton m. Marion **Whitehouse** of Milton 5/4/1917 in Rochester; H - 24, emp. in mill, b. Middleton, s/o Charles W. Evans (Alton, emp. in mill) and Alice M. Tibbetts (Rochester); W - 19, emp. in mill, b. Berwick, ME, d/o Harry F. Whitehouse (Somersworth, emp. in mill) and Lillian G. Blake (Belfast, ME)

Sumner L. of Milton m. Blanche **O'Brian** of Lebanon, ME 7/3/1916 in Rochester; H - 22, laborer, b. Milton, s/o Charles W. Evans (Alton, shoemaker) and Alice M. Tibbetts (Rochester); W - 25, domestic, b. Masonville, PQ, d/o William O'Brian (Masonville, PQ) and Mary L. Stevens (Sutton, PQ)

FAIST,
Robert L. of Barrington m. Jodie A. **Ward** of Milton 7/25/1981

FARNHAM,
Elbridge D. of Milton m. Emma **Sears** of Nashua 8/10/1893 in Wakefield; H - 45, carpenter, b. Milton, s/o David Farnham (Milton) and Rowena; W - 28, shoe stitcher, b. Sh'dica, NB, d/o Harris Sears (Campbellton, clerk) and Synthia

FARRELL,
John F., Jr. of Wakefield m. Kathleen R. **Dee** of Milton 5/9/1970 in Sanbornville; H - b. 8/21/1944; W - b. 2/3/1948
Merlon D. of Lebanon, ME m. Margaret F. **Brown** of Milton 4/5/1942 in Lebanon, ME; H - 27, RR trainman, b. Lebanon, ME, s/o Henry Farrell (Ireland, laborer) and Alice B. Libbey (Berwick, ME, housewife); W - 25, shoe worker, b. Milton, d/o Leslie M. Brown (Glenburn, ME, machinist) and Amy M. Nichols (Dover, ME, housewife)
Merton D. of Milton m. Beulah F. **Jones** of Milton 3/23/1946 in Littleton; H - 31, RR cond., 2nd, b. Lebanon, ME, s/o Henry Farrell (Passaic, NJ, shoe worker) and Alice Libbey (Berwick, ME, deceased); W - 27, office wkr., b. Ossian, IN, d/o Paris Jones (Murray, IN, retired) and Evelyn Sch'busch (Brooklyn, NY, housewife)

FARRINGTON,
Richard W. of Somersworth m. Sharon L. **Elwell** of Milton 2/8/1975; H - b. 7/27/1956; W - b. 3/7/1953
Timothy C. of Weeks Mills, ME m. Shirley J. **Campbell** of Weeks Mills, ME 2/22/1970; H - b. 6/21/1947; W - b. 2/11/1935

FEENEY,
John P. of S. Boston, MA m. Dolores J. **Wyatt** of Milton 6/20/1970; H - b. 8/10/1945; W - b. 7/23/1950

Willard G. of Milton m. Rachel N. **Lamper** of Rochester 5/13/1947 in Rochester; H - 24, carder, b. Milton, s/o Preston Feeney (Saugus, MA, carder) and Minnie Hersom (Sanford, ME, weaver); W - 23, nurse, b. Rochester, d/o Herbert D. Lamper (Alton, fitter) and Hazel D. Littlefield (Dover, shoe worker)

FERGUSON,
Frederick J. of Milton m. Helen F. **Kraus** of Milton 6/18/1954; H - 40, mechanic, 2nd, b. Springvale, ME, s/o Clarence Ferguson and Florence Aharan; W - 34, housewife, 2nd, b. Brooklyn, NY, d/o William Neary and Alma Newcomb

James of Beaver, PA m. Barbara J. **Anderson** of Milton 3/9/1950 in Rochester; H - 31, student, b. Scotland, s/o William Ferguson (Scotland) and Elizabeth Louden (Scotland); W - 26, nurse, 2nd, b. Boston, MA, d/o Norman V. Tilton (Milton) and Eleanor M. Trask (NS)

Scott J. of Milton Mills m. Anne M. **Duggan** of Milton 8/26/1983

FEREIRA,
Frederick J. of Andover, MA m. Merle L. **Stowe** of Milton 4/10/1971; H - b. 3/5/1948; W - b. 9/4/1949

FERLAND,
Rusty M. of Milton m. Cherie A. **Bouchard** of Farmington 6/5/1993

FERNALD,
Frank E. of Milton m. S. Lucy **Watson** of Manchester 3/12/1890 in Manchester; H - 24, shoe stitcher, b. Boston, s/o Eli and Eliza A. (Tamworth, housekeeper); W - 23, shoe stitcher, b. Sandwich, d/o Jeremiah (Gilmanton, blacksmith) and Harriet E. (Sandwich, housekeeper)

Frank E. of Milton m. Lulu A. **Tuttle** of Farmington 4/17/1912 in Rochester; H - 46, supt. shoe factory, 2nd, b. Boston, MA, s/o Eli Fernald and Eliza A. Felch (Tamworth); W - 36, housework, b. Farmington, d/o Charles E. Tuttle (Middleton) and Justina Ham (Dover)

FERRELLI,
James M. of Milton m. Karyn L. **Alberts** of Milton 5/28/1994

FIELDS,
Henry C. of Somersworth m. Arlene M. **Sceggell** of Milton 7/9/1955; H - 33, laborer, 2nd, b. Amherst, s/o Louis Fields and Marion Hillard; W - 23, office worker, b. Milton, d/o Howard L. Sceggell and Anna F. McIntire

FIFIELD,
Cecil M. of Farmington m. Dorothy A. **Frost** of Milton 3/25/1977; H - b. 3/25/1948; W - b. 6/28/1933
Francis H. of Wakefield m. Marjorie V. **Woodes** of Milton 11/3/1945; H - 27, shoe worker, b. Wakefield, s/o George Fifield (Conway, mason) and Blanche E. Penny (Porter, ME, housewife); W - 23, shop worker, b. Rochester, d/o George H. Woodes (Rochester, RR eng.) and Esther Edgerly (Madison, housewife)
Kenneth G. of Milton m. Robbin J. **Genest** of Milton 5/4/1991

FILGATE,
William P. of Laconia m. Margaret **Lover** of Milton 7/14/1928 in Laconia; H - 28, carpenter, b. Plymouth, s/o Levander Filgate (Laconia, carpenter) and Eva Jones (Holderness), W - 23, at home, b. Union, d/o Peter J. Lover (Union, mill operative) and Alice M. Downs (Sanbornville)

FISCHER,
Robert S. of Wells, ME m. Stephanie **Newton** of W. Lebanon, ME 10/28/1989

FITZPATRICK,
George R. of Milton m. Kathleen M. C. **Morash** 5/31/1952; H - 52, unemployed, 2nd, b. NB, s/o Thomas Fitzpatrick and Mary J. MacLellan; W - 46, nurse, b. NS, d/o Benjamin H. Morash and Clara Mossman

FLAGG,
Louis R. of Lynn, MA m. Pauline E. **Smith** of Lynn, MA 4/20/1935; H - 23, shoe findings, b. Saugus, MA, s/o James A. Flagg (NB, retired) and Ethel Flagg (Lynn, MA, housewife); W - 20, at home, b. Lynn, MA, d/o J. G'don Smith (NB, engineer) and Gertrude Turner (NS, shoe findings)

FLANAGAN,
Dennis M. of Somersworth m. Jeanette D. **Marcoux** of Milton 2/7/1959; H - 19, shoe shop, b. Berwick, ME, s/o John Flanagan (NH) and Martha Mathews (ME); W - 23, shoe shop, b. Milton, d/o Napoleon Marcoux (NH) and Hazel Downs (NH)

FLINT,
Stephen F. of Nahant, MA m. Pamela **Mohan** of Swampscott, MA 9/2/1967; H - 21, waiter; W - 20, tech. illustrator

FLOYD,
Melvin of Milton m. Marie **Russell** of Milton 12/2/1912; H - 36, teamster, 2nd, b. Stockton, ME, s/o Joshua Floyd; W - 18, housework, b. Rumford, ME, d/o Sidney A. Russell (Rumford, ME, carpenter) and Lilla A. Goodwin (Rumford, ME)

FLUX,
Robert C. of Milton m. Nancy L. **Inman** of Milton 7/4/1977 in Kingston; H - b. 6/8/1935; W - b. 3/18/1933

FORCIER,
Richard A., Jr. of Milton m. Donna M. **Langley** of Milton 5/22/1981

FORD,
Earl T. of Milton Mills m. Gretchen **Stevens** of Milton Mills 4/13/1985 in Dover
Leroy J. of Milton m. Ella M. **Bliss** of Milton 11/14/1914 in Rochester; H - 23, farmer, b. Dover, s/o William H. Ford (Dover) and Abbie J. Ricker (Milton); W - 29, housework, b. East Windsor, CT, d/o Henry Bliss (Ware, MA) and Minnie Rines (New Durham)

FORTIER,
Leslie W. of Milton Mills m. Laura L. **Dame** of Milton Mills 5/22/1982
Robert R. of Milton m. Sharon A. **Hitchcock** of Milton 1/23/1991
William K. of Milton m. Rena L. **Drew** of Milton 3/13/1951; H - 30, RR clerk, b. Tamworth, s/o Albert J. Fortier (Ossipee) and Nellie W. Lane (Albany); W - 20, student, b. Pittsfield, d/o Dwight S. Drew (Loudon) and Eunice C. Downs (Pittsfield)

FORTIN,
Michael J. of Milton m. Wendy L. **Patriquin** of Milton 10/15/1988

FOSS,
Wade E. of Milton m. Michelle M. **Cormier** of Milton 8/27/1994

FOSTER,
Jeffrey A. of Milton m. Mary A. **Chabot** of Milton 8/4/1984

FOWLER,
William L. of Milton m. Lizzie **Lewis** of Lebanon, ME 9/17/1906 in Rochester; H - 21, paper maker, b. Canada, s/o Silas Fowler (Canada, farmer) and Hannah Kistred (Canada); W - 17, shoe stitcher, b. Lebanon, ME, d/o William J. Lewis (farmer) and Clara B. Brown (Dover)

FOX,
George E. of Acton, ME m. Lucia C. **Plummer** of Milton 9/20/1906; H - 37, farmer, 2nd, b. Acton, ME, s/o Henry L. Fox (Acton, ME, farmer) and Sarah A. Moulton (Milton); W - 29, teacher, b. Milton, d/o Bard B. Plummer (Milton, farmer) and Eliza D. Wentworth (Jamaica Plains, MA)

FRAMPTON,
Michael V. of Milton Mills m. Roberta J. **White** of Kittery, ME 6/15/1985 in Brentwood

FREDETTE,
Frederick, Jr. of Springvale, ME m. Brenda L. **Faber** of Springvale, ME 8/13/1988 in Milton Mills

FREEMAN,
Earland S. of East Rochester m. Eva May **Sanborn** of Milton 4/17/1915; H - 21, emp in mill, b. Rochester, s/o William H. Freeman (Barrington, shoemaker) and Minnie Shattuck (Rowley, MA); W - 16, b. Milton, d/o Walter L. Sanborn (Milton, farmer) and Hattie A. Rines (New Durham)

George L. of Milton m. Annie B. **Kimball** of Milton 2/4/1904; H - 23, civil eng., b. Gray, ME, s/o George H. Freeman (W. Gray, ME, farmer) and Georgie Knapp (Freeman, ME); W - 20, lady, b. Milton, d/o Ralph M. Kimball (Farmington, shoemaker) and Carrie Willey (Middleton)

Lawrence A. of Milton m. Jane G. **Russ** of Milton 9/4/1982

FREETO,

Harry A. of Somerville, MA m. Florence A. **Murray** of Milton Mills 6/19/1916; H - 28, civil engineer, b. Marblehead, MA, s/o John T. Freeto (Marblehead, MA, clerk) and Emma G. Tutt (Marblehead, MA); W - 29, clerk, b. Milton, d/o Daniel Murray (Acton, ME, merchant) and Helen J. Smith (Charlestown, MA)

FRENCH,

Deane N. of Milton m. Judyth **Roberts** of Woburn, MA 5/20/1978 in East Rochester; H - b. 4/9/1950; W - b. 9/1/1956

Forrest S. of Milton m. Gladys L. **Smith** of Milton 3/26/1945 in Franklin; H - 46, garage, b. Roxbury, MA, s/o Elias G. French (Porter, ME, farmer) and Mary A. Kimball (Parsonsfield, ME, housewife); W - 40, housewife, 2nd, b. Milton, d/o Allie Laskey (Milton, farmer) and Elizabeth Weeks (Wakefield, housewife)

Michael A. of Milton m. Kimberley **Ross** of Milton 5/21/1989 in Rochester

FRIEDEL,

Scott T. of Franklin, PA m. Nancy J. **Downs** of Milton 4/27/1990

FROST,

Joseph W. of Milton Mills m. Christina M. **Vedric** of Suffern, NY 8/11/1979

FRYOU,

Richard J. of Milton m. Joyce L. **Gifford** of Milton 5/8/1999

FULTON,

Arthur G. of Farmington m. Marilyn A. **Cleaves** of Milton 9/19/1952 in Farmington; H - 20, shoe worker, b. Farmington, s/o George A. Fulton and Eleanor P. Howard; W - 18, office worker, b. Lynn, MA, d/o Walter T. Cleaves and Frances M. Toomey

GAGNE,
Gary A. of Dover m. Nancy **Day** of Milton 7/24/1982 in Dover

GAGNON,
Donald O. of Dover m. Bonnie J. **McManus** of Milton 6/25/1981
Michael P. of Rochester m. Sheila A. **Routhier** of Milton 7/19/1975; H - b. 5/3/1955; W - b. 6/3/1956

GAITHER,
John E. of Milton m. Krystal M. **Capen** of Milton 11/12/1987 in Dover

GALARNEAU,
Mark A. of Milton m. Stephanie K. **Leavy** of Milton 8/19/1995
Milford of No. Conway m. Madelyn **MacIlvaine** of Milton 8/30/1941; H - 22, shoe worker, b. Union, s/o Joseph Galarneau (Berlin, lumberman) and Cora M. Elliott (Manchester, cook); W - 18, shoe worker, b. Milton, d/o George H. MacIlvaine (Antrim, plumber) and Esther R. Fielder (Beverly, MA, shoe worker)
Milford L., Jr. of Milton m. Sandra J. **Marble** of Milton 6/22/1996

GALLANT,
Paul J. of Rowley, MA m. Alma **Ballam** of Rowley, MA 9/16/1960; H - 24, shoemaker; W - 40, pr. nurse

GARCIA,
Peter A. of Milton m. Kristin A. **Cooper** of Milton 8/26/1989 in Rochester

GARLAND,
Aldo B. of Milton m. Bessie B. **Glass** of Greenland 2/18/1918 in Newcastle; H - 27, US soldier, b. Wolfeboro, s/o George Garland (Brookfield, emp. in mill) and Mary E. Stillings (Ossipee); W - 23, emp. in mill, b. Portsmouth, d/o Elmer E. Glass (Madbury, farmer) and Jeanette M. Dyer (Cape Elizabeth, ME)
Clarence E. of Milton m. Verna M. **Reynolds** of Milton 6/27/1904; H - 31, farmer, b. Wakefield, s/o John F. Garland (Wakefield) and Nellie B. Watts (Canada); W - 21, housekeeper, b. Sanford, ME, d/o Winfield Reynolds (Newfield, ME) and Nellie M. Wentworth (Boston, MA)

David C. of Farmington m. Susan E. **Swett** of Milton 7/18/1964; H - 20, trimmer; W - 18, shoe worker

Forrest A. of Wakefield m. Patricia A. **Witham** of Milton 12/24/1946; H - 26, machinist, 2nd, b. Sanbornville, s/o Arthur A. Garland (Sanbornville, shoe merch.) and Mary Drew (Wolfeboro, deceased); W - 23, mach. oper., b. Dover, d/o Ernest F. Witham (Kittery Pt., ME, mill emp.) and Marguerite Cooley (Wilmington, MA, housewife)

Joseph S. of Wakefield m. Josie M. **Calkins** of Lebanon, ME 11/23/1909; H - 26, surveyor, b. Wakefield, s/o Alvah S. Garland (Wakefield, farmer) and Priscilla L. Lothrop (Cambridgeport, MA); W - 18, teacher, b. Milton, d/o Henry G. Calkins (Trescott, ME, paper maker) and Emma M. Lancaster (Trescott, ME)

Roland P. of West Lebanon, ME m. Wilma A. **Sargent** of West Lebanon, ME 4/7/1979

Terry R. of Wakefield m. Suzanne **French** of Milton Mills 6/28/1962 in Wakefield; H - 19, garage mech.; W - 17, at home

GARNETT,

Reynard of Concord m. Isabelle **McBride** of Milton 3/19/1929 in Northwood; H - 22, student, b. S. Lebanon, ME, s/o John H. Garnett (Stockport, England, weaver) and Mary E. Shorey (S. Lebanon, ME); W - 21, home, b. Watertown, NY, d/o William McBride (Belville, ON, laborer) and Ida Pornell (Belville, ON)

GARRETT,

Hugh of Wakefield m. Eunice T. **Massin** of Milton 10/29/1937 in Wakefield; H - 46, decorator, 2nd, b. Ivoe, England, s/o Frederick Garrett (England, dead) and Lillian Crosfield (Guilford, England, retired); W - 43, at home, 2nd, b. Lynn, MA, d/o Charles K. Tripp (Saratoga, NY, engineer) and Alice Apothecary (Granby, PQ, housewife)

GARVIN,

Josiah D. of Sanbornville m. Annie J. **Perkins** of Milton 12/1/1923 in Dover; H - 24, carpenter, b. Sanbornville, s/o John H. Garvin (Sanbornville, merchant) and Katherine P. Dow (Salem, MA); W - 20, at home, b. New Durham, d/o Harry O. Perkins (Dover, laborer) and Lena G. Willey (Middleton)

GARYAIT,
Barry L. of Milton m. Cynthia F. **Perkins** of Milton 5/26/1984 in Farmington

GATCHELL,
John B. of Milton m. Elaine **McNamara** of Winchester 7/2/1968 in Derry; H - 25; W - 23

GATHMANN,
Paul J. of Chicago, IL m. Catherine R. **Willey** of Milton 4/27/1921; H - 37, mech. engineer, b. Chicago, IL, s/o Louis Gathmann (Chicago, IL, consulting eng.) and Henrietta Ehlert (Chicago, IL); W - 25, secretary, b. Milton, d/o Joseph D. Willey (Wakefield, merchant) and Annie O. Roberts (N. Berwick, ME)

GAULIN,
Richard J. of Rochester m. Deborah J. **Damon** of Milton 6/28/1975; H - b. 6/16/1948; W - b. 10/7/1952
Scott T. of Milton m. Diane M. **Cataldo** of Milton 5/7/1995

GAUTHIER,
Rosary of Milton m. Diana **Dupreis** of Wakefield 8/14/1916; H - 26, emp. in mill, b. St. Sabastien, PQ, s/o Joseph Gauthier (Canada) and Elmer Bernier (Lavie, PQ); W - 19, domestic, b. So. Berwick, ME, d/o Joseph Dupreis (Canada) and Exzilda River (Canada)

GAUTREAU,
Craig E. of Milton Mills m. Vivian E. **Cutter** of Milton 5/31/1980 in Union
Craig E. of Milton Mills m. Twila A. **DuBay** of Rochester 4/25/1987 in Rochester
Eric M. of Milton Mills m. Kim L. **O'Keefe** of Milton 10/25/1980
Mark G. of Milton Mills m. Jean **Worster** of Milton 6/30/1979
Michael W. of Milton Mills m. Evelyn M. **Burrows** of Milton 11/26/1977 in Sanbornville; H - b. 9/10/1954; W - b. 11/18/1958

GAUVREAU,
Donald J. of ME m. Bonita E. **Cross** of ME 3/5/1999

GAYDOS,
John W., Jr. of Milton m. Annette R. **Eldridge** of Rochester 8/28/1976 in New Durham; H - b. 10/18/1942; W - b. 12/21/1947

GAYHART,
John A. of Milton m. Cheryl L. **Fraser** of Milton 6/27/1981

GEARY,
Anthony W. of Milton m. Alice R. **Perkins** of Milton 10/8/1910; H - 21, clerk, b. Waterboro, ME, s/o Samuel R. Geary (Waterboro, ME, weaver) and Carrie B. Thomas (Limerick, ME); W - 18, housework, b. Wolfeboro, d/o Alvaro A. Perkins (Wolfeboro, clerk) and Bertha E. Kimball (Wolfeboro)

Paul A. of Milton m. Lorna **Dall** of Limerick, ME 8/3/1936; H - 21, plumber, 2nd, b. Wolfeboro, s/o Anthony Geary (Waterboro, ME, laborer) and Alice R. Perkins (Wolfeboro, shoe wkr.); W - 20, at home, b. Portland, ME, d/o Edmund Dall (Brunswick, ME, merchant) and Marie Hennessy (Canada, housewife)

GEORGE,
Bernard L. of Milton m. Blanch B. **Sanborn** of Acton, ME 12/10/1921 in Milton Mills; H - 21, mill hand, b. Raymond, s/o Perley E. George (Sandown, farmer) and Florence L. Rand (Auburn); W - 19, weaver, b. Acton, ME, d/o George Sanborn (Acton, ME, farmer) and Stella G. Lane (Wakefield)

Bert D., Jr. of Milton Mills m. Martha L. **Grant** of Milton Mills 8/19/1995

GERARD,
William P. of Wakefield m. Katherine A. **Elwell** of Milton 11/3/1973 in Wakefield; H - b. 10/10/1951; W - b. 3/17/1952

GERRISH,
James F. of Acton, ME m. Emma S. **Archibald** of Milton 10/18/1915; H - 53, farmer, 2nd, b. Acton, ME, s/o Noah R. Gerrish (Acton, ME) and Mary C. Wilson (Londonderry); W - 35, shoe stitcher, b. Milton, d/o John F. Archibald (Milton, carder) and Hannah Greenleaf (Exeter)

William H. of Milton m. Georgie A. **Brown** of Moultonborough 3/10/1888 in Alfred, ME; H - 34, operative, b. Milton; W - 28, b. Moultonborough

GERRY,

Clarence A. of Milton m. L. Belle **Freeman** of Milton 2/19/1930 in Union; H - 71, farmer, 3rd, b. Hardwick, VT, s/o Eli P. Gerry (Cabot, VT, soldier) and Sarah A. Bartlett (Cabot, VT, housewife); W - 59, housekeeper, 2nd, b. Barre, VT, d/o Lucius Thurston (Barre, VT, farmer) and Angeline Cutler (Barre, VT, at home)

Curtis W. of Newfield, ME m. Amy J. **Dunnels** of Newfield, ME 9/19/1917; H - 24, farmer, b. Limerick, ME, s/o Moses Ferry (sic) (Waterboro, ME) and Lillian Roberts (Waterboro, ME); W - 22, at home, b. Newfield, ME, d/o Anson Dunnells (sic) (Newfield, ME, farmer) and Winnie Patch (Newfield, ME)

GHEDONE,

Albert of Acton, ME m. Luella **McDaniel** of Acton, ME 10/29/1912 in Acton, ME; H - 20, laborer, b. Italy, s/o Angelo Ghedone (Italy, laborer) and Katherine Satte (Italy); W - 18, shoe stitcher, b. Sanford, ME, d/o Roy McDaniel (Wakefield, laborer) and Mary Sanborn (Newfield, ME)

GIBBONS,

Wayne S. of Milton Mills m. Shari L. **Rennebu** of Milton Mills 6/18/1994

GIGUERE,

Thomas A. of Sturbridge, MA m. Cheryl L. **Taatjes** of Milton 8/7/1982

GILBERT,

Daniel of Milton m. Ida **Duntley** of Milton 3/16/1889 in Farmington; H - 26, shoe stitcher, b. Farmington, s/o Daniel (Rochester) and Mary (Farmington); W - 18, shoe stitcher, b. Milton, d/o John H. (Milton) and Elizabeth (Milton)

GILE,

Albert of Rochester m. Priscilla A. **Scott** of Milton 7/1/1961 in Rochester; H - 21, student; W - 20, waitress

GILES,

Charles F. of Milton m. Philomen **Sturgeon** of Milton 6/30/1908 in Gonic; H - 46, shoemaker, 2nd, b. Springvale, ME, s/o Jesse Giles (Newfield, ME) and Isabelle Drew (Newfield, ME); W - 29, mill hand, b. Canada, d/o Henry Sturgeon (Canada) and Dorothy Chevotte (Canada)

GILMAN,

John G. of Milton m. Mildred M. **Lake** of Laconia 6/12/1934 in Laconia; H - 23, farmer, b. Lisbon, s/o John S. Gilman (Alton, supt. schools) and Maude Garland (Farmington, housewife); W - 27, nurse, b. Lincoln, d/o Henry Lake (Kent Co., NS, farmer) and Louise Bishop (Woodstock, NB, housewife)

GILMORE,

Frank S. of Milton m. Iva B. **Grace** of Farmington 9/11/1895; H - 27, shoe finisher, 3rd, b. Milton, s/o George A. (Natick, MA); W - 18, lady, b. Farmington, d/o Benjamin (Brookfield, farmer)

Frank S. of Milton m. Clara E. **Tuttle** of Farmington 11/29/1897; H - 32, shoemaker, 4th, b. Milton, s/o George A. Gilmore (Walpole, MA); W - 20, shoe cutter, b. Middleton, d/o Stephen M. Tuttle (Alton, shoemaker)

GLAUSON,

John C. of Milton m. Gay E. **Montanari** of Milton 6/7/1980

GLENNON,

Wesley J., Jr. of Wakefield m. Helen M. **Luscomb** of Milton Mills 5/2/1967; H - 19, laborer; W - 17, student

William R. of Milton m. Gloria A. **Secord** of Farmington 11/5/1949 in Farmington; H - 23, shoe wkr., b. Medford, MA, s/o William E. Glennon (MA) and Lucy E. Staples (Bangor, ME); W - 18, clerk, b. Farmington, d/o Harold B. Secord (MA) and Gertrude McMayes (MA)

GLIDDEN,

Augustus of Farmington m. Hattie J. **Willey** of Farmington 10/31/1891; H - 29, shoemaker, b. Alton, s/o Levi (Alton, farmer) and Alioone

(Alton, housekeeper); W - 26, housekeeper, b. Farmington, d/o Robert (shoemaker) and Mary (Farmington, housekeeper)

Charles A. of Rochester m. Winnie M. **Dorr** of Milton 9/15/1909; H - 48, emp. in mill, 2nd, wid., b. Strafford, s/o Charles A. Glidden (Epping) and Charity Robertson (Rochester); W - 35, housekeeper, 2nd, div., b. Milton, d/o John H. Duntley (Milton) and Elizabeth A. Downs (Milton)

George W. of Milton m. Maude **Nickless** of Leominster, MA 10/4/1913 in Strafford; H - 19, emp. in mill, b. Farmington, s/o Justin Hobbs (Farmington, farmer) and Alma L. Wyatt (Farmington); W - 21, emp. in mill, b. Rochester, d/o Frank Nickless (Hooksett, teamster) and Mary Hildreth (Lunenburg, MA)

Stanley C. of Milton m. Theresa M. **Vachon** of Milton 2/1/1980 in Wakefield

GOLDEN,
Bruce I. of Milton m. Patricia A. **Van Buskirk** of Rochester 8/10/1963 in Rochester; H - 20, salesman; W - 19, office worker

Bruce I. of Milton m. Patricia R. **Loud** of N. Hampton 3/25/1967 in N. Hampton; H - 24, asst. mgr.; W - 20, electric oper.

David E. of Milton m. Barbara E. **Roberts** of Exeter 3/9/1949 in Rochester; H - 26, unemployed, b. C. Barnstead, s/o John E. Golden (Plattsburg, NY) and Nellie B. Locke (Pittsfield); W - 22, unemployed, b. Brooklyn, d/o Sylvester M. Roberts (England) and Marjorie A. Porter (England)

Lawrence of Milton Mills m. Elizabeth J. **Fleming** of Milton Mills 11/25/1978 in Durham; H - b. 3/22/1953; W - b. 5/5/1952

GOLDTHWAITE,
Scott E. of Milton m. Tracy M. **Gardner** of Milton 3/26/1988 in Rochester

GONTHIER,
Paul F. of Somersworth m. Laronda A. **Paey** of Milton 7/1/1989

GOODHEART,
Simon F. of Milton m. Sarah L. **Gane** of Milton 8/24/1916 in Rochester; H - 43, clergyman, 2nd, b. Tilsit, Germany, s/o Herman G. Goodheart (Tilsit, Germany, teacher) and Frieda Walden (Riga, Germany); W -

45, housekeeper, 2nd, b. Plumstead, England, d/o Roger Jones (Dudley, England, retired) and Sarah E. Poulter (Woodford Bridge, England)

GOODWIN,

Carl J., Jr. of Milton m. Margaret J. **Mortensen** of Milton 2/3/1990

Charles H. of Milton m. Stella D. **Hamilton** of Milton 6/4/1910 in S. Acton, ME; H - 25, shoemaker, b. Milton, s/o Benjamin F. Goodwin (Lebanon, ME, painter) and Emma A. Wentworth (Milton); W - 16, shoe stitcher, b. Milton, d/o Edgar F. Hamilton (Milton, farmer) and Carrie A. Hooper (Milton)

Charles W. of Milton m. Eva **Blanch** of Champlain, NY 4/26/1897; H - 23, laborer, b. Milton, s/o Frank Goodwin (Wakefield); W - 26, housekeeper, b. Champlain, NY, d/o Frank Blanch (Champlain, NY)

Frank W. of Milton m. Sarah E. **Brackett** of Milton 4/24/1914 in Milton Mills; H - 33, emp. in mill, b. Milton, s/o Benjamin F. Goodwin (Lebanon, ME, painter) and Emma Wentworth (Milton); W - 29, housework, b. Acton, ME, d/o Levi Brackett (Acton, ME) and Anna G. Gardner (Salem, MA)

Howard W. of Milton Mills m. Frances **Curry** of Sanbornville 10/25/1934 in Acton, ME; H - 19, laborer, b. Milton Mills, s/o Charles H. Goodwin (Milton Mills, laborer) and Stella D. Hamilton (Milton Mills, shoe op.); W - 18, at home, b. Emery Mills, ME, d/o William S. Curry (Stratham, laborer) and Harriette F. Goodwin (Milton Mills, at home)

James R. of Milton m. Elaine M. **Sanborn** of Rochester 6/28/1975; H - b. 7/31/1951; W - b. 2/17/1948

Lloyd E. of Milton m. Barbara J. **Tufts** of Milton 8/28/1942; H - 25, shoe worker, b. Farmington, s/o John F. Goodwin (York, ME, shoe worker) and Inez J. Ham (Alton, housewife); W - 20, shoe worker, b. Milton, d/o John D. Tufts (Middleton, excelsior mill) and Alice M. Hodges (Milton, shoe worker)

GORDON,

Almon of Milton m. Nellie **Cronin** of Milton 12/24/1912 in Acton, ME; H - 24, laborer, b. Shapleigh, ME, s/o Sidney Gordon (Shapleigh, ME, laborer) and Flora Nason (Shapleigh, ME); W - 18, shoe stitcher, b. Acton, ME, d/o William Cronin (Lee, laborer) and Kate Lynch (Marblehead, MA)

Ansel F. of Milton m. Beatrice M. **Bragg** of Milton 4/3/1949; H - 34, woodsman, b. Milton, s/o Almon Gordon (ME) and Nellie Cronin; W - 32, housewife, 2nd, b. Greenfield, d/o Charles Dalphond (VT) and Alice Colby

Glenn A. of Milton m. Wendy A. **Foss** of Milton 2/23/1991

GOSS,

Arthur D. of Boston, MA m. Lucy F. **Cook** of Milton 11/4/1903; H - 41, landlord, 3rd, b. Auburn, ME, s/o Sewell M. Goss (Danville J., ME) and Elmira P. Caville (Kingfield, ME); W - 26, housekeeper, 2nd, b. Acton, ME, d/o Josiah Witham (Acton, ME, farmer) and Mary A. Willey (Salem, MA)

GOSSELIN,

Albert A. of Milton m. Thelma L. **Smith** of Milton 4/21/1934 in Rochester; H - 20, mill op., b. Milton, s/o Joseph A. Gosselin (Canada, retired) and Lucy Bellemeur (Canada, housewife); W - 18, housekeeper, b. Dover, d/o Henry F. Smith (Somersworth, laborer) and Gertrude F. Perkins (Dover, housewife)

Joseph E. of Milton m. Lucy E. **Bellemeur** of Milton 2/20/1906 in Gonic; H - 21, moulder, b. Somersworth, s/o Joseph Gosselin (Canada) and Caroline Cote (Canada); W - 20, at home, b. Canada, d/o Charles H. Bellemeur (Canada, emp. in mill) and Celanire Jellineau (Canada)

Kenneth R. of Rochester m. Linda A. **Knight** of Milton 6/21/1963; H - 20, trucking; W - 18, student

GOWEN,

George W. of Milton m. Annie E. **Baker** of Milton 9/12/1888 in Wakefield

Wesley S. of York Corner, ME m. Lillian M. **Warren** of Rochester 5/26/1910; H - 22, conductor, b. York Corner, ME, s/o William Gowen (York Corner, ME) and Sadie Johnson (York Corner, ME); W - 18, b. Rochester, d/o Wilmer G. Warren (Rochester, sup't. cemetery) and Mabel A. Horne (Rochester)

GRACE,

Bert N. of Milton m. Elsie M. L. **Horne** of Milton 12/24/1910; H - 21, farmer, b. Tamworth, s/o Chandler P. Grace (Chatham, farmer) and

Abbie E. Bean (Conway); W - 25, housekeeper, 2nd, div., b. Milton, d/o Alfred C. Varney (Alfred, ME) and Eva A. Blair (Milton)

Carl L. of Milton m. Mildred P. **Varney** of Milton 7/6/1910; H - 19, farmer, b. Tamworth, s/o Chandler P. Grace (Chatham, farmer) and Abbie E. Bean (Conway); W - 17, housekeeper, b. Farmington, d/o Alfred C. Varney (Alfred, ME) and Eva A. Blake (Milton)

Donald L. of Milton m. Florence E. **Carver** of Farmington 4/16/1971; H - b. 6/18/1949; W - b. 2/20/1952

GRANQUIST,

Karl J. of Lynn, MA m. Ruth O. **Shorey** of Saugus, MA 9/20/1952; H - 39, mach. assembler, 2nd, b. Brockton, MA, s/o Charles Granquist and Hilda Magnuson; W - 50, housewife, 2nd, b. Lynn, MA, d/o Charles O. Darke and Anne Wishart

GRANT,

Angus of E. Rochester m. Margaret **Loughlin** of Milton 9/13/1927 in Farmington; H - 49, shoe oper., b. NS, s/o James E. Grant (NS, farmer) and Mary Frazer (NS); W - 50, at home, b. Cambridge, MA, d/o John Loughlin (Ireland, foreman) and Nellie Callahan (Ireland)

Arthur R. of Lynn, MA m. Olive J. **Copen** of S. Lebanon, ME 8/21/1959; H - 40, civil engineer, 2nd, widower, b. MA, s/o Joseph W. Grant (NS) and Elizabeth A. Strout; W - 40, housework, 2nd, widow, b. S. Lebanon, ME, d/o Frank A. Hall (NH) and Lila B. Wallingford (NH)

Michael M., Jr. of Milton m. Donna A. **Arabia** of Milton 8/16/1992

GRAVES,

Richard A., III of Presque Isle, ME m. Angelika E. K. **Rank** of Gloucester, MA 8/30/1969; H - b. 4/26/1942; W - b. 7/4/1945

GRAY,

Chester E. of Milton m. Arlene I. **King** of Farmington 6/10/1950 in Farmington; H - 19, farmer, b. Farmington, s/o Samuel J. Gray (Gilmanton) and Mildred Marshall (Cambridge, MA); W - 19, shoe wkr., b. Alton, d/o Harry A. King (Alton) and Irene M. Woodman (Alton)

Daniel H. of Rochester m. Sandra J. **Williams** of Milton 3/4/1972; H - b. 9/22/1953; W - b. 10/20/1953

Donald F. of Union m. Charlene B. **Hall** of Milton 4/11/1981

Fred H., Jr. of E. Rochester m. Patricia A. **Williams** of Milton 10/7/1977; H - b. 11/1/1957; W - b. 5/4/1956

Haven J. of Milton m. Almira **Jacobs** of Milton 9/28/1889; H - 24, carpenter, b. Orne, ME, s/o John (St. Johns, NB) and Mary (Oldtown, ME); W - 23, house, b. Lebanon, ME, d/o Isaac (Sanford, ME) and Celissa (Rochester)

Merton F. of Brownfield, ME m. Mildred G. **Moodey** of Boston, MA 3/15/1903; H - 21, laborer, b. Brownfield, ME, s/o Anjavine W. Gray (Eaton, farmer) and Fannie Bickford (Brownfield, ME); W - 22, lady, b. NS, d/o Henry Moodey (NS)

Norman A. of Cary, NC m. Terry L. **Peterson** of Milton 10/7/1989 in Rochester

Perley A. of Milton m. Florence E. **Pope** of Milton 9/10/1954; H - 67, shoe worker, 2nd, b. Lynn, MA, s/o Willis J. Gray and Mary R. Waitt; W - 58, bookkeeper, 2nd, b. Lynn, MA, d/o George W. Wyman and Carrie L. Lewis

Stephen C. of Rochester m. Sharon A. **Appleton** of Milton 6/16/1984

William A. of Milton m. Rita J. **King** of Farmington 9/10/1953 in Farmington; H - 36, shoe worker, b. Alton, s/o Samuel J. Gray and Mildred Marshall; W - 21, at home, b. Alton, d/o Harry A. King and Irene Woodman

GREANEY,

Herbert R. of Amesbury, MA m. Kathleen L. **Bateman** of Newburyport, MA 7/12/1953; H - 36, mechanic, 2nd, b. Amesbury, MA, s/o Martin Greaney and Elsie O'Shea; W - 19, at home, b. Newburyport, MA, d/o Frank Bateman and Elizabeth Leavitt

GREEN,

John F. of Hudson, OH m. Alison L. **Zaeder** of Milton 6/23/1984

GREENE,

Douglas A. of Milton Mills m. Genny P. **Frase** of Wakefield 6/25/1966 in Sanbornville; H - 23, mill worker; W - 24, teacher

James L. of Milton m. Patricia L. **Ferguson** of Milton 7/6/1956 in Newmarket; H - 21, tanner, b. Salem, MA, s/o James C. Greene and Ada M. Hurd; W - 18, student, b. Lynn, MA, d/o Fred J. Ferguson and Louise Downing

GREENLEAF,
Milton C. of Milton m. Alice M. **Henner** of Milton 6/7/1974; H - b. 8/8/1953; W - b. 9/9/1956

GREENWOOD,
Wilfred J. of Milton m. Sarah **Hanscam** of Rochester 7/14/1933 in Rochester; H - 34, mill op., 2nd, b. Somersworth, s/o George Greenwood (Canada, retired) and Marie Rouleau (Canada, housewife); W - 23, at home, b. Marshfield, ME, d/o Charles Hanscam (Machias, ME, mill op.) and Carrie Faulkingham (Jonesport, ME, housewife)

GREGOIRE,
Gerard J. of Milton m. Donna L. **Scala** of Rochester 8/10/1973 in Rochester; H - b. 9/19/1949; W - b. 2/1/1955

GRIFFIN,
John J. of Milton Mills m. Janet L. **York** of Rochester 7/30/1959 in Rochester; H - 17, shoe worker, b. Medford, MA, s/o Thomas F. Griffin (MA) and Frances Fitzpatrick (MA); W - 18, at home, b. Farmington, d/o George A. York (NH) and Barbara T. Wyatt (NH)

Michael E. of Milton Mills m. Robin M. **Bernier** of Milton Mills 11/12/1983 in Wolfeboro

Thomas G. of Milton m. Terri E. **Sanborn** of W. Lebanon, ME 5/4/1963; H - 24, truck driver; W - 18, shoe shop

GRIMES,
Steven P. of Manchester, MA m. Georgeanne L. **Richards** of Salem, MA 10/7/1979

GRISKOWITZ,
Anthony of Garfield, NJ m. Sharon L. **Titcomb** of Rochester 12/22/1962 at Pease AFB; W - 20, USAF; W - 16, student

GRISWOLD,
John of Thompsonville, CT m. Phyllis M. **Connell** of W. Springfield, MA 4/23/1938; H - 24, truck driver, b. Whitman, MA, s/o William Griswold (Whitman, MA, deceased) and Martha Welch (Scatic'k, NY, housewife); W - 24, sales girl, b. Milton, d/o Edward M.

Connell (Littleton, MA, beater eng.) and Ione E. Beaton (Lunenburg, VT, nurse)

GRONDIN,
Leo V. of Milton m. Lesley J. **Liiby** of Milton 6/27/1997

GROVER,
William S. of Dover m. Elizabeth W. **Spencer** of Milton Mills 2/21/1938 in Milton Mills; H - 26, engineer, b. Dover, s/o William A. Grover (Lynn, MA, deceased) and Annie Rutledge (Portsmouth, housewife); W - 20, at home, b. S. Berwick, ME, d/o Frank F. Spencer (Berwick, ME, undertaker) and Ramona Weston (Hanover, housewife)

GUILD,
Frederick A. of Rochester m. Eleanor J. **Masquat** of Milton 8/11/1979

GUSTAFSON,
Carl W. of Milton m. Frances E. **Marsh** of Manchester 3/28/1932 in Manchester; H - 25, tel. oper., b. Milton, s/o Herman Gustafson (Sweden, mason) and Annie Lord (Hingham, MA, housewife); W - 18, operator, b. Manchester, d/o Arthur S. Marsh (Boston, MA, shoeworker) and Grace Rowe (Manchester, shoeworker)

Nicholas H. of Milton m. Sarah A. F. **Miller** of Milton 10/13/1906 in Rochester; H - 42, laborer, b. Sweden, s/o S. Gustafson (Sweden) and Christine ----- (Sweden); W - 36, housekeeper, 2nd, b. Hingham, MA, d/o William H. Lord (W. Quincy, MA, farmer) and Hannah W. Gardner (Hingham, MA)

HAGEMIKE,
Anthony C. of Farmington m. Catherine E. **Appleton** of Milton 5/4/1979

HAGEN,
Stephen G. of Milton m. Paula L. **Allard** of Milton 8/22/1970 in West Milton, H - b. 4/1/1951; W - b. 4/6/1954

HALE,
Albert A. of Rochester m. Mamie C. **Day** of Milton 9/29/1925 in Milton Mills; H - 51, box maker, 2nd, b. Laconia, s/o Samuel Hale (Laconia, farmer) and Susan Durgin (Laconia); W - 35, weaver, b. W.

Newfield, ME, d/o John L. Day (Shapleigh, ME, farmer) and Susan B. Patch (Limerick, ME)

HALL,

Christopher W. of Milton m. Joan E. **Michaud** of Dover 2/11/1994

Gary A. of W. Lebanon, ME m. Sue I. **Moody** of Milton 8/12/1967; H - 22, machinist; W - 20, unemployed

John A. of Milton m. Marion A. **Libby** of Newfield, ME 8/10/1940 in Sanbornville; H - 21, Gen. Elec., b. Milton, s/o John A. Hall (Union, heel shop) and Laura Willey (Milton, housewife); W - 20, at home, b. Granite, d/o Scott D. Libby (W. Newfield, ME, farmer) and Stella Russell (Waterboro, ME, housewife)

Jon L. of Gonic m. Elaine G. **Coburn** of Milton Mills 10/13/1962 in Somersworth; H - 20, shoe shop; W - 18, shoe shop

Kenneth W., Jr. of W. Lebanon, ME m. Brenda J. **Sanborn** of Milton 9/30/1961; H - 20, draftsman; W - 18, clerk

Marshall P. of Epping m. Nancy W. **Chase** of Milton 6/27/1959; H - 23, Navy Yard, b. Newton, MA, s/o Marshall L. Hall (CT) and Melina Filion (NH); W - 22, secretary, b. Rochester, d/o Leslie O. Chase (NH) and Doris Fortier (NH)

Odelon of Milton m. Elsie **Connolly** of Milton 9/26/1906 in Exeter; H - 20, shoemaker, b. Milton, s/o John Hall (Canada, weaver) and Masaline ----- (Canada); W - 18, at home, b. Milton, d/o Timothy Connolly (Milton, painter) and Clara A. Lowd (Acton, ME)

Raymond E. of Milton m. Mary E. **Pires** of Lodi, NJ 4/25/1942; H - 32, salesman, b. Ctr. Effingham, s/o Perley Hall (Sawyers River, VT, deceased) and Myrtle E. Sprague (Shapleigh, ME, housewife); W - 22, at home, b. Peabody, MA, d/o Joseph E. Pires (Lodi, NJ, leather wkr.) and Sarah Martins (Lodi, NJ, housewife)

HAM,

Bernard of Milton m. Rita **Burbank** of Gonic 10/28/1939 in Gonic; H - 22, mill worker, b. Milton, s/o James J. Ham (Dover, mill worker) and Blanche Drew (Brookfield, housewife); W - 18, at home, b. Rochester, d/o Peter Burbank (Canada, box factory) and Annie Dubois (Winthrop, ME, housewife)

Charles E. of Milton m. Lena L. **Varney** of Milton 10/11/1897; H - 37, laborer, 3rd, b. Farmington, s/o Moses Ham (Alton, farmer); W - 21, housekeeper, b. Milton, d/o Eli Varney

Cyrus A. of Milton m. Susie A. **Duffy** of Farmington 3/1/1895; H - 25, mill operative, b. Farmington, s/o Moses Ham (Barnstead, farmer); W - 36, shoe stitcher, b. Brooklyn, NY, d/o John W. Duffy (Dover)

F. Malcolm of Lebanon, ME m. Lilla A. **McCann** of Portland, ME 3/4/1916; H - 23, shoemaker, b. Lebanon, ME, s/o Samuel D. Ham (N. Berwick, ME, farmer) and Alice C. McIntire (Dover); W - 19, teacher, b. Hopedale, MA, d/o Thomas N. McCann (Randolph, supt. heel fact.) and Sarah E. Gilman (Biddeford, ME)

James J. of Milton m. Blanche C. **Drew** of Milton 6/17/1908; H - 20, papermaker, b. Dover, s/o William Ham (Dover) and Margaret Driscoll (Ireland); W - 17, shoe stitcher, b. Brookfield, d/o William H. Drew (Brookfield) and Emeline Drew (Brownfield, ME)

HAMILTON,

Harry of Milton m. Minnie G. **Remick** of Milton 3/5/1902; H - 25, shoemaker, b. Rochester, s/o Edgar F. Hamilton (Milton, shoemaker) and Annie M. Cook (Roxbury, MA); W - 19, shoe stitcher, b. Milton, d/o Charles E. Remick (Milton, shoemaker) and Etta ----- (Newfield, ME)

W. D. E. of Milton m. Anna **Solas** of Roxbury, MA 7/18/1948; H - 50, engineer, 2nd, b. Winthrop, MA, s/o Dave Hamilton (E. Boston, MA, city laborer) and Ellen B. England (NS); W - 34, stenographer, 2nd, b. Greece, d/o Nicholas Kallan (Greece, retired) and Eva Theakou (Greece, housewife)

HAMMOND,

William E. of Portland, ME m. Helen H. **Dexter** of Portland, ME 11/1/1926; H - 46, RR trainman, 2nd, b. Peru, ME, s/o George W. Hammond (Wells, ME, laborer) and Nellie F. Harper (Peru, ME); W - 32, waitress, b. Lewiston Jct., ME, d/o Jesse G. Dexter (Eastport, ME, hotel keeper) and Elva V. Dawes (Bridgton, ME)

HANEY,

David W., Sr. of Milton m. Jeannette O. **Dixon** of Strafford 9/1/1990 in Rochester

HANSCOM,

Teddie S. of Milton m. Wendy A. **Gordon** of Milton 11/27/1999

HANSEN,
William of Wakefield m. Fanny E. **Fletcher** of Milton 10/9/1943 in Wakefield; H - 25, dairy farmer, b. Boston, MA, s/o Dirck Hansen (Copenhagen, Denmark, sales manager) and Mary C. Sullivan (Boston, MA, housewife); W - 23, secretary, b. Acton, ME, d/o Harry P. Fletcher (Caribou, ME, orchard wkr.) and Laura Young (Acton, ME, mill worker)

HANSON,
Lloyd G. of Barnstead m. Natalie L. **Hanson** of Milton 11/26/1945 in Farmington; H - 26, teamster, b. Barnstead, s/o George G. Hanson (Barnstead, farmer) and Alice M. Pickesnell (Dorchester, MA, stenographer); W - 22, housewife, 2nd, b. Farmington, d/o Ralph Wyatt (Farmington, farmer) and Ellen Thompson (Barrington, housewife)

HARDING,
Christopher A. of E. Lebanon, ME m. Cheryl A. **Henderson** of E. Lebanon, ME 4/17/1993

Ralph E. of Milton m. Catherine A. **Boyd** of Milton 6/8/1947; H - 28, bus driver, 2nd, b. NS, s/o Charles S. Harding (VT, engineer) and Edith B. Martin (NS, housewife); W - 25, office wkr., 2nd, b. Dover, d/o Joseph A. Boyd, Sr. (Milton, mechanic) and Catherine R. Lougee (Rochester, housewife)

HARGRAVES,
Carlton J. of Milton m. Lillian R. **Prescott** of Milton 1/19/1904; H - 19, barber, b. Milton, s/o William F. Hargraves (No. Shapleigh, ME, barber) and Alberta J. Cutts (Milton); W - 17, lady, b. Milton, d/o Crosby H. Prescott (Acton, ME, hotel prop.) and Annie Hurd (Acton, ME)

HARMON,
Arthur of Rochester m. Nellie **Ellis** of Milton 11/24/1921; H - 23, boxmaker, b. Sanford, ME, s/o Levi Harmon (Buxton, ME, boxmaker) and Carrie Cate (Biddeford, ME); W - 18, counter maker, b. Milton, d/o George Ellis (Wolfeboro, emp. ice house) and Gertrude Duntley (Milton)

HARRIMAN,
Charles I. of Berwick, ME m. Eva May **Freeman** of Milton 10/30/1921; H - 36, laborer, 2nd, b. Somersworth, s/o James W. Harriman (Somersworth, machinist) and Abbie E. Berry (Waltham, MA); W - 23, housekeeper, 2nd, b. Milton, d/o Walter L. Sanborn (Milton, farmer) and Hattie A. Rines (New Durham)
Eugene E. of Milton m. Isadore **White** of Berwick, ME 9/27/1914; H - 25, carpenter, b. Ossipee, s/o Frank L. Harriman (Ossipee, carpenter) and Sadie A. Hill (Kittery, ME); W - 31, housework, 2nd, b. Berwick, ME, d/o Walter S. Howard (Rochester, shoemaker) and Elizabeth Cooper (Berwick, ME)

HARRIS,
Henry E. of Milton m. Blanche E. **Downs** of Milton 7/17/1894 in Farmington; H - 23, shoemaker, b. Woburn, MA, s/o Otis S. Harris (Woburn, MA, mason) and Jennie L.; W - 18, housekeeper, b. Milton, d/o Hazen W. Downs (Milton, teamster) and Fannie M. (Berwick, ME)
Kenneth W. of Milton m. Emilia J. **Dion** of Wakefield 7/2/1966 in Wakefield; H - 18, shoe worker; W - 16, at home
Timothy J. of Milton m. Donna L. **Leeman** of Milton 8/13/1978; H - b. 9/5/1958; W - b. 8/13/1960

HART,
Lewis P. of Milton m. Addie A. **Bodge** of Milton 9/23/1894; H - 40, farmer, 3rd, b. Worcester, MA, s/o Henry H. Hart (Westboro, MA) and Lucy E.; W - 39, housekeeper, 2nd, b. Wolfeboro, d/o Charles C. [Whitehouse] (Wolfeboro, carpenter) and Laura J. (Effingham)
William P. of Milton m. Donna L. **Hart** of Milton 10/8/1988

HARTE,
Kevin J. of Rochester m. Colleen J. **Cheney** of Milton 1/16/1982 in Rochester

HARTFORD,
Fred S. of Milton m. Hattie E. **Downs** of Milton 7/25/1891; H - 24, shoe cutter, b. Rochester, s/o W. Frank (Rochester, shoemaker) and Esther (Rochester, housekeeper); W - 27, shoe stitcher, b. Milton, d/o Albert F. (Milton) and Dora (Milton, housekeeper)

HARTNETT,
John P. of Milton m. Daisy G. **Douprie** of Milton 2/28/1918; H - 45, ice man, 2nd, b. Lynn, MA, s/o Daniel Hartnett (Ireland, ice man) and Kate Dwyer (Bangor, ME); W - 39, housework, b. Needham, MA, d/o Charles A. Duprie (sic) (Arlington, MA, laborer) and Hattie Shattuck (Peterborough)

HASKELL,
Gerald E. of Kenduskeag, ME m. Nellie M. **Garland** of Wakefield, MA 6/30/1928 in Milton Mills; H - 27, farmer, b. Kenduskeag, ME, s/o Edward E. Haskell (Cornell, ME, farmer) and Fannie R. Everett (Kenduskeag, ME); W - 23, stenographer, b. Milton, d/o Clarence Garland (Wakefield, farmer) and Verna M. Reynolds (Sanford, ME)
Robert P. of Milton m. Catherine C. **Gilkey** of Milton 9/4/1905; H - 27, shoemaker, b. St. Stevens, NB, s/o Robert Haskell (St. Stevens, NB, contractor) and Louise Stanhope (Calais, ME); W - 23, waitress, b. Burlington, VT, d/o John Gildey (sic) (Sidney, CB, miner) and Catherine Stackpole (Spain)

HASTINGS,
Gerald P. of Milton m. Stephanie M. **Dostie** of East Wakefield 9/10/1988 in Sanbornville
Richard M. of Milton Mills m. Ellan M. **Smith** of Ossipee 7/30/1983 in Sanbornville

HATCH,
Francis W. of Milton m. Susie A. **Dyer** of Milton 7/19/1894; H - 32, farmer, b. Lyman, ME, s/o Francis W. Hatch (Lyman, ME) and Margaret; W - 26, housekeeper, 2nd, b. Milton, d/o Jacob F. Staples (Milton, farmer) and A. J. (Boston, MA)
John J. of Malden, MA m. Julie K. **Salaliko** of Lebanon, ME 7/16/1988

HAYES,
Clarence M. of Milton m. Mary A. **Cowan** of Orono, ME 6/14/1904 in Orono, ME; H - 26, mech. eng., b. Milton, s/o Luther Hayes (Lebanon, ME) and Ellen Morrill (Pembroke); W - 28, teacher, b. Orono, ME, d/o Hilborn Cowan (Orono, ME) and ----- Brown (Gorham)

Guy L. of Milton m. Myrtie E. **Clements** of Milton 4/14/1900 in Rochester; H - 22, carpenter, b. Milton, s/o George A. Hayes (Milton, carpenter) and Dora Tuttle (Deerfield); W - 27, shoe stitcher, b. Lebanon, ME, d/o Samuel N. Clements and Charlotte L. Ingalls (Canterbury)

Guy L. of Milton m. Nellie D. **Jones** of Milton 9/5/1938 in Hillsborough; H - 60, carp., mason, 2nd, b. Milton, s/o George A. Hayes (Milton, deceased) and Dora Tuttle (Lebanon, ME, deceased); W - 62, housewife, 2nd, b. Goffstown, d/o Louis T. Daniels (Canada, laborer) and Adeline Garneau (Canada, deceased)

Halton R. of Rochester m. Agnes M. **Townsend** of Milton 4/24/1920 in Milton Mills; H - 26, salesman, b. Rochester, s/o Edwin F. Hayes (Rochester, plumber) and Hattie Pinkham (New Durham); W - 19, at home, b. Milton, d/o John E. Townsend (Milton) and Edna B. Lowd (Acton, ME)

Luther C. of Milton m. Cora E. **McDuffee** of Rochester 9/2/1903 in Rochester; H - 33, farmer, b. Milton, s/o Luther Hayes (Milton) and Sarah D. Coffran (Pembroke); W - 22, teacher, b. Rochester, d/o Daniel S. McDuffee (Rochester, foreman) and Martha J. Pinkham (Rochester)

Maurice L. of Milton m. Grace M. **Stevens** of Ossipee 10/12/1915 in Ossipee; H - 22, inspector, b. Milton, s/o S. Lyman Hayes (Milton, RR clerk) and Annie F. Corson (Milton); W - 22, b. Ossipee, d/o Edwin H. Stevens (Ossipee, farmer) and Lucy Smith (Hamilton, MA)

Milton W. of Milton m. Valna I. **Lover** of Milton 6/28/1930; H - 25, chemist, b. Milton, s/o S. Lyman Hayes (Milton, retired) and Annie F. Corson (Milton, housewife); W - 22, teacher, b. Milton, d/o Peter J. Lover (Wakefield, mill emp.) and Alice M. Downs (Wakefield, housewife)

Norman H. of Allston, MA m. Beatrice C. **Lord** of Milton 6/24/1925; H - 25, mechanic, b. Milton, s/o S. Lyman Hayes (Milton, RR mail clerk) and Annie F. Corson (Milton); W - 22, clerk, b. Biddeford, ME, d/o Frank H. Lord (Huntingville, PQ, merchant) and Harriett A. Lary (Shelburne)

Paul T. of Milton Mills m. Caroline **Wiegman** of Bronx, NY 7/5/1945 in Milton Mills; H - 20, textiles, b. Bradford, MA, s/o Halton R. Hayes (Rochester, textiles) and Agnes Townsend (Rochester, housewife);

W - 20, model, b. Norfolk, VA, d/o Stanley Wiegman (Washington, DC, sea capt.) and Gladys T. Wright (TX, nurse)

Richard W. of Rochester m. Pamela L. **Feyler** of Milton 12/31/1966 in Rochester; H - 19, box shop worker; W - 19, shoe worker

Theodore L. of Milton m. Hattie M. **Ames** of Milton 12/31/1900; H - 27, shoe cutter, b. Milton, d/o George A. Hayes (Milton, carpenter) and Dora E. Tuttle (Deerfield, housewife); W - 29, paper finisher, 2nd, b. Newport, ME, d/o Thomas Smart and Mary E. Smart (New York, NY, housewife)

Walter W. of Somerville, MA m. Gertrude M. **Getchell** of Milton 10/2/1918; H - 32, locom. fireman, b. Milton, s/o S. Lyman Hayes (Milton, RR mail clerk) and Annie F. Corson (Milton); W - 32, music teacher, b. Sanford, ME, d/o William B. Getchell (Putnam, CT) and Dora Higgins (Amesbury, MA)

Warren A. of New Durham m. Virginia L. **Wyatt** of Milton 11/24/1944 in New Durham; H - 21, laborer, b. New Durham, s/o Everett W. Hayes (New Durham, laborer) and Rosana Grenier (Rochester, housewife); W - 19, typist, b. Farmington, d/o Ralph F. Wyatt (Farmington, laborer) and Ellen E. Thompson (Barrington, housewife)

HEATH,

Charles E. of Wakefield m. Marion L. **Hamden** of Milton 5/12/1910 in Brookfield; H - 41, blacksmith, 2nd, div., b. Parsonsfield, ME, s/o Simon B. Heath (Newfield, ME, shoemaker) and Patience J. Stevens (Parsonsfield, ME); W - 22, housekeeper, b. Denmark, ME, d/o Granville Hamden (Denmark, ME, farmer) and Matilda Lord (Stoneham, ME)

HEBERT,

Edgar J., Jr. of Milton m. Laurin A. **Moreau** of Milton 7/9/1994

Edward J. of Milton Mills m. Melodie A. **Hill** of Milton Mills 1/31/1976 in Rochester; H - b. 9/29/1944; W - b. 11/9/1956

HELIE,

Everett C. of Alton m. Carol A. **Marcoux** of Milton 8/11/1962; H - 21, US Navy; W - 17, at home

HEMARD,
Lawrence F. of Milton m. Ann M. **Kenney** of Milton 3/15/1974 in Wakefield; H - b. 11/1/1942; W - b. 11/6/1946

HENDERSON,
Clifford of Rochester m. Geraldine **Horton** of Milton 9/2/1939 in Farmington; H - 20, mill oper., b. Sanford, ME, s/o Charles Henderson (Shapleigh, ME, weaver) and Lillian Hartley (Philadelphia, PA, housewife); W - 22, shoe oper., b. Nashua, d/o George Horton (Nashua, RR emp.) and Albina Labrie (Rochester, housework)
Franklin of Milton m. Leona **Herrick** of Somersworth 8/23/1957 in Somersworth; H - 20, farmer, b. NH, s/o Edwin Henderson (NH) and Ruth Gerrish (NH); W - 18, waitress, b. VT, d/o Charles Herrick (VT) and Esther Proctor (VT)
George F. of Milton m. Hannah A. **Ellis** of Milton 2/16/1889 in Wolfeboro; H - 41, farmer, b. Berwick, ME, s/o Abraham and Caroline; W - 53, house, 2nd, b. Wiscosset
Peter of Milton Mills m. Cara M. **Glidden** of Milton Mills 6/30/1995
Stanley W. of Milton m. Mary M. **Vachon** of Milton 7/17/1982 in Rochester

HENNER,
Richard A. of Milton m. Jane L. **Varney** of Milton 4/24/1964; H - 20, machinist; W - 19, clerk
Robert J. of Milton m. Lorene M. **Steves** of Milton 5/4/1993

HENRY,
Harold of S. Berwick, ME m. Jeannette **Mattress** of Milton Mills 12/1/1956 in Acton, ME; H - 25, shoe shop, b. VT, s/o Hervey Henry and Josephine Croteau; W - 19, nurses aid, b. Rochester, d/o Harold Mattress and Marie Botti

HEON,
Dale P. of Milton Mills m. Michelle L. **Johnson** of Milton Mills 9/27/1997

HERMONAT,
Jason E. of Milton m. Dorothy A. **Vachon** of Milton 2/14/1992

HERSCHEL,
Richard L. of Concord m. Beatrice L. **Horn** of Milton 8/5/1986 in Concord

HERSEY,
Brian E. of Rochester m. Lorraine C. **Fields** of Milton 8/27/1983
Roland D. of Rochester m. Marie J. **Ellis** of Milton 6/11/1977; H - b. 12/5/1954; W - b. 1/14/1958

HERSOM,
Clifton E. of Milton m. Mildred **Weeks** of Milton 5/16/1920 in Milton Mills; H - 19, laborer, b. Lebanon, ME, s/o Elmer F. Hersom (Lebanon, ME, lumberman) and Emily Wilson (Sanford, ME); W - 20, weaver, b. Ossipee, d/o Frank S. Weeks (Porter, ME, physician) and Minnie L. Alley (Porter, ME)
Clifton E. of Milton m. Blanch J. **Walker** of Milton 6/9/1923; H - 22, lumberman, 2nd, b. Sanford, ME, s/o Elmer F. Hersom (Lebanon, ME, lumberman) and Emma Wilson (Sanford, ME); W - 28, housekeeper, 2nd, b. Milton, d/o Moses Chamberlain (Milton, farmer) and Arthie E. Junkins (Wakefield)

HERZOG,
James D. of Bethpage, NY m. Frances E. **Slauenwhite** of Milton 7/17/1982

HESELTON,
Frank I. of Milton m. Georgianna **Palardies** of Canada 9/16/1889 in Rochester; H - 29, mill operative, b. VT, s/o Clifford C. (VT) and Lydia E. (VT); W - 18, house, b. Canada

HESTER,
Frank R. of Dover m. Jacquelyn N. **Kirk** of Milton Mills 4/1/1967; H - 24, factory worker; W - 20, at home

HETT,
Philip E. of Milton m. Jean G. **Fisher** of Milton 7/1/1984 in Rochester

HEWES,
Frederick C. of Rochester m. Helen A. **Dicey** of Milton 4/5/1930 in Springvale, ME; H - 22, shoe oper., b. Norwood, MA, s/o Charles F. Hewes (Lawrence, MA, fac'y supt.) and Harriet Bailey (Newport, VT, housewife); W - 18, shoe oper., b. Milton, d/o Dana M. Dicey (Milton, deceased) and Marion Dixon (Lebanon, ME, housewife)

HEWNER,
Roland J., Jr. of Milton m. Shirley L. **Smith** of Wakefield 11/9/1963; H - 21, mechanic; W - 17, student

HIBBARD,
Gary M. of Milton Mills m. Sharon L. **Lavertue** of Milton Mills 6/17/1978 in Dover; H - b. 10/21/1957; W - b. 1/10/1959

HICKEY,
Daniel of Milton m. Etta **Wentworth** of Milton 2/27/1891; H - 20, weaver, b. Hingham, MA, s/o John (Hingham, MA, carder) and Jane (Augusta, ME, housekeeper); W - 21, weaver, b. Milton, d/o James (shoemaker) and Mary (housekeeper)

HIGGINS,
Daniel E., Jr. of Dorchester, MA m. Evelyn M. **Dallachie** of Brighton, MA 8/23/1949; H - 31, mechanic, 2nd, b. ME, s/o Daniel E. Higgins (ME) and Theresa Garnett (NB); W - 32, secretary, 2nd, b. Needham, MA, d/o James Dallachie (MA) and Lillian Armstrong (MA)
Robert F. of Milton Mills m. Wannetta L. **Crites** of Milton Mills 9/5/1998

HILL,
John W. of Milton m. Cindy K. **Weide** of Milton 7/4/1988
Melvin H. of Milton m. Mildred **Pearl** of Farmington 7/29/1911 in Dover; H - 23, shoemaker, b. Lyman, ME, s/o Freedom R. Hill (Lyman, ME, sawyer) and Ella Cousins (Dayton, ME); W - 18, shoe stitcher, b. Farmington, ME, d/o Preston Pearl (Farmington) and Mattie P. Ricker (NS)
Norman of Boston, MA m. Barbara **Armstead** of Roxbury, MA 6/29/1957; H - 25, janitor, 2nd, black, b. Boston, MA, s/o Clifford Hill (MA) and Anna Hill (MA); W - 24, mechanic, black, b. MA, d/o Robert Armstead (ME) and Catherine Woolen (MA)

Raymond S. of Farmington m. Shirley M. **Lilljedahl** of Milton 6/24/1992
Winfred L. of Milton Mills m. Marjorie **Clough** of Milton Mills 3/9/1940 in Acton, ME; H - 21, truck driver, b. Newton Falls, MA, s/o Joseph H. Hill (NS, painter) and Vera R. Langdale (NS, housewife); W - 23, weaver, b. Acton, ME, d/o Dennis F. Clough (Berwick, ME, boss weaver) and Mamie V. Marsh (Acton, ME, housewife)

HILLAGE,
Benjamin F. of Haverhill, MA m. Geneva M. **Nelson** of Haverhill, MA 6/11/1962; H - 44, coal passer; W - 51, stitcher

HILLSGROVE,
Robert D. of Milton m. Lisa M. **Thurston** of Milton 6/20/1992
W. Merl of Barnstead m. Louise E. **Pike** of Milton Mills 2/6/1933 in Pittsfield; H - 19, farmer, b. Barnstead, s/o Walter J. Hillsgrove (Wilmot, farmer) and Myrtie O. Day (Northwood, housewife); W - 20, stenographer, b. Milton Mills, d/o Philip G. Pike (Milton Mills, storekeeper) and Rosamond E. Piper (Wakefield, school tchr.)

HILTZ,
Willard G. of Ashland m. Garry **Golden** of Ashland 10/4/1952; H - 30, salesman, 2nd, b. NH, s/o Guy M. Hiltz and Mabel Wood; W - 20, clerk, b. NH, d/o John Golden and Blanche Locke

HINTON,
Grant of Milton m. Diane K. **LePage** of Milton 8/31/1999

HISELER,
Stanley W. of Lebanon, ME m. Mary N. **Lessard** of Milton 7/3/1960 in Sanbornville; H - 46, construction; W - 46, shoe worker

HITCHCOCK,
Newell W., Jr. of Milton m. Diedra E. **Barr** of Farmington 5/2/1987 in Farmington

HOBBS,
George W. of Milton m. Angela **Bourgoine** of Rochester 11/20/1982 in Rochester

HOBIN,
Timothy F. of Milton m. Ourania N. **Demetres** of Milton 1/3/1992

HOBLER,
Christopher W. of Milton Mills m. Jennifer M. **Taylor** of Milton Mills 7/12/1997

HODGKINS,
Arthur D. of Milton Mills m. Harriet L. **Fifield** of Milton Mills 9/14/1991

HODSON,
Paul D. of Milton m. Teri J. **Macumber** of Milton 10/24/1992

HOGUE,
Edward J. of Sanford, ME m. Ida **Burnham** of Sanford, ME 6/3/1903; H - 31, steam fitter, b. Malone, NY, s/o Louis D. Hogue (Canada, machinist) and Eliza Gallean (Malone, NY); W - 19, lady, b. Milton, d/o Henry Burnham (Wakefield, teamster) and Sarah A. Mills (Milton)

HOKINSON,
Terry E. of Berwick, ME m. Melissa J. **Redimarker** of South Berwick, ME 7/2/1994

HOLMES,
Arthur E. of Melrose, MA m. Helen M. **Fitzpatrick** of Malden, MA 8/6/1960; H - 21, repairman; W - 18, tel. operator

HOLT,
Brian B. of Portsmouth m. Susan M. **Duggan** of Milton 7/12/1980 in Portsmouth

HOOD,
Leslie J., Jr. of Milton m. Madeline R. **Davis** of E. Rochester 10/26/1944 in E. Rochester; H - 21, Sylvania, b. Springfield, MA, s/o Leslie J. Hood (Lowell, MA, x-ray tech.) and Ida E. Dixon (Lebanon, ME, housewife); W - 20, clerk, b. Acton, ME, d/o Frank E. Davis (Springvale, ME, leatherb'd mill) and Rose M. Comeau (Haverhill, MA, restaurant)

HOPKINS,
Donald A. of Milton m. Frances C. **Hurd** of Rochester 2/12/1943; H - 26, weaver, b. Peterborough, s/o Reuben A. Hopkins (Chelmsford, MA, poultryman) and Chrystabel Hill (Mt. Vernon, shoe oper.); W - 19, spinner, b. Rochester, d/o Robert Eastman (Portland, ME) and Jennie F. Chase (Milan, deceased)

HORN[E],
Charles A. of Milton m. Clara **Knight** of Milton 12/21/1897; H - 42, butcher, b. Milton, s/o Francis D. Horne (Milton); W - 42, housekeeper, b. Milton, d/o Stephen H. Knight (Farmington)
Charles A. of Milton m. Lettie A. **Otis** of Haverhill, MA 10/20/1915 in Nashua; H - 57, merchant, 2nd, b. Milton, s/o Francis D. Horne (Milton) and Sarah A. Ricker; W - 51, milliner, b. Rochester, d/o O. B. Otis (Rochester) and Hannah Worcester (Somersworth)
Clyde H. of Acton, ME m. June E. **Runnels** of Milton 12/6/1947; H - 26, mechanic, b. Acton, ME, s/o Frank G. Horne (Acton, ME, farmer) and Martha M. Treadwell (Acton, ME, housewife); W - 19, tel. oper., b. Milton, d/o Othello D. Runnels (Acton, ME, lumberman) and Pearl E. Wilkinson (Salem, MA, housewife)
George E., Jr. of Milton m. Sandra R. **Woodill** of Milton 9/17/1976 in Rochester; H - b. 5/17/1946; W - b. 12/15/1938
Harold B. of Acton, ME m. Cecelia **Provencher** of Milton 2/18/1939 in Sanbornville; H - 32, laborer, b. Acton, ME, s/o Edgar Horne (Acton, ME, farmer) and Cora Bellzer (UT, housewife); W - 24, shoe worker, b. Sanbornville, d/o Donat Provencher (Canada, ice house) and Melvina Huard (Canada, housewife)
Herman J. of Milton m. Mildred E. **Dow** of Rochester 6/23/1929 in Milton Mills; H - 23, clerk, b. Milton, s/o John E. Horne (Acton, ME, merchant) and Olive A. Moulton (Newfield, ME); W - 25, cashier, b. Dover, d/o Joseph W. Dow (Moultonboro, supt.) and Charlotte Heeney
Jethro E. of Middleton m. Lydia E. **Webber** of Milton 4/28/1900; H - 44, farmer, 2nd, b. Middleton, s/o John D. Horne and Mary E. Chase; W - 36, housekeeper, 2nd, b. Milton, d/o John P. Jones (Milton) and Louisa M. -----
John E. of Milton Mills m. Gertrude M. **Coombs** of Portland, ME 5/1/1926 in Bath, ME; H - 47, merchant, 2nd, b. Acton, ME, s/o John Horne (Acton, ME, lumberman) and Em'e M. B. Meserve

(Wakefield); W - 28, nurse, b. Carbon, IA, d/o Alfred Coombs (W. Bath, ME, farmer) and Amy Howes (Well. Co., Canada)

Orral F. of Milton m. Elsie M. **Varney** of Milton 3/12/1904 in Somersworth; H - 24, shoemaker, b. Rochester, s/o Augustus E. Horne (Wolfeboro, shoemaker) and Nellie S. Johnson (Wolfeboro); W - 18, shoe stitcher, b. Milton, d/o Alfred C. Varney (Milton, shoemaker) and Eva A. Blake

Raymond F., Jr. of Milton m. Mildred K. **French** of Portsmouth 12/31/1956 in Exeter; H - 29, mechanic, b. Milton, s/o Raymond F. Horne and Eva McIntire; W - 22, saleslady, 2nd, b. Laconia, d/o William F. French and Isabel Bunker

Vaun E. of Milton m. Deborah L. **Cheney** of Milton 3/30/1985

HORNER,

Leonard C. of Wilmington, DE m. Janet **Gathmann** of Milton 6/23/1945; H - 29, secretary, b. Hebron, MD, s/o Ira N. Horner (Norristown, PA, barber) and Sarah A. Foskey (Delmar, DE, housewife); W - 23, dietitian, b. Oak Park, IL, d/o Paul A. Gathmann (Chicago, IL, retired) and Catharine Willey (Milton, housewife)

HORTON,

Michael A. of Milton m. Sandra L. **Glichouse** of Milton 8/1/1998

HOULE,

James F. of Raymond m. Tona D. **Hanley** of Milton Mills 9/7/1957 in Sanbornville; H - 21, student, b. NH, s/o Reginald Houle (NH) and Lillian Dockham (NH); W - 22, med. tech., b. MA, d/o Rolla T. Hanley (VT) and Agnes McGibney (ME)

John R. of Farmington m. Mahala J. **Bickford** of Milton Mills 8/7/1970 in Farmington; H - b. 7/23/1941; W - b. 3/27/1949

HOWARD,

Francis O. of Rochester m. Marguerite O. **Downs** of Milton 11/14/1936 in Dover; H - 21, mill oper., b. Rochester, s/o Ormsby L. Howard (Barrington, shoe oper.) and Florence Canney (Rochester, housewife); W - 21, housework, 2nd, b. Milton, d/o Ambrose M. Brown (Brighton, MA, mill oper.) and Ora Blouin (Milton, housewife)

Kevin of Milton m. Christine M. **Fogg** of Milton 5/22/1999

HOWE,
Scott E. of Milton m. Hazel G. **Reed** of Wakefield 5/31/1920 in Union; H - 30, laborer, 2nd, b. Laconia, s/o Willis E. Howe (N. Hatley, PQ, sexton) and Mamie E. Davis (Laconia); W - 18, mill operative, b. Wakefield, d/o Edwin S. Reed (Wakefield, mill operative) and Inez M. Dicey (Effingham)

HOWLAND,
John J. of Carroll m. Lulu A. **Barnes** of Milton 11/1/1899 in Milton Mills; H - 39, hotel prop., b. Canada, s/o John Howland; W - 34, lady, b. Milton, d/o George Barnes

HOYT,
George L. of Milton m. Laura E. **Jones** of Milton 3/23/1918; H - 48, farmer, b. Milton, s/o Rufus A. Hoyt (Rochester, shoemaker) and Lucy A. Drew (Brookfield); W - 34, housework, b. Milton, d/o Alfred W. Jones (Randolph, MA, farmer) and Ella S. Kimball

John F. of Farmington m. Gertrude M. **Paul** of Milton 6/24/1950; H - 20, shoe wkr., b. Belmont, s/o John M. Hoyt (Belmont) and Alice Danforth (Laconia); W - 19, housewife, b. Rochester, d/o Joseph Paul (MA) and Gertrude McNeil (RI)

HUDGINS,
Isaac R. of Milton m. Shannon K. **Kirk** of Milton 8/19/1989

HUGHES,
Edward, Jr. of Natick, MA m. Jeralyn **Wong** of Natick, MA 8/9/1989
Mark A. of Milton m. Kimberly A. **Campbell** of Milton 9/22/1984 in Gonic
Michael K. of Milton m. Teresa A. **Salamy** of San Antonio, TX 7/16/1990
Micheal K. of Milton m. Gail A. **Gage** of Milton 2/14/1978; H - b. 3/23/1957; W - b. 2/14/1952

HULL,
Robert H. of Hampton m. Elizabeth **Pray** of Milton 11/18/1972; H - b. 3/30/1909; W - b. 4/3/1912

HUNT,
James G. of Milton m. Sarah Ann **Wilson** of Milton 2/25/1932 in Union; H - 68, merchant, 2nd, b. Georgetown, DC, s/o James G. Hunt (Boston, MA, merchant) and Jennie E. Elliott (Richmond, VA, housewife); W - 56, nurse, 2nd, b. England, d/o John C. Barker (England, merchant) and Annie A. Atherly (England, housewife)

HUNTER,
Charles O., Jr. of Milton m. Virginia B. **Staples** of New Durham 9/19/1947 in New Durham; H - 23, mill man, b. Somerville, MA, s/o Charles O. Hunter, Sr. (Charlestown, MA, retired) and Jennie Magee (Arlington, MA, housewife); W - 18, at home, b. Tuftonboro, d/o Charles F. Staples (Wolfeboro, millman) and Doris Willard

HUNTLEY,
Charles J. of Wakefield, MA m. Bessie **Pike** of Wakefield, MA 7/31/1938; H - 25, fireman, b. Manchester, s/o Charles J. Huntley (Old Lyme, CT, contractor) and Lillian Bushey (MN, housewife); W - 21, at home, b. Everett, MA, d/o Archibald Pike (NB, carpenter) and Hazel Elms (Lynn, MA, housewife)

HUNTRESS,
Joseph of Shapleigh, ME m. Lovie **Ross** of Sanford, ME 11/18/1891; H - 30, farmer, b. Shapleigh, ME, s/o Ichabod and Mary; W - 27, housekeeper, b. Lebanon, ME

HURD,
Arthur S. of Milton m. Lizzie **Webber** of Milton 8/29/1897 in Wakefield; H - 18, blanket fin., b. Lebanon, ME, s/o Frank J. Hurd (Milton, fireman); W - 16, lady, b. Milton, d/o Parker G. Webber (Shapleigh, ME, carpenter)

Carl R. of Acton, ME m. Sophie E. **Ramsey** of Milton 8/1/1941; H - 23, teacher, b. Acton, ME, s/o Irl R. Hurd (Acton, ME, farmer) and Mary B. Turner (Glasgow, Scotland, housewife); W - 20, maid, b. Saco, ME, d/o Frank E. Ramsey (Somersworth, farmer) and Sophie M. Smith (Schuyler, NE, housewife)

George I. of Acton, ME m. Jennie L. **Ramsey** of Milton 8/22/1947 in N. Berwick, ME; H - 26, farmer, b. Acton, ME, s/o Ire R. Hurd (Acton, ME, farmer) and Mary B. Turner (Glasgow, Scotland, housewife);

W - 23, office wkr., b. Saco, ME, d/o Frank S. Ramsey
(Somersworth, farmer) and Sophie Smith (Schuyler, NE, housewife)

John C. of Milton Mills m. Catherine T. **Daoust** of Rochester 7/22/1946 in Rochester; H - 30, chef, b. Milton, s/o Ralph H. Hurd (Milton Mills, mill emp.) and Florence E. Tuttle (Wakefield, housewife); W - 30, at home, 2nd, b. Clinton, MA, d/o John W. O'Malley (England, gas foreman) and Catherine Ferguson (Ireland, at home)

Mervyn F. of Milton Mills m. Alice E. **Stevens** of Middleton 8/31/1930 in Rochester; H - 20, salesman, b. Milton Mills, s/o Ralph H. Hurd (Milton Mills, fin'r in mill) and Florence E. Tuttle (Wakefield, housewife); W - 18, at home, b. Middleton, d/o Albert Stevens (Middleton, farmer) and Bernice Tufts (Middleton, housewife)

William F. of Milton m. Lillian A. **Richards** of Buxton, ME 12/20/1913; H - 32, emp. in mill, b. Acton, ME, s/o Frank J. Hurd (Acton, ME, farmer) and Cora B. Jenness (Acton, ME); W - 36, weaver, 2nd, b. Buxton, ME, d/o Rias Richards (Buxton, ME) and Nancy Dunn (Buxton, ME)

Willie G. of Milton m. Nellie A. **Varney** of Milton 10/24/1895; H - 27, farmer, b. Tilton, s/o Henry (Farmington, farmer); W - 25, housekeeper, b. Farmington, d/o Beard (Farmington, farmer)

HUSSEY,

Daniel E. of Rochester m. Sandra D. **Hobbs** of Milton 7/29/1978 in Middleton; H - b. 1/1/1957; W - b. 5/30/1958

John S. of Berwick, ME m. Jean **Brown** of Milton 1/14/1989

Kenneth R. of Milton Mills m. Christine P. **Maxfield** of Milton Mills 3/22/1975 in Rochester; H - b. 9/18/1932; W - b. 2/7/1932

Kenneth R., III of Milton Mills m. Pamela L. **Adjutant** of Farmington 6/27/1999

HUTCHINS,

Edwin H. of Wakefield m. Gloria J. **Clough** of Milton 7/27/1947; H - 20, farmer, b. Wolfeboro, s/o Bernard Hutchins (Wakefield, mechanic) and Teresa Hayes (Tuftonboro, housewife); W - 16, spooler, b. Milton, d/o Dennis Clough (Berwick, ME, woolen mill) and Mamie Marsh (Acton, ME, housewife)

James E. of Milton Mills m. Mary J. **Marcoux** of Milton 8/28/1976; H - b. 2/17/1956; W - b. 3/31/1956

James E. of Milton Mills m. Kathy J. **Laurent** of Rochester 2/29/1984 in Rochester

INGALLS,
Edmund J. of Portland, ME m. Marion **Tardiff** of Portland, ME 11/9/1932; H - 28, mechanic, 2nd, b. Denmark, ME, s/o James Ingalls (Denmark, ME, farmer) and Sadie L. Smith (Denmark, ME, housewife); W - 22, at home, b. Bangor, ME, d/o Louis Tardiff (MI, farmer) and Dazarnille Morin (Canada)

INGRAM,
Charles of Hyannis, MA m. Mildred **Reichert** of Hyannis, MA 12/20/1937; H - 29, lawyer, b. Lynn, MA, s/o John Ingram (NB, lawyer) and Julia E. Sarvis (Wyoming, OH, housewife); W - 31, reporter, b. Pawnee, IL, d/o Edward Reichert (Pawnee, IL, fruit grower) and Mary H. Dyson (Auburn, IL, dead)

INNES,
Andrew Ernest of Lebanon, ME m. Ellen M. **Carey** of So. Boston, MA 6/14/1921; H - 29, laborer, b. Restigech, NB, s/o Alexander Innes (Scotland, farmer) and Christena MacNeir (New Mills, NB); W - 27, dressmaker, b. Campbellton, NB, d/o Thomas Carey (Carlton, PQ, farmer) and Jane Smith (PQ)
Hugh M. of Milton m. Mary C. **Jones** of Lebanon, ME 7/1/1950 in Rochester; H - 66, beaterman, 2nd, b. NB, s/o Alexander Innes (NB) and Christine McNair (NB); W - 59, at home, b. Milton, d/o Ira W. Jones (Milton) and Lucia C. Wentworth (Milton)

IRVINE,
William H. of Dover m. Donna L. **Tanner** of Milton 9/19/1981

ISENBERG,
Henry M. of Milton m. Camille R. **Clement** of Milton 12/26/1987 in Tamworth

JACKSON,
Keith F. of Barrington m. Audrey M. **Perry** of Milton 7/15/1967; H - 19, mechanic; W - 17, student

JACOBS,
David J. of Milton m. Allison M. **Ferron** of Candia 8/21/1999
David W. of Milton m. Lauren J. **Joos** of Milton 10/3/1975; H - b. 5/5/1957; W - b. 2/19/1955
John of East Rochester m. Annie **Downs** of Milton 2/15/1930 in East Rochester; H - 22, weaver, b. East Rochester, s/o Moses H. Jacobs (Shapleigh, ME, fireman) and Mary E. Clark (N. Lebanon, ME, housewife); W - 21, housewife, b. Milton, d/o Fred Downs (Lebanon, ME, mill) and Eva West (Wakefield, housewife)
Joseph E. of Lebanon, ME m. Mary J. **Ward** of Lebanon, ME 6/5/1954; H - 21, US Navy, b. Rochester, s/o H. Norris Jacobs and Grace Hersam; W - 20, decorator, b. Milton, d/o Donald F. Ward and Jeanette Blouin
Stephen N. of Lebanon, ME m. Betty J. **Chase** of Milton 5/4/1952 in Rochester; H - 20, US Navy, b. NH, s/o Henry N. Jacobs and Grace R. Hersom; W - 18, at home, b. NH, d/o George H. Chase and Adaline G. Willey
Stephen N. of Milton m. Dorothy J. **Murphy** of Rochester 10/6/1973; H - b. 9/21/1931; W - b. 9/4/1921

JAMES,
Robert E. of Milton m. Sherry L. **Saltzman** of E. Lebanon, ME 7/20/1991
Robin L. of Milton m. Leslie C. **Sirois** of Milton 6/1/1991

JAREST,
Octave J. of Peterborough m. Florence H. **Bigelow** of Milton 7/18/1953; H - 34, basket mkr., b. Peterborough, s/o Remi Jarest and Eva Hill; W - 29, checker, b. VT, d/o E. Lincoln Bigelow and Marian Turner

JENKINS,
Greg J. of Bath, ME m. Sarah L. **Green** of Bath, ME 3/21/1962; H - 21, market; W - 18, student

JENNESS,
Edwin C. of Milton m. Grace S. **Corson** of Milton 11/13/1909 in Acton, ME; H - 25, teamster, b. Milton, s/o Edwin P. Jenness (Milton, laborer) and Alma J. Hawkins (Dover); W - 26, emp. in mill, b. Rochester, d/o James R. Corson (laborer) and Annie L. Smith (Dover)

Joseph C. of Acton, ME m. Sarah M. **Day** of Milton 4/28/1917 in Milton Mills; H - 29, weaver, b. Milton, s/o Edwin P. Jenness (Wakefield, laborer) and Alma J. Hawkins (Dover); W - 28, weaver, 2nd, b. Brookfield, d/o Samuel M. Allen (Brookfield, mason) and Emma Cummings (Wakefield)

Raymond W. of Milton Mills m. Pauline F. **Bellemeur** of Rochester 3/9/1946 in Rochester; H - 23, farm hand, b. Nashua, s/o Daniel W. Jenness (Ayer, MA, fireman) and Alice B. Whitcomb (Brookline, housewife); W - 21, shoe oper., b. Rochester, d/o William N. Bellemeur (Sanbornville, box mill) and Alta M. Jenness (Rochester)

JEWETT,
Charles G. of Rochester m. Marilyn E. **Harrington** of Milton 8/11/1951 in East Rochester; H - 21, lumberman, b. NH, s/o Harold D. Jewett (ME) and Dorothy Grenier (NH); W - 19, at home, b. MA, d/o Herman F. Harrington (NH) and Violet DeMoranville (NH)

Clayton G. of Milton m. June E. **Roberts** of Milton 8/15/1970; H - b. 6/23/1930; W - b. 8/16/1932

Clayton G. of Milton m. Norma R. **Woodbury** of Milton 8/25/1972; H - b. 6/23/1930; W - b. 5/18/1937

Richard I. of Milton m. Sarah D. **Lowd** of Acton, ME 11/24/1909; H - 25, farmer, b. Milton, s/o Haven R. Jewett (Milton, farmer) and Nellie M. Sibley (Boston, MA); W - 34, housekeeper, b. Acton, ME, d/o George W. Lowd (Acton, ME) and Mary E. Hersom (Stoneham, MA)

JOHNSON,
Clarence E. of Rochester m. Josephine L. **Gosselin** of Milton 8/28/1926 in Rochester; H - 21, foreman, b. Rochester, s/o Ellsworth M. Johnson (Strafford, teamster) and Eva Corson (Barrington); W - 20, mill operative, b. Rochester, d/o Joseph Gosselin (Canada, mill operative) and Emma Bellemeur (Milton)

David L. of Milton m. Karen A. **Goodwin** of Rochester 12/9/1984

Ernest of Sanford, ME m. Eva **Bissitt** of Sanford, ME 1/14/1911; H - 21, clerk, b. No. Berwick, ME, s/o Dennis Johnson (Sanford, ME, teamster) and Gertrude R. Haines (Alfred, ME); W - 17, clerk, b. Edmundston, NB, d/o George Bissitt (Lauladois, CB, blacksmith) and Emily Dumont (Revierre Delo'x)

Fred E. of Somerville, MA m. Stella A. **Murray** of Milton 9/20/1911; H - 25, fireman, b. MN, s/o William Johnson (Charlestown, MA, engineer) and Sarah F. Fifield (Stow, ME); W - 24, milliner, b. Milton, d/o Daniel Murray (Acton, ME, merchant) and Helen J. Smith (Charleston, ME)

Jack of Milton m. Kimberly R. **Doucette** of Milton 11/18/1993

Larry A. of Milton m. Shirley A. **Hanson** of Milton 10/28/1978; H - b. 8/31/1947; W - b. 11/19/1946

Larry A. of Milton m. Claire G. **Johnson** of Milton 12/21/1991

Norman H. of Milton m. Darlene L. **Joy** of Wakefield 6/22/1974 in Union; H - b. 6/4/1954; W - b. 9/4/1957

Roland C. of Groveton m. Pauline R. **Eaton** of Groveton 3/10/1973; H - b. 1/18/1928; W - b. 7/22/1939

JONES,

Arthur of Milton m. Hazel M. **Millitte** of Milton 6/17/1932 in Rochester; H - 43, woodsman, 2nd, b. E. Rochester, s/o Samuel Jones (E. Rochester, carpenter) and Etta Rogers (N. Shapleigh, ME, housewife); W - 32, housekeeper, 2nd, b. York, ME, d/o Henry Pineo (Halifax, NS, carpenter) and Etta Perkins (Rollinsford, housewife)

Arthur G. of Lebanon, ME m. Bertha L. **Marsh** of Acton, ME 11/11/1897 in Springvale, ME; H - 21, farmer, b. Lebanon, ME, s/o Gersham Jones (Lebanon, ME, farmer); W - 21, housekeeper, b. Acton, ME, d/o Drew Marsh (farmer)

Bruce D. of Milton m. Judith M. **Robinson** of Milton 7/31/1999

Charles A. of Milton m. Nellie M. **Crocker** of Wakefield 12/6/1898 in Rochester; H - 47, farmer, b. Milton, s/o George H. Jones (Milton, farmer); W - 29, lady, b. Hyde Park, MA, d/o Aldin Crocker

Charles A. of Milton m. Mary E. **Frost** of Milton 2/13/1904; H - 52, farmer, 2nd, b. Milton, s/o George H. Jones (Milton, farmer) and Lucy J. Varney; W - 41, housekeeper, 2nd, b. Wolfeboro, d/o Daniel T. Whitehouse (Wolfeboro, watchman) and Martha A. Burke (Wolfeboro)

Charles A. of Milton m. Nellie E. **Daniels** of Barnstead 6/7/1916; H - 65, farmer, 3rd, b. Milton, s/o George H. Jones (Milton) and Lucy Varney (Milton); W - 40, housekeeper, b. Goffstown, d/o Louis Daniels (St. Monique, PQ) and Adeline P. Gardner (St. Antoine, PQ)

Wilber E. of Middleboro, MA m. Susan F. **Merrow** of Milton 7/2/1906; H - 31, shoemaker, b. Ft. Fairfield, ME, s/o Edward F. Jones (Ft.

Fairfield, ME, farmer) and Ruth J. Webb (Ft. Fairfield, ME); W - 17, shoe stitcher, b. New Durham, d/o Wilber S. Merrow (Ossipee, shoemaker) and Lizzie Mitchell (Middleton)

William E. of Milton m. Sarah A. **Bly** of Acton, ME 11/12/1904 in Acton, ME; H - 42, jeweler, 2nd, b. Middleton, s/o John Jones (Bangor, ME) and Mary S. Burroughs (Middleton); W - 30, shoe stitcher, b. Epping, d/o Jacob M. Bly (Brentwood) and Lydia A. Tuttle

JOOS,

David D. of Milton m. Marlys E. **Newton** of Phoenix, AZ 12/10/1966 in Rochester; H - 31, teacher; W - 29, student

JORDAN,

George Ed. of Milton m. Sarah E. **Waycott** of Milton 12/4/1918 in Rochester; H - 42, shoe cutter, b. Milton, s/o George I. Jordan (Prospect, ME) and Elizabeth A. Downs (Dover); W - 42, housekeeper, 2nd, b. Lynn, MA, d/o Charles W. Brown (Pittsfield) and Mary A. Loge (Lawrenceville, IN)

JOY,

Donald A. of Wakefield m. Gayle J. **Merrill** of Milton 9/9/1974 in Union; H - b. 1/19/1955; W - b. 2/1/1955

Douglas E. of Wakefield m. Cheryl L. **Davis** of Milton 4/15/1960 in Wakefield; H - 17, laborer; W - 16, at home

Leslie E. of Union m. Nancy A. **Pageau** of Milton 8/27/1966; H - 26, NCR service; W - 20, student

Stephen P. of Wakefield m. Lucinda E. **Hicks** of Milton 3/30/1974 in Union; H - b. 9/28/1954; W - b. 10/11/1955

JULIN,

Arnold S. of Milton m. Elsie E. **Williams** of Arlington, MA 7/18/1931 in Arlington, MA; H - 25, poultry farmer, b. E. Boston, MA, s/o Gustav Sigfrid and Vanja Smith; W - 24, teacher, b. Boston, MA, d/o Griffith Williams and Winifred Andrews

Gwyn A. of Milton m. Patricia H. **Kelly** of Union, NJ 6/12/1965 in Durham; H - 25, teacher; W - 22, student

KAPISE,

Donald L. of Farmington m. Mary M. **Pomeroy** of Milton 5/16/1986

KASSA,
Randy J. of Pensacola, FL m. Alison M. **Rouleau** of Milton 8/13/1977 in Wolfeboro; H - b. 7/31/1954; W - b. 6/5/1952

KASSAB,
Shamel A. of Milton m. Denise E. **Richardson** of Milton 9/8/1990 in Exeter

KASZYNSKI,
Dennis P. of Milton m. Helen I. **Brown** of Milton 6/5/1982 in Rochester
Stanley A. of Milton m. Joan B. **Hodgdon** of Milton 7/2/1977; H - b. 12/1/1956; W - b. 9/1/1938

KEAN,
Gerald L., Jr. of Rochester m. Dawn M. **Stacy** of Wakefield 3/27/1999
Kevin J. of Milton m. Wendy L. **White** of Milton 8/31/1996

KEARNEY,
Gordon P. of S. Braintree, MA m. Pearl M. **Drollett** of S. Braintree, MA 11/11/1934; H - 30, oil b. serv., b. Chelsea, MA, s/o Peter Kearney (Canada, electrician) and Jane Lavangie (Canada, housewife); W - 21, salesgirl, b. S. Braintree, MA, d/o George Drollett (Braintree, MA, rubber wks.) and Ada F. Thayer (Braintree, MA, housewife)

KEDDIE,
Arthur W. of Milton m. Lula E. **Britton** 12/25/1923 in Rochester; H - 31, finisher, 2nd, b. Beverly, MA, s/o Robert Keddie (Edenborough, Scotland, carriage trimmer) and Jennie Dease (Edenborough, Scotland); W - 36, housekeeper, 2nd, b. Parsonsfield, ME, d/o George Andrews (Parsonsfield, ME, farmer) and Rose Chase (Parsonsfield, ME)

KEEGAN,
Joseph P. of Milton Mills m. Suzie Jo **Elliot** of Milton Mills 9/29/1990

KEENE,
Carl H. of Milton m. Eva M. **Lessard** of Milton 5/2/1920; H - 32, laborer, b. Boston, MA, s/o Charles H. Keene (Reading, England, laborer) and Catherine M. McKenery (Newfoundland); W - 26, domestic, b.

Rochester, d/o Belaine Lessard (Canada, farmer) and Delvina Dion (Canada)
Nelson B. of Milton m. Lillian E. **Gerry** of Rochester 6/21/1942 in Rochester; H - 25, machinist, 2nd, b. Boston, MA, s/o Earl H. Keene (MA, beaterman) and Eva M. Lessard (Rochester, housewife); W - 23, shoe oper., b. Waterboro, ME, d/o Arthur H. Gerry (Limerick, ME, teamster) and Ethel G. Heath (Limerick, ME, housewife)
Norman G. of Milton Mills m. Eva **Grenier** of Rochester 3/14/1927 in Union; H - 21, bronzesetter, b. Kittery, ME, s/o Oren Keene (Marlboro, MA, shoemaker) and Martha Gooch (Alton); W - 19, housekeeper, b. Rochester, d/o Archie Grenier (Canada, boxmaker) and Mary Silver (Canada)
Robert N. of Rochester m. Irene T. **Castonguay** of Rochester 1/14/1967; H - 23, pipefitter; W - 20, bookkeeper

KELLER,
Stephen E. of Rochester m. Jayne A. **Elliott** of Milton 7/10/1993

KENDALL,
Algen W. of Lebanon, ME m. Marie A. **Tanner** of Lebanon, ME 2/8/1919; H - 34, foreman, 2nd, b. Shirley, MA, s/o Jason T. Kendall and Ida F. Boynton; W - 34, housekeeper, 2nd, b. Clare Morris, Ireland, d/o John Devaney (Clare Morris, Ireland, farmer) and Bessie Beisty (Clare Morris, Ireland)
Steven J. of Rochester m. Diane M. **Tanner** of Milton 6/24/1977; H - b. 4/13/1957; W - b. 3/11/1959

KENNEDY,
Leroy V. of Lebanon, ME m. Vicki L. **Cunningham** of Lebanon, ME 9/28/1996

KENNEY,
Frank A. of Milton m. Nettie M. **Ellis** of Milton 3/19/1908; H - 29, emp. paper mill, b. Burlington, MA, s/o Bernard Kenney (Ireland) and Abbie Young (Eaton); W - 32, housekeeper, 2nd, b. Sanbornville, d/o Charles Dyer (Brownfield, ME, farmer) and Martha A. Drew (Brookfield)
Herbert N. of Milton m. Grace E. **Yeaton** of Milton 12/21/1901; H - 22, laborer, b. Farmington, s/o George H. Kenney (Lebanon, ME,

shoemaker) and Lulu Wentworth (Farmington); W - 18, lady, b. Wolfeboro, d/o John Yeaton (Wolfeboro, laborer) and Eunice S. Black

KENNISTON,
Herbert W. of Lee m. Florence E. **Ellis** of Milton 4/22/1903; H - 28, farmer, b. Lee, s/o Greenleaf C. Kenniston (Epping, farmer) and Mary F. Kenniston (Newmarket); W - 18, lady, b. Milton, d/o Ephraim Ellis and Hannah A. Jones (Middleton)

KETCHAM,
Wesley J., Jr. of Milton m. Polly A. **Gillen** of Milton 9/8/1996

KIERSTEAD,
Charles F. of Milton m. Augusta M. **George** of Milton 4/9/1916 in Acton, ME; H - 24, shoemaker, b. Boston, MA, s/o Charles F. Kierstead (NS, machinist) and Christiana Bradshaw (Canada); W - 19, shoe stitcher, b. Raymond, d/o Perley George (Sandown, shoemaker) and Florence L. Rand (Auburn)

KILGORE,
George L. of Milton m. Lizzie A. **Witham** of Milton 8/24/1890 in Wakefield; H - 23, shoemaker, b. Waterford, ME, s/o Liberty (farmer) and Susan A. (dead); W - 19, mill operative, b. Milton, d/o Josiah (mill operative) and Abbie (dead)

KIMBALL,
Arthur H. of Milton m. Carrie P. **Bragg** of Milton 2/27/1904; H - 45, emp. in mill, b. Farmington, s/o Alvah M. Kimball and Annie M. Hayes (Farmington); W - 39, housekeeper, 2nd, b. No. Shapleigh, ME, d/o Simon Bragg (Acton, ME, farmer) and Mahala Ross (Acton, ME)
Bruce A. of Milton m. Cynthia L. **Veno** of Milton 9/7/1985
Bruce A. of Milton m. Jodie A. **Ward** of Milton 8/4/1996
Charles A., Jr. of Milton m. Annie X. **Daley** of Salem, MA 2/20/1917 in Salem, MA; H - 23, farmer, b. S. Boston, MA, s/o Charles A. Kimball (Middleton, farmer) and Clara F. Tripp (S. Boston, MA); W - 20, mill hand, b. Salem, MA, d/o Edward Daley (Ireland, engineer) and Bridget Grogan (Salem, MA)

David of Milton m. Marie **Lachapelle** of Haverhill, MA 2/1/1899 in Milton Mills; H - 18, shoemaker, b. Middleton, s/o Daniel Kimball (Parsonsfield, ME, shoemaker); W - 20, shoe stitcher, b. Haverhill, MA, d/o Joseph Lachapelle (Canada, policeman)
Nathaniel T., Jr. of Rochester m. Clara E. **Chipman** of Milton 9/7/1923; H - 28, NH forestry, b. Rochester, s/o Nathaniel T. Kimball (Farmington, treas., RCA) and Lizzie G. Trask (Milton); W - 19, stenographer, b. Milton, d/o Edward S. Chipman (Natick, MA, leatherboard finisher) and Bertha M. Drew (Milton)
Ralph W. of Milton m. Gladys M. **Wingate** of Rochester 9/9/1921 in Portsmouth; H - 22, chemist, b. Milton, s/o Ralph M. Kimball (Rochester, shoemaker) and Carrie M. Willey (Middleton); W - 23, at home, b. Rochester, d/o William H. Wingate (Rochester, shoemaker) and Mabel L. French (Gilmanton)

KINDSVATER,
William D. of Haddon Heights, NJ m. Kathy A. **Richards** of Milton Mills 6/10/1978; H - b. 4/1/1958; W - b. 3/14/1958

KING,
David of Milton m. Bella C. **Fernald** of Milton 11/9/1889 in Rochester; H - 23, laster, b. Canada, s/o David (Canada) and Blondine (Canada); W - 18, shoe stitcher, b. Wolfeboro, d/o Albert (Wolfeboro) and Lucy
George H. of Acton, ME m. Grace M. **Rowe** of Acton, ME 6/18/1902; H - 22, mor. dresser, b. Barrington, s/o Patrick King (stone cutter) and Susie M. Rowe (Barrington); W - 22, weaver, b. Alfred, ME, d/o Len Rowe (conductor) and Emma ----- (Alfred, ME)

KIRK,
Elwin R. of Milton Mills m. Susan B. **Logan** of Milton 2/25/1967; H - 19, student; W - 16, student
Elwin R. of Milton Mills m. Louise H. **Oakes** of Milton Mills 8/15/1986
Stephen J. of Milton Mills m. Emily M. **Young** of Milton 11/22/1970; H - b. 9/11/1950; W - b. 7/19/1952

KLADDER,
Matthew J. of Milton m. Denise A. **Fennell** of Milton 4/25/1987

KNIGHT,
Eugene L. of Milton m. Mary F. **Sanford** of Wellesley, MA 2/6/1948 in Farmington; H - 24, emp. in mill, b. Lynn, MA, s/o Lawrence H. Knight (Milton, salesman) and Rachel Erwin (Barre, VT, housewife); W - 27, beautician, b. Wellesley, MA, d/o Frederic L. Sanford (fireman) and Margaret Maloney (housewife)

Roland W. of Milton m. Christine C. **Souter** of Milton 4/12/1935 in Hampton; H - 20, clerk, b. Milton, s/o Wilbur C. Knight (Milton, merchant) and Sarah B. Maddox (N. Shapleigh, ME, housewife); W - 20, at home, b. Somerville, MA, d/o Thomas Souter (Glasgow, Scotland, shoe worker) and Wilhelmina Swanson (Edinburgh, Scotland, housewife)

Wilber C. of Milton m. Sarah B. **Maddox** of Milton 12/9/1896; H - 26, shoemaker, b. Milton, s/o Robert L. (Milton) and Marilla M.; W - 20, shoe stitcher, b. N. Shapleigh, ME, d/o John H. (Newfield, ME, millwright) and Olive F. (N. Shapleigh, ME)

KNOWLES,
Charles of Milton m. Bessie I. **Keyes** of Milton 10/5/1898; H - 23, shoemaker, b. Middleton, s/o Joseph H. Knowles (Milton, farmer); W - 20, shoe stitcher, b. Conway, d/o Everett F. Keyes (Ossipee, cobbler)

KNOX,
Frank I. of Milton m. Laura C. **Stewart** of Milton 6/30/1896; H - 33, shoe cutter, b. Milton, s/o Hosea B. (Milton) and Belinda (Farmington); W - 33, shoe finisher, 2nd, b. Andover, ME, d/o Abel and Matilda Marston

Richard F. of Milton m. Marie A. **Purington** of Dover 7/9/1988 in Dover

KRASNOW,
Stephen J. of Milton m. Susan M. **Valdina** of Milton 12/21/1980

KRIETE,
Ernest A., Jr. of Milton Mills m. Gloria J. **Jordan** of Milton Mills 8/20/1994

Ernest A., Jr. of Milton m. Ellen M. **Ryan** of Milton 10/2/1999

KUSHNER,
Richard I. of Dover m. Gail A. **Walsh** of Milton 8/10/1974; H - b. 9/22/1947; W - b. 11/23/1954

LABRECQUE,
Lionel N. of Rochester m. Diane S. **Schulkind** of Milton 5/4/1985

LABRIE,
Leo M. of Milton m. Anita V. **Lavoie** of Dover 10/9/1948 in Dover; H - 22, mechanic, b. Wakefield, s/o Ludger Labrie (Canada, laborer) and Clara Dubois (Biddeford, ME, housewife); W - 18, M. & M. Co., b. Canada, d/o Antoins Lavoie (Canada, carpenter) and Alexina Lasante (Franklin, housewife)
Stephen M. of Milton m. Cheryl A. **Byrd** of Milton 3/23/1973 in Sanbornville; H - b. 1/6/1953; W - b. 2/15/1954

LACHANCE,
Robert G. of Rochester m. Daisy B. **Drew** of Milton 4/16/1947 in Rochester; H - 20, shoe wkr., b. Rochester, s/o Lewis B. LaChance (Boston, MA, shoe worker) and Marilda Grondin (Rochester, housewife); W - 17, at home, b. Union, d/o Charles A. Drew (Sanbornville, mill worker) and Cora M. Williams (Rochester, housewife)
Robert R. of Springvale, ME m. Brenda L. **Toy** of Milton 2/13/1993

LACOUTURE,
Richard D. of Auburn, ME m. Elizabeth **Plummer** of Auburn, ME 10/5/1985

LACROIX,
Jean Paul of Old Orchard, ME m. Frances A. **MacLachan** of Old Orchard, ME 1/23/1960; H - 36, police officer; W - 39, at home

LAMBERT,
Donald E. of Milton Mills m. Helen B. **Smith** of Woodsville 5/14/1983 in North Haverhill
Michael L. of Milton m. Dawna M. **Woodill** of Milton 8/29/1981
Norbert P. of Milton m. Jacqueline E. **Laferte** of Rochester 10/2/1965 in Rochester; H - 21, US Coast Guard; W - 21, legal sec'y

LAMOUREUX,
Michael R. of Milton m. Nancy E. **Taylor** of Rochester 2/16/1979

LAMSON,
Joseph C. of Milton m. Jenette B. **Meikle** of Milton 11/5/1903; H - 20, piano tuner, b. Manchester, s/o Levi A. Lamson (Amherst, laundryman) and Drusilla Kimball (Parsonsfield, ME); W - 19, shoe stitcher, b. Wakefield, d/o William Meikle (Wakefield, carder)

LANDRY,
Marquis of Milton Mills m. Eileen **Davis** of Acton, ME 9/25/1926 in Sanbornville; H - 21, laborer, b. C. Blomid'n, NS, s/o Charles Landry (Kentville, NS, carpenter) and Marian Coffil (C. Blomid'n, NS); W - 18, at home, b. W. Newfield, ME, d/o Frank Davis (Amesbury, MA, painter) and Rose Comeau (Haverhill, MA)

Rudolph of Sanford, ME m. Germaine **Cloutier** of Chester 9/14/1940 in Derry; H - 23, mill worker, b. Sanford, ME, s/o Alphonse Landry (NB, weaver) and Cecelia Martin (Canada, housewife); W - 23, housework, b. Derry, d/o Joel Cloutier (N. Adams, MA, shoe worker) and Mereda S. Saviour (Canada, housewife)

LANE,
Merrick E. of Rochester m. Deborah A. **Marcoux** of Milton 11/21/1970 in Rochester; H - b. 7/24/1950; W - b. 11/8/1952

LANGLEY,
Thomas F. of Boston, MA m. Mary J. **Cook** of Milton 9/4/1900; H - 60, painter, 2nd, b. Boston, MA, s/o Thomas E. Langley and Elizabeth Parkin; W - 34, shoe stitcher, b. Milton, d/o John I. Cook (Milton, farmer) and Mary A. Davis (Exeter)

Wilmont H. of Milton m. Frances M. **Lewis** of Milton 7/4/1899 in Wakefield; H - 27, shoemaker, b. Skowhegan, ME, s/o Daniel H. Langley (Bingham, ME, laborer); W - 19, lady, b. Milton, d/o James Lewis (England, farmer)

LANTZ,
Christopher J. of Bath, PA m. Kimberly A. **Wood** of Bath, PA 10/23/1993

LAPANNE,
Paul R. of Milton m. Shirley J. **Nadeau** of Milton 10/1/1994

LAPLUME,
Edward J. of Rochester m. Audrey E. **Valley** of Milton Mills 7/5/1969 in Rochester; H - b. 6/20/1947; W - b. 11/17/1946

LARMIE,
Keith J. of Milton m. Samantha J. **Meiklejohn** of Rochester 10/25/1997

LAROCHE,
Albert J. of Rochester m. Frances M. **DeGara** of Milton 1/15/1955 in Farmington; H - 39, shoe worker, 2nd, b. Canada, s/o Willis LaRoche and Mary Tetreault; W - 27, shoe worker, 2nd, b. Athol, MA, d/o Frank M. Cutter and Margaret Phillips

LAROCHELLE,
Arthur of Milton m. Lena **Columbus** of Milton 6/12/1906; H - 26, shoemaker, b. Canada, s/o Adolphe LaRochelle (Canada) and Mary Fortier (Canada); W - 17, shoe stitcher, d/o Odelin Columbus (Canada, laborer) and Melvina Hall (Canada)

LASKEY,
Alan L. of Milton m. Barbara L. **Beckwith** of Wakefield 9/16/1967 in Sanbornville; H - 19, construction wkr.; W - 16, at home
Allie J. of Milton m. Lizzie A. **Weeks** of Wakefield 10/2/1899 in Milton Mills; H - 39, farmer, 2nd, b. Milton, s/o Jonas S. Laskey (Milton, farmer); W - 21, housekeeper, b. Wakefield, d/o Brackett Weeks (Wakefield, farmer)
Clyde of Milton m. Eva May **Richards** of Wakefield 7/21/1934 in Rochester; H - 28, farmer, b. Milton, s/o Allie J. Laskey (Milton, farmer) and Lizzie A. Weeks (Wakefield, housewife); W - 20, mill emp., b. Wakefield, d/o Walter H. Richards (Wakefield, farmer) and Lillian M. Johnson (Lowell, MA, housewife)
Kenneth M. of Milton m. Arlene F. **Bumford** of Wakefield 5/23/1942 in Sanbornville; H - 27, mechanic, b. Milton, s/o Ralph D. Laskey (Milton, farmer) and Maude Philbrick (Milton, housewife); W - 23, waitress, b. Wakefield, d/o Scott H. Bumford (Lebanon, ME, machinist) and Flora A. Hobbs (Lebanon, ME, housework)

Ralph D. of Milton m. Maude **Philbrick** of Milton 12/3/1913 in Dover; H - 20, teamster, b. Milton, s/o Allie J. Laskey (Milton, farmer) and Rose A. Barker (New Vineyard, ME); W - 20, housework, b. Milton, d/o Charles S. Philbrick (Freedom, farmer) and Jennie Applebee (Milton)

Robert P. of Milton Mills m. Agnes A. **Smith** of Milton 2/26/1932 in Brookline; H - 21, bookkeeper, b. Milton Mills, s/o Ralph D. Laskey (Milton Mills, laborer) and Maud Philbrick (Milton Mills, housewife); W - 19, at home, b. Middleton, d/o Guy A. Smith (Franconia, foreman) and Clara Tufts (Middleton, housewife)

Roger C. of Acton, ME m. Beatrice T. **Lavoie** of Milton 3/26/1969 in Rochester; H - b. 12/14/1932; W - b. 3/26/1925

LAURENT,
David W. of Milton m. Susan D. **Boles** of Milton 11/29/1985
Lucien G. of Milton m. Karen J. **Stacy** of Milton 7/13/1985 in Berwick, ME

LAUZE,
Joseph M. of Milton m. Bonnie L. **MacAllister** of Milton 12/28/1970 in Sanbornville; H - b. 7/24/1950; W - b. 11/1/1951

LAVAULT,
Roger E. of Milton m. Anita R. **Baron** of Milton 12/5/1992

LAVERTUE,
John R. of Milton m. Frances L. **Wilson** of Union 3/2/1929 in Rochester; H - 25, laborer, b. Rochester, s/o Henry Lavertue (Montreal, Canada, painter) and Florence Downs (Rochester); W - 20, at home, b. Union, d/o William J. Wilson (Moncton, NB, carpenter) and Edith Hall (Union)

Joseph of Milton m. Margaret **Coran** of Rochester 12/12/1931 in Alton; H - 23, foreman, b. Rochester, s/o Henry Lavertue (Canada, painter) and Florence Downs (Rochester, housekeeper); W - 19, at home, b. Rochester, d/o William Coran (England, shoe cobbler) and Elizabeth Sanderson (England, housewife)

LAVOIE,
Paul L. of Rochester m. Beatrice T. **Lessard** of Milton 12/28/1963; H - 35, Great Falls Prod.; W - 38, Spaulding Fibre

LAWRENCE,
Charles E., Jr. of Milton m. Marie A. **Whitehouse** of Rochester 8/12/1950 in Rochester; H - 26, shoe cutter, b. NH, s/o Charles E. Lawrence (NH) and Florence E. Griffin (NH); W - 28, clerk, b. NH, d/o Merel Whitehouse (NH) and Eva Tumell (NH)

LEARY,
John E., Jr. of Rochester m. Gloria J. **Burroughs** of Milton 5/31/1967; H - 25, shoe worker; W - 21, shoe worker
John E., III of Milton m. Janaya M. **Hall** of Milton 4/12/1997
Rodney V. of Milton m. Virginia R. **Gagnon** of Wakefield 6/2/1962 in Wakefield; H - 17, tannery; W - 15, at home

LEBLANC,
Alfred J. of Dover m. Carolyn F. **Badger** of Milton 12/24/1941 in Dover; H - 18, laborer, b. Newmarket, s/o William LeBlanc (Barton, VT, laborer) and Mary Forrest (Canada, housewife); W - 16, housewife, b. Boston, MA, d/o Charles E. Badger (Winchester, MA, laborer) and Hattie D. Baerd (NS, housewife)
Robert J., Jr. of Milton m. Christine M. **Camerato** of Milton 10/9/1992
Ted J. of Dover m. Mary M. **Henderson** of Milton 1/16/1993

LECLAIR,
Amos R. of Milton m. Nancy L. **Lesure** of Milton 4/16/1983
Stephen M. of Milton m. Susan F. **McDonough** of Manchester 7/11/1981 in Manchester

LECLARE,
Carl of Nottingham m. Margaret **Butler** of Milton 5/31/1937; H - 21, lumbering, b. Epping, s/o Alphonse LeClare (Nottingham, lumbering) and Florence Glover (Nottingham, at home); W - 19, bookkeeper, b. Milton, d/o Edward Butler (Hingham, MA, fireman) and Margaret Burbine (Wakefield, MA, at home)

LEDOUX,
Lucien A. of Manchester m. Helen L. **Eldridge** of Milton 5/24/1968; H - 27; W - 25

LEE,
James E. of Dover m. Lorita A. **Horne** of Milton 6/23/1929 in Milton Mills; H - 25, electrician, b. Portsmouth, s/o James C. Lee (Eastport, ME, machinist) and Florence Johnson (Portsmouth); W - 26, teacher, b. Milton, d/o John E. Horne (Acton, ME, merchant) and Olive A. Moulton (Newfield, ME)

LEEMAN,
Milledge G. of Milton m. Helen M. **DeWolfe** of Milton 4/28/1913 in Somersworth; H - 23, moulder, b. Eastport, ME, s/o George H. Leeman (Moncton, NB) and Addie Spinney (Grand Manan, NB); W - 21, milliner, b. Milton, d/o Charles F. DeWolfe and Hattie Hayes (Milton)

LEFEBVRE,
Robert R. of Rochester m. Thelma J. **Titcomb** of Milton 6/28/1952 in Rochester; H - 24, shoe worker, s/o Joseph Lefebvre and Mary L. Seymore; W - 18, shoe worker, b. Beverly, MA, d/o Charles L. Titcomb and Charlotte M. Gile

LEIGHTON,
Kenneth A. of Milton m. Karen D. **Plaisted** of Rochester 11/3/1984
Kenneth A. of Milton m. Linda J. **Bull** of Milton 5/25/1991
Michael H. of Milton m. Robin D. **Dale** of Dover 3/7/1992

LEMIEUX,
Perley A. of Milton m. Lucille A. **Wood** of Milton 7/10/1954; H - 20, US Army, b. Sanford, ME, s/o Joseph Lemieux and Almie St. Jean; W - 20, shoe shop, b. Lebanon, ME, d/o Fred Wood and Nellie Banker

LEMOUNTHEUE,
Joseph of Tamworth m. Lenora **Clifford** of Milton 7/25/1912 in Wakefield; H - 21, artist, b. Canada, s/o Joseph Lemounthune (sic) (Canada, barber); W - 24, housework, 2nd, b. Tamworth, d/o James Arling (Barrington, ME, farmer) and Emma Bickford (Lowell, MA)

LEMRAUD,
Arthur of Lebanon, ME m. Sadie **Cassidy** of Lebanon, ME 8/21/1911; H - 23, emp. in mill, b. Sanford, ME, s/o William Lemraud (Canada) and Marie LeFlesh (Canada); W - 19, emp. in mill, b. Lubec, ME, d/o Andrew Cassidy (NS) and Mary MacDonald (NS)

LESSARD,
Leo E. of Milton m. Kristin S. **Gordon** of Milton 10/18/1997
Norman E. of Milton Mills m. Brenda L. **Lachance** of Milton Mills 10/10/1998
Walter D. of Milton m. Mary N. **Dupuis** of Milton 8/19/1944 in W. Milton; H - 47, Navy Yard, b. Milton, s/o Benonie Lessard (Canada, retired) and Delvina Dion (Canada, housewife); W - 30, welder, 2nd, b. Milton, d/o Harry Wiggin (Tuftonboro, mill wkr.) and Mabel Drown (Ctr. Ossipee, moulder)

LETOURNEAU,
Ronald R. of Milton m. Kristal J. **Knight** of Milton 5/17/1997
Steven G. of Rochester m. Diane L. **Shevenell** of Milton 9/14/1985

LEVEILLE,
David J. of New Durham m. Vickie L. **Desrosiers** of Milton 10/6/1982 in Wolfeboro

LEVITT,
Walter J. of Milton Mills m. Linda E. **Welch** of Milton Mills 10/19/1990 in Rochester

LEWIS,
Leon, Jr. of Milton m. Edith G. **Buzzell** of Milton 10/20/1989 in Rochester
Philip V., Jr. of Brookfield m. Penney C. **Tirrell** of Milton 8/9/1980 in Union
Walter J. of Lebanon, ME m. Mary **Couture** of Milton 9/28/1895; H - 20, shoemaker, b. Lebanon, ME, s/o William J. (Biddeford, ME, laster); W - 18, shoe stitcher, b. Canada, d/o Lewis (Canada, laborer)
William J. of Lebanon, ME m. Clara B. **Brown** of Dover 8/15/1889; H - 35, shoemaker, widower, b. ME, s/o William and Mary; W - 23, shoe stitcher, b. Great Falls, d/o George B. and Pauline (Acton, ME)

LIBBEY,
Aubrey D. of Milton m. Jennie F. **Gerrish** of Milton 8/6/1891; H - 26, asst P.M., b. No. Berwick, ME, s/o Elijah T. (postmaster) and Ida (housekeeper); W - 25, lady, b. Lebanon, ME, d/o Elisha P. and Elizabeth M. (housekeeper)

Vivian A. of Milton m. Leona E. **Yeaton** of Milton 7/5/1899; H - 26, shoemaker, b. Dover, s/o Alvah M. Libbey; W - 29, housekeeper, 2nd, b. Milton, d/o Stephen W. Yeaton (ME, farmer)

LIBBY,
Donald of Ossipee m. Josephine **Paul** of Milton 10/16/1954; H - 25, tannery, b. Milton, s/o Robert Libby and Helen Eldridge; W - 21, shoe worker, b. Rochester, d/o Joseph Paul and Gertrude McNeal

Ernest L. of Milton m. Ruth M. **Libby** of Ossipee 7/20/1930 in Lebanon, ME; H - 21, motion picture, b. Wolfeboro, s/o Aubrey Libby (N. Berwick, ME, painter) and Florence Hatch (Tuftonboro, housewife); W - 16, at home, b. Portsmouth, d/o James Libby (Oakfield, ME, painter) and Elizabeth Monahan (Ireland, housewife)

Robert F. of Springvale, ME m. Linda L. **Carswell** of Milton Mills 9/15/1967 in Milton Mills; H - 18, dairyman; W - 20, at home

Willard F. of Milton m. Elsie M. **Peterson** of Milton 11/5/1901; H - 23, farmer, b. St. Stevens, s/o James M. Libby (St. Stevens, farmer) and Sarah D. Logan (Calais, ME); W - 18, lady, b. Livingston, d/o Louis J. Peterson (New York, NY, shoemaker) and Emma Bean (Parsonsfield, ME)

LILLJIDAHL,
Carl H., Jr. of Milton m. Thelma I. **Dumont** of Rochester 11/22/1952 in Rochester; H - 25, US Army, b. MA, s/o Carl H. Lilljidahl and Dorothy C. Varney; W - 19, shoe shop, b. NH, d/o Arthur J. Dumont and Marie A. Larochelle

Carl W. of Lynn, MA m. Lydia T. **Hunt** of Lynn, MA 5/1/1948; H - 71, carpenter, 2nd, b. Sweden, s/o Carl A. Lilljidahl (Sweden, court clerk) and Christine Johanson (Sweden, housewife); W - 69, housewife, 2nd, b. Sweden, d/o Lois Schwartz (Sweden, coppersmith) and Emma Pagander (Sweden, housewife)

Robert C. of Milton m. Ann M. **Minnicucci** of Rochester 12/9/1952 in Rochester; H - 23, US Air Force, b. Lynn, MA, s/o Carl H. Lilljedahl and Dorothy C. Varney; W - 21, clerk, b. Lawrence, MA, d/o Joseph V. Minnicucci and Josephine DeIorio

LINCOLN,
Harold G., III of Milton m. Susan M. **Lincoln** of Milton 8/11/1990 in Rochester

LINDH,
David C. of Somersworth m. Louise R. **Lauze** of Milton Mills 7/23/1966 in Sanbornville; H - 20, die maker; W - 17, student

LINDSAY,
Kevin G. of Milton m. Karen L. **Wolforth** of Rochester 8/12/1989 in Rochester

LINDSEY,
George H. of Milton m. Mary A. **Keenan** of Milton 6/15/1889; H - 35, shoemaker, b. MA, s/o George (MA) and Mary (Lynn, MA); W - 24, shoe shop, b. NS, d/o John (MA) and Ann (NS)

LITTLEFIELD,
Delbert W. of Wakefield m. Constance M. **Mollica** of Milton 12/31/1971 in Union; H - b. 4/28/1953; W - b. 6/21/1954
Haven B. of N. Berwick, ME m. Laura J. **Hoyt** of Milton 2/20/1935; H - 73, foundry, 3rd, b. Wells, ME, s/o Joshua Littlefield (N. Berwick, ME, farmer) and Susan Abbott (N. Berwick, ME, housekeeper); W - 51, housekeeper, 2nd, b. Milton, d/o Alfred W. Jones (Randolph, MA, machinist) and Ella S. Kimball (N. Berwick, ME, housekeeper)

LITTLER,
Robert H. of Milton m. Geraldine R. **Evans** of Milton 8/15/1982

LIVINGSTONE,
Fred A. of Wollaston, MA m. Katherine M. **Jones** of Milton 11/1/1910; H - 22, teamster, b. Hampstead, s/o George E. Livingston (sic) (Auburn, veterinary) and Mary A. King (Manchester); W - 23, housekeeper, b. Haverhill, MA, d/o Charles D. Jones (Milton, merchant) and Pauline E. Hart (Milton)

LOCKE,
Brian J. of Milton m. Angela M. **Clark** of Milton 8/31/1996

LOCKHART,
Charles P. of Rochester m. Lorraine F. **Dupuis** of Milton 12/20/1969; H - b. 4/24/1946; W - b. 7/1/1946

LOGAN,
Charles H. of Milton m. Patricia **Parsons** of Rochester 10/18/1943 in Farmington; H - 20, US Army, b. Milton, s/o Charles W. Logan (Lynnfield, WI, laborer) and Florence Y. Welch (Ossipee, housewife); W - 18, at home, b. Rochester, d/o Bernald Parsons (Rochester, mill operative) and Mary E. Regan (Milton, housewife)

Charles M. of Milton m. Bonnie I. **Byrd** of Milton 9/28/1974 "on the bridge" at Lake Chocorua; H - b. 7/16/1954; W - b. 7/28/1955

Charles W. of Milton m. Florence Y. **Emack** of Ossipee 12/14/1919 in Ossipee; H - 38, laborer, 2nd, b. Lynxville, WI, s/o Michael Logan (Baltic, CT, wheelwright) and Elizabeth Featherston (Baltic, CT); W - 32, mill hand, 2nd, b. Ossipee, d/o Moses Welch (Ossipee, farmer) and Sarah Welch (Ossipee)

LONDO,
Erwin N. of Milton m. Lillian C. **Eldridge** of Rochester 12/30/1947 in Rochester; H - 34, mechanic, 2nd, b. Raymond, s/o Nelson Londo (Bucksport, ME, laborer) and Mildred Corson (S. Wolfeboro, shoe shop); W - 21, shoe shop, b. Lebanon, ME, d/o Melvin H. Eldridge (Ossipee, mill worker) and Delia A. Custeau (Milton, housewife)

LONG,
Donald A. of Milton Mills m. Joan M. **Hall** of Wakefield 10/31/1987

Frank of Wolfeboro m. Janice **Gervais** of Lebanon, ME 4/17/1938 in Wolfeboro; H - 21, laborer, b. Bowdoinham, ME, s/o Frank Long (St. George, ME, fish mkt.) and Lula M. Leavitt (Bowdoin, ME, housewife); W - 18, shoe worker, b. Haverhill, MA, d/o Walter Gervais (Isle La Motte, VT, laborer) and Bernice Dearborn (Greenland, deceased)

John H., Jr. of Acton, ME m. Linda E. **Scott** of Milton Mills 12/24/1972 in Milton Mills; H - b. 3/24/1953; W - b. 12/8/1952

Melvin L. of Dover m. Nancy **Harriman** of Milton 11/25/1955; H - 23, service sta., b. IN, s/o James Long and Myrtle Richardson; W - 20, nurse, b. Rochester, d/o Frederick Harriman and Jane Swift

Michael T. of Milton Mills m. Mary E. **Haskins** of Milton Mills 12/31/1977 in Milton Mills; H - b. 1/8/1957; W - b. 12/24/1958

LONGLEY,
George W. of Milton Mills m. Thyra E. **Benson** of Milton Mills 5/21/1938 in Milton Mills; H - 55, hotel clerk, 2nd, b. Bingham, ME, s/o Jonah S. Longley (Solon, ME, deceased) and Anastazia Gilman (Bingham, ME, deceased); W - 54, housewife, 2nd, b. Sweden, d/o Svante Swenson (Sweden, deceased) and Hilda Lungren (Sweden, deceased)

LOONEY,
Harry H. of Milton m. Manola E. **Boston** of N. Berwick, ME 11/2/1915 in Rochester; H - 33, shoemaker, b. Milton, s/o Charles H. Looney (Milton) and Emma E. Miller (Milton); W - 25, domestic, b. Milton, d/o Frederick Boston (N. Berwick, ME, plumber) and Pauline Trafton (N. Berwick, ME)

Ned F. of Milton m. Adelaide C. **Sloan** of Farmington 9/23/1897 in Rochester; H - 24, shoemaker, b. Milton, s/o Charles H. Looney (Milton, merchant); W - 24, shoe stitcher, 2nd, b. Milton, d/o John Waldron (Farmington, shoemaker)

LOPES,
Michael J. of Milton m. Lorraine J. **Lesure** of Milton 10/24/1987

LOPSEY,
Joseph of Milton m. Hazel W. **Gray** of Rochester 3/31/1976; H - b. 8/8/1931; W - b. 1/4/1928

LORD,
Ernest A. of Salem, MA m. Jeannette B. **D'Allesandro** of Lynn, mA 2/20/1965 in Milton Mills; H - 51, pressman; W - 52, boxmaker

John E. of Farmington m. Elaine A. **Woodward** of Milton 7/8/1972; H - b. 1/11/1951; W - b. 4/21/1951

John F. of Lebanon, ME m. Lottie S. **Johanson** of Lebanon, ME 12/25/1888; H - 52, farmer, widower, b. Lebanon, ME; W - 26, b. Sweden

Richard W. of Milton m. Bertha M. **Leathers** of Dover 7/8/1953 in Dover; H - 26, prod. clerk, b. NH, s/o James E. Lord and Ruth Wentworth; W - 34, teacher, b. NH, d/o Frank Leathers and Mary Towle

Robert J. of Portland, ME m. Marlene E. **Savoie** of Milton 6/20/1971; H - b. 8/25/1944; W - b. 5/24/1951

LOUBIER,

Roland L., Jr. of Milton m. Nancy A. **Carlson** of Milton 4/2/1983

LOUGEE,

Robert of Milton m. Doris G. **Ellison** of Exeter 8/20/1937 in Brentwood; H - 33, salesman, b. Rochester, s/o William S. Lougee (Pittsfield, dead) and Mabelle Robie (Bristol, housewife); W - 27, at home, b. Exeter, d/o Forrest Ellison (Exeter, salesman) and Daisy B. Davis (Bradford, VT, saleslady)

William S. of Milton m. Mrs. Annie **Peterson** of Milton 3/27/1890 in Middleton; H - 43, shoemaker, 2nd, b. NH, s/o Jacob (Gilmanton, dead) and Abigail (Loudon, dead); W - 42, housekeeper, 2nd, b. Hiram, ME, d/o William Pendexter (Bridgton, ME, dead) and Elizabeth (No. Berwick, ME, dead)

LOVEJOY,

George A. of East Rochester m. Joyce M. **Rouleau** of Milton 7/4/1953; H - 22, US Navy, b. Portland, OR, s/o John H. Lovejoy, Sr. and Jennie L. Stevens; W - 18, sales clerk, b. Lebanon, ME, d/o Alfred J. Rouleau and Helen E. Duquette

Raymond of Acton, ME m. Jane **Plummer** of Milton 6/15/1948 in Chester, VT; H - 55, orchardist, 3rd, b. Industry, ME, s/o George Lovejoy (New Portland, ME) and Flora Rackliffe (Industry, ME); W - 25, orchardist, b. Dover, d/o Bard B. Plummer (Milton, farmer) and Ruth L. Fall (Milton, housewife)

LOVER,

Richard P. of Milton m. Nancy E. **Swain** of Barrington 2/9/1974 in Portsmouth; H - b. 7/7/1949; W - b. 6/8/1950

Wilbur C. of Milton m. Merle V. **Derby** of Farmington 6/20/1942; H - 27, leather wkr., b. Milton, s/o Peter J. Lover (Wakefield, mill worker) and Alice M. Downs (Wakefield, housewife); W - 21, shoe worker, b. Barnstead, d/o Charles L. Derby (Montpelier, VT, carpenter) and Sylvia V. Cook (Barnstead, housewife)

LOVERING,

George L. of Milton m. Jennie N. **Stevens** of Milton 3/13/1895; H - 49, merchant, b. Tuftonboro, s/o Plummer G. (Tuftonboro); W - 30, teacher, b. Brookfield, d/o Daniel D. (Middleton, farmer)

LOWD,

Freeman H. of Milton m. Mary A. **Wentworth** of Milton 9/19/1917 in Milton Mills; H - 64, lumber dealer, 2nd, b. Acton, ME, s/o Sylvester Lowd (Acton, ME, farmer) and Dorcas Hanson (Acton, ME); W - 38, music teacher, b. Milton, d/o Hiram Wentworth (Milton, carpenter) and Clara J. Hart (Milton)

LOWELL,

Franklin C. of Milton m. Cheri J. **Hemenway** of Milton 8/7/1992

Herbert S. of Milton m. Iola A. **McIntire** of Rochester 10/18/1913; H - 22, ice man, b. Alton, s/o Philomen Lowell (Alton, sawyer) and Eva Rand (Alton); W - 20, housework, b. Dover, d/o Frank B. McIntire (Dover, car inspector) and Ruth E. Cole (Dover)

LOWRY,

Mark K. of Milton m. Doris L. **Arlington** of Milton 8/7/1993

LOZIER,

Bruce P. of Hampden, ME m. Anita **Morgan** of Hampden, ME 9/9/1978; H - b. 2/3/1949; W - b. 11/6/1952

LUCEY,

John of Milton m. Pearl **Hartford** of East Rochester 10/19/1926 in Rochester; H - 25, laborer, b. Melrose, MA, s/o Dennis Lucey (Ireland, laborer) and Catherine Walsh (Ireland); W - 20, mill operative, b. East Rochester, d/o Lewis Hartford (Rochester, laborer) and Annie Webber (York, ME)

LUCIER,
John A. of Milton m. Lisa H. **Aubert** of Milton 10/23/1993
John M., Jr. of Milton m. Paula A. **Regan** of Milton 10/9/1954 in Sanbornville; H - 19, surveyor, b. Hartford, CT, s/o John M. Lucier and Myrtle Granger; W - 18, at home, b. Rochester, d/o James V. Regan and Dorothy Otis

LUMBARD,
Robert of Milton m. Marie **Meyer** of Milton 12/11/1948 in Farmington; H - 36, boiler man, b. Portland, ME, s/o Alfred Russell (Rutland, VT, barber) and Mary Sanborn (Sebago Lake S., ME, housewife); W - 33, mill worker, 3rd, b. Brooklyn, NY, d/o Joseph Botti (Italy, chauffeur) and Gladys Hanscom (NH, housewife)

LUND,
Gary S. of Milton m. Lorraine E. **Provencher** of Milton 6/12/1982

LUNEAU,
Christopher J. of Rochester m. Linda L. **Lucier** of Milton 6/22/1976 in Rochester; H - b. 5/1/1953; W - b. 5/18/1955
Christopher J. of Lansdale, PA m. Linda L. **Mollica** of Milton 6/17/1995

LUSCOMB,
Kenneth K. of Brookfield m. Juanita **Clough** of Milton 4/15/1949 in Wakefield; H - 19, lumberjack, b. MA, s/o Arthur G. Luscomb (MA) and Helen Thompson (MA); W - 15, housekeeper, b. NH, d/o Warren Clough (NH) and Marguerite Weeks (NH)
Kenneth K., Jr. of Milton Mills m. Roxanne M. **Guldbrandsen** of Rochester 4/18/1975 in Rochester; H - b. 10/4/1954; W - b. 5/4/1956

LYGREN,
John of Durham m. Janice L. **Greene** of Milton Mills 12/4/1959 in Newington; H - 25, student, b. Norway, s/o Ole Lygren (Norway) and Marta Traeland (Norway); W - 21, student, b. Salem, MA, d/o James C. Green (sic) (NJ) and Ada Hurd (MA)
John of Milton m. Joan M. **Drago** of Milton 6/13/1981 in Rochester

LYONS,
James E. of Milton m. Ann E. **English** of Milton 11/21/1987

Michael W. of Milton Mills m. Terri E. **Fowler** of Milton Mills 10/18/1991

MACDONALD,
Philip N. of Cairo, Egypt m. Mary N. **Walker** of Milton 8/25/1909; H - 30, manager, b. East Boston, MA, s/o Norman MacDonald (Cape Breton, tool sharpener) and Jane (Cape Breton); W - 22, b. Island Pond, VT, d/o Joseph N. Walker (England, clergyman) and Mary Clayton (Lancashire, England)

MACGOWN,
Darren J. of Milton m. Ellen K. **Brock** of Milton 12/17/1988

MACK,
Gregory E. of Portsmouth m. Betsy R. **Pugh** of Milton 3/17/1968; H - 21; W - 18

MACKENZIE,
Craig B. of Acton, ME m. Leslie R. **Goldstein** of Acton, ME 10/7/1979

MACLEOD,
Herbert M. of Brookline, MA m. Mary A. **Smith** of Brookline, MA 1/20/1962; H - 21, ins. agency; W - 18, clerical

MADDEN,
William J. of Milton m. Beulah N. **Marsh** of Milton 10/2/1920 in Milton Mills; H - 34, farmer, b. Wandsworth, England, s/o Jack Madden (Fulham, England, laundryman) and Anne Otterway (Fulham, England); W - 29, blanket finisher, b. Acton, ME, d/o Edwin E. Marsh (Acton, ME, laborer) and Lucy L. Earl (Acton, ME)

MADDIX,
Roger B., Jr. of Milton Mills m. Cory B. **Goodrow** of Rochester 5/22/1987 in Rochester

MADDOX,
Eugene A. of Milton m. Eva R. **Sleeper** of Milton 12/24/1889; H - 18, mill operative, b. Newfield, ME, s/o John (Newfield, ME) and Olive

(Shapleigh, ME); W - 20, shoe stitcher, b. Alton, d/o Geremy (Alton) and Rose (Bangor, ME)

MAHONEY,
David K. of Milton m. Beverly J. **Swartz** of Milton 2/2/1991
William T., III of Milton m. Susan W. **Moore** of Winthrop, MA 3/14/1997

MAILMAN,
Russell L., Jr. of Weston, MA m. Judith **Storey** of Lexington, MA 1/11/1956; H - 20, US Army, b. Boston, MA, s/o Russell L. Mailman and Alberta Tuthill; W - 19, retailing, b. Boston, MA, d/o John M. Storey and Blanche Bingston

MALDONADO,
Mickey D. of Milton m. Sharon K. **Rothell** of Milton 12/11/1994

MALEHAM,
Mark C. of Milton Mills m. Amanda J. **Crothers** of Milton Mills 9/11/1999
Matthew D. of Dover m. Shoanie L. **Semco** of Milton 8/15/1997

MALLETT,
Elmer W. of Rochester m. Jacqueline P. **Savoie** of Milton 8/28/1952 in Rochester; H - 31, laborer, b. NH, s/o Harry A. Mallett and Jane Quelch; W - 27, nurse, b. NH, d/o Fred P. Savoie and Ruby Ellis

MANNING,
Philip E. of Salem, MA m. Marion L. **Hall** of Salem, MA 6/4/1946; H - 26, unemployed, b. Salem, MA, s/o William A. Manning (Salem, MA, printer) and Lena E. Leduc (Canada, housewife); W - 24, unemployed, b. Haverhill, MA, d/o Perley Hall (Sawyers River, VT, deceased) and Myrtle E. Sprague (Springvale, ME, housewife)
Steven L. of Gilmanton m. Deborah L. **Snyder** of Milton 3/22/1969 in Rochester; H - b. 9/12/1947; W - b. 3/16/1951

MANSFIELD,
Burleigh B. of Milton Mills m. Verda E. **Duplissa** of Milton Mills 10/11/1965 in Milton Mills; H - 75, ret. physician; W - 75, retired

MARCH,
Chris M. of Milton m. Gloria M. **Gray** of Milton 11/8/1986

MARCHAND,
Arthur of Milton m. Felanise **Valley** of Milton 11/26/1893; H - 20, laborer, b. Canada, s/o Lezore Marchand (Canada, laborer) and Celeneo; W - 18, shoe stitcher, b. Canada, d/o Michelle Valley (Canada, laborer) and Rose

MARCIL,
Alfred of Milton m. Emma **Morris** of Milton 5/17/1918; H - 41, shoemaker, 2nd, b. Canada, s/o Octave Marcil (Canada) and Olive Preidum (Canada); W - 36, housekeeper, b. Lebanon, ME, d/o Luke Morris (Canada, shoemaker) and Emma ----- (Canada)

MARCOUX,
Archie M. of Milton m. Irene B. **Marchand** of East Rochester 6/20/1921 in Rochester; H - 25, machine tender, b. Wakefield, s/o Archie G. Marcoux (Canada, mill wright) and Rose Brouillard (Canada); W - 20, shoe operative, b. Milton, d/o Louis Marchand (Canada, laborer) and Arline Theoret (Canada)

Archie P. of Milton m. Beverly M. **Young** of Rochester 1/26/1946; H - 20, l. bd. mill, b. Milton, s/o Napoleon Marcoux (Wakefield, deceased) and Hazel M. Downs (Milton, l.b. mill); W - 18, at home, b. Rochester, d/o Carlton C. Young (Rochester, bus driver) and Dorothy L. Davis (Farmington, shoe shop)

Francis J. of Milton m. Amber L. **Pike** of Milton 6/7/1986

James P. of Milton m. Wendy L. **Horn** of Milton 7/19/1968; H - 20; W - 18

James P. of Milton m. Mary A. **Meattey** of Barrington 11/23/1974; H - b. 2/2/1948; W - b. 3/19/1947

Joseph R. of Milton m. Janet M. **Chapman** of Middleton 5/13/1950; H - 23, mach. tender, b. Milton, s/o Napoleon Marcoux (Wakefield) and Hazel Downs (Milton); W - 18, shoe wkr., b. Laconia, d/o Fred Chapman (Haverhill) and Irene Acton (Laconia)

Joseph R., Jr. of Milton m. Jayne J. **Russell** of Farmington 6/25/1974; H - b. 10/15/1950; W - b. 2/12/1956

Joseph R., Jr. of Milton m. Donna L. **Harriman** of Milton 2/27/1982

Napoleon O. of Milton m. Hazel M. **Downs** of Milton 11/28/1923 in Farmington; H - 25, mill employee, b. Wakefield, s/o Archie Marcoux (Canada, mill emp.) and Rose Storm (Canada); W - 16, at home, b. Milton, d/o C. Fred Downs (Lebanon, ME, laborer) and Eva M. West (Wakefield)

Raymond A. of Milton m. Mary Jane C. **Nadeau** of Somersworth 11/25/1954 in Somersworth; H - 21, drierman, b. Milton, s/o Napoleon Marcoux and Hazel Downs; W - 19, shoe worker, b. NH, d/o Benedict Nadeau and Rose Jacques

Robert D. of Rochester m. Julie A. **Massingham** of Rochester 11/26/1966; H - 29, mach. tender; W - 23, candle insp.

MARGERISON,
Thomas of Milton m. Virena G. **Hollis** of Milton 8/21/1994

MARQUIS,
Scott D. of Milton m. Lisa M. **Adabahr** of Milton 12/26/1998

MARSH,
Forrest L. of Milton m. Mildred J. **Tebbetts** of Newfield, ME 12/19/1899 in Newfield, ME; H - 27, lawyer, b. Milton, s/o Oscar F. Marsh (Milton, foreman); W - 22, lady, b. Newfield, ME, d/o William M. Tebbetts (Newfield, ME, carriage m'r)

Frank L. L. of Milton m. Mary E. **McAdams** of Allston, MA 7/9/1916 in Milton Mills; H - 61, emp. in mill, 2nd, b. Acton, ME, s/o Noah L. Marsh (Acton, ME) and Naomi Joy (Acton, ME); W - 58, nurse, 2nd, b. NS, d/o Thomas Ryan (NS) and Naomi Harding (NS)

Garfield A. of Acton, ME m. Catherine M. **Buzzell** of Acton, ME 12/10/1908; H - 28, farmer, b. Acton, ME, s/o Thomas E. Marsh (Acton, ME, farmer) and Viola Hurd (Acton, ME); W - 34, housekeeper, 2nd, b. Wakefield, d/o Edward B. Farnham (Wakefield, farmer) and Jennie A. Watts (Canada)

George W. of Acton, ME m. Eva M. **Burrows** of Milton 7/11/1908; H - 29, farmer, b. Acton, ME, s/o Drew Marsh (Acton, ME, farmer) and Viola Hurd (Acton, ME); W - 18, b. Milton, d/o Hiram J. Hurd (Lebanon, ME, blacksmith) and Sarah A. Town (Parsonsfield, ME)

Robert E. of Milton m. Marian A. **March** of Rochester 5/10/1952 in Rochester; H - 20, Coast Guard, b. NH, s/o Ithiel E. Marsh and Mary

E. Whitehouse; W - 24, clerk, b. NH, d/o Clifton L. March and Ida M. Junkins
Shawn E. of Ocala, FL m. Kathy L. **Potvin** of Ocala, FL 5/25/1996

MARSTERS,
Lewis F. of Milton m. Eleanor M. **Heskey** of Newton, MA 3/12/1945 in Boston, MA; H - 31, US Navy, b. NS, s/o Lewis Marsters and Elizabeth Fielding; W - 30, clerk, b. Watertown, MA, d/o Wallace Heskey and Leona Westaver
Robie L. of W. Lebanon, ME m. Mary E. **Devore** of W. Lebanon, ME 12/31/1989

MARTIN,
David D. of Milton m. Debra E. **Reid** of Rochester 8/15/1981
David D. of Milton m. Bridget R. **Gordon** of Milton 11/23/1988
David P. of Sanbornville m. Rita A. **Berry** of Sanbornville 8/8/1998
Donald L., Jr. of Milton m. Pamela A. **Dupuis** of Milton 9/5/1992
William C., III of Milton m. Cheryl L. **Brown** of Milton 7/18/1986

MASTEN,
Sydney R. of Suncook m. Wendy L. **Marcoux** of Milton 7/11/1975 in Wakefield; H - b. 6/21/1944; W - b. 8/6/1949

MATHER,
David A. of Milton m. Donna J. **Berry** of Rochester 5/26/1984 in Rochester

MATHEWS,
Dewey F. of Milton m. Karen S. **Bickert** of Milton 7/22/1989 in Merrimack

MATTRESS,
Michel S. of Acton, ME m. Kim E. **Moody** of Milton Mills 4/29/1977; H - b. 1/15/1959; W - b. 8/13/1960

MAXFIELD,
Leland L. of Milton m. Elizabeth Z. **Bronson** of Boston, MA 7/21/1938; H - 29, minister, b. Strafford, s/o Louis A. Maxfield (Rochester, shoe maker) and Mildred Howard (Strafford, housewife); W - 25, nurse,

b. Durham, NY, d/o Jesse B. Bronson (Windham, NY, deceased) and Rose Thompkins (Ashland, NY, deceased)

MAYRAND,
Samuel E. of No. Rochester m. Mavis L. **Page** of Milton 7/29/1919 in Shirley, MA; H - 35, mill hand, b. St. Annie Parade, Canada, s/o Elzeard Mayrand (Canada, mill hand) and Dralice Burichire (Canada); W - 29, mill hand, b. Milton, d/o George W. Page (Dalton, mill hand) and Jennettie A. Rines (Milton)

McCALLUM,
James G., Jr. of Dayton, OH m. Jane F. **Hay[es]** of New York City 2/23/1957; H - 51, chem. engr., 2nd, b. MI, s/o James G. McCallum (MI) and May Williams (MI); W - 31, secretary, b. Boston, MA, d/o Maurice L. Hayes (Milton) and Grace M. Stevens (Ossipee)

McCARTEN,
Hugh J. of Portsmouth m. Mary E. **Kingston** of Milton 6/25/1919; H - 35, steam fitter, b. Ireland, s/o Patrick McCarten (Ireland, laborer) and Jane Doran (Ireland); W - 39, skiver, b. Milton, d/o George Kingston (Ireland, RR foreman) and Nellie Sullivan (Ireland)

McCORMICK,
Robert J., Jr. of Milton m. Brenda L. **Sprowls** of Milton 10/11/1986
Thomas F., Jr. of Milton m. Sandra J. **Fiske** of Milton 8/21/1999

McCOURT,
Raymond Y. of Rochester m. Carol D. **Peloquin** of Milton 8/21/1993

McDANIEL,
Lyman L. of Milton m. Janice E. **Trull** of Raymond 9/19/1998
Sewell H. of Milton m. Ruby Ardelle **Taylor** of Effingham 10/30/1915 in Newfield, ME; H - 24, weaver, b. N. Shapleigh, ME, s/o Samuel L. McDaniel (Wakefield, laborer) and Mary E. Sanborn (Newfield, ME); W - 27, housekeeper, b. Effingham, d/o John B. Taylor (Effingham, farmer) and Mattie Varney (Rochester)

McGARVEY,
Kevin B. of Rangeley, ME m. Christine M. **Welch** of West Lebanon, ME 10/15/1994

McGLAUFLIN,
Robert of Milton m. Sue Marie **Ramer** of Milton 8/27/1988 in Portsmouth

McGRATH,
Thomas J. of Milton m. Mary J. **Gill** of Milton 1/7/1925 in Farmington; H - 42, mill worker, b. Ireland, s/o James McGrath (Ireland, retired policeman) and Mary Fitzgerald (Ireland); W - 30, mill worker, 2nd, b. Ireland, d/o Patrick McCarten (Ireland, laborer) and Jane Doran (Ireland)

McILVAINE,
George H. of Milton m. Esther L. **Fielder** of Milton 8/28/1933 in Sanford, ME; H - 51, plumber, b. Antrim, s/o George F. McIlvaine (Antrim, carpenter) and Sarah E. Boutelle (Dublin, housewife); W - 37, shoe worker, b. Beverly, MA, s/o Albert W. Fielder (Beverly, MA, shoe worker) and Alice M. Caswell (Beverly, MA, housewife)

McINNES,
Daniel E. of West Lebanon, ME m. Deborah M. **Feeney** of Milton Mills 11/19/1976; H - b. 8/24/1941; W - b. 11/1/1953

McINTIRE,
Charles N. of Milton m. Patricia A. **Swebilius** of Milton 4/20/1974; H - b. 5/17/1942; W - b. 10/3/1951

F. Everett of Milton m. Marie E. **McKeagney** of Milton 8/22/1936 in W. Lebanon, ME; H - 21, shoe worker, b. Rochester, s/o Frank B. McIntire (Dover, millwright) and Grace Downing (Farmington, housewife); W - 17, at home, b. Ossipee, d/o Patrick H. McKeagney (Ireland, plumber) and Laura M. Gibson (Boston, MA, office wkr.)

George C. of Milton m. Barbara E. **Heald** of Portland, ME 8/31/1940 in Rochester; H - 31, dryerman, b. Rochester, s/o Frank B. McIntire (Dover, mechanic) and Grace M. Downing (Farmington, housewife); W - 40, teacher, 2nd, b. Lincolnville, ME, d/o Frederick A. Heald (Lincolnville, ME, stone mason) and Addie I. Young (Lincolnville, ME, housewife)

Robert E. of Milton m. Lena I. **Smith** of Union 10/4/1958 in Wolfeboro; H - 19, Navy, b. Rochester, s/o F. Everett McIntire (NH) and Marie C. McKeagney (NH); W - 18, at home, b. Milton, d/o Edmund L. Smith (NH) and Hannah Demeritt (NH)

Walter G. of Milton m. Joyce L. **Cheney** of Milton 1/23/1960; H - 21, student; W - 21, hairdresser

McINTOSH,
Robert of Milton m. Addie C. **Duntley** of Milton 8/26/1897; H - 27, laster, b. Calais, ME, s/o David McIntosh (Calais, ME); W - 29, lady, b. Milton, d/o Ira A. Duntley (Milton, blacksmith)

McKEAGNEY,
George A. of Milton m. Thelma M. **Hill** of Rochester 7/8/1941 in Rochester; H - 32, state trooper, b. Boston, MA, s/o Patrick McKeagney (Ireland, plumber) and Laura A. Gibson (Boston, MA, office clerk); W - 33, dietitian, b. Everett, MA, d/o Frederick Wright (Montpelier, VT, deceased) and Helen Durgin (Halifax, NS)

Robert of Rochester m. Blanche M. **Dorr** of Milton 6/3/1944; H - 23, geologist, b. Quincy, MA, s/o Patrick McKeagney (Ireland, plumber) and Laura M. Gibson (Boston, MA, office wkr.); W - 21, at home, b. Milton, d/o William W. Dorr (Milton, mill wkr.) and Ruth M. Edwards (Temple, housewife)

McKENNEY,
Ira B. of Milton m. Susan B. **Morgan** of Milton 12/7/1975; H - b. 5/23/1956; W - b. 10/7/1951

McKEON,
Martin K. of Milton m. Natalie P. **Kumar** of Milton 8/17/1996

McMULLEN,
Stephen P. of Milton m. Katherine R. **Currier** of Milton 8/27/1994

McNALLY,
James F., Jr. of Milton m. Michelle R. **Moore** of Milton 6/14/1986

McPHERSON,
Jeffery R. of Milton m. Laurie A. **Trzuskowski** of Milton 8/15/1998

Kevin M. of Milton m. Bonnie L. **Casavant** of Milton 12/10/1999
Michel T. of Milton m. Jessica J. **Everett** of Milton 6/5/1999
Roger W. of Milton m. Susan K. **Lund** of Milton 10/14/1972; H - b. 1/26/1950; W - b. 11/3/1952

McQUIRE,
Robert B. of Milton m. Christine M. **Hutchins** of Milton 2/26/1994

MEADER,
James D. of Milton m. Sandra L. **Gelinas** of Milton 7/13/1990

MEDEIROS,
Manuel W. of Arlington, MA m. Janet M. **Cook** of Arlington, MA 11/11/1961; H - 28, taxi dist.; W - 19, stenographer
Richard A. of Cambridge, MA m. Sandra L. **Clough** of Milton 4/5/1969 in Rochester; H - b. 12/21/1942; W - b. 10/26/1949

MEE,
Arthur R. of Acton, ME m. Emily A. **Columbus** of Milton 10/10/1952; H - 34, student, b. Acton, ME, s/o Horace H. Mee and Marcia E. Hurd; W - 39, nurse, b. Milton, d/o Arthur Columbus and Flora Greenwood

MEIKLE,
Alexander of Acton, ME m. Maria E. **Dearden** of Acton, ME 9/30/1895 in Sanbornville; H - 63, block printer, 2nd, b. Glasgow, Scotland; W - 62, housekeeper, 2nd, b. Rockdale, England
William A. of Milton m. Clara E. **Googins** of Milton 4/30/1898 in Acton, ME; H - 24, shoe cutter, b. Acton, ME, s/o William Meikle (Scotland, printer); W - 20, housekeeper, b. Milton, d/o Frank Googins (Hollis, ME, spinner)

MEIKLEJOHN,
Gerald R. of Milton m. Carmen A. **Wyatt** of Milton 11/25/1983 in Rochester

MELLEN,
Gary W. of Milton m. Terri Lyn **Spruce** of Rochester 4/26/1975 in Rochester; H - b. 5/8/1951; W - b. 6/18/1957

MENEGONI,
Frank J. of Milton m. Yvonne M. **Rouleau** of Milton 4/10/1970 in Sanbornville; H - b. 4/13/1917; W - b. 7/4/1933

MERRILL,
Allie E. of Milton m. Nettie E. **Stevens** of Milton 10/8/1898 in Acton, ME; H - 23, shoecutter, b. Albany, s/o Alby E. Merrill (Milton, farmer); W - 20, lady, b. Milton, d/o Freeman E. Stevens (Milton, shoemaker)

Allie E. of Milton m. Esther **Williams** of Milton 11/22/1910; H - 36, machinist, 2nd, wid., b. Albany, s/o Abby Merrill (New Bedford, MA, farmer) and Sarah J. Smyther (NB); W - 26, shoe stitcher, b. Wakefield, d/o Lorenzo Williams and Augusta Williams (Wakefield)

Frank W. of Milton m. Beryl M. **White** of Lebanon, ME 7/29/1919 in East Rochester; H - 21, mill hand, b. Saco, ME, s/o Orion P. Merrill (Saco, ME) and Mary E. Berry (Portland, ME); W - 18, b. Lebanon, ME, d/o Victor White (Lowell, MA, mill hand) and Effie Drew (Lebanon, ME)

Richard H. of Milton m. Linda A. **Blaisdell** of East Rochester 9/23/1967 in East Rochester; H - 19, US Navy; W - 19, bookkeeper

Scott M. of Milton m. Stacy L. **Deschaine** of Milton 5/8/1998

MESERVE,
Irving E. of Milton m. Joan B. **Dodge** of Wakefield 10/4/1947; H - 18, mill emp., b. Milton, s/o Ralph E. Meserve and Cecelia E. Eldridge; W - 16, at home, b. Providence, RI, d/o Raymond L. Dodge (Block Island, RI, laborer) and Evelyn M. Hines (N. Rochester, housewife)

MEYER,
Ernest W. of Milton Mills m. Marie J. **Mattress** of Milton Mills 1/31/1946 in Sanford, ME; H - 32, painter, b. Dover, MA, s/o Fred A. Meyer (Acton, ME, carpenter) and Agda Fredholm (Sweden, housewife); W - 30, housewife, 2nd, b. Brooklyn, NY, d/o Joseph A. Botti (Italy, chauffeur) and Gladys E. Hanscom (NH, housewife)

Fred A., III of Milton m. Wanda G. **Keller** of Wakefield 4/15/1972 in Sanbornville; H - b. 5/23/1953; W - b. 12/6/1953

Frederick A., Jr. of Milton m. Irma J. **Currier** of Milton 6/24/1950 in Wakefield; H - 26, carpenter, b. Needham, MA, s/o Frederick A. Meyer (MA) and Agda A. Fredholm (Sweden); W - 27, spinner, 2nd,

b. Greenfield, MA, d/o Ira Hutchinson (Deerfield, MA) and Ruth
Fuller (Adams, MA)
John of Andover, MA m. Lorri A. **Strait** of Andover, MA 7/11/1992
Robert E. of Milton Mills m. Robina S. **Remich** of Rochester 9/25/1970 in
Rochester; H - b. 3/15/1919; W - b. 5/30/1922
Warren F. of Milton Mills m. Jacqueline D. **Highland** of Milton Mills
6/11/1987

MICHAELS,
Joseph A., Jr. of Milton m. Gail M. **Vaillancourt** of Milton 4/20/1996

MICHALSKI,
Stanley J., III of Milton m. Mary L. **Miner** of Loudon 7/10/1999

MICHAUD,
Mark R. of Milton m. Lauren L. **Munroe** of Milton 2/14/1987 in Center
Strafford
Michael A. of Milton m. Betty L. **King** of Milton 3/10/1973 in Rochester;
H - b. 5/21/1951; W - b. 8/10/1948

MICKELONIS,
Travis L. of Milton m. Shelly A. **Dusseault** of Milton 9/28/1996

MILLER,
Brad D. of Milton m. Laura J. **Hastings** of Strafford 4/24/1993
David Cameron of Milton m. Clara Belle **Tozier** of Milton 7/1/1918 in
Rochester; H - 47, farmer, b. Clinton, MA, s/o William A. Miller
(Glasgow, Scotland) and Janet L. Cameron (Pasley, Scotland); W -
47, teacher, b. Fairfield, ME, d/o Nahum Tozier (Fairfield, ME) and
Julia B. Holt (Fairfield, ME)
George D. of Milton m. Geraldine W. **Webber** of Quincy, MA 8/21/1991
Malcolm W. of Rochester m. Marie Y. **Labrie** of Milton 3/5/1946 in
Farmington; H - 23, barber, b. Rochester, s/o Douglas Miller
(Redstone, grain mill) and Edith Jackson (Rochester, housewife); W
- 21, at home, b. Somersworth, d/o Ludger J. Labrie (Canada, mill
worker) and Clara Dubois (Biddeford, ME, housewife)
Merton H. of Milton m. Blanche M. **Clough** of Farmington 3/30/1913 in
Farmington; H - 20, laborer, b. Hingham, MA, s/o John C. Miller
(Richford, VT) and Sarah A. F. Lord (Hingham, MA); W - 22,

waitress, b. Farmington, d/o Daniel B. Clough (Alton) and Lizzie F. Young

Robert J., Jr. of Milton m. Susan K. **Downs** of Milton 9/23/1978; H - b. 4/29/1945; W - b. 4/21/1949

Scott W. of Milton m. Carol A. **Hatch** of Milton 6/23/1989 in Rochester

MILLS,

Frank A. of Milton m. Emma **Thompson** of Milton 5/14/1902; H - 30, laborer, b. Milton, s/o William F. Mills (Milton, farmer) and Hannah Somes; W - 30, housekeeper, b. NY, d/o Robert T. Thompson (England, gilder) and Julia Blake (Cambridge, MA)

Fred W. of Milton m. Annie **Eaton** of Brookfield 6/16/1897; H - 22, weaver, b. Milton, s/o William F. Mills (Milton, farmer); W - 22, weaver, b. Brookfield, d/o Samuel Eaton (Wolfeboro, farmer)

William F. of Milton m. Amanda M. **Hargraves** of Milton 7/19/1899 in Milton Mills; H - 39, painter, 2nd, b. Hudson, MA, s/o George Mills; W - 36, housekeeper, 2nd, b. Milton, d/o Josiah E. Page (Wakefield, farmer)

William F. of Milton m. Cora E. **Heath** of Ossipee 3/10/1921 in Union; H - 61, farmer, 3rd, b. Hudson, MA, s/o George P. Mills (Portland, ME, farmer) and Rebecca Hunting (Needham, MA); W - 43, teacher, b. Ossipee, d/o Frank W. Heath (Concord, shoemaker) and Ellen Nichols (Ossipee)

MISEK,

Victor A. of Nashua m. Susan **Woodbury** of Milton 6/25/1955 in Nashua; H - 25, engineer, b. OH, s/o Albert B. Misek and Mathilda Chapee; W - 23, draftsman, b. NH, d/o William E. Woodbury and Doris M. Horne

MITCHELL,

Carl E. of Milton Mills m. Gwendolyn M. **Germain** of Milton Mills 2/14/1973; H - b. 4/22/1932; W - b. 12/1/1936

Charles N. of Milton m. Alice I. **Hussey** of Milton 2/16/1931; H - 22, laborer, b. Concord, s/o Albert Mitchell (Canada, truckman) and Lizzie Mitchell (Canada, housewife); W - 20, housework, 2nd, b. Riverdale, d/o Joseph Ritchie (Canada, laborer) and Emma Hildreth (Chelmsford, MA, housewife)

Edward C. of Union m. Allie May **Ricker** of Milton 12/16/1891; H - 23, station agent, b. Wakefield, s/o Jacob (Middleton, carpenter) and Lydia (Middleton, housekeeper); W - 22, lady, b. Milton, d/o Charles E. (Milton, laborer) and Mary (Wakefield, housekeeper)

George A. of Milton m. Gertrude **Tucker** of Milton 11/18/1899 in Rochester; H - 31, foreman, b. Westminster, s/o William C. Mitchell; W - 25, lady, b. Eastport, ME, d/o John Tucker

Ira L. of Portland, ME m. Eva G. **Curtis** of Portland, ME 11/30/1923; H - 34, mechanic, 2nd, b. Portland, ME, s/o Arthur L. Mitchell (Canton, ME, furniture mfr.) and Maria J. Hodsdon (Castine, ME); W - 22, stenographer, b. S. Portland, ME, d/o Lendall L. Curtis (Lewiston, ME, shoemaker) and Maud A. Berry (Freeport, ME)

William P. of Milton m. Lillian M. **Jordan** of Milton 2/12/1889; H - 33, shoemaker, s/o Thomas and Lydia A.; W - 22, lady, b. Milton, d/o George I. and Elizabeth A.

William P. of Milton m. Lillian E. B. **Durkee** of Beverly, MA 8/29/1906; H - 51, janitor, 2nd, b. Dover, s/o Thomas E. Mitchell (New Durham) and Lydia A. Perkins (Middleton); W - 35, b. Yarmouth, NS, d/o Robert Durkee (Yarmouth, NS) and Allene A. Healey (Yarmouth, NS)

MOLLICA,
Philip M. of Milton m. Linda L. **Lucier** of Milton 4/12/1980

MONTEITH,
Frank O., Jr. of Milton m. Brenda J. **Yelle** of Milton 8/14/1994

MONTGOMERY,
Ralph S. of Rochester m. Arline M. **Quint** of Milton 3/16/1950 in Dover; H - 28, welder, 3rd, b. NH, s/o William Montgomery (MA) and Ida E. Chase (NH); W - 25, office wkr., 2nd, b. NH, d/o Leon M. Willey (NH) and Flora M. Downs (NH)

MOODY,
Alfred H. of Milton m. Alice M. **Phinney** of Milton 2/23/1929 in Rochester; H - 20, laborer, b. Tamworth, s/o Joseph Moody (Boston, MA, laborer) and Nettie Williams (Tamworth); W - 18, at home, b. Lynn, MA, d/o William H. Phinney (Pt. Lorne, NS, mill worker) and Georgia A. Reed (C'n'tville, NS)

Ronald A. of Milton m. Susan L. **Bennett** of Sanbornville 6/2/1973 in Sanbornville; H - b. 5/3/1950; W - b. 5/22/1952

Terrence A. of Milton Mills m. Melody J. **Barber** of Milton Mills 7/24/1966 in Sanbornville; H - 19, US Army; W - 20, beautician

Terrence A. of Milton m. Susan E. **Smith** of Lebanon, ME 2/15/1975 in Rochester; H - b. 3/9/1947; W - b. 9/14/1953

MOOERS,

Fred L. of Lebanon, ME m. Arlene M. **Currier** of Milton 7/4/1948; H - 25, machinist, b. Lebanon, ME, s/o Grover C. Mooers (Lebanon, ME, shoe worker) and Ella M. Nickerson (Tamworth, housewife); W - 19, mill worker, b. Milton, d/o Henry S. Currier (Acton, ME, mill fireman) and Alfrida M. Bragg (Acton, ME, housewife)

Leon W. of Milton m. Cynthia A. **Bergeron** of Dover 7/1/1969; H - b. 7/20/1950; W - b. 5/28/1952

MOONEY,

Patrick M. of Milton m. Victoria L. **Haskins** of Milton 9/4/1999

Stanley E. of Wakefield m. Karen K. **Luscomb** of Milton 10/18/1969 in Wakefield; H - b. 11/1/1945; W - b. 6/23/1951

MOORE,

Brian R. of Verona, WI m. Deborah R. **Chase** of Milton 6/14/1980

Lyle K. of Milton m. Hannah E. **Cerley** of Mattapan, MA 5/20/1916 in Farmington; H - 25, ice man, b. Milton, s/o William E. Moore (Lowell, MA) and Sarah E. Downs (Milton); W - 27, bookkeeper, b. Roslindale, MA, d/o Patrick Cerley (Roslindale, MA) and Catherine Butler (Roslindale, MA)

Richard D. of Milton m. Celena E. **Olivarez** of Milton 8/17/1997

MOOREHOUSE,

Thomas F., II of Milton m. Sheri A. **Dexter** of Milton 2/12/1995

MORANN,

Tom W. H. of Milton m. Deborah L. **Hescock** of Milton 7/9/1988

Tom W. H. of Milton m. Kathleen A. **Seavey** of Milton 4/3/1999

MOREAU,
Henry F. of Milton m. Shirley M. **Chapman** of Rochester 7/4/1972 in Rochester; H - b. 12/5/1931; W - b. 11/4/1934
Roland J. of Rochester m. Diana L. **Higgins** of Milton Mills 8/1/1987

MORGAN,
Alan L. of Milton m. June W. **Worster** of Milton 9/9/1989
Donald M. of Milton m. Betty J. **Hackett** of Farmington 9/22/1951 in Farmington; H - 20, US Army, b. Alfred, ME, s/o Harry D. Morgan (Wolfeboro) and Eleanor H. Wentworth (Springvale, ME); W - 18, at home, b. Farmington, d/o George E. Hackett (Farmington) and Velma I. Gooch (Alton)
William R., Jr. of Milton m. Debra M. **Liquore** of Milton 8/21/1975; H - b. 1/7/1939; W - b. 9/29/1952

MORIN,
Charles A. of Milton m. Grace M. **Downs** of Milton 8/29/1891; H - 62, shoemaker, b. Stoneham, s/o David (Canada, shoemaker) and Mary (Stoneham, housekeeper); W - 39, shoe stitcher, b. Milton, d/o Albert F. (Milton) and Dora (Milton, housekeeper)

MORNEAU,
Edward A. of Milton m. Doris A. **Drapeau** of Milton 6/6/1992

MORPHY,
Thomas H. of Milton m. Wilhelmina **Arnold** of Milton 11/29/1939 in Berwick, ME; H - 39, foreman, 2nd, b. Canada, s/o Roland W. Morphy (Canada, deceased) and Eleanor Kidder (Canada, at home); W - 30, at home, 2nd, b. S. Groveland, MA, d/o William H. Cole (W. Boxford, MA, deceased) and Grace E. Morrison (Haverhill, MA, at home)

MORRILL,
Donald W. of Acton, ME m. Betty F. **Lacouture** of Acton, ME 2/12/1983
Donald W., Jr. of Milton Mills m. Faith T. **Dube** of Milton 5/1/1976; H - b. 11/3/1956; W - b. 2/18/1958
Fred M. of Wakefield m. Eva C. **Meyer** of Milton 9/2/1948 in Wakefield; H - 18, truck driver, b. Acton, ME, s/o Harry W. Morrill (Wakefield, laborer) and Phyllis Grant (Acton, ME, housewife); W - 17, at home,

b. Needham, MA, d/o Frederick A. Meyer (Walpole, MA, carpenter) and Adga H. Fredholm (Sweden, housewife)

Fred R., Jr. of Milton Mills m. Denise A. **Provencher** of Milton Mills 10/23/1983 in Milton Mills

Robert E. of Milton Mills m. Maureen B. **Mosher** of Farmington 6/24/1978 in Farmington; H - b. 9/9/1953; W - b. 3/8/1956

Robert E. of Milton Mills m. Maureen B. **Morrill** of Milton Mills 1/1/1985

MORRISON,

Franklin E. of Milton m. Ruth A. **Southwick** of Milton 8/2/1934; H - 24, mill emp., b. Milton, s/o Harry B. Morrison (Eastport, ME, mill emp.) and Vernie R. Leighton (Milton, housewife); W - 28, teacher, b. Franconia, d/o George B. Southwick (Humphrey, NY, clergyman) and Flora L. Weaver (C. Creek, NY, housewife)

MORSE,

George of Springvale, ME m. Edith M. **Wentworth** of Springvale, ME 7/4/1902; H - 21, wool sorter, b. Walpole, MA, s/o Albert Morse (Norfolk, MA) and Fannie Blake (Franklin, MA); W - 21, lady, b. Braintree, MA, d/o Frank J. Wentworth (Shapleigh, ME, farmer) and Abbie Ridley (Alfred, ME)

MORTON,

Kevin L. of Milton m. Stephanie M. **Mickelonis** of Milton 6/3/1995

MOSS,

John W., III of Dover m. Christina M. **Legrand** of Milton 5/2/1992

MOULTON,

Benjamin I. of Sanford, ME m. Flora E. **Burnham** of Sanford, ME 6/1/1902; H - 29, carpenter, b. Sanford, ME, s/o Silas M. Moulton (Sanford, ME, farmer) and Olive A. Whitham (Sanford, ME); W - 23, lady, b. Wakefield, d/o Henry M. Burnham (Wakefield, carpenter) and Sarah A. Miles (Milton)

Seth A. of Milton m. Elfrida M. **Peacock** of Milton 9/3/1903; H - 27, mec. engineer, b. Lowell, MA, s/o Charles E. Moulton (Saxonville, MA, mechanic) and Clara A. Russ (Lowell, MA); W - 22, lady, b.

Solon, ME, d/o Robert M. Peacock (Canada, clergyman) and Ada M. Lee (Riverside, ME)

Stephen B. of Berwick, ME m. Mary Anne **Blackey** of Milton 4/10/1987

MOUZOURAKIS,
Stergos of Milton m. Anthi **Manolakis** of Milton 12/27/1988

MUGRIDGE,
Frank D. of Milton m. Carrie E. **Quimby** of Wakefield 6/15/1912 in Rochester; H - 27, shoemaker, b. Shapleigh, ME, s/o Walter Mugridge (Lebanon, ME, shoemaker) and Elsie Joy (Shapleigh, ME); W - 37, shoe stitcher, 2nd, b. Middleton, d/o George E. Pinkham (Farmington, farmer) and Laura Maine (Milton)

MULLANEY,
Thomas C. of Wrentham, MA m. Sarita **Leppert** of Wrentham, MA 5/27/1966 in Milton Mills; H - 43, mechanic; W - 41, nurse

MUNROE,
Richard A., Jr. of Wolfeboro m. Darlene M. **MacAllister** of Milton 5/1/1971 in Sanbornville; H - b. 2/21/1946; W - b. 11/18/1952

MURPHY,
Walter E. of Old Orchard, ME m. Paulette T. **Desilets** of Old Orchard, ME 9/13/1960; H - 21, mechanic; W - 18, student

MURRAY,
Stephen W. G. of Lebanon, ME m. Lillian **Goodwin** of Lebanon, ME 7/31/1911; H - 24, emp. on RR, b. Parsonsfield, ME, s/o Hubbard G. Murray (Jamaica Plains, MA, farmer) and Annie J. Nelson (Norway); W - 34, housework, b. Lebanon, ME, d/o Plummer Goodwin (Lebanon, ME) and Isabelle M. Trafton (Shapleigh, ME)

MUSE,
James R. of Somerville, MA m. Marion C. **Marshall** of Milton 4/16/1906; H - 29, ice driver, b. Yarmouth, NS, s/o John Muse (Yarmouth, NS, farmer) and Madeline Muse (Yarmouth, NS); W - 20, shoe stitcher, b. Sanbornville, d/o Louis Marshall (Canada, emp. in mill) and Arline Theoret (Canada)

NADEAU,
Audie J. of Milton Mills m. Kris D. **Morrill** of Milton Mills 7/14/1990
George C. of Rochester m. Grace R. **Jacobs** of Milton 9/24/1988 in Rochester

NARY,
Edward A. of Milton m. Ann M. **DesRoches** of Milton 9/14/1952; H - 17, unemployed, b. MA, s/o Elmer E. Nary, Jr. and Elizabeth Osborne; W - 18, unemployed, b. VT, d/o Rolland DesRoches and Mary Ainger

NASON,
Clarence C., Sr. of Milton m. Pauline R. **Hodgdon** of Milton 10/28/1972; H - b. 3/18/1940; W - b. 3/4/1925
Clarence C., Jr. of Milton m. Norrene L. **Provencher** of Milton 8/15/1981
Dave R. of Milton m. Karen M. **Lamper** of Milton 9/29/1990
James E. of Milton m. Karen M. **Santoro** of Milton 9/4/1993
Rodney E. of Middleton m. Betty F. **Provencher** of Milton 3/17/1957 in Sanbornville; H - 20, USAF, b. Wolfeboro, s/o Edward R. Nason (Wakefield) and Ida M. Drapeau (Brookfield); W - 18, laborer, b. Milton, d/o Edward A. Provencher (Wakefield) and Draxa Corson (Milton)
Ronald W. of Wakefield m. Sharon E. **Downs** of Milton 7/2/1957 in Wakefield; H - 20, laborer, b. Gorham, ME, s/o Raymond Nason (Wakefield) and Ada ----- (Gorham, ME); W - 17, at home, b. Rochester, d/o Herbert A. Downs (NH) and Wilma Warnecke (NH)
Ronald W. of Milton m. June L. **Williams** of Milton 6/26/1965 in Wakefield; H - 28, mach, tender; W - 40, homemaker

NESBITT,
James M., IV of Milton m. Jami-Lynn **Bleyl** of Milton 9/6/1997
James P., Jr. of Milton m. Patricia A. **Couture** of Milton 8/30/1986
Todd J. of Milton m. Jackie D. **Patch** of Milton 8/31/1996

NEVIS,
Daniel A., Jr. of Mims, FL m. Kathryn L. **Hermanson** of Mims, FL 8/6/1993

NEWELL,
Milford W. of Milton m. Vera A. **Craig** of Newbury 8/2/1924 in Newbury; H - 23, mill hand, b. Clarks Harbor, NS, s/o Isaiah Newell (Clarks Harbor, NS, fisherman) and Margaret Newell (W. Head, NS); W - 23, teacher, b. Bradford, d/o Frank P. Craig (Newbury, farmer) and Mabel F. Blood (Bradford)

NEWICK,
John W. of Milton m. Tammy F. **Ayer** of Milton 7/21/1984

NICHOLS,
Everett A. of Milton m. Doris A. **Hartford** of Rochester 1/27/1942 in Dover; H - 26, spinner, b. Sunapee, s/o James Nichols (Burke, NY, retired) and Fannie Young (Burke, NY, housewife); W - 31, mill hand, b. Lebanon, ME, d/o Alonzo Hartford (E. Rochester, farmer) and Maude Tibbetts (Haverhill, MA, housewife)

NICKERSON,
James T. of Milton m. Lillian M. **Mason** of Milton 9/12/1894; H - 24, teamster, b. Clyde River, NS, s/o James Nickerson (Barrington, NS) and Sarah (Woodsh'r, NS); W - 22, housekeeper, b. Milton, d/o Albert Mason (Sandwich, farmer) and Mary J. (Tuftonboro)
Ralph of Norwalk, CT m. Elsie C. **Remick** of Milton Mills 9/4/1930 in E. Norwalk, CT; H - 25, pressman, b. Norwalk, CT, s/o Alfred Nickerson and Lettie Hanlon; W - 21, teacher, b. Milton Mills, d/o William Remick and Caroline Hurd
Willis of Milton m. Mertie A. **Welch** of Milton 12/31/1929; H - 32, laborer, b. Milton, s/o James T. Nickerson (Clyde, NS, sawyer) and Lillian M. Mason (Milton); W - 29, housekeeper, 2nd, b. Tamworth, d/o Justus W. Williams (Ossipee, farmer) and Mertie Smart (Tamworth)

NISBET,
James G. of Dexter, ME m. Roxie V. **Page** of Dexter, ME 7/26/1949; H - 66, mechanic, 2nd, b. Houlton, ME, s/o William P. Nisbet (NB) and Mary E. Faulkner (NB); W - 59, mill wkr., 3rd, b. Atkinson, ME, d/o William L. Brown (ME) and Alice C. Levensellor (ME)

NIVEN,
Michael R. of Milton m. Sarah A. **Wallace** of Milton 9/30/1995

NOBBS,
James W. of Acton, ME m. Belle C. **Ord** of Acton, ME 11/2/1924 in Milton Mills; H - 52, farmer, 2nd, b. Gloucester, England, s/o James Nobbs (Gloucester, England, preacher) and Eliza Haynes (Chelturn, England); W - 48, musician, 2nd, b. Malden, MA, d/o Herman Gould (Malden, MA, druggist) and Elizabeth Sumner (Beverly, MA)

NOLAN,
Robert E. of Milton m. Mildred L. **Bragdon** of Milton 7/17/1911 in Sanbornville; H - 37, contractor supt., b. Middleboro, MA, s/o William Nolan (Ireland) and Ellen Flynn (Ireland); W - 31, housekeeper, b. Milton, d/o Stephen M. Bragdon (Milton) and Lydia E. Downs

NORMAN,
Thomas of Milton m. Bessie M. **Corson** of Milton 5/27/1922; H - 49, laborer, 2nd, b. S. Berwick, ME, s/o John Norman (York, ME) and Sarah Varnham (York, ME); W - 31, housekeeper, 2nd, b. Milton, d/o Allie J. Laskey (Milton, farmer) and Rose Barker (New Vineyard, ME)

NORMANDEAU,
Marc R. of Milton m. Aimee M. **Loef** of Milton 6/18/1994

NORRISH,
Stephen E. of Milton m. Tammy A. **Champy** of Wakefield 11/14/1987

NORTON,
Steven S. of Milton m. Rhonda A. **Sowards** of Milton 12/31/1988 in Farmington

NOYES,
Albert P. of Hampstead m. Eliza R. **Mason** of Milton 2/15/1899 in Somersworth; H - 41, photographer, b. Hampstead, s/o Joshua F. Noyes (Hampstead, farmer); W - 35, lady, b. Milton, d/o Albert Mason

NUTE,
Arthur H. of Milton m. Clara B. **Nute** of Alton 9/11/1894 in Wakefield; H - 35, farmer, b. Milton, s/o Stephen Nute (Milton, farmer) and Mary E. (Effingham); W - 31, housekeeper, 2nd, b. New Durham, d/o W. Chamberlin and Sarah (Middleton)

Charles E. of Milton m. Ella May **Jenness** of Milton 6/20/1915; H - 17, pressman, b. Milton, s/o Charles Nute (Farmington) and Emma Pike (Dover); W - 20, weaver, b. Milton, d/o Edwin P. Jenness (Wakefield, laborer) and Alma Hawkins (Dover)

George E. of Milton m. Emma M. **Barber** of Milton 3/29/1919 in Farmington; H - 65, farmer, 2nd, b. Milton, s/o John P. Nute (Milton) and Ann M. Burrows (Stoughton, MA); W - 17, domestic, b. Newport, d/o William Barber (Burlington, VT, shoemaker) and Melvina S. Babbitt (Canada)

Harry Y. of Milton m. Cristie G. **Goodwin** of Milton 10/20/1894; H - 19, shoemaker, b. Milton, s/o John S. Nute (Dover, shoemaker) and Emma (Province Pen.); W - 18, shoe stitcher, b. Acton, ME, d/o Lorenzo D. Goodwin (Lebanon, ME, farmer) and Mary E.

Herbert R. of Milton m. Marie T. **Foley** of Dover 11/6/1954 in Dover; H - 24, shoe worker, b. Milton, s/o Ray H. Nute and Doris Ferland; W - 24, tel. oper., b. Brookline, MA, d/o Martin T. Foley and Trissella O'Gara

Lewis S. of Milton m. Mamie A. **Wilkins** of Milford 4/5/1899 in Lawrence, MA; H - 21, barber, b. Milton, s/o John S. Nute (Dover, shoemaker); W - 19, lady, b. Milford, d/o Thomas J. Wilkins (Milford, laborer)

Ray H. of Milton m. Deloria **Ferland** of Farmington 12/23/1922; H - 27, shoemaker, b. Milton, s/o Arthur H. Nute (Milton, farmer) and Clara Chamberlain (Alton); W - 23, shoemaker, b. Rochester, d/o Thomas Ferland (Canada, shoemaker) and Mary Marcoux (Rochester)

William H. of Milton m. Bertha M. **Pike** of Wakefield 12/24/1901; H - 29, shoemaker, b. Milton, s/o John S. Nute (Dover, laborer) and Emma Moore (Dover); W - 20, shoe stitcher, b. Wakefield, d/o Henry A. Pike (Wakefield, stone mason) and Minnie B. Robinson

NUTTER,
Addis S. of Milton m. Marion G. **Rand** of Milton 6/11/1914 in Farmington; H - 19, emp. ice co., b. Milton, s/o Hartley A. Nutter (Milton, emp. ice co.) and Ada Huntress (Athens, ME); W - 18, b.

Milton, d/o George W. Rand (Cambridge, MA, emp. in mill) and Ida E. Moore (Milton)

F. Reginald of Milton m. Ernestine **Witham** of Milton 6/30/1939; H - 24, radio oper., b. Milton, s/o Frank J. Nutter (Sanford, ME, mill worker) and Gertrude Wentworth (Milton, housewife); W - 20, housekeeper, b. Portsmouth, d/o Ernest F. Witham (Kittery, ME, fireman) and Marguerite Cooley (Wilmington, MA, housewife)

Frank J. of Milton m. Gertrude E. **Wentworth** of Milton 8/27/1905; H - 22, shoemaker, b. Sanford, ME, s/o Frank J. Nutter (N. Berwick, ME) and Julia E. Greenlaw (Deer Is., NB); W - 18, lady, b. Milton, d/o Ernest L. Wentworth (Milton, merchant) and Florence A. Lucas (IA)

Frank R. of Milton m. Jeanette W. **McCallister** of Gonic 8/18/1979

Hartley A. of Milton m. Ada M. **Huntress** of Milton 7/20/1893; H - 19, laborer, b. Milton, s/o L. Sidney Nutter (Milton, fish dealer) and Belle; W - 18, housekeeper, b. Wakefield, d/o Stillman Huntress (painter) and Francina

John M. of Milton m. Ada F. **Whitehouse** of Farmington 5/30/1895 in Rochester; H - 36, farmer, 2nd, b. Milton, s/o Jethro; W - 20, shoe stitcher, b. Middleton, d/o Thomas L.

Malcom of Milton m. Grace E. **Gray** of Ctr. Barnstead 10/2/1940; H - 24, farmer, b. Milton, s/o Addis S. Nutter (Milton, ice man) and Marion G. Rand (Milton, housewife); W - 18, decorator, b. Ctr. Barnstead, d/o Bessie O. Gray (Ctr. Barnstead, shoe worker)

Roscoe C. of Milton m. May E. **Johnson** of Milton 1/8/1896; H - 19, shoemaker, b. Milton, s/o L. Sidney (Milton, fireman) and Belle (Milton); W - 25, shoe stitcher, b. Greenland, d/o John and Annie

NYE,
Philip R. of Milton m. Linda **Timmins** of Milton 12/12/1987 in Dover

O'KEEFE,
John B., Jr. of Milton Mills m. Kimberlyanne **Westfall** of Milton Mills 11/20/1988

O'LAUGHLIN,
James G. of Milton m. Addie F. **Knight** of Milton 4/8/1893 in Wakefield; H - 24, shoemaker, b. Stoneham, MA, s/o Michael O'Laughlin and

Lucy; W - 19, shoe stitcher, b. Milton, d/o Robert L. Knight and Marilla

OAKES,
Elijah P. of Milton m. Lydia F. **Doble** of Milton 3/7/1932; H - 48, carpenter, b. Sangerville, ME, s/o Augustus J. Oakes (Sangerville, ME, veterinary) and Jennie Potter (Brunswick, ME, housewife); W - 34, shoeworker, b. S. Weymouth, MA, d/o George H. Doble (S. Weymouth, MA, shoeworker) and Eva L. Humble (S. Weymouth, MA, housewife)

OECHLER,
Jaret D. of Milton m. Kathryn J. **Alley** of Milton 7/10/1999

OLIVER,
Frederick, III of Milton m. Martha A. **Koch** of Milton 4/29/1989 in Rochester

ORMEZZANI,
Christopher of Milton m. Lelani R. **Evert** of Milton 7/2/1988 in Newmarket

ORRELL,
William I. of Lebanon, ME m. Blanche **Miller** of Hinesburg, VT 8/23/1904; H - 21, meat cutter, b. Lebanon, ME, s/o Charles S. Orrell (Berwick, ME, farmer) and Myra B. Hussey (Milton); W - 20, governess, b. Hinesburg, VT, d/o Eugene Miller and Vallie Degree

ORTIZ,
Perfecto A. of Milton m. Jean D. **Nesbitt** of Milton 8/15/1992

OTIS,
Lawrence of Lebanon, ME m. Alice **Grenier** of Lebanon, ME 6/10/1950; H - 41, mechanic, 3rd, b. Stratham, s/o Robert Otis (Stratham) and Frances Hallowin (Portsmouth); W - 58, housewife, 3rd, b. NB, d/o Josiah Wood (NB) and Lena Bubar (NB)

OXTON,
Mark A. of Milton m. Emily C. **Costa** of Milton 6/20/1992

PAEY,

Bernard of Milton m. Irene **Otis** of Somersworth 10/10/1936 in Exeter; H - 31, shoe oper., b. Milton, s/o George Paey (Stoneham, MA, fmn., shoe) and Josephine Downs (Milton, at home); W - 27, at home, b. Somersworth, d/o Lorenzo D. Otis (Somersworth, painter) and Susanne Newcome (Halifax, NS, at home)

David G. of Milton m. Dorothy M. **Christie** of Wakefield 8/14/1959; H - 23, US Navy, b. Rochester, s/o Clyde W. Paey (Milton) and C. Louise Huntress (MA); W - 24, mill emp., 2nd, b. Wakefield, d/o Carroll F. Bickford (Wolfeboro) and Blanche I. Jenness (NH)

David G., Jr. of Milton m. Robin J. **Sanborn** of Rochester 5/1/1992

George W. of Milton m. Josephine M. **Downs** of Milton 7/15/1899 in Rochester; H - 27, shoemaker, b. Stoneham, MA, s/o George Paey; W - 22, shoe stitcher, b. Milton, d/o Albert F. Downs (Milton)

PAGE,

George W. of Milton m. Clara M. **Sprague** of Rochester 1/28/1949 in Wakefield; H - 21, shoemaker, b. Charleston, VT, s/o Harold J. Page (Charleston, VT) and Kattie N. Sprague (P. Quebec); W - 18, shoe shop, b. Kittery, ME, d/o Stanley I. Sprague (S. Portland, ME) and Evelyn M. Frary (Kittery, ME)

Richard A. of Milton m. Deborah L. **Morann** of Milton 4/25/1998

Robert of Milton m. Ida **Sibley** of Wakefield 3/15/1899 in Acton, ME; H - 22, barber, b. Milton, s/o John W. Page (GA, wool sorter); W - 25, housekeeper, b. Wakefield, d/o Richard F. Sibley (Wakefield)

Robert W. of Milton Mills m. Dorothy **Leeman** of Milton 8/31/1935 in Milton Mills; H - 24, mill worker, b. Milton Mills, s/o Robert Page (Milton Mills, barber) and Ida Sibley (Boston, MA, housewife); W - 18, at home, b. Milton, d/o Milledge G. Leeman (Eastport, ME) and Helen DeWolfe (Milton, housewife)

Robert W. of Milton m. Marion H. **Pike** of Milton 10/31/1942 in Sanbornville; H - 31, mach. oper., 2nd, b. Milton, s/o Robert Page (Milton, mach. oper.) and Ida Sibley (Everett, MA, housewife); W - 42, blanket finish., 2nd, b. Everett, MA, d/o Roy T. Brierley (Acton, ME, deceased) and Hattie E. Webber (N. Shapleigh, ME, housewife)

Wesley L., Jr. of Rochester m. Patricia R. **Tufts** of Milton 2/16/1947 in Rochester; H - 24, laborer, 2nd, b. Rochester, s/o Wesley L. Page (Rochester, fireman) and Margaret O. Johnson (N. Waterboro, ME, housewife); W - 19, shoe wkr., b. Milton, d/o Mose D. Tufts (Middleton, farmer) and Evelyn R. Nutter (Milton, shoe worker)

PAGEAU,
James L. of Milton m. Joyce L. **Hayward** of Union 9/29/1973 in Wakefield; H - b. 3/15/1954; W - b. 10/9/1954
James L. of Milton m. Linda M. **Casey** of Milton 10/1/1994
James W. of Strafford m. Andrea M. **Drake** of Strafford 5/22/1999

PALMER,
David W. of Milton m. Pamela A. **Paquette** of Milton 12/1/1984
Kenneth T. of Albany, NY m. Kim C. **Ferrelli** of Milton 8/6/1988

PAPPAGALLO,
Arthur R. of Milton m. Debra A. **Doucet** of Rochester 8/25/1979

PAPPAS,
Gregory A. of Milton Mills m. Deidre R. **Cartier** of Milton Mills 7/18/1997
Vassileos of Milton m. Edith G. **Mohbat** of Milton 7/14/1917; H - 20, emp. in mill, b. Lavarzon, Greece, s/o Ep'mon'doo Pappas (Levarzon, Greece, farmer) and Kaliaroy Kariakoy (Levarzon, Greece); W - 16, emp. in mill, b. New York, NY, d/o Joseph Mohbat (Beyvont, Syria) and Katherine Koury (Kisba, Syria)

PAQUETTE,
William R. of Milton m. Kimberly C. **Hall** of Milton 9/14/1996

PARADIS,
Henry L. of Milton m. Rebekah **Blake** of Milton 10/7/1989 in Rochester
Lucien G., Jr. of Rochester m. Candise E. **Carignan** of Milton Mills 12/10/1971 in Rochester; H - b. 3/27/1941; W - b. 10/10/1949
Raymond L. of Milton m. Cindy J. **Lyons** of Rochester 7/3/1993
Thomas M. of Milton m. Angela M. **Howe** of Milton 12/28/1996

PARCELL,
Robert D. of Rochester m. Phyllis L. **Sprague** of Milton Mills 4/8/1961 in Rochester; H - 28, shoe shop; W - 19, shoe shop

PARKER,
Michael P. of Somersworth m. Christine M. **McMillan** of Milton Mills 6/30/1990
Philip E. of Rochester m. Louise T. **Dupuis** of Milton 5/29/1954; H - 24, laborer, b. Rochester, s/o Lauren Parker and Evelyn Morrill; W - 23, G.E., b. Milton, d/o Wilfred Dupuis and Gertrude Harrity
Robert L. of Milton m. Elaine A. **Vickery** of Rochester 8/4/1979

PARO,
David J., Jr. of Milford m. Carol A. **Smith** of Milton 8/28/1965 in Sanbornville; H - 21, salesman; W - 20, salesgirl

PARON,
Joseph of Milton m. Celina **Lapoint** of Wakefield 1/22/1908 in Sanbornville; H - 20, shoemaker, b. Canada, s/o Alfred Paron (Canada, farmer) and Melene Jotier (Canada); W - 17, at home, b. Wakefield, d/o Seril Lapoint (Canada, emp. on RR) and Orale Marcoux (Canada)

PARSONS,
Gordon B. of Milton Mills m. Wendy G. **Barber** of Milton Mills 7/2/1998

PARTRICK,
Clinton of E. Norwalk, CT m. Christine **Remick** of Milton Mills 10/3/1937 in Melvin Village; H - 34, printer, b. E. Norwalk, CT, s/o Oscar Partrick (Redding, CT, dead) and Elsie Ainsworth (S. Norwalk, CT, dead); W - 33, at home, b. Milton Mills, d/o William Remick (Milton Mills, dead) and Caroline Hurd (Milton Mills, dead)

PATCH,
Alfred of Rochester m. Margaret **Rouleau** of Milton 2/7/1945 in Sanford, ME; H - 21, truck driver, b. Acton, ME, s/o George Patch (Limerick, ME, mill worker) and Margaret O'Connor (Amesbury, MA, housewife); W - 20, shoe shop, b. Milton, d/o Louis Rouleau (Lebanon, ME, woodsman) and Josephine Burbine (MA, housewife)
Bruce R. of Milton m. Beverly A. **Brierley** of Milton 10/12/1974; H - b. 3/22/1956; W - b. 5/9/1956
Michael J. of S. Lebanon, ME m. Lillian M. **Griffin** of Milton 7/20/1974; H - b. 9/16/1952; W - b. 10/15/1954

Steven W. of Milton m. Brenda L. **Reinhold** of Milton 10/1/1994

PATTON,
James L. of Fremont m. Yvonne M. **Menegoni** of Milton 11/27/1993

PAUL,
George H. of Milton m. Alice **Lord** of Milton 5/30/1895 in Wakefield; H - 29, farmer, b. Lynn, MA, s/o Henry H. (Lynn, MA); W - 30, housekeeper, b. Acton, ME, d/o George W. (Topsham, ME)
Morrill A. of N. Andover, MA m. Natalie E. **Cloyd** of Groveland, MA 7/9/1937; H - 33, meat mgr., b. N. Andover, MA, s/o Walter H. Paul (Canada, dead) and Bertha Etherington (Canada, dead); W - 33, at home, 2nd, b. Exeter, d/o Benjamin Rowell (Brentwood, shoe cutter) and Bernice Gray (Exeter, dead)

PEABODY,
Ernest W. of Rochester m. Ruth E. **Perry** of Milton 4/12/1947; H - 72, shoe cutter, 2nd, b. Peabody, MA, s/o Charles S. Peabody (Hamilton, MA, carpenter) and Lucy Wellington (Gloucester, MA, housewife); W - 27, at home, b. Walpole, d/o Charles E. Perry (Brewster, MA, farmer) and Ruth W. Perry (Brewster, MA, housewife)
William S. of Rochester m. Cheryl A. **Chase** of Milton 9/17/1994

PEARSON,
Craig S. of Milton m. Karen L. **Cheney** of Milton 4/15/1989 in Rochester
Jeffrey D. of Milton m. Janice E. **Charles** of Rochester 8/3/1985 in Rochester

PEASLEY,
James H. of Stralfield, CT m. Patricia J. **Sarne** of Brookline, MA 10/13/1962; H - 20, student; W - 18, student

PEAVEY,
Frank E. of Milton m. Maggie H. **Campbell** of Milton 5/14/1889 in Milton Mills; H - 28, farmer, b. Tuftonboro, s/o William (NH) and Mary L. (NB); W - 25, shop, b. Scotland, d/o George (Scotland) and Hannah (Scotland)

PELKIE,
David E. of Milton m. Doreen L. **Dusseault** of Milton 7/21/1990

PELLETIER,
Donald J. of Dover m. Patricia A. **Marcoux** of Milton 12/30/1977; H - b. 4/29/1954; W - b. 5/10/1957
Gerard R., II of Milton m. Roberta A. **Jarest** of Milton 8/21/1993
Michael K. of Milton m. Jennifer L. **Adjutant** of Milton 9/25/1993
Norman E. of Milton m. Paula D. **Moulton** of Hollis, ME 2/8/1964; H - 22, student; W - 18, student

PELLEY,
William S., Jr. of Milton m. Janette D. **Leavy** of Milton 8/8/1992

PENDROK,
Paul J. of Milton Mills m. Deborah L. **Roach** of Milton Mills 11/7/1983

PENNELL,
Alston E. of Milton m. Gail A. **McCarthy** of Milton 7/10/1965; H - 20, millworker; W - 18, student
James E. of Milton m. April L. **Young** of Rochester 1/5/1985 in Rochester
John W. of Milton m. Rhonda F. **Buck** of Dover 4/11/1976; H - b. 4/6/1951; W - b. 5/31/1957
Reginald of Tamworth m. Helen J. **Remick** of Milton 6/18/1939 in Lebanon, ME; H - 21, furn. wkr., b. Milton, s/o Edward A. Pennell (Tamworth, RR wkr.) and Dora Williams (Tamworth, housewife); W - 16, at home, b. Milton, d/o Arthur F. Remick (Tamworth, mechanic) and Angie E. Page (Milton, housewife)
Reginald E. of Milton m. Anne C. **Morgan** of Rochester 6/18/1965 in Rochester; H - 25, public wks. dept.; W - 17, student
Reginald E., Jr. of Milton m. Pamela A. **Williams** of Milton 8/31/1991

PENNEY,
Robert S. of Milton m. Kelly M. **Laventure** of Milton 6/17/1990

PENNO,
Alan D. of Milton Mills m. Susan A. **Jones** of Lebanon, ME 6/20/1992

PERFECT,
Ernest G. of Exeter m. Grace E. **Brock** of Milton 10/27/1939 in N. Berwick, ME; H - 27, laborer, 2nd, b. N. Berwick, ME, s/o John R. Perfect (Franklin, MA, foreman) and Hazel Moreland (Woburn, MA, housewife); W - 26, packer, 2nd, b. W. Lebanon, ME, d/o Ralph H. Betts (S. Lebanon, ME, farmer) and Myrtie McIntire (W. Lebanon, ME, housewife)

PERKINS,
Donald F. of Rochester m. Karen S. **Webb** of Milton 7/4/1981

Harry A. of Milton m. Daisy G. **Corkery** of Milton 8/28/1905; H - 27, salesman, b. Kenduskeag, ME, s/o Charles B. Perkins (Madison, ME) and Abbie Wentworth (Stetson, ME); W - 25, milliner, b. Milton, d/o Daniel Corkery (St. John, NB) and Martha E. Felch (Reading, MA)

Lloyd A. of Milton m. Mary A. **Lawson** of Milton 9/13/1958; H - 25, pub. serv. co., b. Beverly, MA, s/o Stephen H. Perkins (MA) and Hilda A. Berg (MA); W - 20, secretary, b. Rochester, d/o Henry N. Lawson (IA) and Audrey Y. Tanner (NH)

Mark M. of Farmington m. Lori A. **Putney** of Milton 5/13/1978 in Farmington; H - b. 7/11/1952; W - b. 7/1/1959

Melvin R. of Milton m. Cristine **Putney** of Milton 12/26/1978; H - b. 5/17/1926; W - b. 7/21/1935

Otis I. of Milton m. Clara **Clow** of Acton, ME 10/5/1920 in Milton Mills; H - 21, laborer, b. Wolfeboro, s/o Charles E. Perkins (Middleton, laborer) and Jennie Piper (Alton); W - 21, domestic, b. Portsmouth, d/o Charles A. Clow (N. Berwick, ME, fireman) and Mabel Nichols (Ossipee)

Otis I. of Milton Mills m. Hattie **Twombly** of Sanbornville 6/20/1931 in Union; H - 31, laborer, 2nd, b. Wolfeboro, s/o Charles E. Perkins (Middleton) and Jennie M. Piper (Wolfeboro, housewife); W - 20, at home, b. Wolfeboro, d/o Clarence Twombly (Conway, lumberman) and Bessie Downs (Wolfeboro, housewife)

Patrick S. of Milton m. Lisa M. **Kern** of Milton 9/22/1990

Ralph C. of Rochester m. Gale A. **Halcy** of Milton 11/27/1970; H - b. 7/1/1947; W - b. 7/7/1948

Ralph C. of Acton, ME m. Pamela L. **Maxfield** of Milton Mills 9/27/1975; H - b. 7/1/1947; W - b. 9/25/1951

PERRON,
Gerard L. of Milton m. Linda I. **Allard** of Milton 2/14/1973 in Rochester; H - b. 9/29/1953; W - b. 3/25/1952

PERRY,
James E. of Milton m. Lilla F. **Doyer** of Lowell, MA 8/21/1918 in Lowell, MA; H - 22, emp. in mill, b. Brookfield, s/o John Perry (Wolfeboro, florist) and Lena Eaton (Brookfield); W - 23, weaver, b. Lowell, MA, d/o Andrew Doyer (Canada, carpenter) and Philomen Godin (Canada)

PETERSON,
Christopher R. of Milton m. Judith L. **Lucier** of Milton 10/21/1983 in Rochester
Steve T. of Milton m. Raylene A. **Weekly** of Milton 7/21/1984 in Rochester
Steve T. of Milton m. Kelley L. **Prentice** of Milton 11/21/1989 in Rochester
Thomas O. of Milton m. Dianne E. **Hancock** of Rochester 6/28/1985 in Rochester

PHILBRICK,
Charles S. of Milton m. Jenny **Applebee** of Milton 8/27/1890; H - 30, farmer, b. Freedom, s/o Henry (farmer) and Adeline (housekeeper); W - 26, lady, b. Milton, d/o John (farmer) and Sarah (housekeeper)
Daniel of Milton m. Jennie C. **Hanson** of Milton 6/4/1903; H - 62, farmer, 2nd, b. Freedom, s/o Frederick Philbrick and Clarisa Young; W - 26, housekeeper, b. Milton, d/o John W. Hanson (Milton, farmer) and Hattie Dearborn

PHILIPPI,
Todd L. of Aurora, CO m. Michelle M. **Meattey** of Milton 5/9/1992

PHILLIPS,
Daniel S. of Strafford m. Laura J. **Moore** of Milton 10/17/1981 in Rochester
David B. of Rochester m. Denise A. **Lilljedahl** of Milton 6/29/1979

PHILPOT,
J. Frank of Milton m. Jeanette L. **Columbus** of Milton 4/28/1934 in Farmington; H - 24, laborer, b. S. Windham, ME, s/o Cyrus E. Philpot (New Portland, ME, farmer) and Margaret Quigley (Minudie, NS, housewife); W - 18, beautician, b. Milton, d/o Arthur Columbus (Acton, ME, truckman) and Flora Boisvert (Somersworth, housewife)

PHINNEY,
Bradford C. of Milton m. Nancy A. **Fields** of Milton 10/11/1980
Bradford C. of West Lebanon, ME m. Gloria M. **Garyait** of West Lebanon, ME 9/6/1986
Charles K. of Milton m. Marguerite E. **Brown** of West Lebanon, ME 12/14/1985 in Rochester

PICARD,
Laurent G. of Dover m. Katherine M. **Karcher** of Milton 5/15/1976 in Farmington; H - b. 9/29/1951; W - b. 6/29/1950

PIERCE,
Carl H. of Wakefield m. Mary E. **Drew** of Milton 7/31/1943; H - 29, painter, b. Cornish, ME, s/o Chester L. Pierce (Waterboro, ME, box mill emp.) and Jetta M. Scott (Waterboro, ME, housewife); W - 18, at home, b. Wakefield, d/o Charles A. Drew (Wakefield, chimney clnr.) and Cora M. Dunn (Dorchester, MA, housewife)
Carl H., Jr. of Milton m. Bernadette M. **Cardin** of Milton 2/19/1966; H - 21, dryerman; W - 19, shoe worker
David B. of Milton m. Louann **Mann** of Rochester 7/5/1963 in Rochester; H - 19, meat clerk; W - 19, office worker
Jesse E. of Milton Mills m. Mary E. **Pierce** of Milton Mills 9/20/1975; H - b. 5/4/1931; W - b. 4/6/1926

PIERSON,
George A. of N. Easton, MA m. Helen H. **Healey** of Milton 2/4/1949 in Dover; H - 41, police officer, b. N. Easton, MA, s/o Edwin S. Pierson (Sweden) and Hulda Swanson (Easton, MA); W - 35, social wkr., 2nd, b. Belmont, MA, d/o Hilmer S. Anderson (Sweden) and Ruth H. Swenson (Boston, MA)

PIKE,
Elmer E. of Milton m. Susie F. **Wiggin** of Milton 6/28/1908 in Rochester; H - 47, teamster, 2nd, b. Middleton, s/o John C. Pike (Milton) and Elma E. Whitehouse (Middleton); W - 42, housekeeper, 2nd, b. Shapleigh, ME, d/o Benjamin Day (Augusta, ME) and Anna ----- (Alfred, ME)

Kevin R. of Milton Mills m. Sherrylee M. **Gauthier** of Sanbornville 2/17/1968 in Milton Mills; H - 18; W - 17

Lawrence R. of Rochester m. Dorothy A. **Rouleau** of Milton 6/28/1949 in Wakefield; H - 28, mechanic, b. Rochester, s/o Roland L. Pike (Rochester) and Bessie C. Jenness (Rochester); W - 15, unemployed, b. Milton, d/o Louis Rouleau (Lebanon, ME) and Josephine Burbine (Wakefield, MA)

Lewis F. of Milton m. Vida **Seeley** of Williamstown, MA 2/22/1919 in Williamstown, MA; H - 30, US Army, b. Wakefield, s/o Freeman D. Pike (Brookfield) and Sophia Ricker (Milton); W - 27, b. Bethlehem, PA, d/o Charles F. Seeley and Nanna P. Skoog

Lloyd G. of Wakefield m. Marylin L. **Williams** of Milton 8/21/1954 in Wakefield; H - 21, farmer, b. NH, s/o Forrest Pike and Lois Robinson; W - 18, clerk, b. NH, d/o Ralph Williams and Lillian McCarten

Philip D. of Milton Mills m. Beatrice **Van Buskirk** of E. Rochester 12/17/1937 in Rochester; H - 22, mill hand, b. Milton Mills, s/o Philip G. Pike (S. Lebanon, ME, butcher) and Rosamond Piper (Sanbornville, school tchr.); W - 20, shoe worker, b. Chelsea, MA, d/o Seymour Van Buskirk (NB, mill hand) and Sadie Burke (Lynn, MA, housewife)

Philip G. of Milton m. Rosamond E. **Piper** of Milton 1/3/1912 in Portsmouth; H - 21, butcher, b. Milton, s/o Robert S. Pike (Wakefield, butcher) and Fannie Roberts (Acton, ME); W - 23, teacher, b. Wakefield, d/o James A. Piper (Newfield, ME, carpenter) and Laura Evans (Wakefield)

Philip W. of Milton Mills m. Edith L. **Byrd** of Milton Mills 6/11/1983

Ralph W. of Milton m. Marion H. **Brierley** of Fayetteville, NY 2/26/1921 in Union; H - 27, bookkeeper, b. Milton, s/o Robert S. Pike (Middleton, butcher) and Fannie Roberts (Milton); W - 20, at home, b. Everett, MA, d/o Roy T. Brierley (Milton) and Hattie E. Webber (No. Shapleigh, ME)

Raymond E. of Milton Mills m. Frances **Clough** of Milton Mills 6/24/1928 in Sanbornville; H - 22, laborer, b. Wakefield, s/o David C. Pike (Middleton, farmer) and May E. Miller (Lawrence, MA); W - 18, at home, b. Milton Mills, d/o Dennis F. Clough (N. Berwick, ME, loomfixer) and Mamie V. Marsh (Acton, ME)

Richard A. of Union m. Cynthia A. **Manson** of Milton 6/24/1978 in Milton Mills; H - b. 3/17/1943; W - b. 1/3/1942

Richard A. of Sanbornville m. Emily J. **Pearce** of Milton 12/23/1995

Roland S. of Milton m. Carolyn M. **Drew** of Wakefield 6/7/1947 in Union; H - 22, mechanic, b. Milton, s/o Ralph W. Pike (Milton, salesman) and Marion B. Brierley (Everett, MA, housewife); W - 19, student, b. Union, d/o Harold S. Drew (Union, carpenter) and Charlotte L. Brown (Sanbornville, housewife)

Sumner E. of Milton m. Agnes L. **Wiggin** of Milton 6/15/1908; H - 20, shoemaker, b. East Rochester, s/o Elmer E. Pike (Middleton, teamster) and Etta S. Wallingford (Lebanon, ME); W - 18, mill hand, b. Milton, d/o Elbridge Wiggin (Acton, ME, mill hand) and Susie F. Day (Shapleigh, ME)

Weyland P. of Milton Mills m. Sandra A. **Moody** of Milton 6/14/1959; H - 20, US Navy, b. Rochester, s/o Daman P. Pike (NH) and Beatrice Van Buskirk (MA); W - 18, student, b. Rochester, d/o Walter L. Moody (NH) and Margaret Golden (NH)

PILLSBURY,

John of Acton, ME m. Edith M. **Brackett** of Acton, ME 5/1/1898 in Wakefield; H - 30, farmer, 2nd, b. Acton, ME, s/o Charles Annis (laborer); W - 23, housekeeper, b. Acton, ME, d/o Levi Brackett (Acton, ME)

PINA,

Antonio of Taunton, MA m. Thelma M. **Columbus** of Milton 9/3/1949; H - 27, shipper, b. MA, s/o Manuel Pina (Cape Verde Is.) and Deolinda Alburqueque (Portugal); W - 30, at home, b. Milton, d/o Arthur Columbus (Milton) and Flora Boisvert (Somersworth)

PINFOLD,

Edwin T. of Milton m. Serepta Clara **Eaton** of Milton 8/14/1917 in Milton Mills; H - 24, weaver, b. Milton, s/o William Pinfold (England, laborer) and Annie L. Lewis (England); W - 24, teacher,

b. W. Buxton, ME, d/o Wyman Eaton (Buxton, ME) and Eltora Clarke (Hollis, ME)

PINKHAM,
Carl E. of Milton m. Maude M. **Carter** of Lebanon, ME 10/25/1913 in Boston, MA; H - 27, merchant, b. Milton, s/o James D. Pinkham (Milton, newsdealer) and Sarah A. McGonigle (Ireland); W - 32, b. Wilmington, MA, d/o Fred M. Carter (Wilmington, MA, superintendent) and Barbara E. Cole (England)

Harold of Milton m. Edith W. **Stoehrer** of Berwick, ME 10/21/1938; H - 44, writer, b. Milton, s/o James D. Pinkham (Milton, deceased) and Sarah McGonigle (Ireland, housewife); W - 39, at home, 2nd, b. Milton Mills, d/o Albert E. Wiggin (Acton, ME, mill hand) and Cora B. Day (Newfield, ME, deceased)

Harry W. of Milton m. Fannie I. **Hayes** of Milton 6/29/1909; H - 36, farmer, b. Milton, s/o William H. H. Pinkham (Farmington, farmer) and Sarah A. Pinkham (Farmington); W - 27, teacher, b. Milton, d/o Charles Hayes (Milton) and Nellie M. Parmenter (Farmington)

Harry W. of Milton m. Joyce E. **Sanborn** of Milton 2/3/1957; H - 18, USAF, b. Rochester, s/o Winston Pinkham (Milton) and Muriel Chamberlain (Milton); W - 19, secretary, b. Rochester, d/o William H. Sanborn (Farmington) and Doris Bean (Eaton)

Thomas H. of Milton m. Mary F. **Cushman** of Brattleboro, VT 6/21/1904 in Brattleboro, VT; H - 37, painter, b. Cliftondale, MA, s/o Daniel G. Pinkham and Mary Penny; W - 23, lady, b. Orford, d/o Peleg E. Cushman and Mary E. Piper

Winston of Milton m. M. E. **Chamberlain** of Milton 5/29/1937 in Dover; H - 26, shoe worker, b. Milton, s/o Harry Pinkham (Milton, dead) and Fannie I. Hayes (Milton, housewife); W - 19, shoe worker, b. Milton, d/o Guy Chamberlain (Union) and Elizabeth Cunningham (Scotland, dead)

PINSON,
Christopher L. of Milton m. Jennifer D. **Emerson** of Milton 10/28/1999

PIPER,
Charles E. of Milton m. Catherine J. **Grant** of Manchester 4/29/1967 in Manchester; H - 77, laborer; W - 68, homemaker

Edwin C. of Milton m. Dorothy M. **Gray** of Lebanon, ME 6/12/1936 in Rochester; H - 25, shoe worker, b. Milton, s/o Charles E. Piper (Wakefield, gas station) and Helen Pray (Dover, tele. oper.); W - 19, shoe worker, b. Lebanon, ME, d/o Robert F. Gray (Gonic, carpenter) and Marion Morrison (Somerville, MA, housewife)

Grover C. of Milton m. Grace L. **Flanders** of Lowell, MA 11/26/1914 in Lowell, MA; H - 22, teamster, b. Milton, s/o James A. Piper (Newfield, ME, carpenter) and Laura A. Evans (Wakefield); W - 18, housework, b. Lowell, MA, d/o George H. Flanders (Lowell, MA, shoe cutter) and Annie M. Dugay (NB)

PITT,

John R. of Worcester, MA m. Susan D. **Elms** of Weymouth, MA 12/28/1964; H - 30, teacher; W - 24, teacher

PLACE,

Lawrence E. of Farmington m. Lillian P. **Tarlton** of Milton 4/18/1953 in Rochester; H - 21, US Army, b. Farmington, s/o Percy Place and Esther Dore; W - 19, bench worker, b. Epping, d/o Arthur Tarlton and Jeanette Johnson

PLANTE,

Donald E. of Dover m. Catherine A. **Huckins** of Milton 6/21/1986 in Rochester

Richard E. of Milton Mills m. Kellie Jo **Friedl** of Rochester 10/21/1989 in Rochester

PLAZA,

Keith H. of Dover m. Kelly E. **Sullivan** of Milton Mills 5/10/1986 in Milton Mills

PLOURDE,

Samuel F. of Rochester m. Eleanor J. **Eldridge** of Milton 10/22/1949 in Rochester; H - 24, lumberman, b. NH, s/o Oliver Plourde (Canada) and Alma Dion (NH); W - 17, at home, b. NH, d/o Chauncey Eldridge (NH) and Esther Adjutant (NH)

Samuel F., Jr. of Milton m. Dale N. **Wilkins** of Lebanon, ME 4/5/1969; H - b. 2/7/1951; W - b. 1/20/1951

PLUMMER,
Bard of Milton m. Martha E. **Hefler** of Milton 8/26/1953 in Farmington; H - 42, mach. operator, b. Milton, s/o Bard B. Plummer and Ruth L. Fall; W - 25, teacher, b. Newton, MA, d/o William A. Hefler and Gerardine Doyle

Bard B., Jr. of Milton m. Ruth L. **Fall** of Milton 8/20/1906 in Sanbornton; H - 26, farmer, b. Milton, s/o Bard B. Plummer (Milton, farmer) and Eliza D. Wentworth (Jamaica Plains, MA); W - 19, teacher, b. Milton, d/o George G. Fall (Lebanon, ME, expressman) and Lizzie Lyman (Milton)

Dwight H. of Milton m. Blanch C. **Hayes** of Milton 4/2/1919; H - 22, farmer, b. Milton, s/o Moses B. Plummer (Milton, farmer) and Elizabeth J. Hussey (Acton, ME); W - 23, clerk, b. Milton, d/o S. Lyman Hayes (Milton, RR mail clerk) and Annie F. Corson (Milton)

Hazen of Milton m. Nettie E. **Pike** of Milton 3/14/1891; H - 20, shoemaker, b. Middleton, s/o Daniel (Milton, dead) and Sarah (Milton, housekeeper); W - 20, shoe stitcher, b. Wolfeboro, d/o John S. (Middleton, farmer) and Mary M. C. (Middleton, housekeeper)

Hazen of Milton m. Grace C. **Fogg** of Dover 3/17/1919 in Dover; H - 52, machinist, 2nd, b. Milton, s/o Daniel Plummer (Milton, farmer) and Sarah E. Clements (Milton); W - 36, bookkeeper, 2nd, b. Newmarket, d/o Edsil P. Card (Newmarket, emp. belt factory) and Helen A. Whittier (Dover)

Lyman of Milton m. Ruth E. **Whitehouse** of Farmington 3/21/1942 in Farmington; H - 29, mtr. veh. dept., b. Milton, s/o Bard B. Plummer (Milton, farmer) and Ruth L. Fall (Milton, housewife); W - 26, secretary, b. Farmington, d/o Frank Whitehouse (Farmington, deceased) and Fannie C. Fall (Farmington, shoe worker)

Moses B. of Milton m. Elizabeth J. **Hussey** of Acton, ME 7/28/1890; H - 42, farmer, b. Milton, s/o Joseph (Milton) and Adeline; W - 33, teacher, b. Acton, ME, d/o Ralph R. (Acton, ME, farmer) and Martha L. (West Rosbury, housekeeper)

POLLARD,
Richard L. of Farmington m. Gladys I. **Twombly** of Milton 6/28/1946 in Farmington; H - 20, mill worker, b. Rochester, s/o Richard Pollard (Medford, MA, shoe worker) and Mary B. Bickford (Waterboro, ME, housewife); W - 20, shoe worker, b. Fremont, d/o Albert D.

Twombly (Fremont, sawyer) and Ellen L. Freeman (Somerville, MA, housewife)

POMEROY,
Randy W. of Milton m. Sally E. **Leclair** of Milton 7/29/1989 in Farmington
Richard S. of Milton m. Crystal L. **Messer** of Milton 9/12/1998
Thomas M. of Sanbornville m. Helene S. **Difruscio** of Sanbornville 10/16/1999
William J. of Dover m. Patricia A. **Thompson** of Milton 10/15/1960; H - 23, moulder; W - 20, hairdresser

POMROY,
Donald E., Jr. of Rochester m. Barbara A. **Garyait** of Milton 3/31/1956; H - 25, counterman, 2nd, b. Boothbay, ME, s/o Donald E. Pomroy and Abbie Bailey; W - 20, shoe worker, b. Rochester, d/o Arthur P. Garyait and Charlotte Wiggin

POORMAN,
James D. of Milton m. Laurie L. **Cote** of Milton 5/25/1991

POPOLSKI,
Martin J. of W. Lebanon, ME m. Sylvia L. **Dalessandri** of W. Lebanon, ME 9/27/1980

PORTER,
Brian G. of Milton m. Sandra J. **Nadeau** of Milton 9/20/1997
Stephen M. of Alton m. Elizabeth A. **Carswell** of Milton Mills 8/22/1981 in Sanbornville

POULIN,
Claude J. of Milton m. Cheryl A. **Garland** of Milton 8/23/1996

POULIOT,
Ernest R. of Rochester m. Linda A. **Hoyt** of Milton 5/26/1979
Robert L. of Milton m. Charity A. **Morgan** of Milton 8/2/1997

POWERS,
Thomas A. of Rochester m. Carol **Smith** of Milton 4/26/1980 in Rochester

PRATT,
John C., Jr. of Union m. Paula A. **Menegoni** of Milton 7/28/1979

PRAY,
George W. of Shapleigh, ME m. Delia **Gerry** of Shapleigh, ME 5/8/1891; H - 88, farmer, b. Shapleigh, ME, s/o Charles (Shapleigh, ME, farmer) and Sarah (Shapleigh, ME, housekeeper); W - housekeeper, b. Ireland

PRAYLOW,
Ralph, Jr. of Columbia, SC m. Heidi M. **Drapeau** of Columbia, SC 12/27/1995

PREEPER,
William C., Jr. of Acton, ME m. Charlotte P. **Dorr** of Milton 10/4/1905; H - 30, shoemaker, b. Boston, MA, s/o William C. Preeper (NS, farmer) and Matilda McDonald (PEI); W - 26, milliner, b. Milton, d/o James F. Dorr (Milton, farmer) and Lizzie S. Maddox (Newfield, ME)
William C., Jr. of Milton m. Carrie B. **Remick** of Milton 10/29/1910 in Union; H - 34, painter, 2nd, wid., b. Boston, MA, s/o William C. Preeper (NS, farmer) and Mehitable Macdonald (PEI); W - 27, weaver, 2nd, wid., b. Acton, ME, d/o Frank J. Hurd (Acton, ME, fireman) and Cora B. Jenness (Lebanon, ME)

PRINCE,
George H. of Milton m. Mary E. **Moore** of Milton 3/8/1893; H - 26, laborer, b. Sparta, WI, s/o Joel Prince and H. E.; W - 18, housekeeper, b. Milton, d/o William E. Moore (Lowell, MA, farmer) and Sarah E. (Dover)

PROVENCHER,
Norris L. of Milton m. Dorothy M. **Smith** of Wolfeboro 9/3/1960; H - 25, shoe worker; W - 26, factory
Norris L., II of Milton m. Jennifer J. **Miller** of E. Holden, ME 6/16/1990

PRUNIER,
Scott A. of Milton m. Melinda A. **Paker** of N. Berwick, ME 10/5/1996

PUGLISE,
William, Jr. of Rochester m. Kelly A. **Nicholson** of Milton 1/22/1989

PURVIS,
Douglas R. of Milton Mills m. Sharon A. **Ballou** of Milton Mills 8/15/1981 in Milton Mills

PUTNEY,
Gary W. of Milton m. Jeannette C. **Malone** of Rochester 6/1/1985

Warren C. of Milton m. Cristine **Williams** of Milton 6/29/1957; H - 20, laborer, b. Derry, s/o Warren Putney and Sarah Hescock (ID); W - 21, shoe worker, b. Rochester, d/o Shaber Williams (Tamworth) and Myrtle Ellis (Milton)

Wray A. of Groveton m. Patricia A. **Garland** of Milton 4/21/1961; H - 42, salesman; W - 37, housewife

QUIMBY,
Willard H. of Center Ossipee m. Patricia L. **Ayotte** of Milton Mills 12/29/1989

QUINLAN,
William H. of Rochester m. Annie B. **Plummer** of Milton 5/26/1920 in Rochester; H - 56, farmer, b. Alton, s/o David Quinlan (Ireland, RR employee) and Kate O'Connell (Ireland); W - 56, housework, b. Milton, d/o Daniel Plummer (Milton, farmer) and Sarah E. Clements (Milton)

QUINN,
George of Milton m. Lucy **Caden** of Milton 4/8/1894 in Rochester; H - 29, laborer, b. Canada, s/o Felix Quinn (Canada, laborer) and Adele; W - 21, shoe stitcher, b. Newark, NJ, d/o Luke Caden (Dayton, OH, musician) and Ellen (Newark, NJ)

William J., IV of Rockford, IL m. Ronna E. **Nowill** of Milton Mills 2/14/1979

QUINT,
Robert of Rochester m. Arline M. **Willey** of Milton 10/19/1945 in Rochester; H - 26, mach. oper., b. Rochester, s/o Dalbert Quint (Brownfield, ME, carpenter) and Nellie Kezar (Boston, MA,

housewife); W - 21, office worker, b. Milton, d/o Leon M. Willey (Brookfield, Navy Yard) and Flora M. Downs (Milton, housewife)

RADCLIFFE,
Dale T. of Milton m. Lori A. **Marcoux** of Milton 10/31/1988 in Rochester

RAMSDELL,
Warren of Gardner, MA m. Annie G. **Corson** of Ayer, MA 7/5/1930; H - 31, shipper, 2nd, b. Gardner, MA, s/o Charles Ramsdell (Hub'st'ne, MA, chair mkr.) and Emma Sequist (Sweden, housewife); W - 23, dental hygienist, b. Milton, d/o John M. Corson (Dover, farmer) and Eva M. Postleton (Acton, ME, housewife)

RAMSELL,
Scott H. of Lebanon, ME m. Daisy A. **Dorr** of Milton 11/9/1904; H - 18, shoemaker, b. Milton, s/o Elmer E. Randall (sic) (Gloucester, MA, teamster) and Clara E. Jordan (Wolfeboro); W - 18, housekeeper, b. Milton, d/o Charles C. Dorr (Milton, farmer) and Melissa Jones (Milton)

RAMSEY,
Charles E. of Milton m. Adelia E. **Jenness** of Milton 2/28/1948 in Acton, ME; H - 22, shoe worker, b. Milton, s/o Frank E. Ramsey (Somersworth, farmer) and Sophie M. Smith (Schuyler, NE, housewife); W - 23, stenographer, b. Nashua, d/o Daniel W. Jenness (Ayer, MA, fireman) and Alice B. Whitcomb (Brookline, housewife)
Charles E. of Milton m. Ella M. **Baun** of Milton Mills 4/23/1976 in Somersworth; H - b. 7/29/1925; W - b. 10/8/1937
Earl E. of Milton m. Emma P. **Vachon** of Milton 2/19/1946 in Farmington; H - 37, mill worker, b. Berwick, ME, s/o Frank E. Ramsey (Somersworth, farmer) and Sophie M. Smith (Schulyer, NE, housewife); W - 40, clerk, 2nd, b. Milton, d/o Aldege Custeau (Canada, deceased) and Lizzie Blouin (Canada, housewife)
Lawrence of Milton m. Ruth E. **Stevens** of Farmington 6/4/1938 in Ogunquit, ME; H - 24, mill oper., b. Thompson, CT, s/o Frank Ramsey (Somersworth, farmer) and Sophie Smith (Schuler, NE, housewife); W - 19, waitress, b. Nottingham, d/o Carl Stevens (Rochester, merchant) and Emma Hartford (Rochester, mill oper.)

RAND,

Arthur H. of Milton m. Vera F. **Cooley** of Milton 2/20/1910; H - 25, shoe cutter, b. Wilmington, MA, s/o George H. Rand (Littleton, MA) and Gertrude Thompson (Concord, MA); W - 23, housekeeper, b. Boston, MA, d/o David F. Cooley (Boston, MA) and Bessie S. Stevens (Portland, ME)

Donald E. of Rochester m. Cynthia R. **Sprague** of Milton 7/1/1961; H - 22, painter; W - 22, at home

Earl K. of Milton m. Hazel A. **Hoyt** of Rochester 8/15/1917 in Rochester; H - 19, ice man, b. Milton, s/o George W. Rand (Cambridge, MA, fireman) and Ida E. Moore (Milton); W - 25, emp. in mill, b. Rochester, d/o Frank R. Hoyt (Rochester, emp. of RR) and An'ell'r R. Henward (Portsmouth)

Frank N. of Haverhill, MA m. Fannie L. **Hayes** of Milton 12/25/1919; H - 56, real estate, 2nd, b. Morrisville, VT, s/o Alvinza B. Rand (Woodstock, VT, painter) and Fidelia R. Goodell (Morrisville, VT); W - 54, teacher, b. Milton, d/o Luther Hayes (Lebanon, ME, farmer) and Sarah Coffran (Pembroke)

George W. of Wilmington, MA m. Ida E. **Moore** of Milton 9/16/1893; H - 23, laborer, b. Cambridge, MA, s/o George H. Rand (wood carver) and Mary S.; W - 22, housekeeper, b. Milton, d/o William F. Moore (farmer) and Sarah E.

Harold F. of Milton m. Doris P. **Tibbets** of Farmington 4/23/1955 in Farmington; H - 51, mill worker, b. Milton, s/o George W. Rand and Ida E. Moore; W - 46, shoe worker, 3rd, b. Alton, d/o George R. Prescott and Lillian M. Jones

Leo E. of Milton m. Mabel E. **Sanborn** of Milton 2/1/1936 in Farmington; H - 25, laborer, b. Milton, s/o George W. Rand (Cambridge, MA, laborer) and Ida E. Moore (Milton, housewife); W - 24, at home, b. Milton, d/o Walter L. Sanborn (Milton, farmer) and Esther E. Harnden (Fryeburg, ME, housewife)

RANDALL,

Edgar E. of Sanbornville m. Kathy J. **Logan** of Milton 8/19/1967; H - 20, auto mechanic; W - 19, at home

Jerry L. of Milton m. Mary J. **Marcoux** of Milton 2/13/1981 in East Rochester

RANDLETT,
Ronald L. of Rochester m. Claire M. **Welch** of Milton 8/27/1983

RANKIN,
James of Milton m. Clara **Brackett** of Milton 12/14/1903; H - 24, laborer, b. Houlton, ME, s/o James Rankin (Ireland) and Cordelia Victory (Houlton, ME); W - 16, shoe stitcher, b. Acton, ME, d/o Levi Brackett and Anna G. Perkins (Salem, MA)

RAWSKI,
Dereck of Milton m. Michele R. **Howard** of Milton 6/21/1997

REASON,
Paul A. of Winchester m. Louise E. **Harriman** of Milton 11/27/1976; H - b. 8/7/1953; W - b. 2/12/1955

REED,
Eugene L., Jr. of Milton m. Stacey A. **Sweatt** of Lebanon, ME 10/10/1981

REGAN,
James V. of Milton m. Dorothy A. **Otis** of Sanbornville 3/2/1933 in Alton; H - 26, clerk, b. Milton, s/o Jerome Regan (Ireland, laborer) and Mary Mahoney (Ireland, housewife); W - 20, at home, b. Farmington, d/o Arthur Otis (Rochester, laborer) and Bertha Tibbetts (Sanbornville, housewife)

Raymond J. of Milton m. Dorothy L. **Page** of Milton 6/14/1946; H - 30, mill worker, b. Milton, s/o Jerome J. Regan (Ireland, retired) and Mary A. Mahoney (Ireland, housewife); W - 28, mill worker, 2nd, b. Milton, d/o Milledge G. Leeman (Eastport, ME, deceased) and Helen M. DeWolfe (Milton, housewife)

REMICK,
Arthur F. of Milton m. Angie E. **Page** of Milton 11/18/1910 in Ossipee; H - 28, machinist, b. Tamworth, s/o Frank P. Remick (Sandwich) and Florence Durrell (Tamworth); W - 22, b. Milton, d/o George W. Page (Dalton, mason) and Jeanette A. Rines (Milton)

Edgar B. of Milton m. Carrie E. **Grace** of Milton 12/24/1918; H - 25, emp. in mill, 2nd, b. Milton, s/o Charles E. Remick (Milton, farmer) and Lula E. Kenney (Farmington); W - 19, at home, b. Albany, d/o Frank L. Grace (Chatham, farmer) and Lizzie Willey (Conway)

Willie of Milton m. Carrie B. **Hurd** of Milton 8/12/1903; H - 34, shoemaker, b. Milton, s/o Moses Remick (Milton) and Clara Wentworth (Ossipee); W - 19, weaver, b. Acton, ME, d/o Frank J. Hurd (Acton, ME, fireman) and Cora Jenness (Lebanon, ME)

RENDALL,
Walter E. of Milton m. Maude W. **Gray** of Wells, ME 4/20/1898 in Acton, ME; H - 27, shoemaker, 2nd, b. Newfield, ME, s/o Aaron W. Rendall (Berwick, ME); W - 20, shoe stitcher, b. Rockport, ME, d/o Almon E. Gray (Wells, ME, stonecutter)

REYNOLDS,
Willis L. of Milton m. Alice M. **Treadwell** of Milton 11/3/1947 in Buxton, ME; H - 76, retired, 2nd, b. Acton, ME, s/o Charles A. Reynolds (Acton, ME) and Nellie A. Sanborn (Tamworth); W - 60, housekeeper, b. Buxton, ME, d/o Charles A. L. Treadwell and Luella E. Miller

RHODES,
Charles C. of Lebanon, ME m. Lizzie **Sargent** of Acton, ME 9/4/1897; H - 37, shoemaker, 2nd, b. Cape Vincent, s/o Charles Rhodes (France, brewer); W - 26, housekeeper, 2nd, b. Acton, ME, d/o Elias Miller (farmer)

Joseph C. of Lowell, MA m. Helen **Meikle** of Milton 6/20/1900; H - 26, weaver, b. Medford, MA, s/o Cuthbert A. Rhodes and Elizabeth Ellis (Bradford, England); W - 20, dressmaker, b. Wakefield, d/o William Meikle (Scotland, printer) and Kathryne Steele (Scotland)

RICHARD,
David R. of Milton m. Stacey M. **Pero** of Farmington 10/21/1989 in Dover

Joseph A. of Dover m. Audrey A. **Rawls** of Milton 6/30/1989 in Dover

RICHARDS,
Allan R. of Rochester m. June **Worster** of Milton 7/29/1978; H - b. 10/14/1958; W - b. 6/10/1959

Dean L. of Milton m. Suzette L. **LaChapelle** of Milton 7/3/1993

Douglas C. of Wakefield m. Peggy A. **Moody** of Milton 5/22/1970 in Wakefield; H - b. 10/21/1943; W - b. 12/17/1944

Edward L. of Newton U. Falls, MA m. Anna M. C. **Boland** of Milton 10/28/1925; H - 64, fireman, 2nd, b. Needham, MA, s/o John E. Richards (Needham, MA, farmer) and Sarah A. Stone (Scotland); W - 52, cook, 2nd, b. Bremen, Germany, d/o Henry Weichmann (Oeldenburg, Germany, blacksmith) and Meta Oettken (Mecklenburg, Germany)

RICHARDSON,

Matthew J. of Milton m. Laurie A. **Joy** of Milton 10/12/1996

Theodore G. of Milton m. Heather L. **Estes** of Milton 5/10/1997

RICKER,

Charles E. of Berwick, ME m. Eunice **Plummer** of Milton 12/15/1894; H - 23, tinsmith, b. Berwick, ME, s/o Charles A. Ricker (Lebanon, ME, shoemaker) and Sarah A.; W - 17, b. Milton, d/o Daniel Plummer and Sarah

Melvin C. of Somersworth m. Ellen M. **Wood** of Milton Mills 8/30/1957 in Milton Mills; H - 21, shoe worker, b. Rochester, s/o George Ricker and Grace Arlen; W - 19, shoe worker, b. Lebanon, ME, d/o Fred T. Wood and Nellie Banker

RIDEOUT,

Maynard of Portland, ME m. Nellie M. **Gilman** of Portland, ME 6/7/1944; H - 43, woodworker, 3rd, b. Bucksport, ME, s/o Walter Rideout (Bucksport, ME) and Sadie Leach (Holland, ME); W - 57, housework, 3rd, b. Peaks Island, ME, d/o Charles I. Blake (Portland, ME, mechanic) and Eugenia Hawkesworth (NS)

RIEK,

Christopher J. of Granby, CT m. Nichole A. **Boucher** of Milton 8/5/1995

RIGAZIO,

Richard A. of Rochester m. Amy B. **Chaisson** of Milton 4/6/1991

RILEY,

Raymond F. of Milton m. Pamela J. **Griffin** of Milton 11/18/1988

RINARD,
Daniel L. of Milton m. Roberta C. **Hashem** of N. Berwick, ME 9/23/1995

RINES,
Charles H., Jr. of New Durham m. Mary S. **Webber** of Milton 12/25/1899 in Beverly, MA; H - 39, shoemaker, 2nd, b. New Durham, s/o Charles H. Rines (Alton, farmer); W - 44, weaver, 2nd, b. Milton, d/o Noah Merrow

Ellsworth B. of Milton m. Mabel E. **Goodwin** of Lebanon, ME 7/2/1933 in Lebanon, ME; H - 53, farmer, b. Brookfield, s/o Elihu M. Rines (New Durham, farmer) and Mary E. Dearborn (New Durham, housewife); W - 47, housekeeper, b. Lebanon, ME, d/o Henry H. Goodwin (Lebanon, ME, laborer) and Emma J. Johnson (Fryeburg, ME, housewife)

James (Rev.) of Milton m. Mrs. Nancy **Young** of Milton 11/25/1888

Lafayette of Milton m. Ella **Geyer** of Lebanon, ME 2/11/1896 in Rochester; H - 33, butcher, 2nd, b. New Durham, s/o Charles H. (Alton, farmer) and Sarah L. (Lyman, ME); W - 41, dressmaker, 2nd, b. Lebanon, ME, d/o Samuel (Lebanon, ME, farmer) and Mary A. Jones (Lebanon, ME)

RIOUX,
Roger J. of Milton m. Carrie A. **Barrett** of Milton 10/22/1994

RITCHIE,
J. Raymond of Milton m. Charlotte K. **Betts** of Lebanon, ME 10/25/1933 in Lebanon, ME; H - 20, auto mech., b. Newfield, ME, s/o Joseph Ritchie (Canada, auto business) and Emma Hildrith (Chelmsford, MA, housewife); W - 16, at home, b. Lebanon, ME, d/o Ralph Betts (Lebanon, ME, farmer) and Myrtle McIntire (Lebanon, ME, housewife)

RITZ,
Ernest C., Jr. of Tulsa, OK m. Barbara J. **Burroughs** of Milton Mills 6/3/1958 at Pease AFB; H - 35, USAF, 2nd, b. Tulsa, OK, s/o Ernest C. Ritz, Sr. (Rogers, AR) and Anna Wilburn Ritz (Ft. Worth, TX); W - 26, elec. worker, 2nd, b. Worcester, MA, d/o William I. Colby (Bow) and Lois J. Stillings (Milton Mills)

ROACH,
Robert B. of China, ME m. Eleanor **Hisler** of China, ME 10/12/1935; H - 21, farmer, b. Portland, ME, s/o Daniel Roach (Portland, ME, insurance) and Eva Rackliffe (N. V'boro, ME, housewife); W - 20, teacher, b. China, ME, d/o William C. Hisler (Windsor, ME, farmer) and Elva A. Baker (Richmond, ME, housewife)

ROBBLEE,
Dexter A. of Milton Mills m. Christine L. **Smith** of Rochester 9/8/1990 in Milton Mills

ROBERGE,
Daniel J. of Milton m. Kathleen A. **Durost** of Milton 6/29/1996

ROBERTS,
Alvin B. of Milton m. Marion L. **Downing** of Milton 2/8/1925; H - 28, laborer, 2nd, b. Raymond, s/o Albert B. Roberts (Raymond, shoeworker) and Carrie E. Nutter (Milton); W - 22, teacher, b. Milton, d/o George A. Downing (Farmington, RR foreman) and Alice Hodgdon (Somersworth)

Ernest L. of Rochester m. Sarah A. **Wentworth** of Milton 11/20/1948 in Farmington; H - 64, farmer, 2nd, b. Rochester, s/o Henry K. Roberts (Rochester, farmer) and Rose B. Hill (Rochester, housewife); W - 54, housewife, 2nd, b. England, d/o James Pomfret (England, spinner) and Alice Harkess (England, weaver)

Fred B. of Milton m. Mary J. **Spaulding** of Worcester, MA 10/10/1917; H - 54, lumber dealer, b. Milton, s/o Ira Roberts (Middleton) and Caroline C. Foss (Milton); W - 41, housekeeper, 3rd, b. PEI, d/o John W. Raynor (Travellers Rest, PEI) and Mary A. Raynor (Beldeford, PEI)

Kevin B. of Milton m. Monique R. **Laurion** of Milton 6/24/1995

ROBINSON,
George W. of Rochester m. Gretchen **Phillips** of Milton 7/1/1947 in Farmington; H - 70, painter, 4th, b. Farmington, s/o George E. Robinson (Farmington, shoemaker) and Elizabeth Weeks (Farmington, housewife); W - 54, housewife, 4th, b. Lynn, MA, d/o Herbert W. Waycott (PEI, grocery clk.) and Sarah E. Brown (Lynn, MA, housewife)

Philip G. of Milton m. Deborah J. **Kerlin** of Milton 7/17/1993
William A. of Sanbornville m. June **Valley** of Milton 10/16/1948 in Wakefield; H - 21, mechanic, b. Gloucester, MA, s/o George P. Robinson (Exeter, musician) and Alberta Maddix (Sanbornville, restaurant wk.); W - 18, at home, b. Milton Mills, d/o Paul G. Valley and Mildred R. Weeks (weaver)

ROCHELEAU,
Norman W. of Milton m. Betty R. **Lacasse** of Milton 5/11/1991

ROGERS,
Francis of Milton m. Paula **Beaulieu** of Milton 4/5/1989 in Lincoln
Roy Wesley of Farmington m. Elaine E. **Rouleau** of Milton 4/1/1949; H - 25, truck driver, 2nd, b. NH, s/o George J. Rogers, Sr. (MA) and Irene P. Jones (NH); W - 19, shoe worker, b. ME, d/o Alfred J. Rouleau (ME) and Helen E. Duquette (NH)

ROLLINS,
Donald L. of Rochester m. Gloria M. **Lemire** of Milton 4/17/1974 in Rochester; H - b. 4/4/1949; W - b. 11/8/1947
Robin L. of Mechanic Falls, ME m. Christina D. **Greene** of Milton Mills 3/25/1966 in Milton Mills; H - 28, Northeast Airlines; W - 24, stewardess

ROMAN,
David L. of Saugus, MA m. Barbara L. **Townsend** of Saugus, MA 10/12/1963 in Milton Mills; H - 22, latex comp.; W - 19, at home

RONAYNE,
John J. of Milton m. Kathie J. **Terry** of Berwick, ME 11/25/1988

ROODE,
Malcolm J. of Milton m. Willa L. **Evans** of Rochester 12/28/1935 in Rochester; H - 36, lea. bd. wkr., 2nd, b. Yarmouth, NS, s/o Lucius Roode (Yarmouth, NS, retired) and Mary Giles (Yarmouth, NS, housewife); W - 25, lea. bd. wkr., b. Rochester, d/o Isaac Evans (New Durham, salesman) and Susie Rollins (Rochester, housewife)

ROSEBERRY,
Steven M. of Milton m. Michele S. **Gagne** of Milton 11/5/1983 in Somersworth

ROSS,
Lincoln K. of Dover m. Grace F. **Plummer** of Milton 6/7/1941 in Dover; H - 75, retired, 2nd, b. Biddeford, ME, s/o Benjamin K. Ross (Ipswich, MA, shoe dealer) and Luna Perkins (Barre, VT, housewife); W - 54, at home, 3rd, b. Dover, d/o Edsil Card (Newmarket, belt factory) and Helen A. Whittier (Dover, housewife)

ROSSIGNOL,
Edmond of Milton m. Ellen P. **Fontaine** of Milton 3/17/1990

ROULEAU,
Albert L. of Milton m. Bernice **Tarlton** of Milton 7/15/1950 in Epping; H - 24, trk. driver, b. Lebanon, ME, s/o Alfred J. Rouleau (Lebanon, ME) and Helen Douquith (Milton); W - 23, shoe shop, b. Epping, d/o Arthur S. Tarlton (Chester) and Jeannette Johnson (Epping)

Albert L., Jr. of Rochester m. Alison M. **Boggs** of Milton 6/24/1972 in Rochester; H - b. 9/29/1950; W - b. 6/5/1952

Alfred J. of Lebanon, ME m. Helen E. **Douquette** of Milton 5/4/1925; H - 23, laborer, b. Lebanon, ME, s/o Albert Rouleau (Canada, farmer) and Delia Blouin (Canada); W - 19, shoe stitcher, b. Milton, d/o Leon Douquette (Canada, fireman) and Emma Hall (Canada)

George L., Jr. of Milton m. Carol J. **Silvia** of Farmington 10/7/1946 in Farmington; H - 19, lumb. wkr., b. Ossipee, s/o George E. Rouleau, Sr. (Lebanon, ME, factory wkr.) and Inez E. Eldridge (Ossipee, factory wkr.); W - 21, shoe worker, b. Farmington, d/o John J. Silvia (Oakland, CA, shoe worker) and Gladys T. Wilkes (Barnstead, housewife)

Kenneth D. of Milton m. Kathleen H. **Chapman** of Rochester 7/4/1964 in Rochester; H - 24, truck driver; W - 23, nurse

Louis H. of Lebanon, ME m. Josephine **Burbine** of Milton 12/28/1920; H - 22, laborer, b. Lebanon, ME, s/o Albert Rouleau (Canada, laborer) and Delia Blouin (Canada); W - 19, at home, b. Wakefield, MA, d/o John Burbine (Argyle, NS, foreman) and Margaret Muse (Quinnin, NS)

Norman A. of Milton m. Audrey B. **Merrill** of N. Rochester 2/3/1947 in S. Lebanon, ME; H - 18, laborer, b. Rochester, s/o Alfred Rouleau (Lebanon, ME, millwright) and Helen Duquette (Milton, housewife); W - 17, housework, b. Lebanon, ME, d/o Frank Merrill (Saco, ME, lumberman) and Beryl White (Lebanon, ME, housewife)

Robert N. of Milton m. Maureen L. **White** of Farmington 7/7/1966; H - 26, shoe worker; W - 20, machine operator

Samuel of Lebanon, ME m. Margh'ta **Lavertue** of Lebanon, ME 10/30/1927; H - 26, laborer, b. Lebanon, ME, s/o Albert Rouleau (Canada, farmer) and Delia Blouin (Canada); W - 18, at home, b. Rochester, d/o Henry Lavertue (Canada, painter) and Florence P. Downs (Rochester)

S[amuel] J., Jr. of Milton m. Barbara M. **Herrick** of Sanbornville 6/26/1948 in Lebanon, ME; H - 19, RR worker, b. Milton, s/o Samuel J. Rouleau (Lebanon, ME, poultryman) and Margherita Lavertue (Rochester, housewife); W - 17, at home, b. Wolfeboro, d/o George Herrick (W. Newfield, ME, woodsman) and Edith Nason (Wakefield, housewife)

ROULON,

Albert of Milton m. Delia **Beloin** of Milton 5/26/1894 in Rochester; H - 24, laborer, b. Canada, s/o Lewis Roulon (Canada, paper operative) and Pheby; W - 19, mill hand, b. Canada, d/o Onezime Beloin (Canada, farmer) and Pheby

ROWE,

Jerry L. of Milton m. Deborah L. **Buck** of Milton 2/16/1982

Robert J., Jr. of Milton m. Wendy A. **Hodge** of Rochester 7/17/1982 in Rochester

William P. of Milton Mills m. Elzada S. **Howard** of Milton Mills 8/18/1984 in Wakefield

ROWELL,

Fred W. of Milton m. Viva D. **Swain** of Milton 8/31/1947; H - 66, mortician, 2nd, b. Salisbury, s/o Ben W. Rowell (Webster, retired) and Flora A. Minard (Salisbury); W - 49, housewife, 3rd, b. W. Andover, d/o Selem Ferry and Martha Fish

ROXBY,
Patrick R. of Milton m. Karen K. **Boucher** of Milton 8/28/1999

ROYER,
Paul M. of Milton Mills m. Pamela L. **Poisson** of Milton Mills 10/6/1990 in Dover

RUDOLPH,
Mark N. of Rochester m. Donna S. **Hill** of Milton 7/9/1984

RUFF,
Charles R., III of Milton Mills m. Eugenia B. **Ruff** of Milton Mills 4/4/1998

RUNNEL[L]S,
Eugene of Milton Mills m. Alice L. **Damon** of Milton Mills 12/25/1929 in Acton, ME; H - 55, carpenter, 2nd, b. Acton, ME, s/o Israel Runnels (Acton, ME, farmer) and Mary E. Rodgers (Acton, ME); W - 55, pastor asst., b. Fairfield, VT, d/o Loami C. Damon (Springfield, VT, por. painter) and Achesa M. Parker (Richford, VT)
Eugene E. of Acton, ME m. Carrie A. **Deane** of Milton 4/10/1899 in Milton Mills; H - 24, farmer, b. Acton, ME, s/o Israel Runnells (Acton, ME, farmer); W - 22, housekeeper, b. Millbury, MA, d/o James R. Deans (E. Berkshire, VT, teamster)
Eugene E. of Milton Mills m. Maud R. **Wiltsey** of Milton Mills 12/20/1945; H - 71, carpenter, 3rd, b. Acton, ME, s/o Israel Runnels (Acton, ME, farmer) and Mary E. Rogers (Parsonsfield, ME, housewife); W - 58, nurse, 3rd, b. Worcester, MA, d/o Joseph H. Ralph (Sennet, NY, confectioner) and Luella Watson (Oxford, MA, housewife)
Glenn E. of Milton Mills m. Marie E. **Roberts** of No. Berwick, ME 11/29/1963; H - 20, inspector; W - 20, factory work
Othello D. of Milton Mills m. Pearl E. **Wilkinson** of Sanbornville 5/15/1927 in Rochester; H - 25, carpenter, b. Acton, ME, s/o Eugene E. Runnells (Acton, ME, carpenter) and Carrie Dean (Millbury, MA); W - 22, at home, b. Salem, MA, d/o Frank S. Wilkinson (Freedom, section man) and Lucy M. Roles (E. Wakefield)
Othello D. of Milton m. Bernice I. **Goodwin** of Wakefield 4/13/1975 in Wakefield; H - b. 3/11/1902; W - b. 3/27/1920

Robert D. of Milton Mills m. Virginia S. **Worster** of Wakefield 7/21/1951; H - 19, Navy Yard, b. Wakefield, s/o Othello D. Runnels (Acton, ME) and Pearl Wilkinson (Salem, MA); W - 20, at home, b. MA, d/o Clayton Worster (ME) and Edith Day (RI)

Robert D., Jr. of Milton m. Karen R. **Hill** of Middleton 11/10/1973 in Union; H - b. 2/10/1955; W - b. 1/22/1955

RUSH,

Gary R. of Canton, MI m. Barbara E. **Coleman** of Canton, MI 1/2/1995

RUSS,

David A. of Milton m. Brenda L. **Archer** of Milton 6/25/1983

David A. of Milton m. Kathy J. **Ecker** of Milton 9/21/1985

Stephen A. of Milton m. Stephanie M. **Taplin** of Milton 9/10/1988

Stephen A. of Milton m. Darline D. **Smith** of Milton 2/18/1999

RUSSELL,

James K. of Milton m. Catherine **Gonthier** of Rochester 6/26/1982 in Rochester

Jonathan L. of Farmington m. Peggy E. **Morgan** of Milton 7/11/1980 in Farmington

Lee R. of Farmington m. Patricia A. **Marcoux** of Milton 6/22/1974 in Farmington; H - b. 7/17/1947; W - b. 5/10/1957

Lewis H. of Wolfeboro m. Hazel **Cotton** of Milton 12/29/1934 in Rochester; H - 51, janitor, 2nd, b. Johnson, VT, s/o Henry L. Russell (Cambridge, VT, laborer) and Annie McCaffry (Rouses Point, NY, housewife); W - 21, domestic, b. Brookfield, d/o John A. Cotton (E. Wolfeboro, farmer) and Mary Leona Neal (Brookfield, housewife)

Theodore S. of Rochester m. Bonita L. **Brewer** of Milton Mills 6/17/1973 in Rochester; H - b. 9/30/1947; W - b. 11/27/1950

SAGER,

Arthur F. of Salem, MA m. Lillian V. **Wallace** of Milton 10/10/1897; H - 24, clerk, b. Malden, MA, s/o A. E. Sager (Pigeon Hill, PQ, pat. maker); W - 22, teacher, b. Middleton, d/o Albert S. Wallace (Hanover, farmer)

SALISBURY,
Wayne C. of Farmington m. Sandra J. **Goodwin** of Milton 10/11/1969; H - b. 5/15/1946; W - b. 5/14/1948

SANBORN,
Charles W. of Milton m. Annie L. **Otis** of Somersworth 9/9/1917 in Farmington; H - 45, laborer, b. Middleton, s/o Emma J. Willey (New Durham); W - 49, housekeeper, 3rd, b. Alton, d/o Eben Ellis (Rochester) and Mary G. Watson (Alton)

Clifton I. of Milton m. Lorraine A. **Couture** of Somersworth 2/8/1958 in Somersworth; H - 20, press opr., b. Rochester, s/o Ivory L. Sanborn (NH) and Dorothy Grace (NH); W - 16, shoe worker, b. Rochester, d/o John J. Couture (Canada) and Yvonne C. Pouliot (Rochester)

George A. of Acton, ME m. Florence E. **Ryan** of Milton 10/1/1919 in Milton Mills; H - 19, farmer, b. Acton, ME, s/o George B. Sanborn (Acton, ME, farmer) and Stella J. Lane (Wakefield); W - 19, domestic, b. Lunenburg, NS, d/o Charles Ryan (Sable River, NS, carpenter) and Bessie Dauphiee (Lunenburg, NS)

James A. of Salem, MA m. Elizabeth E. **Locke** of Salem, MA 8/5/1914; H - 71, 2nd, b. Salem, MA, s/o James Sanborn (Salem, MA) and Abigail F. Cate (Salem, MA); W - 56, housekeeper, b. Lewiston, ME, d/o Alpheus C. Locke (Epsom) and Louisa Kimball (Hopkinton)

James W. of Milton m. Elizabeth A. **Rodrigue** of Milton Mills 1/9/1982

Norman G. of Rochester m. Ruth E. **Whitnall** of Milton 5/29/1947 in Rochester; H - 18, poultry dlr., b. Rochester, s/o Guy R. Sanborn (Boston, MA, poultry dlr.) and Florence M. Morrill (Rochester, housewife); W - 19, shoe wkr., b. Worthington, OH, d/o Leroy E. Whitnall (Constitution, OH, woodsman) and Eleanor T. Tanner (Wakefield, housewife)

Norris R. of Sanbornville m. Margaret K. **Regan** of Milton 9/23/1933 in Farmington; H - 21, moving pict., b. Sanbornville, s/o Ansel N. Sanborn (Sanbornville, mov. pictures) and Maude E. Woodus (Haverhill, MA, housewife); W - 21, clerk, b. Milton, d/o Jerome Regan (Ireland, foreman) and Mary Mahoney (Ireland, housewife)

Walter L. of Milton m. Hattie A. **Rines** of Wakefield 2/26/1895 in Wakefield; H - 21, laborer, b. Milton, s/o George H. Pike (Wakefield, teamster); W - 19, housekeeper, b. New Durham, d/o William T. Rines (New Durham, farmer)

Walter L. of Milton m. Esther E. **Day** of Milton 5/22/1912 in Brookfield; H - 39, farmer, 2nd, b. Milton, d/o George H. Pike (Wakefield) and Louisa Sanborn (Milton); W - 39, housework, 2nd, b. Denmark, ME, d/o Granville Harnden (Denmark, ME) and Matilda P. Lord (Stoneham, ME)

William E. of Milton m. Tammy L. **Foss** of Milton Mills 9/8/1984

William H. of Milton m. Doris **Flanders** of Wolfeboro Falls 1/30/1937 in Wolfeboro; H - 21, mill worker, b. Farmington, s/o Roland Sanborn (Rochester, shoe shop) and Alice Gray (Farmington, dead); W - 23, shoe shop, 2nd, b. Eaton, d/o Willis Bean (Conway Ctr., carpenter) and Ellen Thompson (Eaton, housewife)

Winfield S. of Milton m. Etta L. **Johnson** of Milton 10/31/1901 in Lebanon, ME; H - 29, papermaker, 2nd, b. Chatham, s/o Orestes B. Sanborn (Baldwin, ME, farmer) and Mahitable V. McKeen (Chatham); W - 32, housekeeper, b. Stowe, ME, d/o Solomon Johnson (farmer) and Lydia McKeen (Chatham)

SANFACON,
Richard P. of Milton m. Madelyn Y. **Melanson** of Milton 7/11/1987

SANTORO,
Robert G. of Merrimack m. Sylvia M. **Santoro** of Milton 4/16/1977; H - b. 1/4/1932; W - b. 10/17/1934

SARGENT,
Edward A. of Farmington m. Matilda M. **Knight** of Farmington 2/14/1964; H - 38, farmer; W - 37, at home

Warren E. of Gilmanton m. Lizzie **Miller** of Milton 12/11/1890; H - 20, shoemaker, b. Gilmanton, s/o Thomas (Gilmanton, butcher) and Ida (housekeeper); W - 17, weaver, b. Milton, d/o Elias (farmer) and Mary (housekeeper)

SATCHFIELD,
Peter A. of East Rochester m. Beverly J. **Christman** of Milton 10/11/1986

SAVOIE,
Fred J. of Milton m. Ruby **Ellis** of Milton 10/7/1922 in Somersworth; H - 25, laborer, b. Dover, s/o Joseph Savoie (salesman) and Delia Burns

(Philadelphia, PA); W - 17, emp. in mill, b. Milton, d/o George E. Ellis (Wolfeboro, laborer) and Inez G. Duntley (Milton)

Maurice M. of Milton m. Helen D. **Cheney** of Milton 7/2/1949; H - 22, shoe wkr., b. Milton, s/o Fred J. Savoie (Dover) and Ruby Ellis (Milton); W - 18, none, b. Milton, d/o Richard H. Cheney (Whitefield) and Doris V. Brock (Boston, MA)

SAWYER,

Allen R. of Milton m. Pearl L. **Bell** of Gonic 8/20/1956 in Rochester; H - 47, carpenter, 2nd, b. ME, s/o Eugene A. Sawyer and Mary J. Yeaton; W - 40, housework, 2nd, b. NH, d/o Paul N. Britton and Bernadette Lacasse

Kenneth G. of Milton m. Barbara R. **Kern** of Milton 6/6/1992

SCEGGELL,

David A. of Milton m. Doreen P. **Dube** of Milton 6/23/1984 in Union

Forrest of Milton m. Ruth H. **Leeman** of Milton 2/14/1931; H - 20, mill emp., b. Ossipee, s/o Benjamin B. Sceggell (Ossipee, laborer) and Edna M. Demeritt (Conway, housewife); W - 17, at home, b. Milton, d/o Milledge Leeman (Eastport, ME, foreman) and Helen E. DeWolfe (Milton, housewife)

Howard of Milton m. Anna F. **McIntire** of Milton 12/21/1929; H - 24, laborer, b. Ossipee, s/o Benjamin P. Sceggell (Ossipee, laborer) and Edna M. Demeritt (Conway); W - 19, at home, b. Dover, d/o Frank B. McIntire (Dover, millwright) and Grace M. Downing (Farmington)

Howard J. of Milton m. Shirley R. **Tirone** of Dover 8/2/1986

Howard J., Jr. of Milton m. Shirley M. **Lilljedahl** of Milton 6/6/1954; H - 18, mach. oper., b. Rochester, s/o Howard J. Sceggell and Anna F. McIntire; W - 18, unemployed, b. Rochester, d/o C. H. Lilljedahl, Sr. and Dorothy Varney

Stephen H. of Milton m. LuAnn B. **Pratt** of Wakefield 6/11/1977 in Union; H - b. 11/4/1957; W - b. 11/16/1958

SCHINDLER,

Elmer of Milton, MA m. Violet M. **Cooke** of Milton, MA 6/28/1931; H - 21, garage, b. Milton, MA, s/o Albert Schindler (Dorchester, MA, garage) and Bessie Graham (NS, housewife); W - 22, at home, b.

Weymouth, MA, d/o Merrill Cooke (NS, farmer) and Evelyn Hatt (NS, housewife)

SCOTT,
Nathan L. of Milton m. Nancy L. **Varney** of Milton 7/1/1967; H - 23, USAF; W - student
Vincent T. of Milton m. Sandra G. **McBride** of Milton 12/27/1995

SEAVEY,
Dennis G. of Milton m. Kirsten W. **Demott** of Milton 3/26/1994
Elmer L. of Rochester m. Amy T. **Dixon** of Milton 7/3/1938 in Rochester; H - 29, printer, b. Rochester, s/o Fred L. Seavey (Rochester, P.O. clerk) and Flora Wentworth (Rochester, housewife); W - 27, reg. nurse, b. Milton, d/o Stephen E. Dixon (Milton, mill worker) and Georgie Moody (W. Ossipee, mill oper.)
Ronald E. of Alton m. Elsie A. **Tufts** of Milton 11/15/1966 in Middleton; H - 19, student; W - 16, at home

SEELING,
Frederic E. of Sandusky, OH m. Jane **Woodbury** of Milton 5/7/1955 in Wolfeboro; H - 24, truck driver, b. Germany, s/o Heinrich Seeling and Hulda Ossenberg; W - 27, nurse, b. Milton, d/o William E. Woodbury and Doris M. Horne

SEIDEN,
Richard B. of Durham m. Maureen E. **Farrell** of Milton 6/14/1979

SEMCO,
Donald R. of Milton m. Marlene A. **Arigo** of Milton 11/15/1975; H - b. 2/19/1955; W - b. 1/2/1958
Donald R. of Milton m. Linda M. **D'Amore** of Milton 6/29/1998

SENCAR,
Joseph E. of Pawtucket, RI m. Carolyn D. **Bellis** of Pawtucket, RI 10/4/1980

SEXTON,
William H., Jr. of Milton m. Tracy E. **Earl** of Milton 9/11/1999

SHAPLEIGH,
Fred., Jr. of Eliot, ME m. Janet F. **Witham** of Milton 8/23/1947; H - 22, auto b. wks., b. Portsmouth, s/o Fred. A. Shapleigh (Eliot, ME, Stand. Oil Co.) and Gertrude E. Spinney (Eliot, ME, housewife); W - 22, Gen. Elec., b. Rochester, d/o Ernest F. Witham (Kittery Pt., ME, mill worker) and Marguerite Cooley (Wilmington, MA, housewife)

George F. of Eliot, ME m. Emma S. **Dixon** of Chesterville, ME 12/20/1894 in Wakefield; H - 29, farmer, b. Chelsea, MA, s/o Charles A. Shapleigh (Eliot, ME, carpenter) and Mary F. (Lebanon, ME); W - 34, housekeeper, b. Chesterville, ME, d/o Abiel S. Dixon (Farmington, ME, farmer) and Hannah (Jay, ME)

SHAW,
Kevin T. of Milton m. Barbara M. **Mahoney** of Milton 2/14/1992
William N., Jr. of Milton m. Terri L. **Huntress** of Milton 2/20/1987

SHEA,
Alfred H. of Wakefield m. Lois J. **Colby** of Milton Mills 6/10/1935 in Milton Mills; H - 21, laborer, b. Wakefield, s/o Patrick Shea (Somerville, MA, laborer) and Florence Reed (Wakefield, housewife); W - 23, at home, 2nd, b. Milton Mills, d/o Arthur Keddie (Beverly, MA) and Clara Wentworth (Milton Mills, housewife)

Carroll J. of Union m. Susan G. **Burns** of Milton Mills 2/8/1974 in Union; H - b. 8/5/1948; W - b. 5/8/1950

SHEING,
Craig W. of Milton m. Deborah J. **Griffin** of Milton 4/30/1988 in Somersworth

SHERMAN,
Richard F. of Hodgdon, ME m. Mary K. **Tufts** of Milton 6/6/1959; H - 21, US Navy, b. ME, s/o Floyd Sherman (ME) and Virginia Longfellow (VA); W - 28, shoe shop. 2nd, b. Milton, d/o Napoleon Marcoux (NH) and Hazel Downs (NH)

Scott E. of Milton m. Jennifer J. **Moore** of Milton 10/2/1999

SHORT,
Frederick H., III of Eliot, ME m. Marion E. **Fields** of Milton 8/16/1969; H - b. 12/23/1947; W - b. 1/26/1949

SIEMON,
Carl of Milton m. Beverly E. **McCabe** of Concord 12/12/1981

SILVESTRO,
Gerald R. of Milton m. Patricia J. **Golden** of Milton 11/24/1973 in Concord; H - b. 1/22/1945; W - b. 7/22/1951

SIMES,
Albert L. of Milton m. Josie E. **Miller** of Acton, ME 3/12/1898; H - 21, shoemaker, b. Milton, s/o George E. Simes (Milton, carpenter); W - 18, shoe stitcher, b. Acton, ME, d/o Elias Miller (Acton, ME, farmer)

Frederick H. of Milton m. Mary A. **Smith** of Rochester 5/31/1888 in Wakefield

Hervey D. of Milton m. Lulu E. **Manson** of Acton, ME 8/3/1898; H - 24, shoemaker, b. Milton, s/o John U. Simes (Milton, merchant); W - 18, weaver, b. Farmington, d/o George H. Manson (Limerick, ME, baker)

SIMONAULT,
George J. of Sanford, ME m. Alice **Fleurant** of Sanford, ME 8/29/1925 in Rochester; H - 30, mill man, b. Hiram, ME, s/o Edward Simonault (Canada, millman) and Melina Venner (Canada); W - 24, weaver, b. Canada, d/o Napoleon Fleurant (Canada, carpenter) and Julie Morin (Canada)

SINCLAIR,
Milo M. of Dover m. Minnie F. **Ellis** of Milton 6/16/1900; H - 21, shoemaker, b. Stowe, ME, s/o George H. Sinclair and Susie G. Johnson (Stowe, ME); W - 32, shoe stitcher, 2nd, b. Milton, d/o James W. Johnson (Milton, laborer) and Julia -----

SINNOTT,
Winfield B. of Chelsea, MA m. Sadie H. **Willey** of Milton 11/26/1914; H - 29, painter, b. Westboro, MA, s/o Winifred B. Sinnott (Saco, ME)

and Mary J. Brown (Boston, MA); W - 35, housework, b. Milton, d/o Joseph F. Willey (Brookfield) and Mary J. Laskey (Milton)

SIROIS,
Robert J. of Milton m. Adela L. **Martin** of New Bedford, MA 12/14/1973; H - b. 12/12/1949; W - b. 7/21/1948
Victor D. of Milton m. Pauline R. **Worster** of Milton 6/30/1973; H - b. 5/5/1930; W - b. 7/22/1927

SKELTON,
Benjamin E. of Eaton m. Bonnie L. **Bullis** of Milton 9/16/1989 in Wakefield

SKIBICKI,
Anthony W. of Milton m. Darlene E. **Grassie** of Milton 8/18/1990 in Gonic

SLAZENIK,
John C. of Milton m. Linda F. **Coggeshall** of Rochester 5/5/1984
John C. of Milton m. Lynn M. **Staples** of Milton 4/4/1987

SLEEPER,
Fred B. of Milton m. Stella **Dicey** of Milton 8/29/1896; H - 21, shoemaker, b. Alton, s/o Jeremy (Alton) and Rose (Bangor, ME); W - 19, shoe stitcher, b. Wakefield, d/o George W. (Jackson) and Susan (Wakefield)

SMALL,
Arthur H. of Milton m. Helen E. **Lowd** of Acton, ME 3/18/1903: H - 23, b. Rockport, ME, s/o Joseph L. Small (Deer Isle, ME, farmer) and Ellen Weymouth (Appleton, ME); W - 19, lady, b. Acton, ME, d/o John Lowd (Acton, ME, farmer) and Viola Coffin (Newfield, ME)
Chester W. of Milton m. Elsie M. **Nute** of Milton 1/16/1906; H - 21, shoemaker, b. Boston, MA, s/o Albert L. Small (Boston, MA, policeman) and Etta Davison (Nashville, TN); W - 18, shoe stitcher, b. Farmington, d/o John S. Nute (Milton, laborer) and Emma Moore

SMALLIS,
Ernest of Portsmouth m. Laurie J. **Boggs** of Milton 9/22/1984 in Portsmouth

SMART,
Gregory E. of Rutland, VT m. Faith E. **Harriman** of Milton 8/18/1979
Kenneth E. of Milton m. Olive M. **Bent** of Milton 3/14/1953; H - 27, bed laster, 2nd, b. Raymond, s/o Everett Smart and Annie McGall; W - 19, unemployed, b. Norfolk, MA, d/o Halford Bent and Ruth Ormes

SMITH,
Adriel C. of Milton Mills m. Mary L. **Locke** of Barrington 9/25/1960 in Rochester; H - 25, mechanic; W - 18, at home
Albert W. of Dover m. Leona M. **McDonald** of Brookfield 6/13/1954; H - 68, janitor, 2nd, b. MA, s/o J. Albert Smith and Ida Cook; W - 69, housewife, 2nd, b. NH, d/o Edward Hall and Ida Hall
Arthur T. of Cambridge, MA m. Orinda S. **Dickey** of Milton 11/15/1906; H - 31, lawyer, b. Silver City, ID, s/o Arthur N. Smith (Meddybemps, ME, physician) and Mary H. McCann (IA); W - 23, at home, b. Ludlow, MA, d/o Myron P. Dickey (Derry, clergyman) and Louise Shumway (Palmer, MA)
Carl R. of Milton Mills m. Lorraine R. **Gauthier** of Rochester 8/12/1961 in Rochester; H - 20, Navy; W - 18, waitress
Carl R. of Milton Mills m. Lauris R. **Burns** of Milton Mills 11/18/1963 in Milton Mills; H - 21, US Navy; W - 17, waitress
Cecil E. of Milton m. Josephine **Scarpignato** of Fitchburg, MA 1/4/1947 in Fitchburg, MA; H - 25, disch. vet., b. Union, s/o Guy Smith and Clara Tufts; W - 23, secretary, b. Fitchburg, MA, d/o Joseph Scarpignato and Mary Pallavinci
Charles I. of Acton, ME m. Amanda M. **Hussey** of Acton, ME 3/25/1890; H - 23, day laborer, b. Shapleigh, ME, s/o Irving (Waterford, ME) and Christina (Waterford, ME); W - 15, housework, b. Acton, ME, d/o Isaac (Acton, ME) and Harriet (Acton, ME)
Daniel W. of Milton Mills m. Susan M. **Gilliland** of Milton Mills 8/16/1980 in Sullivan
David L. of Rochester m. Anne M. **Swiatocha** of Milton 6/12/1982 in Rochester
David R. of Milton m. Draxine M. **Provencher** of Milton 10/14/1978; H - b. 8/10/1958; W - b. 3/17/1961

Donald T. of Milton m. Joyce M. **Emerson** of Milton 1/22/1972; H - b. 9/13/1950; W - b. 7/9/1951

Earl L. of Milton m. Vera B. **Abbott** of Milton 12/8/1938 in Lebanon, ME; H - 24, laborer, b. Farmington, s/o William A. Smith (Alton, laborer) and Iona Knight (N. Mills, VT, housewife); W - 18, housework, b. Southboro, MA, d/o Jacob N. Abbott (Ossipee) and Tessie Ainsworth (Montpelier, VT, housewife)

Edmund L. of Milton m. Hannah **DeMeritt** of Milton 10/13/1935; H - 27, shoe worker, 2nd, b. Farmington, s/o William A. Smith (Alton, laborer) and Cora B. Knight (Mortonville, VT, housewife); W - 25, clerk, P.O., b. Milton, d/o Berthold DeMeritt (Newfield, ME, foreman) and Musetta A. Dorr (Dover, housewife)

Ernest R. of Milton m. Karen K. **Doherty** of Milton 4/30/1976; H - b. 1/9/1956; W - b. 4/7/1959

Frederick R. of Milton m. Margie M. **Chenette** of Milton 8/4/1990

Guy R. of Milton m. Myrtle L. **Derby** of Farmington 6/25/1938 in W. Milton; H - 22, mill worker, b. Union, s/o Guy A. Smith (Franconia, prod. mgr.) and Clara M. Tufts (Middleton, housewife); W - 18, shoe worker, b. Barnstead, d/o Charles L. Derby (Montpelier, VT, laborer) and Sylvia V. Cook (Barnstead, housewife)

Harry R. of Milton m. Patricia M. **Hill** of Milton Mills 5/3/1960; H - 21, shoe worker; W - 18, student

Harry R., Jr. of Milton Mills m. Tammy J. **Whitten** of Milton Mills 5/28/1983

Irving L. of Milton m. Kathleen M. **Jones** of Lebanon, ME 6/23/1973; H - b. 9/9/1946; W - b. 10/14/1949

John of Milton Mills m. Mary **Bermudz** of Milton Mills 11/8/1941; H - 31, laborer, b. Newfield, ME, s/o William Smith (Newfield, ME, laborer) and Mary Smith (W'db'y M., ME, housewife); W - 22, dress maker, b. Cayey, PR, d/o Hilarion Bermudz (Coamo, PR, storekeeper) and Christina Ortiz (Cedra, PR, housewife)

John R. of Milton m. Toan Thi **Nguyen** of Saigon, South Vietnam 9/9/1972; H - b. 11/13/1953; W - b. 2/1/1950

Kenneth R. of Milton m. Susan M. **Carlson** of Milton 8/15/1973 in Portsmouth; H - b. 7/4/1954; W - b. 12/23/1954

Michael R. of Milton m. Brenda J. **Wessell** of Milton 12/28/1985

Oscar C. of Newburyport, MA m. Mary A. **Hodsdon** of Milton 1/5/1893; H - 28, shoe cutter, b. Kennebunk, ME, s/o Charles F. Smith (So.

Berwick, ME, shoemaker) and Louise S.; W - 21, shoe stitcher, b.
Milton, d/o George F. Hodsdon (painter) and Lucinda
Patrick H. of Milton Mills m. Pamela J. **Foster** of Milton Mills 5/16/1987
Peter W. of Milton m. Quang **Brock** of Milton 7/3/1993
Randy D. of Milton Mills m. Jeannette L. **Pridham** of Milton Mills 11/16/1985
Richard A. of Milton m. Diane M. **Saragian** of Worcester, MA 7/28/1984
Ricky A. of Milton m. Carol A. **Collins** of Rochester 11/15/1969 in Rochester; H - b. 7/17/1950; W - b. 10/8/1949
Robert L. of Milton m. Beulah M. **Leighton** of Middleton 6/2/1955; H - 36, lumberman, 2nd, b. Lebanon, ME, s/o William A. Smith and Iona Richardson; W - 18, at home, b. Middleton, d/o William T. Leighton and Leona Grace
Ronald D. of Milton Mills m. Barbara M. **Dunlap** of Portsmouth 3/21/1960 in Portsmouth; H - 26, USCG; W - 26, none
Shane M. of Milton m. Jennifer E. **Gilman** of Farmington 9/7/1991
Shane M. of Milton m. Amy L. **Hagar** of Milton 9/18/1996
William J. of Milton m. Lorene V. **Wilkinson** of Sanbornville 6/6/1964 in Wakefield; H - 20, textile worker; W - 18, student

SNYDER,

Glen P. of Milton m. Fawn S. **Choate** of Rochester 12/30/1982 in Rochester

SOUCY,

Gary J. of Milton m. Janet D. **Gagnon** of East Lebanon, ME 3/21/1987 in Farmington
Oscar J., Jr. of Wakefield m. Roberta C. **Marcoux** of Milton 9/9/1961; H - 17, shoe worker; W - 24, shoe worker
Oscar J., Sr. of Milton m. Grace L. **Koutzoukis** of Milton 3/28/1992

SOUTER,

Thomas, Jr. of Milton m. Mildred E. **Lucey** of Rochester 6/14/1942 in Farmington; H - 25, shoe cutter, b. Somerville, MA, s/o Thomas Souter (Glasgow, Scotland, ship fitter) and Will'mina Swanson (Scotland, housewife); W - 24, shoe worker, 2nd, b. Farmington, d/o Melvin S. Tirrell (Lebanon, ME, shoe worker) and Mardell E. Howard (Dover, shoe worker)

SPENCER,
Frank F. of Milton Mills m. Lela B. **Colman** of Rochester 2/10/1938 in Rochester; H - 45, fun'l dir., 2nd, b. Berwick, ME, s/o Fred A. Spencer (Berwick, ME, deceased) and Minnie L. Foss (Somersworth, at home); W - 31, at home, 2nd, b. Dover, d/o Eli P. Bessey (Thorndike, ME, deceased) and Grace C. Brownell (Dover, saleslady)

SPINALE,
Frank D. of Milton m. Susan M. **Murphy** of Dover 12/2/1990

SPRAGUE,
Dale R. of New Durham m. Kendra J. **Bruce** of Milton 4/10/1982
Louis R. of Wakefield m. Cynthia R. **Paey** of Milton 5/12/1956 in Wakefield; H - 21, mach. opr., b. NH, s/o Louis E. Sprague and Madeline Adjutant; W - 16, at home, b. NH, d/o Clyde W. Paey and Caroline L. Huntress
Richard E. of Milton m. Linda A. **Lamper** of Milton 9/22/1978; H - b. 11/21/1956; W - b. 7/1/1957
William C. of Milton m. Tammy J. **McKay** of Milton 7/14/1988
William C. of Milton m. Kimberly A. **Grant** of Milton 6/26/1998

STACY,
William R. of Milton m. Georgiella H. **Marston** of Deerfield 9/21/1893; H - 23, bookkeeper, b. Cambridge, MA, s/o George W. Stacy (grocer) and Jennie O.; W - 19, shoe stitcher, b. Deerfield, d/o George Marston (farmer) and Jennie

STANLEY,
Donald E. of Milton m. Mabel R. **Leighton** of Middleton 11/28/1953 in Chichester; H - 34, truck driver, 2nd, b. Berwick, ME, s/o Harry R. Stanley and Ellen Randell; W - 21, shoe worker, b. Middleton, d/o William T. Leighton and Leona M. Grace
Ernest of Milton m. Gertrude **Plummer** of Concord 12/25/1912; H - 23, emp. tel. co., b. Hollis, ME, s/o Randall L. Stanley (Porter, ME, farmer) and Ida B. Bisbee (Ossipee); W - 38, housework, 2nd, b. Bedford, d/o Clark G. Mudge (Bedford) and Emma F. Adams (Bedford)
Robert F., Jr. of Milton m. Brooke C. **Barger** of Milton 9/7/1997

STAPLES,

Harry W. of Milton m. Henrietta M. **Sigler** of New Durham 1/3/1903; H - 30, teamster, b. Milton, s/o Jacob F. Staples (Milton, farmer) and Nancy J. Pike (Boston, MA); W - 18, lady, b. NY, d/o Stephen Sigler and Ella M. Nelson (Denmark)

Harry W. of Milton m. Clara Jordan **Cox** of Milton 7/1/1916; H - 44, farmer, 2nd, b. Milton, s/o Jacob F. Staples (Farmington) and Amancy J. Pike (Boston, MA); W - 45, housekeeper, 3rd, b. Houlton, ME, d/o James Jordan (NY) and Charlotte Daniel (London, England)

Joseph A. of Milton m. Tonda L. **Cumpton** of Milton 8/21/1990

Raymond F. of Milton m. Betty A. **Marra** of Milton 5/23/1987

Wayne D. of Milton m. Patricia A. **Lavoie** of Milton 10/19/1991

STAPLETON,

Mark R. of Milton Mills m. Jane **Mullavey** of Milton Mills 5/24/1997

Robert A. of Milton Mills m. Jill M. **Scott** of Acton, ME 10/9/1993

STEEVES,

Ford O. of Dover m. Janet L. **Philpot** of Milton 5/22/1954 in Dover; H - 42, postal emp., b. Dover, s/o Lloyd A. Steeves and Edith Lutolf; W - 38, insp. G.E., 2nd, b. Milton, d/o Arthur Columbus and Flora Boisvert

STEVENS,

Charles L. of Milton m. Dora **Weeks** of Brookfield 4/30/1889; H - 32, stage driver, b. Brookfield, s/o Daniel D. (Middleton) and Hannah J. (Middleton); W - 20, house, b. Brookfield, d/o John W. (Brookfield) and Nancy E. (Brookfield)

Charles L. of Milton m. Sadie M. **Merrill** of Acton, ME 11/25/1903 in Acton, ME; H - 44, asst. post master, 2nd, b. Brookfield, s/o Daniel D. Stevens (Middleton, farmer) and Hannah J. Cook (Middleton); W - 42, dressmaker, b. Acton, ME, d/o George Merrill (Acton, ME, shoemaker) and Rebecca Downs (Milton)

Chester I. of Acton, ME m. Louise E. **Teel** of Milton Mills 10/8/1932 in Acton, ME; H - 24, farmer, b. Acton, ME, s/o Jacob H. Stevens (Acton, ME, farmer) and Viola A. Preeper (Medford, MA, housewife); W - 23, tel. oper., b. Arlington, MA, d/o Wallace Teel

(Arlington, MA, riding ins.) and Louise Stimson (Lexington, MA, housewife)

Dennis W. of East Lebanon, ME m. Betty U. **Cochrane** of Berwick, ME 12/28/1973; H - b. 5/18/1952; W - b. 10/31/1954

Frank L. of Milton m. Mary **Mikle** of Milton 6/1/1895 in Milton Mills; H - 22, shoe laster, b. Milton, s/o Durrell (Middleton, farmer); W - 18, housekeeper, b. Wakefield, d/o William (Scotland, blanket fin.)

Henry G. of Salem, MA m. Lillie A. **Bickford** of Salem, MA 12/31/1894; H - 41, stablekeeper, b. Middleton, s/o J. B. Stevens (Middleton, farmer) and Sarah I.; W - 34, housekeeper, 2nd, b. Lawrence, MA, d/o J. Libby (Limerick, ME, carpenter) and Anna M.

Howard M. of Milton m. Edna A. **Greenwood** 6/10/1961 in Rochester; H - 55, maintenance; W - 57, repairer

Jonathan E. of Milton m. Janine M. **Washburne** of Milton 5/23/1992

STILES,
James A. of Milton m. Sonya M. **Legere** of Milton 5/13/1995

STILLINGS,
Elmer O. of Milton m. Lois J. **Colby** of Milton 5/10/1952 in Portsmouth; H - 39, contractor, b. Portsmouth, s/o Charles O. Stillings and Susie F. Newell; W - 40, housewife, 4th, b. Milton, d/o Arthur W. Keddie and Clara B. Wentworth

Harold A. of Milton m. Mildred **Cunningham** of Crawfordsville, IN 10/29/1943; H - 33, US Army, b. Portsmouth, s/o Charles Stillings (Ossipee, laborer) and Susie F. Newell (NS, housewife); W - 29, printing plant, 2nd, b. Crawfordsville, IN, d/o Walter Cunningham (Crawfordsville, IN, custodian) and Mary McDaniel (Crawfordsville, IN, housewife)

STODDARD,
Francis E. of Lebanon m. Virginia L. **Fifield** of Lebanon 6/22/1968; H - 23; W - 21

STONE,
Henry A. of Milton m. Lydia E. **Kimball** of Milton 6/27/1928; H - 44, teamster, 2nd, b. Rochester, s/o Peter Stone (Canada, brickmaker) and Diantha Pares (Canada); W - 33, at home, b. S. Boston, MA, d/o

Charles A. Kimball (Middleton, farmer) and Clara F. Tripp (E. Boston, MA)

Henry A. of Milton m. Emma **Richie** of Milton 7/24/1930; H - 46, farmer, 3rd, b. Rochester, s/o Peter Stone (Montreal, Canada, brickmaker) and Annie Pares (Oldtown, ME, housewife); W - 48, housewife, 3rd, b. Chelmsford, MA, d/o Rufus Hildrith (Chelmsford, MA, teamster) and Caroline Root (Monroe, housewife)

STONESIFER,

Jason A. of Milton m. Karen R. **Massey** of Milton 7/24/1999

STOREY,

John M. of Milton m. Vivian D. **Teague** of Nashua 11/3/1961 in Nashua; H - 55, salesman; W - 45, at home

STOWE,

Donald W. of Milton m. Mary A. **Ramsey** of Milton 11/1/1941; H - 23, mould maker, b. Milton, s/o Merle L. Stowe (Dover, ME, deceased) and Amy R. Williams (Alma, NB, housewife); W - 25, shoe worker, b. Thompson, CT, d/o Frank E. Ramsey (Somersworth, farmer) and Sophie M. Smith (Schuyler, NE, housewife)

STOWELL,

Carl D. of Milton m. Mary J. **Stowell** of Milton 10/7/1940 in Sanbornville; H - 26, truck driver, b. Antrim, s/o Irving E. Stowell (Ashburnham, MA, painter) and Theresa Dineen (Ireland, housewife); W - 28, shoe worker, 2nd, b. Milton, d/o John A. Hall (Wakefield, farmer) and Laura Willey (Milton, housewife)

Donald I. of Milton Mills m. Betty Lou **Gallagher** of Sanbornville 9/27/1958 in Gorham; H - 22, laborer, b. Milton, s/o Earl Stowell (NH) and Mary Hale (NH); W - 19, bookkeeper, b. Concord, d/o William D. Gallagher (ME) and Orline Day (NH)

Leon C. of Milton m. Mary J. **Hall** of Milton 3/24/1934 in Milton Mills; H - 24, laborer, 2nd, b. Antrim, s/o Irving E. Stowell (Ashburnham, MA, mill wright) and Teresa Dineen (Ireland, housewife); W - 21, at home, b. Milton, d/o John A. Hall (Wakefield, farmer) and Laura Willey (Milton, housewife)

STRACHAN,
George C. of Milton m. Lola E. **Drew** of Milton 7/2/1959; H - 19, US Navy, b. Rochester, s/o George C. Strachan (Canada) and Mary Bigeau; W - 18, at home, d/o Dwight Drew (NH) and Eunice Downs (NH)

STREETER,
Milton H. of Bernardston, MA m. Barbara **Newton** of Greenfield, MA 7/23/1939 in Milton Mills; H - 21, college stud., b. Bernardston, MA, s/o Harold Streeter (Bernardston, MA, farmer) and Ethel Cairns (Quebec, housewife); W - 21, reg. nurse, b. Greenfield, MA, d/o Henry E. Newton (Bernardston, MA, farmer) and Ruth Parmenter (Bernardston, MA, housewife)

STRONG,
John G., II of Milton m. Susan E. **Foster** of Milton 9/27/1980

STUART,
Richard E. of Milton m. Mary-Lou **Waterhouse** of Rochester 5/5/1953 in Rochester; H - 19, USAF, b. ME, s/o Reginald E. Stuart and Helen A. Tibbetts; W - 19, at home, b. NH, d/o Alfred K. Waterhouse and Hazel A. Heath

STURGEON,
John A. of Acton, ME m. Elizabeth A. **Hammond** of Milton 8/19/1919 in West Newfield, ME; H - 42, shoemaker, b. Acton, ME, s/o Henry Sturgeon (Canada) and Dorothy Chauvette (Canada); W - 37, shoe stitcher, 2nd, b. N. Wakefield, d/o Lorenzo Williams (farmer) and Mary A. Watson (No. Wakefield)

SULLIVAN,
Francis J. of Milton m. Nancy J. **Sigmon** of Milton 7/17/1993

SWAN,
Charles R. of Everett, MA m. Marion G. **Oliver** of Everett, MA 2/22/1993

SWEENEY,
Thomas H. of Medford, MA m. Lisa M. **Tierno** of Medford, MA 7/16/1988

SWEET,
Fred I. of Boston, MA m. Anna V. **Rydberg** of Winthrop, MA 8/15/1934; H - 25, manager, b. Concord, s/o Fred H. Sweet (Boscawen, laborer) and Lenna Nutter (Holyoke, MA, housewife); W - 28, at home, b. Roxbury, MA, d/o Carl I. Rydberg (Sweden, painter) and Alma Beigstraud (Sweden, housewife)

Harry J. of No. Rochester m. Iris **Jangro** of No. Rochester 1/16/1909; H - 21, emp. in mill, b. Boston, MA, s/o John Sweet (Windsor, NS) and Delia MacCumber (Cheverie, NS); W - 18, emp. in mill, b. Hoosac Tunnel, MA, d/o Joseph Jangro (Canada, engineer) and Meta Boupra (Pittsford, VT)

Samuel G. of Milton m. Harriett J. **Bodge** of Wolfeboro 2/23/1895; H - 27, shoemaker, b. Marblehead, MA, s/o Henry P. Sweet (Marblehead, MA, farmer); W - 24, shoe stitcher, b. Wolfeboro, d/o Alfred Bodge (Wolfeboro)

SWINERTON,
George of Shapleigh, ME m. Daisy I. **Gilpatrick** of Limerick, ME 9/12/1912 in Rochester; H - 21, laborer, b. Shapleigh, ME, s/o Eugene Swinerton (farmer) and Eliza Cook; W - 18, b. Limerick, ME, d/o Otis Gilpatrick (Rochester, laborer) and Mabel Clark

Henry of Milton m. Ruth B. **Varney** of Milton 8/26/1931 in Rochester; H - 33, shoe cutter, b. Portsmouth, s/o Jacob Swinerton (Rochester, shoemaker) and Emma A. Melville (Braintree, MA, housewife); W - 32, at home, b. Farmington, d/o Alfred C. Varney (Alfred, ME, shoemaker) and Elva A. Blake (Milton, housewife)

John B. of Milton m. Anita M. **McFarlane** of Milton 9/11/1950 in Rochester; H - 46, carder, b. Kingston, s/o Amos Swinerton (ME) and Emma Bryant (Ayer, MA); W - 21, at home, b. MA, d/o Charles S. M. McFarlane (Scotland) and Anna Cahill (Ireland)

Richard of Milton m. Laura **Duchano** of Sanbornville 10/20/1930 in Sanbornville; H - 22, shoemaker, b. Milton, s/o Jacob Swinerton (Somersworth, shoemaker) and Emma Melville (Worcester, MA, housewife); W - 19, at home, b. Sanbornville, d/o Moses Duchano (Canada, mason) and Marie Welch (Salmon Falls, housewife)

SYLVESTRE,
Bernard E. of Dover m. Kim L. **McVicar** of Milton 6/21/1986 in Dover

SZWYD,
Robert F. of Rochester m. Lorraine B. **Archer** of Rochester 1/31/1998

TAATJES,
Brian S. of Milton m. Kathleen M. **Fennell** of Haverhill, MA 8/2/1980
Brian S. of Milton m. Stacy I. **Ferris** of Milton 10/19/1996
Michael R. of Milton m. Amy B. **Parenteau** of Rochester 12/18/1993

TAFFE,
Joseph L., Jr. of Milton m. Jacqueline A. **Shea** of Newmarket 2/2/1991
Joseph L., Sr. of Milton m. Barbara M. **Spencer** of Milton 5/23/1992

TAGGETT,
William H. of Meredith m. Ann E. **Moore** of Milton 3/21/1992

TALON,
Ronald W. of Milton m. Pamela J. **Dumont** of Milton 11/25/1998

TANDY,
Wilbert C. of Athol, MA m. Florence M. **Hunter** of Arlington, MA 6/20/1925; H - 50, machinist, b. Athol, MA, s/o Charles F. Tandy (Hancock, painter) and Priscilla E. Fay (Athol, MA); W - 41, file clerk, b. Woburn, MA, d/o Harvey Hunter (W. Medway, MA, painter) and Laura A. Smith (Bradley, ME)

TANNER,
Charles E. of Milton m. Vila L. **Kimball** of Middleton 3/27/1919 in Rochester; H - 24, mill hand, b. Rochester, s/o Hervey A. Tanner (Farmington, carpenter) and Mary O'Hare (Belfast, Ireland); W - 18, b. Middleton, d/o George Kimball (Middleton, mill hand) and Eliza S. Hanscom (Dover)
Charles E. of Milton m. Helen **Johnson** of Rochester 1/20/1940 in Rochester; H - 45, postmaster, 2nd, b. Rochester, s/o Hervey E. Tanner (Farmington, carpenter) and Mary A. O'Hare (Ireland, housework); W - 32, clerk, 2nd, b. Rochester, d/o Ellsworth Johnson (Barrington, teamster) and Eva Corson (Strafford, housework)
Floyd I. of Farmington m. Edna L. **Marcoux** of Milton 7/4/1959; H - 45, shoe worker, b. NH, s/o George I. Tanner and Gertrude Smart (NH);

W - 35, shoe worker, b. NH, d/o Napoleon Marcoux (NH) and Hazel Downs (NH)
George L. of Milton m. Rita E. **Piper** of Milton 10/17/1931 in Rochester; H - 43, garage, b. Farmington, s/o Hervey E. Tanner (Farmington, carpenter) and Mary O'Haire (Belfast, Ireland, housewife); W - 20, at home, b. Milton, d/o James A. Piper (Newfield, ME, carpenter) and Laura A. Evans (Wakefield, housewife)
George L., Jr. of Milton m. Therese A. **Sampson** of Farmington 7/10/1954 in Farmington; H - 20, com. artist, b. Rochester, s/o George L. Tanner and Rita Piper; W - 20, bank teller, b. N. Cambridge, MA, d/o Francis Sampson and Adelaide Beaulieu
Herbert of Milton m. Evelyn A. **Marchand** of Rochester 1/1/1965 in Somersworth; H - 54, carpenter; W - 37, hosp. kitchen
Hervey C. of Milton m. Yvonne **Lessard** of Rochester 12/11/1933 in Rochester; H - 29, barber, b. Whitefield, s/o Hervey E. Tanner (Farmington, carpenter) and Mary O'Hare (Ireland, housewife); W - 23, clerk, b. Rochester, d/o Joseph Lessard (Rochester, clerk) and Lydia Turcotte (Canada, housewife)
Patrick P. of Milton m. Frances A. **Michel** of Rochester 10/28/1961 in Rochester; H - 24, shoe cutter; W - 22, clerk-typist
Philip J. of Milton m. Jessica L. **Pitman** of Rochester 4/14/1984 in Rochester
Stanley C. of Milton m. Cordelia **Davidson** of Milton 11/15/1931; H - 39, garage, b. Farmington, s/o Hervey E. Tanner (Farmington, carpenter) and Mary O'Haire (Belfast, Ireland, housewife); W - 35, nurse, b. Bethel, PQ, d/o Frank Davidson (Bascobel, PQ, farmer) and Maud Waterson (R'xt'n F., PQ, housewife)
Vincent of Lebanon, ME m. Ruth **Ramsey** of Milton 9/25/1936 in Acton, ME; H - 23, laborer, b. Lebanon, ME, s/o Herbert Tanner (Farmington, farmer) and Marie Devaney (Ireland, housewife); W - 25, bookkeeper, b. Berwick, ME, d/o Frank Ramsey (Somersworth, farmer) and Sophia Smith (Schuyler, NE, housewife)

TARBOX,
Harry F. of Jericho, VT m. Florence E. **Pierce** of W. Newbury, MA 9/27/1960; H - 71, retired; W - 64, at home

TARDIF,
Andrea of Milton m. Victoria **Whitehouse** of Milton 1/8/1923; H - 22, shoemaker, b. St. Calixe, PQ, s/o Agenor Tardif (St. Calixte, PQ, farmer) and Clara Martineau (St. Julie, PQ); W - 28, shoe operative, 2nd, b. Union, d/o Leon Douquette (Canada, fireman) and Emma Houle (Canada)
Donald of Middleton m. Carrie E. **Remick** of Milton 5/11/1925 in Union; H - 27, woodsman, b. Plassisville, Canada, s/o Joseph Tardif (Plassisville, Canada, farmer) and Azilda Martineau (Canada); W - 25, housekeeper, 2nd, b. Albany, d/o Frank L. Grace (Chatham, farmer) and Lizzie B. Willey (Albany)

TARLTON,
Richard of Milton m. Betty J. **Salyards** of Milton 4/3/1948 in Rochester; H - 19, box maker, b. Epping, s/o Arthur S. Tarlton (Chester, box maker) and Jeanette A. Johnson (Epping, housewife); W - 22, shoe shop, b. Huntington, PA, d/o Harry Salyards and Ruth H. Varney (housewife)

TARMEY,
Michael P. of Rochester m. Kelly A. **Logan** of Milton 6/5/1982 in New Durham

TASKER,
Theodore L., Jr. of Milton m. Elaine R. **Childs** of Milton 12/7/1986
Theodore L., III of Milton m. Theresa M. **Whelan** of Milton 1/31/1986 in Barrington

TAY,
Mark H. of Methuen, MA m. Carylyn V. **Grondin** of Milton 9/7/1985 in Rochester

TAYLOR,
David C. of Ogden, UT m. Joanne P. **Moody** of Milton 3/23/1956; H - 21, US Navy, b. Ogden, UT, s/o Alfred L. Taylor and Blanche Baird; W - 20, student, b. Rochester, d/o Alfred H. Moody and Alice M. Phinney

TEBBETTS,
Ronald C. of Rochester m. Judith K. **Tully** of Milton 4/12/1969; H - b. 4/4/1940; W - b. 9/19/1946

TERCYAK,
Michael F. of Milton m. Deborah J. **Savoie** of Milton 1/25/1974; H - b. 5/27/1954; W - b. 6/1/1954

TESSIER,
Albert J. of Rochester m. Katherine B. **Ham** of Milton 2/8/1936 in Farmington; H - 22, bus driver, b. Wakefield, s/o Louis Tessier (Suncook, shoe oper.) and Lucy Pouliot (Wakefield, housewife); W - 24, nurse, b. Milton, d/o James Ham (Dover, truck driver) and Blanche Drew (Wakefield, housewife)

TEVES,
David J. of Milton m. Cheryl A. **Goodwin** of Milton 2/13/1993

THAYER,
Benjamin P. of Milton m. Linda D. **McGivern** of Milton 9/19/1992

THERIAULT,
Reginald, Jr. of E. Lebanon, ME m. Jonice **Perry** of E. Lebanon, ME 6/6/1992

THEROUX,
David L. of Milton m. Kari A. **Michalski** of Milton 8/28/1997

THIBAULT,
Arthur of Milton m. Hattie M. **Burke** of Lebanon, ME 9/5/1908; H - 20, papermaker, b. Dover, s/o C. T. Thibault (Canada, emp. woolen mill) and Olive M. Douchane (Canada); W - 22, shoe stitcher, b. Wolfeboro, d/o Charles F. Burke (Milton, farmer) and H. Clara Tibbetts (Wolfeboro)

THIBODEAU,
James W. of Milton m. Jeanne D. **Zeller** of E. Providence, RI 8/1/1973 in Montville, CT; H - b. 3/11/1946; W - b. 2/18/1943

Patrick J. of Grand Isle, ME m. Lucy E. **Pinfold** of Milton 9/26/1917 in Milton Mills; H - 31, machinist, b. Grand Isle, ME, s/o Thomas Thibodeau (Caribou, ME, machinist) and Mary A. Thibodeau (Grand Isle, ME); W - 30, school supervisor, b. Reading, England, d/o William Pinfold (Reading, England, prop. boarding house) and Annie E. Lewis (Windsor, England)

THIVIERGE,
Roger O. of E. Lebanon, ME m. Maxene M. **Marble** of Berwick, ME 6/29/1974; H - b. 6/20/1954; W - b. 3/20/1956

THOMAS,
Charles L. of Milton m. Kazecho **Nakahara** of Tokyo, Japan 1/28/1957 in Tokyo, Japan; H - 20, US Army, b. Rochester, s/o Wilfred Thomas (NS) and Blanche Dadman (MA); W - 27, at home, b. Japan, d/o Toshi Nakahara (Japan) and Fuker Nakahara (Japan)

James G. of Milton m. Janice L. **Russell** of Rochester 9/20/1988 in Rochester

Wilfred of Milton m. Blanche M. **Dadmun** of Milton 9/27/1936; H - 24, emp. mill, b. NS, s/o Elias Thomas (G. Mt., NS, farmer) and Elizabeth Young (Paradise, NS, housewife); W - 18, at home, b. Allston, MA, d/o Ales H. Dadmun (Baltimore, MD, photographer) and E. Lita Guilford (Thornton, housewife)

THOMPSON,
Cornelius of Milton m. Nellie T. **Sullivan** of Milton 3/7/1905 in Gonic; H - 31, laborer, b. PEI, s/o Charles Thompson and Mary Quark (Ireland); W - 26, weaver, b. Ireland, d/o Daniel Sullivan (Ireland, farmer) and Mary ----- (Ireland)

Dennis T. of Milton m. Leona M. **Moore** of Dover 1/4/1968 in Dover; H - 31; W - 33

Edwin C. of Milton m. Thelma **Warnecke** of Milton 7/3/1934 in Alton; H - 25, mill emp., b. Milton, s/o Cornelius Thompson (PEI, laborer) and Nellie T. Sullivan (Ireland, housewife); W - 18, clerk, b. Milton, d/o William Warnecke (Germany, machinist) and Francina I. Nutter (Milton, housewife)

Edwin C. of Milton m. Joan F. **Ahern** of Rochester 6/28/1958 in Rochester; H - 22, student, b. Lewiston, ME, s/o John F. Thompson

(NH) and Mary A. McLaughlin (MA); W - 21, secretary, b. Newton, MA, d/o Richard E. Ahern (MA) and Mary C. MacPherson (NS) Edwin F., Jr. of Milton m. Barbara E. **Seaward** of Milton 12/28/1991 Steven D. of Milton m. Susan J. **Burrows** of Milton 6/2/1984 Wendell L., Jr. of Rochester m. Cynthia A. **Evans** of Milton 5/1/1983

THORNLEY,
James F., Jr. of Rehoboth, MA m. Marlena T. **Gebo** of Rehoboth, MA 7/11/1996

THORNTON,
John P. of S. Boston, MA m. Marie A. **Bartz** of S. Boston, MA 8/29/1926; H - 21, medical stud., b. Dublin, Ireland, s/o Patrick A. Thornton (Dublin, Ireland, postmaster) and Katherine A. Canney (Dublin, Ireland); W - 18, at home, b. Lowell, MA, d/o Frank A. Bartz (Germany, sausage mfgr.) and Augusta M. Heincke (New York, NY)

THURLO,
Perley E. of Milton m. Bertha Q. **Delano** of Fall River, MA 6/16/1934 in E. Providence, RI; H - 26, soldier, 2nd, b. Newburyport, MA, s/o Clemens Thurlo (Newburyport, MA, retired) and Ida M. Carpenter (Rollinsford); W - 24, at home, b. Berkeley, MA, d/o Warren R. Delano (Berkeley, MA) and Medeline M. Tripp (Boston, MA)

THURSTON,
Charles H. of Milton m. Eubie **Leighton** of Farmington 3/11/1897; H - 34, stablekeeper, 2nd, b. Gilmanton, s/o Hananiah Thurston (watchman); W - 18, lady, b. Farmington, d/o Charles H. Leighton

TIBBETTS,
Albert M. of Milton m. Mary E. S. **Bray** of Ipswich, MA 11/4/1904; H - 29, emp. in mill, b. Milton, s/o Walter S. Tibbetts (New Durham, farmer) and Hattie L. Downing (Milton); W - 35, housekeeper, 2nd, b. Ipswich, MA, d/o Samuel Stevens (Saco, ME)
Louis E. of Milton m. Arlene R. **Laskey** of Milton Mills 6/12/1937 in Farmington; H - 33, farmer, 2nd, b. Brookfield, s/o Everett Tibbetts (Brookfield, farmer) and Susie L. Weeks (Wakefield, postmistress);

W - 20, at home, b. Milton Mills, d/o Ralph D. Laskey (Milton Mills, laborer) and Maud Philbrick (Milton Mills, housewife)

Rick E. of Berwick, ME m. Mary M. **Allen** of Berwick, ME 12/11/1993

Robert of Milton m. Gladys **Woodman** of Parsonsfield, ME 11/19/1940 in Farmington; H - 26, trucking, b. Somerville, MA, s/o Christopher Tibbetts (Milton, farmer) and Theresa Stevens (Boston, MA, housewife); W - 22, at home, b. Parsonsfield, ME, d/o Herman Woodman (Wakefield, farmer) and Susie Wiggin (Ossipee, housewife)

Robert A. of Milton m. Agnes F. **Martin** of Loudon 10/22/1954 in Pittsfield; H - 40, lumbering, 2nd, b. MA, s/o Chris H. Tibbetts and Theresa V. Stevens; W - 34, nurse, 2nd, b. MA, d/o William J. Rogers and Agnes F. Graham

TILTON,

Glen W. of Milton m. Matilda **Whitehouse** of Milton 3/23/1922 in Wolfeboro; H - 18, box maker, b. East Rochester, s/o Clark A. Tilton (St. Johnsbury, VT, farmer) and Sadie Jones (East Rochester); W - 21, domestic, b. Farmington, d/o Nicholas Whitehouse (Middleton, laborer) and Margaret Cassidy (Boston, MA)

TIRRELL,

Carleton W. of Milton m. Sylvia J. **Merrill** of Farmington 6/19/1953 in East Rochester; H - 18, shoe worker, b. Dover, s/o Carl W. Tirrell and Gertrude Currier; W - 19, at home, b. Lebanon, ME, d/o Frank W. Merrill and Beryl M. White

TITCOMB,

Harvey L. of Milton m. Marie **Casey** of Milton 6/21/1947; H - 24, s. metal wkr., b. Newburyport, MA, s/o Charles L. Titcomb (W. Newbury, MA, carpenter) and Charlotte M. Gile (Conway, shoe worker); W - 21, shoe wkr., b. Boston, MA, d/o William E. Casey (Ireland, farmer) and Hazel M. Emery (N. Gloucester, ME, shoe worker)

TOMPSON,

Michael A. of Rochester m. Pamela J. **Pouliot** of Milton 7/9/1988 in Rochester

TOPLIFFE,
David B. of Milton m. Claudia M. **Lodge** of Milton 8/29/1980 in Union

TOUSSAINT,
Shawn P. of North Berwick, ME m. Sandra A. **Constantine** of East Lebanon, ME 9/6/1986

TOWLE,
Joseph A. of Milton m. Ann M. **Turmelle** of Dover 9/7/1974; H - b. 7/31/1954; W - b. 5/5/1958
Thomas S. of Milton m. Susan M. **Nesbitt** of Milton 9/5/1984

TOWNSEND,
John C. of Saugus, MA m. Grace M. **Townsend** of Milton 6/17/1896; H - 24, clerk, b. E. Wilton, ME, s/o Joseph (England) and Ruth P. (Acton, ME); W - 22, lady, b. Milton, d/o Henry H. (Dorchester, MA, woolen mfr.) and Agnes J. (Lowell, MA)
John E. of Milton m. Eda B. **Lowd** of Acton, ME 1/28/1896; H - 24, clerk, b. Milton, s/o Henry H. (Dorchester, MA, woolen mfr) and Agnes J. (Lowell, ME); W - 24, milliner, b. Acton, ME, d/o Elbridge (Acton, ME) and Melissa (Acton, ME)

TOY,
Harold E. of Milton m. Brenda L. **Bowley** of Milton 9/28/1974 in Acton, ME; H - b. 3/7/1954; W - b. 5/7/1956

TOZER,
Granville of Milton m. Annie M. **Wiggin** of Milton 8/14/1909; H - 19, teamster, b. Danvers, MA, s/o Edward Tozer (Norton, MA, teamster) and Maretta McCallin (Windham Hill, NS); W - 20, emp. in mill, b. Milton, d/o Elbridge Wiggin (Acton, ME, emp. in mill) and Susie F. Day (Shapleigh, ME)

TRAFTON,
Eugene C. of Milton m. Marion E. **Maleham** of Wakefield 3/5/1966 in Sanbornville; H - 19, state hgy. worker; W - 18, student
Harold A., Jr. of Milton m. Cynthia S. **Lee** of Milton Mills 12/29/1984

TRAINOR,
William P., Jr. of Rochester m. Cynthia A. **St. Hilaire** of Milton 11/7/1992

TRENT,
Laurence E. of Sn'dville, TN m. Patricia E. **Butler** of Milton 10/28/1944 in Rochester; H - 20, farmer, b. Sn'edv'e, TN, s/o James E. Trent (farmer) and Kitty Rhea (housewife); W - 20, factory wkr., b. Milton, d/o Edward T. Butler (Hingham, MA, fireman) and Margaret Burbine (Wakefield, MA, housewife)

TRIPP,
F. Leroy of Milton m. Nellie F. **Merison** of Milton 6/18/1916 in Farmington; H - 24, farmer, b. Milton, s/o Edwin P. Tripp (Sanford, ME, shoemaker) and Lucy E. Howe (Milton); W - 21, domestic, b. Rochester, d/o Marcellus Merison (Barrington, farmer) and Ida C. Hill (Newton, MA)

F. Leroy of Milton m. Florence A. **Hayes** of Portland, ME 9/20/1921 in Rochester; H - 29, farmer, 2nd, b. Milton, s/o Edwin P. Tripp (Sanford, ME, shoe sorter) and Lucy A. Howe (Milton); W - 38, nurse, b. Milton, d/o Charles Hayes (Milton, farmer) and Nellie Parmenter (Farmington)

TRUMP,
Richard W. of Milton m. Nancy I. **Kern** of Milton 1/19/1985 in Dover

TUCK,
David L. of Milton m. Irene M. **Loesch** of Germany 3/16/1977 in Farmington; H - b. 10/22/1942; W - b. 6/24/1939

Donald L. of Rochester m. Draxa C. **Provencher** of Rochester 6/27/1959; H - 45, Gen. Elect., 2nd, s/o Percy H. Tuck (MA) and Florence Griffin (NH); W - 48, Gen. Elect., 2nd, d/o George N. Corson (NH) and Betsy Laskey (NH)

TUCKER,
Charles of Lebanon, ME m. Edna N. **Calkins** of Milton 6/17/1905; H - 29, emp. in mill, b. Lebanon, ME, s/o George Tucker (Burlington, VT, farmer) and Augusta Ellis (Lebanon, ME); W - 22, teacher, b.

Trescott, ME, d/o Henry G. Calkins (Trescott, ME, paper maker) and Emma M. Lancaster (Trescott, ME)

Ernest S. of Lynn, MA m. Annie E. **Wall** of Lynn, MA 5/9/1931; H - 20, photographer, b. Lynn, MA, s/o Ernest E. Tucker (Lebanon, ME, shoemaker) and Alice Shorey (Lebanon, ME, housewife); W - 20, at home, b. Lynn, MA, d/o Alex B. Wall (Sweden, moulder) and Ida H. Anderson (Finland, housewife)

Kenneth D. of Milton m. Gloria J. **LeBlanc** of Milton 6/19/1999

Paul D. of Dover m. Claire E. **Douglas** of Milton 2/18/1967 in Dover; H - 53, nuclear power insp.; W - 45, homemaker

TUFTS,

Charles E. of Milton m. Alexandrina **German** of Milton 4/10/1895; H - 33, shoe operative, b. Dover, s/o Charles C. Tufts (Somersworth); W - 27, shoe stitcher, 2nd, b. Canada, d/o Barrome German (Canada)

Joseph S. of Milton m. June B. **Rand** of Rochester 2/26/1977; H - b. 9/27/1951; W - b. 8/1/1953

Lauriston of Milton m. Elizabeth A. **Pomerleau** of Gonic 3/21/1953 in Gonic; H - 19, US Air Force, b. NH, s/o Evelyn B. Tufts; W - 17, at home, b. MA, d/o Joseph N. Pomerleau and Elsie Tremblay

Maurice W. of Milton m. Mary J. **Stanley** of Milton 11/12/1955; H - 26, construction, b. Middleton, s/o Moses Tufts and Evelyn Nutter; W - 22, shoe worker, b. Laconia, d/o Harry Stanley and Ellen Otis

Moses D. of Middleton m. Evelyn R. **Nutter** of Milton 1/12/1927 in Union; H - 29, farmer, 2nd, b. Middleton, s/o Wright Tufts (Middleton, farmer) and Cora B. Cook (Milton); W - 20, teacher, b. Milton, d/o Frank J. Nutter (Berwick, ME, mill operative) and Gertrude Wentworth (Milton)

Stephen J. of Middleton m. Mary K. **Marcoux** of Milton 11/11/1947 in Farmington; H - 21, lineman, b. Rochester, s/o Leon G. Tufts (Farmington, farmer) and Addie Kimball (Farmington, housewife); W - 17, at home, b. Milton, d/o Napoleon Marcoux (Wakefield, mill emp.) and Hazel M. Downs (Milton, mill emp.)

Stephen J. of Middleton m. Rita A. **Marcoux** of Milton 8/31/1957; H - 31, foreman, 2nd, b. Rochester, s/o Leon Tufts (NH) and Addie Kimball (Farmington); W - 25, shoe worker, b. Milton, d/o Napoleon Marcoux (NH) and Hazel Downs

TURCOTTE,
Norman A. of Durham m. Phyllis L. **Lavertue** of Milton 5/14/1964; H - 37, watchmaker; W - 23, housewife

TURNER,
Robert H. of Milton Mills m. Rita J. **Davis** of Milton 4/3/1964 in Dover; H - 26, const. worker; W - 27, at home

Willard F. of N. Reading, MA m. Alberta **Bowman** of Medford, MA 10/10/1931; H - 24, clerk, b. N. Reading, MA, s/o Willard P. Turner (Halifax, NS, farmer) and Annie Sutherland (R. John, NS, housewife); W - 19, secretary, b. Boston, MA, d/o David H. Bowman (Springfield, MA, salesman) and Cora F. Guirrard (Fall River, MA, housewife)

TUSEO,
John A. of Lawrence, MA m. Geneva E. **Comparine** of Lawrence, MA 7/20/1926; H - 22, student, b. Lawrence, MA, s/o Antonio Tuseo (Italy, mill operative) and Anna Perotta (Italy); W - 20, student, b. Lawrence, MA, d/o Antonio Comparine (Italy, mill operative) and Caremila Dimonti (Italy)

TUTTLE,
Dana C. of Milton m. Essie I. **Dorr** of Milton 5/4/1916; H - 27, clerk, b. Wakefield, s/o Daniel Tuttle (Wakefield, farmer) and Ora F. Tibbetts (Wolfeboro); W - 23, bookkeeper, b. Farmington, d/o Herbert W. Dorr (Wakefield, shoemaker) and Flora E. Burnham (Farmington)

Jason A. of Milton m. Christy M. **Harrison** of Milton 12/27/1998

Mark O. of Rochester m. Sonya R. **Dore** of Milton 10/25/1980

Samuel F. of Milton m. Cecelia E. **Meserve** of Milton 12/5/1936 in W. Milton; H - 25, shoe worker, b. Dover, s/o Frank H. Tuttle (Dover, retired) and Almie Austin (Dover, housekeeper); W - 25, housekeeper, 2nd, b. Ossipee, d/o Orodon J. Eldridge (Ossipee, retired) and Lucy Welch (Ossipee, housekeeper)

Willie M. of Rochester m. Ruth M. **Lessard** of Milton 2/24/1940 in Berwick, ME; H - 17, laborer, b. Farmington, s/o Eugene A. Tuttle (Alton, laborer) and Maude R. Smart (Farmington, housework); W - 19, at home, b. Dorchester, MA, d/o Charles E. Dore (Milton, laborer) and Bertha Lessard (Milton, housework)

TWITCHELL,
Harris E. of Rochester m. Charlotte L. **Tanner** of Milton 7/2/1960 in Rochester; H - 23, painter; W - 21, student

TWOMBL[E]Y,
Bertrand E. of Milton m. Bessie A. **Plumer** of Milton 6/30/1903; H - 25, emp. in mill, b. Milton, s/o James H. Twombly (Milton, farmer) and Ellen H. Wentworth (Rochester); W - 22, lady, b. Milton, d/o George H. Plumer (Milton, gx) and Mary P. Hayes (Milton)

Lawrence W. of Wakefield m. Kathy L. **Moody** of Milton 8/22/1964 in Sanbornville; H - 20, group foreman; W - 18, at home

ULMER,
Fred L. of Milton m. Deborah J. **Fortin** of Milton 10/10/1982 in Wolfeboro

UNFONAK,
James E. of Milton m. Beverly I. **Haynes** of Milton 5/22/1971; H - b. 4/29/1947; W - b. 3/10/1946

UPTON,
Jeffrey D. of Milton m. Sharlene E. **Dube** of Milton 3/16/1974; H - b. 8/3/1956; W - b. 4/25/1956

URRUTIA,
Thomas B. of Milton m. Dorothy M. **Plaisted** of Milton 9/27/1997

VACHON,
Daniel J. of Rochester m. Pamela D. **Pomroy** of Milton 9/24/1983

Homer E. of Milton m. Eileen M. **Hourihan** of Rochester 4/27/1957 in Rochester; H - 24, dry cleaner, b. Milton, s/o Emile Vachon (NH) and Emma Custeau (NH); W - 19, dental asst., b. Dover, d/o Stephen Hourihan, Jr. (Somersworth) and Caroline E. O'Neil (Somersworth)

J. Martin of Lebanon, ME m. Sandra J. **Whitehouse** of Lebanon, ME 3/29/1958; H - 21, welder, b. Orlando, FL, s/o Edmund Vachon (NH) and Edith Carrigan (NH); W - 18, none, b. Rochester, d/o James Waterhouse (sic) and Emma Gerrish (ME)

John W. of Somersworth m. Barbara J. **Brown** of Portsmouth 12/16/1961; H - 27, shoe worker; W - 19, shoe worker

Joseph A. of Milton m. Marjorie E. **Hale** of Newmarket 7/21/1951 in Durham; H - 24, teacher, b. Milton, s/o Emile Vachon (Somersworth) and Emma Custeau (Milton); W - 23, teacher, b. Exeter, d/o Alfred Hale (MA) and Margaret Norton (Newmarket)

Richard E. of Milton m. Olive G. **Davis** of Milton 12/1/1962; H - 31, painter; W - 28, at home

Richard R. of Somersworth m. Darlene P. **Cheney** of Milton 8/20/1982 in Rochester

Robert A. of Milton m. Theresa **Duchesneau** of Wakefield 8/30/1947 in Sanbornville; H - 19, box mkr., b. Milton, s/o Emile J. Vachon (Somersworth, mill worker) and Emma P. Custeau (Milton, housewife); W - 18, waitress, b. Wolfeboro, d/o Oscar J. Duchesneau (Wakefield, mason) and Doris E. Pratt (Ossipee, housewife)

Valmore R. of Milton m. Donna M. **Breeden** of Milton 12/2/1992

VAILLANCOURT,
Armand P. of Milton Mills m. Marie A. **Pappagallo** of Milton Mills 9/14/1985 in Rochester

VALLEY,
Norman E. of Milton m. Blanche E. **Williams** of Milton 11/26/1949; H - 23, finisher, b. Milton, s/o Paul G. Valley (Ossipee) and Mildred Weeks (Moultonville); W - 17, at home, b. Wakefield, d/o Jefferson Williams (Ossipee) and Cora Dunn (MA)

VARNEY,
Adelbert of Milton m. Evelyn **Swinerton** of Milton 8/30/1935; H - 30, shoe worker, b. Lowell, MA, s/o William H. Varney (Lowell, MA, electrician) and Mary J. Moore (England, housewife); W - 34, shoe worker, b. Farmington, d/o Herbert Swinerton (Somersworth, shoe worker) and Esther Blaisdell (Farmington, housewife)

Charles E. of Milton m. Jennie M. **Remick** of Milton 6/21/1898 in Farmington; H - 28, laborer, b. Milton, s/o Orrin Varney (Milton, engineer); W - 23, mill operative, b. Milton, d/o Charles D. Remick (farmer)

Charles H. of Milton m. Iva B. **Gilmore** of Gilford 12/22/1906; H - 38, emp. in mill, 2nd, b. Tamworth, s/o Charles T. Varney (Berwick, ME, farmer) and Hannah J. Hutchins (Albany); W - 25, housekeeper, 2nd, b. Farmington, d/o Quincy B. Grace (Kittery, ME, farmer) and Adaline G. Frost (Belfast, ME)

George A. of Milton m. Ida M. **Whittier** of Milton 10/30/1905 in Sanborville; H - 19, farmer, b. Milton, s/o Albion F. Varney (Alfred, ME, farmer) and Sarah E. Prescott (Madbury); W - 16, housekeeper, b. Wolfeboro, d/o Andrew J. Whittier (Wolfeboro, laborer) and Ida Brown (Boston, MA)

Guy G. of Wakefield m. Eliza E. **Jenness** of Milton 12/1/1909; H - 20, teamster, b. Wakefield, s/o John F. Varney (Milton, painter) and Nancy Prescott (Milton); W - 17, housekeeper, b. Milton, d/o Edwin P. Jenness (Milton, laborer) and Alma J. Hawkins (Dover)

Kenneth M., Jr. of Newmarket m. Shirley Ann **Pugh** of Milton 3/17/1956; H - 23, salesman, b. Boston, MA, s/o Kenneth M. Varney and Harriet Carpenter; W - 19, checker, b. Rochester, d/o Ralph W. Pugh and Rachel M. Doe

Lewis M. of Milton m. Edella **Webster** of East Rochester 9/19/1921 in East Rochester; H - 51, laborer, b. Farmington, s/o Beard P. Varney (Farmington, farmer) and Clara M. Twombly (Farmington); W - 45, housekeeper, 3rd, b. Jefferson, d/o Mark Rines (Jefferson, lumberman) and Georgia Ford (Jefferson)

Nathaniel B. of Milton m. Ella M. **Champion** of Lebanon, ME 4/16/1891; H - 19, blacksmith, b. Milton, s/o Ira (Milton, dead) and Lydia (Wolfeboro, dead); W - 18, housekeeper, b. Newfield, ME, d/o Daniel (farmer) and Filena (dead)

VAUGHN,
Jeffrey A. of Tulsa, OK m. Ruth-Ellen **Hopkins** of Tulsa, OK 6/24/1989

VENO,
David A. of Milton m. Sara C. **Bishop** of Milton 3/23/1974 in Portsmouth; H - b. 10/2/1948; W - b. 12/10/1952

Ernest W. of Milton m. Debra J. **Laurent** of Milton 11/26/1977 in Rollinsford; H - b. 6/29/1956; W - b. 8/1/1959

VERVILLE,
William P. of Hopkinton m. Martha E. **Plummer** of Milton 6/20/1980 in Contoocook

VETTER,
Norman P. of Rochester m. Stacia R. **Picard** of Milton 4/8/1988 in Rochester

WAGNER,
Kenneth C. of Milton m. Laura A. **Boudreau** of Milton 6/12/1993

WAINWRIGHT,
Raymond of Needham, MA m. Frances **Lewis** of S. Boston, MA 12/6/1936 in Milton Mills; H - 23, laborer, b. Newton Falls, MA, s/o John Wainwright (England, retired) and Lucy Keegin (Newton, MA, housekeeper); W - 22, at home, b. Waverley, MA, d/o Fred Lewis (ME, retired) and Luella Smith (Canada, housekeeper)

WALBRIDGE,
Charles H. of Milton m. Marion L. **Lessard** of Milton 6/14/1936 in Farmington; H - 29, salesman, b. Peterborough, s/o Charles F. Walbridge (VT, clerk) and Lucille Paquet (W. Peterborough, housewife); W - 24, at home, b. Milton, d/o Bennoni Lessard (Canada, farmer) and Delvina Dion (Canada, farmer)
Charles H. of Milton m. Louise M. **Hayes** of Milton 10/12/1976; H - b. 2/4/1907; W - b. 7/14/1935

WALDRON,
Fred E. of Milton m. Annie B. **Pinkham** of Milton 3/2/1891; H - 20, spinner, b. Wolfeboro Jct., s/o Enoch B. (Wakefield, card stripper) and Addie (Berwick, ME, housekeeper); W - 17, shoe stitcher, b. Milton, d/o George W. and Ella (housekeeper)

WALKER,
Allie F. of Acton, ME m. Blanch **Chamberlin** of Milton 6/29/1910 in Union; H - 23, teamster, b. Limerick, ME, s/o William Walker (Limerick, ME) and Mary A. Reynolds (MA); W - 18, b. Milton, d/o Moses G. Chamberlin (Milton, farmer) and Arthie Junkins (Wakefield)
Burton M. of Milton m. Marion I. **Chute** of Milton 11/3/1944; H - 32, farmer, b. Milton, s/o Allie F. Walker (Limerick, ME, woodsman) and Blanche Cham'er'n (Milton, housewife); W - 26, housewife, b.

Newfield, ME, d/o Sidney W. Chute (Old Orchard, ME, road work) and Bessie M. Libbey (Old Orchard, ME, housewife)

Thomas E. of Denver, CO m. Danette L. **Collins** of Milton 10/4/1986

WALL,

James A. of Milton m. Rita M. **Remick** of Somersworth 2/28/1986 in Somersworth

WALLACE,

James S. of Parsonsfield, ME m. Cora J. **McKinney** of Lebanon, ME 9/19/1900 in Sanbornville; H - 53, teamster, 2nd, b. Jefferson, s/o William Wallace and Matilda Worthing; W - 43, housekeeper, 3rd, b. Augusta, ME, d/o George A. Bragg and Christena Wilson

WALLINGFORD,

Amos of Milton m. Helen N. **Burnett** of Somerville, MA 10/28/1929; H - 40, farmer, 2nd, b. Milton, s/o C. M. Wallingford (Milton, farmer) and Ida E. Downs (Milton); W - 43, at home, 2nd, b. Raleigh, NC, d/o Albert H. Tarr (Prospect, ME, gardener) and Susan A. Foster (NC)

Forrest A. of Milton m. Pauline L. **Marsden** of Milton 3/27/1965; H - 25, stripper; W - 29, at home

Forrest A. of Milton m. Carolyn N. **Dow** of Milton 4/20/1968 in Exeter; H - 29; W - 24

WALSH,

Glenn I. of East Rochester m. Myrtle E. **Dickie** of Milton 9/11/1948; H - 29, truck driver, b. S. Lebanon, ME, s/o John E. Walsh (Somersworth, retired) and Grace E. Smith (Pittsfield, MA, housewife); W - 24, nurse, 2nd, b. Salem, MA, d/o Porter J. Durkee (Danvers, MA, real estate) and Estella A. Swinerton (Farmington, housewife)

John P. of Milton m. Susan M. **Russo** of Milton 7/21/1979

John P. of Milton m. Susan M. **Russo** of Milton 9/30/1988

John P. of Milton m. Ann L. **Taylor** of Exeter 6/26/1999

Robert E. of Milton m. Alice S. **Ramsey** of Milton 8/27/1988

WALTER,
Elmer E. of Milton m. Eva R. **Maddox** of Milton 2/24/1897 in Warren, ME; H - 34, shoemaker, b. Warner, ME, s/o William E. Walter (Waldoboro, ME); W - 25, shoe stitcher, 2nd, b. Alton, d/o Jeremy B. Sleeper (Alton)

WALTERS,
Charles M. of Milton m. Elaine F. **Nailor** of Milton 2/16/1985
Jeff R. of Farmington m. Sharon E. **Steeves** of Milton 7/7/1984 in Rochester
John M. of Milton m. Michele C. **Tipton** of Milton 8/20/1983

WARBURTON,
David F. of No. Rochester m. Delores I. **Perkins** of Milton 10/29/1960 in Middleton; H - 20, mill worker; W - 18, shoe worker
Robert E. of Milton m. Rebecca J. **Burrows** of Milton 6/28/1986

WARD,
Ronald P., II of Milton m. Judith M. **Remick** of Rye 7/28/1984 in Rye

WARNECKE,
Donald of Milton m. Marion L. **Rouleau** of Lebanon, ME 12/18/1944 in Farmington; H - 21, US Army, b. Milton, s/o W. Warnecke (Germany, millwright) and Francena Nutter (Milton, housewife); W - 20, mill wkr., b. Ossipee, d/o George Rouleau (Lebanon, ME, mill wkr.) and Inez Eldridge (Ossipee, housewife)
W. H., Jr. of Milton m. Ruth Anna **Dixon** of Milton 1/4/1941; H - 20, mill hand, b. Milton, s/o William H. Warnecke (Gronen, Germany, mill wright) and Francina I. Nutter (Milton, housewife); W - 18, at home, b. Milton, d/o Stephen E. Dixon (Milton, retired) and Georgie Moody (Ossipee, housewife)
William H. of Milton m. Francina I. **Nutter** of Milton 12/6/1915; H - 30, ice man, b. Groneur, Germany, s/o Fred E. Warnecke (Alfelt, Germany, miller) and Anna Rodr (Brcenkersen, Germany); W - 13, b. Milton, d/o Hartley A. Nutter (Milton, ice man) and Ida Huntress (Athens, ME)

WARNOCK,
Chandler R. of Milton m. Mildred **Rogers** of Medford, MA 6/8/1912 in Rochester; H - 21, RR fireman, b. Medford, MA, s/o William Warnock (Newalk, NY) and Florence C. Preeper (Roxbury, MA); W - 18, student, b. Medford, MA, d/o John S. Rogers (Boston, MA, chief clerk, B&M Fire Dept) and Christina McIntire

WARREN,
Arlie of Milton m. Roberta **Canney** of Milton 5/16/1969; H - b. 6/28/1942; W - b. 2/25/1937
Edward R. of Westbrook, ME m. Ada S. **Hawkes** of Westbrook, ME 5/21/1943; H - 38, ship yard, 2nd, b. Cornish, ME, s/o Preston Warren (Hiram, ME, retired) and Maude Witham (Cornish, ME, retired); W - 33, welder, 2nd, b. Gorham, ME, d/o Horace Stevens (Windham, ME, farmer) and Thora Tanberg (Portland, ME, deceased)

WASSON,
Robert W. of Milton m. Brenda J. **Huntress** of Milton 4/26/1997

WATSON,
Gary B. of Alton m. Marie O. **Brown** of Milton 6/24/1984
Millard O. of E. Parsonsfield, ME m. Lois I. **Day** of E. Parsonsfield, ME 5/8/1935; H - 29, truck driver, b. E. Parsonsfield, ME, s/o Armand E. Watson (Parsonsfield, ME, farmer) and Ina B. Norton (Cornish, ME, housewife); W - 20, at home, b. E. Parsonsfield, ME, d/o Elmer F. Day (E. Parsonsfield, ME, laborer) and Ramona Bickford (E. Parsonsfield, ME, housewife)
Richard E. of Milton m. Frances A. **Benton** of Milton 7/3/1948; H - 19, mill worker, b. Farmington, s/o William M. Watson (Alton, shoe worker) and Dorothy Garside (Dover, shoe worker); W - 19, student, b. Rochester, d/o Maynard Benton (Sanbornton, mill worker) and Lucilla Stillings (Wolfeboro, housewife)

WATTS,
Richard W. of Rochester m. Ann M. **Cormier** of Milton 9/16/1989 in Rochester

WEARE,
Donald E. of Milton m. Rita M. **Welch** of Rochester 6/22/1946 in Rochester; H - 25, leather ctr., b. Rochester, s/o Charles Weare (Rochester, heel scourer) and Bertha Jenness (Rochester, housewife); W - 19, shoe worker, b. Tamworth, d/o Russell Welch (Tamworth, farmer) and Hester Clark (Alton, housewife)

WEAVER,
John T. of Milton m. Cora M. **Heath** of Milton 9/21/1957 in Farmington; H - 56, retired, 2nd, b. CA, s/o John T. Weaver (IL) and Viola Ferguson (MI); W - 50, cook, 3rd, b. Alfred, ME, d/o Unknown and Ida Maxwell (Lebanon, ME)

WEBB,
George L. of New Castle m. Elizabeth L. **Smith** of Milton 6/23/1962; H - 21, Coast Guard; W - 20, office
Norman of Lower Sackville, NS m. Mary L. **Perkins** of Milton 7/8/1989

WEBBER,
Bruce L. of Milton m. Shirley **Hersey** of Portsmouth 9/5/1989
Royal K. of Milton m. Nellie B. **Tasker** of Milton 9/24/1890 in Farmington; H - 30, carpenter, b. Shapleigh, ME, s/o Greenleaf (Shapleigh, ME) and Sarah C. (Acton, ME); W - 24, shoe stitcher, b. Milton, d/o George W. (Milton, shoe cutter) and Lydia S. (Milton, dead)

WEBSTER,
Ralph S. of Milton m. Elva M. **Gowen** of Milton 9/8/1909; H - 24, draughtsman, b. Lakeport, s/o John A. Webster (Lakeport, machinist) and Fannie E. Hendley (Alton); W - 18, telephone operator, b. Milton, d/o George W. Gowen (Berwick, ME, laborer) and Eva M. Baker (Gloucester, MA)
Robert F. of Haverhill, MA m. Paulette D. **Landry** of Haverhill, MA 8/31/1962; H - 38, counter work; W - 18, at home

WEDGEWOOD,
Irving S. of Brighton, ME m. Francis E. **Kenniston** of Farmington 10/13/1897; H - 19, shoemaker, b. Brighton, ME, s/o Sylvanus

Wedgewood; W - 16, housekeeper, b. Farmington, d/o Samuel Kenniston (Boston, MA, shoemaker)

WEEKS,
Albert of Milton m. Phylura **Dame** of Rochester 11/27/1902 in Rochester; H - 21, farmer, b. Wakefield, s/o Brackett M. Weeks (Wakefield, farmer) and Matilda Allen (Blue Hill, ME); W - 24, teacher, b. Rochester, d/o Charles Dame (Boston, MA, farmer) and Emily Perkins (Farmington)

WELCH,
Charles of Milton m. Lydia **Marcoux** of Milton 4/4/1904 in Rochester; H - 20, emp. in mill, b. Salmon Falls, s/o Joseph Welch (Canada, engineer) and Exzilda Rivers (Canada); W - 20, shoe stitcher, b. Canada, d/o Joseph Marcoux (Canada, laborer) and Lida Sear (Canada)

Fred of Milton m. Lydia **Marchand** of Milton 10/19/1903; H - 21, emp. in mill, b. So. Berwick, ME, s/o Joseph Welch (Canada, engineer) and Exzilda River (Canada); W - 19, lady, b. Wakefield, d/o Louis Marchand (Canada, emp. in mill) and Ellen Nailor (Canada)

John E. of Milton m. Clara E. **Ramsell** of Milton 11/11/1903 in Lebanon, ME; H - 26, machinist, b. Townsend, MA, s/o Morris C. Welch (Townsend, MA, cooper) and Mary E. Buckley (Townsend, MA); W - 20, lady, b. Milton, d/o Elmer E. Ramsell (Gloucester, MA, teamster) and Clara E. Jordan (Wolfeboro)

Napoleon of Milton m. Florence **Codey** of Milton 3/5/1904 in Rochester; H - 21, laborer, b. So. Berwick, ME, s/o Joseph Welch (Canada, engineer) and Exzilda River (Canada); W - 18, housekeeper, b. Farmington, d/o Edward Codey and Emma Ham (Barnstead)

Wilfred D. of Milton m. Mary **Wiggin** of Lebanon, ME 12/5/1930 in S. Berwick, ME; H - 24, mill help, b. Milton, s/o Fred Dupuis (S. Berwick, ME, mill help) and Annie Marchand (Sanbornville); W - 17, mill help, b. Milton, d/o Harry Wiggin (Tuftonboro, mill help) and Mabel Drowns (Ossipee, mill help)

WENTWORTH,
Carl of Milton m. Jean **McInerney** of Rochester 6/1/1940 in Rochester; H - 22, laborer, b. Milton, s/o Homer Wentworth (Wakefield, laborer) and Marjorie Drown (Ossipee, housework); W - 21, secretary, b.

Brighton, MA, d/o John McInerney (NB, accountant) and Josephine Baker (Harwichport, MA, housework)

Charles E. of Milton m. Clara L. **Place** of Middleton 7/12/1890; H - 24, shoemaker, b. Milton, s/o Charles H. (Milton, farmer) and Arvilla (Milton, housekeeper); W - 19, lady, b. Middleton, d/o William (farmer) and Lydia (Milton, housekeeper)

Earl R. of Milton m. Virginia **Kimball** of Union 8/2/1941 in Union; H - 20, shipper, b. Wakefield, s/o Homer Wentworth (Union, mill worker) and Marjorie Drown (Wakefield, mill worker); W - 19, at home, b. Rochester, d/o George B. Kimball (Middleton, foreman) and Gladys F. Corson (Milton, deceased)

Fred S. of Acton, ME m. Mary C. **Barker** of Milton 5/2/1891 in Wakefield; H - 35, carpenter, b. New Vineyard, ME, s/o James E. (Shapleigh, ME, farmer) and Lizzie (housekeeper); W - 34, dressmaker, b. Rochester, d/o Dyer (farmer) and Matilda (housekeeper)

G. C. S. of Milton m. Alberthana **Pinkham** of Milton 1/19/1910 in Reading, MA; H - 70, retired, 3rd, wid., b. S. Berwick, ME, s/o Samuel Wentworth and Sarah Varney; W - 63, housekeeper, 2nd, wid., b. Milton, d/o Hazen Duntley (Bow) and Phoebe Leighton (Farmington)

George A. of Milton m. Maude A. **Clements** of Milton 11/28/1901; H - 33, shoemaker, b. Milton, s/o John A. Wentworth (Milton, farmer) and Hannah E. Gray (Strafford); W - 29, teacher, b. Lebanon, ME, d/o Samuel N. Clements and Charlotte L. Ingalls (Canterbury)

George C. S. of Milton m. Tryphena A. **Lord** of Milton 10/18/1893; H - 53, shoe cutter, 2nd, b. So. Berwick, ME, s/o Samuel Wentworth and Sarah; W - 48, clerk, b. W. Lebanon, ME, d/o Ezekiel R. Lord and Draxa D. (W. Lebanon, ME)

Grover C. of Milton m. Mildred **Smith** of Rochester 7/3/1948 in Dover; H - 57, box shop, 2nd, b. Milan, s/o Henry Wentworth (Portland, ME, woodsman) and Abbie Webster (Albany, housewife); W - 53, shoe shop, 3rd, b. Everett, MA, d/o Walter C. Jensen (Denmark, steam fitter) and Bessie M. Blackadar (Yarmouth, NS, housewife)

Harry of Milton m. Martha L. **Tuttle** of Milton 2/20/1948; H - 22, student, b. Milton, s/o Horace A. Wentworth (Albany, lumberman) and Sarah A. Pomfret (England, housewife); W - 21, shoe worker, b. Rochester, d/o Fred L. Tuttle (Wakefield, mill worker) and Ruth E. Dickson (Boston, MA, housewife)

Horace of Milton m. Emma M. **Nute** of Milton 7/2/1938 in Newport; H - 44, mill wright, 3rd, b. Albany, s/o Henry Wentworth (Portland, ME, deceased) and Abbie Webster (Albany, deceased); W - 36, shoe worker, 2nd, b. Newport, d/o William Barber (Canada, deceased) and Melvina Babbitt (Canada, at home)

John E. of Milton m. Ida S. **Emery** of Milton 3/23/1899 in Milton Mills; H - 42, blacksmith, 2nd, b. Milton, s/o Eli Wentworth; W - 34, shoe stitcher, 2nd, b. Waterboro, ME, d/o Stephen Chick (Ross Corner, ME, merchant)

Linwood of Lebanon, ME m. Lena A. **Smith** of Milton 10/31/1929 in Springvale, ME; H - 41, lineman, 2nd, b. Lebanon, ME, s/o William Wentworth (Lebanon, ME, mason) and Emily Kenney (Lebanon, ME); W - 23, housekeeper, b. Alton, d/o Albert Smith (Alton, teamster) and Cora B. Richardson (Alton)

Thomas C. of Milton m. Linda J. **Arsenault** of Rochester 5/7/1983 in Rochester

Timothy W. of Milton m. Patricia M. **Doyon** of Rochester 7/16/1977 in Rochester; H - b. 10/4/1953; W - b. 4/5/1959

Wilber of Milton m. Etta M. **Hall** of Milton 9/5/1891; H - 23, shoemaker, b. Farmington, s/o George E. and Emma E. (Milton, housekeeper); W - 22, shoe stitcher, b. Dover, d/o Charles (dead) and Lizzie (housekeeper)

WEST,
Carl B. of Beebille, OH m. Marie T. **Vachon** of Milton 9/2/1972 in Sanbornville; H - b. 4/16/1951; W - b. 4/26/1952

WESTCOTT,
Brian R. of North Kingstown, RI m. Joyce E. **Grinnell** of Milton 9/6/1969 in Sanbornville; H - b. 1/20/1945; W - b. 3/31/1948

WESTPHAL,
Mark R. of Milton m. Donna M. **Turcotte** of Milton 7/20/1996

WHEELER,
Mark A. of Milton m. Karen L. **McVicar** of Milton 11/8/1986
Walter A., Jr. of Rochester m. Jane B. **Doliber** of Milton 2/16/1991

WHIPPLE,
Fred E. of Rochester m. Cora B. **Welch** of Milton 11/19/1905; H - 36, farmer, b. Rochester, s/o John Whipple (Moultonboro) and Mary D. Smith (Moultonboro); W - 43, nurse, 2nd, b. Ossipee, d/o Daniel Kimball (Ossipee) and Zulema Chase (Parsonsfield, ME)

WHITCOMB,
Howard H. of Milton m. Ruth B. **McGuire** of Rochester 3/18/1972 in Rochester; H - b. 2/21/1944; W - b. 9/1/1943

WHITE,
Arthur J. of Milton m. Linda F. **Coggeshall** of Milton 4/24/1993
Brian N. of Milton m. Tammie R. **Pebeahsy** of Lawton, OK 4/2/1990
Brian N. of Milton m. Candis L. **Magee** of Vidor, TX 8/14/1993
Charles H., Jr. of Wakefield m. Gloria F. **Allaman** of Milton 4/22/1978; H - b. 4/17/1956; W - b. 1/1/1956
William F. of Milton m. Mary E. **Perkins** of Milton 7/8/1914; H - 33, emp. in mill, 2nd, b. Boston, MA, s/o William White (Boston, MA, mechanic) and Elizabeth Hervey (Brighton, MA); W - 17, housework, b. Berwick, ME, d/o William W. Perkins (Dover, carpenter) and Evelyn M. Allen (So. Berwick, ME)

WHITEHOUSE,
Charles R. of Milton m. Ruth Elsie **Staples** of Milton 2/19/1921; H - 27, laborer, b. Portsmouth, s/o Nicholas W. Whitehouse (Middleton, laborer) and Margaret M. Cassidy (Boston, MA); W - 17, student, b. Milton, d/o Harry W. Staples (Milton, farmer) and Henrietta M. Sigler (New York, NY)
Daniel H. of Lebanon, ME m. Pauline **Baker** of Milton 7/29/1933 in Rochester; H - 20, mechanic, b. Lebanon, ME, s/o Herbert F. Whitehouse (Berwick, ME, merchant) and Eva M. Burke (Wolfeboro, housewife); W - 19, mill op., b. Moultonboro, d/o Paul F. Baker (Tilton, cook) and Bertha Evans (Moultonboro, housewife)
Donald of Milton m. Barbara A. **Michalski** of Milton 9/18/1999
Eugene W., Jr. of Milton m. Michele A. **Trainor** of Milton 5/6/1995
John W. of Milton m. Grace M. **Thurston** of Effingham 9/17/1923 in Wolfeboro; H - 20, laborer, b. Farmington, s/o Nicholas Whitehouse (Middleton, laborer) and Margaret Cassidy (Boston, MA); W - 18, at

home, b. Effingham, d/o Edward Thurston (Effingham, laborer) and Sidney Stokes (Effingham)

Paul A. of Milton Mills m. Ella M. **St. Laurent** of Milton Mills 11/8/1986 in Rochester

Ralph H. of Milton m. Bonibell I. **DeMeritt** of Milton 11/9/1912; H - 19, shoemaker, b. Wolfeboro, s/o Charles Whitehouse (So. Berwick, ME) and Mary B. Hodgdon (Tuftonboro); W - 18, b. Milton, d/o Berthold I. DeMeritt (Newfield, ME, foreman) and Musetta A. Dorr (Dover)

Ralph T. of Milton m. Arleene L. **Frechette** of Milton 11/26/1977; H - b. 5/21/1956; W - b. 11/6/1955

Stephen J. of Rochester m. Betty L. **York** of Milton 7/7/1979

WHITMAN,

Ward B. of Plymouth, MA m. Carlyne P. **Dickson** of Milton 9/2/1928; H - 23, floorman, b. Stonington, ME, s/o Newell Whitman (Armenia, clergyman) and Edith Fifield (Stonington, ME); W - 20, at home, b. Milton, d/o William A. Dickson (Lunenburg, MA, supt. mill) and Hattie Newell (Harvard, MA)

WHITMORE,

Paul J. of Portland, ME m. Karen J. **Parker** of Milton 6/25/1977 in Concord; H - b. 4/1/1950; W - b. 8/25/1951

WHITNALL,

Leroy of Westerville, OH m. Eleanor T. **Tanner** of Milton 12/26/1925; H - 26, iron worker, b. Constitution, OH, s/o Charles E. Whitnall (minister) and Elizabeth Leigh (Harpers Ferry, WV); W - 24, at home, b. Wakefield, d/o Hervey E. Tanner (Farmington, carpenter) and Mary O'Haire (Ireland)

WHITTEN,

Willis D. of Milton Mills m. Janet E. **Keeney** of Milton Mills 9/1/1990

Willis D. of Milton Mills m. Shirley F. **Veino** of Milton Mills 5/14/1994

WICHER,

Edgar R. of Sanford, ME m. L. Frances **Pease** of Sanford, ME 12/6/1936 in Milton Mills; H - 20, mill worker, b. Alfred, ME, s/o Ansel C. Whicher (sic) (Sanford, ME, mill wkr.) and Fannie A. Swett

(Sanford, ME, mill wkr.); W - 19, housekeeper, b. Cornish, ME, d/o
Ralph M. Pease (Cornish, ME, retired) and Bertha M. Chick
(Cornish, ME, housekeeper)

WIEBELHAUS,
Virgil F. of Salem, MA m. Marie D. F. **Soucy** of Salem, MA 4/21/1946; H
- 31, contractor, b. Hart'ton, NE, s/o Joseph Wiebelhaus (Hartington, NE, retired) and Johanna Minke (Germany, retired); W - 31, unemployed, 2nd, b. Salem, MA, d/o Lorenzo Soucy (Canada, retired) and Antoinette Dumont (Canada, deceased)

WIGGIN,
Albert L. of Milton m. Marlene S. **Dent** of Dover 11/28/1953 in Rochester; H - 18, shoe shop, b. NH, s/o Luther D. Wiggin and Irene E. Tatro; W - 18, M & M bakery, b. ME, d/o George F. Dent and Iona M. Garvey
Bradley M. of Lebanon, ME m. Patricia A. **Moody** of Milton 3/23/1956 in Lebanon, ME; H - 19, shoe worker, b. ME, s/o Raymond Wiggin and Anita Gerry; W - 18, clerk, b. NH, d/o Alfred H. Moody and Alice M. Phinney
Elmer A. of Milton Mills m. Elizabeth C. **Jenkner** of Auburn, MA 12/1/1933 in Milton Mills; H - 32, textile op., b. Acton, ME, s/o Albert E. Wiggin (Acton, ME, gas sta. atd.) and Cora E. Day (Newfield, ME, housewife); W - 20, textile op., b. Worcester, MA, d/o Richard M. Jenkner (Wiel'fels, Germany, machinist) and Elizabeth Eilmers (Stan'h'm, Germany, housewife)
Luther E. of Wakefield m. Carrie E. **Wentworth** of Milton 6/20/1895 in Milton Mills; H - 29, lumber dealer, b. Boston, MA; W - 20, b. Milton
Maurice E. of Milton m. Mary E. **Cooke** of Wakefield 5/12/1917 in Sanbornville; H - 21, emp. in mill, b. Tuftonboro, s/o John W. Wiggin (Wakefield, laborer) and Mary A. Elliott (Tuftonboro); W - 20, emp. in mill, b. Wakefield, d/o Elmer Cook (sic) (Wenham, MA, teamster) and Lillian Clow (Wolfeboro)

WILBAR,
Carl P. of Brockton, MA m. Allie M. **Hodgdon** of Milton 6/29/1898; H - 24, shoemaker, b. Brockton, MA, s/o Dexter E. Wilbar (Brockton,

MA, shoe mfgr.); W - 24, lady, b. Milton, d/o George F. Hodgdon (Boston, MA, painter)

WILDER,

Robert F. of Wakefield m. Doris M. **Page** of Milton 5/16/1920 in Rochester; H - 23, lineman, b. Dennysville, ME, s/o Charles E. Wilder (Dennysville, ME, carpenter) and Margaret M. Farnsworth (Pembroke, ME); W - 25, tel. operator, b. Milton, d/o George W. Page (Dalton, laborer) and Jennette A. Rines (Milton)

WILKINS,

Arthur W. of Milton m. Violet M. **Sliney** of Milton 7/13/1922 in Union; H - 27, carder, b. Acton, ME, s/o Homer W. Wilkins (Acton, ME, farmer) and Mary B. Hutchins (Wakefield); W - 22, weaver, 2nd, b. Skowhegan, ME, d/o Seth M. Devol (Brighton, MA, laborer) and Teresa McCollor (Bingham, ME)

Arthur W. of Milton m. Minnie E. **Feeney** of Milton 7/3/1947 in Farmington; H - 52, weaver, 2nd, b. Acton, ME, s/o Homer W. Wilkins (Acton, ME, farmer) and Mary B. Hutchins (S. Wakefield, housewife); W - 54, weaver, 2nd, b. Sanford, ME, d/o Elmer F. Hersom (Lebanon, ME, lumberman) and Emily J. Wilson (Fall River, MA)

Richard R. of Milton m. Irma L. **Wilkins** of Milton 8/30/1939 in Berwick, ME; H - 21, shoe worker, b. Farmington, s/o Salon Wilkins (Ossipee, deceased) and Grace Haddock (Ossipee, shoe worker); W - 20, shoe worker, 2nd, b. Springvale, ME, d/o Dean A. Place (Middleton, shoe worker) and Lena Bachelder (Springvale, ME, shoe worker)

WILKINSON,

Durwood F. of Milton Mills m. Linda M. **Worster** of Wakefield 7/8/1966 in Wakefield; H - 21, construction worker; W - 18, at home

Melbourne of Milton Mills m. Carlene E. **Gould** of Milton Mills 8/16/1960 in Milton Mills; H - 20, shipping clerk; W - 18, waitress

Melbourne A., Jr. of Milton Mills m. Betty L. **Ferris** of Sanford, ME 11/4/1966; H - 26, foreman; W - 25, marker

Wilfred A. of Middleton m. Nellie E. **Wood** of Milton Mills 7/21/1960 in Rochester; H - 47, truck driver; W - 49, tannery

WILLEY,
Glendon L. of Milton m. Susan C. **Scott** of Portland, ME 12/20/1968; H - 18; W - 24

Herbert F. of Milton m. Winifred **Pearce** of Syracuse, NY 7/24/1943 in Keene; H - 22, US Navy, b. Milton, s/o James H. Willey (Salmon Falls, druggist) and Grace Fletcher (Cape Neddick, ME, housewife); W - 23, H. E. teacher, b. Syracuse, NY, d/o Wilbur E. Pearce (Delhi, NY, inspector) and Kathleen Sweeney (Little Falls, NY, girl scout dir.)

James H. of Milton m. Grace C. **Fletcher** of Waterville, ME 1/4/1919 in Waterville, ME; H - 43, druggist, b. Rollinsford, s/o James P. Willey (Wakefield, retired) and Frances P. Savis (Trenton, ME); W - 22, teacher, b. Cape Neddick, ME, d/o William Fletcher (Newport, clergyman) and Winnifred E. Roundy (Hermon, ME)

Moses D. of Milton m. Maria **Mattress** of Acton, ME 7/24/1917 in Milton Mills; H - 62, carpenter, 2nd, b. Salem, MA, s/o James L. Willey (Acton, ME) and Mary A. Applebee (Milton); W - 62, housekeeper, 2nd, b. Ossipee, d/o Samuel Williams (NS) and Esther Welch (Ossipee)

Nelson F. of Milton m. Haroldine P. **Howe** of Milton 12/–/1948; H - 39, mill worker, 2nd, b. Wakefield, s/o Clarence D. Willey (Wakefield, farmer) and Charlotte Twombly (Wakefield, housewife); W - 23, shoe worker, 2nd, b. Oxford, ME, d/o Harold Gagne (Oxford, ME, farmer) and Fay Cousins (Lewiston, ME, housewife)

Paul G. of Manchester m. Irene L. **Whitehouse** of Milton 9/25/1948; H - 27, insurance, b. Manchester, s/o Howard M. Willey (Auburn, dry cleaner) and Julia Cunningham (W. River Jct., VT, housewife); W - 24, telephone opr., b. Milton, d/o Charles R. Whitehouse (Portsmouth, truck driver) and Ruth E. Staples (Milton, housewife)

Richard M. of Milton m. Cecelia L. **Colby** of Rochester 11/22/1947 in Rochester; H - 27, Navy Yard, b. Milton, s/o Leon M. Willey (Brookfield, Navy Yard) and Flora Downs (Milton, housewife); W - 33, beautician, 3rd, b. Rochester, d/o Louis Carter (Cambridge, MA, retired) and Herminni M. Courtici (Canada, housewife)

WILLIAMS,
Anthony R. of Milton m. Judith H. **Michaud** of Milton 9/12/1986

Arnold of Milton m. Claire E. **Montgomery** of Milton 7/5/1954; H - 18, US Army, b. Rochester, s/o Shaber Williams and Myrtle Ellis; W -

18, at home, b. Rochester, d/o Melvin Montgomery and Ruth Wentworth
Hugh D. of Truckee, CA m. Denise R. **Heon** of Truckee, CA 5/30/1992
Jefferson of Milton m. Gertrude A. **Smith** of Milton 9/5/1942; H - 42, wood chopper, 3rd, b. Ossipee, s/o Frank P. Williams (Ossipee, retired) and Sarah J. Eldridge (Ossipee, houskeeper); W - 37, housewife, 2nd, b. Strafford, d/o Edgar E. Huckins (Madbury, deceased) and Addie M. Hill (Strafford, deceased)
Jeffrey A. of Milton m. Carolyn D. **Smith** of Milton 8/20/1994
Mark A. of Milton m. Madolyn L. **Warner** of Kennebunk, ME 8/10/1985
Ralph, Jr. of Milton m. Jacqueline L. **Marcoux** of Rochester 3/5/1954 in Wakefield; H - 30, unemployed, 2nd, b. Milton, s/o Ralph A. Williams and Lillian McCarten; W - 15, at home, b. Rochester, d/o Alfred Marcoux and Mary Maddox
Ralph A. of Milton m. Eleanor P. **Smart** of Farmington 2/14/1950 in Farmington; H - 26, US Army, b. Tamworth, s/o Ralph J. Williams (Tamworth) and Lillian McCarton (Ireland); W - 20, at home, 3rd, b. Franklin, MA, d/o George A. Fulton (Franklin, MA) and Eleanor P. Howard (Farmington)
Ralph J. of Milton m. Lillian **McCarten** of Milton 9/1/1923; H - 22, laborer, b. Tamworth, s/o William H. Williams (Tamworth, retired) and Susie Welch (Ossipee); W - 23, emp. in mill, b. Ireland, d/o Dennis McCarten (Ireland, laborer) and Janet Doran (Ireland)
Shaber W. of Milton m. Myrtle M. **Ellis** of Milton 11/15/1933; H - 36, mill op., b. Ossipee, s/o William H. Williams (Ossipee, lumberman) and Susie Welch (Ossipee); W - 26, mill op., b. Milton, d/o George E. Ellis (Wolfeboro, laborer) and Inez G. Duntley (Milton, mill op.)
William E. of Milton m. Lisa M. **Verville** of Milton 2/9/1991

WILLIS,
Perley of Milton m. Alice **Douquette** of Milton 3/31/1925 in Dover; H - 24, laborer, b. St. Albans, VT, s/o George Willis (E. Richford, VT, laborer) and Carrie Perry (St. Albans, VT); W - 17, at home, b. Milton, d/o Leon Douquette (Canada, fireman) and Emma Hall (Canada)

WILLS,
Glen A. of Nantucket, MA m. Heidi L. **Drew** of Milton 10/19/1986 in Meredith

WILSON,
Charles W., Jr. of Milton m. Lucille E. **Druecker** of Alexandria, VA 5/10/1949; H - 31, US Army, 2nd, b. Portland, ME, s/o Charles W. Wilson (ME) and Florence E. Blake (ME); W - 31, clerk, b. MO, d/o August Druecker (Germany) and Clara Schurinke (IA)

Danny R. of Milton m. Lindi L. **Defalco** of Milton 7/20/1996

Gary A. of Milton m. Molly A. **Perkins** of Milton 6/21/1986

James O. of Rochester m. Vaina A. **Filgate** of Milton 3/28/1953 in Rochester; H - 26, salesman, 2nd, b. NH, s/o George F. Wilson and Beatrice Osborne; W - 24, nurse, b. NH, d/o William P. Filgate and Margaret Lover

Lester A. of Wakefield m. Joanne L. **Dupuis** of Milton 9/1/1962; H - 19, laborer; W - 18, shoe worker

Robert H. of Bedford, MA m. Evamae **Marsh** of Lebanon, ME 10/4/1958; H - 26, USAF, b. Dover, s/o Elizabeth Williamson (VT); W - 22, home dem. agt., b. Rochester, d/o Ithill E. Marsh (ME) and Mary E. Whitehouse (NH)

Ronald R. of Milton m. Elizabeth **Bodenstedt** of Milton 6/15/1989

WILVER,
Gene M. of Milton m. Barbara E. **Balestrier** of Milton 12/31/1992

WINKLEY,
Forrest of Strafford m. Thelma W. **Feeny** of Milton Mills 1/1/1938 in C. Strafford; H - 25, truck driver, b. Strafford, s/o Hiram Winkley (Strafford, farmer) and Carrie Preston (Barrington, at home); W - 20, at home, b. Milton Mills, d/o Preston H. Feeny (Saugus, MA, mill oper.) and Minnie Hersam (Sanford, ME, at home)

WINTON,
Kenneth A. of East Wakefield m. Paula J. **Vachon** of Milton 9/16/1972; H - b. 12/16/1950; W - b. 8/23/1954

WITHAM,
Arthur R. of Acton, ME m. Margaret F. **Day** of Milton 4/28/1919 in Acton, ME; H - 22, farmer, b. Acton, ME, s/o Josiah W. Witham (Acton, ME, farmer) and Georgianna Sanborn (Acton, ME); W - 17, weaver, b. Newfield, ME, d/o John L. Day (Shapleigh, ME, laborer) and Susan B. Patch (Limerick, ME)

Ernest F. of Milton m. Marguerite A. **Cooley** of Milton 12/24/1917 in Rochester; H - 22, emp. in mill, b. Kittery, ME, s/o George W. Witham (Boston, MA, carpenter) and Arabella Goodspeed (Gardiner, ME); W - 19, at home, b. Wilmington, MA, d/o David F. Cooley (Boston, MA) and Bessie L. Stevens (Saco, ME)

Perley D. of Milton m. Mabel **Woodman** of Milton 4/25/1900 in Alton; H - 24, shoemaker, b. Milton, s/o Everett Witham (Milton, farmer) and Jennie Colomy (Newfield, ME); W - 19, weaver, b. Alton, d/o Henry Woodman (New Durham, farmer) and Susan E. Chamberlin

Robert R. of Rochester m. Connie L. **Meserve** of Milton 9/14/1968; H - 22; W - 20

WOOD,

Kirby R. of Milton m. Joyce **Nutter** of Farmington 8/18/1990 in Farmington

Neal D. of Milton m. Lori A. **Entwistle** of Milton 8/5/1989

WOODBURY,

Ernest P. of Rochester m. Norma R. **Burroughs** of Milton 9/3/1955; H - 27, shoe worker, b. Rochester, s/o Carl Woodbury and Gladys Andrews; W - 18, shoe worker, b. Rochester, d/o Wilfred Burroughs and Emily Wallingford

Stephen H. of Milton m. Eleanor S. **Connorton** of Milton 8/27/1950 in Acton, ME; H - 22, radio tech., b. Milton, s/o William E. Woodbury (Hudson) and Doris Horne (Milton); W - 19, at home, b. Melrose, MA, d/o William H. Connorton (Somerville, MA) and Hilda Hillsman (Everett, MA)

William of Durham m. Doris M. **Horne** of Milton 6/25/1922 in Wakefield; H - 25, farmer, b. Hudson, s/o Edgar C. Woodbury (Londonderry, carpenter) and Eva J. Wheeler (Nashua); W - 22, teacher, b. Milton, d/o John E. Horne (Acton, ME, merchant) and Olive A. Moulton (Newfield, ME)

WOODILL,

Rodney J. of Milton m. Dolores E. **Ellis** of Milton 7/24/1976; H - b. 10/18/1957; W - b. 10/7/1956

Roland L. of Worcester, MA m. Julie A. **Hart** of Long Beach, CA 2/12/1966; H - 23, welder; W - 20, office clerk

WOODRUFF,
David R. of W. Concord, MA m. Janet **Tibbetts** of Milton 8/27/1960; H - 25, ass't mgr.; W - 25, teacher

WOODRUM,
Glenn M. of Milton m. Joy L. **Bostrom** of Milton 7/4/1991

WOODWARD,
Steven R. of Milton m. Lisa M. **Raymond** of Milton 8/8/1998

WOOTEN,
Charles E. of Milton m. Jennie **Wentworth** of Milton 12/27/1910; H - 20, vamper, b. London, England, s/o Osborne C. Wooten (England, mason) and Alice Huggett (England); W - 23, shoe stitcher, b. Milton, d/o Charles S. Wentworth (Milton, farmer) and Hattie Patch (Newfield, ME)

WORMHOOD,
Herbert of Rochester m. Elizabeth A. **Cleveland** of Milton 8/24/1945 in Portsmouth; H - 72, carpenter, 2nd, b. Ossipee, s/o Charles Wormhood (Kennebunk, ME, painter) and Huldah Eldridge; W - 72, housewife, 2nd, b. Lynn, MA, d/o R. W. Walker (Manchester) and Emily F. Beedee (Sandwich)

WORSTER,
Don H. of Milton m. Marie A. **McPherson** of Farmington 6/26/1971; H - b. 8/23/1952; W - b. 3/12/1951

WRIGHT,
Edward of Milton m. Lulie M. **Rowe** of Milton 2/15/1899; H - 22, paper maker, b. Hadley, NY, s/o John Wright (Hadley, NY, barber); W - 18, lady, b. Lebanon, ME, d/o David T. Rowe
Kevin J. of Epping m. Rose Anna **Dumas** of Milton 7/24/1981
Robert M. of Milton m. Mary E. **Yardley** of Milton 7/29/1977; H - b. 6/15/1947; W - b. 8/7/1949

WUESTHOFF,
Raphael J. of Boston, MA m. Betty J. **Bowen** of Boston, MA 7/3/1965; H - 27, student; W - 25, teacher

WYATT,
Clarence T., Jr. of Milton m. Carmen A. **Hamel** of Gonic 9/9/1967 in Rochester; H - 22, laborer; W - 20, factory worker
Clarence T., Sr. of Milton m. Merlyn E. **Appleton** of Milton 6/15/1991
Edgar J. of Farmington m. Hattie E. **DeWolfe** of Milton 4/25/1903; H - 31, teamster, b. Farmington, s/o Asa Wyatt (Farmington, farmer) and Arabella C. Ricker (Milton); W - 34, housekeeper, 2nd, b. Milton, d/o Luther Hayes (Milton, farmer) and Sarah D. Coffran (Milton)
Richard D. of Rochester m. Marion P. **Currier** of Milton Mills 6/29/1973; H - b. 9/9/1946; W - b. 10/14/1949

WYETH,
John H. of Dover m. Linda A. **St. Hilaire** of Milton 9/18/1993

YEATON,
Maurice A. of Epsom m. Nettie P. **Holmes** of Milton 6/23/1928 in Milton Mills; H - 22, farmer, b. Epsom, s/o Samuel R. Yeaton (Epsom, farmer) and Mabel E. Stewart (Epsom); W - 21, school tchr., b. Milton, d/o Clarence Holmes (Buxton, ME, prin., HS) and Winnifred B. Dorr (Milton)

YOUNG,
Albert of Rochester m. Nellie S. **Wiggin** of Acton, ME 9/7/1897 in Wakefield; H - 17, shoemaker, b. Lebanon, ME, s/o Charles Young (Lebanon, ME, carpenter); W - 16, shoe stitcher, b. Acton, ME, d/o Mark Wiggin (Milton, farmer)
David W. of Milton m. Lavina B. **Fifield** of Milton 8/29/1964 in Winchendon, MA; H - 43, carpenter; W - 33, homemaker
Ivory H. of Milton m. Alfreda M. **Carindon** of Milton 5/9/1956 in Rochester; H - 28, truck driver, b. Rochester, s/o Ivory L. Young and Nancy E. Brock; W - 26, housewife, 2nd, b. Rochester, d/o Albert W. Smith and Iona Richardson

YURICK,
Joseph S., Jr. of Somersworth m. Deborah E. **Bickford** of Milton 7/14/1979

ZANGARINE,
Dennis A., Sr. of Milton m. Tammy A. **Tripp** of Milton 8/17/1996

ZELLER,
Kurt P. of Milton m. Kimberly A. **Jenness** of Milton 10/31/1990

ZEOLI,
Vincent D. of Milton m. Ann G. **Morganelli** of Milton 10/12/1979

ZERBINOPOULOS,
Lance T. of Milton m. Holly A. **King** of Acton, ME 10/29/1994

DEATHS

[UNKNOWN],
male, d. 7/14/1896 at 35; run over by train

ABBOTT,
Arthur B., d. 2/12/1941 at 59/3/29 in Lynn, MA
Clifton O., d. 4/2/1976 at 70; machine operator; b. NH; Wilbur F. Abbott and Florence Cook
Eva W., d. 12/3/1943 at 65/0/20 in Lynn, MA
Florence I., d. 4/22/1954 at 71/3/10 in North Conway; housewife; widow; b. Ossipee; James Cook and Mary Bunker
Gertrude A., d. 11/29/1980 in Rochester; Alexander Miles and Violetta Hutchinson
Ralph Emerson, d. 2/5/1990 in Wolfeboro
Wilbur F., d. 2/10/1949 at 69/8/23 in Fryeburg, ME

ABRAMS,
John L., d. 6/9/1935 at 83/9/28 in Dover
Mary J., d. 3/22/1956 at 80 in Boston, MA

ADAMS,
Grant L., d. 8/13/1965 at 69 in Manchester; manager, ret.; b. Bedford, PQ; James Adams and Jennie Carter
Robert R., d. 4/18/1985 in Dover; Joseph Adams and Mary Carver

ADJUTANT,
child, d. 1/7/1966 at 1 hr. in Rochester
child, d. 1/7/1966 at 1 hr. in Rochester
son, d. 8/22/1968 at 6 hrs. in Wolfeboro; b. NH; Ronald H. Adjutant and Susan E. Kelly
Carl, d. 2/25/1969 at 74 in Rochester
Ervin F., d. 7/20/1981 in Rochester
Evelyn G., d. 8/2/1973 at 62 in Wolfeboro
Foster W., d. 8/13/1994 in Acton, ME
Jennie M., d. 3/7/1963 at 67 in Wolfeboro
Joseph C., d. 8/21/1979 in Wolfeboro
Lester Ervin, d. 2/18/1992 in Sanbornville
Rachel White, d. 10/8/1992 in Acton, ME
Russell D., d. 4/14/1984 in Sanford, ME

Scott P., d. 5/20/1970 at 0/0/0 in Rochester; b. Rochester; Ronald H.
Adjutant and Susan E. Kelly

AGRI,
Joseph M., d. 4/9/1990 in Milton; Michael Agri and Lucy Bencale

ALDRICH,
Ethel M., d. 10/18/1987 in Rochester; John Ballard and Nettie Munson
William R., d. 7/10/1993 in Dover; Averill Aldrich and Agnes Ray

ALLARD,
Aileen L., d. 5/16/1994 in Portland, ME
Antoinette M., d. 8/14/1997 in Dover; Charles F. Descary
Normand D., d. 9/15/1986 in Portland, ME
Paul A., d. 3/23/1980; Louis Allard and Rose Blis

ALLEN,
Annie E., d. 6/5/1908 at 0/0/1; premature birth; b. Milton; George W.
Allen (Wakefield) and Hattie M. Cook (Brookfield)
Katherine A., d. 6/18/1948 at 78/7/26 in Lowell, MA
Mary H., d. 12/15/1913 at 0/1/12; asphyxia accidental; John M. Allen
(Ireland) and Sarah Shackford (Gorham, ME)

AMAZEEN,
Abigail, d. 3/19/1905 at 75/11/9; bronchitis; widow; b. Milton; William
Wentworth and Abigail
Henry C., d. 4/29/1897; cancer; farmer; married; b. New Castle; William
Amazeen and Jane Jones
Warren, d. 5/14/1929 at 7/11/21; student; b. Milton; Walter Amazeen
(Milton) and Lillian F. Parkhurst (Lynnhurst, MA)

AMES,
Frank H., d. 5/26/1964 at 69; cem. caretaker; b. Rochester; William Ames
and Lydia York
Ida M., d. 5/27/1977 at 67 in Rochester; homemaker; b. NH; Elmer
Junkins and Jessie Remick

AMORY,
Henry F., d. 9/11/1932 at 73/9/6; salesman; married; b. Medford, MA; George Amory (Marblehead, MA) and Lydia Skinner (Malden, MA)

ANDERSEN,
Marion D., d. 4/26/1994 in Santa Paula, CA (1995)

ANDERSON,
Hazel A., d. 7/6/1958 at 60; housewife; married; b. Middleton; Harry O. Perkins and Lena G. LaBonte
Hazel D., d. 7/30/1973 at 75 in Sanford, ME
Maude B., d. 3/12/1964 at 69 in Rochester; housewife; b. Mansfield, MA; Earl Baker and Vesta Morse
Raymond C., d. 12/21/1976 at 80 in Portland, ME

ANDREWS,
Eva T., d. 7/14/1982; Joseph Trottier and Marie -----
Joseph, d. 7/23/1938 at 76/4/3 in Dover; laborer; widower; b. SD; Joseph Andrews (Black Hill, SD) and Mary ----- (Black Hill, SD)
Rose A., d. 2/7/1926 at 66/11/10 in Milton Mills; housewife; married; b. North Parsonsfield, ME; Edmond Chase (No. Parsonsfield, ME) and Ruth Edwards (No. Parsonsfield, ME)
Rose E., d. 6/11/1948 at 81/11/8 in Union; housewife; widow; b. New Durham; Charles H. Rhines (New Durham) and Sarah L. Boston
Russell J., d. 4/9/1966 at 77; foundryman; b. Canada; James O. Andrews and Ella Wentworth

ANGELL,
Harold G., d. 8/14/1932 at 73/10/17 in Rochester; single; b. Yonkers, NY; Henry F. Angell and Annie B. Jackson (Providence, RI)

ANNIS,
Ai S., d. 2/23/1927 at 70/1/25; grocer; widower; b. Bethlehem; Amasa Annis (Bath) and Mercy Palmer (Lunenburg, VT)
Lucy M., d. 1/18/1925 at 55/7/13; housewife; married; b. Roxbury, VT; William Henry Walbridge (Roxbury, VT) and Hannie Burnham (Roxbury, VT)

APPLEBEE,
Charles H., d. 9/19/1946 at 83/9/23 in Franklin; mill worker; widower; b. Milton; William H. Applebee (Milton) and Susan Miller (Acton, ME)
Esther M., d. 3/30/1986 in Ossipee
James W., d. 1/13/1931 at 86/6/4 in Lynn, MA; retired; married; b. Milton; James Applebee (Milton) and Sally Rines (Alton)
John S., d. 11/6/1902 at 65/7/23; cirrhosis of liver; farmer; widower; b. Milton; James Applebee (Milton) and Sally Rines (Milton)
Sally F., d. 2/20/1917 at 80/11; widow; b. Acton, ME; John Miller (Acton, ME) and Lydia Varnham (Acton, ME)
Sarah, d. 7/14/1935 at 86/0/18; housekeeper; married; b. Salem, MA; Lyman Willey (Acton, ME) and Mary A. Applebee (Milton Mills)
Sarah E., d. 3/18/1900 at 61/9; fatty degeneration of heart; housekeeper; married; b. Wakefield; Joseph Evans (Madbury) and Abigail Pickering (Wakefield)

APPLETON,
Roland R., d. 12/18/1990 in Dover; Roland L. Appleton and Lillian V. Taylor

ARCHIBALD,
Alzina, d. 8/5/1924 at 75; retired; married; b. Newfield, ME; Lafayette Davis (ME) and Mary Burnham (Parsonsfield, ME)
Ecelyn M., d. 10/10/1980 in Wolfeboro; John J. Hines and Ida B. Otis
George D., d. 4/1/1896 at 39/7/7; tuberculosis; spinner; married; b. Milton; J. W. Archibald (Acton, ME) and Mary Waldron (Acton, ME)
Hannah H., d. 11/27/1942 at 87/11/3; housewife; widow; b. Exeter; Jabez Greenleaf (Effingham) and Hulda Rowell (Exeter)
J. Frank, d. 6/12/1924 at 72/1/14; retired; married; b. Milton; John Archibald and Mary Waldron
Mary, d. 10/8/1898 at 77/0/9; apoplexy; housekeeper; widow; b. Acton, ME; Stephen Waldron (Acton, ME) and Hannah Horne (Acton, ME)
Mott L., d. 8/19/1953 at 79; carpenter; single; b. Acton, ME; Reuben Archibald and Abzina Davis
Stewart G., d. 4/6/1976 at 78; lumberman; b. Canada; Ambrose Aulenback and Janet -----

ARIGO,
Rosario, d. 12/8/1983 in Rochester; Giacomo Arigo and Pasquelina Aloisi

ARKERSON,
Leonard E., III, d. 2/2/1969 at 17; student; b. Lawrence, MA; Leonard E. Arkerson and Gladys M. Blood

ARLIN,
John, d. 9/23/1905 at 56; apoplexy; farmer; widower

ARLING,
John, d. 6/6/1999 in Rochester; John Arling and Mildred Kaulback

ARMSTEAD,
Henry or Harry E., d. 4/11/1962 at 73; factory; b. Lynn, MA; Henry P. Armstead and Everetta Rich

Maud E., d. 3/29/1971 at 84 in Milton Mills; secretary; b. MA; Harry Armstead and Evie Tufts

ARMSTRONG,
Dana W., d. 12/28/1974 at 60 in Rochester; marine machinist; b. ME; Lester Armstrong and Clara Ingalls

AUSTIN,
Gladys M., d. 8/22/1959 at 77 in Rochester; retired; divorced; b. Peru, ME; Sumner Knox and Mary E. Martin

AVERY,
Brackett F., d. 5/30/1911 at 82/10/7; chronic valv. heart; farmer; widower; b. Wolfeboro; Walter Avery (Wolfeboro) and Sallie Cotton (Wolfeboro)

Elsie G., d. 2/6/1902 at 19/9/9; typhoid fever; student; single; b. Milton; Joseph H. Avery (Acton, ME) and Emma C. Hanscom (Milton)

Emma, d. 1/10/1990 in South Windsor, CT

Emma B., d. 6/3/1949 at 82; housewife; widow; b. Lawrence, MA; Edward Getchell and Cynthia Shaw

Emma C., d. 11/14/1933 at 81/11/6 in Milton Mills; housewife; married; b. Milton; James Hanscam (Milton) and Sarah Jones (Milton)

Flora F., d. 3/22/1942 at 64/3; housewife; married; b. Milton; Walter S. Tibbetts (New Durham) and Harriett Downing (Milton)

Harry L., d. 9/30/1936 at 72/8/2; merchant; widower; b. Milton; Brackett Avery (Wolfeboro) and Susan Varney (Milton)

Hattie L., d. 12/21/1922 at 63/10/23; at home; married; b. Milton; Nathaniel G. Pinkham (Milton) and Emily C. Corliss (Sandwich)

John S., d. 11/15/1954 at 69 in Rochester; farmer; widower; b. Barnstead; John Avery and Mary Staples

John W., d. 2/5/1936 at 66/6/18; shoe cutter; married; b. Wolfeboro; Brackett Avery (Wolfeboro) and Susan Varney (Milton)

Joseph H., d. 9/27/1937 at 93/2/28; ret. merchant; widower; b. Acton, ME; John Avery (Acton, ME)

Louise P., d. 5/12/1942 at 44/11/20; town clerk; single; b. Milton; Harry Avery (Milton) and Hattie Pinkham (Milton)

May E., d. 3/12/1948 at 78/11/19 in Wakefield

Norman E., d. 10/29/1954 at 34 in Rochester; accountant; single; b. Laconia; Theron Avery and Emma Piper

Oscar, d. 11/27/1945 at 80/6/11 in Barrington; farmer; widower; b. Barnstead; Stephen Avery (Rumney) and Mary Straw (Rumney)

Sallie C., d. 2/26/1960 at 92 in Rochester; practical nurse; b. Wolfeboro; Brackett F. Avery and Susan Varney

Susan V., d. 1/2/1895 at 70/1/25; cardiac dropsy; housekeeper; married; b. Milton; John H. Varney (Milton) and Betsy Cloutman

Theron W., d. 4/26/1965 at 69 in Manchester, CT

AYER,

Charlotte H., d. 12/29/1946 at 83/1/24; mgr. tel. o.; widow; b. New York, NY; Henry Hanscom (E. Wakefield) and Mariah Edwards (London, England)

Gladys H., d. 9/26/1966 at 67 in Wolfeboro; tel. exch. agt.; b. Maplewood, ME; Eugene Ayer and Charlotte Hanscom

Hannah T., d. 2/25/1907 at 63/10/10; meningitis; housework; single; b. Newfield, ME; Lewis Ayer (Newfield, ME) and Nancy Tibbetts (Newfield, ME)

Harry E., d. 9/10/1935 at 82/5 in Milton Mills; retired; married; b. Newfield, ME; Lewis Ayer (Newfield, ME) and Nancy Tibbetts

Priscilla G., d. 12/4/1996 in Laconia; Wallace H. Garrett and Elizabeth Perkins

Richard E., d. 11/11/1973 at 87 in Wolfeboro

Theodore H., d. 5/18/1995 in Wolfeboro; Harry E. Ayer and Charlotte Hanscom

William R., d. 1/2/1954 at 64/8/21; farmer; single; b. Newfield, ME; Harry E. Ayer and Charlotte Hanscom

BABB,
Alma D., d. 5/16/1948 at 70/2/0 in Madbury; housewife; widow; b. Strafford Corners; Levi Miller (Croydon) and Sarah A. Babb (Strafford Corners)

BACHAND,
Edward P., d. 12/21/1988 in Rochester; Peter Bachand and Marie L. Larouche

BAILEY,
Alden H., d. 2/10/1964 at 74; laborer; b. Sandown; Isaiah Bailey and Ida Hoyt

Alice W., d. 6/8/1977 at 85 in Rochester; homemaker; b. NH; Clarence Wallingford and Ida -----

Clifford F., d. 10/8/1899 at 28/4/12; consumption; shoemaker; married; b. Wells, ME; Frank Bailey (Natick, MA) and Lydia Horne (Bethel, ME)

Jessie A., d. 10/12/1969 at 81 in Wolfeboro; housewife; b. ME; Alfred Ham and Jane A. Duncan

Lillian J., d. 3/10/1916 at 71 in Rochester; housewife; b. Brooklyn, NY; James Jeffery and Orina -----

William A., d. 1/20/1988 in Jupiter, FL

BAKER,
Debra A., d. 6/22/1995 in Dover; Kenneth Lessard and Stella Tackett

BALCH,
Joseph T., d. 12/27/1981 in Rochester

BALENTINE,
Emily W., d. 2/13/1913 at 74/10/1; intestinal obstruction; widow; b. Somersworth; John Brackett and Mary Pitman

BALLANTINE,
Fred, d. 10/27/1891 at 26/11/9; typhoid fever; loom fixer; married; b. Peabody, MA; Hugh Ballantine and Emily Brackett

BALODIS,
Anna, d. 6/8/1965 at 61 in Rochester; housewife; b. Latvia; John Landouskis and Anna Grunte
Vilhelms E., d. 1/30/1978 at 79 in Stoneham, MA; mill worker; b. Latvia; Karlis Balodis and Grieta -----

BANFIELD,
Elizabeth L., d. 1/21/1915 at 91/11; widow; b. Alton; David Place (Rochester) and Susan Perkins (Alton)

BANKS,
Michael J., d. 11/27/1964 at 0/0/29; b. Milton; George J. Banks and Virginia M. Potts

BANNISTER,
Fred, d. 10/11/1940 at 70/2/14; ret. minister; married; b. England; John Bannister (England) and Sarah Thornton (England)

BARBOUR,
Arthur W., d. 2/17/1962 at 42 in Los Angeles, CA
Blanche H., d. 1/7/1972 at 81 in Sanford, ME

BARKER,
Harriet Symes, d. 3/23/1897 at 78/2/16; apoplexy; widow; b. Plymouth

BARLOW,
Thomas P., d. 7/15/1908 at 0/8/7; cholera infantum; b. Milton; Thomas J. Barlow (Waltham, MA) and Mary A. McCormack (Ireland)

BARNARD,
Melvin L., d. 12/5/1965 at 70 in Rochester; night watchman; b. Milltown, ME; William A. Barnard and Martha Collins

BARNES,
Harriet R., d. 1/17/1991 in Rochester; William B. Dewhirst and Anna Richmond

BARNEY,
Nellie E., d. 8/10/1973 at 90 in Concord; homemaker; b. VT; Henry Eastman

BARRETT,
Louise P., d. 9/9/1983 in Rochester; William Stern and Blanche Resch

BARRYMAN,
James, d. 7/21/1976 at 84 in Rochester; prop. trucking co.; b. MA; James R. Barryman and Ida A. Woodworth

BARTLETT,
Everett E., d. 8/29/1988 in Middleton
Frederick H., d. 10/20/1923 at 63/6/7; farmer; widower; b. Annapolis, NS; John H. Bartlett (England) and Albenia S. Bent (NS)
Josephine M., d. 11/28/1975 at 70 in Farmington

BARTSCH,
Pauline M., d. 1/29/1969 at 39 in Wolfeboro

BASSETT,
Ivis M., d. 10/1/1954 at 38/11/11; nurse; married; b. Corinth, VT; Willie W. Moulton and Lillian Johnson
John L., d. 3/10/1984 in Rochester; Alston Bassett and Irene Chapman

BEAN,
Herbert L., d. 10/31/1908 at 49/1/7; nervous exhaustion; mill operative; married; b. Ossipee; Stephen Bean (Tuftonboro) and Martha J. Abbott (Ossipee)
John I., d. 5/14/1987 in Rochester
Richard F., d. 2/23/1938 at 16/1/5; single; b. Milton; Henry E. Bean (Moultonboro) and Ethel M. Ellis (Milton)
Roland F., d. 10/30/1948 at 0/2/2; b. Rochester; Clayton Bean (Milton) and Lucille Goodrow (New Durham)

Stephen, d. 1/11/1908 at 79/11/27; senility; married; b. Tuftonboro; James Bean and Sally Bennett

BEARD,
Mary J., d. 9/5/1933 at 22/3/1 in Dover; at home; married; b. Milton; Clarence G. Goodwin (Milton) and Agnes Mulligan (Lynn, MA)

BEATON,
Hazel Leola, d. 9/21/1900 at 0/7/17; cholera infantum; b. Milton; Hugh A. Beaton (Jefferson, OH) and Myrtle Hartshorne (Lunenburg)
Hugh A., d. 2/12/1940 at 66/7/4; B. M. agt; married; b. Jefferson, OH; Charles Beaton (Guildham, VT) and Eliza Hill (Sandusky, OH)

BEAUDRY,
Doris M., d. 9/24/1969 at 49 in Dover

BEAULIEU,
Cecile E., d. 2/20/1983; Damais Martin and Diana -----
Nike Tomas, d. 6/3/1992 in MA

BEAUREGARD,
Dorothy A., d. 5/6/1994 in Milton; Parker MacFaun and Ada Underwood

BEDARD,
Joseph D., d. 7/6/1961 at 70 in Wolfeboro; millworker; b. Groton, VT; Joseph S. Bedard and Angeline St. Louis

BEGIN,
Wilfred J.O., d. 1/7/1976 at 55 in Rochester; contractor; b. MA; Joseph G. Begin and Olivine Gamache

BELANGER,
Conrad, d. 12/5/1995 in Rochester; Edmond Belanger and Ruth Theriault

BELL,
Lena, d. 4/9/1913 at 0/1/12; meningitis; b. Milton; Amedey Bell (Canada) and Phoebe Bonsent (Canada)

BELLAMAR,
Rosa, d. 12/16/1895 at 4/11/5; peritonitis; single; b. Milton; Charles Bellamar and Selvia Galenon

BELLEMEUR,
Celina, d. 6/20/1929 at 71/2/17; housewife; married; b. Canada; Jean Baptist Gelineau (Canada) and Lucie M. Parrain (Canada)
Charles, d. 9/11/1937 at 76/4/27; retired; widower; b. Canada; Antonio Bellemeur (Canada) and Marie Prevost (Canada)

BELLEVILLE,
Louise, d. 1/8/1923 at 84/8; widow; b. Canada
Theodore W., d. 7/10/1967 at 63 in Milton Mills; laborer; b. Milton; Fred Belleville and Marie Simard

BENNER,
Florence P., d. 8/6/1983; Albinus Tebbetts and Mary Amazeen
Mark L., d. 2/19/1971 at 1 ½ hrs. in Rochester; b. Rochester; Robert Benner and Marie Downs

BENNETT,
George A., d. 10/12/1921 at 68/0/1; clergyman; married; b. Groton, MA; Alfred L. Bennett (Groton, MA) and Mary A. Nutter (New Ipswich)

BENTON,
Edward M., d. 7/7/1972 at 68 in Rochester; factory supt.; b. NH; Albert Benton and Alma Morse
Lucilla M., d. 4/4/1990 in Rochester

BEODOIN,
Ernest, d. 7/19/1913 at 18/11/5; accidental drowning; emp. ice co.; single; b. Canada; Gedeon Beodoin (Canada) and Mary Gigiare (Canada)

BERRY,
Arthur II., d. 3/22/1981 in Rochester; Hiram Berry and Mary J. Hanson
Charles J., d. 3/17/1933 at 96/1/3 in Portland, ME; retired; widower; b. Milton Mills; James Berry (Milton Mills) and Nancy Jewett (Milton Mills)
Clifford, d. 5/5/1937 at 57/2/24 in Brockton, MA

Estella G., d. 11/20/1936 at 56/4/10 in Haverhill, MA

George E., d. 4/12/1927 at 39/9/24 in Boston, MA; painter; divorced; b. Milton; Hiram H. Berry (Milton) and Mary J. Hanson (Milton)

Hannah R., d. 6/12/1905 at 42/6/10; nephritis; housekeeper; single; b. Milton; Jonathan Berry (Milton) and Sarah G. Cloutman (Wakefield)

Hiram H., d. 7/22/1940 at 86/9/18 in Milton Mills; farmer; married; b. Milton; Jonathan Berry (Milton) and Eliza W. Hussey (Milton)

John W., d. 2/17/1921 at 84/9/27 in Chester; single; b. Milton; John Berry (Milton) and Betsy Farnham (Acton, ME)

Jonathan, d. 7/20/1907 at 89/7/24; broken compensation; widower; b. Milton; James F. Berry and Betsy P. Hard

M. Augusta, d. 1/10/1923 at 87/8/18; at home; single; b. Milton; James Berry (Milton) and Eliza Jewett (Milton)

Martha M., d. 7/28/1930 at 79/4/3 in Wakefield; housewife; widow; b. Wakefield; Asa Farnham (Wakefield) and Mary Jones (Wakefield)

Mary E., d. 2/18/1926 at 65/6/18 in Milton Mills; at home; single; b. Milton Mills; Jonathan Berry (Milton) and Sarah Cloutman (Wakefield)

Mary J., d. 5/12/1941 at 90/1/8; housewife; widow; b. Milton; Moses Hanson (Dover) and Olive Dearborn (Milton)

Roxie Q., d. 7/9/1894 at 28/3/1; consumption; shoe shop; single; b. Milton; Jonathan Berry (Milton) and Sarah Cloutman (Wakefield)

Sarah G., d. 11/22/1904 at 77/7/15; chronic pneumonia; housekeeper; married; b. Wakefield; Joshua Cloutman (Wakefield) and Mary Hanson (Middleton)

William, d. 4/4/1929 at 86/0/22 in Wakefield; married; b. Wakefield; Francis Berry (Milton) and Temperance Wiggin (Acton, ME)

William A., d. 3/22/1967 at 0/0/2 in Rochester; b. Rochester; John Berry, Jr. and Linda Perkins

BERRYMAN,

George W., d. 12/20/1913 at 62/9/16; pneumonia; laborer; single; b. W. Buxton, ME; James Berryman (W. Buxton, ME) and Margaret Hanna

BESHAW,

Fred J., d. 6/17/1993 in Dover; Fred Beshaw and Anna LaPointe

BESSON,
Felix, d. 4/11/1896 at 0/1/9; premature birth; b. Milton; Frank Besson (Canada) and Odelia Lochance (Canada)

BEST,
Harriett K., d. 11/2/1941 at 82/0/0 in Acton, ME
William C., d. 5/10/1930 at 71 in Chelsea, MA; meat business; married; b. Newfoundland; George Best (England) and Mary A. Chipman (Newfoundland)

BETTS,
Charlotte F., d. 3/5/1923 at 65/8/5; widow; b. Lebanon, ME; Charles Chamberlain (Lebanon, ME) and Sarah Hooper (Wakefield)
Richard M., d. 4/19/1999 in Milton; Harold Betts and Mildred Thresher

BEVARD,
son, d. 7/29/1967 at 0/0/0 in Sanford, ME; b. Sanford, ME

BICKFORD,
Bruce L., d. 11/30/1998 in Dover; Lewis Bickford and Jeannette Turcotte
Donald, d. 3/16/1927 at 18/11/6 in Danvers, MA; clerk; single; b. Brockton, MA; Thomas E. Bickford (Dover) and Bessie M. Chipman (Milton)
Harry, d. 7/1/1935 at 53/10/8; store keeper; married; b. Farmington; Isaac Bickford (Rochester) and Julia Hatch (Lincoln)
Richard, d. 8/7/1937 at 15/9/20; scholar; single; b. Somersworth; Charles Bickford (Somersworth) and Angelina Jacques (Somersworth)
Sharon J., d. 6/22/1978 at 26 in Dover; shoe worker; b. NH; Clarence Perkins and Louise Colbroth

BLACKEY,
Frank A., d. 1/4/1954 at 81; caretaker; married; b. Sandwich; Elijah Blackey and Carrie Blanchard
Gertrude C., d. 12/15/1972 at 93 in Rochester; homemaker; b. NH; Edwin Henderson and Ada Forrest

BLAIR,
Amelia M., d. 7/31/1956 at 67 in Rochester; housewife; married; b. Newark, NJ; Frank Clifford and Kate Shelly

Leonard G., d. 10/22/1989 in Portland, ME; Gould K. Blair and Rene D. Paey

Rena D., d. 1/5/1980; George Paey and Josie Downs

BLAISDELL,
Ethel M., d. 3/31/1972 at 71 in Rochester; homemaker; b. NH; George Ellis and Inez Duntley
Flora, d. 1/21/1939 at 73/4/7; housewife; married; b. Acton, ME; Lorenzo Goodwin (Lebanon, ME) and Mary E. Butler (Lebanon, ME)
Samuel G., d. 11/1/1953 at 74/7/8; laborer; married; b. Somersworth; George Blaisdell and Katherine Morey

BLAKE,
Alma U., d. 2/2/1942 at 87/3/24; forelady; widow; b. Gilmanton; Charles W. Gilman (Gilmanton) and Judith A. Bennett (Barre, VT)

BLISS,
Minnie L., d. 4/27/1931 at 72/11/9; at home; widow; b. New Durham; Charles H. Rines (New Durham) and Sarah Boston (Lunenburg, VT)

BLOUIN,
Mary, d. 11/29/1899 at 20/0/4; cerebral coma; shoestitcher; single; b. Canada; Onesime Blouin (Canada) and Philomene Bison (Canada)
Mary J.E., d. 8/24/1903 at 0/1/14; inanition; b. Milton; Onesime Blouin (Canada) and Emma Joyal (Canada)
Onesime, d. 4/9/1900 at 0/2/20; pneumonia; b. Milton; Onesime Blouin (Canada) and Ema Goyal (Canada)
Phelomen, d. 4/9/1900 at 49; cerebral embolus; housekeeper; married; b. Canada; Tomma Beson (Canada) and Angelique Vachon (Canada)

BODIO,
James L., d. 1/22/1995 in Rochester; Louis E. Bodio and Stella B. Pocius
Susan M., d. 2/23/1978 at 20; student-homemaker; b. MA; James L. Bodio and Margaret A. Ryan

BODLEY,
Charles G., d. 7/7/1938 at 52/4/2; salesman; married; b. No. Adams, MA; Harry I. Bodley (KY) and Annie Gillespie (New York, NY)

BODWELL,
Charles L., d. 5/5/1913 at 55/0/9; chronic nephritis; hotel keeper; married; b. Acton, ME; John Bodwell and Louisa Goodwin (Sanford, ME)
Mildred G., d. 8/31/1996 in Dover; Roscoe C. Wentworth and Blanche Tufts
Raleigh V., d. 2/12/1910 at 0/1/3; probably suffocation; b. Lebanon, ME; Linwood C. Bodwell (Somersworth) and Myrtle G. Schofield (White Rock, NS)
Wilbur A., d. 8/4/1987 in Dover; Albion W. Bodwell

BOHAN,
Gerald J., d. 4/10/1998 in Milton

BOISCLAIR,
Peter, d. 3/12/1940 at 70/2/17 in Milton Mills; carp., bldr.; married; b. Canada; Lewis D. Boisclair and Elizabeth Murphy

BOISVERT,
Viola A., d. 12/28/1987 in Dover; George Wiggin and Marcella Vern

BOODEY,
Tamson L., d. 8/16/1901 at 80/7/13; apoplexy; widow; Nathaniel Howe and Clarissa Chamberlin

BORGKVIST,
Sybel D., d. 4/28/1973 at 78 in York, ME; worker

BORZILLO,
Anthony E., Jr., d. 6/21/1981; Anthony E. Borzillo, Sr. and Mary Serraro

BOSLEY,
John C., d. 6/1/1975 at 18; b. NH; Charles E. Bosley and Roberta F. Nason

BOUCHARD,
Antoinette, d. 7/4/1924 at 15/8/16; student; single; b. Somersworth; Auguste Bouchard (Canada) and Melvina Ruel (Canada)

BOUCHEE,
son, d. 8/5/1903 at 0/0/0; stillborn; Sifrais Bouchee (Canada) and Julia Hagarty (Ireland)
Julia, d. 8/5/1903 at 45; acute nephritis; housekeeper; married; b. Ireland; Patrick Hagarty (Ireland)

BOUCHER,
Almira E., d. 4/24/1979 in Stoughton, MA
John W., d. 9/11/1963 at 74 in Wolfeboro; machinist; b. Quebec; Joseph Boucher and Edith Griffith

BOUSQUIN,
Myrtle O., d. 3/19/1907 at 0/1/25; congenital heart dis.; b. Milton; William Bousquin (Canada) and Leona S. Stevens (Biddeford, ME)

BOUTIN,
Benjamin, d. 11/29/1899 at 0/6/21; hydrocephalus; b. Milton; Joseph Boutin, Jr. (Canada) and Zelim Morin (Canada)

BOUTWELL,
Warren C., d. 1/17/1943 at 35/5/26 in Dover; navy yard; married; b. Milton; Stephen Boutwell (Temple) and Grace M. Fish (Temple)

BOWDEN,
Violetta, d. 10/6/1891 at 42/8/1; heart disease; housekeeper; married; b. Milton; James Hanscam (Milton) and Sarah Jones (Milton)

BOWLEY,
Lydian E., d. 9/5/1990 in Wolfeboro; Edward Coolidge and Mabel Cook

BOYD,
Abbie E., d. 5/5/1963 at 86; housewife; b. Milton Mills; Eratus B. Shaw and Sarah E. Rhines
Joseph, d. 5/2/1946 at 72/6/9 in Dover; carpenter; married; b. Boston, MA; Joseph Boyd (Ireland) and Catherine Barrett (NB)
Joseph, d. 8/26/1996 in Syracuse, NY
Joseph A., Sr., d. 2/22/1959 at 57; mechanic; married; b. Milton Mills; Joseph Boyd and Abbie Shaw

Patricia A., d. 12/20/1947 at 4 hrs., 47 mins. in Rochester; b. Rochester; Joseph A. Boyd, Jr. (Dover) and Thelma Murphy (Wilmington, DE)

BOYLE,
Martin, d. 7/24/1975 at 44; MBTA lineman; b. MA; John Boyle and Anastiatia Toomey

BOYNTON,
James R., d. 8/25/1931 at 80/0/23 in Milton Mills; retired m. clk.; widower; b. Weymouth, MA; Haskel Boynton and Martha Walker

BRACKETT,
Annie F., d. 2/17/1948 at 83/3/20 in Alfred, ME
Elmer, d. 4/16/1936 at 75/10/26 in Alfred, ME; married
Eva, d. 8/29/1977 at 89 in Somerville, MA
Helen M., d. 2/20/1995 in North Berwick, ME
John C., d. 12/17/1902 at 41/11/14; fibroid phthisis; shoemaker; married; b. Milton; Moses D. Brackett (Acton, ME) and Sarah J. Perkins (Middleton)
Lillian, d. 4/2/1940 at 71/0/12 in Acton, ME; housekeeper; single; b. Acton, ME; Jacob Brackett (Acton, ME) and Belinda Folsom (Ossipee)
Lydia, d. 3/14/1894 at 88/10/25; cardic dropsy; housekeeper; single; b. Acton, ME; Joshua Brackett (Acton, ME) and Mary Tibbetts (Acton, ME)
Norris F., d. 5/26/1987 in Biddeford, ME

BRADSTREET,
Charles O., d. 11/9/1967 at 61; laborer, GE; b. Gloucester, MA; Ralph E. Bradstreet and Agnes E. Burgess

BRAGAW,
Richard, d. 10/6/1942 at 58/11/8 in Wayne, MI; married

BRAGDON,
Ann M., d. 11/12/1912 at 80/11/19; pneumonia; widow; b. No. Wakefield; Edmund Wentworth (No. Wakefield) and Lavinia Wentworth (Conway)

James A., d. 6/23/1906 at 73/4/14; functional dis. of heart; married; b. Milton; James Bragdon (York, ME) and Lucy Ricker (Milton)

Laura F., d. 2/13/1948 at 81/10/15 in Dover; single; b. Milton; James A. Bragdon and Ann -----

Stephen M., d. 3/4/1909 at 72/2/8 in Farmington; heart disease; farmer; widower; b. Milton; George L. Bragdon and Betsey Henderson (Milton)

BRAGG,
George L., d. 8/19/1901 at 30; Bright's disease; blacksmith; married; b. Shapleigh, ME; Jefferson Bragg and Abbie F. Sherborn (Shapleigh, ME)

BRAGOW,
Alice B., d. 6/12/1971 at 87 in Bloomfield Hills, MI

BRAILEY,
Fred B., d. 10/15/1937 at 72/2/16; married; b. Canaan; Alvin W. Brailey (Danbury) and Anne W. Annis (Groton)

BRAINARD,
Ama R., d. 7/7/1984 in Dover; Frank Brainard and Harriet Buch

BRAMAN,
Alfred E., d. 6/26/1953 at 61 in Rochester; hotel business; married; b. Canada; Samuel Braman and Alberta Varwart

BRAUDIS,
daughter, d. 8/30/1918 at 0/0/0; b. Milton; Arthur E. Braudis (Rochester) and Bernis L. Page (Milton)

BRAWN,
Edith M., d. 10/5/1918 at 43/5/24; housekeeper; married; b. Milton; George E. Nute (Milton) and Abbie M. Russell (Canton, MA)

BRETON,
Iris I., d. 3/8/1999 in Portsmouth

BREWER,
Leslie S., d. 11/26/1963 at 78; laborer; b. Royalston, MA; Elgernon Brewer and Myra Bosworth

BREWSTER,
Charles B., d. 8/6/1920 at 35; salesman; single; b. Rynland, NY; Charles A. Brewster (Goshen, NY) and Gertrude Taylor (Brookline, MA)

BRIERLY,
Hannah E., d. 9/17/1927 at 78/10/20 in Acton, ME; at home; widow; b. Acton, ME; Sylvester Lowd (Acton, ME) and Dorcas Libby (Lebanon, ME)

BRINKMAN,
Jeremie E., d. 3/31/1986; Edward C. Brinkman and Barbara J. Staples
Joshua E., d. 3/31/1986; Edward C. Brinkman and Barbara J. Staples

BROCHU,
Bonnie J., d. 3/30/1987 in Newburyport, MA
Eli J., d. 6/24/1997 in Rochester; Leger Brochu and Odelie Paradis
Linda, d. 3/4/1951 at 1/7/14 in Rochester; b. Milton; Paul Brochu and Jane Durgin
Michael J., d. 7/22/1982 in Rochester

BROCK,
Annie M., d. 6/30/1930 at 59/8/15; housewife; married; b. Brownfield, ME; Charles H. Dyer (Brownfield, ME) and Martha A. Drew (Brookfield)
John B., d. 12/5/1948 at 74/3/15 in Union; laborer; widower; b. Pittsfield; John Brock (Strafford)
Leon L., d. 5/29/1981; Roscoe A. Brock and Jennie Bickford
Warren R., d. 3/3/1987 in Rochester; Warren H. Brock, MD and Gail Anderson

BRONSON,
Stanley C., d. 1/21/1977 at 61 in Wolfeboro; ret. shoe foreman; b. PA; Eli Bronson and Minnie Coss

BROOKS,
Abbie D., d. 10/1/1947 at 78 in Norwell, MA
John M., d. 8/2/1938 at 74/0/0 in Medford, MA
Sandra D., d. 12/29/1995 in Dover; Carlyle G. Brooks and Martha K. Hill

BROUILLETTE,
Rosalie, d. 8/5/1940 at 93/1/26; housewife; widow; b. Canada; -----
    Marcellais (Canada) and Rosalie ----- (Canada)

BROULARD,
Rose, d. 9/30/1902 at 67/7; shock; married; b. Canada; Entoine Belimeur
    (Canada) and Marie Provo (Canada)

BROULERD,
Alvenor, d. 3/21/1913 at 63/4; cerebral hemorrhage; married; b. Canada

BROULLERD,
Isadore, d. 8/1/1915 at 86; farmer; widower; b. Canada

BROWN,
Abbie F., d. 2/26/1927 at 76; milliner; single; b. Amesbury, MA; William
    C. Brown (Amesbury, MA) and Cornelia Weeks (Waterville, ME)
Addie M., d. 9/22/1913 at 45/4/15; cirrhosis of liver; married; b. Milton;
    Joseph H. Avery (Acton, ME) and Thesta Hanscom (Milton)
Ambrose, Jr., d. 5/26/1944 at 20/8/15 in Italy; US Army; single; b.
    Milton; Ambrose M. Brown (Brighton, MA) and Ora M. Blouin
    (Springvale, ME)
Ambrose M., d. 2/12/1946 at 61/4 in Rochester; F. M. worker; widower;
    b. Somerville, MA; John B. Brown (NS) and Marguerite Fay
    (Boston, MA)
Amy M., d. 4/29/1959 at 78; housewife; married; b. Dover, ME; Thomas
    Nichols and Agustie Silver
Everett, d. 7/9/1921 at 67/0/22; retired; single; b. Milton; Robert Brown
    (Ossipee) and Sarah A. Reynolds (Tuftonboro)
George L., d. 7/9/1894 at 9/4/21; scrofulous consumption; single; b.
    Farmington; John H. Brown (Farmington) and Cora E. Witham
    (Wolfeboro)

Georgie A., d. 4/9/1900 at 55/4/23; paralysis; housekeeper; widow; b. Newfield, ME; Mark F. Piper (Newfield, ME) and Elizabeth C. Davis (Newfield, ME)

Helen W., d. 6/30/1936 at 18/3/27; housewife; married; b. W. Somerville, MA; Perley Whitehouse (Farmington) and Victoria Douquette (Union)

John M., d. 2/20/1916 at 63/0/17; ice deliverer; married; b. Port George, NS; Ambrose Brown (Port George, NS) and Catherine Winer (Port George, NS)

Lawrence H., d. 11/12/1998 in Rochester

Lois Ernell, d. 12/15/1924 at 0/11/16; b. Milton; Lloyd E. Brown (Glenburn, ME) and Josephine Fabian (Mapleton, ME)

Marguerite H., d. 5/13/1984 in Rochester; Thomas E. Howard and Gertrude Fetherston

Mary E., d. 9/28/1889 at 60/0/11; chr. diarrhea, heart disease; house; widow; b. New Durham; Aaron Palmer and Annie M. Clough

Ora M., d. 2/7/1933 at 37; married; b. Springvale, ME; James Blouin (Canada) and Nellie Lessard (Canada)

Rita M., d. 7/10/1996 in Milton; John F. Kennedy and Cecilia McGovern

Robert, d. 8/24/1905 at 76/1; cerebral hemorrhage; widower; b. Ossipee; Hoitt Brown

Sarah Abba, d. 11/26/1901 at 77/10/20; senility; housewife; married; b. Tuftonboro; Paul Reynolds (Farmington) and Sally Ranlet (Farmington)

William R., d. 1/14/1991 in Milton; James E. Brown and Clara Greely

BRUCE,

Alice May, d. 9/12/1898 at 24/3/6; exopthalmic goitre; housekeeper; single; b. Boston, MA; Henry J. Bruce (Boston, MA) and Mary F. Thompson (Ossipee)

David K., d. 12/14/1996 in Sanbornville

Kenneth R., d. 4/8/1975 at 58; machine operator; b. ME; Fred F. Bruce and Affie A. Guptill

Mary F., d. 11/12/1900 at 56/5/16; strangulated hernia; housekeeper; widow; b. Ossipee; John Thompson (Newfield, ME) and Mary Wormwood (Kennebunkport, ME)

BRYANT,
A. H. C., d. 12/1/1935 at 79/11/24; b. Effingham; Asill M. Carr (Ossipee) and Hannah Chalgon (Sweden)
John M., d. 10/29/1940 at 90/3/4; ret. mach.; widower; b. Tamworth; John Bryant (Tamworth) and Susan E. Gilman (Tamworth)

BUCCI,
Maude M.P., d. 8/9/1975 in Northridge, CA

BUCK,
Alice C., d. 10/20/1944 at 76/4/14 in Marblehead, MA; widow
Grace B., d. 8/17/1959 at 71 in NJ
Herman L., d. 11/6/1961 at 86 in Bloomfield, NJ
Horatio B., d. 10/12/1941 at 68/3/6 in So. Boston, MA
Nellie D., d. 10/24/1969 at 90 in Topeka, KS

BUGUEY,
Mary E., d. 4/22/1896 at 51/1/21; apoplexy; housekeeper; married; b. England; James Keating (England) and Margaret Pendergist (England)

BULLIS,
Bertha M., d. 8/3/1975 at 57 in Wolfeboro

BUMPUS,
Marcella, d. 8/11/1942 at 88; housewife; widow; b. NS; Archie MacLellan (Scotland) and Isabel MacLellan (Scotland)

BURBINE,
David H., d. 4/16/1917 at 0/0/5; b. Milton; David H. Burbine (Wakefield, MA) and Marietta Doucette (NS)
William C., d. 8/3/1923 at 7/1/20; b. Milton; David H. Burbine (Wakefield, MA) and Mary E. Doucette (Yarmouth, NS)

BURGESS,
Joseph E., d. 10/1/1978 at 73; ret. oil dealer; b. Canada; Frederick Burgess and Mary Furness

BURKE,
Anna N., d. 4/8/1939 at 22/0/20 in Rochester; shoe worker; married; b. Milton; Clarence Goodwin (Dover) and Agnes Mulligan (Lynn, MA)
Franklin, d. 2/3/1899 at 79/2; senile gangrene; farmer; married; b. Wolfeboro; James Burke (Wolfeboro) and Hannah French (Wolfeboro)
Lila, d. 5/16/1900 at 3/6; typhoid pneumonia; b. Wolfeboro; Edwin A. Burke (Wolfeboro) and Ethel Rollins (Wolfeboro)
William E., d. 2/26/1900 at 25/10/13; diabetes mellitus; shoemaker; married; b. Wolfeboro; Charles F. Burke (Milton) and Hattie M. Tibbetts (Wolfeboro)

BURKHART,
Jeanne M., d. 11/12/1987; Marcus L. Bergsten and Elizabeth Gaden

BURNHAM,
Eliza M., d. 7/18/1888 at 84/0/25; heart failure from old age; housekeeper; widow; b. Durham

BURNS,
James G., d. 6/25/1995 in Wolfeboro
Robert I., d. 6/13/1980 in Wolfeboro; George Burns and Annie Iredale
Sarah R., d. 10/3/1976 at 53 in Rochester; homemaker; b. Sweden, ME; George Ridlon and Eva Bonney

BURROUGHS,
Emily W., d. 3/9/1991 in Rochester; Charles Wallingford and Rose Dumont
Eugene, d. 10/30/1944 at 19/3/11 on USS Franklin; US Navy; single; b. Milton; Warren D. Burroughs (Wolfeboro) and Madelene G. White (Rochester)
Howard W., d. 5/17/1978 at 72 in Rochester; mill worker; b. NH; Howard W. Burroughs and Mercy M. Kimball
James, d. 10/30/1899 at 76/5; pernicious anemia; farmer; married; b. Lebanon, ME; David Burroughs (Lebanon, ME) and Mary Shorey
Lorania, d. 10/1/1910 at 83/2/20; acute nephritis; housework; widow; b. Parsonsfield, ME; Benjamin Blaisdell (Lebanon, ME) and Zubia Mathes (Thomaston, ME)

Madelene G., d. 12/8/1997 in Rochester; Chester White and Isadore Harriman

Marion G., d. 6/28/1978 in Rochester; Guy Chamberlain and Elizabeth Cunningham

Roy, d. 8/8/1975 at 71 in Rochester; fireman; b. NH; Howard Burroughs and Mercy Kimball

Warren D., Sr., d. 10/22/1979 in White River Jct., VT; Howard Burroughs and Mercy Kimball

BURROWS,

Alvah G., d. 4/9/1893 at 52/3/4; suicide; shoemaker; married; b. Lebanon, ME; Jonathan Burrows (Lebanon, ME)

Carl M., d. 3/10/1967 at 72; mill worker; b. Middleton; David Burrows and Miria Pinkham

Hiram, d. 10/9/1938 at 83/8/13 in Acton, ME; blacksmith; married; b. Lebanon, ME; Edward Burrows (Lebanon, ME) and Mary Ricker (Lebanon, ME)

Lincoln, d. 7/21/1923 at 0/5/9; b. Milton; Carl M. Burrows (Middleton) and Marion G. Rand (Milton)

Lincoln, d. 5/17/1963 at 4 in Rochester; b. Rochester; Luman Burrows and Ruth Ann Blanchard

Lucille M., d. 10/9/1950 at 22 in Dover; housewife; married; b. Wolfeboro; Andrew Goodrow and Jessie Goodrow

Sarah E., d. 5/10/1955 at 93/1/10 in Acton, ME; housewife; widow

Willard C., d. 10/15/1918 at 1/1/28; b. Milton; Carl M. Burrows (Middleton) and Marion G. Rand (Milton)

BUSSEY,

Phyllis, d. 3/21/1991 in Rochester; Walter C. Caswell and Effie Miner

BUTLER,

son, d. 8/8/1927 at 0/0/1; b. Milton; Edward T. Butler (Hingham, MA) and Margaret J. Burbine (Wakefield, MA)

Abbie D., d. 8/13/1910 at 79/0/3; cerebral hemorrhage; housekeeper; widow; b. Milton; Joseph Dearborn and Harriet Drew

Conrad V., d. 5/14/1936 at 2/5/5; b. Milton; Edward T. Butler (Hingham, MA) and Margaret Burbine (Wakefield, MA)

Edward T., d. 2/5/1957 at 69 in Dover; boiler attendant; widower; b. Kingston, MA; Pierce Butler and Mary McCurthy

John, d. 6/14/1889 at 76/8; apoplexy; farmer; married; b. Berwick, ME; Benjamin Butler and Sarah Gowell

Margaret J., d. 11/27/1949 at 53; housewife; divorced; b. Wakefield, MA; John Burbine and Margaret Thrashwell

Richard A., d. 5/27/1907 at 28; convulsions; trained nurse; single; b. Valley Falls; William Butler and Catherine

BUZZELL,
Alice S., d. 3/23/1941 at 74/11/29 in Milton Mills; at home; widow; b. Acton, ME; James H. Buzzell (Acton, ME) and Sarah Littlefield (Springvale, ME)

Edwin E., d. 5/12/1934 at 71/2/18 in Wolfeboro; married

Florence M., d. 7/27/1958 at 79 in Wakefield; housewife; married; b. W. Newfield, ME; John L. Day and Susan B. Patch

George A., d. 6/8/1972 at 95 in Rochester; farmer; b. ME; Lyman R. Buzzell and Jane Lord

James H., d. 12/31/1909 at 79/11/11; exhaustion; farmer; married; b. Acton, ME; Jacob Buzzell (Alfred, ME) and Mary Roberts (Alfred, ME)

Raymond, d. 6/26/1935 at 56/0/22 in Wakefield; farmer; married; b. Milton; James H. Buzzell (Acton, ME) and Sara F. Littlefield (Springvale, ME)

Sarah F., d. 3/5/1932 at 94/8/5 in Milton Mills; widow; b. Springvale, ME; Moses Littlefield (Springvale, ME) and Ruth -----

BYRD,
Donald L., d. 4/30/1986 in Rochester; Walter O. Byrd and Arlene Richardson

BYRON,
Beulale A., d. 9/11/1896 at 3/1/29; membraneous croup; b. Berwick, ME; Jeremie P. Byron (Manchester) and Annabel J. Brewster (Tamworth)

CALLAHAN,
James G., d. 12/24/1909 at --; natural causes; laborer

John R., d. 2/16/1966 at 39 in Boston, MA; school principal; b. Concord; John P. Callahan and Evelyn Bjork

CAMERON,
John B., Jr., d. 1/17/1991 in Rochester; John B. Cameron, Sr. and Marion E. Haycock
Melvin, d. 2/10/1924 at 58; laborer; married; b. Milton

CAMPBELL,
Hattie E., d. 8/31/1907 at 34/3/30; cere'o spinal meningitis; teacher; single; b. Sanford, ME
Irma G., d. 3/6/1996 in Milton; Harold Dunnifer and Ruth Crooker
William J., d. 5/5/1976 at 76 in Rochester; prop. nursing home; b. VT; John Campbell and Mary -----

CARAN,
David, d. 8/21/1905 at 0/0/28; pertussis; b. Milton; Conrad Caran (Canada) and Marie L. Caron (Canada)

CARLL,
Stephen A., d. 6/13/1997 in Portsmouth; Robert W. Carll and Joan P. Cotton

CARLTON,
Helen S., d. 3/12/1991 in Rochester; Nathaniel E. Spinney and Iza Stone

CARMICHAEL,
Helen F., d. 11/17/1971 at 90 in Rochester; housewife; b. NH; Everett F. Fox and Carolyn B. Ricker

CARON,
Edward L., d. 2/20/1970 at 74 in Milton Mills; side laster; b. Rochester; Edward Caron and Celina St. Hillaire
Ernest E., d. 8/29/1951 at 48 in Rochester; painter; married; b. Rochester; Edward Caron and Celina St. Hilaire
James, d. 3/1/1978 at 102; teamster; b. Canada; Pierre Gagnon and Phelonise Caron

CARPENTER,
Ernest L., d. 12/14/1943 at 84/2/7; carpenter; married; b. Berwick, ME; George L. Carpenter (Berwick, ME) and Laura L. Jenkins (Rollinsford)

Hattie, d. 7/8/1955 at 87/6/9; housewife; widow; b. So. Berwick, ME; Charles Cheney

John, d. 11/18/1941 at 56/1/13; painter; married; b. So. Berwick, ME; Ernest Carpenter (So. Berwick, ME) and Genevive Webber (Portland, ME)

Lydia M., d. 9/5/1920 at 28/0/24; housekeeper; married; b. Milton; Oscar B. Dixon (Milton) and Nellie Doe (Ossipee)

Maude L., d. 7/17/1980; John Wentworth and Belle S. Hussey

CARR,

George Edward, d. 1/22/1990 in Dover; Frank S. Carr and Olive M. Chase

James G., d. 8/5/1991 in Rochester; George E. Carr and Betty -----

CARSWELL,

Clifton F., d. 11/23/1999 in Milton; Fred Carswell and Frances Ayer

Dorothy L., d. 6/22/1967 at 39 in Milton Mills; housewife; b. Fitchburg, MA; Fred Wilder and Flora Daby

Frances E., d. 11/9/1980 in Wolfeboro; Harry E. Ayer and Charlotte Hanscomb

Fred E., d. 10/4/1957 at 65/11/26; postmaster; married; b. Denver, CO; Luther Carswell and Eva Titus

Natalie B., d. 10/26/1981 in Milton Mills; Raymond H. Blake and Bertha Bennett

CARTER,

Frank E., d. 5/11/1949 at 59; grocer; married; b. Parkton, MD; George Carter and May Kennedy

CASEY,

Catherine H., d. 12/2/1981 in Rochester

William E., d. 7/14/1958 at 77 in Rochester; farmer; married; b. Ireland; Michael Casey and Honora Howard

CASWELL,

James H., d. 5/3/1991 in Rochester; Henry E. Caswell and Julia E. Scott

CATANZANO,
Salvatore F., d. 9/26/1963 at 36; chauffeur; b. Everett, MA; Salvatore F. Catanzano, Sr. and Mary Dillion

CATE,
Aaron J., d. 3/15/1945 at 71/6/12; toolmaker; married; b. Salem, MA; Doniran J. Cate (Haverhill, MA) and Henrietta Batchelder (Salem, MA)
Hiram S., d. 8/25/1903 at 82/3/19; arterio sclerosis; emp. in mill; married; b. Franklin; Simeon Cate and Dorothy Call
Mary E., d. 1/17/1938 at 71/7/3; housekeeper; married; b. Milton; John Wentworth (Milton) and Hannah E. Gray (Strafford)

CHAGNON,
Maurice L., d. 2/28/1985 in Rochester; Arthur Chagnon and Casey Bishop

CHAMBERL[A]IN,
Abbie M., d. 5/24/1915 at 77/10; single; b. Lebanon, ME; James B. Chamberlain (Lebanon, ME) and Almira Force (Lebanon, ME)
Arthie, d. 12/28/1943 at 81/11/13 in Rochester; housewife; married; b. Wakefield; James Junkins (Wakefield) and Sally Wentworth (Wakefield)
Elizabeth, d. 10/4/1918 at 33/10/9; housewife; married; b. Scotland; Alexander Cunningham (Scotland)
Ernest W., d. 6/25/1963 at 85 in Alton
F. M., d. 5/30/1935 at 77/0/1 in Union; patrolman; widower; b. Milton; S. G. Chamberlain (Milton) and Mary E. Fall (Lebanon, ME)
Gardner M., d. 12/24/1979 in Rochester; Guy Chamberlain and Elizabeth Cunningham
Hannah E., d. 5/12/1915 at 69/8/22; housework; widow; b. Tuftonboro; J. C. Seavey (Pittsfield) and Esther Hooper (Tuftonboro)
Howard R., d. 5/19/1963 at 49; supervisor; b. Brockton, MA; Guy Chamberlain and Elizabeth Cunningham
Mary E., d. 11/4/1890 at 67/1/13; pneumonia; housekeeper; married; b. Milton; Daniel Fall and Lucy Fall
Moses G., d. 7/11/1951 at 89; lumber dealer; widower; b. Milton; Samuel G. Chamberlain and Mary E. Fall

Samuel G., d. 1/2/1911 at 83/5/23; cerebral hemorrhage; farmer; married; b. Milton; Samuel Chamberlain (Milton) and Mary M. Moody (Lebanon, ME)

Sarah E., d. 7/11/1926 at 79/10/24 in Wakefield; housewife; married; b. Wakefield; Robert Corson and Sarah Nay (Ossipee)

Winifred G., d. 1/9/1973 at 94 in Rochester

CHANDLER,
son, d. 2/10/1921 at 0/0/0; b. Milton; Joseph L. Chandler (Groton) and Gladys A. Hoyt (Rochester)

Gladys A., d. 9/23/1923 at 29/10/7; housewife; married; b. Rochester; Frank R. Hoyt (Rochester) and Armneller Howard (Portsmouth)

CHAPLIN,
Margaret I., d. 12/23/1992 in Milton; George Leonard and Elsie Robbins

CHAPMAN,
daughter, d. 6/25/1938 at 0/0/0; b. Milton; Fred Chapman, Jr. (Haverhill) and Irene Acton (Laconia)

CHASE,
Adaline W., d. 12/23/1944 at 58/11/20; housewife; married; b. Wakefield; John D. Willey (Wakefield) and Olivia Demerritt (Lee)

Arthur L., d. 3/8/1976 at 64 in Manchester; carpenter; b. NH; George H. Chase and Adeline Willey

Doris F., d. 9/6/1995 in Rochester; Albert J. Fortier and Nellie Lane

George H., d. 11/30/1967 at 86 in East Lebanon, ME; shoe worker; b. Cambridge, MA; George F. Chase and Harriet G. Wright

Helen E., d. 8/3/1988 in Dover; Neils A. Bastberg and Laura Dimmock

Henry L., d. 1/2/1970 at 79 in Ossipee

Inga J., d. 1/21/1987 in Rochester; Charles E. Joy and Emma Satterlee

Leslie Oliver, d. 3/11/1992 in Milton; George H. Chase and Adeline Willey

CHASSE,
Marc G., d. 9/16/1993 in Rochester; Raymond Chasse and Dorene Deschenes

CHAUVETTE,
Lawrence, d. 1/23/1905 at 35; accident, killed in saw mill; teamster; single; b. Canada

CHECK,
Abbie R., d. 11/17/1962 at 91 in Rochester; housewife; b. Shapleigh, ME; Samuel Batchelder and Lucy Trafton

CHENEY,
Albert A., d. 12/21/1984 in Rochester; Arthur Cheney and Mary Ducharme
Richard H., d. 8/13/1953 at 47/2/12; laborer; married; b. Whitefield; Arthur Cheney and Mary Duchaume

CHESBROUGH,
Gladys M., d. 12/31/1982 in Wolfeboro
Walter, d. 6/22/1958 at 77 in Wakefield; moulds; married; b. Gaines, NY; Chauncey Chesbrough and Jennie M. Bennett

CHESLEY,
Havilah, d. 1/9/1903 at 89/1/6; heart failure; farmer; widower; b. Middleton; Benjamin Chesley and Abigail Page

CHICK,
Everett A., d. 10/11/1923 at 53/0/18; contractor; married; b. Shapleigh, ME; Winslow O. Chick (Shapleigh, ME) and Sarah A. Murray (Shapleigh, ME)

CHIKREOTIS,
James, d. 11/11/1914 at 0/0/3; convulsions; b. Milton; Michael Chikreotis (Greece) and Deni Mikrees (Greece)

CHIPMAN,
Edward, d. 9/13/1933 at 66/0/20 in Dover; laborer; married; b. Natick, MA; John Chipman (NS) and Jessie Rockwell (NS)
Mary B., d. 1/2/1957 at 90; housewife; widow; b. Milton; Asa Drew and Hannah Pinkham
Ralph L., d. 11/24/1894 at 1/4/26; meningitis; single; b. Milton; Edward Chipman (Natick, MA) and Mary B. Drew (Milton)

CHRESTENSEN,
Chris C., d. 9/26/1999 in Milton; Arthur Chrestensen and Judith Tuxsbury

CHRISTMAN,
Evelyn, d. 8/14/1997 in Milton; Henry Murphy and Bridget Reagan

CILLEY,
Gertrude G., d. 10/16/1945 at 39/6/29; housewife; married; b. Exeter

CLAPP,
Anne E., d. 8/17/1985 in Rochester; John Monahan and Helen -----
Charles M., Sr., d. 8/16/1989 in Rochester; Elmer A. Clapp and Katherine K. Dolan

CLARK,
Catherine, d. 4/23/1956 at 84/8/20 in Boston, MA
Deborah M., d. 1/12/1996 in Rochester; Joseph Minnon and Jean Kimball
Julia A., d. 7/1/1917 at 54/11/26; housekeeper; widow; b. NB; John Adams (NB)
Lew B., d. 7/17/1963 at 72; US government; b. Lynn, MA; George Clark and Unice Newhall
Mary E., d. 1/29/1935 at 70/8/29; at home; widow; b. New York, NY; John Rafferty (Ireland) and Catherine Splaine (Ireland)
Mary E., d. 5/17/1965 at 90 in Milton Mills; housewife; b. Buxton, ME; Charles A. Treadwell and Mary E. Peacock
Mary P., d. 12/4/1978 at 57 in Wolfeboro
Raymond D., d. 6/15/1996 in Dover
Willard L., Jr., d. 8/22/1992 in Lyman, ME
Willard L., Sr., d. 10/8/1982 in Sanford, ME

CLAY,
Harold E., d. 4/24/1959 at 59 in Sanford, ME; card tender; married; b. Haverhill, MA; Edward Clay and Mabel Long

CLAYTON,
Fred, d. 3/7/1932 at 62/7/18 in Milton Mills; mechanic; married; b. England; George Clayton (England) and Sarah Wilson (England)
Letty A., d. 11/8/1983; Richard A. Clayton and Almena A. Bissett

CLEAVES,
Alta D., d. 7/6/1938 at 42/9/18; op. emp. office; divorced; b. Ms; Edwin Chipman (Natick, MA) and Bertha M. Drew (Milton)
Thomas L., d. 12/26/1922 at 6/1/9; b. Rochester; George N. Cleaves (Milton, MA) and Vivian McGregor (Roxbury, MA)

CLEMENT,
son, d. 10/10/1895 at 0/0/1; inanition; b. Milton; Charles Clement

CLEMENTS,
daughter, d. 7/5/1896 at 0/0/1; inanition; b. Milton; Charles Clements (Wakefield) and Harriet Goodwin (Milton)
Charlott L., d. 2/4/1920 at 81/11/6; housekeeper; widow; b. Canterbury; Calvin Ingalls (Canterbury) and Nancy Sanborn (Sanbornton)
George W., d. 8/12/1894 at 0/3/29; cholera infantum; b. Milton; James W. Clements and Lena King (Canada)
Hanson E., d. 9/25/1914 at 62/1/17; typhoid fever; carpenter; married; b. Berwick, ME; Hanson Clements (Berwick, ME) and Lydia Guptill (Berwick, ME)
John B., d. 6/1/1932 at 68/5/24 in Dover; widower; b. Milton; Leander Clements (Milton) and Susan Stevens (Tuftonboro)
Leander, d. 6/14/1914 at 83/10/20; atheroma; farmer; widower; b. Milton; Samuel Clements (Berwick, ME) and Sally Staples
Martha B., d. 10/4/1944 at 89/0/22; housewife; widow; b. Farmington; Paul Twombly (Farmington) and Melinda A. ----- (Rochester)
Susan A., d. 3/16/1906 at 75/3/23; apoplexy; housewife; married; b. Tuftonboro; Nathan Stevens and Susan Berry

CLEVELAND,
Elizabeth R., d. 4/24/1949 at 0/0/0 in Rochester; b. Rochester; Raymond Cleveland and Lucille M. Pontbriand
John, d. 11/25/1929 at 63/2/17; shipping clerk; married; b. Otisfield, ME; Edwin Cleveland (Oxford, ME) and Melinda Edwards (Otisfield, ME)
Louise C., d. 4/1/1991 in Rochester
Lucille M., d. 2/8/1990 in New York
Melinda E., d. 10/4/1925 at 90/7/1; retired; widow; b. Otisfield, ME; John Edwards (Casco, ME) and Mary Smitts (Otisfield, ME)

Ruth O., d. 10/22/1948 at 48/0/21; shoe worker; married; b. Boston, MA; Charles O. Stillings (Ossipee) and Susie Newhall (NS)

Willard C., d. 12/16/1985 in Rochester

CLOUGH,

Celina M., d. 2/7/1949 at 55/9/1 in Rochester; housewife; widow; b. Newmarket; Frank Larose and Mary Minor

Dennis F., d. 11/22/1976 at 90 in Rochester; boss weaver; b. ME; Franklin Clough and Mary Piper

Elsie M., d. 6/18/1910 at 18/11/23; tubercular tonsilitis; housewife; married; b. Wolfeboro; Charles A. Tinker (Ellsworth, ME) and Elizabeth Whiteworth (Lawrence, MA)

Fred E., d. 12/5/1984 in Manchester; Warren Clough and Marguerite Weeks

Herman, d. 7/19/1981 in Rochester

Kerry W., d. 5/29/1965 at 2 hrs. in Sanford, ME

Leon E., d. 6/1/1979 in Portland, ME

Mamie V., d. 5/10/1973 at 84 in Wolfeboro; homemaker; b. ME; Thomas Marsh and Viola -----

Marguerite D., d. 2/15/1972 at 69 in Rochester; homemaker; b. NH; Dr. Frank S. Weeks and Minnie Alley

Melva G., d. 2/11/1984; Frank Kehoe and Margaret Hunter

CLOUTMAN,

Emma, d. 12/26/1938 at 87/7/27 in Farmington; housewife; widow; b. Milton; Henry Downs (Canada) and Elizabeth Drew (Dover)

CLOW,

Charles, d. 12/20/1936 at 56/2/3 in Sanford, ME; farm laborer; married; b. Wolfeboro; Franklin Clow and Mary Jane Piper (Alton)

CLUFF,

Lulu Rowena, d. 9/7/1899 at 0/0/3; inanition; b. Milton; Asa W. Cluff (Alfred, ME) and Lizzie E. Morton (Augusta, ME)

COATES,

Daniel G., d. 5/15/1968 at 47 in Dover; truck driver; b. MA; Albert Coates and Madeline Allen

COATY,
Emma J., d. 6/29/1915 at 59/4/23; widow; b. Barnstead; Moses Ham and Elizabeth Locke

COCHEY,
Arthur G., d. 9/18/1973 at 81; lea. mfg.; b. MA; James Cochey and Elizabeth Bixby

COFFRIN,
Francis, d. 10/17/1906 at 78/3/6; Bright's disease; wool sorter; widower; b. Sandwich; Francis Coffrin (Sandwich) and Lydia Plummer (Sandwich)

COLBY,
Beatrice J., d. 2/24/1991 in Dover; David Pinkham and Flora Belle Furber

COLE,
Grace B., d. 11/2/1956 at 86 in Lebanon, ME
Grace F., d. 6/14/1977 at 48 in Wolfeboro; homemaker; b. ME; Charles Hartford and Etta Haddock
Henry W., d. 9/15/1948 at 84/9/19 in No. Lebanon, ME
John B., d. 6/30/1980 in Hiram, ME
Lula M., d. 10/29/1971 at 79 in Rochester; housewife; b. NH; ----- Brown

COLES,
Abbie M., d. 3/31/1952 at 98; housewife; widow; b. Milton; Benjamin Foss and Lavina Downs
Harry D., d. 8/29/1930 at 73/6/20; clerk; married; b. PEI; James Coles and Margaret E. Coles

COLLINS,
son, d. 11/19/1935 at 0/0/1 in Rochester; b. Rochester; George W. Collins (Sanford, ME) and Mattie Randall (East Rochester)
Ethel M., d. 6/21/1990 in Milton; James Z. Collins and Mary Hatch
Fred W., d. 10/29/1953 at 43 in Rochester; mill worker; married; b. Swampscott, MA; Walter Collins and Elsie Waldron
James Z., d. 11/27/1962 at 88 in Dover; painter; b. Alton; Lewis Collins and Mary Young

Nora K., d. 6/27/1917 at 26/7; school teacher; single; b. Rochester; James Collins (Ireland) and Minnie Murray (Ireland)

Sylvia E., d. 9/24/1933 at 0/1/20 in Rochester; b. Rochester; George Collins (Sanford, ME) and Mattie Randall (E. Rochester)

COLLURA,
Corinne P., d. 4/25/1996 in Wolfeboro; George W. Porter and Frances Saltonstall

COLMAN,
Charles D., d. 11/20/1984 in Manchester
Ramona, d. 3/18/1975 at 77 in Manchester

COLOMBE,
Odilon, d. 2/6/1943 at 80/0/24; farmer; widower; b. Canada; Joseph Colombe (Canada)

COLOMY,
Annie F., d. 4/14/1891 at 96/7; old age; housewife; widow; b. Farmington; Daniel French and Abby Roberts

Carold R., d. 9/2/1895 at 0/7/21; cholera infantum; b. Farmington; Horatio Colomy and Florence F. Tibbetts

Earlan A., d. 3/23/1908 at 0/4/29; pneumonia; b. Milton; John K. Colomy (Dover) and Cora E. Allen (Brookfield)

COLUMBUS,
Albert H., d. 1/18/1985 in Brookline, MA; Odilon Columbus and Melvina Houle

Alexander B., d. 4/11/1905 at 4/5/8; diphtheria; b. Lebanon, ME; Odelon Columbus (Canada) and Melvina Hall (Milton)

Arthur N., d. 10/6/1971 at 84 in Dover; owner truck bus.; b. NH; Odilon Columbus and Melvina Hall

E., d. 8/2/1905 at 0/3/4; whooping cough; b. Milton; O. Columbus (Canada) and Melvina Hall (Milton)

Flora H., d. 4/10/1921 at 35/6/29, housewife; married; b. Somersworth; George Boisvert (Canada) and Mary Ballon (Canada)

Marjorie, d. 2/12/1963 at 48; housewife; b. Jamaica Plains, MA; Howard Benner and Esther Hurd

Melvina, d. 6/18/1931 at 61/11/14; housekeeper; married; b. Milton; Nasaire Houle (Milton) and Celina St. Cyr (Milton)

COMEAU,
Elizabeth F., d. 1/30/1920 at 36/0/20; married; b. Salem, MA; John Gorman (Ireland)

COMOSA,
Mary K., d. 4/21/1979 in Rochester; James Tobin and Elizabeth Canavan

CONDON,
Ralph G., d. 1/27/1973 at 75 in Rochester; shoe worker; b. NS; George Condon and Delia -----

CONNELLY,
Raymond W., d. 10/7/1960 at 69 in Rochester

CONNERS,
Harold, d. 8/4/1901 at 0/2/24; cholera infantum; b. Milton; Michael Conners (Ireland) and Carrie Schroeder (Boston, MA)

CONNERTON,
Hilda E., d. 9/28/1961 at 59 in Rochester; housewife; b. Everett, MA; Ralph Hulsman and Vesta Witham

CONNOLLY,
Mary J., d. 2/18/1947 at 88/0/18; housewife; married; b. Acton, ME; Lyman Buzzell (Acton, ME) and Jane Lord (Shapleigh, ME)
Timothy J., d. 2/15/1950 at 93 in Portsmouth; painter; widower; b. Union; Timothy Connolly and Annie Trindel

CONSTANTINE,
John A., d. 3/1/1998 in Rochester

CONWAY,
Kathleen F., d. 3/23/1979 in Rochester; Patrick Byrnes and Mary Lane

COOK,
Clarence E., d. 6/10/1961 at 55; truckman; b. Middleton; Edward Cook and Ennie Jones
Frank P., d. 8/14/1913 at 60/2/2; acute indigestion; farmer; married; b. Milton; Elias S. Cook (Milton) and Hannah Twombly
Hannah, d. 1/11/1899 at 82/4/27; old age; housekeeper; widow; b. Milton; Jonathan Howe and Mehitable
Ira A., d. 4/3/1898 at 54/4/21; heart failure; farmer; married; b. Milton; William H. Cook (Milton) and Mary Beaton (Wolfeboro)
Lizzie S., d. 6/4/1914 at 75/8/23 in Wakefield; inst'rst'l nephritis; housekeeper; widow; b. Acton, ME; Luther Sanborn (Acton, ME) and Abigail Berry (Milton)
Lucy J., d. 7/30/1914 at 64/1/10; cancer of uterus; widow; b. Rochester; Lewis Hoyt and Clarisa
Lydia, d. 10/28/1890 at 83/5/27; congestion of lungs; housekeeper; married; b. Lebanon, ME; Enoch Blaisdell (Lebanon, ME)
Martin V. B., d. 12/21/1891 at 53/1; Bright's disease; farmer; married; b. Milton; Joseph Cook and Rebecca Ricker
Mary B., d. 3/31/1909 at 51/4/9; cerebral hemorrhage; single; b. Milton; Elias S. Cook (Milton) and Hannah Howe (Milton)
May, d. 12/31/1890 at 88/0/27; bronchitis; housekeeper; widow; b. Wolfeboro; George Yeaton (Portsmouth) and Abigail Wentworth (Milton)

COOKE,
Elwin S., d. 4/8/1900 at 53; la grippe; farmer; single; b. Milton; Elias S. Cooke (Milton) and Hannah Howe (Milton)

COOPER,
Ada S., d. 7/31/1937 at 76/11/6; at home; married; b. England; Henry Mills (Birmingham, England) and Rebecca -----

COPLEY,
son, d. 7/27/1984 in Wolfeboro
son, d. 7/31/1984 in Lynn, MA

CORBETT,
John K., d. 2/3/1907 at 81/5/28; senility; ship carp.; widower; b. NS; John Corbett (NS)

CORKERY,
Daniel, d. 9/15/1902 at 59/8/16; pyaemia; flagman; married; b. St. Johns, NB; Daniel Corkery (England) and Mary Blake (England)

CORMIER,
Evelyn S., d. 8/17/1997 in Milton; George Filiau and Anna Levens
Florence L., d. 10/15/1977 at 69 in Rochester; homemaker; b. MA; Michael Vienneau and Caroline Martin

CORNETTE,
Grace May, d. 8/15/1958 at 75 in Arlington, MA

CORSETTI,
June, d. 5/20/1988 in Lexington, MA

CORSON,
Alonzo, d. 12/23/1889 at 58/8; chr. diarrhea; laborer; married; b. Milton; Thomas Corson and Eliza Jewett
Annie B., d. 12/7/1923 at 79/1/13 in Haverhill, MA; married; b. Buxton, ME; ----- Berryman and Augusta Whitehouse
Carl E., d. 12/29/1896 at 0/4; pneumonia; b. Milton; Leroy F. Corson (Milton) and Winora W. Jones (Lebanon, ME)
Charles E., d. 10/20/1905 at 19/9/12; typhoid; emp. in mill; b. Milton; George M. Corson (Lebanon, ME) and Draxy H. Pierce (Lebanon, ME)
Clara M., d. 5/9/1928 at 83/8/8; at home; widow; b. Milton; James Downs (Milton) and Abigail Ware (Leominster, MA)
Draxa H., d. 10/30/1914 at 75/0/1; lobar pneumonia; housewife; married; b. Lebanon, ME; Noah Pierce (Lebanon, ME) and Ada Goodwin (Lebanon, ME)
George M., d. 10/4/1917 at 75/0/23; retired; widower; b. Lebanon, ME; John Corson (Lebanon, ME) and Eliza Jones
George N., d. 10/14/1917 at 35/3/21; farmer; married; b. Milton; George M. Corson (Lebanon, ME) and Draxa Pierce (Lebanon, ME)
John E., d. 8/20/1940 at 85/10/25 in Sanbornville; retired; married; b. Wakefield; Robert Corson (Milton) and Sarah ----- (Ossipee)
John M., d. 8/6/1935 at 62/6/20 in Dover; George M. Corson (Lebanon, ME) and Draxa H. Pierce (Lebanon, ME)

Lilla M., d. 10/29/1958 at 69 in East Rochester; married; b. Bristol; Aaron Southard and Cora Knowles

Mary, d. 2/14/1907 at 75/3/2; senility; widow; b. Milton; Ivory Hanscom (Milton) and Huldah Goodwin (Milton)

Nellie, d. 3/19/1959 at 86 in Concord; housewife; widow; b. New Hampton; Gardner Knight and Jane Jenness

Royal W., d. 4/30/1974 at 83 in East Rochester; florist; b. NH; Elihu Corson and Mirriam Noyes

Sumner J., d. 12/22/1889 at 3/2/28; meningitis; b. Lebanon, ME; Leroy F. Corson and Winora W. Jones

Vina A., d. 12/1/1960 at 85 in Wolfeboro; housewife; b. Westville, NS; Robert Simpson and Charlotte Higgins

COTTON,

Abigail, d. 7/20/1893 at 73/9; congestion of brain; housekeeper; widow; b. Milton; Hayes Nute (Milton)

Maria, d. 4/16/1909 at 45; cerebral hemorrhage; housekeeper; single; b. Hiram, ME; John Cotton (Hiram, ME) and Maria Cotton (Hiram, ME)

COTY,

Louis J., d. 3/21/1947 at 64/11/20 in Sanford, ME

Louis R., d. 11/1/1987 in Lebanon, ME

Mabel E., d. 4/4/1974 at 86 in Sanford, ME

COUCHEE,

Caroline, d. 11/7/1913 at 78/10/7; intestinal carcinoma; housewife; married; b. Canada; Frank Lambert (Canada) and Josephine Couchee (Canada)

COULOMBE,

Harvey A., d. 9/30/1985 in Rochester; Eugene Coulombe and Imelda Guilmette

Marion A., d. 1/3/1988; Moses Peavey and Ella Fogg

COUSINS,

Mary E., d. 3/3/1928 at 75/11/1; retired; widow; b. Milton; Isaac Wentworth (Milton) and Abby Watson (Tamworth)

COUTURE,
Lucien G., d. 9/19/1992 in Dover

COWELL,
Elizabeth J., d. 5/18/1923 at 93/5/24; widow; b. Milton; Samuel Chamberlain (Milton) and Mary Moody (Lebanon, ME)

COX,
Albert W., d. 8/6/1920 at 37/11/3; salesman; single; b. Philadelphia, PA; Albert W. Cox (Philadelphia, PA) and Anna Holson (Philadelphia, PA)
Bertha E., d. 11/10/1984 in Rochester; Lyle F. Hartford and Josie M. Glidden

CRAIG,
Franklin, d. 9/10/1929 at 64/8/9; married; b. Newbury; James Craig (Newbury) and Alphia Colby (Warner)

CRAWFORD,
Jeffery T., d. 8/27/1981; Ronald I. Crawford and Phyllis Duplissa

CRETEAU,
George A., d. 7/23/1959 at 59; merchant; married; b. Sanbornville; Charles Creteau and Marie Drouin

CROCKETT,
Addie R., d. 7/27/1890 at 29/0/2; tumor of lymp glands; housekeeper; married; b. Mt. Vernon; Judson Locke (Mt. Vernon) and Ruth Wells (Biddeford, ME)

CRONIN,
Michael J., d. 8/27/1995 in Milton; Richard J. Cronin and Barbara A. Denicola

CRONK,
Richard O., d. 1/25/1983 in Manchester; Ansel Cronk and Ruth Hersey

CROSSMAN,
Eleanor, d. 8/3/1997 in MA

CRUM,
M. Eliza, d. 3/1/1947 at 79/1/6 in Wakefield; housewife; widow; b. Acton, ME; Josiah Witham (Acton, ME) and Abbie Willey (MA)
Samuel, d. 5/22/1924 at 65/1/13; mill operative; married; b. Matteawan, NY; Henry Crum (Scotland) and Elizabeth (Ireland)

CRUZ,
Edward, d. 12/25/1993 in Lowell, MA

CULLEN,
Steven K., d. 9/15/1995 in Milton (approx.); Roland P. Cullen and Betty J. Busbee

CUMMINGS,
Clyde, d. 12/6/1956 at 63/6/0 in Rochester; designer; single; b. Roxbury, MA; Henry N. Cummings and Elizabeth Felt

CUNNINGHAM,
Elbridge, d. 7/5/1905 at 42; natural causes; laborer; single; b. ME

CURLL,
Margaret, d. 1/11/1942 at 63/5/21 in Rochester; at home; widow; b. Portland, ME; Charles H. Towle (Portland, ME) and Bridget Schofield (Portland, ME)

CURRIER,
Alfreda M., d. 5/17/1993 in Rochester
Blanche C., d. 4/14/1982 in Acton, ME
Damon R., d. 9/10/1974 at 57 in Rochester; night watchman; b. ME; Joseph Currier and Delia -----
Delia, d. 6/30/1938 at 63/0/27 in Acton, ME; at home; married; b. Ossipee; Gilbert Mattress (Canada) and Maria Williams (Ossipee)
Edna G., d. 10/13/1950 at 52/5; housewife; married; b. Acton, ME; Elmer Nason and ----- Abbott
Harry, d. 4/25/1937 at 26/3/22 in Rochester; single; b. Acton, ME; Joseph Currier (Ossipee) and Delia Mattress (Canada)
Henry S., Sr., d. 7/13/1983 in Rochester; Joseph Currier and Delia Mattress

Joseph, d. 8/21/1948 at 83/1/22 in Wolfeboro; mill hand; married; b. Canada; Patrick Currier (Canada) and Mary ----- (Canada)

Joseph, d. 10/14/1965 at 67 in Acton, ME

Linda, d. 4/9/1959 at 0/7 in Sanford, ME

Ralph H., d. 12/25/1949 at 30/3/28 in Rochester; mule spinner; married; b. Acton, ME; Joseph Currier and Delia Mattress

Raymond H., d. 8/1/1973 at 76 in Danvers, MA

CURRY,

Doreda G., d. 1/10/1977 at 84 in Quincy, MA

Everett W., d. 8/21/1900 at 0/2/14; val. disease of heart; b. Milton; William S. Curry (Stratham) and Hattie Goodwin (Milton)

John E., d. 11/4/1957 at 71 in Dover; widower; b. Acton, ME; John T. Curry and Ada Ricker

John T., d. 6/13/1945 at 93/1/15 in Wakefield; carpenter; widower; b. Lenox, MA; Alex Curry (Scotland) and Mary Cusudu (Ireland)

Lena M., d. 12/11/1941 at 55/7/13 in Rochester; housewife; married; b. Lynn, MA; William J. Feeny (Lynn, MA) and Leona M. Tibbetts (Portland, ME)

Thomas J., d. 2/24/1977 at 80 in Quincy, MA

William S., d. 1/6/1952 at 73; laborer; widower; b. Newfields; John T. Curry and Ada E. Ricker

CURTIS,

Lucretia, d. 4/17/1928 at 88/6/12; at home; widow; b. Newcastle; John Vennard (Newcastle) and Hannah Batson (Newcastle)

Patrick, d. 8/5/1937 at 68/4/19; blacksmith; married; b. NS; Lawrence Curtis (Ingonish, NS) and Susan Duphine (Ingonish, NS)

Rufus, d. 2/5/1903 at 74/1/27; apoplexy; farmer; widower; b. Newcastle; Benjamin Curtis (Newcastle) and Sarah Amazeen (Newcastle)

Sophia A., d. 7/26/1898 at 69/1/11; cerebral softening; housekeeper; married; b. Middleton; Moses Place

CUSTEAU,

Charles, d. 5/22/1973 at 90 in Tilton; hotel manager; b. ME; George Custeau and Delvina Marcoux

Clesilda B., d. 8/21/1965 at 83; skiver; b. Canada; Onesime Blouin and Philomene Bisson

Eldredge E., d. 10/11/1907 at 0/6/24; acute meningitis; b. Milton; Eldredge Custeau (Canada) and Lizzie Blouin (Canada)
George A., d. 2/10/1985 in Rochester; Aldege Custeau and Clesilda Blouin
Mildred B., d. 1/30/1990 in Rochester

CUTLER,

Charles F., d. 7/10/1939 at 76/8/7 in Milton Mills; farmer; married; b. Lexington, MA; Thomas E. Cutler (Lexington, MA) and Melinda Houghton (Lexington, MA)
Marilla C., d. 3/21/1941 at 74/6/14 in Milton Mills; housewife; widow; b. Charlestown, MA; William Teel (Arlington, MA) and Melissa Otis (ME)

CUTTER,

Jean W., d. 6/22/1995 in Rochester
Michael F., d. 1/23/1956 at 0/0/0 in Rochester; b. Rochester; Mearl L. Cutter and Norma M. Drew
Norma M., d. 2/23/1994 in Farmington

CUTTS,

Charles, d. 3/9/1958 at 93/4/9 in Haverhill, MA; col. teacher, ret.; widower; b. Milton Mills; William F. Cutts and Abigail Sanborn
Fred H., d. 3/30/1902 at 37/4/26; septisemia; farmer; married; b. Milton; William F. Cutts (No. Berwick, ME) and Mary A. Sanborn (Acton, ME)
Julia A., d. 11/8/1903 at 75/6/26; apoplexy; housekeeper; single; b. No. Berwick, ME; Thomas J. Cutts (No. Berwick, ME) and Hulda Chadburn (No. Berwick, ME)
Lydia M., d. 5/19/1922 at 79/7/27; at home; married; b. Milton; Asa Jewett (Milton) and Mary A. Richards (Somersworth)
Mary A., d. 10/13/1893 at 58/0/15 in Portland, ME; removal of tumors; housekeeper; married; b. Acton, ME; Luther Sanborn (Acton, ME) and Abigail Berry (Milton)
Nellie W., d. 11/14/1955 at 89/0/17 in Haverhill, MA; married; b. Bowdoin, ME; David Curtis and Rachel Merriman
Thomas J., d. 3/15/1933 at 93/8/9; retired; widower; b. Berwick, ME; Thomas J. Cutts (Berwick, ME) and Hulda Chadbourne (Berwick, ME)

William F., d. 2/24/1910 at 79/2/2; heart syncope; farmer; widower; b. No. Berwick, ME; Thomas J. Cutts (No. Berwick, ME) and Hulda Chadborne (No. Berwick, ME)

D'ANNA,
Katherine Mary, d. 2/25/1989 in Rochester; Robert A. D'Anna and Carol Parks

DAGNINO,
Inez A., d. 7/8/1916 at 16/8/10; single; b. Boston, MA; John R. Dagnino (Italy) and Emily Currotti (NY)

DAILEY,
David L., d. 2/25/1945 at 67/10/17 in Togus, ME; barber; married; b. KY; David Dailey (MO) and Amelia Vermillion (KY)

DALEY,
John H., d. 5/18/1913 at 57/6; acute alcoholism; laborer; single; b. Natick, MA

DAME,
Daniel O., d. 7/19/1958 at 60 in Wolfeboro
Gladys E., d. 12/23/1972 at 71 in Rochester
Howard E., d. 12/27/1975 at 60 in Rochester; wood working; b. NH; Daniel E. Dame and Josephine Pinkham
Virginia A., d. 4/4/1991 in Ossipee

DANFORTH,
Edward S., d. 3/27/1950 at 78/7/23 in Dover; retired; widower
Elizabeth, d. 12/31/1943 at 72 in Wellesley, MA; housework; married; b. NS; Reuben McAdams (NS) and Mary J. Chivers (NS)

DANIELS,
Robert A., Jr., d. 7/3/1986 in Milton Mills; Robert A. Daniels and Sandra H. Taylor

DAVIS,
daughter, d. 10/2/1939 at 0/0/0 in Rochester; b. Rochester; Daniel Davis (Newfield, ME) and Helen Colby (Springvale, ME)

Addie S., d. 2/2/1899 at 38/3/28; hemiplegia; housekeeper; married; b. Alton; Charles W. Duntley (Ossipee) and Lovina Watson (Alton)

Daniel N., d. 8/5/1985 in Milton Mills; Eugene Davis and Rose Comeau

Ella, d. 4/7/1971 at 87 in No. Berwick, ME

Flora May, d. 12/15/1891 at 0/1/15; cancer; b. Milton; John F. Davis and Ida M. Place

Frank H., d. 1/23/1957 at 83 in Dover

Helen R., d. 6/21/1958 at 43 in Sanford, ME; spinner; married; b. Springvale, ME; Fred Colby and Edith Pike

Mary, d. 4/6/1914 at 83/4/14; cerebral hemorrhage; widow; b. Lebanon, ME; John Corson (Lebanon, ME) and Eliza Jones (Wells, ME)

Sharon D., d. 4/30/1942 at 0/4/20 in Rochester; b. Rochester; Daniel N. Davis (Newfield, ME) and Helen Colby (Springvale, ME)

Teresa W., d. 3/11/1997 in Rochester

DAWSON,

Edith A., d. 10/14/1918 at 32/3; married; b. Warsaw, NY; George E. Ackerman (Bath, NY) and Eugenia Van Warner (Cohorton, NY)

Giles E., d. 5/18/1993 in Rochester; William Dawson and May A. Duncan

Ruth H., d. 8/15/1985 in Wolfeboro; Svante Swenson and Milda Lundgren

Seth F., d. 4/15/1955 at 75 in Rochester; ret. manuf.; married; b. Lawrence, MA; Seth F. Dawson

Wilfred E., d. 1/20/1988; John Dawson and Clara Macomber

DAY,

Alden A., d. 3/23/1992 in Rochester (1993)

Aurena M., d. 7/26/1908 at 75/2/16; tuberculosis; housework; widow; b. ME; Aaron Goodwin (Acton, ME)

Austin M., d. 3/2/1990 in Laconia

Frances M., d. 6/26/1923 at 12/0/26 in Rochester; b. Brookfield; Alden Day (Newfield, ME) and Sarah Allen (Brookfield)

Freeman H., d. 11/3/1907 at 46/2/12; internal injuries; farmer; married; b. Porter, ME; James E. Day (Brownfield, ME) and Lydia J. Lowell (Hiram, ME)

Horace, d. 6/2/1893 at 29/6/18; pulmonary consumption; hostler; single; b. Shapleigh, ME; Benjamin Day (Shapleigh, ME) and Annie Goodwin (Sanford, ME)

Jeremy L., d. 4/27/1983 in Rochester; Kenneth J. Day and Deborah Bickford

Susan, d. 3/23/1917 at 62/10/8; married; b. Parsonsfield, ME; Plummer Patch (Shapleigh, ME) and Sarah (Acton, ME)

DEANGELIS,
Angelo P., d. 5/17/1981 in Chelsea, MA

Edward, Jr., d. 12/18/1971 at 2 in Rochester; b. NH; Edward DeAngelis and Jean A. Hutchins

Mary E., d. 4/27/1983 in Lowell, MA

DEARBORN,
Everett, d. 3/16/1945 at 66 in Dover; laborer; divorced; b. Dover; Horace E. Dearborn (Canada) and Leona Chapman (Canada)

DEEGAN,
Margaret T., d. 6/5/1972 at 60; homemaker; b. MA; William Mahoney and Nora McCarthy

DELLECHAIE,
Judith M., d. 10/1/1965 at 0/0/3 in Rochester; b. Rochester; John F. DelleChaie and Eleanor Mells

DELUCA,
Rena, d. 12/15/1985 in Rochester; Phillip Regali and Aldane Ferranti

DEMER[R]ITT,
daughter, d. 3/26/1941 at 0/0/0; b. Milton; Delphin DeMeritt (Milton) and Carrie S. Tobey (Dover)

Berthold I., d. 6/14/1949 at 74; shoe shop; widower; b. Newfield, ME; David Demerritt and Hannah Nason

Bertie, d. 8/10/1899 at 0/0/11; tetanus; b. Milton; B. J. Demeritt (Newfield, ME) and Musetta A. Dorr (Milton)

Lloyd A., d. 9/4/1896 at 0/3; enterocolitis; b. Milton; B. I. Demeritt (Newfield, ME) and Musetta A. Dorr (Eliot, ME)

Mary A., d. 2/26/1903 at 32/10/3; tuberculosis; housekeeper; married; b. Boston, MA; Parker Spinney (Wakefield) and Abigail A.M. Hanson (Somersworth)

Merribah A., d. 7/28/1904 at 10/11/22; peritonitis; b. Milton; Berth. I. Demeritt (Newfield, ME) and Musetta A. Dorr (Milton)

Musetta A., d. 4/12/1946 at 70/9/3 in Rochester; housewife; married; b. Dover; Frank Raitt (Eliot, ME) and Caroline George (Dover)

DESCARY,
Charles F., d. 2/15/1967 at 84; laborer; b. Stoneham, MA; Joseph Descary and Martha Marr

DEVOID,
Clarence E., d. 8/19/1962 at 61 in Manchester; woodsman; Frank L. Devoid and Hattie M. LaRose

DEXTER,
Gilwin, d. 5/18/1936 at 33/2/22 in Rochester; laborer; married; b. Dover, ME; Leslie Dexter (Dover, ME) and Amy M. Nichols (Dover, ME)

DIACK,
Oliver J., d. 5/30/1957 at 47 in Manchester; dry cleaner; single; Alfred Diack and Jeannie Wilson

DICEY,
George W., d. 9/23/1894 at 52/9/6; consumption and malaria; carpenter; married; b. Gilmanton; C. Dicey

Gertrude S., d. 1/14/1895 at 12/8/26; meningitis; single; George W. Dicey (Gilmanton) and Susan Durrell (Wakefield)

Jessie, d. 9/30/1893 at 19/8; dysentery; single; b. Wolfeboro; George W. Dicey (Jackson) and Susan Durrell (Union)

Susan A., d. 9/5/1899 at 53/10/22; pernicious anemia; housekeeper; widow; b. Wakefield; Nathaniel Durrell and Mahaley Whitehouse

DICKEY,
Nellie W., d. 12/4/1918 at 42/11/11; teacher; widow; b. Milton; John A. Wentworth (Milton) and Hannah E. Gray (Strafford)

DICKSON,
Allie May, d. 5/2/1978 at 96 in Rochester; homemaker; b. NH; George M. Corson and Draza Pierce

Ernest, d. 9/7/1900 at 0/4/26; cholera infantum; b. Milton; Ernest F. Dickson (Lunenburg) and Allie M. Corson (Milton)

Ernest F., d. 9/15/1956 at 77 in Rochester; mill supt.; married; b. Lunenburg, MA; William F. Dickson and Sylvia Lacey

Franklin, d. 11/14/1969 at 67 in Hanover; foreman; b. NH; Ernest Dickson

Grace H., d. 3/21/1963 at 80 in Rochester; housewife; b. Boston, MA; Walter Harwood

Hattie M., d. 12/20/1914 at 39/6/3; Bright's disease; housekeeper; married; b. Still River, MA; William V. Newell (Boston, MA) and Lucy Mullen (Skowhegan, ME)

Mary J., d. 4/21/1907 at 79/6/8; apoplexy; widow; b. Lowell, MA; Jonathan Morse and Eliza Marble

Mary T., d. 7/15/1999 in Lee; Henry Timmins and Hannah Tuck

William A., d. 10/26/1952 at 78 in Rochester; ret. supt.; married; b. Lunenburg, MA; William F. Dickson and Myrtle Lancey

William F., d. 5/9/1941 at 87/4/15; retired; widower; b. Charlestown, MA; William Dickson (Charlestown, MA) and Mary Morse (Medford, MA)

DIONNE,
David J., d. 8/30/1986 in Hanover; Raymond Dionne and Jo-Anne Marion

DIPRIZIO,
Albert C., d. 11/30/1970 at 21 in Rochester; student; b. NH; John H. DiPrizio and Enid Lowd

DIXON,
Clemence C., d. 5/10/1951 at 63/0/26 in Rochester; mail messenger; single; b. So. Boston, MA

George, d. 8/13/1890 at 41/4/13; cirrhosis of liver; laborer; single; b. Milton; Ichabod Dixon and Nancy J. Harmon

Herman, d. 8/8/1937 at 34/4/17; pipe fitter; married; b. Eliot, ME; George P. Dixon (Eliot, ME) and Mabel Spinney (Eliot, ME)

Lizzie M., d. 4/12/1903 at 66/1/4; schirrhus cancer; housekeeper; widow; b. Milton; William W. Cook (Milton) and Mary Yeaton (Wolfeboro)

Nancy Jane, d. 3/11/1898 at 74/10/13; cardiac syncope; housekeeper; widow; b. Cornish, ME; Simon Harmon and Lydia

Stephen E., d. 6/7/1946 at 82/8/6; watchman; married; b. Milton; Ichbold Dixon (Milton) and Nancy Harmon (Cornish, ME)

DOE,
Arthur N., d. 1/11/1900 at 0/1/23; inanition; b. Milton; James F. Doe (Milton) and Edith Witham (Brookfield)
Chester A., d. 5/13/1901 at 2/7/11; chronic gastritis; b. Milton; James F. Doe (Milton) and Edith M. Witham (Brookfield)
Edith M., d. 5/5/1900 at 25/2/23; consumption; housekeeper; married; b. Brookfield; Charles H. Witham (Milton) and Rosa Hardy (Newport)
Etta F., d. 3/29/1963 at 89; nurse; b. Brockton, MA; Bartholomew Martin and Margaret Henderson
James F., d. 4/5/1920 at 48; farmer; married; b. Milton; Mark D. Doe (Newfield, ME) and Rachal Horne (Milton)
Mark D., d. 11/16/1904 at 77/6; senility; farmer; widower; b. Newfield, ME; Ebenezer Doe (Parsonsfield, ME) and Orinda Dam (Newfield, ME)
Ralph A., d. 2/2/1916 at 18/7/15; single; b. Milton; James F. Doe (Milton) and Edith M. Whitham (Brookfield)

DOHRN,
Fannie R., d. 12/2/1933 at 69/8/15; housewife; widow; b. Dilhollsie, NS; John Carter (Bear River, NS) and Rebecca Snell (London, England)

DOKRN,
Gustave W., d. 9/21/1933 at 70/1/11; chef; married; b. Germany

DONALDSON,
David, d. 1/23/1900 at 39/7/6; internal hemorrhage; farmer; married; b. Canada; Charles Donaldson (Scotland) and Sarah Mould (Canada)

DONDERO,
Louis F., d. 1/16/1999 in Milton; Louis Dondero and Loretta Gagne

DONNELL,
Ethel R., d. 1/27/1906 at 25/3; pulmon. tuberculosis; single; b. Biddeford, ME; George W. Donnell (Biddeford, ME) and Victoria L. Waterhouse (Scarboro, ME)
Lewis, d. 5/3/1930 at 78/10/3; ret. brass moulder; married; b. Canada

DONNELLY,
Colleen G., d. 9/7/1963 at 3 in North Rochester; b. Biloxi, MS; John J. Donnelly, Jr. and Ella Tanner

DONOHUE,
Elizabeth, d. 1/14/1956 at 67/7/27 in Weymouth, MA; married; b. Milton; Bertha Drew

DOOR,
Ella M., d. 6/21/1889 at 39/8/14; ovarian tumor; house; single; b. Milton; Eliphet P. Door and Augusta H. Fox
Nathaniel H., d. 8/18/1889 at 46/2/11; consumption; farmer; single; b. Milton; Eliphet P. Door and Augusta H. Fox

DORE,
son, d. 5/16/1932 at 0/0/1; b. Milton; Charles E. Dore (Milton) and Blanch Nickerson (Milton)
Abbie, d. 4/21/1895 at 73/11; cancerous tumor; housekeeper; widow; b. Newfield, ME; Phineas Howe (Newfield, ME) and Hannah Ham (Newfield, ME)
Augusta, d. 4/2/1914 at 100/10/27; heart failure; widow; b. Acton, ME; James Fox and Sallie Thompson
Blanche E., d. 8/25/1983 in Rochester; James T. Nickerson and Lillian M. Mason
Charles E., d. 5/24/1964 at 71 in Manchester; laborer; b. Milton; Charles Dore and Winnifred Duntley
Herbert W., d. 6/28/1912 at 52/4/20; accident drowning; shoemaker; married; b. Wakefield; Hanson Dore and Mary Morrison
James F., d. 11/24/1912 at 69/1/21; Bright's disease; farmer; married; b. Milton; Eliphlet Dore (Milton) and Augusta (Milton)

DORNAN,
Aaron J., d. 6/27/1998 in Milton
John Wright, d. 3/26/1989 in Rochester

DORR,
daughter, d. 12/1/1913 at 0/0/2; premature birth; b. Milton; William W. Dorr (Milton) and Ruth M. Edwards (Temple, ME)

Alfranzo F., d. 5/3/1927 at 53/10/27; laborer; married; b. Milton; Stephen D. Dorr (Milton) and Melvina Staples (Farmington)

Augusta M., d. 12/2/1953 at 77/1/1 in Dover; shoe worker; widow; b. Wolfeboro; Charles F. Burke and Hattie M. Tibbetts

Charles C., d. 9/24/1913 at 84/4/27; senile gangrene; farmer; widower; b. Milton; George W. Dorr (Milton) and Jane Frost (Eliot, ME)

Charles H., d. 10/6/1923 at 70/9/8; laborer; divorced; b. Milton; Amasa Dorr (Lebanon, ME) and Sarah A. Ellis (Middleton)

Dana C., d. 4/30/1890 at 11; severed femoral artery; school; single; b. Milton; C. C. Dorr (Milton) and Mary Watson (Milton)

Fred H., d. 9/19/1941 at 64/4/1; shoe worker; single; b. Milton; Stephen D. Dorr (Milton) and Melvina Staples (Farmington)

Hannah W., d. 4/6/1911 at 72/6/7; pneumonia; housework; married; b. Milton; Daniel Hill (Lebanon, ME) and Sallie Downs (Milton)

Hattie A., d. 8/13/1939 at 83/5/6 in Norway, ME; ret. secretary; single; b. Milton; John C. Dorr (Sandwich) and Julia Corliss (Milton)

Hervey W., d. 11/11/1956 at 82/5/23; farmer; married; b. Milton; Charles C. Dorr and Melissa Jones

Irving G., d. 7/6/1922 at 38/4/7; shoe cutter; single; b. Milton; Stephen D. Dorr (Milton) and Melvina F. Staples (Farmington)

Isaac B., d. 7/1/1891 at 70/0/7; heart failure; laborer; married; b. Milton; Beriah Dorr and Mary Pray

Lizzie S., d. 9/13/1920 at 74/6/25; housekeeper; widow; b. No. Shapleigh, ME; Stephen Maddox (Newfield, ME) and Sally Moore (Newfield, ME)

Melissa, d. 8/7/1889 at 34/10/17; chr. hepatitis; house; married; b. Milton; Nathan Jones and Vesty B. Davenport

Melvina F., d. 10/4/1919 at 74/6/24; housewife; widow; b. Farmington; Jacob Staples (Whitefield) and Temperance Watson (Farmington)

Simon C., d. 10/2/1913 at 73; heart failure, senility; farmer; widower; b. Milton; George W. Dorr (Milton) and Jane Frost (Eliot, ME)

Stephen D., d. 5/14/1916 at 85 in Dover; divorced; b. Milton; George W. Dorr (Milton) and Jane Frost (Eliot, ME)

Theodore Lyman, d. 3/12/1899 at 0/11; hydrocephalus; b. Milton; Charles H. Dorr (Milton) and Mary W. Duntley (Milton)

Theodore Lyman, d. 12/8/1899 at 0/8/13; hydrocephalus; b. Milton; Charles H. Dorr (Milton) and Mary E. Duntley (Milton)

DOUGLAS,
Kenneth, d. 12/1/1962 at 57 in Dover; machinist; b. Dover; William Douglas and Lillian G. Lancaster
Ronald G., d. 3/13/1991 in Kissimmee, FL
Shirley L., d. 3/30/1982 in Rochester; Ralph Williams, Sr. and Lillian ----

DOWE,
Elizabeth M., d. 6/25/1895 at 51/5/26; pulmonary phthisis; housekeeper; married; b. Raynham, MA; Baylies Richmond (Taunton, MA) and Dora Smith (Rehoboth, MA)

DOWNING,
Alice H., d. 2/5/1923 at 58/7/21; married; b. Somersworth; George W. Hodgdon and Mary Hobbs
Charles L., d. 10/29/1932 at 50/6/28 in Fayette, ME; laborer; married; b. Farmington; Charles W. Downing and Sarah Page
Daisy A., d. 1/7/1900 at 30/9/9; mastobitis; married; b. No. Hampton; Oliver Page (Hampton) and Susan Rowe (Seabrook)
Elizabeth, d. 8/5/1899 at 78/6/24; chronic nephritis; housekeeper; widow
Fannie G., d. 10/19/1893 at 80; bronchial pneumonia; housekeeper; widow; b. Holderness; David Prescott (Holderness) and Polly Glines (Moultonboro)
Jeremiah, d. 10/3/1911 at 66/7/12; pneumonia; ice business; married; b. Kennebunkport, ME; John Downing (Kennebunkport, ME) and Mary Roberts (Waterboro, ME)
Sarah, d. 11/11/1933 at 74/8/12 in Hiram, ME

DOWNS,
A. Jennie, d. 4/1/1898 at 49/3/9; carcinoma; housekeeper; single; b. Milton; James D. Downs (Milton) and Abbie B. Weare (Leominster, MA)
Abbie B., d. 10/1/1893 at 78/11/13; dysentery; housekeeper; widow; b. Leominster, MA
Albert F., d. 6/28/1909 at 60/11/1; acute cardiac dilation; divorced; b. Milton; Moses Downs (Dover) and Lavina Hanson (Alton)
Anna L., d. 9/13/1951 at 58 in Rochester; housewife; married; b. Portsmouth, OH; Thomas R. Adams and Lydia A. Rice
Annette, d. 9/9/1936 at 73/2/28; at home; widow; b. Wolfeboro; David T. Piper (Alton) and Maria Charles (Fryeburg, ME)

Arthur F., d. 10/9/1891 at 34/0/20; consumption; shoemaker; married; b. Milton; Henry Downs (Canada) and Elizabeth Drew (Canada)
Arthur L., d. 2/15/1956 at 67 in Rochester; farmer; widower; b. Center Barnstead; Herbert A. Downs
Augusta, d. 11/30/1940 at 76/5/9; housekeeper; married; b. Middleton; John B. Kimball (Augusta, ME) and Sabrina Downs (Berwick, ME)
Carrie W., d. 11/29/1986 in Ossipee
Dora M., d. 1/11/1924 at 75/4/30; widow; b. Strafford; Jonathan Tuttle (Barrington) and Sarah Waterhouse (Barrington)
Emily P., d. 12/5/1897 at 68/8/22; angina pectoris; housekeeper; married; b. Farmington; Hazen Duntley (Bow) and Phoebe Leighton (Farmington)
Eva M., d. 6/12/1960 at 74; counter moulder; b. Wakefield; Charles F. West
Fannie M., d. 10/17/1894 at 46/9/2; complication of diseases; housekeeper; married; Jesse R. Hursom (Lebanon, ME) and Mary E.
Frank L., d. 3/11/1948 at 87/6/14 in Dover; janitor; widower; b. Milton; John T. Downs (Canada) and Olive A. Wentworth (Milton)
Fred C., d. 4/1/1963 at 87 in Dover; sup't; b. Waltham, MA; Charles Downs
George A., d. 6/11/1924 at 54/2/17; laborer; married; b. Milton; Albert F. Downs (Milton) and Dora M. Tuttle (Strafford)
George F., d. 6/18/1921 at 65/5/3; butcher; married; b. Milton; Simon T. Downs (Milton) and Clara Rankins (Milton)
George Q., d. 1/24/1935 at 81/2; retired; single; b. Milton; James Downs (Milton) and Abigail Ware (Leominster, MA)
Hannah M., d. 5/18/1973 at 92 in Rochester
Hazen W., d. 11/10/1916 at 68/9/16; married; b. Milton; Joshua H. Downs (Milton) and Emily Duntley (Milton)
Herbert A., d. 6/3/1993 in Portland, ME; Arthur Downs and Maude -----
J. Hanson, d. 12/14/1898 at 72/9/7; heart disease; shoemaker; widower; b. Milton; Moses Downs and Lavina Hanson
James M., d. 5/21/1982 in Union
John, d. 3/22/1898 at 68/5/8; heart disease; laborer; widower; b. Milton; Moses Downs and Lavina Hanson
John A., d. 10/5/1935 at 74/11/2; laborer; married; b. Barrington; John Downs (Milton) and Sophia Seavey (Rochester)
John T.H., d. 5/2/1900 at 70/2/20; pneumonia; farmer; married; b. Canada; James Downs (Rochester) and Judith Wentworth (Milton)

Lizzie M., d. 2/6/1938 at 68/2/3; housewife; widow; b. Auburn, ME; Otis Thompson (Chesterville, ME) and Lizzie S. Pettee (E. Sullivan, ME)

Lura M., d. 12/31/1903 at 22/3/3; pulmonary tuberculosis; single; b. Milton; Hazen W. Downs (Milton) and Fannie Hersom (Waterboro, ME)

Olive A., d. 8/16/1905 at 76/1/18; senility; widow; b. Milton; Jacob Wentworth (Milton) and Sally Hanson (Alton)

Raymond F., d. 6/26/1950 at 36/2/15 in Rochester; laborer; married; b. Milton; Fred Downs and Eva West

Raymond L., d. 12/26/1977 at 16 in Hanover; student; b. NH; Raymond F. Downs and Helen Kraus

Rebecca E., d. 5/4/1896 at 79/9/6; cerebral congestion; widow; b. Milton; John P. Jenkins (Milton) and Nancy Patten (Dover)

Roy M., d. 3/24/1968 at 74; mill worker; b. NH; John A. Downs and May Thompson

Sophia A., d. 5/21/1897 at 70/5; erisypelas; housekeeper; married; b. Rochester; Richard Savory and Lydia Savory

Wilma F., d. 1/19/1998 in Dover

Winifred E., d. 11/5/1968 at 80 in Wolfeboro

DRAPER,

Stacey A., d. 9/10/1960 at 72; carpenter, ret.; b. Tilton; Alva E. Draper and Mary Alma Dustin

DRAWBRIDGE,

son, d. 6/28/1899 at 0/0/0; stillborn; b. Milton; Edward Drawbridge (Worcester, MA) and Bertha E. Cook (Milton)

Bertha C., d. 7/6/1899 at 22/3/21; Bright's disease; milliner; married; b. Milton; M.V.B. Cook (Milton) and Sarah E. Sanborn (Acton, ME)

DREW,

Angie M., d. 6/24/1916 at 68/5/22; housewife; married; b. Shapleigh, ME; Ivory Ridley (Shapleigh, ME) and Eliza Norton (Alfred, ME)

Catherine, d. 3/14/1988 in Benton

Clara E., d. 2/11/1902 at 44/11/7; influenza; shoe stitcher; single; b. Milton; Asa B. Drew (Acton, ME) and Hannah Pinkham (Milton)

Clarence L., d. 2/21/1970 at 83; laborer; b. NH; John Drew and Ada Tibideau

Cora A., d. 6/4/1935 at 52/7/26; at home; married; b. Conway; Harding
Nason (ME) and Lucinda Thorne (ME)
Donald K., d. 8/10/1986 in Acton, ME
Dwight S., d. 2/19/1998 in Dover
Emeline, d. 1/25/1915 at 66/2/25; widow; b. Porter, ME; Simeon Dyer
(Hollis, ME) and Nancy Day (Brownfield, ME)
Fannie M., d. 2/9/1933 at 69/11/18 in East Providence, RI
George, d. 11/23/1943 at 68 in Ossipee
Hannah M., d. 9/28/1914 at 82/3/4; cerebral hemorrhage; widow; b.
Milton; James Pinkham and Sally Jewett
Harriet L., d. 8/8/1960 at 71 in Rochester; housewife; b. No. Adams, MA;
Augustus Locke and Martha Perkins
Henry, d. 9/23/1946 at 76/7/29; laborer; widower; b. Brookfield; William
H. Drew (Brookfield) and Emily Dyer (Brownfield, ME)
Henry W., d. 2/1/1912 at 75/8/23; chronic nephritis; married; b.
Brookfield; Benjamin Drew (Milton) and Hannah Drew (Dover)
Herbert M., d. 8/6/1951 at 52; brick mason; married; b. Bow; Frederick E.
Drew and Mary E. Baker
Ida L., d. 7/14/1979 in Rochester; Richard Cornell and Isabelle -----
Ina F., d. 5/6/1922 at 47/10/10; at home; married; b. Milton; G.C.S.
Wentworth (So. Berwick, ME) and Mary C. Hanson (Milton)
Joanna H., d. 4/8/1943 at 82/3/2 in Wakefield; housework; married; b.
Wolfeboro; Amos E. Bradley (Wolfeboro) and Sarah F. Kenney
(Wolfeboro)
Lyle S., d. 10/1/1961 at 70 in Wakefield; manufacturer; b. Union; George
W. Drew and Malie E. Drew
Malie E., d. 8/30/1938 at 71/0/8 in Wakefield; housewife; married; b.
Middleton; Thomas J. Stevens (Middleton) and Mary Whitehouse
(Middleton)
Patsy L., d. 2/9/1995 in Rochester
Pearl M., d. 11/29/1993 in Rochester
Roscoe C., d. 1/12/1924 at 27/11/14; single; b. Brookfield; William H.
Drew (Brookfield) and Emeline Dyer (Porter, ME)
Tamson, d. 1/20/1895 at 86/7/26; pneumonia; widow; b. New Durham;
Reuben Whitehouse (Durham) and Dorcas Lang (Portsmouth)
Thelma, d. 11/23/1897 at 1/4/28; meningitis; b. Milton; Samuel E. Drew
(Stoneham) and Ina F. Wentworth (Milton)
William, d. 10/26/1904 at 0/6/17; broncho pneumonia; b. Milton; William
F. Drew (Tamworth) and Kate M. Hardy (Tamworth)

William S., d. 3/7/1928 at 73/9/5; mill operator; single; b. Milton; Asa B. Drew (Acton, ME) and Hannah Pinkham (Milton)

Zenas F., d. 3/23/1929 at 82/6/5; farmer; widower; b. Acton, ME; Edmund Drew (Acton, ME) and Caroline Levan (Watertown, MA)

DRISCOLL,
Nellie, d. 9/27/1961 at 62 in Jersey City, NJ

DUBY,
Arthur G., d. 5/9/1958 at 70/11/28; building; married; b. Canada

DUDLEY,
Frances H., d. 1/27/1988 in Rochester
Pauline M., d. 1/13/1981 in Rochester; Arthur P. Moulton and Maude Smith
Sarah E., d. 1/30/1961 at 86; housewife; b. Westfield, VT; Thomas L. Gilbert and Mary Killian

DUEZ,
Agnes R., d. 11/16/1996 in Rochester; Joseph Bernier and Margaret Gagnon
Robert L., d. 7/12/1986 in Rochester; Clemant Duez and Isabelle Stevens

DUGGAN,
Charlotte E., d. 12/6/1986 in Rochester; Frederick Dunham and Elvera Milliken
James G., d. 1/14/1992 in Rochester; John M. Duggan and Catherine Brazile

DUNNELLS,
Annette J., d. 1/13/1986 in Rochester
Clinton E., d. 8/20/1967 at 57 in Sanford, ME

DUNTLEY,
Clarence W., d. 1/8/1918 at 47/7; farmer; single; b. Milton; John H. Duntley (Milton) and Elizabeth A. Downs (Milton)
Elizabeth A., d. 7/12/1907 at 61/11/24; chronic nephritis; housework; widow; b. Milton; Henry Downs (Canada) and Elizabeth Drew (Dover)

Hattie, d. 12/1/1936 at 67/3/24 in Scituate, MA; housekeeper; single; b. Milton; Ira W. Duntley (NH) and Sarah Hodgeman (NH)

Herbert, d. 2/28/1966 at 83 in Dover

Ira W., d. 3/20/1916 at 74/4; blacksmith; widower; b. Milton; Hazen Duntley (Bow) and Phebe Leighton (Farmington)

John H., d. 8/8/1896 at 50/6/13; hemorrhage; shoemaker; married; b. Milton; Arial Duntley (Sandwich) and Mary Ricker (Somersworth)

Sarah A., d. 1/1/1914 at 69/11; ch. int'rs nephritis; married; b. Walpole, MA; Samuel Hodgman and Adeline A. Tibbetts

DUPONT,
Elzear, d. 6/16/1981 in Rochester; Alphonse Dupont and Destonges LaBranche

DUPUIS,
Carrie B., d. 2/21/1980 in Wolfeboro; Frank Blackey and Gertrude Henderson

Euclide R., d. 10/10/1995 in Rochester; Fred W. Dupuis and Lydia Marchand

Gertrude T., d. 10/17/1984 in Rochester; Peter Harrity and Phoebe Sylvain

DUQUETTE,
Emma, d. 4/25/1958 at 86 in Wakefield; housewife; married; b. Canada; Nazaire Houle and Marie St. Cyr

Leon, d. 9/25/1958 at 87 in Wakefield; mill operative; widower; b. Canada

DURKEE,
Estella A., d. 3/20/1998 in Milton

Porter J., d. 10/15/1979 in Rochester; George Durkee and Rose Gould

DUSABLON,
Alfred J., d. 1/31/1984 in Rochester; Alfred J. Dusablon, Sr. and Mary L. Therrien

DWYER,
Peter W., d. 4/7/1939 at 85/9/22 in Dover; single; b. So. Boston, MA; Lawrence Dwyer (So. Boston, MA) and Catharine Ford (So. Boston, MA)
Richard J., d. 10/30/1961 at 44; dealer; b. Lynn, MA; Richard I. Dwyer and Ruth Aulson

DYER,
Benjamin, d. 3/6/1901 at 27/8/9; Bright's disease; mill hand; single; b. Wakefield; Charles H. Dyer (Brownfield, ME) and Martha A. Drew (Brookfield)
Charles, d. 9/18/1911 at 68/3/23; chronic myocarditis; farmer; married; b. Brownfield, ME; Simeon Dyer (Brownfield, ME) and Nancy J. Day (Hiram, ME)
Martha A., d. 4/18/1918 at 74/9/2; widow; Benjamin Drew (Milton) and Hannah Drew (Dover)

EARLY,
Ann C., d. 12/12/1996 in Dover; Joseph Sinclair and Catherine O'Rourke

EASTMAN,
Charles F., d. 10/15/1950 at 67 in Rochester
Mary A., d. 8/13/1948 at 58/0/18 in Middleton
Robert E., d. 8/31/1946 at 15/8/22 in Rochester; student; single; b. Wolfeboro; Anna Eastman (Middleton)

EATON,
Charles A., d. 5/10/1996 in Springvale, ME
Doris C., d. 8/25/1974 at 57 in Dover
Doris M., d. 8/8/1962 at 61 in Arlington, MA
Douglas L., d. 5/9/1992 in Hillsboro
Emma E., d. 3/6/1998 in Dover
Ernest A., d. 2/13/1969 at 80
Harriet R., d. 12/12/1972 at 82 in Sanford, ME
Henry O., d. 11/11/1967 at 39 in Rochester; laborer; b. Wells, ME; Daniel Eaton and Gertrude Russell
Roger, d. 11/30/1936 at 0/2/8 in Sanford, ME; b. Sanford, ME; William Sourman (Portsmouth) and Frances Eaton (Acton, ME)
Yvonne D., d. 1/9/1979 in Portland, ME

EAVES,
Emery D., d. 5/25/1973 at 43 in Greenland; state highway emp.; b. MA; Hollis A. Eaves and Constance Cole

EDGERL[E]Y,
Addie C., d. 4/24/1902 at 37/5/28; pul. tuberculosis; shoemaker; widow; b. Middleton; John S. Pike (Middleton) and Mary M. Cloutman (Middleton)
Helen P., d. 5/18/1904 at 18/6/18; consumption; single; b. Milton; Benjamin W. Edgerley (Wakefield) and Addie C. Pike (Middleton)
Hiram V.R., d. 6/22/1909 at 87/8/27; senility; carpenter; widower; b. Alton
Lydia Ann, d. 2/20/1906 at 77/4; senility; married; b. Milton; Jesse Knox and Lydia Dore
Mary M., d. 12/19/1898 at 87/6/24; old age; widow; b. Milton; Jediah Leighton (Farmington) and Sarah (Farmington)

ELDREDGE,
John A., d. 10/18/1916 at 80/2/1; machinist; married; b. Orrington, ME; John Eldredge and Caroline Wood

ELDRIDGE,
Arthur, d. 1/12/1929 at 0/1/27; b. West Lebanon, ME; Melvin H. Eldridge (Ossipee) and Delia Custeau (Milton)
Chauncey J., d. 6/15/1994 in Farmington
Donald, d. 4/27/1941 at 0/2/22; b. Milton; Moses O. Eldridge (Ossipee) and Lillian M. Johnson (W. Lebanon, ME)
Doris G., d. 9/20/1990 in Rochester; Walter Caswell and Effie Minor
Esther L., d. 8/13/1974 at 59 in Rochester; electrical wkr.; b. NH; Harry Adjutant and Jennie Dore
Everett, d. 12/7/1941 at 0/0/15; b. Milton; Chauncey Eldridge (Ossipee) and Esther Adjutant (Wolfeboro)
Fred R., d. 12/19/1988 in Wolfeboro; Everett Eldridge and Nettie Pike
Lillian M., d. 12/28/1968 at 64 in East Rochester
Louise, d. 11/7/1917 at 75/2/11; widow; b. Orrington, ME; John B. Polland (Orrington, ME) and Hannah D. Snow (Orrington, ME)
Lucy C., d. 10/19/1963 at 90; housewife; b. Ossipee; Moses P. Welch and Sarah J. Welch

Moses, d. 6/3/1964 at 64 in Rochester; laborer; b. Ossipee; Oradon Eldridge and Lucy Welch

Orodon J., d. 6/20/1951 at 89; laborer; married; b. Ossipee; Simon Eldridge and Robeline Johnson

ELLIOTT,

Flora P., d. 12/31/1918 at 16/7/18; at home; single; b. Alton; Charles F. Elliott (Rumney) and Martha J. Brooks (Dorchester)

ELLIS,

Abbie H., d. 1/15/1905 at 62/7/23; peritonitis; housewife; widow; b. Middleton; John Jones (Middleton) and Mary Burroughs (Middleton)

Arthur G., d. 10/24/1945 at 64/6/16 in Dover; edge trimmer; married; b. Milton; Ephraim Ellis and Abagail Jones

Charles E., d. 4/25/1916 at 69/2/5; barber; widower; b. Milton; William S. Ellis (Milton) and Hannah L. Bragdon (Milton)

Edward G., d. 1/24/1958 at 42 in Rochester; mill worker; married; George Ellis and Inez Duntley

Erwin E., d. 11/19/1996 in Rochester; Lloyd Ellis and Eleanor Londo

Evelyn May, d. 2/17/1899 at 0/2/2; pneumonia; b. Milton; George E. Ellis (Wolfeboro) and Inez G. Duntley (Milton)

Gary A., d. 1/5/1997 in Milton; Erwin Ellis and Doris Stevens

George E., d. 9/17/1933 at 64/4/7; laborer; married; b. Wolfeboro; Moses Ellis (Sandwich) and Hannah Somes (Somersworth)

George W., d. 2/5/1941 at 78/8/12 in Concord; shoemaker; widower; b. Milton; William Ellis (Milton) and Hannah Bragdon (Milton)

Ida M., d. 4/15/1935 at 69; housewife; married; b. Lebanon, ME; Moses Varney and Sarah Blaisdell

Inez G., d. 11/8/1963 at 83 in Rochester; housewife; b. Milton; John H. Duntley

John, d. 3/14/1893 at 26/8/14; cirrhosis of liver; carpenter; married; b. Middleton; Ephraim Ellis (Middleton) and Hannah A. Jones (Middleton)

Lillian R., d. 9/29/1913 at 4/9/7; pneumonia; b. Milton; George E. Ellis (Wolfeboro) and Inez G. Duntley (Milton)

Lloyd F., d. 5/14/1973 at 77 in Rochester; fibre worker; b. NH; George Ellis and Inez G. Duntley

Lucretia, d. 4/19/1905 at 54/2/17; uraemia; housewife; married; b. Milton; John Marsh (Acton, ME) and Sarah Runnels (Acton, ME)

Nettie, d. 5/19/1911 at 0/6/11; pneumonia; b. Milton; George E. Ellis (Wolfeboro) and Inez G. Duntley (Milton)

Robert H., d. 2/21/1905 at 31/11/21; pernicious anemia; paper maker; married; b. Milton; Ephraim Ellis (Middleton) and Abbie J. Jones (Middleton)

William M., d. 1/6/1942 at 61/1 in Glendale, CA; married; b. Milton; Charles E. Ellis (Milton) and Lucretia Marsh (Milton)

ELWELL,
Becky S., d. 6/8/1984 in Rochester; Larry D. Elwell and Gloria J. Downs

EMERSON,
Burton E., d. 6/22/1999 in Milton; Charles Emerson and Nellie Shelby

E. W., d. 3/9/1927 at 71/2/1 in Milton Mills; druggist; widower; b. Pittsfield; Charles Emerson (NH) and Harriett Newell (Barnstead)

Frances C., d. 7/19/1919 at 62/5/26; housewife; married; b. New Durham; William Chamberlain and Harriet Elkins

Horten C., d. 7/6/1950 at 77 in Lebanon, ME; retired; widower; b. Alton; John Emerson and Abbie Emerson

Sadie W., d. 5/28/1967 at 87 in Wolfeboro

EMERY,
Abigail, d. 3/26/1894 at 68/10/7; age and apoplexy; housekeeper; married; b. Middleton; Amos Whitehouse (Middleton) and Abagail Cotton (Wolfeboro)

Daniel C., d. 2/4/1898 at 74/2/12; heart disease; farmer; widower; b. Milton; Timothy Emery (Dover)

EVANS,
Calvin J., d. 10/21/1959 at 84 in Sanbornville; laborer; widower; b. Wakefield; John Evans and Melvina Farnham

Carrie M., d. 7/29/1960 at 56 in Wakefield; housework; b. Milton; Calvin J. Evans and Flora B. Rines

Flora B., d. 11/20/1920 at 46/4/13; housekeeper; married; b. New Durham; William T. Rines (New Durham) and Ellen Boston (Lunenburg, VT)

Grace E., d. 8/4/1950 at 73 in Acton, ME; housewife; married; Freeman Dorr
Laura W., d. 6/4/1956 at 74 in Rochester; housewife; married; b. Milton; Joseph Willey and Mary Laskey
Madeline D., d. 6/29/1980 in Rochester; Perley Hall and Myrtle Sprague
Mattie C., d. 12/5/1949 at 62; housewife; married; b. Wakefield; Bracket Weeks and Matilda Arlen
Reuben J., d. 7/14/1956 at 64 in Wolfeboro; ret'd textile worker; married; b. Holyoke, MA; Edwin S. Evans and Caroline Hecker
Richard, d. 7/10/1984 in Wolfeboro
Victor C., d. 7/13/1953 at 69; laborer; widower; b. Wakefield; John Evans and Melvina Farnham
Yvonne, d. 1/15/1934 at 0/0/1 in Rochester; b. Rochester; Richard Evans (Wakefield) and Miriam Paschal (Boston, MA)

FALL,
Clarabel, d. 3/31/1936 at 81/5/14; retired; single; b. Lebanon, ME; Ebenezer Fall (Lebanon, ME) and Dorcas Horne (Lebanon, ME)
George G., d. 5/27/1933 at 76/9/17; retired; married; b. Lebanon, ME; Ebenezer Fall (Lebanon, ME) and Dorcas Horne (Lebanon, ME)
Lizzie L., d. 6/4/1943 at 84/0/25 in Rochester; housewife; widow; b. Milton; George Lyman (Milton) and Hannah Plummer (Rochester)

FARMER,
Mary, d. 4/5/1924 at 72/9/3; housewife; married; b. England; John Dearden (England) and Maria Ellsworth (England)
Thomas, d. 4/29/1935 at 88/0/23 in East Rochester; widower

FARNHAM,
Elbridge, d. 3/25/1928 at 79/10/18 in Milton Mills; carpenter; divorced; b. Milton; David Farnham (Acton, ME) and Rowena Dearborn (Milton)
Fannie, d. 7/8/1891 at 89/9/2; dis. thigh and apoplexy; housewife; widow; b. Acton, ME; Enoch Wood and Dorothy Hurd
Harriet, d. 3/10/1929 at 92/1/22 in Haverhill, MA; widow
J. Frank, d. 2/17/1933 at 72/9/27 in Wakefield; retired; married; b. Acton, ME; Ezra Farnham (Acton, ME) and Harriet A. Hubbard (Acton, ME)
Marjorie A., d. 2/8/1951 at 75 in New York, NY

Ora E., d. 3/12/1944 at 85/3 in Old Orchard Beach, ME; at home; widow; ----- Cutts

Rowena S., d. 9/6/1900 at 86/5/6; paralysis; housekeeper; widow; b. Milton; Nathaniel Dearborn (Greenland) and Mary Whidden (Greenland)

Washington, d. 12/26/1909 at 70/7/3; coma; laborer; single; b. Milton; David Farnham (Milton) and Rowena S. Dearborn (Milton)

FARRELL,

Linda M., d. 4/7/1946 at 1/9/26; b. Rochester; Merlon Farrell (Lebanon, ME) and Margaret Brown (Milton)

Margaret F., d. 6/11/1944 at 27/7/12 in Rochester; housewife; married; b. Milton; Leslie M. Brown (Glenburn, ME) and Amy M. Nichols (Dover, ME)

FARWELL,

Ross, d. 9/1/1908 at 0/7/25; meningitis; b. Lawrence, MA; Walter W. Farwell (ME) and Edela Rines (Jefferson)

FEENY,

George H., d. 11/23/1939 at 84/0/15; hand laster; divorced; b. Lynn, MA; James Feeny (Pearsonville, NY) and Lorana Johnson (Lynn, MA)

Preston H., d. 2/25/1944 at 48/10/25; carder; married; b. Saugus, MA; George H. Feeny (Lynn, MA) and Winona E. Parker (Reading, MA)

FELISATH,

Italia, d. 1/14/1932 at 65/5/3; housekeeper; widow; b. Italy; Tito Rossi (Italy) and Mary Balognessi (Italy)

FENNER,

Edith A., d. 10/9/1942 at 56/2/3 in Sanford, ME

Evelyn K., d. 11/28/1973 at 62 in Sanford, ME

FERGUSON,

Clarence L., d. 6/9/1949 at 64; carpenter; married; b. Alfred, ME; Willie F. Ferguson and Sarah Bird

Florence A., d. 10/31/1973 at 89 in Milton Mills; homemaker; b. Canada

Margaret G., d. 1/4/1993 in Lynn, MA

FERNALD,
Eliza A., d. 8/22/1894 at 72; old age; housewife; widow; b. Tamworth; Robert Felch
Frank E., d. 12/14/1944 at 78/11/11; retired; married; b. Melrose, MA; Eli Fernald and Eliza A. Felch
Lula A., d. 7/18/1964 at 88 in Rochester; housewife; b. Farmington; Charles E. Tuttle and Justina Ham

FERRELL,
James H., d. 10/8/1890 at 31/5/9; heart disease; harness maker; single; b. Liverpool; Patrick Ferrell (Newcastle) and Mary A. Shea (Liverpool)

FIELDS,
Arlene M., d. 6/27/1987 in Dover; Howard Sceggell and Anna F. McIntire

FIFE,
Marion R., d. 6/3/1995 in Milton

FIFIELD,
George R., d. 11/22/1963 at 38; laborer; b. Wakefield; George Fifield and Blanche Penny

FILGATE,
William, Jr., d. 4/26/1930 at 0/0/1; b. Milton; William Filgate (Plymouth) and Margaret Lover (Union)

FINEGAN,
Abbie A., d. 11/24/1921 at 73/9/21; widow; b. Troy; Levi B. Bent and Sarah Lawrence
Dorothy B., d. 2/9/1906 at 9/5/7; tuberculosis, meningitis; b. Townsend, MA; Herbert F. Finegan (Rindge) and Clara B. Wakefield (Townsend, MA)
Herbert F., d. 11/17/1933 at 64/10/28 in Boston, MA; retired bkpr.; married; b. Rindge; John D. Finegan (St. Albans, VT) and Abbie Bent (Fitzwilliam)

FISHTINE,
Helen, d. 5/12/1996 in Dover; Matthew Piper and Ethel -----

FISKE,
Albert L., d. 7/7/1951 at 91; farmer; widower; b. Rutland, VT; Albert O. Fiske

FLAGG,
Carl A., d. 7/8/1950 at 69/8/3 in Rochester; engineer; married; b. Hollis; George Flagg
Emily C., d. 8/21/1909 at 72/2/16; pulmonary oedeima; widow; b. Dover; Moses Hussey (Somersworth) and Clarissa Ham (Dover)

FLANAGAN,
Edward J., Jr., d. 10/5/1951 at 24; draftsman; single; b. Hoboken, NJ; Edward J. Flanagan and Florence M. Monaghan
Michael, d. 9/16/1961 at 62 in Boston, MA
Ruth (Wentworth), d. 9/15/1978 at 94 in Natick, MA

FLANDERS,
Cora E., d. 5/22/1942 at 81/4/27; widow; b. Alton; Samuel E.P. Gilman (Alton) and Nancy J. Cooper (Alton)

FLETCHER,
Clinton, d. 7/7/1981 in Dover
Harry P., d. 12/9/1975 at 83 in Ossipee
Laura E., d. 12/12/1966 at 68 in Rochester

FLINT,
Ernest E., d. 11/18/1984 in Wolfeboro

FOGG,
Elizabeth M., d. 8/16/1945 at 19/3/26; student; single; b. Wolfeboro; Raymond D. Fogg (Ossipee) and Lois Chipman (Milton)
Maude R., d. 9/29/1958 at 81 in Rochester; housewife; widow; b. Waterford, ME
Raymond D., d. 12/9/1969 at 66 in Wolfeboro; carpenter; b. NH; Daniel Fogg and Mary Collins

FOLLEY,
Cranston W., d. 7/18/1983 in Biddeford, ME

FORD,
Abbie J., d. 2/21/1933 at 79/11/11 in Lebanon, ME; housekeeper; widow; b. Milton; William W. Ricker (Milton) and Sarah Downs (Milton)
Arthur G., d. 6/10/1958 at 39; mechanic; married; b. Nashua; Arthur J. Ford and Emma P. Glover
Ella B., d. 2/10/1972 at 86 in Concord; homemaker; b. CT; Henry Bliss and Minnie Rines
Leroy J., d. 12/14/1966 at 75 in Rochester; farmer; b. Dover; William H. Ford and Abbie J. Ricker
William H., d. 5/21/1907 at 66/7/25; abscess of lung; farmer; married; b. Dover; Jacob Ford (Dover) and Sarah Mitchell (New Durham)

FORTIER,
William K., d. 11/4/1976 at 56; machinist; b. NH; Albert J. Fortier and Nellie W. Hobbs

FOSS,
Benjamin W., d. 9/13/1913 at 92/9/18; old age; widower; b. Milton; John Foss (Rochester) and Lydia Wingate (Rochester)
Eli W., d. 4/3/1952 at 96 in Rochester; laborer; widower; b. Milton; Benjamin Foss and Lavina Downs
Laura G., d. 5/28/1893 at 30/1/11; cancer of stomach; housekeeper; married; b. Strafford
Levina, d. 7/30/1897 at 70/3/2; tabes mesenterica; housewife; married; b. Milton; Moses Downs (Milton) and Levina Hanson (Alton)

FOSTER,
Augustus, d. 8/18/1951 at 83 in Middleton; married
Flora M., d. 4/12/1984 in Rochester
Frederick L., d. 4/30/1951 at 89/4/1; sawyer; widower; b. Waterford, ME; Jeremiah Foster and Bianca Lovejoy
Sarah E., d. 4/21/1948 at 81/3/18; housewife; married; b. Milton; Albert Mason (Sandwich) and Mary Whitehouse (Ossipee)
Walter J., d. 6/19/1957 at 49 in Sanford, ME; teacher; married; John F. Foster and Rosilda Cyr

Ida F., d. 7/31/1916 at 54/10/6; housewife; widow; Harrison W. Chesley (East Gilford) and Mary E. Laker (Tewksbury, MA)

Mary J., d. 8/13/1901 at 71/8/15; debility; housekeeper; widow; b. Milton; Joseph Nute (Milton) and Rebecca Kenney (Lebanon, ME)

Thomas M., d. 8/10/1930 at 74/11/13 in Lebanon, ME; laborer; single; b. Milton; Thomas French (Farmington) and Mary J. Nute (Milton)

FROST,
Kathryn S., d. 4/26/1973 at 67 in Rochester; tel. & tel.; b. MA; George Warford and Fannie O'Connor

FULLER,
Raymond G., d. 2/17/1978 in Rochester; Frank Fuller and Maude -----

FURLONG,
Flora, d. 4/2/1937 at 84/7/19 in Milton Mills; at home; widow; b. Northfield, VT; Reuben Smith (VT) and Fannie Chamberlain (Randolph, VT)

Frank W., d. 6/5/1934 at 78/11/16 in Sanford, ME; retired; married; b. Limerick, ME; Sylvester Furlong (Limerick, ME) and Adelia ----- (Randolph, VT)

GAGE,
James M., d. 12/29/1914 at 68 in East Rochester; heart disease; shoe cutter; widower; b. Dover; Gerry R. Gage (Dover) and Abigail B. Tuttle (Dover)

GAGNE,
Evelyn C., d. 3/1/1989; Adolph Raab and Marie Kopp

Harold P., III, d. 3/29/1952 at 0/1/9 in Rochester; b. Rochester; Harold P. Gagne, 2d and Frances Weeman

Harold P., Jr., d. 7/5/1987 in East Cleveland, OH

Ivan E., Sr., d. 12/23/1991 in Rochester

Jerome W., d. 7/28/1980 in Rochester; Robert Gagne and Madeline Fournier

GAGNON,
Oscar E., d. 5/18/1962 at 64 in Wolfeboro; maintenance; b. Sanbornville; Ernest Gagnon and Georgiana Lepary

Viola R., d. 8/23/1987 in Concord

GALARNEAU,
Milford L., d. 2/28/1990 in Hawaii

GARDNER,
Edwin D., d. 11/3/1927 at 59/0/15; laborer; single; b. Tamworth; Daniel Gardner and Margaret Woodman
Lennie A., d. 8/20/1989; Putman Kinser and Lillie Eley
Peter, d. 12/9/1944 at 59/7/11; woodman; married; b. Canada

GARLAND,
daughter, d. 2/5/1923 at 0/0/0; b. Milton; Bernice M. Garland (Wolfeboro)
Ann A., d. 12/25/1921 at 84/3/21; housekeeper; widow; Luther Pinkham
Cora B., d. 2/12/1944 at 85/4/27 in Laconia; at home; widow; b. Farmington; Mark D. Goodall (Farmington) and Almarette Edgerly (Wolfeboro)
George, d. 11/17/1946 at 79/2/16 in Rochester; retired; widower; b. Brookfield; John T. Garland (Ossipee) and Fannie Ricker (Greenland)
Jacob D., d. 9/22/1897 at 66/5/13; nerv. prostration; farmer; married; b. Middleton; Alfred Garland (Rochester) and Abagail Horne (Middleton)
Llewellyn, d. 6/18/1929 at 72/1/3; farmer; married; b. Farmington; Dudley Garland and Ann Pinkham
Mary E., d. 9/28/1946 at 74/3/11 in Rochester; housewife; married; b. Ossipee; Charles H. Stillings (Ossipee) and Mary S. Thompson (Ossipee)
Robert D., d. 9/6/1997 in Milton; Robert W. Garland and Kathryn Donnelly
Ruth W., d. 5/17/1917 at 1/2/4; b. Wakefield; Bernice M. Garland (Wolfeboro)
Sumner G., d. 1/9/1913 at 63/5/10; chronic nephritis; farmer; married; b. Ossipee; John Garland (Wakefield) and Hannah Gile (Effingham)
Verna M., d. 10/8/1933 at 50/11/1 in Milton Mills; housewife; married; b. Sanford, ME; Winfield Reynolds (Newfield, ME) and Nellie Wentworth (Boston, MA)

GARNETT,
Isabelle, d. 4/4/1980 in Portland, ME
William, d. 8/23/1985 in Portsmouth

GARRAN,
Charles S., d. 8/22/1953 at 46/5; dr. of osteo.; married; b. Malden, MA; Charles E. Garran and Florence Winchell

GARRATT,
Eunice Tripp, d. 2/4/1966 at 73 in Norwalk, CT; interior dec.; b. Lynn, MA; Charles K. Tripp and Alice R. Taylor
Hugh B., d. 6/12/1975 at 78 in Wolfeboro; inter. decorator; b. England; Frederick Garratt and Lillian West

GARVIN,
Maggie J., d. 10/4/1894 at 35/5; pulmonary phthisis; housewife; married; b. Scotland; Charles Mahoney (Scotland)
Nellie C., d. 4/22/1903 at 45/5/12; cardiac dropsy; housekeeper; married; b. Fal. V., Canada; George McElroy (Sheffield, MA) and Almira Clark (Sheffield, MA)

GARYAIT,
Arthur P., d. 9/22/1984 in Rochester; Frederick Garyait and Elizabeth Roukey

GATELY,
Alice M., d. 5/9/1958 at 80 in Dorchester, MA
John F., d. 8/27/1960 at 43 in MA

GATHMANN,
Catherine W., d. 5/23/1970 at 74 in Wolfeboro; housewife; b. NH; Joseph Willey and Olive Roberts
Paul J., d. 11/18/1955 at 71 in Wolfeboro; merchant; married; b. Chicago, IL; Louis Gathmann and Henrietta Eklert

GAUTREAU,
Edward D., d. 9/28/1996 in Milton; Edward D. Gautreau, Sr. and Anna Dozzi

Scott A., d. 6/29/1984 in Wells, ME; Edward D. Gautreau and Catherine -
----

GAYDOS,
John W., d. 5/29/1987 in Dover; John Gaydos and Anna Hymics
John W., d. 9/7/1994 in Rochester; John W. Gaydos and Florence Henry

GEARY,
Bessie K., d. 10/8/1979 in Wolfeboro; Charles Eastman and Mary Tufts
Susan A., d. 2/28/1933 at 79/0/2; shoe worker; widow; b. Milton; Henry
  C. Amazeen (New Castle) and Abigail Wentworth (Milton)

GENEST,
Thomas J., d. 8/13/1981 in Pownal, ME; Emile Genest and Trissie -----

GERMAIN,
Clifford P., III, d. 8/19/1977 at 19 in Rochester; construction wkr.; b. NH;
  Clifford P. Germain, Jr. and Gwendolyn M. Turner

GERRISH,
Elisha, d. 6/5/1935 at 86/0/25 in Milton Mills; farmer; widower; b. Acton,
  ME; Joshua W. Gerrish (Berwick, ME) and Susan Sanborn
  (Wakefield)
Elizabeth M., d. 5/18/1914 at 82/2/4; influenza; widow; b. Lebanon, ME;
  Nahum Hersom (Lebanon, ME) and Betsy Pray (Lebanon, ME)
Ella M., d. 6/17/1913 at 66/3/5; carcinoma of breast; housewife; married;
  b. Hingham, MA; George W. Hersey (Hingham, MA) and Jane P.
  Davis (Rockport, MA)
Jane S., d. 4/7/1908 at 68/6/11; chronic bronchitis; housework; widow; b.
  Acton, ME; Zebulon Gilman (England) and Eliza Hanson
Josiah W., d. 6/13/1903 at 78/5/13; cystitis; farmer; widower; b. Berwick,
  ME; Nathaniel Gerrish (Berwick, ME) and Abigail Randlet
  (Stratham)
Myra H., d. 3/17/1947 at 86/0/27 in Rochester; widow
Susan R., d. 9/2/1891 at 70/5/17; pulmonary consumption; housekeeper;
  b. Wakefield; Elisha Sanborn and Susan Leighton

GERRY,
Clarence A., d. 11/21/1935 at 81/3/19; retired; married; b. W. Danville, VT; Eli P. Gerry (VT) and Sarah ----- (VT)

GEYER,
Madeline, d. 2/2/1972 at 80 in Newbury, MA

GIAMPA,
Alphonse J., d. 10/15/1997 in Rochester; Joseph R. Giampa and Mary Prestia

GIBSON,
Mary H., d. 3/28/1928 at 79/8/26; widow; b. Newfoundland; Joseph Hackett (Newfoundland) and Mary Quigley (Newfoundland)

GILBERT,
daughter, d. 7/11/1910 at 0/0/0; premature birth; Daniel Gilbert (Farmington) and Ida M. Duntley (Milton)
Wilfred, d. 9/5/1965 at 69 in Manchester; stock fitter, ret.; b. Milton; Daniel Gilbert and Ida Duntly

GILE,
Abbie C., d. 7/15/1899 at 75/10/27; paralysis; housewife; widow; b. Wolfeboro; William Furber (Wolfeboro) and Abigail Randall

GILMAN,
Harriett J., d. 1/24/1920 at 77/2/16 in Wolfeboro; widow; b. Denmark, ME; James Richardson (Denmark, ME) and Betsy Warren (Denmark, ME)
John G., d. 1/1/1987; John S. Gilman and Maude Garland
Mildred Lake, d. 7/22/1989 in Rochester; Henry Lake and Louise Bishop
Olga G., d. 4/4/1962 at 51 in Milton Mills; housewife; b. Barnstead; Orin Littlefield

GILMORE,
son, d. 5/27/1933 at 0/0/0; b. Milton; William E. Gilmore (Worcester, MA) and Doris M. Goodwin (Laconia)
Charles A., d. 11/29/1936 at 75/8/5; retired; widower; b. Milton; Albert Gilmore (Natick, MA) and Malinda Corson (Milton)

Eliza, d. 11/10/1936 at 77; housekeeper; married; b. Milton; Stephen Twombly (Middleton) and Susan L. Turner (Hamilton, MA)
Frank S., d. 6/27/1905 at 40/2/12; intestinal obstruction; painter; married; b. Milton; George A. Gilmore (Walpole, MA) and Melinda K. Corson (Milton)
Melinda K., d. 4/13/1906 at 72/11; senility; widow; b. Milton; Thomas Corson (Lebanon, ME) and Eliza G. Jewett (Milton)

GILSON,
Alice S., d. 10/12/1931 at 63/4/22; widow; b. Farmington; James Downing (Farmington) and Addie S. Smith (Rochester)
Rachel E., d. 7/24/1899 at 47/7/15; cancer of uterus; housewife; married; b. England

GLASZ,
Anton, d. 1/28/1962 at 52; laborer; b. No. Adams, MA; Anton Glasz and Mary D. Fuchs

GLEASON,
Addie E., d. 7/19/1918 at 71/0/14; widow; b. Hopkinton, MA; Joseph Gamage (Hopkinton, MA) and Mary Taft (Upton, MA)

GLIDDEN,
Ada May, d. 9/8/1913 at 1/3/11; convulsions; b. Gonic; Charles A. Glidden (Barrington) and Winnie Duntley (Milton)
Mary W., d. 4/7/1936 at 58/4 in Rochester; widow; b. Milton; John H. Duntley (Milton) and Elizabeth Downs (Dover)

GOING,
Agnes, d. 9/10/1938 at 84/10/3; at home; widow; b. Ontario; William Gilchrist (England)

GOLDEN,
David E., d. 2/25/1978 at 55 in Rochester; plumber; b. NH; John Golden and Blanche Locke

GOLDTHWAIT,
Fred H., d. 1/14/1961 at 72 in Milton Mills; laborer; b. Lynn, MA; William Goldthwait

GOLTY,
Agnes E., d. 6/21/1954 at 51/8/2; housewife; married; b. Brookfield; Fred Garland and Hattie West

GOODALE,
Earl S., d. 8/9/1996 in Milton; Glendon Goodale and Lillian Tongren

GOODALL,
Almarette S., d. 7/26/1915 at 84/1/6; retired; widow; b. Wolfeboro; Nathaniel Edgerly (Wolfeboro) and Mary Furber (Wolfeboro)

GOODELL,
Mark B., d. 6/18/1999 in Milton; George Goodell and Caroline Fischer

GOODRICH,
Evelyn B., d. 1/8/1989; Samuel Buchanan and Agnes Layden

GOODWIN,
Agnes Mary, d. 2/12/1966 at 78 in Los Angeles, CA
Albert J., d. 2/8/1921 at 60; farmer; divorced
Augustus P., d. 11/14/1903 at 53/5/2; cerebral mollities; single; b. Milton; Shepard K. Goodwin (Middleton) and Sophronia P. Young (Milton)
Charles, d. 7/4/1935 at 52/6/28 in Milton Mills; laborer; married; b. Milton Mills; Benjamin Goodwin (Lebanon, ME) and Emma Wentworth (Milton)
Clarence, d. 2/11/1935 at 54/1/16; shoe worker; married; b. Dover
Daniel B., d. 10/10/1888 at 77/7/18; clergyman; married; b. Middleton; Joseph Goodwin and A. H. Goodwin
Emma A., d. 7/8/1910 at 53/2/4; cerebral hemorrhage; widow; b. Milton; William H. Wentworth (Milton) and Emerline Blaisdell (Milton)
Everett E., d. 10/18/1942 at 67/8/13; retired; married; b. Providence, RI; Charles A. Goodwin (Newfield, ME) and Ida E. Chillis (W. Newfield, ME)
Frank W., d. 7/2/1962 at 82 in Milton Mills; caretaker; b. Milton Mills; Benjamin Goodwin and Emma Wentworth
George H., d. 1/23/1930 at 83/8/13 in Rochester; farmer; single; b. Milton; Shepard Goodwin (Middleton) and Sophronia Young (Milton)
Hilton S., d. 9/27/1941 at 82/0/28 in Rochester

Sarah, d. 7/21/1965 at 80 in Rochester; housewife; b. Acton, ME; Levi H. Brackett and Anna R. Gardner

Shepard K., d. 12/31/1891 at 69/2/25; pneumonia; farmer; married; b. Milton; Joseph Goodwin and Anna Hanson

Sophia J., d. 6/12/1903 at 78/5/20; pneumonia; housekeeper; widow; b. Milton; Isaac Young (Alton) and Mary Pinkham (Milton)

GOOGINS,

Margaret, d. 3/28/1940 at 85/11/4 in Rochester; at home; widow; b. Salmon Falls; Timothy Connolly (Ireland) and ----- Trumble (Ireland)

GORDON,

Agnes C., d. 8/15/1979 in Boston, MA

Almon F., d. 3/1/1970 at 82 in Wolfeboro

Ansel, d. 8/19/1977 at 63 in Wolfeboro; woodsman; b. NH; Almon F. Gordon and Nellie E. Cronin

Ansel F., d. 12/31/1961 at 18; laborer; b. Exeter; Beatrice Dalphand

Casey, d. 7/23/1983 in Dover

Clyde A., d. 5/26/1973 at 57 in Togus, ME

Ellsworth F., d. 1/15/1997 in ME

James R., d. 12/21/1991 in Milton; Lee M. Gordon, Sr. and Rachel M. Cates

Leon, d. 7/13/1930 at 10/2 in Acton, ME; b. Acton, ME; Almon Gordon (Shapleigh, ME) and Nellie Cronin (Acton, ME)

Marekay M., 12/21/1991 in Milton; John Brackett and Marie Cummings

Marion, d. 6/14/1930 at 0/0/2 in Acton, ME; b. Acton, ME; Almon Gordon (Shapleigh, ME) and Nellie Cronin (Acton, ME)

Nellie F., d. 6/1/1989 in Milton Mills; William Cronin and Katie Lynch

GORTON,

Ellen, d. 12/15/1973 at 84 in Rochester

William E., d. 12/12/1986 in Laconia

GOULD,

Burton G., d. 3/4/1990 in Rochester

Evelyn, d. 2/24/1958 at 50 in Hanover; folder; married; b. Lancaster; Andrew Hodgdon and Alice Perkins

Flora, d. 4/12/1985 in Rochester; Frank L. Grace and Lizzie Willey

GOUPIL,
Roger A., d. 2/2/1969 at 17; student; b. Dover; Arthur Goupil and Marie A. Chouinard

GOWEN,
son, d. 7/1/1902 at 0/0/0; stillborn; George W. Gowen (Berwick, ME) and Eva Baker (Gloucester, MA)
son, d. 12/10/1904 at 0/0/0; premature birth; George W. Gowen (Berwick, ME) and Eva A. Baker (Gloucester, MA)

GRACE,
Bert N., d. 10/28/1975 at 87; woodsman; b. NH; Chandler Grace and Abigail Bean
Carl L., d. 1/28/1960 at 69 in Rochester
Chandler T., d. 4/14/1970 at 67 in Manchester; mer. seaman; b. NH; Joseph Grace and Lucy L. Cates
Elsie M., d. 12/31/1962 at 77 in Rochester; shoe worker; b. Milton; Alfred Varney and Eva Varney
Frank L., d. 4/19/1933 at 73/5/11 in Wakefield; farmer; married; b. Chatham; Franklin Grace (Chatham) and Elizabeth Johnson (Chatham)
Joseph E., d. 2/23/1999 in Rochester; Joseph Grace and Lodema Cates
Lizzie B., d. 12/17/1958 at 88 in Rochester
Mildred P., d. 7/20/1979 in Rochester; Alfred ----- and Eva Blake

GRANT,
Abbie E., d. 9/30/1971 at 84 in Wolfeboro; homemaker; b. ME; Frank Hammond and Miriam Marsh

GRAY,
Arlene I., d. 6/15/1955 at 25 in Wakefield; housewife; married; b. Farmington; Harry King and Irene Woodman
Jean C., d. 4/26/1998 in Milton
Kenneth O., d. 7/4/1984 in Rochester; Samuel Gray and Mildred Marshall
Natalie J., d. 2/7/1990 in Rochester; John T. Weaver and Sarah B. Gerrish
Perley A., d. 9/30/1956 at 69; shoeworker; married; b. Lynn, MA; Willis J. Gray and Mary R. Waitt

GREEN,
Josephine S., d. 8/8/1898 at 48/2/19; consumption; housekeeper; married; b. Alton; Andrew Davis (New Durham) and Sarah Cate (Barrington)

GREENE,
Ada M., d. 3/19/1989 in Milton Mills; George W. Hurd and Elizabeth Manning
James C., d. 9/3/1987 in Rochester; Thomas E. Greene and Lillian Cote

GREENWOOD,
Jennie N., d. 8/21/1951 at 89/1/30 in Shrewsbury, MA; housewife; widow; b. Port Clyde, NS; Jeremiah Nickerson and Mary A. Johnson

GREGSON,
Betsey, d. 12/22/1940 at 79/1/13 in Westminster, MA
Robinson, d. 6/4/1932 at 70/6/2 in Wakefield; merchant; married; b. England; Robert Gregson (England) and Alice Gregson (England)

GRENIER,
Louis Wilfred, d. 3/17/1899 at 0/7/5;bronchitis; b. Milton; Joseph Grenier (Canada) and Alphonsine Croteau (Canada)

GREY,
Elsie E., d. 1/28/1974 at 49 in Rochester; homemaker; b. RI; Robert J. Grey and Clara Moore
Eva L., d. 9/28/1908 at 0/3/24; acute meningitis; b. Milton; George H. Grey (Sheffield, VT) and Eva A. Gray (Sheffield, VT)

GRIFFIN,
child, d. 3/12/1963 at 0/0/0 in Rochester; b. Rochester; John J. Griffin and Janet L. York
child, d. 3/12/1963 at 0/0/0 in Rochester; b. Rochester; John J. Griffin and Janet L. York
Anthony G., d. 4/11/1987 in Rochester
Frances V., d. 9/11/1966 at 56; restaurant prop.; b. Medford, MA; John Fitzpatrick and Mary Griffin
Guy L., d. 11/28/1969 at 82 in Milton Mills; laborer; b. ME; Luther Griffin and Kate Day

Mary E., d. 10/27/1916 at 81/4/1; housekeeper; widow; b. Tuftonboro;
David Goodwin (Melvin Village) and Mary S. Eaton (Melvin
Village)
Thomas F., d. 8/26/1973 at 62 in Wolfeboro
Yvonne V., d. 11/24/1995 in Salem, MA

GRISWOLD,
Ruth I., d. 9/7/1967 at 52 in Kittery, ME; b. MA; Charles M. Hosmer and
Rosens Barry

GRONDIN,
son, d. 12/6/1961 at 0/0/0 in Rochester
Sterling L., Sr., d. 11/6/1995 in Rochester; Samuel Grondin and Mary
Borden

GROVER,
son, d. 9/23/1905 at 0/0/0; stillborn; Harry C. Grover (Barrington) and
Mary F. Emerson (Wakefield)

GRUNER,
Reet, d. 1/19/1999 in Milton Mills; Erich Vaherun and Marta Sepp

GULLIFORD,
Karl R., d. 8/8/1973 at 69 in Milton Mills; carpenter; b. MA; George
Gulliford

GURNEY,
Lillian M., d. 2/17/1985; Charles E. Woodman and Annie Cummings

GUSTAFSON,
Herman L., d. 11/12/1905 at 0/4/28; pneumonia; b. Milton; Nicholas H.
Gustafson (Sweden) and Sarah A.F. Lord (Hingham, MA)

HAGEN,
Carin Lee, d. 7/14/1972 at 0/3 in Rochester; b. NH; Stephen Hagen and
Paula Allard
Joy, d. 9/21/1964 at 12 in Rochester; student; b. Lawrence, MA; George
E. Hagen and Edna Scranton

HAINES,

Calvin S., d. 11/30/1932 at 71/4/12 in Milton Mills; undertaker; married; b. Wakefield; George W. Haines (Wakefield) and Susan A. Nichols (Wakefield)

Cora H., d. 1/10/1945 at 81/3/18 in Exeter; housewife; widow; b. Lebanon, ME; Zackarial Knox (Ossipee) and Sarah Newcomb (Buxton, ME)

HALE,

Albert A., d. 3/12/1948 at 73 in Biddeford, ME

Harry, d. 7/19/1912 at 62/11/4; acute nephritis; RR engineer; single; b. Rochester; John B. Varney (Lebanon, ME) and Almira S. Clarke (Lyman, ME)

Mamie C., d. 12/10/1980 in Waltham, MA

HALEY,

Catherine, d. 8/6/1966 at 82; housewife; b. Ireland; Thomas Sweeney and Ellen Keating

Ernest J., d. 10/3/1971 at 77 in Dover; laborer; b. NH; George Haley and Edith Avers

Frank, d. 3/29/1904 at 69/1/9; Bright's disease; clergyman; married; Enoch Haley (Tuftonboro) and Cynthia Piper (Tuftonboro)

Sarah P., d. 4/10/1931 at 83/2/23; at home; widow; b. Milton; Enoch Plummer (Milton) and Orinda Ayers (Wakefield)

Susan P., d. 12/18/1955 at 76 in Concord; cashier; single; b. Seabrook; Frank Haley and Sarah Plummer

HALL,

Elsie M., d. 6/20/1972 at 83 in Portsmouth; homemaker; b. NH; Timothy Connolly and Clara Lowd

Elvira, d. 1/31/1934 at 83/3; housekeeper; widow; b. Eaton; Daniel Thurston (Eaton) and Mary Littlefield (Eaton)

Eslette, d. 7/7/1891 at 3; diphtheria; Fred Hall (Canada) and Mary Duquette (Canada)

Frank G., d. 8/18/1953 at 79/8/28 in No. Berwick, ME

Frank H., d. 10/1/1924 at 52/8/16; laborer; widower; b. Lebanon, ME; Allen Hall

George L., d. 12/31/1959 at 65; married; b. Melrose, MA; George M. Hall and Addie W. Temple

George W., d. 8/1/1952 at 66 in Wakefield; executive; married; b. Bar Mills, ME; Frank J. Hall and Abagail Junkins
John A., d. 9/22/1923 at 63/9/18; farmer; married; b. Wakefield; Andrew G. Hall (Wakefield) and Harriet J. Moulton (Wakefield)
John G., d. 12/8/1963 at 77 in Rochester; paper mfg.; b. Somerville, MA; John E. Hall and Elizabeth Rymes
John W., d. 12/10/1924 at 73/8/22; farmer; married; b. Jackson; Andrew L. Hall (Jackson) and Clarissa Gray (Jackson)
Josephine W., d. 1/23/1978 at 91 in Rochester; homemaker; Frank I. Nute and Elizabeth Trow
Kenneth W., Jr., d. 9/12/1989 in Rochester; Kenneth W. Hall, Sr. and Barbara Rhodes
Laura G., d. 3/23/1957 at 83 in Middleton
Laura V., d. 9/13/1912 at 8/11/17; diphtheria; b. Milton; John Hall (Canada) and Marcell Moren (Canada)
Margaret P., d. 2/16/1986; James F. Pope and Maude L. Fuller
Mary, d. 8/1/1952 at 67 in Wolfeboro; housewife; widow; b. Bar Mills, ME; Thomas Berry and Elizabeth Deering
Odelon J., d. 12/25/1979 in Portsmouth
Percy E., d. 12/11/1942 at 82/9/25; retired; widower; b. Union; Andrew G. Hall (Union) and Harriett Moulton (Wakefield)

HAM,
Blanche C., d. 2/14/1946 at 54/5/14; housewife; married; b. Brookfield; William H. Drew (Brookfield) and Emily Dyer (Brownfield, ME)
Dolores J., d. 6/8/1979 in Portland, ME
Eleanor M., d. 8/12/1993 in Dover; William R. Aldrich and Ethel M. Ballard
Francis H., d. 4/15/1977 at 68 in Rochester; truck driver; b. NH; James Ham and Blanche Drew
James J., d. 11/18/1972 at 85 in Dover; maintenance wkr.; b. NH; William Ham and Margaret Driscoll
Mildred T., d. 10/8/1918 at 5/8/9; b. Milton; James J. Ham (Dover) and Blanch C. Drew (Brookfield)

HAMILTON,
Arthur, d. 8/6/1949 at 65 in MI; retired; married
Beatrice, d. 9/27/1906 at 0/3/6; gastric enteritis; b. Milton; Harry Hamilton (Rochester) and Minnie G. Remick (Milton)

Joanne L., d. 4/26/1969 at 32 in Honolulu, HI

HAMMOND,
Clarence, d. 11/17/1912 at 0/2/1; meningitis; b. Acton, ME; Joseph Hammond (Acton, ME) and Lizzie Williams (Wakefield)
Hazel P., d. 3/20/1915 at 1/0/13; b. Milton; Joseph Hammond (Acton, ME) and Lizzie Williams (Wakefield)

HANLEY,
Rolla T., d. 11/24/1969 at 73 in Manchester; machinist; b. VT; Frank Hanley and Mary Kelley

HANSCOM,
Frank, d. 7/2/1936 at 65/7/22 in Acton, ME
Sarah, d. 9/24/1889 at 68/11/23; apoplexy; house; married; b. Milton; Nathan Jones and Susan Davis

HANSON,
Elizabeth R., d. 2/8/1943 at 80/8/9 in Hull, MA; widow; b. Milton; Jonas Laskey and Mary J. Willey
Elmer D., d. 3/7/1951 at 84; farmer; widower; b. Methuen, MA; John Hanson and Harriet Dearborn
Frank A., d. 2/13/1933 at 81/3/3 in Boston, MA; fireman painter; married; b. Lowell, MA; Richard R. Hanson (Brookfield) and Sarah A. Ford (Nottingham)
Harriette, d. 10/7/1940 at 49/7/6 in Milton Mills; housekeeper; single; b. Rollinsford; Elmer Hanson (Methuen, MA) and Florence Norwood (Dover)
John W., d. 3/16/1921 at 77/11; farmer; widower; b. Wakefield; John Hanson (Wakefield) and Mary Jane Cook (Wakefield)

HAPGOOD,
Carrie M., d. 6/22/1902 at 20/8/12; heart disease; single; b. Milton; Wilbur Hapgood (Hudson, MA) and Maria E. Mills (Hudson, MA)
Maria E., d. 5/29/1920 at 79/8/2; widow; b. MA; George P. Mills (ME) and Elizabeth Stickney (MA)
Wilber, d. 11/6/1908 at 71/0/8; valvular lesion of heart; farmer; married; b. Hudson, MA; Moses Hapgood (Hudson, MA) and Sally Wetherbee (Harvard, MA)

HARDY,
Robert P., d. 8/30/1989; Robert E. Hardy and Irene Gregoire

HARGRAVES,
Alberta J.C., d. 3/26/1917 at 53/11/23; married; b. Milton; Thomas J. Cutts (No. Berwick, ME) and Lydia Jewett (Milton)
John, d. 8/2/1889 at 67/1; apoplexy; mill operative; married; b. England; William Hargraves and Mary McClaren
Mary O., d. 1/15/1890 at 69; pneumonia; widow; b. Boston, MA; James McClaren and Mary -----

HARMON,
Albert A., d. 6/8/1921 at 48/11/16; mill operative; single; b. Freedom; Reuben Harmon (Eaton) and Olive Moulton (Freedom)

HARNDEN,
Matilda C., d. 12/30/1914 at 62/3/24; chronic enteritis; widow; b. Stoneham, ME; William Lord (Alfred, ME) and Mary Cotton

HARRIMAN,
Carl E., III, d. 11/19/1985; Carl E. Harriman, Jr. and Faith E. Brooks
Eugene E., d. 10/16/1926 at 37/1/5; carpenter; married; b. Ossipee; Frank L. Harriman (Ossipee) and Sadie Hill (Kittery, ME)
Frank L., d. 7/22/1923 at 67/10/11; carpenter; married; b. Ossipee; Moses P. Harriman (Ossipee) and Elizabeth Welch (Eaton)
Hannah M., d. 11/26/1904 at 21/11/23; apnoea; housekeeper; single; b. Somersworth; James W. Harriman (Somersworth) and Abbie E. Berry (Waltham, MA)
Isadore, d. 7/31/1934 at 50/11/11 in No. Berwick, ME; practical nurse; widow; b. Berwick, ME; Walter S. Howard (Rochester) and Elizabeth Cooper (Berwick, ME)
Sadie A., d. 8/5/1923 at 61/9/17; at home; widow; b. Kittery Point, ME; Joseph H. Hill (Kittery Point, ME) and Mary A. Allen (Kittery Point, ME)
William J., d. 2/4/1981 in Rochester; Cyrus Harriman and Doria DePatra

HARRINGTON,
Anna M., d. 12/31/1984 in York, ME
Walter, d. 6/15/1975 at 90 in Wolfeboro

HARRIS,
Blanche E., d. 3/31/1900 at 23/8/16; phthisis pulmonalis; housekeeper; widow; b. Dover; Hazen W. Downs (Milton) and Fanny M. Hersom (Waterboro, ME)
Fanny Louise, d. 11/11/1898 at 1/11/13; paralysis; b. Milton; Henry Harris (Woburn, MA) and Blanche Downs (Milton)
Kenneth W., d. 3/27/1993 in Concord; Delbert W. Harris and Lillian E. Beaulieu
Lillian E., d. 4/4/1996 in Rochester; Edgar Beaulieu and Cecile Martin
Ruth L., d. 9/16/1978 at 77 in Malden, MA
Stephen F., d. 4/5/1982 in Rochester

HARRISON,
Maybelle F., d. 7/25/1962 at 86 in Wakefield; b. West Epping

HART,
son, d. 4/2/1893 at 0/0/½; premature birth; b. Milton; M.A.H. Hart (Milton) and Estella L. Draper (Fair Haven)
Bertha L., d. 4/23/1897 at 37/10/4; pyonephrosis; single; b. Milton; Simon Hart (Rochester) and Mary Wentworth (Farmington)
Cyrus F., d. 7/27/1902 at 81/1/24; paralysis; farmer; married; b. Milton; John Hart (Newington) and Elizabeth Nutter (Milton)
Estelle L., d. 6/20/1946 at 82/11/14 in Concord; housewife; married; b. Fairhaven, VT; Hiram Draper (NY) and Elizabeth Lewis (VT)
Lydia, d. 2/1/1907 at 83/4/5; pneumonia; housewife; widow; b. Milton; John Witham (Milton) and Lydia (Sanford, ME)
Malcolm A.H., d. 1/24/1949 at 87/0/27 in Bedford, MA; physician; widower; b. Milton; Simon Hart and Mary A. Wentworth
Mary A., d. 9/13/1891 at 58; gastric fever; housekeeper; married; b. Milton; James M. Twombly
Sally, d. 5/22/1897 at 76/10/19; la grippe; housekeeper; b. Acton, ME; Jonathan Fox and Betsy Wentworth

HARTFORD,
Stephen A., d. 8/23/1967 at 18; student; b. Portsmouth; Chester P. Hartford and Geraldine Connor
William F., d. 11/19/1913 at 65/7/15; gastric carcinoma; shoemaker; widower; b. Rochester; Solomon Hartford and Ruth Tibbetts

HARVEY,
Ethelyn M., d. 7/23/1996 in Dover; Sewall Johnson and Gladys Douglas

HASELTON,
Elsie, d. 2/28/1972 at 72 in Rochester; musician-singer; b. ME; Frank Newton

HASKEY,
Rose A., d. 5/16/1897 at 36/3; pul. consumption; housekeeper; married; b. New Vineyard, ME; D. Barker (New Vineyard, ME) and Matilda Mitchell (New Vineyard, ME)

HASTINGS,
A. J., d. 3/2/1957 at 87/1/15 in Rochester; widow; b. Hudson, MA; ----- Gleason
Richard T., Sr., d. 11/3/1982 in Rochester; Gerald Hastings and Sarah Gorman

HATCH,
Elijah, d. 7/25/1897 at 84/8/8; senile gangrene; farmer; widower; b. Wells, ME; Elijah Hatch (Wells, ME) and Dorcas Perkins (Wells, ME)
George A., d. 2/25/1924 at 80/10/1; shoeworker; married; b. No. Berwick, ME; Elijah Hatch and Eliza W. Hanson
Lydia W., d. 2/23/1903 at 82/0/8; old age; housekeeper; widow; b. Alton; David Place and Susan Perkins
Winifred, d. 1/26/1982 in Rochester; Roland Carpenter and Hazel Trumbel

HAWKES,
Almira, d. 1/8/1922 at 87/2/0; at home; widow; b. Pittsburg

HAWKSWORTH,
James, d. 4/28/1930 at 71/3/15; ret. shoeworker; married; b. Digby, NS; Joshua Hawksworth (England)

HAYES,
daughter, d. 3/20/1906 at 0/0/0; premature birth; b. Milton; Guy L. Hayes (Milton) and Myrta Clements (Lebanon, ME)

Abbie, d. 4/10/1913 at 86/5/7; acute indigestion; widow; b. Wakefield; Parker Spinney (Kittery, ME) and Mary Dearborn (Milton)

Abbie L., d. 6/17/1927 at 69/9/12; at home; single; b. Milton; Charles C. Hayes (Milton) and Abbie P. Spinney (Wakefield)

Abigail V., d. 6/4/1904 at 78/1/1; cerebral hemorrhage; housekeeper; widow; b. Milton; Moses Nute and Eunice Varney

Agnes T., d. 10/10/1970 at 70 in St. Petersburg, FL

Alice L., d. 8/27/1895 at 21/0/1; saero ilica abscess; single; b. Milton; George A. Hayes (Milton) and Eldora Tuttle (Deerfield)

Alvie W., d. 2/19/1980 in FL

Andrew R., d. 6/23/1903 at 66/6; bron. and rheumatism; shoemaker; married; b. Lebanon, ME; A. C. Hayes (Lebanon, ME) and Lovie Rankin (Lebanon, ME)

Annie C., d. 2/19/1955 at 89/4/12; housewife; widow; b. Milton; Henry Corson and Clara M. Downs

Asa H., d. 12/24/1897 at 76/10/22; pneumonia; farmer; single; b. Milton; James Hayes (Milton) and Dorothy Leighton

Benjamin F., d. 10/8/1902 at 85/6/15; strangulated hernia; farmer; married; b. Milton; James Hayes (Milton) and Affie Card (Seavey's Island)

Charles T., d. 1/31/1969 at 78 in Rochester; farmer; b. NH; Charles Hayes and Nellie Parmenter

Cora E., d. 4/8/1954 at 73/0/1; housewife; widow; b. Rochester; Daniel McDuffee and Cora Pinkham

Daisy, d. 7/21/1935 at 47/10/15; widow; b. England; James Warner (England) and Mary A. Baker (England)

Doris, d. 4/8/1969 at 52 in Rochester; housewife; b. NH; Charles Ross and Florence Arlin

Eliza A., d. 10/31/1908 at 80/11/28; ileo colitis; housework; widow; b. Rochester; Beard Wentworth (Rochester) and Sarah A. Roberts (Rochester)

Ellen R., d. 5/2/1909 at 68/10/26; functional dis. of heart; widow; b. Pembroke; Asa F. Morrill (Pembroke) and Rachel F. Page (Raymond)

George A., d. 1/13/1924 at 71/10/29; carpenter; married; b. Milton; Luther Hayes (Lebanon, ME) and Louisa Bragdon (Milton)

George W., d. 10/26/1957 at 70 in Barnstead; b. Milton; Charles Hayes and Nellie Parmenter

Gertrude G., d. 5/10/1954 at 66/4/22; housewife; married; b. Sanford, ME; William Getchell

Guy L., d. 1/10/1949 at 70/10/27 in Rochester; carpenter; married; b. Milton; George A. Hayes and Eldora Tuttle

Halton R., d. 10/7/1981 in St. Petersburg, FL

Hattie, d. 6/22/1937 at 75/7/15 in Milton Mills; widow; b. New Durham; Justin Pinkham and Muvina Kemp

Henry B., d. 3/1/1933 at 79/9/5; farmer; single; b. Milton; Leonard Hayes (Milton) and Eliza Wentworth (No. Rochester)

Ira W., d. 11/17/1928 at 78/7/17 in Dover; farmer; single; b. Milton; Thomas Hayes (Milton) and Abigail V. Nute (Milton)

John, d. 4/18/1900 at 25; pneumonia; single; b. Ireland; Timothy Hayes (Ireland) and Mary Dailey (Ireland)

John E., d. 11/13/1901 at 69/2; carcinoma bowels; farmer; married; b. Lancaster; Samuel Hayes (Lebanon, ME) and Betsey Hersom (Lebanon, ME)

John P., d. 5/28/1926 at 79/9/24; farmer; married; b. Milton; Ephraim Hayes (Milton) and Rosmond Dame (Farmington)

Luther, d. 3/28/1895 at 75/2/16; chronic cystitis; farmer; married; b. Lebanon, ME; George Hayes (Rochester) and Lydia Jones (Lebanon, ME)

Luther C., d. 6/25/1952 at 82/7/22; farmer; married; b. Milton; Luther Hayes and Sarah D. Coffran

Mary E., d. 10/30/1903 at 70/6/24; pulmonary tuberculosis; housekeeper; widow; b. Lebanon, ME; James Clark (Lebanon, ME) and Betsy Hayes

Mary L., d. 3/3/1904 at 44/9/28; obstruction of bowels; housekeeper; single; b. Milton; Charles C. Hayes (Milton) and Abbie Spinney (Wakefield)

Myrta E., d. 5/5/1935 at 62/8/15 in Pittsfield; shoe stitcher; married; b. Lebanon, ME; Samuel Clements (Milton) and Charlotte Ingalls (Canterbury)

Nellie M., d. 8/12/1937 at 80/6/17; at home; widow; b. Farmington; Warren Parmenter and Emma Thurston (Brookfield)

Ormsby L., d. 1/11/1971 at 80 in Togus, ME

Philip G., d. 4/29/1990 in Rochester; Guy L. Hayes and Myrta E. Clements

Phoma E., d. 5/19/1930 at 75/2/8; housekeeper; widow; b. Deerfield; Ezra Tuttle (Nottingham) and Mary E. Savage (Charlestown, MA)

S. Lyman, d. 9/29/1946 at 83/9/19; ret. mail carrier; married; b. Milton; Luther ----- (Lebanon, ME) and Sarah Cofran (Suncook)

Walter W., d. 10/18/1959 at 73 in Rochester; engineer; widower; b. Milton; S. Lyman Hayes and Annie Corson

HAYNES,
John S., d. 4/25/1922 at 75/4/28; farmer; married; b. Concord; John Haynes and Sybil Fisher

HAYS,
Mae, d. 5/10/1982 in Orlando, FL
William E., d. 9/18/1978 in Orlando, FL

HAYWARD,
Charles H., d. 8/29/1957 at 79 in Rochester; ret. contractor; married; b. Scituate, MA

HEALEY,
Amy O., d. 9/13/1956 at 63/5/12 in Sanford, ME; married

HEALY,
Albert E., d. 9/2/1972 at 79 in Sanford, ME

HEATH,
Caddie M., d. 7/10/1916 at 42/5/11; housewife; married; b. Newfield, ME; Calvert Stevens (Newfield, ME) and Delia Benson (Parsonsfield, ME)

Edward C., d. 9/22/1952 at 74 in Wakefield; shoe worker; widower; b. Old Town, ME; Charles Heath and Marie -----

Ida, d. 3/19/1952 at 74 in Concord; housewife; married; b. Milton; Everett Witham and Jennie Colomy

Thelma P., d. 2/27/1912 at 3/4/22; accidental poisoning; b. Dover; Charles E. Heath (Kingman, ME) and Ida J. Witham (Milton)

Walter E., d. 8/24/1956 at 80 in Rochester; ret'd watchman; single; b. Old Town, MA (sic); Charles W. Heath and Maria M. -----

HEAVNER,
Frances E., d. 7/14/1978 at 76; homemaker; b. NY; Augustus Spetti and Bertha -----

HEIDLER,
Lena A., d. 3/12/1975 at 50 in Wolfeboro; waitress; b. Haverhill, MA; Leslie W. Anderson and Hazel A. Perkins

HELIE,
Scott E., d. 10/28/1970 at 0/0/0 in Rochester; b. Rochester; Everett C. Helie and Carol Marcoux

HELLMAN,
Eric H., Jr., d. 6/19/1993 in Manchester

HENDERSON,
Arthur A., d. 9/16/1945 at 67/15/19; farmer; married; b. Waterboro, ME; Alphonso Henderson (Waterboro, ME) and Martha Keirstead (NS)
Augusta, d. 8/19/1958 at 75 in Milton Mills; weaver in mill; widow; b. Milton Mills; Freeman Dorr and Lizzie Maddox
George F., d. 5/19/1919 at 75 in Dover; widower

HENNER,
Roland J., Jr., d. 12/14/1984; Roland J. Henner, Sr. and Lillian Normandin
Roland J., Sr., d. 12/28/1968 at 47 in West Milton; mechanic; b. MA; Jean M.C. Henner and Rosealma Frechette

HERRON,
Daisy E., d. 2/3/1956 at 71 in Lebanon, ME; married
Evangeline, d. 9/11/1977 at 68 in Laconia; chambermaid; b. NH; Fred R. Herron and Daisy Tilton
Helen G., d. 10/6/1975 at 74 in Rochester; secretary; b. MA; Daniel Gibbons
Lewis R., d. 2/11/1981 in Rochester; Fred E. Herron and Daisy Tilton

HERSOM,
Annie, d. 2/10/1974 at 97 in Rochester; homemaker; b. NH; Daniel K. Lovell and Lydia Hussey
Clifton E., d. 7/14/1960 at 59 in Rochester; lumbering; b. Sanford, ME; Elmer F. Hersom and Emily Jane Wilson
Clifton F., d. 8/4/1979 in Rochester
Elmer F., d. 7/29/1946 at 81/2/23 in Sanford, ME

Emily J., d. 4/26/1932 at 61/10/13 in Sanford, ME; housekeeper; married; b. Fall River, MA; Isaac Wilson (England) and Jane Hardy (England)

Herman L., d. 10/31/1956 at 82/6/29; laborer; married; b. Acton, ME; John S. Hersom and Martha Jones

Lyman H., d. 11/16/1906 at 50; apoplexy; married; b. Lebanon, ME

HERSUM,

Ann, d. 12/20/1910 at 68/4/29; fatty degeneration of heart; housekeeper; widow; b. Wakefield; Simeon Wiggin (Shapleigh, ME) and Sarah Wentworth (Milton)

George L., d. 2/7/1890 at 54/7; malaria and organic heart disease; shoemaker; married; b. Milton; Elihu Hersum (Milton) and Druscilla Wakeman (Milton)

HICKMAN,

Earl E., d. 3/10/1981 in Rochester; Silas Hickman and Aretia Cook

HIGGINS,

Helen I., d. 7/27/1996 in Milton Mills; Frederick Gorse and Lora B. Morton

John A., d. 9/14/1995 in Exeter; George E. Higgins and Verna Clough

HILDRETH,

Bertha, d. 9/9/1957 at 74 in Rochester; housewife; married; b. NS; Judson Cockum

James R., d. 7/23/1962 at 78 in Rochester; accountant; b. Reo Grand, NJ; Harry Hildreth and Mary Reeves

Louella, d. 3/12/1969 at 73 in Rochester; housewife; b. NJ; Benjamin McKergan and Angeline Graham

HILL,

Anna B., d. 4/1/1965 at 50 in Ossipee

Annette, d. 11/17/1936 at 74/0/4; at home; single; b. Milton; Daniel W. Hill (Lebanon, ME) and Betsey Rankin (Rome, ME)

Annie M., d. 4/8/1982 in Union

Betsey, d. 12/23/1902 at 74/3/22; cirrhosis of liver; housekeeper; married; b. Rome, ME; John Rankins and Lydia Furbush (Lebanon, ME)

Catherine M., d. 5/23/1929 at 55/9/11 in Wakefield; at home; married; b. Ireland

Daniel W., d. 1/13/1903 at 75/10/9; apoplexy; farmer; widower; b. Lebanon, ME; Daniel S. Hill (Lebanon, ME) and Sally Downs (Milton)

Elnora, d. 11/23/1927 at 70/2/24; at home; single; b. Milton; Daniel W. Hill (Lebanon, ME) and Betsy Rankins (Rome, ME)

Joseph H., d. 6/19/1968 at 79 in Wolfeboro; painter; b. NS; Isiah Hill and Almira Marshall

Leon, d. 7/10/1964 at 80 in Concord; pipe cutter; b. ME; Leonard Hill and Gertrude Barney

Leslie, d. 11/12/1982 in Rochester

Marjorie L., d. 6/5/1989 in Rochester; Dennis F. Clough and Mamie V. Marsh

Owen R., d. 6/19/1979 in Manchester; Leslie Hill and Helena Willey

Penny Lee, d. 1/13/1961 at 0/0/28 in Middleton

Reginald, d. 10/27/1979 in Rochester; Arthur R. Hill and Mildred Monteth

Vera R., d. 5/12/1974 at 76 in Rochester; homemaker; b. NS; James W. Langdale and Elizabeth E. Rines

Vila L., d. 12/7/1984 in Wakefield

Waldo L., d. 9/8/1976 at 71 in Rochester; logger (ret.); b. NH; Leon Hill and Ellen Willey

Winfred L., d. 4/12/1987 in Rochester; Joseph Hill and Vera Langdale

HISELER,
Elizabeth E., d. 6/26/1988 in Wolfeboro
Mary N., d. 10/2/1988 in Dover; Harry L. Wiggin and Mabel Drown
Stanley W., d. 12/10/1989; Leslie Hiseler and Elizabeth E. Tappin

HOBBS,
Geraldine, d. 4/12/1996 in Portland, ME
Howard G., d. 12/23/1974 at 59 in Milton Mills; bus driver; b. NH; Henry B. Hobbs and Bettina Moulton
John L., d. 10/9/1994 in Portland, ME
Lester N., d. 9/14/1985 in Sanford, ME
Ruth L., d. 5/18/1969 at 69 in Acton, ME

HODGDON,
Chauncey, d. 11/7/1994 in Rochester; John Otto and Ida Lord
Cora A., d. 10/1/1934 at 73/4/29; at home; married; b. Milton; Stephen W. Main (Milton) and Hannah Horne (Middleton)
Elsworth, d. 10/13/1949 at 88/0/27 in Wakefield; retired; widower; b. Lebanon, ME; Chandler Hodgdon and Mary -----
George F., d. 4/24/1902 at 73/4/12; arterial sclerosis; painter; married; b. Boston, MA; Jacob Hodgdon (Lebanon, ME) and Lucretia Codman (Boston, MA)
Lucinda J., d. 6/22/1926 at 86/8/1; at home; widow; b. Roxbury, MA; William Jones (Roxbury, MA) and Mary Ross (Roxbury, MA)
Paul A., d. 3/30/1970 at 40 in Hanover; manager Spaulding Fibre; b. VT; Philip Hodgdon and Gertrude Sutherland

HODGES,
Carrie L., d. 6/30/1945 at 70/10/5 in Rochester; housewife; widow; b. Lebanon, ME; George M. Corson (Lebanon, ME) and Draxa Pierce (Lebanon, ME)
Edgar C., d. 6/2/1942 at 72/10/29 in Rochester; retired; married; b. Ossipee; John Hodges (Ossipee) and Laura E. Garland (Ossipee)

HODSDON,
Jeremiah G., d. 10/21/1925 at 82/9/26 in Milton Mills; retired; widower; b. Milton; Jonathan Hodsdon (Acton, ME) and Lydia Goodwin (Milton Mills)

HOFF,
Betty J., d. 10/2/1998 in Milton

HOLDER,
Ralph F., d. 4/21/1986; Ralph C. Holder and Blanche E. Leighton

HOLMAN,
George D., d. 11/14/1956 at 58 in Rochester; laborer; married; b. Lincoln, MA; Amos Holman and Catherine Butcher
Lillian M., d. 7/12/1983 in Ossipee

HOLMES,
Pauline W., d. 10/1/1923 at 16/3/23; single; b. Tariffville, CT; Clarence W. Holmes (Buxton, ME) and Winnie B. Dorr (Milton)

HOLT,
Richard T., II, d. 11/22/1978 at 31 in Farmington; underwater diver; b. CT; Richard T. Holt and Evelyn Fenn

HOOGHKIRK,
daughter, d. 8/22/1944 at 0/0/3 in Wolfeboro; b. Wolfeboro; Harold F. Hooghkirk (W. Haven, CT) and Marilyn Walsh (Milton Mills)

HOOPER,
Ann B., d. 9/16/1908 at 56/2/15; exhaustion; widow; b. Stow, ME; Franklin Reed (Concord, MA) and Emily Crosby (Burlington, MA)
George, d. 7/14/1968 at 91 in Rochester; shoe worker; b. NH; Samuel Hooper and Annie Riad
Samuel, d. 9/8/1893 at 65/11/8; apoplexy; carpenter; married; b. Sanford, ME; Samuel Hooper (Sanford, ME) and Olive Stanley (Shapleigh, ME)

HOPKINS,
Chrystabel F., d. 2/1/1986 in Rochester; Cleon Hill and ----- Robinson
Reuben A., d. 12/31/1966 at 82 in Rochester; poultry farmer; b. Chelmsford, MA; John Hopkins and Sarah Garnsby

HORN,
Carr G., d. 12/25/1961 at 79 in St. Petersburg, FL
Clyde H., d. 6/25/1998 in Milton

HORNE,
Betsy P., d. 2/24/1908 at 87/7/12; cancer; housework; widow; b. New Durham; John Burleigh (Newmarket) and Betty Page
Carrie A., d. 6/18/1913 at 60/2/20; carcinoma of breast; housewife; married; b. Milton; Stephen H. Knight (Farmington) and Louisa Clary (Brooks, ME)
Charles A., d. 10/10/1938 at 79/3/26; meat market; widower; b. Milton; Francis D. Horne (Milton) and Sarah A. Ricker (Milton)

Charles W., d. 5/21/1900 at 56/9/27; pneumonia; emp. mill; married; b. Middleton; Henry B. Horne (Middleton) and Eliza Young (New Durham)

Charlotte A., d. 9/22/1893 at 74/2/7; pneumonia; housekeeper; single; b. Milton; James H. Horne (Milton) and Hulda Roberts (Salmon Falls)

Elijah C., d. 12/29/1906 at 63/2; aortic aneurysm; hotel clerk; widower; b. Milton; Francis D. Horne (Milton) and Sarah A. Ricker (Milton)

Emeline M.B., d. 3/4/1924 at 86/10/14; retired; widow; b. Wakefield; Nathaniel Meserve and Sarah D. Horne (Wakefield)

Ernest G., d. 3/7/1895 at 13/3/1; peritonitis; b. Milton; Frank G. Horne (Milton) and Mary C. Weeks (Somersworth)

Eva A., d. 3/14/1997 in Dover

Frank G., d. 11/27/1923 at 72/2/13; retired; married; b. Milton; Francis D. Horne (Milton) and Sarah A. Ricker (Milton)

Gertrude C., d. 5/3/1974 at 78 in Acton, ME

Ginger M., d. 7/31/1996 in Milton; Fred Britton and Ruth Simms

James H., d. 5/9/1935 at 81/5/11; single; b. Brookfield; Edmund Horne (Brookfield) and Betsy P. Burley (New Durham)

John, d. 5/17/1995 in Wolfeboro

John E., d. 12/15/1953 at 75/7/7; merchant; married; b. Acton, ME; John Horne and Emerline Meserve

John R., d. 4/11/1938 at 85/1/19; farmer; widower; b. Milton; Francis D. Horne (Milton) and Sarah B. Ricker (Milton)

Lettie O., d. 6/3/1929 at 67/11/25 in Rochester; housewife; married; b. Rochester; Orange B. Otis (Kittery, ME) and Hannah Worcester (Canton, MA)

Martha, d. 10/22/1938 at 83/9/3; housekeeper; single; b. Milton; Francis D. Horne (Milton) and Sarah A. Ricker (Milton)

Maude F., d. 2/3/1939 at 61/6/24; at home; single; b. Milton; John R. Horne (Milton) and Olive Corson (Milton)

Octavia P., d. 12/4/1993 in Wolfeboro

Olive Ann, d. 6/9/1924 at 46/7/20 in Rochester; at home; married; b. Newfield, ME; Charles Moulton (Newfield, ME) and Clara Garland (Newfield, ME)

Raymond F., Jr., d. 4/12/1991 in Portsmouth

Ruth M., d. 4/25/1994 in Sanford, ME

Sarah A., d. 6/24/1890 at 72; congestion of brain; housekeeper; widow; b. Milton; Elmer Ricker and Molly Lord

Susie F., d. 10/13/1906 at 64/1/5; strangulated hernia; housekeeper; single; b. Milton; Francis Horne (Milton) and Sarah A. Ricker (Milton)

HORTON,
Bessie F., d. 9/13/1958 at 71 in Acton, ME
Charles H., d. 5/17/1956 at 65/2/19 in Acton, ME

HORWITZ,
Roy, d. 8/21/1988 in Rochester; Sidney Horwitz and Lucille Lander

HOUGHTON,
Elizabeth M., d. 12/26/1991 in Sanford, ME
Fred, d. 11/28/1982 in Sanford, ME

HOUSTON,
Janette Eve, d. 3/30/1992 in Milton Mills; Kenneth Houston and Evelyn Sceggell

HOWARD,
Costilla A., d. 5/24/1934 at 63/8 in Rochester; housewife; married; b. Strafford; Diman Scruton (Strafford) and Betsy A. Foss (Strafford)
Esther M., d. 12/10/1993 in Dover
Fred, d. 2/1/1950 at 83/3/24 in Rochester; retired; widower; b. Rochester; Elbridge W. Howard and Sarah E. Howard
Hannah M., d. 4/30/1919 at 85/0/24; housekeeper; widow; b. Rochester; Joseph Brown (Rochester) and Jane Hodgdon

HOWE,
Dorothy, d. 3/28/1906 at 82/9/26; exhaustion; widow
Maglone F., d. 12/26/1981 in Rochester; George W. Howe and Hattie Blouin
Mary A., d. 9/9/1928 at 92/4/1; housekeeper; single; b. Milton; Ira F. Howe (Milton) and Mary York (Middleton)
Mary Ann, d. 11/8/1922 at 90/10/27; at home; widow; b. Milton; James Plummer (Milton) and Betsey Dealand (Wakefield)
Phineas L., d. 9/15/1900 at 74/8/13; Bright's disease; laborer; married; b. Newfield, ME; George Howe (Newfield, ME) and Hannah Lowe (Shapleigh, ME)

Thomas J., d. 1/24/1915 at 83/5/24; farmer; married; b. Milton; Ira F. Howe (Milton) and Mary N. York (Middleton)

HOWLAND,
Lura A., d. 3/9/1950 at 85 in Portsmouth; widow; b. Milton Mills; ----- Booth and Belle Booth
Vianna, d. 3/24/1923 at 82/3/28; housekeeper; widow; b. W. Dennis, MA; Aaron Baker (W. Dennis, MA) and Lydia Welch (W. Harwich, MA)

HOYT,
Benjamin G., d. 8/17/1893 at 53/5/11; suicide; laborer; married; b. Portland, ME; William G. Hoyt (Gorham) and Arabella D. Elliot (Bristol)
Dean, d. 1/28/1946 at 75/4/27 in Kittery, ME; retired; married; b. Milton; Rufus A. Hoyt (Rochester) and Lucy Drew (Brookfield)
Eliza W., d. 9/10/1936 at 82/4/28 in Portsmouth; at home; widow; b. Milton; Josiah Hussey (Milton) and Phoebe Goodwin (Milton)
George L., d. 1/1/1933 at 63/6/24; farmer; married; b. Milton; Rufus A. Hoyt (Rochester) and Lucy A. Drew (Brookfield)
Hannah, d. 12/25/1936 at 85/3/21 in Milton Mills; housekeeper; widow; b. Milton Mills; Joshua Gerrish (Berwick, ME) and Susan Sanborn (Wakefield)
John F., d. 1/21/1987 in Rochester; Marshall J. Hoyt and Alice Danforth
Katherine, d. 10/24/1946 at 74; housewife; widow; b. Buffalo, NY; Daniel Sullivan (Ireland) and Nancy Harrington (Ireland)
Lucy A., d. 3/29/1909 at 61/8/22; apoplexy; housekeeper; widow; b. Brookfield; Benjamin Drew (Milton) and Hannah Drew (Dover)

HUBBARD,
Aaron, d. 6/25/1890 at 81/10; heart disease; widower; b. Acton, ME

HUCKINS,
Anita M., d. 4/7/1997 in Milton; Wesley W. Stone and Loletta M. Webster

HULBIG,
Mavins F., d. 12/12/1947 at 61/4/25 in Roslindale, MA

HUME,
James O.W., d. 1/15/1980 in Exeter

HUNT,
Annie P., d. 6/16/1929 at 81/4/26; widow; b. Bradford, England; James Irish (Bradford, England) and Annie P. (England)
Emma F., d. 1/25/1931 at 63/2; at home; married; b. Wakefield, MA; George H. Kidder (Saugus, MA) and Matilda Lee (Wakefield, MA)

HUNTER,
Ada A., d. 3/16/1986 in Rochester
Frederick O., d. 3/1/1961 at 31 in Rochester; paine furniture; b. Braintree, MA; James L. Hunter and Elizabeth Martha
George S., d. 6/14/1944 at 16/8/24 in Wolfeboro; shoe worker; single; b. Somerville, MA; Charles O. Hunter (Charlestown, MA) and Jennie E. Magee (Arlington, MA)

HURD,
Abigail, d. 7/8/1889 at 86/2/13; consumption; farmer; widow; b. Rochester; Eleza Rand and Sarah Thompson
Cora B., d. 5/30/1931 at 69/11/15 in Rochester; widow; b. Acton, ME; Charles G. Jenness and Sarah Wallingford
Florence E., d. 11/22/1947 at 65/1/19; blanket fin.; married; b. Wakefield; Daniel N. Tuttle (Wakefield) and Ora Tibbetts (Wolfeboro)
Frank J., d. 10/2/1930 at 78/6/3 in Acton, ME; ret. engineer; married; b. Acton, ME; William Hurd (NS) and Caroline Blaisdell (NS)
George H., d. 12/11/1912 at 84/2/26; influenza; farmer; married; b. Farmington; Jonathan Hurd and Abigail Rand (Farmington)
Marietta, d. 2/7/1916 at 67/3/6; married; b. New Durham; Harrison Boody (New Durham) and Tamson Ham (New Durham)
Olive, d. 9/20/1943 at 90 in Brockton, MA; widow; Nathaniel Rines and Olive Remick

HURLBURT,
Myra, d. 3/19/1921 at 88/8/1; widow; b. NS; John Hurlburt (Young's, NS) and Mary Phymbia (Young's, NS)

HURLICK,
Harry, d. 5/12/1920 at 35; junk dealer; married; b. Russia; Reuben Hurlick (Russia)

HURON,
Frederick B., d. 5/9/1957 at 84/0/12 in Lebanon, ME

HUSE,
Mabel H., d. 2/22/1971 at 87 in Milton Mills; housewife; b. MA; Moses Ridgway and Mary Hale

HUSSEY,
Bathsheba H., d. 11/30/1889 at 69/2/16; nephritis; house; married; b. Milton; Jeremiah Goodwin and Bathsheba Spinney
Edward R., d. 4/18/1900 at 80/1/8; la grippe; farmer; widower; b. Wakefield; Joseph Hussey (Acton, ME) and Anne Wiggins (Wakefield)
Isaac, d. 3/31/1930 at 86/6 in Milton Mills; farmer; married; b. Sanford, ME; Isaac Hussey (Sanford, ME) and Lydia Merrow (Acton, ME)
Mary F., d. 1/13/1932 at 64/9/20 in Rochester; at home; widow; b. Acton, ME; James H. Buzzell (Acton, ME) and Sarah Littlefield (Springvale, ME)
Mrs., d. 3/15/1890 at –; chronic hepatitis; housekeeper; married

HUTCHINS,
Mary, d. 3/21/1939 at 90/6/26 in Union; housewife; widow; b. Union; Robert Corson and Sarah Nay (Ossipee)

INNES,
Hattie M., d. 12/14/1938 at 54/10/18; housewife; married; b. Cambridge, MA; Charles Snow (Waltham, MA) and Elizabeth Pickering (Newington)

ISACKES,
Charles F., d. 7/18/1994 in Milton; Mervin L. Isaccs (sic) and Helen French

JACOBS,
Betty J., d. 8/28/1968 at 35 in Boston, MA; housewife; b. Milton; George H. Chase and Adeline Willey

JAPPE,
Henri V., d. 8/6/1971 at 76 in Wolfeboro; electronics eng.; b. Denmark; Fritz Jappe
Rosa, d. 2/17/1979 in Malden, MA

JENNESS,
Alma J., d. 2/9/1916 at 65/9/8; at home; married; b. Dover; John Hawkins (Dover) and Nancy M. Foss (Dover)
Ann J., d. 6/21/1918 at 75/5/18; widow; b. Berwick, ME; Samuel Randall and Ann Wallingford
Annie, d. 1/20/1962 at 85 in Rochester; housewife; b. Milton Mills; Frank Pinkham
Arthur A., d. 8/5/1941 at 56/4/21 in Milton Mills; shoemaker; married; b. Rochester; Isaac B. Jenness (Rochester) and Sarah Howard (Rochester)
Arthur M., d. 11/28/1904 at 7/4/24; valv. disease of heart; b. Milton; Edwin P. Jenness (Wakefield) and Alma J. Hawkins (Dover)
Charles W., d. 2/18/1941 at 51/1/17 in Wakefield; US Army; single; b. Milton; Edwin P. Jenness (Wakefield) and Alma J. Hawkins (Dover)
Clara E., d. 3/29/1911 at 65/11/22; acute tuberculosis; housework; single; b. Wakefield; Hiram Jenness (Wakefield) and Sarah Welch (Ossipee)
Edgar Joseph, d. 9/28/1921 at 0/1/12; b. Milton; Joseph C. Jenness (Milton) and Sarah M. Allen (Brookfield)
Edwin P., d. 4/26/1923 at 66/9/19; farmer; widower; b. Wakefield; Chesley Jenness and Mary Burnham
Fred W., d. 12/2/1946 at 65/1/7; carder; married; b. Milton; Edwin P. Jenness (Wakefield) and Alma J. Hawkins (Dover)
Joseph C., d. 4/4/1945 at 57/9/11 in Lewiston, ME; tex. worker; married; b. Milton; Edward Jenness (Milton) and Alma Hawkins (Milton)
Sarah M., d. 4/1/1973 at 84 in Rochester; woolen worker; b. NH; Samuel Allen and Emma Cummings
Susan A., d. 3/22/1911 at 70/2/23; pneumonia; single; b. Wakefield; Hiram Jenness (Wakefield) and Sarah Welch (Ossipee)

JENSEN,
Jane A., d. 11/6/1965 at 85 in Wolfeboro; housewife; b. Scotland; Andrew Holmes and Elizabeth Pettigrew

JEWETT,
Haven R., d. 2/5/1924 at 67/5/3; farmer; married; b. Milton; John Jewett (Milton) and Clara Page (Milton)
Mary A., d. 8/7/1910 at 97/3/17; nephritis; widow; b. Wakefield
Richard I., d. 11/24/1946 at 62/4/6 in Rochester; farmer; married; b. Milton; Haven R. Jewett (Milton) and Nellie M. Sibley (Boston, MA)
Sarah L., d. 1/24/1970 at 95 in Sanford, ME

JOHNSON,
Clarence W., d. 7/3/1903 at 0/2/18; cholera infantum; b. Milton; Ralph Johnson (Lowell, MA) and Rosie Dulage (Nashua)
Elinor V., d. 10/24/1996 in Rochester; Charles Hathaway and Messina Lanfile
Ernest V., d. 1/31/1951 at 73 in So. Berwick, ME; fireman; widower; b. Fryeburg, ME; Issachar Johnson and Jennie Jones
Ernest W., d. 6/2/1998 in Rochester
F. Lester, d. 2/22/1935 at 68/11/16 in Whitefield; married; b. Stow, ME; Joseph Johnson and Sarah -----
Fred E., d. 12/11/1955 at 70/2/11 in Somerville, MA; married
Harold D., d. 2/26/1919 at 44/0/15; RR conductor; married; b. Milton; James W. Johnson (New Durham) and Julia Hatch (No. Berwick, ME)
Henry, d. 10/1/1964 at 78 in Rochester; insp. US Army; b. Boston, MA; Herman Johnson
James W., d. 9/5/1920 at 82/9/27; farmer; widower; b. Wolfeboro; Ezra Johnson and Nancy Perkins (New Durham)
Myrtie, d. 3/25/1955 at 75 in Rochester; housewife; widow; b. No. Conway; Moores G. Brown
Nellie M., d. 6/22/1966 at 78; housewife; b. Laconia; Edward D. Hale
Nettie H., d. 7/20/1966 at 60 in Concord; teacher; b. Milton; Clarence W. Holms and Winifred B. Dorr
Stella A., d. 12/12/1963 at 76 in LaHavre, CA
Stephen L., d. 12/28/1988; David H. Johnson and Sherry A. Wyman
William P., d. 4/9/1928 at 79/0/1; warp dresser; widower; b. Milton; Henry Johnson (Cornelius, NY) and Irene Potter

JOHNSTON,
Gertrude, d. 5/20/1912 at 42/8/22; acute indigestion; married; b. Somerville, MA; Edward E. Winslow (Charlestown, MA)

JONES,
Abbie D., d. 1/21/1902 at 81/0/2; apoplexy; widow; b. Milton; Josiah Moulton (Hampton) and Mary Watson (Milton)
Alfred W., d. 2/5/1913 at 64/3/5 in Concord; asphyxia; machinist and farmer; married; b. Randolph, MA; William Jones (Randolph, MA) and Sallie W. Ellis (Alton)
Alice V., d. 8/21/1958 at 62 in Milton Mills; rest. mgr. ret.; single; b. Milton; Fred P. Jones and Emma Cowell
Arthur C., d. 3/22/1938 at 81/9/21 in Wolfeboro; carpenter; widower; b. Lewiston, ME
Bessie E., d. 11/1/1947 at 85/6/27; widow; b. Saco, ME; Rufus Stevens (Portland, ME) and Anastatia Paul (Portland, ME)
Charles A., d. 11/27/1934 at 83/1; farmer; married; b. Milton; George H. Jones (Milton) and Lucy J. Varney (Milton)
Charles D., d. 7/2/1908 at 44/9/10; typhoid fever; merchant; married; b. Milton; Charles Jones (Milton) and Betsey Varney (Milton)
Christie L., d. 3/6/1914 at 72; chronic nephritis; single; George R. Jones (Lebanon, ME) and Mary J. Bragdon (Milton)
Clara E., d. 9/12/1939 at 79/1/0 in Dover; single; b. Milton; George R. Jones (Lebanon, ME) and Mary J. Bragdon (Milton)
Dorothy Betsy, d. 3/8/1908 at 5/11/22 in So. Pines, NC; entero colitis; b. So. Pines, NC; Charles D. Jones (Milton) and Pauline H. Hart (Milton)
Edith E., d. 6/9/1932 at 39/10/14 in Rochester; widow; b. Canada
Elizabeth, d. 3/1/1901 at 81/9; bronchopneumonia; domestic; single; b. Lebanon, ME
Elizabeth, d. 10/23/1975 at 81 in Rochester; b. NH; Fred P. Jones and Emma Cowell
Ella S., d. 2/18/1935 at 84/2/16; housekeeper; widow; b. No. Berwick, ME; John B. Kimball and Sabrina Downs (Berwick, ME)
Emma C., d. 4/13/1941 at 81/7/16; housewife; married; b. W. Lebanon, ME; Edmond E. Cowell and Elizabeth Chamberlain (Milton Mills)
Fred P., d. 11/8/1941 at 82/0/20; retired; widower; b. Milton; Charles Jones (Milton) and Betsey Varney (Milton)

George H., d. 10/23/1918 at 92/6/17; farmer; widower; b. Milton; Joshua Jones (Lebanon, ME) and Sallie Crowell (Lebanon, ME)

George R., d. 3/22/1900 at 82/11/2; hemiplegia; shoemaker; widower; b. Lebanon, ME

John P., d. 1/30/1901 at 82/3/12; apoplecia cerebri; widower; b. Milton; Nathan Jones (Milton) and Susan Davis (Barnstead)

Julian S., d. 9/18/1910 at 2/4/25; convulsions; b. Southern Pines, NC; Charles D. Jones (Milton) and Pauline E. Hart (Milton)

Levi D., d. 5/19/1932 at 40/11/18 in Middleton, MA; tel. oper.; married; b. Milton; Charles D. Jones (Milton) and Pauline Hart (Milton)

Loisa M., d. 11/1/1889 at 69/7/9; chr. bronchitis; house; married; b. Milton; John Wentworth and Abigail Wingate

Lucia C., d. 9/3/1949 at 82; housewife; widow; b. Milton; G.C.S. Wentworth and Mary Hanson

Lucy Jane, d. 3/20/1897 at 70/7/28; bronchitis; housekeeper; married; Bard Varney and Lydia Horne

Marjorie, d. 4/30/1900 at 1/1/15; capillary bronchitis; b. Milton; Fred P. Jones (Milton) and Emma J. Cowell (Lebanon, ME)

Mary E., d. 3/25/1906 at 63/11; heart disease; housewife; married; b. Farmington; ----- Young

Mary E., d. 5/3/1987 in Hamilton, OH

Nellie, d. 4/7/1900 at 30/7/29; pneumonia; housekeeper; married; Aldin Crocker (NS) and Janette McMaster (NS)

Pauline H., d. 2/12/1910 at 44/0/3; pneumonia; housekeeper; widow; b. Milton; John F. Hart (Dover) and Mary A. Twombly (Milton)

Reuben D., d. 5/3/1930 at 72/6/20 in Rochester; caretaker; married; b. Milton; Nathan Jones (Milton) and Vashte Davenport (VT)

Robert E., d. 11/26/1954 at 66/11/14; widower; b. Milton; Fred P. Jones and Emma Cowell

Sally W., d. 12/5/1896 at 74/11/7; intestinal stoppage; housekeeper; married; John Ellis (Rochester) and Olive Ellis

William, d. 6/17/1899 at 80/7/5; carbuncle; farmer; widower; b. Randolph, MA; Obediah Jones (Randolph, MA) and Abigail Madden (Canton, MA)

JOOS,

Joseph, d. 7/12/1972 at 64 in Rochester; maintenance wkr.; b. Belgium; Augustine Joos and Marie VanDaele

Victor J., Sr., d. 1/6/1982 in Rochester; Augustine Joos and Marie VanDahl

JORDAN,
Elizabeth A., d. 10/13/1904 at 63/9/16; chronic gastritis; housekeeper; married; b. Dover; Moses Downs (Milton) and Lavina Hanson (Alton)
George E., d. 2/26/1961 at 84 in Wolfeboro; gas sta. operator; b. Milton; George I. Jordan
George I., d. 9/2/1915 at 79/3/17; widower; b. Prospect, ME; Joseph Jordan
Sarah E., d. 6/27/1967 at 92; housewife; b. Lynn, MA; Charles Brown and Mary Lodge

JOY,
son, d. 2/2/1937 at 0/0/0 in Rochester; b. Rochester; Nelson Joy
Alice P., d. 2/7/1968 at 80 in Union
Dorothy A., d. 7/5/1993 in Union
Emmie L., d. 5/27/1982 in Concord
Frank D., d. 2/23/1948 at 66/0/1 in Wolfeboro
Fred E., d. 9/10/1960 at 22 in Milton Mills; shoe worker; b. Pittsfield; George E. Joy and Maude A. Locke
George E., d. 6/22/1955 at 12/0/28 in Wakefield; student; single; b. Rochester; Lester Joy and Gladys Horne
Gerald P., d. 10/23/1938 at 0/0/1 in Rochester; b. Rochester; Nelson Joy (Middleton) and Mildred Pike (Rochester)
Jessie-Ann, d. 8/22/1998 in Sanbornville
Lawrence I., d. 6/15/1966 at 54 in Union; b. Union; Frank Joy and Alice Kimball
Leah A., d. 5/21/1982 in Union
Marian E., d. 12/26/1936 at 22/8/19; housewife; married; b. Lebanon, ME; Linnie Wentworth (Lebanon, ME) and Carrie Wentworth (Acton, ME)
Nelson M., d. 4/23/1975 at 67 in Rochester; self-emp. carpt.; b. NH; Frank D. Joy and Alice P. Kimball
Sarah, d. 5/30/1943 at 91/3/19 in Berwick, ME
Stephen P., d. 5/21/1982 in Union
Sylvia L., d. 4/28/1992 in Union

JULIN,
Arnold S., d. 8/14/1984; Gustaf Julin and Vanja Smith
Elsie E., d. 4/30/1997 in Rochester

JUNKINS,
Helen, d. 10/30/1929 at 89/10 in Woburn, MA; housewife; widow; b. Wolfeboro; Mark R. Dockum (Greenland) and Betsy Seavey (Wolfeboro)
Sally A., d. 5/23/1903 at 73/11/28; pulmonary tuberculosis; housekeeper; widow; b. Wakefield; Albra Wentworth (Wakefield) and Rhoda Cook (Wakefield)

KASPRZYK,
Louis G., d. 10/8/1969 at 53 in Manchester; merchant; b. MA; John Kasprzyk and Josephine Idzik

KASZYNSKI,
Alexander, d. 9/20/1978 at 57 in Dover; tool & dye maker; b. MA; Ignacy Kaszynski and Cornelius Cybulski
Joan B., d. 11/11/1985 in Dover; Francis Brewer and Doris Etheridge

KATWICK,
Alice C., d. 1/11/1985 in Dover; Herbert W. Smith and Alberta E. Gilmore
Arthur D. (Dr.), d. 4/4/1986 in West Milton; John K. Katwick and Ellen Lynch
Peter J., d. 7/31/1963 at 18 in Brookfield
Robert T., Jr., d. 5/17/1978 at 36 in Wolfeboro; carpenter; b. MA; Robert T. Katwick, Sr. and Mary Lortie
Robert T., Sr., d. 9/11/1972 at 51 in Wolfeboro

KEATING,
R. J., d. 9/16/1948 at 23/5/28 in Milton Mills; mill worker; single; b. Cambridge, MA; James F. Keating (Somerville, MA) and Jane E. Flynn (Leominster, MA)

KEAY,
Olive J., d. 12/22/1903 at 74/3/1; senility; housekeeper; widow; b. Wakefield; Timothy Emery (Limington, ME) and Olive H.K. Wentworth (York, ME)
Winona E., d. 6/26/1949 at 83 in Wakefield; housewife; widow; b. Reading, MA; James H. Parker and Helen Guild

KEEFE,
Julia E., d. 8/8/1943 at 82/0/3; housewife; widow; b. Ireland; Patrick Galvin (Ireland) and Hanna Leary (Ireland)

KEEGAN,
Nancy J., d. 1/22/1991 in Rochester

KEENE,
Eva M., d. 9/10/1963 at 69 in Rochester; housewife; Benoit Lessard and Delvina Dion

KELLEY,
Abigail G., d. 2/28/1907 at 83/0/19; senility; widow; b. Haverhill; William O.S. Chase (Haverhill) and Zelenda Gage (Bradford, MA)
Edward H., d. 10/27/1934 at 76/9/17; retired; married; b. Plymouth, CT; Henry R. Kelley (Goshen, CT) and Sarah E. Bloss (Bethlehem, CT)

KENDALL,
Algin W., d. 7/21/1944 at 58/10/9 in Kittery, ME; electrician; married; b. Shirley, MA; Thomas J. Kendall (Milford, MA) and ----- Boyden (NJ)

KENDZERSKI,
Stephen E., d. 4/15/1991 in W. Milton; Stephen Kendzerski and Blanche Wlatkowski

KENNEY,
son, d. 10/31/1911 at 0/0/1; premature birth; b. Milton; Frank A. Kenney (Burlington, MA) and Nettie M. Dyer (Wakefield)
Abbie A., d. 5/5/1908 at 0/2/12; marasmus; b. Milton; Frank A. Kenney (Burlington, MA) and Nettie M. Dyer (Sanbornville)

Dennis E., d. 11/10/1996 in Rochester; William Kenney and Grace Staples

Frank A., d. 4/1/1954 at 74/10/23; laborer; married; b. MA; Bernard A. Kenney and Abbie Young

Nettie M., d. 4/15/1955 at 79/5/22; housewife; widow; b. Wakefield; Charles Dyer and Martha Drew

KENSTA,
Evelyn M., d. 7/12/1986 in Milton Mills; John J. DiNatale and Mary C. Fopiano

KEYES,
Nancy, d. 2/13/1898 at 79/0/14; intestinal obstruction; housekeeper; widow; b. Wolfeboro

KIBBE,
Richard L., d. 11/9/1991 in Dover; Mirro G. Kibbe and Helen A. Keyes

KIDDER,
Charles N., d. 8/25/1910 at 51; rheumatism of heart; b. Charlestown, MA

KILGORE,
son, d. 1/27/1897 at 0/0/0; inanition; b. Milton; George L. Kilgore (Norway, ME) and Elizabeth A. Witham (Acton, ME)

son, d. 2/7/1897 at 0/0/11; inanition; b. Milton; George L. Kilgore (Norway, ME) and Elizabeth A. Witham (Acton, ME)

KIMBALL,
son, d. 5/15/1926 at 0/0/0 in Rochester; b. Rochester; Elmer B. Kimball (Middleton) and Margaret Wentworth (Milton Mills)

Alice W., d. 7/1/1971 at 77 in Chicopee, MA

Angeline, d. 7/1/1956 at 72 in Union; housewife; widow; b. Epping; George Perkins and Mabel Perkins

Annie M., d. 12/10/1917 at 81/5/10; housekeeper; widow; b. Farmington; Richard R. Hayes (Farmington) and ----- Edgerley (Farmington)

Arthur H., d. 11/3/1907 at 49/7/26; chronic nephritis; emp. in mill; married; b. Rochester; Alvah Kimball (S. Groveland, MA) and Annie M. Hayes (Farmington)

Charles A., d. 12/31/1927 at 65/2/2; farmer; married; b. Middleton; John B. Kimball (Augusta, ME) and Sabina Downs (Somersworth)

Clara C., d. 12/8/1990 in Milton; Edwin Chipman and Bertha -----

Clarence A., d. 1/13/1910 at 9/6/28; cardiac dilation; b. Cambridgeport, MA; Charles A. Kimball (Middleton) and Clara F. Tripp (East Boston, MA)

Eliza, d. 3/31/1930 at 75/8 in Middleton; married

Elmer B., d. 12/7/1971 at 75 in Rochester; US mail carrier; b. NH; George B. Kimball and Eliza Hanscom

George Byron, d. 3/21/1992 in Wolfeboro

George M., d. 11/22/1976 at 62 in Manchester; lumberjack; b. NH; Walter Kimball and Angeline Perkins

Gladys, d. 1/31/1937 at 39/3/14 in Wakefield; housewife; married; b. Milton; John M. Corson (Dover) and Eva Postleton (Acton, ME)

Helen M., d. 12/31/1979 in New Durham; Andrew Kleczek and Mary Brederski

John W., d. 9/10/1983 in Wolfeboro

Margaret, d. 7/5/1987 in Saugus, MA

Marion E., d. 8/8/1983 in Wolfeboro

N. T., d. 1/15/1936 at 80/5/3; widower; b. Farmington; Joshua B. Kimball (Bradford, MA) and Eliza Trask (Milton)

Phillip A., d. 9/2/1944 at 54/10/24 in Northampton, MA; physician; married

Ralph M., d. 2/16/1922 at 62/6/19; laborer; married; b. Rochester; Alvah M. Kimball (So. Groveland, MA) and Annie M. Hayes (Farmington)

Sabina, d. 3/15/1912 at 93/10/29; capillary bronchitis; widow; b. Berwick, ME; Edmund Downs (Berwick, ME) and Sally Downs (Berwick, ME)

Sylvia M., d. 10/1/1996 in Dover

Thomas C., d. 8/11/1959 at 0/0/3; b. Rochester; John W. Kimball and Sylvia Hill

Ward C., d. 10/12/1977 at 75 in Wolfeboro; farmer-lumberman; b. ME; John W. Kimball and Violet Cummings

Woodbury, d. 9/20/1963 at 51 in Wolfeboro

KING,

Frank L., d. 4/26/1978 at 67 in Rochester; woodsman; b. MA; Silas King and Violetta Hutchinson

Guerdon E., d. 4/15/1984 in Dover; Silas King and Violet Hutchenson

Marjorie H., d. 4/19/1996 in Wolfeboro
Marjorie J., d. 7/11/1987 in Sanford, ME

KINGSTON,
Ellen, d. 11/18/1929 at 76/4/24; widow; b. Ireland; John Sullivan (Ireland) and Ellen Connolly (Ireland)
George, d. 8/3/1904 at 54/1/25; intestinal obstruction; emp. RR; married; b. Ireland; William Kingston (Ireland) and Elizabeth (Ireland)
George L., d. 1/12/1935 at 52/0/12; retired; single; b. Milton; George Kingston (Ireland) and Ellen Sullivan (Ireland)
Nellie F., d. 8/20/1915 at 25/3/20; housekeeper; single; b. Milton; George Kingston (Ireland) and Nellie Sullivan (Ireland)

KIRK,
Elwin, d. 10/28/1966 at 54 in Hanover; carpenter; b. Canada; Herbert Kirk and Ada Carr
Millen E., d. 10/20/1965 at 46 in Manchester; heel opr.; b. Colebrook; Herbert A. Kirk and Ada M. Carr

KITFIELD,
Edward H., d. 6/26/1936 at 77/0/22; retired; married; b. Lynn, MA; Thomas H. Kitfield (Manchester, MA) and Mary E. Tilton (Lynn, MA)

KLUTZ,
Robert A., d. 2/14/1950 at 0/1/12; b. Rochester; Jacob A. Klutz and Rita Dupuis

KNAPP,
Virgie M., d. 4/5/1991 in Concord; George Kingsbury and Chloe Kimball

KNIGHT,
Elbridge G., d. 11/16/1920 at 71/0/6; retired; single; b. Milton; Stephen Knight (Farmington) and Louise Clary (Brooks, ME)
Eugene L., d. 10/23/1953 at 30/8/12; machine tender; married; b. Lynn, MA; Lawrence Knight and Rachel Allen
Louise, d. 6/8/1899 at 78/11/20; heart failure; housekeeper; widow; b. Brooks, ME; Joshua Clary (Brooks, ME) and Nancy Rich (Brooks, ME)

Robert L., d. 11/6/1888 at 40 in Somersworth; drowned; shoemaker; married; b. Milton

Sarah B., d. 12/13/1960 at 84 in Rochester; housewife; b. No. Shapleigh, ME; John H. Maddox and Frances F. Webber

Wilbur C., d. 1/5/1969 at 98 in Rochester; merchant; b. NH; Robert L. Knight and Marilla Leighton

KNOWLES,
Harriet M., d. 4/29/1953 at 96/8/29; housewife; widow; b. Milton; John B. Kimball and Sabrina Downs

Sumner J., d. 2/28/1986 in Togus, ME

KNOX,
Forest E., d. 7/15/1918 at 47/7/7; single; b. Milton; Hosea B. Knox (Milton) and Belinda Q. Leighton (Farmington)

Hosea B., d. 10/2/1895 at 65/4/16; consumption; teamster; widower; b. Milton; Jesse Knox

Ira S., d. 6/2/1911 at 81/4/16; intestinal nephritis; shoemaker; married; b. Lebanon, ME; John Knox (Lebanon, ME) and Betsey Jones (Lebanon, ME)

Sarah L., d. 12/8/1942 at 82/0/26 in Concord; housekeeper; single; b. Milton

KOLEY,
Edward G., d. 4/16/1957 at 68 in Newington, CT

KOUTZOUKIS,
Ernest P., d. 7/19/1986 in Rochester; Peter K Koutzoukis and Mary Lemneos

KUPCS,
Maria, d. 11/7/1988 in Rochester; Janis Landovskis and Anna Grunte

Mikelis, d. 5/19/1998 in Rochester

LABRIE,
Clara M., d. 6/5/1972 at 70 in Rochester; homemaker; b. ME; Napoleon Dubois and Lea Goulet

Ludger, d. 8/8/1970 at 69 in Rochester; rag cutter; b. Canada; Joseph Labrie and Florida Cote

LACASSE,
Pauline M., d. 2/10/1994 in Dover; Carl E. Christensen and Mary Devove

LACHANCE,
Lucien J., d. 7/28/1980; Adelard Lachance and Olivine Sylvain

LADD,
Gordon C., d. 1/11/1998 in Rochester

LAIRD,
Doris E., d. 10/7/1995 in Dover; Ezra H. Balmforth and Irene F. Pride
Earl, d. 1/13/1996 in Rochester; Eric Laird and Emmaline Powers

LAMB,
Andross N., d. 1/4/1979; Nelson Lamb and Hazel A. Andross

LANE,
Frank H., d. 7/7/1954 at 83/11; machinist; widower; b. Gray, ME

LANGDALE,
Elizabeth, d. 4/1/1943 at 79/11/24; housework; widow; b. NS; Charles
  Timothy and Margaret Rines (NS)

LANGIELL,
Alfred, d. 10/26/1939 at 67/0/14; retired; married; b. Taunton, MA;
  Alfred Langiell (NS) and Eliza Roulard (NS)

LANGLEY,
daughter, d. 3/17/1902 at 0/0/1; inanition; b. Milton; Hiram W. Langley
  (Fairfield, ME) and Mamie F. Lewis (Milton)
Charles A., d. 4/15/1961 at 83 in Wolfeboro; grocery store; b. Shapleigh,
  ME; George W. Langley and Julia Maddox
Fannie A., d. 7/17/1953 at 74 in Wolfeboro; housewife; married; b.
  Limerick, ME; Frank Furlong and Flora Smith
Mary L., d. 8/23/1958 at 77/8/27 in Plymouth, MA
William H., d. 6/25/1976 at 78 in Rochester; salesman; b. ME; Charles A.
  Langley and Fanny Furlong

LAPORTE,
Antoine J., d. 1/22/1976 at 92 in Sanford, ME
Lettie A., d. 10/24/1963 at 76 in East Lebanon, ME

LAROCHELLE,
Arthur, d. 3/10/1916 at 35/9/28; laster; married; Adolph Larochelle (Canada) and Marie Fortier (Canada)
Richard P., d. 11/21/1990 in Milton; Thomas Larochelle and Emma Gagne

LASKEY,
Agnes Smith, d. 1/1/1990 in Dover; Guy A. Smith and Clara M. Tufts
Allie J., d. 1/7/1937 at 77/7/16; lumberman; married; b. Milton; Jonas Laskey (New Durham) and Sarah Vinal (Dover)
Arlene B., d. 1/11/1987 in Dover
Brackett M., d. 2/5/1909 at 1/2/25; acute nephritis; b. Milton; Allie J. Laskey (Milton) and Lizzie A. Weeks (Wakefield)
Clyde, d. 12/16/1983 in Albany, NY
Cora E., d. 5/7/1936 at 69/0/28 in Acton, ME; married; b. Acton, ME; Isaac Hanson (Acton, ME) and Elizabeth A. Stillings (No. Berwick, ME)
Crosby T., d. 6/22/1994 in Sanford, ME
Elizabeth A., d. 5/16/1955 at 76/0/22; housewife; widow; b. Wakefield; Brackett M. Weeks and Matilda Allen
Eva M., d. 12/11/1995 in Wolfeboro
George H., d. 10/17/1948 at 89/3/15 in Wolfeboro; farmer; widower; b. Milton; Warren Laskey (Milton)
Ida, d. 1/10/1935 at 45/5/9 in Rochester
Ira S., d. 9/14/1961 at 73 in Milton Mills; laborer; b. Milton; Allie J. Laskey and Rose Barker
John O., d. 5/2/1938 at 73/1/17 in Acton, ME; farmer; widower; b. Milton; Jonas S. Laskey (New Durham) and Sarah Vinol (Dover)
Jonas S., d. 12/6/1911 at 82/11/9; nephritis; farmer; widower; b. New Durham; Peltiah Laskey (New Durham) and Judith Miller (New Durham)
Joseph L., d. 2/1/1978 at 0/2 in Dover; b. ME; Alan L. Laskey and Barbara L. Beckwith
Kenneth, d. 1/12/1998 in FL
Mary T., d. 12/3/1942 at 67/3/8 in Sanford, ME; widow

Maude P., d. 4/15/1988 in Sanford, ME
Mildred E., d. 2/26/1989 in Citra, FL
Oscar, d. 6/20/1953 at 61 in Rochester; millwright; married; b. Acton, ME; George H. Laskey and Bertha Lowd
Ralph D., d. 2/17/1981 in Sanford, ME
Robert P., d. 11/12/1976 at 65 in Rochester; salesman (ret.); b. NH; Ralph D. Laskey and Maude Philbrick
Ronald D., d. 11/11/1959 at 0/0/5 in Rochester; b. Rochester; Roger C. Laskey and Mildred L. Hersom
Russell L., d. 2/15/1950 at 46/9/20 in Lowell, MA; George Laskey
Sarah A., d. 3/21/1910 at 69/5/24; Bright's disease; housekeeper; married; b. Dover; James Vinal (Scituate, MA) and ----- Mason
William F., d. 2/29/1936 at 63/7/1 in Milton Mills; farmer; single; b. Milton; Jonas S. Laskey (New Durham) and Sarah Vinal (Dover)

LASSELL,
Jane N., d. 3/14/1970 at 31 in Wolfeboro

LAVALLEY,
Henry J., d. 1/21/1984 in Rochester; Henry Lavalley and Josephine LaRock
William E., d. 11/9/1957 at 67 in Sanford, ME

LAVERTUE,
John R., d. 11/15/1967 at 64 in Rochester; custodian, UNH; b. Rochester; Joseph Lavertue and Florence P. Downs
Phyllis M., d. 9/28/1968 at 27 in Rochester; inspector; b. NH; Harry W. Morrill and Phyllis L. Grant
Rosalie A., d. 1/17/1992 in Milton; George Ellis and Inez Duntley

LAVOIE,
Antoine D., d. 9/11/1977 at 80 in Rochester; carpenter; b. Canada; Jules Lavoie and Laetitia LeBlanc

LAWRENCE,
John E., d. 10/11/1989 in Rochester

LAWSON,
Audrey Y., d. 2/15/1986 in Dover; Hervey E. Tanner and Mary O'Hara

Charles, d. 3/9/1937 at 75/7/6 in Foxboro, MA; storekeeper; widower; b. Londonderry; George Lawson and Ellen Hazeltine

Henry N., d. 7/30/1946 at 53/11/26; mechanic; married; b. Dow City, IA; Alec Lawson (Scotland) and Christiana Nelson (Denmark)

LEADEN,

Theresa, d. 12/21/1992 in Milton Mills; Gustav Dertinger and Elinor Rycktta

LEARY,

John E., d. 2/1/1986 in Rochester

LEAVITT,

Bertha E., d. 11/29/1966 at 73; housewife; b. Moultonboro; Otis M. Evans and Edith Garland

Charles E., d. 10/26/1897 at 40/5/10; carcinoma bladder; farmer; married; b. Wolfeboro; John C. Leavitt (Wolfeboro) and Betsy S. Rust (Wolfeboro)

LEBEAU,

Henry L., Jr., d. 7/31/1956 at 30; shipping clerk; married; b. Worcester, MA; Henry L. LeBeau, Sr. and Irene Kneeland

LEBLANC,

Arthur J., d. 4/4/1995 in Rochester; Basil L. Leblanc and Emma Goguen

Mary T., d. 3/1/1988 in Rochester; Henry Brunelle and Sarah Forcier

LEDOUX,

Yvonne, d. 11/21/1994 in Rochester; Oscar Lacourse and Almina Perrout

LEE,

John P., d. 9/14/1935 at 31/0/16; electrician; married; b. Quincy, MA; John J. Lee (Ontario) and Josephine Wilson (Van Buren, ME)

LEIGHTON,

Adelbert O., d. 5/24/1923 at 70/10; flagman; married; b. Milton; Louis L. Leighton (Farmington) and Lucinda J. Jones (Lebanon, ME)

Carrie B., d. 11/11/1972 at 100; homemaker; b. NH; Charles D. Remick and Susan J. Smallcorn

Doris Thelma, d. 8/6/1992 in Wolfeboro
Edwin, d. 2/19/1935 at 69/6/19; shoe worker; married; b. Milton; Cyrus Leighton (Milton) and Sophia Hayes (Rochester)
Gladys E., d. 11/9/1982 in Union
Lucinda, d. 6/15/1911 at 89/2/11; senility; widow; b. Lebanon, ME; Thomas Jones (Lebanon, ME) and Hannah Hayes (Lebanon, ME)
Mary, d. 3/22/1927 at 76/1/17; housekeeper; widow; b. Boston, MA; Anthony J. Amerald (Portugal) and Mary Cavanaugh (Ireland)
Oscar W., d. 3/3/1956 at 67/2/13; farmer; widower; b. Middleton; Charles Leighton and Lucy Drew
Presco F., d. 3/31/1968 at 68 in Rochester; carpenter; b. NH; Walter F. Leighton and Elizabeth Drew
Sophia M., d. 5/20/1905 at 81/0/28; apoplexy; housewife; widow; b. Rochester; George Hayes (Rochester) and Lydia Jones (Lebanon, ME)

LEJEUNE,
Germain E., d. 3/14/1993 in Rochester; Albert J. LeJeune and Felecite Frennette

LEPENE,
Donald M., d. 6/11/1985; Lawrence O. Lepene and Nellie Miles

LESSARD,
Arthur J., d. 1/19/1915 at 0/11/15; b. Milton; Eva M. Lessard (Rochester)
Benonie, d. 8/24/1943 at 86/11/29; farmer; married; b. Canada; Richard Lessard (Canada) and ----- Pare (Canada)
Elizabeth R., d. 3/26/1952 at 79 in Rochester; housewife; widow; b. Milton; Elias Miller and Mary Pinkham
Joseph A. Norman, d. 1/9/1963 at 44 in Rochester; dyecast opr.; b. Rochester; Joseph A. Lessard and Lydia Turcotte
Lanson, d. 8/19/1907 at 8/4/1; drowning; b. Milton; Benoni Lessard (Canada) and Delvina Dion (Canada)
Lydia, d. 9/1/1959 at 75 in Rochester; housewife; married; b. Canada; Augusta Turcotte and Sylvia Labbe
Marie C., d. 5/29/1898 at 0/3/4; hydrocephalus; b. Milton; Belaine Lessard (Canada) and Delvina Dion (Canada)

LEVESQUE,
Lucien E., d. 3/10/1986 in Manchester

LEWIS,
Alfred W., d. 8/19/1959 at 80 in Wolfeboro; farmer; married; b. Acton, ME; John Lewis and Elizabeth Jones
Bessie M., d. 12/28/1974 at 90 in Sanford, ME
Frank T., d. 9/3/1985 in Lincoln, MA
Hannah G., d. 7/18/1964 at 94 in Rochester; housewife; married; b. Acton, ME; John F. Titcomb and Abbie Gray
James, d. 8/6/1935 at 88/3/24 in Los Angeles, CA; farmer; married
Mary R., d. 3/19/1974 at 74 in Wolfeboro

LIBBEY,
Elizabeth P., d. 7/2/1979; James Phalen and Helen Dempsey
Leon, d. 7/4/1913 at 6/11; acute alcohol poisoning; b. Berwick, ME; Charles Libbey (Somersworth) and Mabel Bennett (So. Berwick, ME)
Lucy Maria, d. 7/16/1958 at 78 in Portsmouth; cook; single; b. Wakefield; Washington Libbey and Ellen Farnham

LIBBY,
Audrey D., d. 1/1/1950 in Grove City, PA; widow
Christine C., d. 2/20/1988 in Rochester; Everett A. Chamberlain and Annie Albrecht
Elijah T., d. 11/19/1918 at 72/0/1; jeweler; married; b. Brownfield, ME; Hall Libbey and Almeda Tibbetts
Florence E., d. 10/13/1944 at 56/11/1 in Wolfeboro; housewife; married; b. Tuftonboro; Albert Hatch (Wolfeboro) and Georgia A. Wendall (Tuftonboro)
Ida A., d. 4/5/1930 at 76/1/1 in Milton Mills; at home; widow; b. Parsonsfield, ME; Charles Eastman (Parsonsfield, ME) and Lydia Day (Parsonsfield, ME)
Laura B., d. 4/29/1938 at 91/0/18 in Wolfeboro; at home; widow; b. Salisbury, MA; Luther Tibbetts (Sanford, ME) and Thurga Tibbetts (Sanford, ME)
Olive M., d. 5/26/1961 at 83 in Portsmouth; manager hotel; b. Wakefield; Washington Libby and Ellen Farnham

Thomas P., Jr., d. 3/8/1964 at 85 in Concord; b. Lawrence, MA; Thomas P. Libby, Sr. and Rosanna York

LIBERI,
Bernard H., Jr., d. 9/22/1992 in Rochester; Bernard H. Liberi, Sr. and Bertha M. Vernava

LILLJEDAHL,
Carl H., d. 2/14/1968 at 64; cont.-builder; b. MA; Carl W. Lilljedahl and Anna Yaderbery
Thelma I., d. 5/19/1996 in Rochester; Arthur Dumont and Maria Anna Larochelle

LIPSETT,
Isabelle M., d. 6/18/1997 in Wolfeboro
Robert George, d. 1/24/1993 in Wolfeboro

LITTLEFIELD,
female infant, d. 11/20/1952 in Waltham, MA (1993)
Alice E., d. 12/22/1964 at 81 in Rochester; housewife; b. Dover
Fanny W., d. 5/3/1956 at 77/9/13 in Dover; housewife; widow; b. Milton; Bard B. Plummer and Eliza D. Wentworth
Frances L., d. 3/16/1998 in Rochester
Grace F., d. 5/18/1972 at 87 in Sanbornville; homemaker; b. ME; Edward P. Eastman and Elizah N. Sawyer
Haven, d. 3/14/1940 at 78/8/26; ret. farmer; widower; b. Wells, ME; Joshua Littlefield (Wells, ME)
Laura J., d. 8/21/1968 at 84 in Rochester; homemaker; b. NH; Alfred W. Jones and Ella Kimball
Madeline A., d. 1/15/1977 at 69 in Rochester; homemaker; b. ME; Richard Hoxie and Kate Rolff
Maynard J., d. 5/22/1977 at 77 in Rochester; prop. Milton Ice Co.; b. ME; Josiah Littlefield and Lillian Sibley
Nathan, d. 3/26/1958 at 73 in Rochester; chef; married; b. York, ME; Jothan Littlefield and Martha Allen
Payson E., d. 8/14/1979 in Rochester; Nathan Littlefield and Grace Eastman

LOBBERT,
daughter, d. 10/30/1970 at 15 hrs. in Rochester; b. Rochester

LOCKE,
Joseph T., d. 11/4/1927 at 76/5/13 in Milton Mills; widower; b. Barrington; Alfred Locke and Mary Seavey
Mary W., d. 11/14/1917 at 76/2/27; widow; b. Somersworth; William Perkins (Barrington) and Abigail Fuller (Exeter)
Rose B., d. 4/18/1926 at 66/8/1 in Milton Mills; housewife; married; b. Somersworth; William Perkins (Barrington) and Abigail Fuller (Exeter)

LOCKHART,
Daniel, d. 2/25/1935 at 66/1/10; farmer; married; b. So. Boston, MA; John Lockhart (NS) and Elizabeth Frazier (NS)
Geneva E., d. 6/19/1980 in Rochester

LOGAN,
Charles H., d. 12/25/1997 in Rochester; Charles W. Logan and Florence Y. Welch
Charles W., d. 6/1/1965 at 84 in Wolfeboro; laborer; b. WI; Michael Logan and Elizabeth Featherstone
Florence Y., d. 5/18/1961 at 72 in Wolfeboro; housewife; b. Ossipee; Moses Welch and Sarah Welch

LONDO,
Erwin, d. 4/21/1992 in Dover; Nelson London and Mildred Corson
Mildred G., d. 5/18/1966 at 73 in Dover; housewife; b. Wolfeboro; George Corson and Nellie Knight

LONG,
Frank L., d. 11/11/1951 at 66 in Dover; clergyman; widower; b. St. George, ME; Leslie Long and Martha Nelson
Frank L., d. 10/29/1979 in Manchester; Frank Long and Lula -----
John H., Jr., d. 12/30/1982; John H. Long, Sr. and Cathrin Perkins
John II., Sr., d. 4/19/1996 in Acton, ME
Martha A., d. 11/2/1948 at 90/1/1 in Wolfeboro

LONGLEY,
A. Mae, d. 5/25/1932 at 72/9/17 in Rochester; at home; widow; b. Brighton, MA; Leonard Gilman (Bingham, ME) and Elvira Eames (Madison, ME)
Asenath, d. 6/15/1935 at 52/6/5 in Rochester; mill op.; married; b. Milton Mills; Edward A. Hargraves (Shapleigh, ME) and Amanda Page (Milton Mills)
George W., d. 5/21/1975 at 93 in Rochester; mgr. motel; b. ME; Jonas Longley and Annastazzia M. Gilman
Thyra E., d. 12/22/1956 at 77/5/7 in Rochester; housewife; married; b. Sweden; Hulda Lundgren and Suante Swenson

LOONEY,
Charles H., d. 4/23/1902 at 52; apoplexy; U.S. Customs Coll.; married; b. Milton; Francis C. Looney and Rhoda Leighton
Emily E., d. 4/22/1921 at 66/6/24; at home; widow; b. Milton; Robert Miller (Frederickton, NB) and Sarah M. Hodgdon (Lebanon, ME)
Rhoda A., d. 6/22/1896 at 79/3/28; apoplexy; widow; b. Milton; Thomas Leighton (Farmington) and Nancy Jones (Berwick, ME)
Robert M., d. 7/22/1932 at 52/1/12 in Newtonville, MA; retired; single; b. Milton; Charles H. Looney (Milton) and Emily E. Miller (Milton)
Walter, d. 10/1/1928 at 50/4/17 in Portsmouth; US collector; married; b. Milton; Charles H. Looney (Milton) and Emily E. Miller (Milton)

LORD,
son, d. 1/27/1936 at 0/0/0; b. Milton; James E. Lord (W. Lebanon, ME) and Ruth Wentworth (E. Lebanon, ME)
Albert J., d. 1/31/1986 in Milton Mills; Fred Lord and Ludine Nadeau
Beatrice V., d. 4/10/1925 at 0/6/8; single; b. Milton; James E. Lord (West Lebanon, ME) and Ruth G. Wentworth (East Lebanon, ME)
Charles L., d. 5/30/1917 at 74/0/22; shoemaker; widower; b. Lebanon, ME; Ezekiel R. Lord (Lebanon, ME) and Draxa Dixon (Lebanon, ME)
Christine B., d. 11/19/1988 in Rochester; William Uzzell and Margaret Mattheson
Dora P., d. 1/21/1916 at 96/8/23; housekeeper; widow; b. Topsham, ME; Alden Quint
Draxa A., d. 12/20/1909 at 90/2/27; senility; widow; b. Lebanon, ME; Stephen Dixon (Lebanon, ME) and Mary Stevens (Lebanon, ME)

Elsie, d. 6/19/1966 at 60; housewife; b. Sanford, ME; Melvin Burnham and Sarah Mills

Ezekiel R., d. 5/6/1891 at 72/8; congestion of brain; farmer; married; b. Lebanon, ME; Nathaniel Lord and Polly Ricker

Francis J., d. 3/16/1981 in Manchester; Arthur Richardson and Roseann Sullivan

Frank, d. 1/17/1938 at 50/8/20 in Dover; saw mill; single; b. Acton, ME; Charles Lord (Acton, ME) and Vesta A. Earle (Acton, ME)

Frank H., d. 10/24/1922 at 54/9/15; married; b. Huntorville, Canada; David Lord (No. Waterford, ME) and Hannah Higgins (Livermore Falls, ME)

Henry, d. 9/3/1931 at 6 hrs; b. Milton; J. Edwin Lord (W. Lebanon, ME) and Ruth Wentworth (E. Lebanon, ME)

Isaac L., d. 3/15/1956 at 85 in Sanford, ME; widower

James E., d. 3/25/1980 in Rochester; James F. Lord and Sarah Warburton

John, d. 9/3/1931 at 6 hrs; b. Milton; J. Edwin Lord (W. Lebanon, ME) and Ruth Wentworth (E. Lebanon, ME)

Josephine D., d. 10/22/1914 at 64/10; cerebral hemorrhage; single; b. Lebanon, ME; Ezekiel R. Lord (Lebanon, ME) and Draxa D. Dixon (Lebanon, ME)

Luella E., d. 3/6/1983 in Rochester

Martin L., d. 6/11/1973 at 63 in Rochester; salesman; b. NH; Shubeal Lord and Ella Grant

Maynard E., d. 10/10/1967 in Sanford, ME

Pauline, d. 5/31/1985 in Portland, ME

Ruth G., d. 4/3/1982 in Rochester; Melvin Wentworth and Clara Goodwin

Susan S., d. 11/17/1905 at 78/3/12; senile debility; divorced; b. Milton; John Hart (Newington)

LOSEE,

Margaret S., d. 7/1/1917 at 87/11/22; retired; widow; b. Pleasant Valley, NY; Hulett Peters (Banghall, NY) and Angeline Simmons (NY)

LOUD,

Lillian B., d. 1/6/1936 at 54/11/7 in Haverhill, MA; single; b. Merrimac, MA; Charles Loud and Addie -----

Ray A., d. 2/18/1969 at 73 in Rochester; engineer; b. NH; George W. Loud and Emlie E. Otis

LOUGEE,
William S., d. 7/7/1931 at 56/10/26 in Rochester; manager; married; b. Pittsfield; Sewell N. Lougee (Gilmanton I.W.) and Sarah E. Smith (Gilmanton I.W.)

LOUGHLIN,
son, d. 6/24/1890 at 0/0/4; heart disease; b. Milton; John Loughlin (Ireland) and Ellen Callahan (Ireland)
Ellen M.J., d. 12/8/1910 at 59/10/23; angina pectoris; housewife; married; b. Ireland; John Callaghan (Ireland) and Margaret Devine (Ireland)

LOVER,
Alice M., d. 6/20/1970 at 81 in Rochester; housewife; b. NH; Charles S. Downs and Isabelle Ellis
Merle V., d. 6/6/1998 in Rochester
Peter J., d. 8/30/1969 at 82; plumber; b. NH; John A. Lover and Selina Cloutier
Richard A., d. 12/10/1910 at 0/4/22; inanition; b. Milton; Peter J. Lover (Union) and Alice M. Downs (Sanbornville)
Wilbur C., d. 10/15/1985 in Concord; Peter J. Lover and Alice M. Downs

LOVERING,
George S., d. 12/21/1912 at 67/2/9; chronic nephritis; merchant; widower; b. Tuftonboro; Plumer G. Lovering (Loudon) and Lydia Burbank (Tuftonboro)
Jennie S., d. 3/26/1901 at 35/9/20; uremia; housewife; married; b. Brookfield; Durrell D. Stevens (Middleton) and Hannah Cook (Middleton)

LOWD,
Albert P., d. 12/2/1975 at 73 in Acton, ME
Archie T., d. 8/17/1930 at 60/6/1 in Acton, ME; mill oper.; married; b. Acton, ME; Wentworth Lowd (Acton, ME) and Sarah Tasker (Milton)
Clara P., d. 1/22/1956 at 85/10/7 in Acton, ME; widow
Clinton S., d. 8/21/1903 at 53/4; Bright's disease; farmer; married; b. Acton, ME; Sylvester Lowd (Acton, ME) and Dorcas Hanson (Berwick, ME)

Cora M., d. 10/3/1930 at 73/9/13 in Wakefield; retired; widow; b. Dover; Simon Ricker and Eliza Kenney

Dorothy L., d. 9/17/1998 in ME

Effie M., d. 1/3/1928 at 54/9/27 in Rochester; weaver; single; b. Acton, ME; George W. Lowd (Acton, ME) and Mary E. Hersom (Stoneham, MA)

Flora D., d. 3/28/1903 at 25/8/3; tuberculosis; weaver; single; b. Acton, ME; Clinton S. Lowd (Acton, ME) and Cora S. Ricker (Dover)

Freeman H., d. 5/1/1933 at 79/7/26; retired; widower; b. Acton, ME; Sylvester Lowd (Acton, ME) and Dorcas Hanson (Lebanon, ME)

George F., d. 5/11/1989 in Springvale, ME

George S., d. 7/17/1939 at 69/4/11 in Springvale, ME; superintendent; married; b. Acton, ME; George W. Lowd (Stoneham, MA) and Mary E. Hersom (Acton, ME)

John, d. 3/6/1922 at 76/9/20; retired; widower; b. Acton, ME; Sylvester Lowd (Acton, ME) and Dorcas Hanson (Acton, ME)

Mary E., d. 6/1/1920 at 69/10/14 in Acton, ME; housekeeper; widow; b. Stoneham, MA; Samuel Hersam (MA) and Martha Hersam (VT)

Mary W., d. 10/27/1927 at 47/6/15 in Rochester; at home; married; b. Milton Mills; Hiram Wentworth (Milton) and Clara J. Hart (Milton)

Melissa, d. 6/21/1915 at 72/10/26; widow; Ansel Buck (Acton, ME) and Adeline Dore (Acton, ME)

Nellie A., d. 9/12/1952 at 76 in Springvale, ME

Stella M., d. 8/31/1940 at 61/2/14 in Lawrence, MA

Viola, d. 10/10/1910 at 55/2; tuberculosis; housework; married; Francis Coffran (Sandwich) and Sarah Ham (Newfield, ME)

LOWE,

Adelia E., d. 8/15/1938 at 82/11/6 in Wakefield; at home; married; b. Milton Mills; Gardner Chamberlain (Milton) and Mary Fall (Lebanon, ME)

Charles W., d. 5/2/1939 at 83/6/9 in Union; retired; widower; b. No. Shapleigh, ME; John Lowe (Newfield, ME) and Hannah Hargraves (Amesbury, MA)

Doris R., d. 4/6/1965 at 62 in Rochester; housewife; b. Solon, ME; Perly A. Rowell and Myrtle Cooley

Eva May, d. 5/31/1963 at 75 in Wakefield

Hannah, d. 9/17/1938 at 76/4/16 in Rollinsford

Homer C., d. 6/3/1951 at 65 in Wakefield; married; Charles Lowe and
Adelia Chamberlain

Ruby E., d. 4/9/1975

LOWELL,

Eliza A., d. 11/2/1917 at 90/0/16; widow; b. Portland, ME; Amos Nichols
(Ossipee) and Eliza Titcomb (Effingham)

LOWELL-WALLACE,

Margaret T., d. 5/11/1984 in Dover; George E. Wallace and Neva S.
Lowell

LOZEY,

Henry, d. 1/22/1948 at 75 in Milton Mills; mill operative; widower; b.
Canada

LUCIER,

Elba H., d. 10/24/1946 at 90/10/7 in Somerville, MA

Max J., d. 4/18/1987 in Wolfeboro

Myrtle I., d. 2/14/1995 in Wolfeboro

LUMBARD,

Marie J., d. 10/19/1969 at 54 in Sanford, ME; P.O. clerk; b. NY; Joseph
Bottie and Gladys Hanscom

Robert, d. 10/1/1995 in Wolfeboro; Alfred R. Lumbard and Mary Sanborn

LUND,

Herbert C., d. 12/6/1970 at 49 in Rochester; fibreboard worker; b. NH;
Frederick Lund and Luri Johnson

LUSSIER,

Elvira O., d. 2/12/1996 in Rochester; Antonia Pecci and Jonina Cavelli

LYMAN,

Andrew R., d. 9/14/1906 at 67/9/9; heart disease; retired; married; b.
Milton; Theodore Lyman (Milton) and Betsy Bragdon (Milton)

George, d. 6/19/1900 at 72/6; chr. Bright's disease; farmer; widower; b.
Milton; Micah Lyman (Milton) and Mary Kelly (Rochester)

Hannah, d. 11/16/1886 at 59/11/16; housekeeper; married; b. Rochester; Jeremiah Plumer (Rochester) and Tamson Twombly (Farmington) (1941)

Theodore, d. 8/1/1891 at 78/11/9; heart disease and dropsy; farmer; widower; b. Milton; Theodore C. Lyman and Dorothy Allan

MACDONALD,

Herbert D., d. 1/6/1954 at 73 in Portsmouth; garageman; divorced; b. NB; Finley MacDonald and Elizabeth Gunn

MACGREGOR,

Walter N., d. 7/6/1986 in Rochester; Fred MacGregor and Fanny Morrison

MACH,

Evelyn A., d. 9/29/1986 in Belleville, IL

MACILVAINE,

Esther L., d. 2/17/1984 in Dover; Albert Fielder and Alice M. Caswell

George H., d. 1/17/1968 at 86; plumber; b. NH; Henry F. MacIlvaine and Sarah Boutwell

Linwood L., d. 6/28/1979 in Lynn, MA

MACKENZIE,

John A., d. 3/20/1975 at 53; gun assembler; b. ME; John A. MacKenzie, Sr. and Ethel Judkins

Waneta A., d. 7/1/1978 at 58 in Rochester; shoe worker; b. ME; Fred Tibbetts and Louisa Cummings

MACLEOD,

child, d. 7/15/1969 at 0/0/0 in Rochester; b. NH

daughter, d. 3/29/1978 at 0/3 in Boston, MA

Daniel M., d. 3/30/1966 at 86 in Wolfeboro; truckman; b. Canada; Duncan MacLeod and Sarah Hayden

MACRAE,

Arleen E., d. 11/8/1989 in Rochester; Ernest Carpenter and Hattie Wentworth

MADDOX,
Eugene A., d. 9/3/1893 at 22/4/22; pulmonary phthisis; clerk; married; b. Newfield, ME; John H. Maddox (Newfield, ME) and Olive F. Webber (Shapleigh, ME)
John H., d. 10/11/1931 at 82/11/11; millwright; married; b. Newfield, ME; John W. Maddox and Susan Benson (Saco, ME)
Olive F., d. 1/28/1946 at 96/7/11; housewife; widow; b. No. Shapleigh, ME; Greenleaf Webber (W. Newfield, ME) and Sarah C. Grant (Acton, ME)

MAGNAN,
Minnie E., d. 9/9/1919 at 51/9/18; housewife; married; b. Pierpont, NY; J. A. Hale (Pierport, NY) and Harriet (Pierport, NY)

MAHONEY,
William G., d. 8/2/1914 at 35; pulm. tuberculosis; laborer; married; b. Ireland; George Mahoney (Ireland) and Mary Driscoll (Ireland)

MAIN,
Fanny, d. 12/14/1973 at 79 in Rochester; homemaker; b. Scotland
Robert, d. 12/19/1965 at 66; refrigeration; b. Nairn, Scotland; James Main and Elizabeth Cope

MAINE,
Hannah, d. 8/17/1907 at 71/3/16; shock; housewife; married; b. Middleton; John D. Horne (Middleton) and Mary Chase (Brookfield)

MALLOY,
Edward F., d. 6/16/1947 at 52/5/27; retired; married; b. Marblehead, MA; Edward F. Malloy (Waltham, MA) and Mary Mahoney (NB)

MALONE,
William J., d. 8/30/1937 at 18/0/5; printer; single; b. Boston, MA; Thomas Malone (Ireland) and Nellie McMahan (Ireland)

MANGAN,
W. A., d. 11/12/1948 at 69; sheet metal worker; widower; b. So. Boston, MA; William A. Mangan (Ireland) and Josephine Walsh (So. Boston, MA)

MANNETTE,
Thomas Russell, d. 8/6/1992 in Milton; Russell T. Mannette and Marguerite A. Rousseau

MANSFIELD,
Ann, d. 2/11/1965 in Ipswich, MA
Dr. Burleigh B., d. 2/19/1968 at 77 in Rochester; physician, MD; b. ME; Ferdanand Mansfield and Julia -----

MANSUR,
Lizzie, d. 4/14/1937 at 79/7/2 in Milton Mills; retired; widow; b. Wakefield; Samuel Cummings (So. Paris, ME) and Nancy Neal (Brookfield)

MARCH,
Lauri M., d. 9/28/1979 in Portland, ME

MARCHAND,
Aurea, d. 1/3/1898 at 0/3/18; inanition; b. Milton; Oscar Marchand (Canada) and Emma Pouliot (Somersworth)
Helen, d. 1/4/1912 at 54; cerebral hemorrhage; married; b. Canada

MARCOUX,
daughter, d. 7/3/1963 at 0/0/0 in Rochester; Robert D. Marcoux and Mary Ann Smith
Charles, d. 3/4/1928 at 0/4/5; b. Milton; Napoleon Marcoux (Wakefield) and Hazel M. Downs (Milton)
David B., d. 8/25/1956 at 21 hrs. in Rochester; b. Rochester; Archie P. Marcoux and Beverly Young
Dora, d. 12/8/1909 at 0/7/1; pneumonia; b. Milton; Archie Marcoux (Canada) and Rosa Storm (Canada)
Hazel M., d. 4/8/1997 in Rochester
Joseph, d. 7/28/1905 at 0/10/26; whooping cough; b. Milton; Archie Marcoux (Canada) and Rosa Storm (Canada)
Joseph, d. 7/5/1984 in Rochester; Napoleon Marcoux and Hazel Downs
Joseph R., d. 9/18/1989 in Rochester; Joseph R. Marcoux, Sr. and Janet M. Chapman
Louis A., d. 10/26/1902 at 0/1/27; inanition; b. Milton; Archie Marcoux (Canada) and Rose Storne (Canada)

MARGERISON,
Virena G., d. 2/28/1998 in Rochester

MARION,
Betty, d. 2/1/1995 in Dover; Francis Fall and Hattie Furbush
Henry J., Sr., d. 8/5/1994 in Rochester; Gideon Marion and Rosilda Laventure

MARK,
Annette G., d. 11/26/1891 at 69; pneumonia; widow; b. Brunswick

MARR,
Agnes M., d. 1/30/1998 in Dover

MARSH,
Anne M., d. 7/23/1954 at 68 in NJ
Bertha B., d. 3/7/1972 at 68 in Westboro, MA
Eddie E., d. 11/11/1926 at 69/7/21 in Milton Mills; farmer; married; b. Acton, ME; Noah Marsh (Acton, ME) and Naomi Joy (Acton, ME)
Eva M., d. 5/18/1969 at 78 in Sanford, ME
Everett C., d. 4/18/1901 at 29/8/18; paralysis; mill hand; single; b. Acton, ME; John E. Marsh (Milton) and Carrie F. Cater (Manchester)
Forrest L., d. 7/17/1945 at 65/10/5 in Kearny, NJ; buyer; married; b. Milton Mills; Oscar Marsh and Georgia Reed
Frank L., d. 9/15/1929 at 76/0/11; retired; married; b. Acton, ME; Noah L. Marsh (Acton, ME) and Naomi Joy (Acton, ME)
Garfield A., d. 12/19/1960 at 79 in Wolfeboro; carpenter; b. Acton, ME; Thomas D. Marsh
George W., d. 4/2/1953 at 74 in Acton, ME
Georgia W., d. 12/29/1918 at 73/2/1; housewife; married; b. Somersworth; Lewis D. Reed (Dover) and Annette W. Randall (Lebanon, ME)
Henry D., d. 9/20/1899 at 48; heart disease; saloon keeper; b. Rockville; Hiram Marsh
Ithiel E., d. 12/28/1980 in West Lebanon, ME
Julia E., d. 12/1/1915 at 62/1/23; at home; married; b. Acton, ME; Joshua B. Sanborn (Acton, ME) and Esther Applebee (Acton, ME)
Katherine M., d. 8/9/1957 at 83/0/8 in Acton, ME; married

Lester, d. 6/2/1965 at 54 in Newton, MA; ret. stock keeper; b. Acton, ME; George Marsh and Eva Burroughs
Letitia, d. 7/12/1908 at 57/5/20; cerebral hemorrhage; single; b. Milton; John Marsh (Acton, ME) and Lulyetta Reynolds (Acton, ME)
Lucy L., d. 3/12/1935 at 79/2/25; at home; widow; b. Acton, ME; John Earl (Acton, ME) and Sally Witham (Acton, ME)
Mary E., d. 6/16/1973 at 64 in W. Lebanon, ME
Mildred T., d. 11/11/1921 at 43/10/26; at home; married; b. Newfield, ME; William M. Tebbetts (Newfield, ME) and Mary Wyatt (Boston, MA)
Oscar F., d. 12/13/1928 at 82/10/20 in Dover; retired; widower; b. Milton Mills; John Marsh (Acton, ME) and Asenath Runnels (Acton, ME)

MARSHALL,
Edward L., d. 11/14/1906 at 0/0/1; premature birth; b. Milton; George B. Marshall (N. Easton, MA) and Rosalie B. Tozin (Waldo, ME)
Ruth A., d. 4/19/1989 in Dover; Charles Fuller and Amelia James

MARTEL,
Jeremy I., d. 5/23/1997 in Milton Mills (approx.); Donald Landry and Lorra M. Newhall

MARTIN,
Augusta T., d. 3/27/1951 at 84 in Wolfeboro; housewife; widow; b. Newfield, ME; William Tibbitts and Mary Wyatt
Elmer, d. 6/13/1924 at 50/10/4; laborer; single; b. Westville; Israel Martin (Canada) and Adelia Stone (E. Middleboro, VT)
Jesse, d. 5/16/1990 in Rochester; John Martin and Gloria Cadera
Meagan L., d. 4/4/1979 in Hanover; Michael Martin and Angelica Brooks

MARTINDALE,
Nikki M., d. 12/26/1996 in Milton; Donald R. Martindale and Shirley M. Coffin

MARTINEAU,
Clifford, d. 6/4/1949 at 44 in Chelsea, MA
Josephine, d. 2/2/1961 at 87 in Rochester; housewife; b. Center Ossipee; John Brown and Mary J. Hayes
Lawrence, d. 3/19/1946 at 31 in Concord

Napoleon, d. 7/19/1941 at 73/11/25 in Rochester; section hand; married; b. Quebec; Peter Martineau (Canada) and Sophie Perrault (Canada)

MASON,
Albert, d. 5/23/1897 at 79/5; chronic bronchitis; farmer; widower; b. Sandwich; Andrew Mason (Tamworth) and Sally Thrasher
Calvin P., d. 10/15/1934 at 89/11/27; farmer; widower; b. Sandwich; Albert Mason (Sandwich) and Sarah Parker (Sandwich)
Lydia A., d. 1/31/1933 at 87/1/13; housewife; married; b. Ossipee; Bradbury Quint (Ossipee) and Sally Tuttle (Ossipee)
Marjorie E., d. 4/15/1980 in Dover
Mary Jane, d. 3/27/1897 at 63/11/15; pneumonia; housekeeper; married; b. Tuftonboro; Henry Whitehouse (Tuftonboro) and Rebecca Whitehouse (Tuftonboro)

MATHENA,
Charles, d. 11/4/1983; Charles M. Mathena and Olive A. Hazzard

MATHES,
son, d. 7/–/1891 at 0/0/0; premature birth; b. Milton; Samuel Mathes and Lottie Leonard
Mary F., d. 9/8/1907 at 90/4; acute indigestion; widow; b. Milton; Josiah Moulton (Hampton) and Mary Watson (Milton)
Robert, d. 7/31/1894 at 82/1/16; valvular heart disease; farmer; married; b. Milton; Robert Mathes (Milton) and Sally (Milton)

MATHEWS,
Hazel, d. 8/1/1913 at 6/11/21; diptheria; black; b. Springvale, ME; Oscar S. Mathews (Brunswick, ME) and Hattie Jackson (Fall River, MA)
Mildred, d. 8/5/1913 at 5/4/21; pneumonia; black; b. Milton; Oscar S. Mathews (Brunswick, ME) and Hattie Jackson (Fall River, MA)

MATTRESS,
Emma, d. 7/20/1962 at 87 in Sanford, ME
Harold E., d. 1/23/1967 at 55 in Hanover
John E., d. 3/13/1960 at 84 in Acton, ME

MAYO,
Leroy S., d. 7/31/1909 at 58/3/8; mitral insufficiency; lumber mfr.; married; b. Standish, ME; William D. Mayo (Standish, ME) and Eunice Moreau (Standish, ME)

MAYRAND,
Mavis, d. 10/4/1938 at 49/1/20 in Dover; housewife; married; b. Milton; George W. Page (Dalton) and Jennette Page (Milton)

McCANNON,
Thomas, d. 4/21/1939 at 66/3/20; retired; married; b. Salem, MA; Thomas McCannon (Salem, MA) and Matilda Fanning (Salem, MA)

McCARTAN,
Patrick W., d. 10/2/1960 at 70 in Rochester; fireman; b. Ireland; Patrick McCartan and Jean Doran

McCAULEY,
Alexander S., d. 10/15/1902 at 60; accident; seaman; married; b. PEI; Anges Macauley (PEI) and Annie Maginnis (PEI)

McCORRISON,
Lizzie, d. 5/1/1945 at 95/1/3 in Appleton, ME; housewife; widow; b. Milton; Hiram W. Ricker (Dover) and Caroline Meserve (Rochester)

McCRELLIS,
Daniel, d. 4/16/1906 at 70/4; acute alcoholism; farmer; widower; b. Lebanon, ME; John McCrellis and Sally

McCULLAGH,
Bella, d. 3/21/1947 at 87/6/8; widow; b. B. Verte, NB; Edwin Hamilton (Ireland) and Eleanor Goodwin (Canada)

McDANIEL,
Priscilla M., d. 8/19/1997 in Milton; Samuel Brideau and Simone Charland

McDONALD,
Emma V., d. 9/8/1972 at 76 in Rochester; homemaker; b. ME; George Laskey and Martha Lowd
Finley R., d. 4/6/1972 at 82 in Rochester; cabinet maker; b. Canada; John McDonald and Mary Morrison

McGLAUFLIN,
Alice C., d. 2/24/1981 in Farmington, ME
Wallace H., d. 7/1/1974 at 84 in Rochester

McGRATH,
Thomas J., d. 11/8/1951 at 69/6/7; millhand; married; b. Ireland; James McGrath and Mary Fitzgerald

McGREGOR,
Ferne C., d. 6/23/1970 at 76 in Rochester; school teacher; b. NH; Fred McGregor and Roseltha Chesley
Fred, d. 6/19/1947 at 74/5/21; farmer; widower; b. Bangor, ME; Archibald McGregor (Scotland) and Maud McGregor
Roseltha S., d. 3/25/1942 at 75/10/3; housewife; married; b. Lowell, MA; Harrison W. Chesley (Gilford) and Mary E. Loker (Tewksbury, MA)

McHUGH,
Donald R., d. 7/10/1960 at 44 in VT

McINNIS,
Murdock N., d. 11/15/1947 at 48/2/5; electrician; married; b. PEI; Alexander McInnis (PEI) and Anne McLeod (PEI)

McINTIRE,
Barbara E., d. 4/21/1983; Frederick Heald and Adelaide Young
Frank B., d. 12/19/1949 at 81/0/14; mechanic; married; b. Dover; Samuel C. McIntire and Isabel Sanborn
Frank Everett, d. 1/14/1993 in Rochester; Frank B. McIntire and Grace Downing
George C., d. 6/12/1995 in Milton; Frank B. McIntire and Grace Downing
Grace M., d. 7/24/1951 at 76/6/29; housewife; widow; b. Farmington; George T. Downing and Hannah Aikens

Robert E., d. 7/2/1965 at 26 in Durham; truck driver; b. Rochester; Frank E. McIntire and Marie McKeagney

McINTOSH,
Robert A., d. 7/17/1933 at 61/11/22; merchant; divorced; b. Calais, ME; David McIntosh (NB) and Margaret McIntosh (NB)
Robert D., d. 8/31/1905 at 7/8; drowned; b. Milton; Robert A. McIntosh (Calais, ME) and Addie C. Duntley (Milton)

McKEAGNEY,
Patrick, d. 2/21/1956 at 73 in Boston, MA; married

McKENERY,
Ellen, d. 5/19/1915 at 74/6/1; widow; b. Newfoundland; Richard Dinn (Newfoundland) and Elizabeth Kane (Newfoundland)

McKENZIE,
Lizzie, d. 5/22/1900 at 19; fibroid consumption; chambermaid; single; John McKenzie (NS) and Frances Twombly (Gilmanton)

McKERGAN,
Ann, d. 5/23/1964 at 66 in Rochester; seamstress; b. Williamsburg, NJ; Benjamin McKergan and Angeline Graham

McLAUGHLIN,
Albina R., d. 6/21/1989 in Dover; Joseph Corriere and Marie Giganti
William P., d. 4/25/1975 at 62 in Rochester; brakeman (RR); b. MA; William A. McLaughlin and Mary Barry

McLEOD,
John A., d. 10/29/1949 at 89; farmer; widower; b. NB; Alic McLeod and Jane Snow

McNEIL,
George F., Jr., d. 3/23/1975 at 43 in Milton Mills; mechanical; b. MA; George F. McNeil

McPHERSON,
Norman E., d. 12/1/1973 at 64; retailer fruit-veg.; b. MA; Isaac McPherson and Melinda Seymour

MEADER,
Amasa R., d. 9/11/1900 at 56/0/13; aneurysm of aorta; paper maker; married; b. Gardiner, ME; Henry Meader (Gardiner, ME) and Mary Stone (Mt. Vernon, ME)

MEIKLE,
Annie B., d. 3/6/1931 at 40/5/22 in Lowell, MA
Cathrene, d. 10/19/1932 at 85/7/27 in Lowell, MA
Clara E., d. 8/10/1957 at 79 in Rochester; housewife; married; b. Milton Mills; Frank Googins and Margaret Connolly
Emma E., d. 5/22/1956 in Lafayette, IN
George S., d. 3/30/1960 at 72 in IN
John S., d. 2/28/1954 at 82 in Rochester
Louise J., d. 7/31/1965 at 83 in Lafayette, IN
Maria, d. 3/7/1910 at 79/7/3; apoplexy; housekeeper; widow; b. England; John Elsdon (England) and Johanna Egelston (Holden, England)
William, d. 9/6/1911 at 69/4/21; Bright's disease; printer; married; b. Denny, Scotland; James Meikle (Sterling, Scotland) and Jane Blaine (Glasgow, Scotland)
William A., d. 6/16/1955 at 81 in Rochester; shoe worker; married; b. Union; William A. Meikle, Sr. and Catherine Steele

MEISNER,
Despy, d. 3/30/1989 in Methuen, MA

MEISSNER,
Edna M., d. 11/12/1994 in Milton; Edward Walters and Mary Buchwald

MELVILLE,
Charles J., d. 11/30/1996 in Milton; Bruce K. Melville, Sr. and Elsie Chrigstrom

MENEGONI,
Antoinette S., d. 1/6/1970 at 51 in Rochester; factory worker; b. MA; Constantine Konsevich and Mary Westom

Frank J., d. 12/25/1988 in Portland, ME

MERCHANT,
Patricia L., d. 9/27/1997 in Milton Mills; Jesse Junkins and Verna Call

MERRICK,
Gordon F., d. 2/6/1953 at 56/0/13 in Haverhill, MA

MERRIFIELD,
George, d. 5/21/1904 at 80/1/16; senility; widower

MERRILL,
George W., d. 3/7/1907 at 84/4/17; exhaustion; widower; b. Acton, ME; Nathan Merrill (Acton, ME) and Sally Brackett (Acton, ME)
Sarah J., d. 11/22/1903 at 63/2/16; la grippe; housekeeper; married; b. NY; Samuel Smyth (Ireland) and ----- Cotton

MERROW,
Elisha, d. 5/8/1893 at 80; heart disease; farmer; married; b. Lebanon, ME
Ida S., d. 1/19/1957 at 97/9/25 in Acton, ME; housewife; widow
Mary, d. 9/10/1901 at 83; dysentery; widow
Mary A., d. 1/2/1905 at 89/3/19; malignant la grippe; housewife; widow; b. Gilford; Jerry H. Rowe (Gilford) and Sarah Jenness (Meredith)
Noah, d. 10/7/1897 at 80/4/22; typhoid dysentery; farmer; b. Milton; James Merrow and Sarah Rogers (Rochester)
Sumner, d. 4/20/1933 at 86/4/16; farmer; single; b. Milton; Noah Merrow (Milton) and Mary A. Rowe (Gilford)

MESERVE,
Fred, d. 2/13/1907 at 36/4/27; meningitis; shoemaker; married; b. Newington; John C. Meserve (Dover) and Sarah Vennia (Madbury)
Irving, d. 5/26/1992 in Portland, ME

MESSER,
Milton R., d. 2/27/1923 at 0/7/18; b. Milton; William Messer (Troy, NY) and Blanche Weatherwax (Glenville, NY)

MEYER,
Agda H., d. 9/5/1964 at 75 in Wolfeboro; housewife; b. Sweden; Hugo Fredholm and Clara Fry
Agnes B., d. 3/1/1990 in Sanford, ME
Brenda J., d. 1/1/1951 at 0/3/5; b. Sanford, ME; George W. Meyer and Elsie Waycott
Carl H., d. 7/5/1984 in Manchester; Frederick A. Meyer and Agda Freedholm
Carl H., Jr., d. 2/12/1994 in Acton, ME
Ernest W., d. 4/23/1953 at 39/5/6 in Berwick, ME
Fred A., Sr., d. 2/2/1966 at 80 in Milton Mills; carpenter; b. Walpole, MA; Fredrick Meyer and Eva Weitz
Frederick A., Jr., d. 11/12/1995 in Milton Mills; Frederick A. Meyer, Sr. and Agda Fredholm
George W., d. 10/30/1996 in Sanford, ME
Irma J., d. 6/18/1993 in Rochester
Robert E., d. 2/14/1995 in Rochester
Warren F., d. 6/27/1963 at 51; groc. store; b. Needham, MA; Frederick A. Meyer and Adna Friedholm

MICHAUD,
Michael A., d. 12/28/1980; Donald Thurston and Betty Cardinal

MICKELONIS,
Agnes, d. 1/8/1971 at 48 in Rochester; housewife; b. ME; William Smith and Iona Knights
Peter M., d. 5/8/1976 at 67 in Rochester; construction wkr.; b. MA; Felix Mickelonis and Antoinette -----

MILES,
Violetta M., d. 5/7/1952 at 67 in Farmington

MILLER,
Blanche E., d. 4/12/1986 in East Wakefield
Clara B., d. 6/19/1946 at 75/4/15; housewife; widow; b. Fairfield, ME; Nahum Tozier (Fairfield, ME) and Julia Holt (Fairfield, ME)
David C., d. 4/20/1930 at 59/4/11; farmer; married; b. Clinton, MA; William Miller (Glasgow, Scotland) and Janet Cameron (Pasley, Scotland)

Fanny W., d. 1/30/1897 at 71/1/23; la grippe; housekeeper; b. Acton, ME; Asa Merrill (Shapleigh, ME) and Fanny Wood (Shapleigh, ME)

Ira, d. 12/12/1902 at 75/11/30; typhoid pneumonia; merchant; widower; b. Acton, ME; Caleb Miller (Acton, ME) and Mary (Acton, ME)

James E., d. 10/7/1914 at 0/4/4; inanition; b. Milton; James W. Miller (Dover) and Katherine M. Ham (Dover)

Josephine, d. 8/30/1932 at 74/9/6; housewife; widow; b. Lowell, MA; Edwin Whitesides (England) and Francis Thompson (Scotland)

Katherine M., d. 2/23/1918 at 25/10/17; housewife; married; b. Dover; William Ham (Dover) and Margaret Driscoll (Lewiston, ME)

Kenneth E., d. 2/12/1993 in Acton, ME

Neil M., d. 10/18/1958 at 72; shipyard; married; b. Scotland; Andrew Miller and Christina MacDonald

Sarah M., d. 3/23/1916 at 79/4/5; housewife; widow; Isaac Hodgdon (Lebanon, ME) and Mary Knox (Lebanon, ME)

Walter F., d. 4/5/1916 at 0/1/19; b. Milton; James W. Miller (Dover) and Katherine Ham (Dover)

Wendell H., d. 2/2/1969 at 17; student; b. Dover; Wendell H. Miller and Marguerite Grant

Winfield S., d. 10/17/1931 at 81/7/13; retired; married; b. Acton, ME; Ira Miller (Acton, ME) and Fannie Wood (Acton, ME)

MILLS,
Albert F., d. 2/8/1985 in Rochester; Albert J. Mills and Esther Gertrude

Amanda M., d. 6/17/1918 at 55/6/21; married; b. Milton; Josiah Page (Wakefield) and Hannah E. Marsh (Milton)

Emma, d. 7/15/1919 at 47/6/11; housewife; married; b. NY; Robert T. Thompson (England) and Julia Blake (Cambridge, MA)

Frank A., d. 6/10/1928 at 68/1; widower; b. Milton; William Mills (Milton) and Hannah Somes (Wiscasset, ME)

Nettie O., d. 3/4/1951 at 86 in Dover; housework; divorced; b. Milton; Frank A. Mills and Hannah Soames

Rebecca, d. 2/6/1904 at 85/0/16; insufficiency of heart; housekeeper; widow; b. Needham, MA; Israel Hunting and Rebecca Platt

William F., d. 5/2/1913 at 74/6/22; pyloric carcinoma; farmer; married; b. Milton; John Mills (Milton) and Albra Ham (New Durham)

William F., d. 3/16/1947 at 87/3/16; painter; married; b. Hudson, MA; George P. Mills (Portsmouth) and Rebecca Hunting (Wellesley, MA)

MILNE,
Louis E., d. 9/5/1982 in Manchester; James Milne and Mary Pines

MINNON,
Joseph C., d. 8/18/1987 in Manchester; Joseph Minnon and Emma Pickard

MITCHELL,
daughter, d. 4/27/1900 at 0/0/0; stillborn; George A. Mitchell (Fitchburg, MA) and Gertrude A. Tucker (Trescott, ME)
Allie M., d. 11/18/1935 at 66/11/27; housekeeper; widow; b. Milton; Charles E. Ricker (Milton) and Mary Hodgdon (Lebanon, ME)
Charles N., d. 6/3/1896 at 6/9/8; appendicitis; single; b. So. Boston, MA; James N. Mitchell (Ashby, MA) and Minnie C. French (Boston, MA)
Harriet, d. 3/17/1928 at 91/2/15 in Rochester; widow; b. Otistown, ME; Reuben Sampson and Mary Smith
Joseph F., d. 10/26/1922 at 79/9/27; farmer; married; b. New Durham; Samuel Mitchell (New Durham) and Sally Drew (Brookfield)
Lillian M.J., d. 6/14/1898 at 32/2/8; cerebral congestion; housekeeper; married; b. Milton; George I. Jordan (Oldtown, ME) and Elizabeth A. Downs (Dover)
Sarah L., d. 5/15/1907 at 80/7/8; senility; single; b. New Durham; William P. Mitchell (New Durham) and Lydia Libby (Rochester)

MITELHOFS,
Olga, d. 1/4/1974 at 76; shoe worker; b. Latvia; Janis Landovskis and Anna Grunte

MOLLEUR,
Francis J., d. 9/30/1980 in Rochester

MONTGOMERY,
Hannah, d. 6/27/1898 at 71/8/18; heart disease; housekeeper; widow; b. Milton; James Applebee (Milton) and Sally Rines (Milton)

MOODY,
child, d. 7/18/1969 at 0/0/0 in Rochester; b. NH

Alice M., d. 10/9/1947 at 37/5/0; housewife; married; b. Lynn, MA; William Phinney (NS) and Georgie O. Reed (NB)

Theodore, d. 6/12/1974 at 54 in Hanover; lab. technician; b. NH; Joseph Moody and Nettie Williams

Virginia, d. 12/25/1937 at 7/0/2; b. Rochester; Alfred Moody (Tamworth) and Alice Phinney (Lynn, MA)

MOOERS,
Fred L., d. 10/8/1993 in Milton; Grover Mooers and Etta Nickerson

James P., d. 10/3/1952 at 0/1/8; b. Rochester; Fred L. Mooers and Arline M. Currier

MOONEY,
Clara, d. 3/4/1959 at 89 in Concord; housewife; widow; b. IL; Abil Griffins and ----- Rosengrantz

Geneva M., d. 9/22/1984; Wesley Perry

MOORE,
Charles W., d. 1/22/1971 at 80 in Middleton

Frank H., d. 11/26/1941 at 77/0/2 in Portsmouth; retired; married; b. Effingham; John Moore (Parsonsfield, ME) and Sarah Leavitt (ME)

George A., d. 10/16/1983; William Moore and Lela Pray

Hattie S., d. 2/13/1944 at 79/4/16 in Portsmouth; at home; widow; George W. Burley and Susan Moulton

Myrtle E., d. 10/14/1960 at 73 in MA

Sarah E., d. 8/1/1917 at 70/0/27; widow; b. Dover; Henry Downs (Canada) and Elizabeth Drew (Dover)

William E., d. 2/13/1916 at 82/8/6; farmer; married; b. Lowell, MA

MORGAN,
Eleanor H., d. 8/21/1976 at 82 in Ossipee

Florence J., d. 6/3/1999 in Rochester; Edward Brown and Margaret MacDonald

Harry D., Jr., d. 11/8/1982 in Rochester

Jeffrey E., d. 11/22/1973 at 18 in West Lebanon, ME

MORIN,
Arthur, d. 5/19/1893 at 2/4; pneumonia; b. Lawrence, MA; Antoine Morin (Canada) and Belzimer DeMars (Canada)

Henry L., d. 1/10/1980; Peter Morin and Ida Maxwell
Lewis J., d. 8/11/1990 in Wolfeboro; Henry Morin and Beatrice Kenney

MORRILL,
Betty F., d. 9/22/1996 in Sanford, ME
Charlotte E., d. 6/21/1966 at 83 in Rochester; housewife; b. Fairfield, ME; Edward P. Eastman and Eliza N. Sawyer
Ethel L., d. 2/28/1926 at 57/5/26 in Dover; housewife; married; b. New Durham; Charles H. Rines (New Durham) and Sarah Boston (New Durham)
George W., d. 1/31/1939 at 75/7/18 in Union; carpenter; married; b. Moultonboro; William H. Morrill (Moultonboro) and Susan E. Brown (Tuftonboro)
Phyllis L., d. 2/19/1982 in Wolfeboro; Fred Grant and Abbie Hammond
Stewart A., d. 4/29/1965 at 3 in Rochester; b. Rochester; Fred R. Morrill and Eva Meyer

MORRISON,
Frances May, b. 5/7/1989 in Port Charlotte, FL
Harry A., d. 10/6/1986 in Port Charlotte, FL
Harry B., d. 6/29/1950 at 77; laborer; married; b. Eastport, ME; Eben Morrison and Josephine Catherine
Vernie, d. 10/12/1973 at 84 in Townsend, MA

MORSE,
Clare M., d. 3/--/1983
Harold E., d. 4/1/1980 in Rochester; Frank Morse and Rosa -----
Velma A., d. 10/29/1976 at 72 in Wolfeboro; sales clerk; b. Lynn, MA; Harry L. Morse and Maude McIntyre

MORTON,
Annie M., d. 4/15/1926 at 34/8/26; housewife; married; b. Gorham, ME; William Skillings (Gorham, ME) and ----- (NS)
Catherine, d. 1/5/1894 at 78/1/14

MOULTON,
Charles, d. 10/25/1921 at 77/11/23; saw mill bus.; widower; b. Newfield, ME; Samuel Moulton (Newfield, ME) and Elizabeth Gilpatrick (Limerick, ME)

MOUNTAIN,
Ethel L., d. 1/26/1954 at 68 in Beverly, MA; housewife; married; b. Lowell, MA; George Lovejoy

MUCCI,
son, d. 6/20/1909 at 0/0/0; hydrencephaloid; b. Milton; Angelo Mucci (Italy) and Julia Lorenzi (Italy)

MUGRIDGE,
Carrie E., d. 8/9/1949 at 74 in Dover; housewife; married; b. Middleton; George E. Pinkham and Laura J. Main

MUIR,
John A., d. 4/19/1910 at 92; old age; ship carpenter; b. Shelburne, NS

MURPHY,
Donna L., d. 10/11/1951 at 3; b. Berlin; Cornelius R. Murphy and Leah B. Cousens
Lynn, d. 10/11/1951 at 2; b. Berlin; Cornelius R. Murphy and Leah B. Cousens

MURRAY,
Abbie M., d. 9/15/1894 at 38/7/2; heart disease; housekeeper; married; b. Brookfield; Daniel M. Lang (Brookfield) and Mary A. Glidden (Ossipee)
Ethel G., d. 12/20/1891 at 9/8/8; heart failure; single; J. W. Murray and Abbie Lang
Nellie F., d. 6/7/1988 in Kissimmee, FL
Ruth D., d. 9/17/1964 at 39; nurse; b. Beverly, MA; Nathaniel C. Chase and Ruth Bowden
Thomas, d. 3/15/1891 at 68/4/1; diabetes; laborer; married; b. Ireland

MURRY,
Daniel, d. 8/10/1917 at 59/5/18; merchant; married; b. Acton, ME; Thomas Murry (Ireland) and Sarah Ernshaw (England)

MYERS,
Bernard T., d. 12/16/1934 at 24/4/4 in Milton Mills; laborer; married; b. Worcester, MA; John T. Myers (Boylston, MA) and Nellie E. Curry (Stratham)
Nellie E., d. 12/8/1939 at 59/11/8; housekeeper; widow; b. Stratham; John T. Curry (Leicester, MA) and Ada Ricker (Dover)
Russell, d. 10/24/1942 at 34/3/19 in Pembroke; single; John T. Myers and Nellie E. Currie (Stratham)

NASON,
Glenn A., d. 11/4/1983; Ernest R. Nason and Shirley L. Adjutant
Maude E., d. 2/18/1988 in Ossipee
Rodney E., d. 10/19/1996 in Milton; Edward R. Nason and Ida M. Drapeau
Willis L., d. 6/23/1976 at 74 in Wolfeboro

NEAL,
Sarah P., d. 2/8/1894 at 72/2/23; pneumonia; married; Joseph Plummer (Milton) and Sally Brown (Hampton Falls)

NEARY,
Alma R., d. 5/31/1955 at 60 in Rochester; nurse; married; b. Norwood, MA

NELSON,
Patricia, d. 8/30/1937 at 16/9; waitress; single; b. Boston, MA; James V. Nelson (Boston, MA) and Sarah A. Baker (Boston, MA)

NEWELL,
Lucilla, d. 4/1/1940 at 88/2/6; at home; widow; b. NS; James Cunningham (NS) and Debra Smith (NS)
Lucy H., d. 1/14/1916 at 71/9/4; widow; b. Boston, MA; Nathaniel Miller (Portsmouth)
William V., d. 12/19/1914 at 71/5/14; arterio sclerosis; laborer; married; b. Boston, MA; Norman Newell (Skowhegan, ME) and Adline Burrows (Derry)

NIBLOCK,
Clifton H., d. 3/27/1969 at 70 in Wolfeboro; gas sta. operator; b. VT; Robert Niblock and Ethel Stanard

NICKERSON,
son, d. 7/30/1895 at 0/0/0; premature birth; b. Milton; James T. Nickerson and Lillian Mason
Converse E., d. 6/26/1977 at 82 in No. Reading, MA
Edward O., d. 6/5/1949 at 76/9/17; painter; married; b. Providence, RI; John Nickerson
James T., d. 2/9/1917 at 46; laborer; married; b. NS; James Nickerson and Sarah Fitzgerald
Mabel E., d. 12/29/1950 at 79 in Portsmouth; housewife; widow; b. Milton; Daniel K. Lovell and Lydia Hussey
Mary, d. 5/3/1938 at 66/3/0; at home; widow; b. Milton; Albert Mason (Milton) and Mary Jane -----

NODDIN,
Arthur E., d. 5/29/1977 at 64 in Milton Mills; shoe wkr.; b. Canada; John Noddin

NORMAN,
Bessie, d. 10/1/1929 at 38/10/26 in Rochester; housewife; married; b. Milton; Allie J. Laskey (Milton) and Rose A. Barker (New Vineyard, ME)
Thomas, d. 3/9 or 10/1933 at 67; lumbering; widower; b. So. Berwick, ME; John Norman (So. Berwick, ME) and Sarah Farnham (So. Berwick, ME)

NORMANDIN,
Pierre, d. 11/21/1969 at 85 in Dover; boat builder; b. Canada; Francois X. Normandin and Eleanor Quinton

NORRISH,
Virginia L., d. 2/2/1997 in Rochester; Rembrandt Wilson and Mary Barnes

NORTON,
James, d. 8/14/1925 at 58; shoe cutter; single; b. Portsmouth; James Norton (Ireland) and Annie Hanley (Ireland)

NORWOOD,
Mabel L., d. 2/13/1964 at 69 in Milton Mills; housekeeper; b. Providence, RI; Frank D. Norwood and Mabel F. Harden

Mary A., d. 7/24/1976 at 75 in Rochester; office worker (ret.); b. MA; James McQuaid and Susan Riley

NUTE,
Abbie M., d. 7/29/1917 at 64/3/11; housewife; married; b. Canton, MA; George Russell (Stoughton, MA) and Martha Tilden (Canton, MA)

Alonzo E., d. 4/1/1921 at 73; farmer; single; b. Dover; Stephen Nute (Milton) and Eleanor Abbott (Tuftonboro)

Arthur H., d. 9/7/1932 at 65/9/26; farmer; widower; b. Milton; Stephen Nute (Milton) and Mary Abbott (Tuftonboro)

Aubrey B., d. 2/3/1900 at 0/11/14; enteritis; b. Milton; Harry Y. Nute (Milton) and Christie Goodwin (Acton, ME)

Aubrey Y., d. 5/27/1899 at 0/3/7; inanition; b. Milton; Harry Y. Nute (Milton) and C. B. Goodwin (Acton, ME)

Charles E., d. 12/7/1940 at 64/0/5 in Rochester; laborer; married; b. Milton; Charles E. Nute (Farmington) and Emma Pike (Dover)

Clara B., d. 9/6/1921 at 58/0/17; housewife; married; b. Alton; William Chamberlain (Alton) and Sarah Tufts (Brookfield)

Edwin E., d. 10/28/1925 at 60/11/19 in Manchester; superintendent; married; b. Milton; John P. Nute (Milton) and Ann M. Busselll (Stoughton, MA)

Ella M., d. 11/10/1973 at 78 in Rochester; shoe worker; b. NH; Edwin Jenness and Alma Hawkins

Fred S., d. 8/22/1950 at 82 in Union; married

Gardner A. W., d. 6/14/1891 at 35/7/24; consumption; farmer; married; b. Milton; Stephen Nute and Mary E. Abbott

George E., d. 11/17/1933 at 82/3/12; farmer; married; b. Milton; John P. Nute (Milton) and Ana Burrell (Stoughton, MA)

George W., d. 5/1/1947 at 94/9/28 in Appleton, ME; butcher; widower; b. Milton; George F. Nute and Irene Main

Harry G., d. 2/5/1952 at 60; laster; single; b. Alton; Gardner Nute and Clara Chamberlin

Herbert R., d. 6/1/1965 at 35 in Rochester; purchasing agt.; b. Milton; Ray Nute and Doria Ferland
Lewis W., d. 10/20/1888 at 68/9/3; Bright's disease; shoe manu'r; widower; b. Milton; Ezekiel Nute and Dorcas Nute
Lizzie A., d. 1/28/1895 at 29/1/18; consumption; housework; single; b. Milton; Stephen Nute (Milton) and Mary E. Abbott (Moultonboro)
Mary Eleanor, d. 1/8/1897 at 73/4/10; pneumonia; housekeeper; widow; Taylor Abbott (Tuftonboro) and Eleanor Lear (Tuftonboro)
Olive A., d. 9/4/1975 at 79 in Wakefield; housewife; b. NH; George Garland and Mary E. Stillings
Ray H., d. 7/26/1974 at 79; shoe worker; b. NH; Arthur H. Nute and Clara Chamberlain
Stephen, d. 2/14/1894 at 73/7; chronic Bright's disease; farmer; married; b. Milton; Moses Nute (Milton) and Eunice Varney (Milton)

NUTTER,
Ada F., d. 11/20/1954 at 79; shoe worker; widow; b. Wolfeboro; Thomas Whitehouse and Ellen Alexandria
Ada H., d. 1/31/1966 at 90; housewife; b. Athens, ME
Addis S., d. 10/4/1915 at 20/7/15; ice man; married; b. Milton; Hartley A. Nutter (Milton) and Ada Huntress (Athens, ME)
Annie F., d. 4/17/1896 at 0/3/8; pneumonia; b. Milton; Roscoe C. Nutter (Milton) and May E. Johnson (Greenland)
Belle, d. 4/5/1932 at 78/6/19; housekeeper; widow; b. Milton; Alonzo Corson (Milton) and Mary Hanscom (Milton)
Edith G., d. 9/15/1956 at 69/0/19; housewife; widow; b. Milton; Ernest Wentworth and Florence Lucas
Frank J., d. 4/18/1945 at 61/8/2; scaler; married; b. Sanford, ME; Frank J. Nutter (No. Berwick, ME) and Julietta Greenleaf (NB)
Hartley A., d. 12/31/1933 at 59/11/7; laborer; married; b. Milton; Luman S. Nutter (Milton) and Belle Corson (Milton)
Jeanette M., d. 10/31/1992 in Rochester; Walter Wood and Mabel Munson
John M., d. 5/21/1928 at 69/4/22; farmer; married; b. Milton; Jethro Nutter and Lucinda Maine
Luman S., d. 9/16/1907 at 61/5/25; angina pectoris; married; b. Milton; Thomas Nutter (Milton) and Mary E. Pinkham (Milton)
Malcom L., d. 11/29/1910 at 10/10/11; pneumonia; b. Wilmington, MA; Hartley A. Nutter (Milton) and Ada M. Huntress (Athens, ME)

Ruth V., d. 5/16/1913 at 82/11; uterine carcinoma; widow; b. Milton; John H. Varney (Milton) and Betsey Cloutman (Rochester)

O'BRIAN,
Joseph, d. 6/27/1917 at 43/0/10; hotel manager; single; b. Lynn, MA; James O'Brian (Ireland) and Mary Kilcarney (England)

O'CONNOR,
Walter A., d. 9/6/1896 at 0/3/15; enterocolitis; b. Sanford, ME; Michael O'Connor (Salem, MA) and Carrie Schroeder (Boston, MA)

O'DONNELL,
Katherine M., d. 1/29/1961 at 80 in Wolfeboro; b. PEI; Loughlin McDonald and Nancy McCray

O'DRISCOLL,
William F., d. 7/14/1964 at 69 in Manchester; store mgr.; b. Worcester, MA; Peter O'Driscoll and Jane Deveroux

O'LAUGHLIN,
Ronald M., d. 1/26/1904 at 1/11/13; diphtheria; single; b. Milton; James G. O'Laughlin (Stoneham, MA) and Addie F. Knight (Milton)

O'NEAL,
George, d. 7/6/1905 at 37; acute indigestion

OLIVER,
Fred H., d. 2/8/1951 at 74; cashier; married; b. Portland, ME; Charles H. Oliver and Lizzie M. Waitt
Marian E., d. 3/28/1955 at 33 in Rochester; housewife; married; b. Hartford, CT; Arthur E. Dudley and Della Merrill

OLSEN,
John G., Jr., d. 12/14/1986 in Rochester; John G. Olsen, Jr. and Mildred P. Nelson

ORRELL,
Rebecca F., d. 5/17/1973 at 73 in Dover

OTIS,
Bertha E., d. 10/13/1970 at 85 in Rochester; cook; b. Wakefield; Thomas B. Tibbetts and Etta Hamilton

OTTERWAY,
Susan S., d. 4/28/1920 at 88/1/27; housekeeper; widow; b. Milton; James Moulton
William, d. 11/30/1911 at 83/8/21; cerebral hemorrhage; farmer; married; b. England; Richard Otterway (England) and Elizabeth Davis (England)

PAEY,
Clyde W., d. 6/24/1995 in Dover; George W. Paey and Josephine Downs
George W., d. 3/20/1956 at 84; shoe worker; widower; b. Stoneham, MA; George Paey and Lizzie Hurld
Josephine M., d. 7/6/1945 at 67/7/9; housewife; married; b. Milton; Albert Downs (Milton) and Dora Tuttle (Strafford)

PAGE,
son, d. 11/23/1899 at 0/0/1; inanition; b. Milton; Robert Page (Milton) and Ida Sibley (Boston, MA)
Annette A., d. 12/23/1916 at 68/0/15; widow; b. Milton; John Marsh (Acton, ME) and Asenath Runnells (Acton, ME)
Esther N., d. 7/11/1999 in Rochester; Arthur Long and Doris Britton
Frank, d. 11/26/1895 at 0/1/1; b. Milton; Edward F. Page (W. Gardiner, ME) and Vena Ray (Canada)
George W., d. 9/26/1910 at 46/8/25; chronic nephritis; mason; married; b. Dalton; Rondyn E. Paige and Ann E. Melcher
George W., d. 12/18/1910 at 84/3/1; senility; laborer; widower; b. VT
Hannah E., d. 2/5/1925 at 84/2/21 in Milton Mills; at home; widow; b. Milton Mills; John Marsh (Acton, ME) and Asenath Runnells (Acton, ME)
Ida S., d. 12/27/1954 at 80; housewife; widow; b. Boston, MA; Richard Sibley and Emma Buzzell
Irma S., d. 3/7/1967 at 58 in Sanford, ME
John W., d. 12/17/1912 at 70/11/23; pneumonia; farmer; married; b. GA; John W. Page
Josiah E., d. 2/9/1911 at 76/9/9; Bright's disease; farmer; married; b. Wakefield; Joseph Page (Milton) and Lydia Remick (Milton)

Marion B., d. 4/28/1990 in Rochester; Roy Brily and Hattie Webber

Mary A., d. 2/1/1902 at 82/1/19; old age; housework; single; b. Milton; Joseph Page (Wakefield) and Lydia Remick (Milton)

Robert, d. 7/30/1951 at 74/7/17 in Rochester; retired; married; b. Milton; John W. Page and Annette Marsh

Robert W., Sr., d. 8/24/1996 in Milton Mills; Robert Page and Ida Sibley

Ruth E., d. 6/30/1920 at 8/0/19; b. Milton; Robert Page (Milton) and Ida F. Sibley (Boston, MA)

PAGEAU,
Rolland A., d. 6/15/1970 at 51; foreman; b. Canada; Elzeor Pageau and Elzebeth Coyer

PAKKALA,
John M., d. 7/23/1965 at 75; wire worker; b. Alavuus, Finland

PALLARINO,
Pamela P., d. 7/29/1983 in Keene

PALMER,
Elizabeth A., d. 2/14/1919 at 77/10/14; widow; b. Danville, VT; Lewis Loveland (Goffstown) and Laura J. Shaw

Jennie G., d. 2/13/1919 at 55/8/1; housewife; married; b. Rumney; Gilman Avery and Lydia Chase (VT)

John N., d. 2/20/1899 at 72; tabes mesenterica; widower; b. Milton; Aaron Palmer and Annie Cloutman

Maude A., d. 5/29/1976 at 86; shoe worker (ret.); b. MA; John Parker and Martha Farley

PAQUETTE,
Everest A., d. 2/21/1997 in Rochester; Harry Paquette and Evelyn Connley

PARCELL,
Robert D., d. 5/11/1990 in Milton; James J. Parcell and Catherine E. Thompson

PARKER,
Earl S., d. 2/16/1952 at 27 in Rochester; weaver; married; b. Union; Lauren Parker, Sr. and Evelyn Morrill
Herman W., d. 6/12/1946 at 68/2/18; retired; married; b. Lynn, MA; George Parker (Fair Valley, VT) and Martha Davis (Lynn, MA)
Marion M., d. 12/20/1967 at 70 in Dover; bookkeeper; b. East Boston, MA; William Brown and Anna Pierce
Wilbert J., d. 3/10/1919 at 73/0/28; retired; married; b. NS; Danford Parker (NS) and ----- Wright

PARSONS,
Elisabeth Ann, d. 3/14/1993 in Rochester; Frank J. Fuoco and Mary Jean Schlichting

PASCHAL,
Benjamin F., d. 1/30/1930 at 61/10/22; sea captain; married; b. Antigonish, NS; Michael Paschal (France)
Emma F., d. 3/1/1941 at 60/5/0 in Milton Mills; housewife; widow; b. Stonington, ME; Gilman L. Bray (Stonington, ME) and Florence A. Clark (Malden, MA)

PASJKOWSKA,
Idroiga L., d. 8/12/1925 at 4/5/17; Joseph E. Pasjkowska (Russia) and Mary Kerryskoi (Russia)

PASQUILL,
William A., Sr., d. 6/11/1996 in Milton; William Pasquill and Beatrice Jones

PATCH,
Delia, d. 10/3/1993 in Milton; Phillias Potvin and Emma Duprey
Edwin F., d. 8/11/1908 at 0/5/25; cholera infantum; b. Farmington; John Patch (Newfield, ME) and Gertie Clark (Gilmanton)
George A., d. 7/12/1941 at 65/7/15 in Wolfeboro; millhand; married; b. Limerick, ME; Sarah Copps
John, d. 3/6/1915 at 36/9/14; farmer; married; b. Newfield, ME; Samuel Patch (Parsonsfield, ME) and Mary Kent (Sandwich, ME)

John, d. 4/7/1946 at 45/8/12 in Wakefield; mill worker; single; b. Wakefield; John Patch (Farmington) and Gertrude Clark (Farmington)

Margaret D., d. 1/1/1962 at 83 in Rochester; housewife; b. Amesbury, MA; Christopher Conners

Margaret M., d. 2/11/1958 at 33 in Rochester; housewife; married; b. Milton; Louis Rouleau and Josephine Burbine

PAUL,

Alice, d. 12/10/1911 at 47/0/3; Bright's disease; housewife; married; b. Acton, ME; George W. Lord

Angeline G., d. 3/23/1956 at 50 in Hanover; shoe worker; married; b. Fall River, RI (sic); Malcolm McNeil and Julia Radloff

Frank L., d. 11/16/1900 at 0/1/3; non-closure heart; b. Milton; George H. Paul (Lynn, MA) and Alice Lord (Acton, ME)

George H., d. 5/23/1936 at 71/4/10 in Lebanon, ME; widower; b. Lynn, MA; Henry H. Paul (Lynn, MA) and Sarah -----

George W., d. 7/19/1969 at 73 in Wakefield; laborer; b. NH; George W. Paul, Sr. and Alice Loud

Henry H., d. 4/25/1900 at 1/10/29; la grippe; b. Milton; George H. Paul (Lynn, MA) and Alice Lord (Acton, ME)

Joseph, d. 5/2/1972 at 79 in Rochester; b. MA; Walter A. Paul and Mary Fitzgerald

Julia A., d. 5/11/1904 at 79/0/27; cerebral hemorrhage; housekeeper; widow; b. Somersworth; Samuel C. Mudgett and Nancy Crain

PAWLOSKY,

Shirley V., d. 2/26/1991 in Weymouth, MA

PEABODY,

Ernest W., d. 12/31/1966 at 91; shoe worker; b. Peabody, MA; Charles S. Peabody and Lucy Wellington

Josephine B., d. 5/31/1945 at 73/9/14; housewife; married; b. Gilmanton; Charles W. Gilman (Gilmanton) and Ann Bennett (Northfield, VT)

Ruth E. (Rev.), d. 5/18/1980 in West Milton; Charles E. Perry, Sr. and Ruth W. Perry

PEACOCK,
son, d. 5/21/1902 at 0/0/0; stillborn; Robert M. Peacock (Ontario) and Ada M. Lee (Riverside)
Ada M., d. 11/17/1930 at 71/2/12 in Melrose, MA; housework; widow; b. Riverside, MA; Alfred Lee (Phippsburg, ME) and Nancy Goodwin (Dresden, ME)
Margaret, d. 10/6/1909 at 63/6/25; catarrhal dysentery; dressmaker; single; b. Canada; Robert Peacock (Scotland) and Catherine McQueen (Scotland)

PEARCE,
Wellesley A., d. 11/3/1981 in Wolfeboro; Arthur Pearce and Clara Stamm

PEARSON,
Cora, d. 6/19/1966 at 70; housewife; b. Chocorua; William Williams and Susie Welch
John, d. 5/31/1970 at 82 in Rochester; factory worker; b. MA; John H. Pearson and Carrie L. Davis
Robert W., d. 8/21/1977 at 66 in Milton Mills; banker; b. MA; Hermon Pearson and Grace Eberhardt

PEASLEE,
Clarence E., d. 10/18/1973 at 64 in Wakefield; funeral director; b. NH; Arthur E. Peaslee and Dorothea Guimond

PELHANK,
daughter, d. 11/14/1928 at 4 hrs. in Boston, MA; b. Boston, MA; James H. Pelhank (IL) and Rosalie Finegan (Milton)

PELTIER,
Florence K., d. 2/12/1983

PENNELL,
daughter, d. 2/8/1927 at 0/0/0; b. Milton; Edward Pennell (Tamworth) and Dora Williams (Tamworth)
Alston E., d. 1/31/1997 in MA
Dora L., d. 6/3/1944 at 51/0/21; housewife; widow; b. Tamworth; William Williams (Ossipee) and Susie Welch (Ossipee)

Lura, d. 12/18/1900 at 0/5/4; pulmonary congestion; b. Rochester; Willis Pennell (St. Albans, VT) and Rosie Baladu (Canada)

Reginald E., d. 1/22/1985 in Manchester; Edward Pennell and Dora Williams

PERKINS,

Alice A., d. 6/15/1934 at 72/6/9 in Northport, ME; housewife; widow; b. Liberty, ME; Jacob Cain (Liberty, ME) and Eleanor Northrop (Digby, NS)

Anna G., d. 10/17/1913 at 61/8/12; heart failure; housewife; widow; b. Salem, MA; George A. Goodwin (Salem, MA) and Hannah S. Hazeltine (Marblehead, MA)

Arthur M., d. 4/2/1967 at 78 in Manchester; meat cutter; b. Northwood; George S. Perkins and Mabel G. Perkins

Asa D., d. 9/4/1910 at 57/6/8; drowning; laborer; b. Wolfeboro; Asa C. Perkins (Alton) and Eliza F. Parker (Wolfeboro)

Bridget, d. 2/9/1966 at 90 in Rochester

Charles E., d. 4/4/1949 at 86/7/22 in Wakefield; laborer; widower; b. New Durham; Augustus J. Perkins and Annie Wallace

Chester E., d. 5/15/1934 at 71/8/17 in Northport, ME; merchant; married; b. Belfast, ME; Daniel Perkins (Belfast, ME) and Harriet Stevens (Northport, ME)

Clarence L., d. 10/10/1980 in W. Lebanon, ME

George D., d. 10/10/1913 at 76/3/11; pneumonia; farmer; married; b. New Durham; Stephen Perkins (Middleton) and Susan Willey (Middleton)

Kate, d. 6/7/1916 at 23/1; married; red; b. Kingman, ME; Joseph Andrews and Esther Frasier (NS)

Lester A., d. 8/17/1973 at 78 in Rochester; woodsman; b. NH; Charles E. Perkins and Mary Jane Piper

Lizzie L., d. 3/13/1931 at 37/10/26 in Acton, ME; at home; married; b. Acton, ME; Charles Lord (Acton, ME) and Vesta Earl (Acton, ME)

Louise D., d. 2/6/1972 at 46 in Rochester; homemaker; b. NH; William Colbroth and Minnie McLaughlin

Margaret E., d. 5/22/1990 in Wolfeboro

Meredith E., d. 8/25/1996 in Exeter

Mildred, d. 5/20/1981 in Portsmouth

Otis I., d. 2/17/1990 in Rumford, ME

Stanley R., d. 11/9/1981 in Wolfeboro; James Perkins and Margaret Swinerton

Stephen H., d. 12/25/1975 at 71 in Rochester; school teacher; b. MA; James Perkins and Mildred Trask

Violet L., d. 8/31/1925 at 0/2/8; Lester A. Perkins (Wolfeboro) and Elizabeth Lord (Acton, ME)

PERKONS,

Milda, d. 9/25/1992 in Milton; Alexander Buss and Frida Purvit

PERRY,

Annie M., d. 3/8/1968 at 87 in Winthrop, MA; housewife; b. Quebec; William Povey and Katherine Morgan

Charles E., d. 1/25/1947 at 57/1/13 in Kittery, ME; laborer; married; b. Brewster, MA; Francis Perry (Brewster, MA) and Lydia Ellis (Brewster, MA)

Chester M., d. 6/10/1986 in Chelsea, MA

Clara L., d. 2/23/1955 at 79; housewife; widow; b. So. Dennis, MA; Elkanah Howland and Vianna Baker

Eva M., d. 9/18/1982 in Rochester; John Pearson and Cora Williams

Francis W., d. 12/24/1944 at 22/5/21 in Luxembourg; US Army; single; b. Milton; Charles E. Perry (Brewster, MA) and Ruth W. Perry (Marston's Mills, MA)

Ruth W., d. 9/29/1955 at 61; housewife; widow; b. Marston Mills, ME; Willard S. Perry and Clara Howland

Walter M., d. 6/14/1956 at 74 in Rochester; dairyman; married; b. NB; William H. Perry and Grace Ruddock

PETERSON,

Carl L., d. 12/21/1973 at 82 in Wolfeboro; fibre worker; b. NE; Elises Peterson and Charlotte -----

Carrol H., d. 8/21/1984 in Rochester; Oliver Peterson and Ethel Folsom

Ronald F., d. 4/3/1989 in Rochester; Oliver Peterson and Ethel Folsom

Selma S., d. 6/23/1971 at 80 in Dover; housewife; b. NH; Leslie M. Seavey and Lizzie G. Perkins

PHILBRICK,
Adaline M., d. 11/2/1900 at 56/6/10; cancer of intestines; housekeeper; married; b. Madison; James Burke (Madison) and Charlotte Jackson (Madison)
Bertha, d. 11/2/1915 at 24/3/23; teacher; single; b. Milton; Charles S. Philbrick (Freedom) and Jennie H. Applebee (Milton)
C[harles] S., d. 12/2/1933 at 73/6/16 in Milton Mills; farmer; married; b. Freedom; Henry Philbrick (Freedom) and Adeline Burke (Madison)
Daniel, d. 2/1/1923 at 81/6/28; retired; married; b. Freedom; Frederick Philbrick (Freedom) and Clarissa Young (Freedom)
Henry, d. 3/17/1909 at 69/7/10; pneumonia; farmer; married; b. Freedom; Frederick Philbrick (Freedom) and Clarissa Young (Freedom)
Jennie, d. 2/21/1939 at 60/6/16 in Dover; housewife; widow; b. Milton; John Hanson (Wakefield) and Harriette Dearborn (Milton)
Jennie H., d. 3/26/1949 at 84/8/21; housewife; widow; b. Milton; John S. Applebee and Sarah E. Evans
Lucy A., d. 2/23/1919 at 74/0/2; housework; widow; b. Littleton, MA; Benjamin Fletcher and Ann Blaisdell
Ruth, d. 7/7/1902 at 65/3/23; cancer of stomach; housekeeper; married; b. Freedom; William Sanborn (Freedom) and Betsy Taylor (Newfield, ME)

PHILIBERT,
Arthur J., d. 2/23/1919 at 0/1/16; b. Milton; Augustine Philibert (Barnet, VT) and Florence Greenwood

PHILPOTT,
Joseph, d. 1/24/1950 at 40/2/18 in Dover; laborer; married; b. So. Windham, ME; Cyrus Philpot and Alicia Quinkley

PHINNEY,
Carol S., d. 1/11/1985 in Rochester; Walter B. Scribner and Carrie E. Wyman

PIERCE,
Carl H., d. 3/20/1975 at 60 in Milton Mills; maintenance; b. ME; Chester Pierce and Zeta -----
Elvira V., d. 3/30/1909 at 83/3/10; senility; housekeeper; widow; b. Milton; Thomas Leighton (Milton) and Hannah Jones (Milton)

Ernest L., Jr., d. 12/20/1990 in Milton; Ernest L. Pierce, Sr. and Carrie Pendleton

Gladys Eleanor, d. 3/16/1993 in Milton; George Grover and Josephine Sargeant

Lester W., d. 8/8/1942 at 49/2/10; bookkeeper; married; b. Salem, MA; Willard Pierce (Danvers, MA) and Estelle Nutting (Gloucester, MA)

Mary Ellen, d. 2/22/1989 in Lancaster

PIKE,

Arthur L., d. 4/2/1973 at 67 in E. Waterboro, ME

Beatrice L., d. 7/19/1982 in Wolfeboro; Seymour VanBuskirk and Sadie Burke

Cory, d. 4/21/1959 at 8 hrs. in Rochester; b. Rochester; Lloyd Pike and Marilyn L. Williams

David Allen, d. 10/4/1961 at 0/3/29 in Lawrence, MA

Esther L., d. 5/27/1932 at 32/8/23 in Concord; mill operative; single; b. Wakefield; David Pike (Wakefield) and Mary E. Miller (Lawrence, MA)

Fannie R., d. 10/13/1942 at 83/7/17; housewife; widow; b. Acton, ME; Millett Roberts and Hannah Butler

Freeman D., d. 3/9/1913 at 70/11/13; arterio sclerosis; carpenter; married; b. Brookfield; Dudley Pike (Middleton) and Adeline Chamberlain (Brookfield)

Judith A., d. 7/24/1941 at 0/4/26 in Milton Mills; b. Rochester; Philip D. Pike (Milton) and Beatrice Van Buskirk (Chelsea, MA)

June A., d. 12/5/1940 at 0/5/26; b. Ossipee; James A. Pike (Wells, ME) and Katherine Fletcher (Shapleigh, ME)

Lincoln, d. 12/4/1950 at 89/7/25 in Rochester

Mariana G., d. 4/29/1950 at 32/0/7 in Rochester; waitress; married; b. Warnocker, PA; Joseph Garzo and Elizabeth -----

Philip G., d. 1/16/1960 at 69 in Wakefield; meat cutter; b. Lebanon, ME; Robert S. Pike and Fanny Roberts

Phillip Damon, d. 11/29/1971 at 56 in Rochester; garage owner; b. NH; Phillip Pike and Rosamond Piper

Ralph W., d. 11/11/1938 at 45/3/7 in Milton Mills; salesman; married; b. Milton; Robert S. Pike (Middleton) and Fannie Roberts (Milton Mills)

Raymond E., d. 1/18/1949 at 42 in Danvers, MA; widower

Robert, d. 3/21/1932 at 31/3/13 in Concord; single; b. Milton Mills;
    Robert S. Pike (Middleton) and Fanny Roberts (Milton Mills)
Robert S., d. 12/16/1933 at 74/2/11 in Milton Mills; merchant; married; b.
    Middleton; George C. Pike (NH) and Maria S. Cook (NH)
Roger L., d. 12/13/1978 at 52 in Cambridge, MA
Rosamond E., d. 1/19/1972 at 83 in Sanford, ME
Susan H., d. 4/7/1968 at 70 in Concord; homemaker; b. NH; David Pike
    and Mary E. -----
Weyland P., d. 9/21/1966 at 27 in Milton Mills; auto mech.; b. Rochester;
    Damon Pike and Beatrice VanBuskirk

PILLSBURY,
Edith M., d. 3/13/1964 at 88 in Rochester; housewife; b. Acton, ME; Levi
    H. Brackette and Anna R. Gardner
William E., d. 2/9/1907 at 61/10/6; pneumonia; physician; married; b.
    Shapleigh, ME; John M. Pillsbury

PINFOLD,
Annie E., d. 10/24/1921 at 52/10/16 in Rochester; housekeeper; widow; b.
    Windsor, England; John Lewis (Midgham, England) and Elizabeth
    Jones (England)
Edwin T., d. 9/18/1920 at 27/7/8 in Rochester; electrician; married; b.
    Milton; William Pinfold (England) and Anna Lewis (England)
Sarepta E., d. 12/28/1984 in Westbrook, ME
William, d. 10/28/1920 at 55/6/1 in Acton, ME; laborer; married; b.
    Reading, England; Joseph Pinfold (Reading, England) and Lucy E.
    Lewis (Magliam, England)
William F., d. 4/1/1951 at 56 in Manchester; textile worker; married; b.
    NH; William Pinfold and Annie Lewis

PINKHAM,
Bernard B., d. 3/4/1973 at 65 in Rochester; school custodian; b. NH;
    Thomas Pinkham and Frances Cushman
Carl, d. 7/3/1971 at 84 in Coral Gables, FL; real est. broker; b. Milton;
    James D. Pinkham and Sarah McGonigle
Clara A., d. 2/24/1920 at 70/9/17; housekeeper; single; b. Rochester;
    Wells R. Pinkham and Martha P. Gray
David, d. 11/19/1939 at 52/0/0; divorced; b. Manchester; George Pinkham
    (Farmington) and Minnie ----- (England)

Edith E., d. 7/28/1984 in Dover; Albert Wiggin and Cora Day
Emily C., d. 1/27/1913 at 74/2/2; Bright's disease; widow; b. Sandwich; John C. Corliss and Louisa Hubbard
Harry W., d. 6/8/1917 at 44/10/5; farmer; married; b. Milton; William H.H. Pinkham (Farmington) and Sarah Pinkham (Farmington)
Hazel M., d. 12/12/1984 in Farmington
James, d. 12/15/1937 at 71/4/25; ret. merchant; married; b. Milton; Nathaniel Pinkham (Milton) and Emily Corliss (Sandwich)
John P., d. 2/11/1907 at 69/10/23; valvular dis. of heart; married; b. Milton; James Pinkham (Milton) and Sally Jewett (Milton)
Mary F., d. 7/9/1952 at 69 in Norwood, MA
Nathaniel G., d. 5/29/1906 at 71/8/19; chronic nephritis; newsdealer; married; b. Milton; James Pinkham (Milton) and Sally Jewett (Milton)
Sarah, d. 6/28/1908 at 90/5; la grippe and pneumonia; housework; widow
Sarah A., d. 8/15/1919 at 76/10/7; housewife; widow; b. Farmington; Thomas Pinkham (New Durham) and Adeline Hodsdon (Farmington)
Sarah A., d. 12/11/1942 at 79/5; housekeeper; widow; b. Ireland; ----- McGonigle
Thomas, d. 11/7/1929 at 64/6/12 in Dover; painter; married; b. Cliftondale, MA
Willard H., d. 12/3/1889 at 85/7/16; endocarditis; farmer; widower; b. Lebanon, ME; Willard Pinkham and Bridget Bony
William H.H., d. 7/25/1915 at 74/9/14; farmer; married; b. Farmington; William Pinkham (Farmington) and Sabrina Colbath (Middleton)

PIPER,

Anna L., d. 3/4/1938 at 72/0/3 in Milton Mills; housekeeper; married; b. Milton Mills; Moses H. Remick (Kittery, ME) and Clara Wentworth (Ossipee)
Charles E., d. 5/22/1969 at 79 in Goffstown; ret. fac. worker; b. NH; James A. Piper and Laura Evans
Edith, d. 5/27/1960 at 67; housewife; b. NH; David C. Tire and May B. Miller
Edwin C., d. 7/23/1955 at 44/5/12; laborer; married; b. Milton; Charles E. Piper and Helen Pray
Elinor M., d. 9/20/1891 at 0/8/17; cholera infantum; b. Wakefield; James A. Piper and Laura A. Evans

Elizabeth C., d. 5/29/1903 at 84/4/29; paralysis; housekeeper; widow; b. Newfield, ME; Daniel Davis (Newfield, ME) and ----- Campbell (Newfield, ME)

Frank, d. 6/12/1911 at 58/8/11; pulmonary tuberculosis; mason; single; b. Newfield, ME; Mark F. Piper (Newfield, ME) and Elizabeth C. Davis (Newfield, ME)

Fred L., d. 7/7/1940 at 82/5/7 in Wolfeboro; minister; widower; b. Tuftonboro; Thatcher Piper (Tuftonboro) and Nancy Allen (Tuftonboro)

Helen P., d. 9/26/1965 at 77; housewife; b. Dover; John I. Pray

James A., d. 5/31/1938 at 80/4/23; carpenter; widower; b. Newfield, ME; Mark F. Piper (Newfield, ME) and Elizabeth Davis (Newfield, ME)

June F., d. 1/14/1978 at 60 in Sanford, ME

Laura A., d. 5/17/1946 at 76/7/16; housekeeper; widow; b. Wakefield; John W. Evans (Wakefield) and Melvina Farnham (Reading, MA)

Lewis P., d. 11/15/1972 at 55 in Rochester; electrician; b. NH; Charles E. Piper and Helen Pray

PIPPIN,
Dorothy E., d. 4/26/1989 in Wolfeboro

Florida, d. 10/4/1928 at 33/9/6 in Milton Mills; housewife; widow; b. Ossipee; Joseph Currier (Canada) and Delia Mattress (Ossipee)

Harold F., d. 7/2/1991 in Ossipee

PITKIN,
Lillian, d. 7/17/1954 at 77/0/6 in Dover; housewife; widow; b. Enfield

William E., d. 6/28/1951 at 67; laborer; married; b. West Hartford, VT; William Pitkin and Ella Clement

PLACE,
Addie R., d. 7/25/1930 at 61/2/1; at home; married; b. Lebanon, ME; Nathaniel Kenney (Lebanon, ME) and Elizabeth Wentworth (No. Berwick, ME)

Norman W., d. 9/30/1993 in Milton Mills; Percy Place and Freena Lover

PLOWMAN,
Jeffrey J., d. 2/1/1993 in York, ME

PLUMER,
Agnes H., d. 11/14/1959 at 86 in Rochester; single; b. Milton; George L. Plumer and Ada E. Burroughs

Charles A., d. 10/22/1896 at 37/1/14; cardiac dropsy; farmer; single; b. Milton; Daniel Plumer (Milton) and Sarah E. Clements (Milton)

Charles A., d. 1/1/1930 at 93/1/17; farmer; single; b. Milton; Lewis Plumer (Rochester) and Lydia Chamberlain (Rochester)

Enoch W., d. 6/18/1896 at 81/2/14; cirrhosis of the liver; farmer; widower; b. Milton; Joseph Plumer (Milton) and Sally Brown (Hampton Falls)

Etta A., d. 4/18/1980 in Derry; George L. Plumer and Ada E. Burrough

George L., d. 1/5/1935 at 88/9/25; retired; widower; b. Milton; Lewis Plumer (Milton) and Lydia Chamberlain (Rochester)

Minnie R., d. 7/1/1913 at 35/11/15; epilepsy; single; b. Milton; George L. Plumer (Milton) and Ada E. Burroughs (Milton)

PLUMMER,
Ada E., d. 1/2/1931 at 75/8/4; at home; married; b. Milton; James Burroughs (Lebanon, ME) and Lorania Blaisdell (Parsonsfield, ME)

Bard, d. 6/12/1977 at 66; emp. Town of Milton; b. NH; Bard B. Plummer, Jr. and Ruth F. Plummer

Bard B., d. 10/22/1919 at 73/4/4; farmer; married; b. Milton; Enoch W. Plummer (Milton) and Orinda Ayers (Wakefield)

Bard B., d. 11/20/1970 at 91 in Rochester; farmer; b. NH; Bard Plummer and Eliza Wentworth

Eliza D., d. 3/12/1931 at 79 in Sharon, MA; widow; b. Jamaica Plain, MA; John Wentworth (Ossipee) and Elizabeth Current (Boston, MA)

Elizabeth, d. 7/4/1910 at 1/5/27; acute indigestion; b. Milton; Bard B. Plummer, Jr. (Milton) and Ruth L. Fall (Milton)

Elizabeth J., d. 5/15/1918 at 61/0/2; married; b. Acton, ME; Ralph R. Hussey (Acton, ME) and Martha J. Lyon (Roxbury, MA)

Ephraim, d. 11/9/1923 at 78/5/22; farmer; single; b. Milton; Samuel Plummer (Milton) and Eliza Ricker (Milton)

Francis B., d. 2/4/1950 at 58/9/1 in Newport Beach, CA; single; b. Milton; Moses B. Plummer and Elizabeth J. Hussey

George H., d. 10/5/1915 at 80/6/9; farmer; married; b. Milton; John J. Plummer (Milton) and Betsy Q. Deland (Brookfield)

Hannah, d. 9/2/1912 at 81/8/15; chronic val. heart; widow; b. Sanbornton; John Clark (Sanbornton) and Betsey Taylor (Sanbornton)

Hazen, d. 4/6/1935 at 68/11/9; foreman; married; b. Milton; Daniel Plummer (Milton) and Sarah E. Clements (Milton)

John, d. 6/13/1891 at 12; membranous croup; single; Daniel Plummer and Sarah Clements

Joseph, d. 3/5/1907 at 5/11/25 (?); prog. muscular atrophy; farmer; married; b. Milton; Joseph Plummer (Milton) and Sally Brown (Hampton Falls)

Joseph, d. 8/15/1912 at 72/2/9; old age; farmer; single; b. Milton; Samuel Plummer (Milton) and Eliza Ricker (Milton)

Joseph, Jr., d. 4/11/1907 at 56/6/13; typhoid; farmer; married; b. Milton; Joseph Plummer (Milton) and Adaline F. Baker (Somersworth)

Joseph L., d. 10/7/1957 at 63 in Manchester; mechanic; single; b. Milton; Isaacs B. Plummer and Elizabeth Hussey

Lewis, d. 4/13/1903 at 93/10/7; senility; farmer; widower; b. Milton

Lyman, d. 8/29/1959 at 47; MVD inspector; married; b. Milton; Bard B. Plummer and Ruth L. Fall

Mary P., d. 11/2/1916 at 73/6/10; housekeeper; widow; b. Milton; Ephraim Hayes (Milton) and Rosamond Dame

Moses, d. 9/27/1938 at 90/5/20; farmer; widower; b. Milton; Joseph Plummer (Milton) and Adeline F. Baker (Somersworth)

Nettie E., d. 9/14/1916 at 53/0/19 in Acton, ME; housewife; married; b. Middleton; Smith Pike (Middleton) and Mary Cloutman (Middleton)

Orinda A., d. 4/18/1895 at 77/6/12; abscess of liver; housekeeper; married; b. Wakefield; Joseph Ayers (Greenland) and Ruth Nudd (Greenland)

Ruth L., d. 7/11/1960 at 73; housewife; b. Milton; George G. Fall and Lizzie Lyman

Ruth Whitehouse, d. 10/10/1992 in Rochester; Frank I. Whitehouse and Fannie Fall

Samuel, d. 2/1/1932 at 81/9/20; farmer; single; b. Milton; Samuel Plummer (Milton) and Eliza Ricker (Milton)

Sarah E., d. 2/23/1920 at 83/6/4; housekeeper; widow; b. Milton; Samuel Clements (Berwick, ME) and Sally Staples

Susan E., d. 2/29/1920 at 80/6; housekeeper; widow; b. East Concord; William Pecker (East Concord) and Susan Chandler (Concord)

PRIEST,
Henry C., d. 7/28/1905 at 54/10/18; schlerosis of liver; foreman; married; b. Gardner, MA; Henry H. Priest (Marlborough, MA) and Martha Coolidge (Gardner, MA)

PRINCE,
Armon L., d. 9/3/1901 at 1/0/1; acute entero colitis; b. Milton; George H. Prince (Sparta, WI) and Mary E. Moore (Milton)
Amie, d. 1/25/1905 at 2/2/20; convulsions; b. Milton; George H. Prince (Sparta, WI) and Mary E. Moore (Milton)

PRITCHARD,
Lilian J., d. 2/5/1975 at 59 in Wolfeboro

PROCTOR,
Edwin, d. 3/31/1951 at 87/10/25 in Wakefield; laborer; widower; b. Swampscott, MA; David Proctor and Margaret Pinkham

PROULX,
Louis, d. 5/26/1938 at 24/9/9; chef; single; b. Long Island; Louis Proulx (Taunton, MA) and Sophia Fisher (Albany, NY)

PROVENCAL,
Michael, d. 5/30/1978 at 1 in Portland, ME

PROVENCHER,
Dale, d. 3/2/1957 at 20/9/23 in Rochester; mechanic; single; b. Milton; Edward A. Provencher and Draxa Corson

PRUSSEN,
Dennis T., d. 8/15/1996 in Rochester; Dennis H. Prussen and Marie Orlando

PUGH,
Ralph W., Sr., d. 11/29/1982 in Rochester; Charles A. Pugh and Amelia Rockwood

POSTLETON,
Francina M., d. 7/24/1918 at 69/7/23; housewife; widow; b. John Paul (Acton, ME) and Julia A. Mudgett (Acton,

POULIN,
James C., d. 8/2/1980; Clement Poulin and Louise Maxfield

POWLES,
Harry A., d. 4/11/1984 in Rochester

PRATT,
George H., d. 11/23/1967 at 77 in Wolfeboro
John C., d. 10/13/1988 in Rochester
Ruth W., d. 6/21/1970 at 70 in Hanover; homemaker; b. NH; Wentworth and Clara Place

PREBLE,
Vida E., d. 10/9/1922 at 8/0/25; b. Lebanon, ME; Stephen E. (Portsmouth) and Jessie N. Calkins (Trescott, ME)

PREEPER,
Antoinette, d. 2/10/1912 at 0/4/14; intussusception; b. Milton; Preeper (Boston, MA) and Carrie Hurd (Acton, ME)
Charlotte, d. 10/8/1909 at 30/4/8; tuberculosis; housewife; marr Milton; James F. Dorr (Milton) and Lizzie Maddox (Newf
William C., d. 10/24/1924 at 82/7/23; retired; widower; b. Truro Fred Preeper (NS)

PRESCOTT,
Adelle J., d. 4/30/1936 at 88/1/2 in Rochester; housekeeper; wid Milton Mills; David Jewett (Milton Mills) and Susan Fox (Mills)
Benjamin F., d. 2/7/1959 at 86 in Dover
Hattie E., d. 5/9/1901 at 0/5/8; epilepsy; b. Milton; Charles E. Pre (Milton) and Mary E. Evans (Nottingham)
Leola I., d. 9/2/1931 at 77/1/13; widow; b. Randolph, MA; Willia (Stoughton, MA) and Sally Ellis (Alton)
May E., d. 7/15/1948 at 67/1/4 in Dover

PULSIFER,
George A., d. 9/26/1898 at 33/6/12; debility; invalid; single; b. Durham; Charles H. Pulsifer (Minot, ME) and Harriet E. Pinkham (Durham)
Sarah E., d. 2/17/1914 at 16/024; broncho pneumonia; single; b. No. Yarmouth, ME; Seth H. Pulsifer (Yarmouth, ME) and Grace M. Royal (No. Yarmouth, ME)

PUTNEY,
Cris A., d. 3/3/1967 at 0/3; b. Rochester; Warren Putney and Christine Williams

QUAGAN,
Arthur E., d. 12/8/1973 at 68 in Rochester; machinist; b. MA; James Quagan and Mary Giblin
Edna, d. 9/23/1983 in Waltham, MA

QUARNSTROM,
Herbert C., d. 4/15/1963 at 67 in Wakefield; contractor; b. Somerville, MA; Andrew Quarnstrom and Agnes Johanson

QUIMBY,
Ella M., d. 2/1/1925 at 70/3/11; housekeeper; widow; b. Wakefield; James L. Wentworth (Wakefield) and Ruth Steward (Wakefield)
Forrest G., d. 8/10/1909 at 26/3/10; natural causes; emp. in mill; married; b. Newfield, ME; Joseph W. Quimby (Newfield, ME) and Ella A. Wentworth (Newfield, ME)
Jessica L., d. 7/11/1986 in Boston, MA

QUINLAN,
Annie B., d. 11/9/1923 at 59/9/19; housewife; married; b. Milton; Daniel Plummer (Milton) and Sarah E. Clements (Milton)

QUINT,
Wilhelmina M., d. 2/6/1914 at 57/8/14; apoplexy; housewife; married; b. Wolfville, NS; William Forsythe (Wolfville, NS) and Keziah Bishop (Wolfville, NS)

RABBITT,
Frances R., d. 2/9/1998 in Milton

John L., d. 8/23/1995 in Rochester; William T. Rabbitt and Frances R. Delfino

RAFFERTY,
Thomas F., d. 9/7/1948 at 78/9/14 in Rochester; bldg. supt.; single; b. W. Roxbury, MA; Patrick J. Rafferty (Ireland) and Catherine Spain (Ireland)

RAMSEY,
Adella, d. 11/15/1962 at 37 in Hanover; housewife; b. Nashua; Daniel Jenness and Alice W. Whitcomb
Charles E., d. 9/12/1981 in Rochester; Frank Ramsey and Sophie Smith
Earl E., d. 9/10/1970 at 62 in Rochester; trimmer; b. Berwick, ME; Frank Ramsey and Sophia Smith
Frank E., d. 6/10/1977 at 93 in Rochester; caretaker; b. NH; Charles Ramsey and Jennie Moss
Sophie E., d. 9/27/1957 at 71/7/26; housewife; married; b. Schuyler, NE; Ephraim Smith and Annie Gerber

RAND,
son, d. 5/1/1919 at 0/0/0; b. Milton; Earl K. Rand (Milton) and Hazel A. Hoyt (Rochester)
Alice S., d. 12/13/1956 at 57/5/27; laborer; single; b. Milton; George W. Rand and Ida Moore
Earl K., d. 4/30/1964 at 66; laborer; b. Milton; George W. Rand and Ida Moore
Ernest W., d. 7/27/1924 at 29/11/21; shoeworker; married; b. Milton; George W. Rand (Cambridge, MA) and Ida Moore (Milton)
George W., d. 11/19/1934 at 64/7/29; watchman; married; b. Cambridge, MA; George Rand (Littleton, MA) and Mary S. Willott (Cambridge, MA)
Ida E., d. 6/19/1952 at 80; housewife; widow; b. Milton; William E. Moore and Sarah E. Downs
Leo E., d. 8/2/1979 in Rochester; George W. Rand and Ida Moore
Mabel E., d. 2/26/1996 in Dover; Walter Sanborn and Esther Harden

RANDALL,
son, d. 9/2/1893 at 0/0/1; heart failure; b. Milton; Herman Randall (Great Falls) and Abbie Batchelder (Shapleigh, ME)

Aaron W., d. 10/3/1896 at 57/9; heart failure; farmer; married; b. Berwick, ME; Samuel Randall (Berwick, ME) and Ann Wallingford (Berwick, ME)

Harry E., d. 8/25/1914 at 38/4/10; heart failure; laborer; married; b. Berwick, ME; Milton Randall (Sanford, ME) and Nellie J. Foote (Lewiston, ME)

Herman, d. 4/3/1923 at 54/5/19 in Dover; laborer; married; b. Berwick, ME; Ann J. Randall (Berwick, ME)

Walter E., d. 2/10/1950 at 78/4/1 in Haverhill, MA; farmer; married; b. Berwick, ME; Aaron Randall

RAYNOLDS,

James O., d. 3/9/1900 at 73/3/9; pneumonia; farmer; married; b. Tuftonboro; Paul Raynolds and Sally Randlett (Farmington)

REAGAN,

John, d. 9/5/1908 at 34; struck by locomotive engine; laborer; single; b. Ireland; John Reagan (Ireland) and Catherine Goggin (Ireland)

REED,

Alice B., d. 3/16/1906 at 53/10/18; Bright's disease; married; b. Wakefield; Warren Nutter (Wakefield) and Roxanna Robbins (Milton)

Carrie D., d. 3/13/1929 at 71/1/13; at home; widow; b. Fryeburg, ME; Elbridge Osgood (Fryeburg, ME) and Emily M. Osgood (Fryeburg, ME)

Edwin S., d. 12/15/1953 at 89/4/13 in Wakefield; laborer; widower; b. Newfield, ME; Aunnon Reed and Elizabeth Waldron

Exzena, d. 8/20/1982 in Wolfeboro

Hattie E., d. 5/20/1901 at 57; fractured vertebra; housekeeper; married; b. Boston, MA; Jonas Lakin (New Bedford, MA) and Harriett Cushing (Groton, MA)

Inez M., d. 12/10/1939 at 68/4/8 in Union; housewife; married; b. Wakefield; George W. Dicey (Jackson) and Susan Durrell (Wakefield)

James A., d. 2/11/1971 at 83 in Concord; retired; b. MA

Leonard C., d. 2/14/1918 at 63/3; widower; b. Newfield, ME; Silas H. Reed (Newfield, ME) and Hannah A. York (Newfield, ME)

Mae A., d. 3/11/1985 in Dover

Theodore E., d. 3/5/1981 in Wolfeboro

REGAN,
Dorothy A., d. 11/9/1984 in Dover; Arthur Otis and Bertha -----
George V., d. 8/8/1914 at 6/0/12; diphtheria; b. Milton; Jerome Regan (Ireland) and Mary Mahoney (Ireland)
James Y., d. 11/18/1959 at 53; leatherboard mfr.; married; b. Milton; Jerome Regan and Mary Mahoney
Jeremiah J., d. 6/3/1947 at 74/2/10; retired; married; b. Ireland; James Regan (Ireland) and Mary Sullivan (Ireland)
Mary Ann, d. 3/23/1954 at 80/2/17; housewife; widow; b. Ireland; George Mahoney and Mary Driscoll
Raymond J., d. 5/24/1969 at 53 in Milton Mills; truck dr.; b. NH; Jerome Regan and Mary Mahoney

REGESTER,
Hyatt F., d. 12/16/1993 in Milton; Hyatt Regester and Beatrice Formano

REID,
Florence L., d. 6/23/1993 in Rochester; Ole Linstad and Ethel Clinton
Warren H., d. 7/27/1961 at 70 in Wolfeboro; traffic eng'r NET&T; b. Cambridge, MA; Robert J. Reid and Mary Ford

REMICK,
daughter, d. 10/19/1924 at 0/0/1 hour; b. Milton; Edgar A. Remick (Milton) and Carrie E. Grace (Albany)
Andrew J., d. 2/22/1895 at 59/2/19; carcinoma ratum; farmer; married; b. Tamworth; Nathaniel Remick and Esther Nickerson (Parsonsfield, ME)
Arthur F., d. 6/2/1956 at 73/5/6; laborer; widower; b. Tamworth; Frank T. Remick and Florence E. Durrell
Etta S., d. 4/25/1910 at 53/6/2; cancer of stomach; married; b. Acton, ME; Louisa Horne (Acton, ME)
Harold L., d. 4/12/1921 at 0/0/1; b. Milton; Edgar B. Remick (Milton) and Carrie E. Grace (Albany)
June D., d. 10/4/1999 in Dover
Lydia A., d. 6/17/1906 at 80/0/15; chronic nephritis; widow; b. Milton; Mark Hart (Rochester) and Betsy Downs (Milton)

Samuel, d. 8/24/1910 at 87/4/23; cancer of stomach; farmer; single; b. Milton; John Remick (Milton) and Abra Applebee (Berwick, ME)

Timothy, d. 5/25/1906 at 77/11/27; valvular dis. of heart; painter; widower; b. Acton, ME

Willie, d. 12/22/1909 at 41/4/7; anuria; farmer; married; b. Milton; Moses H. Remick (Milton) and Clara Wentworth (Milton)

RENDELL,
Emily S., d. 9/28/1913 at 69/11/28; angina pectoris; housewife; widow; b. Dover; Isaac Colomy (Durham) and Lydia Smith (Dover)

RENY,
Frank J., d. 6/7/1986; Richard E. Reny and Rose Tellier

REYNOLDS,
Addie G., d. 5/5/1891 at 1/11/25; concussion of brain; b. Milton Mills; Winfield Reynolds and Mary McCarthy

Alice M., d. 8/19/1978 at 91 in Rochester; school teacher; b. ME; Charles Treadwell and Luella Miller

Annie M., d. 7/9/1946 at 85/7/13 in Wakefield; housewife; widow; b. Acton, ME; Henry L. Fox (Acton, ME) and Sarah A. Moulton (Milton)

Paul, d. 4/2/1889 at 90/8/22; old age; farmer; married; b. Farmington; John Reynolds and Mary Horne

Willis L., d. 6/12/1954 at 83/2/18 in Wakefield; elec. engineer; married; b. Acton, ME; Charles A. Reynolds and Nellie Sanborn

RHINE,
Douglas A., d. 10/25/1993 in Sanford, ME

RHINES,
Emma A., d. 10/28/1918 at 63/0/9; housewife; widow; b. Milton; Hosea B. Knox (Milton) and Belinda Q. Leighton (Farmington)

Marjorie M., d. 4/14/1973 at 74 in Rochester; hairdresser; b. NH; William Meikle and Clara Googins

RHODES,
Harry Cecil, d. 10/8/1989 in Portland, ME

Virginia P., d. 2/7/1979 in Rochester; Clifford White and Olive Johnson

RICE,
Nevada F., d. 7/7/1966 at 73; housewife; b. Cambridge, MA; James J. Worden

RICH,
Mary Ann, d. 12/10/1889 at 72/10; consumption; house; widow; b. Lebanon, ME; David Jones and Mary M. Roberts

RICHARDS,
Anna, d. 10/2/1938 at 67/4/28; cook; widow; b. Germany
Edward, d. 9/19/1938 at 76/4/13; fireman; married; b. Needham, MA; John E. Richards (Needham, MA) and Sarah A. Stone (Cambridgeport, MA)
Lena G., d. 3/23/1936 at 60/7/5; at home; single; b. Wakefield; Charles Richards (Wakefield) and Keziah Quimby (Newfield, ME)

RICHARDSON,
Nathan J., d. 8/31/1987 in Gonic

RICKER,
Charles E., d. 2/10/1913 at 79/7/11; chronic cystitis; married; b. Milton; Charles Ricker (Milton) and Mary Lord (Lebanon, ME)
Eliza J., d. 5/17/1894 at 63/1/23; apoplexy; housekeeper; widow; b. Barnstead; John N. Canney (Barnstead) and Betsy Clark (Barnstead)
Jeremiah, d. 12/6/1891 at 78/5/6; fatty degeneration of heart; farmer; married; b. Acton, ME; Nathaniel Ricker and Mehitable Tebbetts
Mary, d. 11/28/1913 at 79/7/21; senility; widow; Abram Dearborn (Wakefield) and Melinda Stillings (No. Berwick, ME)
Mary F., d. 9/24/1938 at 91 in Beverly, MA

RIDLEY,
Eliza Jane, d. 9/24/1901 at 90/5/18; la grippe; housewife; widow; b. Shapleigh, ME; Joseph Norton (York, ME) and Esther Webber (Shapleigh, ME)

RIDLON,
George H., d. 2/8/1962 at 81 in Milton Mills; laborer; b. Fryeburg, ME; Steven H. Ridlon and Lucy Kimball

RILEY,
Rita M., d. 5/24/1998 in Milton
Robert, d. 3/16/1956 at 10/11/27 in Boston, MA

RINES,
Ada M., d. 12/19/1971 at 80 in Wolfeboro; school teacher; b. NH; Mark Rines and Mary Horne
Carrie May, d. 7/18/1891 at 7/11/26; diphtheria; single; b. Milton; James H. Rines and Emma A. Knox
Charles H., d. 4/28/1924 at 64/2/28; shoe salesman; married; b. New Durham; Charles Rines (Alton) and Sarah Boston (Lunenburg, VT)
Ellen, d. 4/13/1906 at 68/11/8; cancer of stomach and breast; housewife; married; b. Lunenburg, VT; Joseph Boston and Ellen Miller (New Durham)
Hattie M., d. 12/2/1941 at 83/1/0 in Milton Mills; housekeeper; single; b. Milton Mills; Nathaniel Rines (Milton Mills) and Olive Remick (Milton)
J. Harris, d. 9/24/1914 at 59/2/16; acute indigestion; policeman; married; b. New Durham; James Rines (New Durham) and Melissa Boston (New Durham)
Joseph G., d. 6/10/1907 at 83/0/2; chronic bronchitis; mason; married; b. Milton; Joseph Rines (Lebanon, ME) and Sally Remick (Wakefield)
Mark, d. 10/11/1943 at 96/0/29; retired; widower; b. Milton; Nathaniel Rines (Milton) and Olive Remick (Milton)
Mary E., d. 10/6/1928 at 79/7/25 in Milton Mills; housewife; married; b. Brookfield; Edmond Howe (Brookfield) and Betsey P. Burley (New Durham)
Mary S., d. 3/12/1928 at 72/3/9 in Milton Mills; at home; widow; b. Milton; Noah Merrow (Milton) and Mary A. Rowe (Gilford)
Nathaniel, d. 12/15/1900 at 84/9/20; softening of brain; blacksmith; married; b. Milton; Joseph Rines (Berwick, ME) and Sally Remick (Kittery, ME)
Olive, d. 8/28/1908 at 86/1/10; heart lesion; housework; widow; b. Milton; Thomas Remick (Milton) and Olive Abbott (Ossipee)
Samuel Fall, d. 12/18/1897 at 79/6/25; pneumonia; blacksmith; married; b. Milton; Joseph Rines (Milton) and Sally Remick (Kittery, ME)
Sarah Jane, d. 8/28/1916 at 79/11/2; housewife; widow; b. Acton, ME; William Sanborn and Sally Crockett

Susan, d. 9/23/1890 at 69/5/10; ententis; housekeeper; married; b. Milton; John Remick (Milton) and Abbie Applebee (Milton)

William T., d. 1/6/1926 at 80/11/9 in Milton Mills; farmer; widower; b. New Durham

RINGER,
Kenneth C., Jr., d. 3/13/1990 in Wolfeboro
Viola B., d. 4/20/1985 in Rochester; William Sprague and Gladys Hillsgrove

ROBBINS,
Hanibal, d. 3/31/1932 at 73/4/8; retired; widower; b. Milton; Horace Robbins (Acton, ME) and Lydia D. Dearborn (Milton)
Helen L., d. 8/13/1902 at 45/9/28; aneurism of heart; housekeeper; married; b. Spencer, NY; William B. Post and Eliza
Horace T., d. 12/16/1906 at 82/8/25; fatty degeneration of heart; widower

ROBERGE,
Roland R., d. 8/7/1994 in Milton; Omer Roberge and Dora T. Toussaint

ROBERTS,
daughter, d. 1/14/1895 at 0/10/4; pneumonia; Lena Roberts
Alice L., d. 8/13/1961 at 86 in Milton Mills; housewife; b. Dover; Jonas Laskey and Sarah H. Vinal
Amos M., d. 8/10/1907 at 72/2/3; exhaustion; grocer; married; b. Milton; James C. Roberts (Milton) and Lydia Scates (Milton)
Bard P., d. 11/–/1890 at 75/5/2; chronic cystitis; traveling agent; married; b. Milton; James Roberts and Mercy Wentworth
Bertha G., d. 6/20/1957 at 80
Caroline C., d. 1/31/1899 at 75/5/3; pneumonia; housekeeper; widow; b. Milton; John Foss (Rochester) and Lydia Wingate (Farmington)
Clara E., d. 8/23/1938 at 94/4/21; at home; widow; b. Milton Mills; James Berry (Milton) and Eliza Jewett (Milton)
Clara M., d. 6/8/1931 at 91/10/26; widow; b. Milton; Robert Mathes (Milton) and Mary Moulton (Milton)
Dora E., d. 12/13/1956 at 84/6/21 in Boston, MA; single
Earl F., d. 2/10/1986 in Sanford, ME

Eunice A., d. 12/20/1895 at 22; progressive parglycis; lady; single; b. Farmington; James Roberts (Farmington) and Ann M. Thompson (Gilford)

Fred B., d. 10/31/1943 at 80/7/6; lumber dealer; married; b. Milton; Ira Roberts (Middleton) and Caroline Foss (Milton)

James L., d. 6/22/1942 at 47/0/21 in Sanford, ME

John H., d. 4/11/1955 at 80/1/2; farmer; married; b. Somersworth; Thomas H. Roberts and Eliza J. Hilton

Luther, d. 2/1/1977 at 70 in Concord; b. NH; John Roberts and Alice Laskey

Luther B., d. 8/5/1933 at 87/10/22; retired; married; b. So. Waterboro, ME; Jeremiah Roberts (Waterboro, ME) and Olive Roberts (Waterboro, ME)

Margaret G., d. 7/7/1999 in Rochester; John Roberts and Alice Laskey

Mary, d. 6/13/1899 at 87/6/11; cerebral coma; widow; b. Plaistow

Mary Jane, d. 5/22/1960 at 83 in Rochester; housewife; b. PEI

Merton L., d. 11/6/1995 in Milton Mills; Delbert Roberts and Cora Moulton

Millard P., d. 5/11/1901 at 4/10; bronchopneumonia; b. Waldo, ME; Wellington Roberts (Frankfort, ME) and Lizzie Smart (Newburgh, ME)

Sadie B., d. 8/5/1940 at 71/7/29 in Dover; housekeeper; single; b. Milton; Ira Roberts (Middleton) and Caroline C. Foss (Milton)

William A.C., d. 2/1/1921 at 87/10; carpenter; widower; b. So. Berwick; John N. Roberts (Rollinsford) and Eliza Sherburne (Rollinsford)

ROBINSON,
Harold, d. 11/28/1978 at 58; b. NH; Leon Robinson and Bessie Moulton

Ronald M., d. 12/2/1978 at 24 in Rochester; debarker operator; b. ME; Joseph M. Robinson and Ethel Hatch

Scott, d. 11/7/1973 at 0/2-1/2 in Rochester; b. NH; Stephen J. Robinson and Rena L. Drew

ROCHELEAU,
Betty R., d. 12/15/1997 in Rochester

ROGERS,
Laurence, d. 9/19/1995 in Manchester; Joseph Rogers and Mary Compos

ROLLINS,
Julia A., d. 1/9/1899 at 77/0/9; cardiac syncope; housekeeper; widow; Benjamin C. York and Martha Weeks

ROODE,
Wilhelmina D., d. 8/13/1972 at 71 in Rochester; homemaker; b. MA; William Bousley and Edah Ladd

ROONEY,
Hilda, d. 7/20/1922 at 12/9/28; b. Ireland; John Rooney (Ireland) and Agnes McCarten (Ireland)

ROSAMOND,
Mildred V., d. 3/11/1964 at 69 in Rochester; housewife; b. Philadelphia, PA; John Dearborn and Alice Bowker

ROSS,
Edith E., d. 3/14/1999 in Milton; Henry Hanson and Cora Hilton
Margaret R., d. 9/11/1927 at 47; housekeeper; married; b. Ireland; James Regan (Ireland) and Mary Sullivan (Ireland)

ROUKEY,
son, d. 2/13/1916 at 0/0/0; b. Milton; George E. Roukey (New Zealand) and Mary M. Labille (Rollinsford)

ROULEAU,
son, d. 4/20/1895 at 25; Albert Rouleau and Delia Beloin
son, d. 9/4/1921 at 0/0/0; b. Milton; Louis H. Rouleau (Lebanon, ME) and Josephine Burbine (Wakefield, MA)
Delia B., d. 1/19/1956 at 81 in Rochester; housewife; widow; b. Canada; James Blouin
Joseph, d. 8/6/1896 at 0/1/26; congestion of brain; b. Milton; Albert Rouleau (Canada) and Delia Blouin (Canada)
Josephine M., d. 4/24/1979 in Rochester
Louis H., d. 4/14/1990 in Rochester; Albert Rouleau and Delia Blouin
Margherita P., d. 11/18/1992 in Wolfeboro; Henry Lavertue and Florence Pearl
Samuel J., d. 9/18/1991 in Rochester; Albert Rouleau and Delia Blouin

ROWE,
Blanche I., d. 2/15/1939 at 51/9/20; housewife; married; b. Charlestown, MA; Charles Laskey (Milton) and Ida Libby (Boston, MA)
David T., d. 9/17/1896 at 60/2/4; fatal syncope; shoemaker; married; b. Somersworth; Ichabod Rowe and Lydia Berry

ROWELL,
Myrtle C., d. 3/8/1959 at 78 in Acton, ME; housewife; widow; b. Brighton, ME; Leander Cooley and May Gilman
Perley A., d. 7/20/1948 at 71/0/26 in Milton Mills; mail carrier; married; b. Solon, ME; Sumner Rowell (Solon, ME) and Caroline Roundy (Bangor, ME)

ROYCE,
Bertha L., d. 4/20/1993 in Rochester; William Smith and Dorothy -----

ROYER,
Randy A., d. 10/1/1996 in Milton Mills; Roland Royer and Germaine Dionne

RUNNELS,
Alice D., d. 1/11/1940 at 65/5/5 in Milton Mills; housewife; married; b. Richford, VT; Loammi Damon (VT) and Acshah Parker (VT)
Eugene E., d. 12/21/1956 at 82/6/22; carpenter; married; b. Acton, ME; Israel Runnels and Mary -----
Flora N., d. 3/4/1960 at 94 in Wakefield; teacher; b. Acton, ME; Israel Runnells and Mary E. Rogers
Othello D., d. 8/1/1981 in Wolfeboro
Pearl E., d. 12/30/1973 at 69 in Rochester; homemaker; b. NH; Frank Wilkinson and Lucy Roles

RUSS,
Alfred F., d. 5/21/1989 in Rochester; Alfred H. Russ and Marion Johnson

RUSSELL,
Arthur P., d. 2/2/1946 at 67/6/25; wood piler; married; b. Danvers, MA; James N. Russell (Danvers, MA) and Augusta M. Tibbetts (Danvers, MA)
Frederick, d. 12/20/1994 in Milton (approx.)

Horace, d. 8/11/1978 at 59 in Rochester; car inspector - RR; b. Canada; Frederick Russell and Jean Prince

Iva M., d. 9/21/1973 at 77 in Rochester; homemaker; b. NH; Edwin Reed and Inez Dicey

James A., d. 10/16/1954 at 48 in Farmington; laborer; married; b. Danvers, MA; Arthur Russell and Mary Kimball

Mary, d. 2/27/1966 at 88 in Rochester

RUSSO,

Louis R., Sr., d. 7/7/1982 in Rochester; Anthony Russo and Nina Paglia

Rose A., d. 10/20/1995 in Rochester

RYAN,

Edward, d. 12/4/1905 at 34/5; apoplexy; paper maker; married; b. Lima, OH; Michael Ryan (Ireland)

Joseph H., d. 3/7/1976 at 70 in Rochester; machinist; b. NY

SABEAN,

Ruby S., d. 8/17/1961 at 77; housewife; b. Portage Lake, MI; Adelbert Sutherland and Eleanor Ross

SANBORN,

Abram, d. 4/13/1902 at 80/7/1; fatty degeneration of heart; harness maker; widower; b. Tamworth; Daniel Sanborn (Tamworth) and Lydia Cushing (Brentwood)

Carlton I., d. 3/29/1988 in Portland, ME

Dorothy, d. 6/15/1975 at 56 in Rochester; housewife; b. MA; Carl Grace and Mildred Varney

Esther E., d. 9/29/1943 at 70/11/9; housewife; married; b. Denmark, ME; Granville Harnden (Denmark, ME) and Matilda Lord (Cumberland, ME)

Frank, d. 7/12/1951 at 74/7/7 in Sanford, ME

Fred W., d. 3/19/1980 in Rochester; Walter Sanborn and Esther Harden

George A., d. 5/30/1926 at 26/3/17 in Milton Mills; laborer; married; b. Acton, ME; George B. Sanborn (Acton, ME) and Estella Lane (Dover)

Hattie A., d. 3/18/1912 at 36/7/11; pneumonia; married; b. New Durham; William Rines (New Durham) and Ellen Boston (Littleton)

Isabel E., d. 8/27/1984 in Dover

Josephine, d. 4/15/1942 at 86/3/25 in Rochester; housewife; widow; b. Sanbornton; William Woodman (Sanbornton) and Mary Fox (Meredith)

Martin W., d. 11/12/1896 at 0/8/27; diphtheria; b. Milton; Walter L. Sanborn (Milton) and Hattie A. Rines (New Durham)

Mary E., d. 1/27/1899 at 77/5; fractured hip; housekeeper; married; b. No. Berwick, ME; ----- Estes

Moses, d. 4/29/1905 at 70/5/1; valvular disease of heart; farmer; single; b. Avon, ME; Moses Sanborn (Vienna, ME) and Sarah Dow (Durham)

Myrtle M., d. 9/23/1992 in Wolfeboro; Fred Nute and Olive Garland

Sally, d. 12/24/1893 at 87/9/18; enteritis; housekeeper; widow; b. Shapleigh, ME; John Crockett (Shapleigh, ME) and Jane Ridley (Shapleigh, ME)

Walter L., d. 11/26/1945 at 72/8/10; retired; widower; b. Milton; William Sanborn (Acton, ME) and Louisa Sanborn (Milton)

William, d. 6/7/1891 at 87/3/24; pneumonia; farmer; married; b. Acton, ME; Joseph Sanborn

William H., d. 6/8/1997 in Milton; Roland Sanborn and Alice Gray

SANFACON,
Doris L., d. 12/15/1993 in Rochester; Harold B. Butler and Laura Perkins
Robert A., Sr., d. 9/2/1980 in Manchester; Walter Sanfacon and Grace Stevens

SANINI,
William A., d. 10/28/1987 in Dover

SANSONE,
Angelo R., d. 7/20/1991 in Milton; Anthony Sansone and Dorothy Deterranto

SARGENT,
Adam, d. 1/1/1945 at 75/9/17 in Plymouth
Aldo L., d. 4/1/1918 at 0/0/6; b. Milton; Adan L. Sargent (Franklin) and Bertha F. Garland (Wolfeboro)

SAVOIE,
son, d. 12/21/1922 at 0/0/0; b. Milton; Fred J. Savoie (Dover) and Ruby Ellis (Milton)

son, d. 12/21/1922 at 0/0/5 mins.; b. Milton; Fred J. Savoie (Dover) and
    Ruby Ellis (Milton)
Elaine M., d. 5/28/1997 in Milton; Frederick J. Savoie and Ruby Ellis
Frederick J., d. 1/22/1946 at 49/1/24 in Kittery, ME; fire fighter; married;
    b. Dover; Joseph Savoie (St. Anne, Canada) and Delia Burns (Gonic)
Jacqueline, d. 8/21/1948 at 2 hrs., 33 mins. in Rochester; b. Rochester;
    Elaine Savoie (Milton)
Marie E., d. 8/22/1948 at 1 hr., 43 mins. in Rochester; b. Rochester;
    Elaine Savoie (Milton)
Ruby E., d. 9/23/1996 in Rochester; George F. Ellis and Gertrude I.
    Duntley

SCATES,
Henry B., d. 10/31/1919 at 88/8/21; retired; married; Benjamin Scates
    (Milton) and Lovey Lyman

SCEGGELL,
Benjamin, d. 5/20/1938 at 72/9/6; lea. bd. mill; married; b. Ossipee;
    Benjamin Sceggell (Ossipee) and Abbie Nichols (Ossipee)
Edna M., d. 9/22/1957 at 72; housewife; widow; b. Conway; Daniel
    Demeritt and Hannah Whitaker
Forrest B., d. 5/16/1982 in Rochester
Howard J., d. 3/20/1963 at 58 in Rochester; navy yard; b. Ossipee;
    Benjamin P. Sceggell
Stephen H., d. 10/31/1979 in Hanover; Stephen Sceggell and LuAnn Pratt

SCOTT,
Ernest E., d. 11/12/1958 at 72 in Wolfeboro; agent RR; married; b.
    Springvale, ME; Edward Scott and Argie Yeaton
Frances W., d. 3/18/1975 at 84 in Rochester; English teacher; b. MA;
    Francis F. Wadleigh and Mary Gilmour
Jean M., d. 7/13/1991 in Milton; Williard Price and Rubie Nelson

SCRIBNER,
Carrie L., d. 1/17/1978 at 79 in Rochester; homemaker; Fred H. Wyman
    and Lizzie Berry

SCRUTON,
Helen A., d. 11/11/1905 at 20/11/18; septic peritonitis; housewife; married; b. Farmington; Charles Cotton (Wolfeboro) and Viola Edgerly (New Durham)

SEAMANS,
Earl H., d. 3/8/1999 in Rochester; Arthur Leach and Jeanette Sawyer

SEMCO,
Mary G., d. 3/28/1997 in Rochester

SERBERG,
Edith S., d. 9/14/1966 at 89 in Swampscott, MA
Victor E., d. 2/11/1966 at 87 in Weymouth, MA

SERVETAS,
Joanne, d. 6/4/1963 at 16; student; b. Dover; Nicholas Servetas and Mildred Downs

SEWARD,
Berryemal, d. 3/23/1918 at 84; widower; b. Canada

SHAPLEIGH,
Sarah, d. 12/26/1893 at 87; erysipelas; widow; b. Milton; Samuel Bragdon

SHAW,
Aratus B., d. 7/21/1909 at 68/4/1; pernicious anemia; farmer; married; b. Newfield, ME; Aratus Shaw (Newfield, ME) and Eliza Howe (Newfield, ME)
Sarah E., d. 10/15/1933 at 90/3/9 in Dover; dressmaker; widow; b. Milton; Samuel F. Rines (Milton) and Susan Remick (Milton)

SHEA,
Carroll M., d. 7/14/1991 in Wolfeboro
Florence D., d. 6/7/1974 at 83 in Wolfeboro
Patrick J., d. 11/23/1944 at 67/6/25 in Wakefield; driller; married; b. Somerville, MA; Daniel Shea (Ireland) and Abbie Lawton (Ireland)
Russell F., d. 2/18/1984 in Manchester

SHEING,
Elizabeth S., d. 10/30/1992 in Rochester

SHELDON,
Alan R., d. 2/2/1969 at 15; student; b. Quincy, MA; Robert T. Sheldon and Barbara D. McIntosh

SHEPARD,
Ina M., d. 7/24/1932 at 44/2/23 in Acton, ME; at home; married; b. Provincetown, MA; James A. Prince (Orleans, MA) and Eliza M. Phillips (England)

SHOREY,
Abby, d. 4/19/1909 at 73/7/8; pneumonia; widow; b. So. Berwick, ME; Webster Miller (So. Berwick, ME) and Louisa Roberts (Salmon Falls)
Gilbert, d. 8/4/1899 at 72/6/12; val. dis. of heart; farmer; married; b. So. Berwick, ME; Simeon Shorey (So. Berwick, ME) and Sabina Earle (So. Berwick, ME)

SHORTRIDGE,
Carrie M., d. 9/15/1895 at 58/2/1; blood poisoning; housewife; married; b. Newport, ME; John Mason

SHURTLEFF,
Eleanor L., d. 9/8/1993 in Milton; William D. Eldridge and Doris G. Caswell

SIBLEY,
Annie M., d. 8/1/1935 at 71/8/28 in Concord; weaver; widow; b. Dover; Simon Ricker (Dover) and Eliza J. Canney (Dover)
Annie S., d. 9/5/1908 at 63/5; heart syncope; housework; widow; b. NS; Robert Preper (NS) and Susan Fletcher (NS)
Harry H., d. 2/4/1933 at 64/1/19; mill op.; married; b. Boston, MA; Mark Sibley (Wakefield) and Antoinette Preeper (NS)
Mark N., d. 10/2/1907 at 66/1/12; pleuro pneumonia; farmer; married; b. Wakefield; Mark N. Sibley (Meredith) and Mehitable Wiggin (Wakefield)

SIEMBAB,
Adele A., d. 4/6/1996 in Wolfeboro; Joseph Dobolek and Mary -----
Michael A., d. 7/31/1997 in Milton Mills; Anthony Siembab and Anges Pubrat

SIEMON,
David B., d. 12/29/1973 at 19 in Milton Mills; student; b. CT; Carl Siemon and Mary Berdl

SILLER,
Arnold F., d. 1/30/1987; Adolf Siller and Frances Fairchild

SIMES,
Albert L., d. 12/16/1948 at 71/9/9 in Milton Mills; shoemaker; widower; b. Milton; George E. Simes (Milton) and Ann Lowe (Newfield, ME)
Andrew F., d. 9/21/1979 in Rochester; Andrew V. Simes and Abbie Tucker
Ann E., d. 2/26/1905 at 66/3/2; apoplexy; housewife; married; b. Newfield, ME; Phineas Lowe (Newfield, ME) and Elizabeth Shaw (Newfield, ME)
Eda, d. 3/12/1899 at 35/2/3; pul. consumption; dressmaker; single; b. Milton; John U. Simes (Milton) and Nancy Jewett (Milton)
Edward S., d. 9/9/1927 at 84/11/9 in Rochester; carpenter; widower; b. Milton Mills; Bray U. Simes (Portsmouth) and Martha Spinney (Kittery, ME)
Elizabeth C., d. 4/4/1922 at 93/4/26; at home; single; b. Wakefield; Bray U. Simes (Portsmouth) and Martha Spinney (Kittery, ME)
Florence, d. 10/22/1910 at 38/9/28; tuberculosis; single; b. Milton; John U. Simes (Milton) and Nancy Jewett (Milton)
Fred H., d. 4/11/1953 at 85; supt. w. mill; widower; b. Milton; Edward S. Simes and Nancy E. Lowd
George E., d. 11/14/1914 at 82/2/14; act. inst'l nephritis; carpenter; widower; b. Milton; Bray U. Simes (Portsmouth) and Martha Spinney (Kittery, ME)
Hervey D., d. 5/5/1901 at 27/1/27; acute tuberculosis; shoemaker; divorced; b. Milton; John U. Simes (Milton) and Nancy R. Jewett (Milton)

John U., d. 9/30/1927 at 91/3/23 in Milwaukee, WI; retired; widower; b. Milton Mills; Bray U. Simes (Portsmouth) and Martha Spinney (Kittery, ME)

Josephine, d. 10/30/1954 at 74 in Rochester; housewife; widow; b. Milton Mills; Elias Miller and Mary Pinkham

Judith E., d. 7/6/1999 in FL

Mary A., d. 12/13/1943 at 73/8/27 in CA

Mary E., d. 12/25/1920 at 75/11/27; married; b. Acton, ME; Sylvester Lowd (Acton, ME) and Dorcas Hanson

Nancy R., d. 4/4/1904 at 65/2/4; la grippe and pneumonia; housekeeper; married; b. Milton; Asa Jewett (Milton) and Mary A. Richards (Wakefield)

Sarah, d. 5/15/1933 at 53/4 in Everett, MA; at home; married; b. Rawdow, NS; John J. Withrow (Rawdow, NS) and Mary Oxley (Stanley, NS)

SIMPSON,
Maude, d. 1/3/1961 at 83 in Concord; practical nurse; b. NS; Robert Simpson and Charlotte Huggins

SINCLAIR,
Neil L., d. 8/23/1920 at 18/2/16; laborer; married; b. Dover; Colan C. Sinclair (Stowe, ME) and Etta Burse (Concord)

SINDORF,
John H., d. 9/17/1998 in Manchester

SINNOTT,
Winfield B., d. 10/7/1918 at 35/0/25; farmer; married; b. Westboro, MA; Winfield B. Sinnott (Saco, ME) and Mary J. Brown (Boston, MA)

SIROIS,
Clifford E., d. 5/3/1985 in West Milton; William A. Sirois and Rose Foxx

SLACK,
George L., d. 8/6/1967 at 83 in Wolfeboro; elec. engineer; b. NS; David Slack and Henrietta Betts

Helen G., d. 4/30/1982 in Rochester; Wallace Greenwood and Jennie Nickerson

SLEEPER,
daughter, d. 11/1/1889 at ½ day; premature birth; b. Milton; May Sleeper

SLOAN,
Frances M., d. 3/13/1994 in Rochester; Archibald W. Hepworth and Jane M. Parker

SLOUENWHITE,
Victorine, d. 12/19/1960 at 81 in Wakefield; actress; b. Leone, France

SMALL,
Helen, d. 5/10/1925 at 41/0/8 in Pembroke; widow; b. Acton, ME; John Lowd (Acton, ME) and Viola Cofran (Newfield, ME)
Lillian C., d. 9/13/1986; Joseph Lunt and Hazel Annis

SMALLEY,
Barbara R., d. 9/2/1996 in Rochester
Mabel C., d. 5/11/1948 at 64/6/6 in So. Berwick, ME

SMART,
Leon Frank, d. 12/6/1994 in Dover

SMITH,
son, d. 4/17/1925 at 0/0/0; b. Milton; LaForrest Smith (Barrington) and Gladys Laskey (Milton)
Alfred J., d. 11/24/1969 at 61 in Wolfeboro
Amanda, d. 12/12/1938 at 63/6/4 in Union; housekeeper; widow; b. Acton, ME; Isaac Hussey (Acton, ME) and Harriett Miller (Acton, ME)
Arthur Melvin, d. 6/19/1993 in Rochester; Arthur Smith and Maude Howe
Carrie L., d. 1/22/1939 at 76/9/15 in Union; housewife; married; b. Cambridge, MA; Levi Perkins (Limerick, ME) and Elizabeth Sands
Chareleine D., d. 12/7/1988 in Wolfeboro
Clarissa M., d. 1/16/1956 at 71/6/21; housework; married; b. Middleton; George Tufts and Emma Whitehouse
Edmund L., d. 8/6/1970 at 62 in Rochester; laborer; b. NH; William L. Smith and Iona Knight

Eleanor J., d. 9/9/1992 in Rochester; Chauncey J. Eldridge and Esther L. Adjutant

George A., d. 10/18/1943 at 85/11/8; retired; married; b. Dover; Amos D. Smith (Providence, RI) and Harriet P. Ross (Dover)

George H., Sr., d. 9/26/1984 in Rochester; William Smith and Iona Knight

Gerald F., d. 5/1/1953 at 0/10/13 in Rochester; b. Rochester; George H. Smith and Janet Williams

Guy A., d. 2/21/1956 at 74 in Concord; shipping clerk; widower; b. Franconia; Warren S. Smith

Guy R., d. 8/30/1991 in Rochester; Guy A. Smith and Clara Tufts

Iona B., d. 10/3/1955 at 67; housewife; married; b. Norton Mills, VT; Weldon Knight and Lydia Holden

Julius L., d. 6/4/1914 at 53/9/26; chron. myocarditis; painter; married; b. Somersworth; Linus E. Smith (Sandwich) and Emeline S. Beal (Sanford, ME)

Leona, d. 12/27/1968 at 84 in Wolfeboro; homemaker; b. NH; Malcolm Hall and Mary -----

Mabel H., d. 10/6/1985 in W. Lebanon, ME

Marshall W., d. 11/16/1976 at 52 in North Rochester; machine operator; b. NH; William A. Smith and Iona Richardson

Mary A., d. 3/27/1956 at 64 in Rochester

Mary E., d. 2/11/1925 at 80/8; housekeeper; widow; b. Milton

Orpheus, d. 6/22/1960 at 80 in Farmington

Shirley, d. 4/12/1945 at 2 wks.; b. Rochester; George Smith (Farmington) and Janet Williams (Milton)

William, d. 8/25/1935 at 34/7/24 in Wakefield; ice dealer; married; b. Acton, ME; Charles I. Smith (Shapleigh, ME) and Amanda Hussey (Acton, ME)

William R., d. 9/8/1973 at 60 in Manchester; boilerman; b. RI; William R. Smith and Elizabeth Plum

SNYDER,

Lucilla E., d. 8/3/1990 in Milton; John H. Stickroth and Lucilla E. Watson

SOMERS,

Edah A., d. 4/13/1943 at 64/0/5; housework; widow; b. Newburyport, MA; Charles W. Ladd (Saco, ME) and Clara Bessey (Augusta, ME)

Patrick, d. 9/19/1917 at --; laborer

SONA,
Charles M., d. 12/4/1977 at 81 in Rochester; tool & dye maker; b. NJ; Frank Sona and Mary Schnitzler
Jeannette E., d. 4/1/1973 at 71 in Rochester; homemaker; b. RI; Stephen Slocum and Sarah Smith

SOUSA,
Joseph F., d. 7/22/1989 in Rochester; Anthony Sousa and Mary Morgan

SOUTER,
Thomas, d. 4/26/1958 at 77 in Rochester; ship fitter; widower; b. Glasgow, Scotland; William Souter and Margaret Souter
Williamina, d. 5/12/1954 at 80/2/14; housewife; married; b. Scotland; William Swanson

SPENCER,
Sophia D., d. 7/5/1951 at 84/1/7 in Sanford, ME

SPIERS,
Millicent, d. 4/14/1931 at 53/4/19 in Rochester; married; b. Union; John C. Penney (New Durham) and Belle E. Stevens (Middleton)

SPINALE,
Francesco N., d. 1/30/1995 in Rochester

SPINNEY,
Cora B., d. 12/5/1906 at 16/6/3; uraemic convulsions; single; b. Eastport, ME; William L. Spinney (St. George, NB) and Helen A. Gray (Eastport, ME)
Eugene, d. 1/19/1936 at 69/9/13; retired; married; b. Rochester; Joseph F. Spinney (Wakefield) and Helen Wentworth (Rochester)
Fanny D., d. 9/20/1958 at 76 in Pasadena, CA; married; b. MA
Harry L., d. 4/2/1973 at 72 in Wolfeboro; metal finisher; Harry L. Spinney and Jessie Bucknam
Helen A., d. 10/31/1897 at 52/8/19; chronic gastritis; housewife; b. Rochester; L. B. Wentworth (Rochester) and Parmelia Hayes (Rochester)

Nathaniel D., d. 4/7/1900 at 65/2/12; paralytic apoplexy; hotel business; married; b. Wakefield; Parker Spinney (Kittery, ME) and Mary Dearborn (Milton)

SPRAGUE,
daughter, d. 6/28/1954 at 4 ½ hrs. in Sanford, ME; b. Sanford, ME
daughter, d. 11/20/1959 at 0/0/0 in Sanford, ME
Annie M., d. 6/15/1948 at 81/5/22; housewife; married; b. Richmond, ME; ----- Purington (Lewiston, ME) and Hannah Purington (Lewiston, ME)
Bernard G., d. 1/3/1959 at 38 in Rochester; laborer; married; b. Waterboro, ME; William H. Sprague and Gladys Hillsgrove
Charles H., d. 6/18/1948 at 78/5/11; farmer; widower; b. Shapleigh, ME; Levi Sprague (Shapleigh, ME) and Liddy Treadwell (Kennebunk, ME)
Constance H., d. 10/29/1998 in Rochester
Fred E., d. 8/1/1974 at 61 in Wolfeboro
Gladys L., d. 8/30/1973 at 78 in Wolfeboro
Irving, d. 5/24/1940 at 0/3/6 in Acton, ME; b. Acton, ME; Bernard Sprague and Virginia Smith
Louis E., d. 1/8/1985 in Rochester
Louis R., d. 3/11/1961 at 25 in Farmington
Richard E., d. 12/1/1990 in MA
Simon S., d. 9/20/1933 at 61/7/20 in Milton Mills; merchant; widower; b. Shapleigh, ME; Hugh Sprague (Shapleigh, ME) and Emyline Treadwell (Shapleigh, ME)
Virginia M., d. 3/17/1961 at 40 in Sanford, ME
William H., d. 11/26/1960 at 65 in Acton, ME

STACKPOLE,
Lucy E., d. 5/4/1910 at 32/8/23; pulmonary tuberculosis; married; b. St. John, NB; Duncan Sinclair (NB) and Lucy Macglinsky (NB)

STANLEY,
Ellen M., d. 5/21/1956 at 74; housewife; married; b. Somersworth; James B. Otis and Emma Burbank

STAPLES,
Amancy J., d. 9/1/1919 at 73/10/18; housewife; widow; b. Boston, MA; George Pike (Middleton) and Lucy Ricker
Harry W., d. 3/14/1951 at 78/9/23 in Rochester; teamster; divorced; b. Milton; Jacob Staples and Amancy Pike
Jacob, d. 5/13/1896 at 91/1/24; progressive paralysis; farmer; widower; b. Randolph, MA; Jacob Staples (Randolph, MA)
Lovina, d. 12/8/1906 at 67/10/18; biliary colia; housekeeper; married; b. Farmington; James Watson
William G., d. 8/13/1959 at 29; lumbering; single; b. Wolfeboro; Christopher Staples and Ada F. Kenison

STAYLOR,
Ruth G., d. 2/26/1999 in Milton; Archie Colburn and Grace Barrington

STETSON,
Gordon, d. 6/1/1920 at 0/2/20 in Boston, MA; b. Milton; Louis O. Stetson (Piermont) and Bessie Drury (Worcester, MA)

STEVENS,
Anna D., d. 2/1/1900 at 97/4/13; old age; housekeeper; widow; b. Middleton; Jonathan Buzzell (Middleton) and Martha Pike (Middleton)
Aurore P., d. 3/21/1957 at 50/10/20 in Rochester; housewife; single
Bertha F., d. 7/14/1978 at 97 in Dover; homemaker; b. NH; Samuel Runnels and Edna Platt
Charles L., d. 3/3/1923 at 65/11/7; retired; married; b. Middleton; Durell Stevens and Hannah Cook (Middleton)
Daniel D., d. 12/8/1895 at 73/0/16; consumption; farmer; married; b. Middleton; Samuel L. Stevens (Middleton) and Anna D. Bussell (Middleton)
Doris A., d. 1/27/1934 at 0/0/2 in Dover
Earl W., d. 2/2/1972 at 63 in Malden, MA
Edna A., d. 8/15/1984; Louis Labrie and Obeline Turmelle
Edward M., d. 12/11/1902 at 0/1/7; pneumonia; b. Milton; William F. Stevens (Kennebunkport, ME) and Addie S. Daniels (Kennebunkport, ME)
Elizabeth L., d. 5/11/1960 at 63; housewife; b. Somerville, MA; Alexander Dadmun and Edith L. Gilford

Elsie R., d. 1/18/1994 in Dover

Frank, d. 12/25/1939 at 67/2/2 in Medford, MA; garage prop.; married; b. Milton; Daniel D. Stevens (Middleton) and Hannah J. Cook (Middleton)

Freeman E., d. 1/10/1925 at 75/6/14 in Lynn, MA; insurance agent; widower; b. Brookfield; Durrell Stevens (Middleton) and Hannah Cook (Middleton)

Hannah J., d. 5/12/1907 at 75/8/4; uraemia; housework; widow; b. Middleton; Lewis Cook (Barton, VT) and Nancy Jones (Middleton)

Hattie, d. 10/12/1961 at 92 in Dover; housework; b. Addison, ME; John Ross and Francis Wass

Henry, d. 5/1/1940 at 66/11/21 in Boston, MA; married

Hiram S., d. 10/6/1942 at 78/9/24 in Middleton; retired; married; b. Freeport, ME; Benjamin Stevens (Middleton) and Statira Wilson (ME)

Howard N., d. 5/30/1964 at 57; millwright; b. Boston, MA; Herman Stevens and Ursula Stevens

Jacob H., d. 8/16/1955 at 73/4/21 in Acton, ME; farmer; married

John I., d. 6/12/1977 at 71 in Rochester; B&M RR foreman; b. NH; Byron Stevens and Louise Webber

Louise E., d. 12/28/1977 at 69 in Rochester; telephone operator; b. MA; Wallace Teel and Louise Wood

Louise M., d. 3/28/1975 at 86 in Rochester; housewife; b. NH; George Webber and Lydia E. Jones

Mabel A., d. 5/28/1985 in Wolfeboro

Mary M., d. 10/23/1959 at 83/2/7 in Cambridge, MA

May S., d. 10/22/1950 at 60 in Middleton; widow

Robert D., d. 6/8/1944 at 38 mins. in Sanford, ME; b. Samford, ME; Chester Stevens (Acton, ME) and Louise Teel (Arlington, MA)

Roland R., d. 11/16/1941 at 49/3/13 in Dover; mechanic; married; b. Wakefield; Hiram S. Stevens (Freeport, ME) and Hattie Ross (Harrington, ME)

Roy A., d. 6/11/1991 in Union

Sadie M., d. 11/8/1942 at 81/4/18; housekeeper; widow; b. Acton, ME; George Merrill (Shapleigh, ME) and Nancy Merrill (Acton, ME)

Samuel, d. 1/2/1988 in Dover

Sarah E., d. 5/23/1894 at 40/2/23; Bright's disease; housewife; married; b. Newfield, ME; George Horne (Newfield, ME) and Elizabeth Reed (Newfield, ME)

Viola I., d. 6/10/1920 at 8/8/24 in Boston, MA; b. Acton, ME; Jacob H. Stevens (Acton, ME) and Viola A. Preeper (Boston, MA)
Viola P., d. 8/18/1961 at 83 in Acton, ME
Walter R., d. 5/10/1958 at 61 in Wakefield; lineman, ret.; married; b. Middleton; Albert M. Stevens and Bernice Tufts

STEVENSON,
Lizzie A., d. 4/2/1952 at 97 in Sanford, ME

STEWAD,
Albert W., d. 5/30/1957 at 80 in Shapleigh, ME

STEWART,
Charlotte T., d. 4/2/1998 in Milton
Glenn W., d. 6/16/1996 in Milton; Lloyd Stewart and Maude Adams
Sadie, d. 7/16/1964 at 78 in Milton Mills; housewife; b. Charlestown, MA; Nivan Burkett and Amanda Laskey

STICKROTH,
Lucilla E., d. 12/26/1985 in Portsmouth; Thomas Watson and Maude Newell

STILES,
Charles, d. 11/12/1909 at 56; natural causes; farmer; single; b. Sanford, ME

STILLINGS,
Charles O., d. 3/7/1947 at 70/8/7; mill worker; married; b. Ossipee; Charles Stillings (Tamworth) and Mary S. Thompson (Ossipee)
Elmer O., d. 12/28/1985 in Rochester; Charles Stillings and Susie Newell
Susie F., d. 6/26/1958 at 82/9/4; housewife; widow; b. Cape Sable Island; Izah Benton and Lucilla Cunningham

STILLWAGON,
Nancy G., d. 11/4/1983; George Hogue and Anna E. Trufant

STONE,
Amey A., d. 3/10/1960 at 68 in MA
Donald Otis, d. 5/7/1993 in Rochester; Wallace Stone and Annie Pike

Edward R., d. 9/29/1961 at 68/9/12 in Orange, MA

Etta Maria, d. 1/4/1913 at 60/0/27; strangulated hernia; widow; b. Gardiner, ME; George W. Fall (Ossipee) and Elizabeth Stafford (Harmony, ME)

Gary D., d. 5/21/1994 in Milton (estimated); Donald O. Stone and Lucille F. Howard

Louise M., d. 5/8/1950 at 84/7/20; housewife; widow; b. MA; James Mellen and Christine Davis

Marguerite D., d. 8/16/1984 in Sanford, ME

STONEBRAKER,

Leslie M., d. 5/14/1952 at 38 in Rochester; housewife; married; b. Boston, MA; Ralph I. Underhill and Marion D. Matthew

Louis V., d. 7/27/1972 at 58 in Newburyport, MA

Marian, d. 4/16/1947 at 0/1/4 in Boston, MA; b. Rochester; Louis Stonebraker (Indianapolis, IN) and Leslie Underhill (Indianapolis, IN)

STOWE,

Amy R., d. 10/8/1964 at 70 in Wolfeboro; housewife; b. Alma, NB

Mary A., d. 6/26/1993 in Milton; Frank Ramsey and Sophia Smith

Merle I., d. 2/10/1925 at 35/0/14; laborer; married; b. Dover, ME; Frank Stowe and Effie Nichols

STOWELL,

Carl D., d. 11/29/1989 in Milton Mills; Irving Stowell and Teresa Dineen

STRANG,

Mary W., d. 7/31/1954 at 74/8/26; housewife; married; b. Troy, NY; Michael Wade and Nora Wade

STUART,

Reginald E., d. 9/23/1975 at 64 in Rochester; store owner; b. NH; Jed Stuart

SULLIVAN,

John T., d. 3/13/1952 at 74/3/4; mill worker; single; b. Salmon Falls; Timothy Sullivan and Mary Sullivan

Nellie, d. 9/4/1897 at 22; acute phthisis; spinner; single; b. Berwick, ME; Timothy Sullivan (Ireland) and Mary Sullivan
William, d. 12/27/1911 at --; hit by locomotive engine; brick mason; b. Ireland

SUSKA,
Joseph J., d. 12/21/1997 in Rochester; Charles Suska and Teoftla Wyszinski

SUSMAN,
Marie H., d. 6/25/1959 at 32; teacher; single; b. Lowell, MA; Arthur H. Susman and Annie V. Lewis

SUSMANN,
Anne L., d. 2/7/1983 in West Milton; Isaac Lewis and Levina J. Hopper
Anne V., d. 11/14/1985; Arthur H. Susmann and Anne Lewis
Arthur H., d. 10/31/1986 in Rochester; Arthur W. Susmann and May Cowan

SWAN,
Frances H., d. 5/10/1997 in Lancaster; Cleve Hemingway and Bertha Abbott

SWANSON,
Hilda, d. 2/18/1931 at 78/10/6 in Houston, TX; married; b. Sweden; Gustof Lundgren (Sweden)
Svante, d. 2/22/1935 at 83/2/4 in Milton Mills; retired; widower; b. Sweden; Olaf Swanson (Sweden) and Maria ----- (Sweden)

SWASEY,
Henry, d. 5/--/1972
Henry C., d. 6/1/1980 in Biddeford, ME
Rena, d. 12/20/1931 at 38/1/7 in Dover; widow

SWEENEY,
Henry L., d. 5/21/1912 at 0/0/24; unknown; b. Milton; Colton H. Sweeney (NY) and Maud Burke (Somersworth)
Henry R., d. 1/25/1954 at 57/10/9; electrician; married; b. East Boston, MA; William Sweeney and Fanny Plummer

Timothy P., d. 3/26/1995 in Rochester; Thomas H. Sweeney and Nancy A. Mcelhinney

SWENSON,
Karl W., d. 5/30/1956 at 80 in Rochester; married; b. Sweden; Hulda Lundgren and Suante Swenson

SWIFT,
Arthur J., d. 1/2/1946 at 78/10/24 in Wakefield; teamster; widower; b. Windham, ME; Harrison Swift and Lucy Ring

Harrison I., d. 1/22/1946 at 52/0/13 in Portland, ME; retired; married; b. Waterford, ME; Arthur J. Swift (Windham, ME) and Maude Russell (Skowhegan, ME)

SWINERTON,
daughter, d. 6/17/1911 at 0/0/1; inanition; b. Milton; Jacob M. Swinerton (Rochester) and Emma A. Melville (New Braintree, MA)

son, d. 6/17/1911 at 0/0/1; inanition; b. Milton; Jacob M. Swinerton (Rochester) and Emma A. Melville (New Braintree, MA)

Bernice, d. 7/15/1989 in Rochester

Emma, d. 7/16/1936 at 68/8/21; housekeeper; widow; b. Braintree, MA; Charles Melville and Rhoda McKinstrey

Esther M., d. 5/16/1956 at 74 in Rochester; housewife; married; b. Farmington; Orrin N. Blaisdell and Ada Jones

Henry M., d. 11/17/1971 at 73 in Rochester; shoeworker; b. NH; Jacob Swinerton and Emma Melville

Herbert B., d. 6/12/1972 at 92 in Rochester; shoe worker; b. NH; Richard G. Swinerton and Agusta Whitehouse

Jacob M., d. 12/31/1923 at 64/8; shoemaker; married; b. Rochester; Richard Swinerton (Newfield, ME)

James, d. 7/31/1928 at 81/10; farmer; widower; b. Somersworth; Andrew Swinerton (Newfield, ME) and Phydelia Stone (Sanford, ME)

Marie, d. 4/18/1924 at 66/8/11; housewife; widow; b. Digby, NS; Nicholas Debeau (France) and Catherine Ganett (Holland)

Oren H., d. 12/18/1916 at 3/8/20; b. Farmington; Herbert B. Swinerton (Somersworth) and Esther M. Blaisdell (Farmington)

Reginald C.V., d. 4/25/1917 at 13/11/30; b. Milton; Jacob M. Swinerton (Rochester) and Emma A. Melville (New Braintree, MA)

Richard, d. 4/29/1914 at 79/0/11; hyp's'te pneumonia; farmer; married; b. Newfield, ME; Andrew Swinerton (Newfield, ME) and Phidelia Stone (Sanford, ME)

Richard G., d. 1/5/1891 at 28/10/8; pulmonary consumption; shoemaker; married; b. Great Falls; R. G. Swinerton and Augusta Whitehouse

William M., d. 6/14/1921 at 83/10/28; engineer; married; Andrew Swinerton (Newfield, ME) and Phidelia Stone (Sanford, ME)

SWOPE,
Warren L., d. 12/10/1991 in Rochester; James B. Swope and Margaret Yeager

TAFT,
Idamae R., d. 1/25/1970 at 80 in Rochester; housewife; b. ME

TALBOT,
Pauline M., d. 11/25/1995 in Middleton

TANNER,
Charles E., d. 6/5/1974 at 80 in Manchester; carpenter; b. NH; Edward Tanner and Mary A. O'Hare

Cordelia D., d. 8/6/1985 in Rochester

George L., d. 2/8/1954 at 64 in Manchester; laborer; married; b. Farmington; Edwin Tanner and Mary O'Hara

Helen R., d. 3/18/1991 in Dover

Herbert E., d. 5/26/1984 in Manchester; Herbert E. Tanner and Marie Devaney

Hervey, d. 12/25/1929 at 66/4/25 in Dover; carpenter; married; b. Farmington; ----- Tanner and Martha Wiggin (Farmington)

Hervey C., Sr., d. 7/4/1982 in Rochester; Hervey E. Tanner and Mary O'Hare

Lloyd C., d. 12/30/1990 in Wolfeboro

Mary A., d. 5/26/1952 at 87; housewife; widow; b. Ireland

Mildred E., d. 10/8/1974 at 87 in Rochester; shoe worker; b. NH; Edward Tanner and Mary A. O'Hare

Oliver, d. 10/23/1918 at 2/9/14; b. Lebanon, ME; Herbert E. Tanner (Farmington) and Marie Devaney (Ireland)

Patrick J., d. 2/7/1921 at 22/6/21 in Pembroke; laborer; single; b. Wakefield; Erving E. Tanner (Farmington) and Mary A. O'Hare (Ireland)

Ruth A., d. 1/30/1945 at 4 mins. in Rochester; b. Rochester; Vincent Tanner (Lebanon, ME) and Ruth Ramsey (Berwick, ME)

Stanley C., d. 11/24/1971 at 79 in Manchester; auto mechanic; b. NH; Edward Tanner and Molly O'Hare

Yvonne M., d. 3/2/1996 in Rochester; Joseph A. Lessard and Lydia Turcotte

TARBELL,
Walter E., d. 1/9/1936 at 77/5/18; machinist; married; b. Lunenburg, MA; Walter Tarbell (Groton, MA) and Martha Adams (Lunenburg, MA)

TASKER,
George W., d. 3/13/1911 at 81/4/15; chronic valv. heart; shoe cutter; married; b. Milton; Nahum Tasker (Strafford) and Mary Wallingford (Milton)

Lydia S., d. 4/3/1890 at 58/8/4; Bright's disease; housekeeper; married; b. Milton; Joshua Jones (Milton) and Sally Cowell (Lebanon, ME)

Theodore L., Jr., d. 2/22/1997 in Rochester

TASSARD,
Tiboril, d. 10/12/1895 at 0/6/6; hydrocephalus; b. Rochester; Benonie Tassard (Canada) and Delvina Dion

TATRO,
Frank A., d. 10/30/1937 at 62/4/6; retired chef; married; b. No. Adams, MA; Francis Tatro (No. Adams, MA)

Mary A., d. 2/15/1947 at 71/10/26; widow; b. So. Berwick, ME; Joseph Ducharme (Canada) and Alice ----- (Canada)

TAYLOR,
Charles B., d. 11/1/1951 at 68 in Middleton
Mary Ann, d. 11/13/1962 at 77 in Meriden, CT

TEMPLETON,
Theodora C., d. 11/10/1975 at 63 in Wakefield; real estate; Thomas P. Libby and Daisey Hensen

THAYER,
Carrie B., d. 11/19/1960 at 85 in MA
Frank, d. 3/2/1946 at 72/6/5 in Boston, MA; groceries; married; b. Turner, ME; Charles Thayer (ME) and Helen M. Lowe (ME)

THEORET,
Joseph, d. 5/21/1894 at 19/8; phthisis; weaver; single; b. Canada; Alfred Theoret (Canada) and Salima Tapier (Canada)

THERRIEN,
Eleanor Durgin, d. 12/7/1994 in Exeter

THIBEDEAU,
Thelma J., d. 8/15/1987 in Rochester

THOITS,
Elsie, d. 2/5/1989 in Palm Beach Gardens, FL
Walter H., d. 6/3/1973 at 71 in West Palm Beach, FL

THOLLEFSEN,
Mary J., d. 7/9/1979; Thomas Kelley and Mary J. Turbitt

THOMAS,
Blanche M., d. 11/27/1984 in Wolfeboro
Elias B., d. 1/28/1936 at 74/9/24; barber; married; b. Gates Mt., NS; Isaac Thomas (NS) and Louise Durling (NS)
Joseph C., d. 10/31/1981; Gordon Thomas and Lorna Griffin
Wanda, d. 12/25/1964 at 3 in Boston, MA
Wilfred L., d. 11/6/1985 in Wolfeboro; Elias Thomas

THOMPSON,
daughter, d. 6/24/1927 at 0/0/0; b. Milton; Mark L. Thompson (Jay, ME) and Mary E. Smith (Brookline, MA)
Allen T., d. 8/10/1987 in Rochester
Almeda P., d. 5/5/1991 in Brookline, MA; Charles Ward and Florence Kershaw
Andrew J., d. 2/7/1908 at 75/5/27; cerebral hemorrhage; married; b. Jay, ME

Charles E., d. 10/13/1918 at 12/1/4; b. Milton; Cornelius Thompson (PEI) and Nellie Sullivan (Ireland)

Cornelius, d. 4/1/1943 at 69/10/20; mill laborer; married; b. PEI; Charles Thompson (PEI) and Mary Quirk (PEI)

Edna E., d. 7/1/1980 in Rochester

Frank G., d. 12/18/1974 at 83 in Rochester

John F., d. 6/7/1980 in Rochester; Cornelius Thompson and Nellie Sullivan

Kathleen J., d. 6/27/1979 in Rochester; Henry Currier, Sr. and Freda Bragg

Mary A., d. 8/26/1989 in Wolfeboro; Arthur McLaughlin and Julia Toomey

Nancy J., d. 1/23/1907 at 81/11/11; senility; widow; b. Kennebunkport, ME; Ivory Wormwood (Kennebunkport, ME) and Nancy (Kennebunkport, ME)

Nellie T., d. 7/12/1963 at 85; housewife; b. County Cork, Ireland; Daniel Sullivan and Mary Sullivan

Otis S., d. 7/1/1911 at 71/10/16; valv. dis. of heart; married; Aratus Thompson (Chesterville, ME) and ----- Ingham (Chesterville, ME)

Thelma A., d. 5/13/1975 at 59; housewife; b. NH; William Warnecke and Francena Nutter

THURLO,

Dorothy C., d. 6/18/1926 at 20/7/12; housewife; married; b. Manchester; Herbert N. Kenney (Farmington) and Grace E. Yeaton (New Durham)

THURLOW,

Ida M., d. 10/3/1974 at 90 in Rochester; homemaker; b. ME; Ernest Carpenter

THURSTON,

Aphia, d. 6/20/1903 at 93/8; old age; housekeeper; widow; b. Alton; Nehemiah Sleeper and Hannah Bean

Caroline A., d. 7/24/1926 at 86/7/7; at home; widow; b. Alton; Isaac Stockbridge (Alton) and Matilda Lucy (Jackson)

Hananiah, d. 10/27/1922 at 86/11/11; farmer; married; b. Gilford; Benjamin Thurston (Gilford) and Aphia Sleeper (Gilford)

THYNG,
Raymond E., d. 4/16/1900 at 0/5/1; capillary bronchitis; b. Milton; John S. Thyng (Shapleigh, ME) and Nellie G. Trafton (Shapleigh, ME)

TIBBETTS,
Abbie, d. 2/4/1921 at 79/8/9; housekeeper; widow; b. South Sanford, ME; James Ellis (Alton) and Roxana Jacobs (So. Sanford, ME)
Catherine B., d. 10/29/1972 at 85 in Dover
Charles, d. 3/22/1938 at 63/9/20 in Rochester; ice cutter; single; b. Rochester; Luke Tibbetts (Rochester) and Susan A. Ellis (Sanford, ME)
Christopher H., d. 6/19/1963 at 75; lumberman; b. Milton; Walter S. Tibbetts and Harriet Downing
Frank M., d. 1/27/1922 at 52/0/21; laborer; single; b. Rochester; Luke Tibbetts (Rochester) and S. Abbie Ellis (Sanford, ME)
Luke, d. 9/17/1893 at 50/5/7; paralysis; farmer; married; b. Rochester; Jonathan Tibbetts and Phoebe Varney
Sarah E., d. 3/4/1913 at 59/2/9; pneumonia; housework; divorced; b. Alton; Robert W. Evans (Alton) and Mary A. Colomy (New Durham)
Walter S., d. 9/30/1923 at 73/1/21; farmer; married; b. Gilmanton; Thomas Tibbetts

TILTON,
Earlon C., d. 12/8/1916 at 22/8/19; laborer; married; b. Lebanon, ME; Clark A. Tilton (W. Concord, VT) and Sadie Jones (East Rochester)
Norman V., d. 8/29/1961 at 55; lumberman; b. Lebanon, ME; Clark Tilton and Sadie Jones

TINGLEY,
James W., d. 7/11/1920 at 68/1/18; clergyman; married; b. Cape Breton

TITCOMB,
Abbie, d. 4/22/1937 at 79/6/17 in Wakefield; at home; widow; b. Wakefield; Daniel Morse (England) and Elizabeth Wiggin (Wakefield)
Charlotte M., d. 7/20/1953 at 56; housewife; married; b. Conway; Benjamin Gile and Annie Prosser
Dorothy R., d. 6/20/1998 in Milton

Helen, d. 2/27/1978 at 87 in Wolfeboro; school teacher; b. NH; Alonzo Remick and Hattie Maleham

TODD,
Angel, d. 3/19/1977 at 4 hrs. in Rochester; James R. Todd, Jr. and Carole A. Loughnane

TOWNSEND,
Eda B., d. 2/2/1932 at 62/0/3 in Haverhill, MA; housewife; widow; b. Acton, ME; Elbridge Lowd (Acton, ME) and Melissa Buck (Acton, ME)
Frank H., d. 1/19/1969 at 70 in Rochester; b. MA; John C. Townsend and Grace Townsend
George R., d. 11/22/1932 at 74/2/3 in Milton Mills; farmer; married; b. Wakefield, MA
Grace M., d. 9/7/1953 at 79 in Rochester; housewife; widow; b. Milton; Henry H. Townsend and Agnes Brierley
Henry A., d. 4/2/1932 at 34/3/1 in New Orleans, LA; manufacturer; married; b. Milton; John E. Townsend (Milton) and Eda B. Lowd (Acton, ME)
Henry H., d. 6/25/1904 at 61/10/13; cancer of liver; woolen mfg.; widower; b. Dorchester, MA; John Townsend (Wl'n, England) and Jane M. (Milton)
Ingeborg V., d. 3/6/1981 in Rochester; Svanta Swenson and Hilda -----
John C., d. 2/14/1916 at 44/4/27; married; b. East Wilton, ME; Joseph Townsend (Wilton, England) and Ruth Wentworth (Acton, ME)
John E., d. 9/8/1914 at 42/11/30; Bright's disease; manufacturer; married; b. Milton; Henry H. Townsend (Dorchester, MA) and Agnes J. Brierley (Lowell, MA)

TOY,
Edward B., d. 11/11/1986 in Nashua

TRAFTON,
Everett, d. 5/7/1940 at 75/10/7; shoe worker; widower; b. Shapleigh, ME; George H. Trafton (Shapleigh, ME) and Mary Stiles (Shapleigh, ME)
Harold A., Sr., d. 5/6/1989 in Portsmouth; Ashton R. Trafton and Bertha M. Lord

Iva M., d. 1/1/1970 at 92 in East Rochester

Reuben, d. 9/25/1938 at 63/6/20 in Rochester; barber; married; b. Wakefield; Charles Trafton (Acton, ME) and Emily Archibald (Acton, ME)

Virginia L., d. 12/3/1990 in Dover; Harold L. Annis, Sr. and Phyliss E. Dean

TRAINOR,

Charles P., d. 2/17/1947 at 58/11/0; laborer; married; b. Brownfield, ME; ----- Trainor (Ireland) and Ruth Hartford (Brownfield, ME)

John H., d. 4/25/1934 at 59/2/10 in Acton, ME; laborer; married; b. Brownfield, ME; Michael Trainor (Brownfield, ME) and Ruth T. Hartford (Brownfield, ME)

Lisa Ann, d. 1/12/1967 at 0/0/4 in Dover; b. Dover; Eugene C. Trafton and Marion E. Maleham

Mabel, d. 6/21/1944 at 73/3/8 in Augusta, ME; housewife; widow

Norman, d. 11/25/1976 in St. Petersburg, FL

William, d. 6/3/1948 at 65/11/9 in Acton, ME; laborer; single; b. Brownfield, ME; Michael Trainor (Ireland) and Ruth Hartford (Brownfield, ME)

TRASK,

Alfred W., d. 1/20/1888 at 57/11; heart disease; farmer; married

TREADWELL,

Charles, d. 12/19/1929 at 69/2/22 in Acton, ME; farmer; widower; b. Buxton, ME; Charles L. Treadwell (Buxton, ME) and ----- Peacock (Keene)

Kate G., d. 2/4/1978 at 77 in Sanford, ME

Ralph, d. 3/3/1937 at 45/9/22 in Sanford, ME; farmer; married; b. Buxton, ME; Charles Treadwell (Buxton, ME) and Luella Miller (Acton, ME)

TREFETHEN,

Thomas A., d. 12/28/1921 at 75/0/1; ret'd foreman; married; b. Dover; Archillus Trefethen (Kittery, ME) and Mary S. Abrams (Near Portland, ME)

TREMBLE,
Lucille M., d. 10/15/1998 in Dover

TRICKEY,
John, d. 3/19/1952 at 63; supt. lith. co.; married; b. Boston, MA; Newell C. Trickey and Mabel Rogers

TRIPP,
Florence, d. 12/1/1931 at 48/9/29; housewife; married; b. Milton; Charles Hayes (Milton) and Nellie Parmenter (Dover)
Lucy A., d. 3/21/1899 at 38/3/11; cholera morbus; housewife; married; b. Milton; Thomas J. Howe (Milton) and Mary A. Plumer (Milton)
M. Geneva, d. 8/18/1950 at 78/0/3 in Rochester; housewife; married; b. Rochester; Nahum L. Berry and Jane Scruton
Nellie F., d. 3/10/1918 at 22/8/17; housewife; married; b. Rochester; Marcellus A. Merrison (Barrington) and Ida C. Hill (Newton, MA)

TRITES,
Katheryn M., d. 2/25/1985 in S. Weymouth, MA

TRYON,
Alice, d. 3/19/1971 at 84 in Boscawen; housewife; b. MA; ----- Lowd and ----- Miller
George E., d. 4/9/1969 at 73 in Gainesville, FL

TUCK,
L. C., d. 9/14/1894 at 48; cancer; laborer; married; James M. Tucker (W. P'd, ME) and Abagail

TUFTS,
Emma F., d. 1/4/1937 at 80/9/19; at home; widow; b. Middleton; Robert Whitehouse (Middleton) and Clarissa Frost (Middleton)
George D., d. 6/16/1970 at 64 in Middleton
Marion E., d. 5/3/1988 in Portsmouth
Robert L., d. 7/12/1992 in Rochester

TURCOTTE,
Ernest P., d. 1/18/1988 in Dover
Eva M., d. 7/3/1988 in Dover

TURNER,
Annie B., d. 5/13/1950 at 85; housewife; widow; b. NS; John Sutherland and Mary McKenzie
Lydia, d. 11/21/1890 at 78/10; heart failure; housekeeper; widow; b. Sanford, ME; Alvam Houston (ME) and Sally Littlefield (ME)
Marilyn L., d. 3/10/1977 at 56; homemaker; b. ME; Lewis Fletcher and Della Cressey

TURSCHMANN,
E. Blanche, d. 3/21/1988 in Ossipee
Emil H., d. 3/16/1976 at 90 in Rochester; boss weaver; b. Germany; Herman Turschmann

TUTTLE,
Andrew S., d. 1/31/1945 at 66/10/29; laborer; single; b. Newmarket; Jasper Tuttle (Newmarket) and Mary Stevens (Gardiner, ME)
Anna H., d. 7/29/1938 at 15/11/30; student; single; b. Dedham, MA; Fred L. Tuttle (Wakefield) and Ruth E. Dickson (Somerville, MA)
Ceceilia E., d. 2/28/1972 at 61 in Wolfeboro; homemaker; b. NH; Oradon Eldridge and Lucy Welch
Frank H., d. 7/8/1940 at 72/10/21; ret. fireman; widower; b. Newmarket; Jasper Tuttle (Newmarket) and Mary E. Stevens (Gardiner, ME)
Frank S., d. 12/18/1980 in Sharon, VT
Fred L., d. 10/3/1958 at 74; mill worker; married; b. Wakefield; Daniel Tuttle and Ora Tibbetts
Irving W., d. 8/6/1893 at 32/8/9; enteritis; bookkeeper; single; b. Milton; Ezra Tuttle
Lois, d. 3/20/1889 at 70/1/2; consumption; house; widow; Joshua Wingate and Polly McNiel
Mary H., d. 1/31/1907 at 85/9/26; senility; widow; b. Charlestown, MA; John Savage and Mary Harris
Robert D., d. 5/4/1926 at 6/8/21 in Rochester; pupil; b. Dedham, MA; Fred L. Tuttle (Wakefield) and Ruth Dickson (Boston, MA)
Ruth E., d. 3/31/1955 at 69 in Rochester; housewife; married; b. Boston, MA; ----- Dickson and ----- McNutt

TWOMBLY,
Allen Sumner, d. 6/27/1992 in MA

Annie, d. 8/7/1927 at 75/3/29; retired; single; b. Milton; Stephen Twombly

Bessie, d. 5/24/1948 at 67/10/12 in Rochester; housewife; widow; b. Milton; George H. Plumer (Milton) and Mary P. Hayes (Milton)

Callie F., d. 5/5/1917 at 72/0/26; single; Paul Twombly (Farmington) and Melinda A. Kimball (Rochester)

Ellen, d. 5/2/1927 at 78/1/7; housekeeper; widow; b. Rochester; Eri Wentworth (Milton) and Jane Shute (Effingham Falls)

James H., d. 10/30/1922 at 76/6/29; farmer; married; b. Milton; Stephen Twombly and Mary J. Goodwin

James L., d. 9/2/1921 at 85/2/5 in Concord; farmer; married; b. Milton; Lewis Twombly (Milton) and Jane Ford (Berwick, ME)

Lizzie A., d. 1/3/1903 at 58/1/15; chronic gastritis; housekeeper; married; b. Rochester; Otis P. Downs (Milton) and Rebecca E. Jenkins (Rochester)

Susan L., d. 10/20/1902 at 61/5; cerebral apoplexy; housekeeper; widow; b. Hamilton; William Turner (Rochdale) and Lydia Houston (Sanford, ME)

Villa M., d. 4/13/1997 in Rochester

UNDERHILL,

Marion D., d. 11/23/1954 at 72 in Danvers, MA; housewife; widow; b. Brooklyn, NY; Robert Matthew and Christina Diller

VACHON,

Alfred J., d. 7/6/1923 at 42/2/14; moving pictures; married; b. Somersworth; Marjorique Vachon (Canada) and Heloise Robert (Canada)

Phoebe M., d. 9/26/1996 in Milton; Joseph LaFlamme and Delina Couture

Richard E., d. 8/22/1996 in Rochester; Emile Vachon and Emma Custeau

VALLEY,

Mildred R., d. 1/26/1994 in Dover; Frank Weeks and Minnie -----

Paul G., d. 4/12/1940 at 43 in Rochester; fibre worker; divorced; b. Wolfeboro; Michel Valley and Amanda Valley

VAN VLIET,

Ethel, d. 6/28/1935 at 40/10/2 in Goffstown; domestic; married; b. Milton; Frank L. Downs (Milton) and Augusta Kimball (Middleton)

VANASSE,
Roger G., d. 3/9/1992 in Milton; Albert Vanasse and Jeanne Perron

VANDERSLICE,
Miriam, d. 8/31/1977 at 84 in Wolfeboro; accountant; b. MA; Charles H. Vanderslice and Nellie Humphrey

VARNEY,
Abbie, d. 5/19/1908 at 70/6/29; myocarditis; housework; widow; b. Middleton

Albion F., d. 10/29/1921 at 67/4/19; farmer; married; b. Alfred, ME; John B. Varney (Lebanon, ME) and Elmira S. Clark (Lyman, ME)

Carole, d. 12/23/1940 at 0/3/26; b. Lebanon, ME; George W. Varney (Lynn, MA) and Evelyn Tufts (Alton)

Charles, d. 7/18/1961 at 76 in Rochester; shoe worker; b. Milton; John F. Varney and Nancy M. Prescott

Charles E., d. 4/28/1932 at 62/8/14; laborer; married; b. Milton; Orin Varney (Milton) and Annie Leighton (Milton)

Charles L., d. 3/2/1901 at 65/6/19; Bright's disease; shoemaker; single; b. Milton; John C. Varney (Milton) and Hannah (Milton)

Doris E., d. 4/7/1926 at 0/11/17 in Wakefield; b. Wakefield; Gerald G. Varney (Wakefield) and Eliza Jenness (Milton)

Eliza J., d. 9/26/1973 at 81 in Rochester; homemaker; b. NH; Edwin Jenness and Alma Hawkins

Elizabeth E., d. 10/3/1909 at 76/8/13; cerebral hemorrhage; widow; b. Lynn, MA; James E. Gowen (Kittery, ME) and Sally N. Lewis (Lynn, MA)

Elvin V., d. 12/23/1942 at 70/0/20; shoeworker; divorced; b. Farmington; Ira C. Varney (Farmington) and Tamson Varney (Farmington)

Eva A., d. 11/26/1934 at 75/11/22; housewife; married; b. Milton; George Blake (Milton) and Mary Leighton (Dexter, ME)

Evelyn B., d. 12/27/1954 at 41 in Rochester; shoe worker; married; b. Alton; Isaac F. Tufts and Lucy E. Goodwin

Gerald G., d. 6/22/1963 at 73 in Wolfeboro

Harry H., d. 4/8/1982 in Dover

Ira, d. 8/29/1888 at 85/7/24; dropsy; farmer; widower; b. Milton; James Varney and Elizabeth Varney

Jennie M., d. 1/2/1966 at 91; housewife; b. Milton; Charles Remick and Susan Smallcorn

John, d. 5/11/1941 at 69/1/8 in Dover; farmer; single; b. Milton; Eli Varney (Milton) and Abbie Ellis (Middleton)

Josiah W., Sr., d. 10/8/1987 in Rochester; Charles Varney and Catherine Hall

Kim A., d. 9/15/1977 at 19 in Rochester; student; b. NH; Kenneth M. Varney and Shirley Pugh

Lillian, d. 8/26/1989 in Boscawen

Mabel, d. 1/30/1911 at 0/1/2; marasmus; b. Milton; Gerald G. Varney (Wakefield) and Eliza Jenness (Milton)

Martha A., d. 10/11/1890 at 59/9/7; dropsy; housekeeper; married; b. Rochester; Thomas Randall (Rochester) and Lucinda Perkins (Dover)

Mary J., d. 8/12/1959 at 79; housewife; married; b. Gomersal, England; Thomas Moore and ----- Briggs

Pauline, d. 3/20/1967 at 70 in Manchester; retired; b. Lynn, MA; Clarence Hardy and Everetta Rich

Sarah A., d. 2/7/1948 at 81/4/2 in Dover; at home; widow; b. Madbury; Benjamin Prescott (Durham) and Rebecca Foss (Madbury)

Sophia J., d. 7/12/1927 at 85/2/18; widow; b. Milton; John C. Nute

William H., d. 9/27/1968 at 85 in Rochester; b. MA; Ambrose Varney and Cora Niles

VENNURD,
John G., d. 11/3/1971 at 76 in Dover

VENO,
Stella A., d. 10/11/1987 in Rochester; William Veno and Mary Laverture

VINNARD,
Dorothy S., d. 1/29/1979 in Rochester; Reuben B. Trafton and Iva M. Ham

VIOLA,
Anthony J., d. 4/26/1984 in Dover

Sheila J., d. 10/23/1981 in Rochester; Raymond H. Barrett, Sr. and Frances Caldwell

WADLEIGH,
Charlotte K.A.C., d. 6/14/1985 in Dover

Joseph E., d. 5/26/1920 at 30/7/29; undertaker; married; b. Lynn, MA; Francis F. Wadleigh (Wakefield) and Mary J. Gilman (NS)

WAITT,
Florence P., d. 8/17/1947 at 34/8/7 in Rochester; housewife; married; b. Revere, MA; Archibald W. Pike (St. John's, Newfoundland) and Hazel Elms (Lynn, MA)

WAKEFIELD,
Roscoe A., d. 8/6/1918 at 73/9/4; widower; b. Belfast, ME; Paul P. Wakefield (Cape Porpoise, ME) and Jane N. Trickey (Saco, ME)

WALBRIDGE,
Charles H., d. 12/29/1982 in Rochester; Charles F. Walbridge and Lucienne Paquet
Marion L., d. 11/2/1996 in Rochester; Joseph Lessard and Delvina Dion

WALEZOK,
Joseph, d. 7/19/1913 at 33; accidental drowning; emp. ice co.; married; b. Poland

WALKER,
Burton M., d. 6/1/1966 at 53 in Acton, ME
Delbert C., d. 5/22/1925 at 42/9/3 in Milton Mills; meat dealer; married; b. Norway, ME; Ephraim C. Walker (Denmark, ME) and Hannah J. Reed (MA)
Lewis, d. 2/18/1998 in Rochester; Joseph Walker and Helen Kittell
Marion I., d. 11/23/1992 in Sanford, ME
Reuben W., d. 2/10/1918 at 72/10/28; blacksmith; married; b. Concord; Joseph Walker (Milton) and Elizabeth Hildreth (Newburyport, MA)

WALL,
James A., d. 6/22/1974 at 27 in Dover

WALLACE,
Abbie A., d. 12/31/1890 at 59/3/20; pneumonia; housekeeper; single; b. Milton; William B. Wallace (Wakefield) and Abbie M. Dearborn (Milton)

Dora, d. 2/27/1932 at 69/7/8 in New Durham; housewife; married; b. Middleton; Joseph L. Perkins (Middleton) and Sarah Perkins (Dover)

Elsie M., d. 12/21/1953 at 69/0/14 in Boston, MA; single; b. Milton; William F. Wallace and Addie Gilman

John W., d. 10/13/1988 in West Milton; Nathan R. Wallace and Charlotte Melville

Lawrence E., d. 7/24/1943 at 20/11/15; US Army; Anice W. Wallace

Regnald, d. 10/3/1891 at 12/2/10; entero colitis; single; b. Dover; Albert S. Wallace and Elvira Whitehouse

Sadie, d. 10/23/1905 at 19/11/11; anorecia nervosa; single; b. Middleton; Charles F. Wallace (Middleton) and Dora Perkins (Middleton)

Sarah F., d. 1/2/1939 at 82/7/0; housewife; widow; b. Milton; James Downs (Milton) and Abigail Ware (Leominster, MA)

WALLINGFORD,

Amos D., d. 3/8/1956 at 67/2/4; farmer; married; b. Milton; Clarence Wallingford and Ida Downs

Clarence M., d. 1/6/1920 at 67/1/17; farmer; married; b. Milton; David Wallingford (Milton) and Susan Jones (Milton)

David, d. 2/22/1903 at 83/10/18; old age; farmer; widower; b. Milton; Samuel Wallingford (Milton) and Sallie Worster (Milton)

David W., d. 10/18/1926 at 77/10/26 in Rochester; farmer; married; b. Milton; David Wallingford (Milton) and Mary A. Tasker (Strafford)

Helen, d. 5/11/1964 at 78 in Concord; housewife; b. Raleigh, NC; Albert Tarr and Susan -----

Ida G., d. 10/22/1925 at 69/4/10; at home; widow; b. Milton; J. Hanson Downs (Milton) and Emily P. Duntley (Farmington)

Ira, d. 9/28/1909 at 56/1/24; pulmonary tuberculosis; carriage agent; married; b. Milton; Ira Wallingford (Milton) and Delane Thompson (Sandwich)

James W., d. 2/17/1909 at 40; suicide; laborer; single; b. Berwick, ME; Eben Wallingford (Berwick, ME) and Mary Wallingford (Berwick, ME)

Mary, d. 9/22/1939 at 95/0/15 in Manchester; housewife; widow; b. Milton; Enoch Plummer (Milton) and Orinda Ayers (Wakefield)

Samuel W., d. 5/25/1899 at 61/5/28; pyacmia fol. abscess; farmer; married; b. Milton; D. Wallingford (Milton) and Mary A. Tasker (Strafford)

Susan A., d. 2/11/1902 at 81/11/19; old age; married; b. Milton; Joshua Jones (Milton) and Sally Cowell (Milton)

Wayne D., d. 10/11/1982 in Union; Collis E. Wallingford and Beatrice Bunker

WALSH,
Carrie M., d. 3/18/1935 at 62/7; housewife; married; b. Paris, ME; Leonard Briggs and ----- Fields

George L., d. 2/10/1949 at 78/4/28 in Wolfeboro; marker; widower; b. Milton; William E. Walsh and Mary A. Hodsdon

Glenn I., d. 3/20/1983 in Concord; John E. Walsh and Grace E. Smith

Myrtle E., d. 7/13/1986; Porter Durkee and Estella Swinerton

WAMPLER,
Carl F., d. 12/27/1980 in Rochester; Rufus W. Wampler and ----- Blanton

Flora O., d. 8/22/1980 in Rochester; Willie J. Allen and Willie M. Stumbridge

WARD,
Jeanette E., d. 4/20/1998 in Dover

Richmond E., d. 7/23/1959 at 59; merchant; married; b. Rochester; Charles Ward and Mary C. Greenfield

Troy M., d. 5/24/1983; Ralph Ward and Opal Daniels

WARDLEY,
Edwina Elvira, d. 10/28/1961 at 68/2/27 in Lynn, MA

WARNECKE,
daughter, d. 6/12/1947 at 0/0/0 in Rochester; b. Rochester; William Warnecke (Milton) and Ruth Dixon (Milton)

Francena I., d. 7/25/1996 in Rochester; Hartley Nutter and Ada Huntress

Ruth, d. 7/28/1976 at 54 in Rochester; homemaker; b. NH; Stephen Dixon and Georgia Moody

William H., d. 4/13/1960 at 74; machinist; b. Groneau, Germany; Frederick Warnecke and Anna -----

WARREN,
Dorothy, d. 7/3/1936 at 25/1/19; school teacher; married; b. Kittery, ME; Charles E. Woods (Rye) and Julia E. Brown (Kittery, ME)

WATERMAN,
Fred, d. 3/17/1891 at 4/9/10; disease of kidneys; single; b. Dover; Fred Waterman and Julia Sweeney

WATSON,
Dorothy E., d. 1/25/1979 in Rochester; William Garside
Gladys E., d. 1/5/1992 in Milton; Asa A. Abbott and Marantha F. Grant
John, d. 8/24/1970 at 64 in Dover; rigger; b. NY; Thomas Watson and Maud Newell
Margaret E., d. 11/5/1948 at 80/10/1 in Exeter; widow; b. Hopkinton, MA; Adam Dahl (Germany) and Anna Block (Germany)
Richard E., Jr., d. 1/29/1987 in Greenland
Silomon R., d. 11/4/1944 at 75 in Boston, MA

WEAVER,
John T., d. 7/14/1961 at 70; shoe worker; b. Watsonville, CA; John T. Weaver and Sarah Ferguson
Sara G., d. 5/9/1956 at 62; housewife; married; b. Newburyport, MA; Orin B. Gerrish and Josephine McCaslin

WEBB,
George L., d. 9/21/1978 at 38 in Rochester; machine tender; b. MA; George L. Webb, Sr. and Helen Bernier

WEBBER,
Bruce L., d. 10/14/1990 in Portsmouth; Lincoln D. Webber and Geraldine Wood
Fannie M., d. 7/15/1890 at 28; ner. pros'n and con. brain; housekeeper; married; b. Parsonsfield, ME; Elijah Whiting (Ossipee) and Mary Watson (Ossipee)
Nellie B., d. 5/7/1955 at 88 in Orlando, FL; housewife; widow; b. Milton; George W. Tasker and Lydia Jones
Parker, d. 6/9/1940 at 59/8/17 in Wolfeboro
Royal K., d. 7/16/1928 at 68/9/1; carpenter; married; b. Shapleigh, ME; Greenleaf Webber (Shapleigh, ME) and Sarah Grant (Acton, ME)
William W., d. 3/27/1901 at 49/7/26; gen'al tuberculosis; physician; married; b. Shapleigh, ME; Greenleaf Webber (Shapleigh, ME) and Sarah C. Grant (Acton, ME)

WEBSTER,
Almon H., d. 2/10/1941 at 81/0/18; carpenter; married; b. Albany; Horace Webster and Mary Chesley
Maude R., d. 2/27/1961 at 67 in Rochester; dietitian; b. Boston, MA; George Webster and Fanny Carter

WEEKS,
Frank S., d. 4/28/1952 at 81 in Wolfeboro; ret. physician; married; b. Porter, ME; William Weeks and Mary Parker
Josephine, d. 3/28/1904 at 0/0/2; inanition; b. Milton; Albert Weeks (Wakefield) and Phylura Dame (Rochester)
Margaret L., d. 3/21/1993 in Wolfeboro
William S., d. 1/20/1913 at 89/3/28; pneumonia; widower; b. Porter, ME; Joshua Weeks (Grindland, ME) and Jemima Libbey (Porter, ME)

WEEMAN,
Ella S., d. 10/22/1987 in Rochester
Forrest E., d. 5/22/1966 at 35 in Union
Harris, d. 9/24/1963 at 34 in Boston, MA
Howard A., d. 12/2/1960 at 65 in Wakefield; shipfitter; b. W. Buxton, ME; Horinto Weeman and Belle Mackie
Roger R., d. 4/10/1987 in Rochester

WEINERT,
Howard L., d. 6/12/1962 at 68 in East Kingston

WELCH,
Annie M., d. 3/30/1926 at 41/10/24; housewife; married; b. Sanbornville; Louis Marchand (Canada) and Arline Theorette (Canada)
Evelyn Louise, d. 2/26/1921 at 0/0/26; b. Milton; Leon J. Welch (Ossipee) and Mertie A. Williams (Tamworth)
Fred J., d. 5/14/1960 at 78; millwright; b. So. Berwick, ME; Joseph Welch and Celia Nealey
Harriet M., d. 3/19/1907 at 19/3/12; companion; single; b. Ossipee; Peter Welch (Ossipee) and Cora B. Kimball (Parsonsfield, ME)
Harry K., d. 3/23/1960 at 62 in Manchester
Lillian E., d. 2/6/1963 at 53 in Rochester; housework; b. Milton; Fred Welch and Annie Marchand

Odell, d. 5/29/1907 at 0/2/9; inanition; b. Milton; Fred Welch (So. Berwick, ME) and Lydia Marchand (Wakefield)

Sarah J., d. 11/25/1926 at 79/5/13; housework; widow; b. Ossipee; John Welch (Ossipee) and Susie Welch (Ossipee)

WELLS,

Marcia B., d. 1/27/1944 at 72/7/30 in Rochester

WENTWORTH,

son, d. 7/3/1896 at 0/0/1; inanition; b. Milton; Charles S. Wentworth (Wakefield) and Hattie B. Patch (Newfield, ME)

son, d. 5/7/1916 at 0/4/11; b. Milton; Linwood J. Wentworth (Lebanon, ME) and Carrie S. Wentworth (Acton, ME)

daughter, d. 11/21/1924 at 0/0/2 hrs; b. Milton; Grover C. Wentworth (Milan) and Lena A. Miles (Bethlehem)

son, d. 9/13/1925 at 0/0/0; b. Milton; Grover C. Wentworth (West Milan) and Lena Miles (Bethlehem)

A. L., d. 3/23/1933 at 86/9/3; housekeeper; widow; b. Somersworth; John B. Conner and Susan Hodgdon

Abbie, d. 7/18/1900 at 62/8/29; malignant tumor; housekeeper; single; b. Milton; Dudley Wentworth (Milton) and Lucy J. Place (Alton)

Abbie A., d. 4/13/1907 at 83/7; acute indigestion; married

Albertha, d. 3/18/1912 at 66/0/11; pernicious vomiting; housewife; married; b. Milton; Hazen Duntley (Bow) and Phoebe Leighton

Almon E., d. 3/24/1902 at 27/0/12; consumption; shoemaker; single; b. Wolfeboro; John Wentworth (Somersworth) and Sarah Mathews (Ossipee)

Almon H., d. 7/26/1953 at 81/11/21 in Lebanon, ME; married; Hiram Wentworth

Annie F., d. 11/19/1966 at 92 in New Haven, CT

Arville F., d. 5/16/1917 at 83 in Concord; widow; b. Acton, ME; Durina Farnham (Acton, ME) and Anna Miller (Acton, ME)

Bessie H., d. 4/7/1979 in Rochester; Robert Hines and Gertrude Varney

Charles, d. 3/12/1940 at 78/5/4 in Wolfeboro; laborer; widower; b. Newfield, ME; William Wentworth (Newfield, ME)

Charles E., d. 7/28/1945 at 79/9/7 in Wakefield; widower

Charles H., d. 7/2/1904 at 65/6/3; cancer of liver; farmer; married; b. Milton; Phineas Wentworth (Milton) and Nancy Witham (Milton)

Clara, d. 2/1/1894 at 47/0/12; tuberculosis; housekeeper; married; b. Milton; Cyrus Hart (Milton) and Lydia Witham (Milton)

Clara A., d. 11/28/1894 at 23/9; pulmonary tuberculosis; housewife; married; John C. Penney (New Durham) and Belle E. Stevens (Middleton)

Clara P., d. 7/10/1921 at 58/7/24; at home; widow; b. Shapleigh, ME; Caleb S. Pierce (Lebanon, ME) and Lovisa Jellison (Shapleigh, ME)

Clyde, d. 3/8/1900 at 0/1; heart failure; b. Milton; Elroy Wentworth (Milton) and Ethel Hargraves (Somersworth)

Cora, d. 11/11/1940 at 84/8/6 in Stow, MA

David, d. 5/3/1915 at 81/5/23; shoemaker; married; b. Lebanon, ME; Benjamin Wentworth (Lebanon, ME) and Mary Ricker (Lebanon, ME)

Delbert R., d. 4/9/1927 at 57/3/27; millwright; single; b. Milton; Charles H. Wentworth (Milton) and Arvilla Farnham (Acton, ME)

Edgar, d. 12/9/1932 at 76/11/2; retired; married; b. Milton; Levi Wentworth and Elizabeth -----

Edward E., d. 9/26/1899 at 0/7/1; cholera infantum; b. Milton; Elroy E. Wentworth (Milton) and Ethel M. Goodwin (Somersworth)

Edward S., d. 1/10/1950 at 55/2/17 in Rochester; painter; married; b. Somerville, MA; William E. Wentworth and Eleanor Law

Eli, d. 10/31/1894 at 64/6/23; pneumonia; farmer; married

Eliza K., d. 4/10/1898 at 75/6; burned; housekeeper; married; b. Tamworth; George Woodman (Tamworth) and Margaret Brewster (Tamworth)

Eliza M., d. 4/11/1926 at 63/9/7; at home; widow; b. Tuftonboro; John Hanson (Tuftonboro) and Emily Whitehouse (Tuftonboro)

Ella, d. 1/16/1937 at 68/1/29; shoe stitcher; single; b. Milton; David Wentworth (Lebanon, ME) and Lydia Palmer (New Durham)

Ella B., d. 6/21/1947 at 76/10/2 in Acton, ME; housewife; married; b. Acton, ME; John C. Buck (Acton, ME) and Hannah Brackett (Acton, ME)

Emma B., d. 11/13/1979 in Rochester; Joseph W. Barber and Melvina Babbit

Ernest, d. 12/13/1944 at 80/3/18; sta. eng.; widower; b. Milton; David Wentworth (Lebanon, ME) and Lydia J. Palmer (Milton)

G. C. S., d. 2/1/1934 at 94/3/13; retired; widower; b. So. Berwick, ME; Samuel Wentworth and Sarah Varney

Georgia, d. 3/4/1940 at 74/7/26; housewife; married; b. Lebanon, ME; Elisha Gerrish (Lebanon, ME) and Mary E. Hersom (Lebanon, ME)

Hannah, d. 12/17/1931 at 91/0/18; housekeeper; widow; b. Strafford; Jethro Gray (Strafford) and Lucretia Pottle (Strafford)

Harriet, d. 12/25/1929 at 60/6/24; at home; married; b. Limerick, ME; Plummer Patch (Shapleigh, ME) and Sarah Copp (Newfield, ME)

Harry E., d. 12/10/1955 at 86/1/27 in Acton, ME; widower; Hiram Wentworth

Henry H., d. 5/9/1920 at 76/5/6; widower; b. Milton; Hiram V. Wentworth (Milton) and Mary J. Nute (Milton)

Herbert A., d. 3/10/1967 at 79; farmer; b. Farmington; Martin G. Wentworth and Georgia A. Gerrish

Hiram, d. 1/12/1917 at 73/0/28; carpenter; married; b. Milton; Levi Wentworth (Milton) and Mary Witham

Hiram V., d. 9/29/1890 at 71/10/17; widower; b. Milton; I. H. Wentworth (Milton) and Peace Varney (Milton)

Homer R., d. 4/16/1972 at 75 in Rochester; maintenance wkr.; b. NH; Charles Wentworth and Carrie Place

Horace A., d. 2/26/1962 at 68; mill wright; b. Albany; Henry Wentworth and Abbie Webster

Isaac, d. 2/12/1909 at 85/2/6; pneumonia; farmer; widower; b. Milton; Isaac Wentworth (Milton) and Lucy Twombly (Milton)

John, d. 5/26/1905 at 76/5/24; angina pectoris; farmer; married; b. Somersworth; Ezekiel Wentworth (Rochester) and Rebecca (Dover)

John A., d. 2/13/1904 at 72/6/6; chronic nephritis; farmer; married; b. Milton; Jacob Wentworth (Milton) and Sally Hanson (Alton)

John E., d. 2/23/1920 at 64/0/26; widower; b. Milton; Eli Wentworth (Milton) and Naomi Witham

John M., d. 10/20/1893 at 0/2/20; capillary bronchitis; b. Milton; George E. Wentworth (Milton) and Lillian Maddox (N. Shapleigh, ME)

John S., d. 11/17/1909 at 52/11/16; chronic nephritis; shoemaker; married; b. Milton; John Wentworth and Olive Downs

Louisa M., d. 1/21/1915 at 68/1/9; housewife; married; b. Milton; Luther Hayes (Rochester) and Louisa M. Bragdon (Milton)

Lucretia M., d. 7/14/1888 at 82/2/2; old age

Lucy J., d. 3/20/1897 at 71/5/6; pneumonia; single; b. Milton; Dudley Wentworth (Milton) and Lucy J. Place (Alton)

Lula M., d. 1/24/1958 at 88/10/11 in Boston, MA

M. Jane, d. 4/30/1895 at 72/6/20; apoplexy; housewife; widow; b. Milton; John Howe and Mehitable Twombly

Martin G., d. 6/17/1947 at 84/5/5; farmer; widower; b. Milton; John Wentworth (Milton) and Hannah E. Gray (Strafford)

Mary C., d. 10/13/1890 at 45/9/9; apoplexy; housekeeper; married; b. Milton; John M. Hanson (Lebanon, ME) and Nancy R. Pinkham (Milton)

Mary W., d. 6/1/1915 at 85/5/16; married; b. Cape Cod, MA; Edmund Lord

Max, d. 7/4/1891 at 0/0/0; convulsions; b. Milton; Luther H. Wentworth and Flora Nelson

Merl T., d. 2/14/1958 at 62; storekeeper, ret.; married; b. W. Lebanon, ME; Melvin Wentworth and Clara Goodwin

Naomi, d. 12/12/1906 at 75/4/25; exhaustion; widow

Norman L., d. 12/15/1991 in Sanford, ME

Richard A., d. 5/7/1976 at 33 in Sarasota, FL

Roland G., d. 5/18/1893 at 2/1/2; gas. intes. catarrh; b. Milton; Ernest L. Wentworth (Milton) and Florence Lucas (IA)

Roscoe C., d. 7/3/1950 at 59 in Union; married; Charles Wentworth and Clara Place

Russell G., d. 11/20/1972 at 73; farmer; b. NH; Martin G. Wentworth and Georgia A. Gerrish

Ruth J., d. 10/28/1915 at 88/9/2; widow; b. Wakefield; Samuel Seward and Betsy Wentworth

Samuel E., d. 2/11/1908 at 73/6/9; chronic nephritis; farmer; married; b. Bradford, MA; Edward J. Wentworth and Eliza Stiles

Sarah A., d. 10/29/1910 at 69/7/16; nephritis; single; b. Rochester; Beard Wentworth (Rochester) and Sarah Roberts (Rochester)

Sarah E., d. 1/17/1900 at 5/0/20; Bright's disease; b. Acton, ME; John I. Wentworth (Milton) and Augusta Laskey (Milton)

Stella, d. 7/7/1935 at 59/5/12; housekeeper; single; b. Ossipee; Samuel Wentworth (Bradford, MA) and Asenath H. Conner (Somersworth)

Warren T., d. 10/28/1980 in Lynn, MA

WESSELL,

John E., d. 1/15/1994 in Dover; James A. Wessell and Barbara E. Hutchinson

WETLEY,
Maria, d. 3/6/1941 at 87/8/2 in Barrington

WHALEN,
son, d. 9/16/1972 at 0/0/0 in Rochester; Henry F. Whalen and Shirley A. McNeil

WHEELER,
Ruby, d. 7/25/1979 in Rochester; Frank Brainard

WHETNALL,
Colleen, d. 2/3/1932 at 0/3/9; b. Rochester; Leroy Whetnall (Constitution, OH) and Eleanor Tanner (Wakefield)

WHIDDEN,
Shirley S., d. 11/27/1974 at 85 in Rochester; homemaker; b. NH; F. Charles Stevens and M. Alice Campbell

WHITCOMB,
Madeline J., d. 9/8/1995 in Rochester; Perley Hurd and Grace Cooper

WHITE,
Adam K., d. 7/20/1979 in Madbury; Kenneth H. White and Linda Perkins
Gardiner C., d. 4/15/1949 at 87 in Rochester; retired; widower; b. Stoughton, MA
Roberta L., d. 12/15/1997 in FL
William F., d. 2/12/1915 at 35/7; mill hand; married; b. Boston, MA; William White (Boston, MA) and Elizabeth Hervey (Brighton, MA)

WHITEHOUSE,
son, d. 5/23/1910 at 0/0/0; suffocation; Nicholas Whitehouse (Middleton) and Maggie Cassidy (Boston, MA)
C. M., d. 6/24/1934 at 52/8/11 in Milton Mills; at home; married; b. Farmington; James A. Fletcher (New Durham) and Elizabeth ----- (New Durham)
Charles R., d. 1/21/1982 in Manchester; Nicholas Whitehouse and Margaret Cassidy
Fannie C., d. 7/27/1961 at 73 in Rochester; housewife; b. Farmington; Charles F. Fall and Emma Richardson

Florence, d. 10/27/1908 at 0/4/12; entero colitis; b. Milton; N. W. Whitehouse (Middleton) and Margaret Cassidy (Boston, MA)

John W., d. 6/28/1944 at 80/2/3; farmer; single; b. Wolfeboro; Thomas Whitehouse (Middleton) and Ellen Alexandria (Burlington, VT)

Margaret, d. 5/29/1913 at 40/0/6; mitral regurgitation; housewife; married; b. Boston, MA; James Cassidy (Ireland) and Annie (Ireland)

Ruth Elsie, d. 10/4/1989 in Rochester; Harry Staples and Henrietta Hastings

Sarah A., d. 12/18/1919 at 76/4/16; housekeeper; widow; b. Middleton; Davis Tufts (Middleton) and Adeline Horne (Middleton)

WHITHAM,

Sarah A., d. 12/17/1902 at 88/8; exhaustion; housekeeper; widow; b. Milton; Joseph Walker (Rochester) and Sally Pray (Rochester)

WHITING,

Cora, d. 3/4/1952 at 89 in Rochester; housewife; widow; b. Ossipee; George H. Smith and Mary Bunker

WHITTEN,

Henry A., d. 7/9/1903 at 77/6/19; heart failure; brick mason; widower; b. Wolfeboro; Jesse A. Whitten (Wolfeboro) and Betsy J. Drew (Wolfeboro)

William H., d. 11/6/1925 at 68 in Milton Mills; laborer; single; b. Newfield, ME

WHITTIER,

Doris L., d. 4/2/1993 in Dover; Arthur B. Lewis and Mabel Pearl

WHITTON,

Jesse A., d. 1/2/1906 at 50/5/29; natural causes; teamster; single; b. Wolfeboro; Henry A. Whitton (Wolfeboro) and Lydia Drew (Wolfeboro)

WHITTIKER,

Anna D., d. 10/24/1902 at 66/1/1; chronic nephritis; widow; b. Trenton; Peter Howell (Trenton) and Adaline Pratt (Philadelphia, PA)

WIGGIN,
daughter, d. 3/4/1907 at 0/0/0; stillborn; Harvey Wiggin (Wakefield) and Myra L. Witham (Milton)
Albert, d. 11/19/1939 at 66 in Branford, CT; widower; b. Acton, ME; Mark N. Wiggin (Wakefield) and Susan ----- (Acton, ME)
Charles, d. 1/31/1932 at 69/7/9 in Acton, ME; mill employee; widower; b. Acton, ME; Mark N. Wiggin (Wakefield) and Ellen Farnham (Acton, ME)
Cora B., d. 4/4/1934 at 63/1/16 in Rochester; at home; married; b. Newfield, ME; John Day (Newfield, ME) and Susan Patch (Newfield, ME)
Ethel M., d. 6/7/1910 at 4/4/15; peritonitis; b. Wakefield; Harvey F. Wiggin (Wakefield) and Myra L. Witham (Milton)
Everett, d. 1/7/1932 at 63/7/10 in Portsmouth
Harvey F., d. 4/4/1946 at 61/6/21 in Wakefield; farmer; married; b. Wakefield; Frank J. Wiggin (Wakefield) and Augusta C. Farnham (Wakefield)
Irene E., d. 6/16/1944 at 27/4/27 in Rochester; housewife; married; b. Milton; Frank Tatro (No. Adams, MA) and Mary Ducharme (Berwick, ME)
Laura E., d. 4/12/1949 at 83/7/16 in Lynbrook, NY; housewife; widow; b. Acton, ME; Henry L. Fox and Sarah A. Moulton
Luther P., d. 11/10/1915 at 82/7/4; widower; b. Milton; Simeon Wiggin (Milton) and Sarah Wentworth (Milton)
Lydia J., d. 12/21/1915 at 80/5/14; widow; b. New Durham; Aaron Palmer (New Durham) and Anna Cloutman (Rochester)
Marion, d. 8/29/1912 at 8/1/29; acute nephritis; Albert E. Wiggin (Acton, ME) and Cora B. Day (Newfield, ME)
Mary A., d. 3/17/1916 at 63/0/10; housewife; married; b. Tuftonboro; Albert Elliott (Moultonboro) and Mahitable Caverly (Tuftonboro)
Myra L., d. 4/25/1950 at 68/8/1 in Wolfeboro; widow; Everett Witham and Jennie Witham
William E., d. 9/7/1931 at 65/8/20 in Rochester; lumber mill; married; b. Acton, ME; Mark Wiggin (Wakefield) and Ellen Farnum (Rochester)

WIGNOT,
Alena C., d. 5/29/1963 at 93 in Medway, MA

Jacob, d. 7/6/1937 at 61/4/20 in Wakefield; supt. schools; married; b. Natick, MA; John Wignot (Alsace-Lorraine) and Melvina Lindanau (Germany)

WILKINS,
Arthur W., d. 11/28/1971 at 77 in Wolfeboro; maintenance oper.; b. ME; Homer Wilkins and Mary B. Hutchins
Mary B.H., d. 12/19/1914 at 51/3/12; uterine carcinoma; housekeeper; married; b. Wakefield; Hiram Hutchins (Wakefield) and Mary Neal (Ossipee)
Minnie H., d. 10/23/1981 in Milton Mills; Elmer F. Hersom and Emily J. Wilson
Virginia B., d. 4/13/1997 in Milton Mills; Harry W. Wade and Mildred Sanborn

WILKINSON,
Durwood Fred, d. 2/25/1993 in Union
Melbourne A., d. 3/14/1998 in Milton Mills
Wilfred A., d. 6/25/1997 in ME

WILLEY,
daughter, d. 6/8/1924 at 0/0/0; b. Milton; Edwin F. Willey (Wakefield) and Marion P. Hinkley (Gloucester, MA)
son, d. 6/16/1925 at 0/0/0 in Milton Mills; b. Milton; E. Farnham Willey (Wakefield) and Mariam Hinckley (Gloucester, MA)
Charles A., d. 4/21/1954 at 58; mechanic; married; b. Auburn; George Willey and Melvina J. Kelley
Charles P., d. 5/9/1985 in Rochester
Cortez W., d. 3/23/1969 at 85; farmer; b. NH; William H. Willey and Maria Jones
Dorothy H., d. 10/18/1944 at 55/6/23 in Wolfeboro; housewife; married; b. New Bedford, MA; George M. Allen (Dover) and Minnie F. Howe (Dorchester, MA)
Edwin F., d. 7/14/1954 at 66; RR engineer; married; b. Wakefield; William H. Willey, 2d and Maria Jones
Everett C., d. 2/2/1949 at 3/8/7; b. Wolfeboro; Charles A. Willey and Phoebe C. Whitten
Frances, d. 6/15/1936 at 83/9/3; housewife; widow; b. Taunton, MA; John B. Davis and Elmira Stanley (Mt. Desert, ME)

Fred K., d. 5/19/1926 at 62/7/10; farmer; single; b. Milton; Joseph F. Willey (Brookfield) and Mary J. Laskey (Milton)

Grace, d. 2/13/1986 in Newton, NC

Herbert, d. 2/17/1940 at 71/5/19; farmer; single; b. Milton; Joseph F. Willey (Brookfield) and Mary J. Willey (Milton Mills)

James H., d. 4/27/1946 at 70/11 in Rochester; druggist; married; b. Salmon Falls; James P. Willey (Wakefield) and Frances Davis (Trenton, ME)

James P., d. 12/25/1932 at 80/10/11 in Rochester; retired; married; b. Wakefield; Aziah C. Willey (Brookfield) and Martha Dearborn (Milton)

John D., d. 5/18/1926 at 66/9/13; farmer; widower; b. Wakefield; Aziah Willey (Brookfield) and Martha Dearborn (Milton)

Joseph A.C., d. 7/30/1955 at 65 in Wakefield; farmer; widower; b. Wakefield; William H. Willey and Maria Jones

Joseph D., d. 9/4/1931 at 77/7/20; merchant; married; b. Wakefield; Aziah C. Willey (Brookfield) and Martha Dearborn (Milton)

Joseph E., d. 11/27/1942 at 56/5; merchant; single; b. Milton; Joseph D. Willey (Wakefield) and Olive A. Roberts (No. Berwick, ME)

Joseph F., d. 3/8/1912 at 76/3/6; chronic nephritis; farmer; married; b. Brookfield; William Willey (Brookfield) and Susan Henderson (Dover)

Lillian E., d. 2/24/1988; Samuel Burnley and Minnie Mawson

Maria J., d. 5/14/1934 at 83/7/7 in Wakefield; at home; married; b. Randolph, MA; William Jones (Randolph, MA) and Sally W. Ellis (Alton)

Marion E., d. 9/13/1977 at 69 in Rochester; teacher; b. ME; Archie T. Lowd and Clara M. Page

Mary J., d. 11/3/1918 at 73/8/16; housewife; widow; b. Milton; Pelatiah J. Laskey (Lee) and Judith A. Miller (New Durham)

Miriam P., d. 5/23/1955 at 68; housewife; widow; b. Gloucester, MA; Elias G. Hinckley and Elizabeth Hillier

Nelson F., d. 5/11/1973 at 63 in Milton Mills; tannery worker; b. NH; Clarence D. Willey and Charlotte G. Twombly

Olive A., d. 4/12/1937 at 77/1/22; at home; widow; b. No. Berwick, ME; William Roberts (No. Berwick, ME) and Catherine Guptill (So. Berwick, ME)

Richard M., d. 11/29/1988 in Rochester; Leon Willey and Flora Downs

William, d. 1/14/1997 in FL

William, 2d, d. 11/16/1935 at 81/11/2 in Wakefield; farmer; widower; b. Wakefield; Aziah C. Willey (Wakefield) and Martha Dearborn (Milton)

WILLIAMS,
Augusta, d. 1/25/1908 at 53/2/21; septicemia; housework; widow; b. No. Wakefield; Isaac Watson (Wolfeboro) and Esther J. Deane (England)
Clifford J., d. 3/6/1999 in Rochester; Ralph Williams and Lillian McCarthy
Donald, d. 10/6/1991 in Rochester
Dorothy A., d. 7/23/1986 in Rochester; Andrew Anderson and Anna Jacobson
Fred S., d. 7/17/1997 in Milton; Thomas Williams and Dora Nanze
George H., d. 12/6/1976 at 68 in Wolfeboro; lumber laborer; b. CT; Alonzo M. Williams and Minnie J. McNorton
Gertrude A., d. 4/7/1989 in Fall River, MA
Harry P., d. 9/12/1993 in Rochester
Harry R., d. 12/9/1991 in Rochester (1992)
Hattie, d. 1/13/1925 at 69/7/3; single; b. Bowdoinham, ME; Hiram Williams (Bowdoinham, ME) and Eliza Toothaker (Litchfield, ME)
Jefferson N., d. 6/27/1979 in Rochester; Frank R. Williams and Sarah J. Eldridge
John E., Jr., d. 11/6/1985 in Rochester; John E. Williams, Sr. and Florence Hickey
Justus W., d. 4/29/1926 at 73/2/13; widower; b. Ossipee; Shaber Williams (Ossipee) and Lydia Welch (Ossipee)
Lillian J., d. 9/28/1982
Mae F., d. 8/2/1985 (1992)
Myrtle M., d. 8/10/1966 at 59 in Hanover; mill worker; b. Milton; George Ellis and Gertrude Duntley
Penelope F., d. 4/9/1995 in Portland, ME; William W. Kruetz and Doris Smith
Ralph J., d. 2/18/1977 at 75 in Rochester; mill wkr.; b. NH; William Williams and Susie Welch
Shaber W., d. 8/3/1975 at 79 in Rochester; woodsman; b. NH; Willis Williams and Susie Welch
Susie, d. 5/13/1955 at 86/6/15; housewife; widow; b. Ossipee; Moses P. Welch and Sarah Welch

William H., d. 3/12/1923 at 65/1/11; retired; married; b. Ossipee; Shaber Williams (Ossipee) and Lydia Welch (Ossipee)

WILLIAMSON,
Geraldine M., d. 2/27/1953 at 67; housewife; married; b. Rochester; Eli W. Foss and Laura Scruton
John S., d. 10/14/1957 at 80/3/21; painter; widower; b. So. Boston, MA; William Williamson and Mary Winn

WILSON,
Charles W., d. 1/12/1958 at 68; millwright; married; b. Portland, ME; Francis Wilson and Margaret Gallagher
George W., d. 8/17/1952 at 84; farmer; widower; b. Beverly, MA; Moses Wilson
Valna A., d. 2/8/1996 in Rochester

WINN,
Keith W., d. 3/1/1988 in Beverly Hills, FL

WINSLOW,
Edward L., d. 11/26/1949 at 77 in Wolfeboro; RR conductor; married; b. Lynn, MA; John Winslow
Emma, d. 5/15/1936 at 88/8/23 in Rochester; widow; b. Salem, MA
John T., d. 1/21/1931 at 84/6/12; doll repairer; married; b. Northam; Ephraim Winslow (Nottingham) and Sally Grave (Pittsfield)

WITHAM,
Alma, d. 12/31/1918 at 32/5/19; housewife; married; b. Industry, ME; Charles Oliver (Stark, ME) and Ida B. Merry (Industry, ME)
Arthur R., d. 5/12/1978 at 81 in Milton Mills; machine operator; b. ME; Josiah W. Witham and Georgianna Sanborn
Charles W., d. 9/30/1920 at 47/4/22 in Beverly, MA; married; b. Milton; Josiah Witham (Acton, ME) and Mary A. Willey (Salem, MA)
Clifton M., d. 3/3/1920 at 0/0/27; b. Milton; Perley D. Witham (Milton) and Florence P. Locke (Boston, MA)
Connie L., d. 2/8/1998 in Rochester
Edward J., d. 9/1/1959 at 77 in North Rochester; married
Ernest F., d. 3/26/1977 at 82 in Rochester; fireman; b. ME; George W. Witham and Arabella Goodspeed

Everett T., d. 2/21/1922 at 69/5/21; laborer; married; b. Melrose, MA; Ira Witham (Milton)

Florence P., d. 2/20/1920 at 40; housekeeper; married; b. Boston, MA

Grace E., d. 5/14/1972 at 57 in Portland, ME

Margaret F., d. 1/19/1980 in Rochester; John Day and Susan Patch

Marguerite A., d. 10/2/1964 at 66; housewife; b. Wilmington, MA; David Cooley and Bessie Stevens

Mary A., d. 4/13/1909 at 80/9/27; pneumonia; widow; b. So. Berwick, ME; Webster Miller (So. Berwick, ME) and Louisa Roberts (Salmon Falls)

Nellie, d. 4/1/1949 at 79 in Acton, ME; housewife; widow; b. Biddeford, ME; Thomas H. Rodgers and Ida Jane Hood

Nettie, d. 4/10/1959 at 72 in Hanover; housewife; married; b. Saco, ME; Onie Merrill and Mary Berry

Perley D., d. 2/3/1949 at 73/1/4 in Acton, ME; laborer; widower; b. Milton; Everett Witham and Jennie -----

Perley I., d. 1/15/1974 at 56 in Manchester

Raymond O., d. 3/13/1989 in Rochester

WOOD,
Edith B., d. 5/13/1978 at 83 in Wolfeboro; hosp. dietician; b. ME; William E. Dornan and Ethel Mahoney

June K., d. 3/1/1994 in Portland, ME

WOODBURY,
Doris H., d. 4/5/1983 in Milford

William E., d. 4/21/1947 at 50/6/29 in Kittery, ME; poultryman; married; b. Hudson; Charles E. Woodbury and Eva J. Wheeler

WOODRUFF,
Frank C., d. 10/3/1996 in Milton; George H. Woodruff and Cordelia J. Sneden

WOODWARD,
Orista, d. 2/5/1938 at 89/1/10 in Rochester

WORLEY,
Elsie May, d. 11/2/1958 at 75/7/18 in East Orange, NJ

WORMHOOD,
Elizabeth, d. 7/2/1949 at 76/7/9 in Rochester; housewife; married; b. Lynn, MA; Reuben Walker and Emily F. -----

WRIGHT,
Harriett R., d. 8/23/1951 at 74 in Manchester; widow; b. MA; William C. Preeper and Matilda McDonald

WYATT,
Brian J., d. 2/2/1995 in Rochester; Douglas Wyatt and Vivian Watson
Charles H., Jr., d. 3/2/1993 in Middleton
Clarence T., Sr., d. 4/18/1993 in Milton; Ralph F. Wyatt and Ellen Thompson
Edgar J., d. 10/1/1941 at 69/11/16; farmer; married; b. Haverhill, MA; Asa Wyatt (Farmington)
Hattie E., d. 12/5/1951 at 83/7/5; housewife; widow; b. Milton; Luther Hayes and Sarah Coffran
Pearl T., d. 6/22/1984 in Rochester; Perley Thurlow and Dorothy Kenney

WYMAN,
Carrie L., d. 10/25/1950 at 82; housewife; widow; b. Weymouth, NS; Christine Wyman

YANOFF,
Nicholas G., d. 7/24/1962 at 64 in Milton Mills; custodian; b. Russia; Nicholas Yanoff

YEATON,
Arthur B., d. 7/1/1942 at 67/7 in Sanford, ME; carpenter; married; b. Wolfeboro; John Yeaton (Alfred, ME) and Eunice S. Black (Gray, ME)
Herbert, d. 1/12/1932 at 55/3; laborer; widower; b. Wolfeboro; John Yeaton (Alfred, ME) and Eunice S. Black (Gray, ME)

YORK,
Randy A., d. 5/22/1993 in Rochester; Richard A. York, Sr. and Florence M. Pratt

YOUNG,
Albert C., d. 4/8/1963 at 82 in Acton, ME
Annie R., d. 11/5/1897 at 36/11/20; consumption; housekeeper; widow
Byron R., d. 4/17/1903 at 18/7/11; acute tuberculosis; single; b. Milton; Horace E. Young (Candia) and Annie Remick
Cyrus T., d. 10/9/1896 at 32/9; consumption; shoemaker; married; b. Canada; John H. Young (Farmington) and Melissa Downing (Holderness)
Dorothy R., d. 11/18/1984 in Sanford, ME
Horace F., d. 11/30/1890 at 34/4/5; phthisis pulmonalis; minister; married; b. Candia; Aaron Young and Laura Hall
John, d. 6/24/1905 at 80/4/15; chronic nephritis; marble worker; widower; b. Waterboro, ME; John Young (Waterboro, ME) and Nancy Horne (Acton, ME)
Louis A., d. 12/9/1990 in Portland, ME
M. H., d. 2/19/1895 at 59/6; shock; single; b. Milton; Isaac Young (Alton) and Mary Pinkham (Milton)
Nellie E., d. 12/12/1963 at 82 in Sanford, ME; own home; b. Acton, ME; Mark Wiggin and Ellen Farnham
Peleg, d. 1/23/1921 at 80/6/28; retired; married; b. Bar Harbor, ME; Eben G. Young (Bar Harbor, ME) and Prudence Hamer (Bar Harbor, ME)
Scott W., d. 8/23/1968 at 14; student; b. NH; William L. Young and Edith M. Wentworth
Willard A., d. 7/28/1962 at 21; shoe worker; b. Rochester; Willard J. Young and Beatrice L. Wilkinson
William D., d. 8/28/1987 in Rochester; Lineus E. Young and Catherine R. Jones

ZIMNOCH,
Frederick A., d. 3/10/1988 in Rochester; Alexander Zimnoch and Josefa Truskowska

Other Heritage Books by Richard P. Roberts:

Alton, New Hampshire Vital Records, 1890–1997

Barnstead, New Hampshire Vital Records, 1887–2000

Barrington, New Hampshire Vital Records

Dover, New Hampshire Death Records, 1887–1937

Gilmanton, New Hampshire Vital Records, 1887–2001

Marriage Records of Dover, New Hampshire, 1835–1909

Marriage Records of Dover, New Hampshire, 1910–1937

Milton, New Hampshire Vital Records, 1888–1999

Moultonborough, New Hampshire Vital Records

New Castle, New Hampshire Vital Records, 1891–1997

New Hampshire Name Changes, 1768–1923

New Hampshire Name Changes, 1923–1947

Ossipee, New Hampshire Vital Records, 1887–2001

Rochester, New Hampshire Death Records, 1887–1951

Vital Records of Durham, New Hampshire, 1887–2002

Vital Records of Effingham and Freedom, New Hampshire, 1888–2001

Vital Records of Farmington, New Hampshire, 1887–1938

Vital Records of Lyme and Dorchester, New Hampshire, 1887–2004

Vital Records of New Durham and Middleton, New Hampshire, 1887–1998

Vital Records of North Berwick, Maine, 1892–2002

Vital Records of Orford and Piermont, New Hampshire, 1887–2004

Vital Records of Pittsburg, New Hampshire, 1904–2008

Vital Records of Sandwich, New Hampshire, 1887–2007

Vital Records of Tamworth and Albany, New Hampshire, 1887–2003

Vital Records of Tuftonboro and Brookfield, New Hampshire, 1888–2005

Vital Records of Wakefield, New Hampshire, 1887–1998

Vital Records of Warren, New Hampshire, 1887–2005

Wolfeboro, New Hampshire Vital Records, 1887–1999

www.ingramcontent.com/pod-product-compliance
Lightning Source LLC
Chambersburg PA
CBHW071230300426
44116CB00008B/975